Fighting Patton

ABOUT THE AUTHOR

Harry Yeide is an international affairs analyst with the federal government. He has worked primarily with political and security/military issues, writing assessments for the president of the United States and other senior policymakers. He is the author of *The Longest Battle, The Tank Killers, Steel Victory, Weapons of the Tankers, Steeds of Steel,* and *The Infantry's Armor* and the coauthor, with Mark Stout, of *First to the Rhine.* Yeide lives with his wife, Nancy, and three cats in Hyattsville, Maryland.

Fighting Patton

George S. Patton Jr.
Through the Eyes of His Enemies

Harry Yeide

ZENITH PRESS

First published in 2011 by Zenith Press, a member of Quayside Publishing Group, 400 First Avenue North, Suite 400, Minneapolis, MN 55401 USA

Zenith Press titles are also available at discounts in bulk quantity for industrial or sales-promotional use. For details write to Special Sales Manager at Quayside Publishing Group, 400 First Avenue North, Suite 400, Minneapolis, MN 55401 USA.

To find out more about our books, join us online at www.zenithpress.com.

Library of Congress Cataloging-in-Publication Data

Yeide, Harry.
    Fighting Patton : George S. Patton Jr. through the eyes of his enemies / Harry Yeide.
        pages cm.
    Includes bibliographical references and index.
    ISBN 978-0-7603-4592-4 (softcover)
    1. Patton, George S. (George Smith), 1885-1945. 2. Patton, George S. (George Smith), 1885-1945--Military leadership. 3. Patton, George S. (George Smith), 1885-1945--Adversaries. 4. Generals--United States--Biography. 5. United States. Army--Biography. 6. World War, 1939-1945--Campaigns--Western Front. 7. World War, 1939-1945--Campaigns--Africa, North. I. Title. II. Title: George S. Patton Jr. through the eyes of his enemies.
    E745.P3Y45 2014
    355.0092--dc23
    [B]
                                    2013042771

Credits
Maps: Harry Yeide
On the cover: Lt. Gen. George S. Patton Jr., March 30, 1943.
U.S. Army Signal Corps
On the back cover: Four-star General Patton following World War II.
National Archives

Printed in the United States of America

10 9 8 7 6 5 4 3 2 1

To Bob Ovelmen, who is the master
of the other fellow's point of view.

PRAISE FOR *FIGHTING PATTON*

"Harry Yeide has written a powerful book that looks at General George S. Patton Jr. from the enemy's perspective. This truly unique view of one of America's greatest military leaders benefits from superb research and previously unpublished material from enemy archives and is all woven together by a compelling narrative."
—Brian M. Sobel, author of *The Fighting Pattons*

"Known for his work on American armored units in WWII, Yeide combines extensive research in published and archival materials to render a unique sketch of General Patton as seen through the eyes of his enemies."
—*Publishers Weekly*

"For students of the German armed forces, the publication of *Fighting Patton* is especially significant, because of the depth and breadth of the German material utilized by Mr. Yeide. Suffice it to say that there are many professional historians writing in the same general field of investigation who would profit from learning and utilizing Harry Yeide's research methods. . . . The result is that the reader gains a comprehensive insight into the personalities and battlefield experiences of Patton's principal enemies."
—*New York Journal of Books*

"During the last seven or eight years, Harry Yeide has emerged as a prolific and increasingly important author of WWII-related books. With this title, his most recent, the author takes his work to a new level, producing a big, solid, serious book that transcends all his earlier output. . . . Quite a nice addition to anyone's library."
—Stone & Stone Second World War Books

"A book that is absolutely essential for anyone interested in the U.S. Army in World War II, the campaign in northwestern Europe, and George S. Patton."
—New York Military Affairs Symposium

"Harry Yeide has written an absorbing account of Patton and the adversaries he faced during both conflicts."
—*WWII* magazine

"This book offers a unique survey that considers German thinking about Patton's military might, and deserves a place in any serious military history holding."
—*Midwest Book Review*

"Dozens of books have profiled the charismatic, outspoken American general, George S. Patton Jr. What makes Harry Yeide's 528-page *Fighting Patton* a different story is that Yeide, a military historian, has written the book from the perspective of his enemies, a unique twist that provides the reader a new historic viewpoint . . ."
—*News-Review*

"Well documented from official reports and personal accounts and with extensive endnotes. Useful for its perspective from the other side, for both interested general readers and specialists."
—*Library Journal*

"[*Fighting Patton*] is a fresh look at one of the U.S. military's most colorful characters."
—*Tucson Citizen*

Contents

Preface

Seeing the battle through the opponent's eyes is the most dramatic way of seeing it. It is different in one important respect from "looking at it through the opposite end of the telescope." For instead of being minimized, the picture is magnified—with startling vividness.

B. H. Liddell Hart

M ANY BOOKS HAVE BEEN WRITTEN about Gen. George S. Patton Jr. This is the book that hasn't.

I have exploited vast and entirely new resources to reveal Patton's story through the eyes of his enemies. No published history of Patton that I could find reveals the identity of the German units that fought him in the St. Mihiel salient and Meuse-Argonne or what those soldiers experienced. Yet I tracked down those documents, some of which are still as crisp as when they were first placed in filing boxes, at all echelons of command, ranging from army-group level down to the battalion level. Those documents revealed who commanded the machine guns that shot at Patton at Pannes when he advanced alone on foot with a tank. I have used hundreds of unpublished accounts by German officers to show you the great American general through their eyes. I have burrowed through the original battle accounts of Patton's future enemies on the eastern front to explain why they learned to fight the way they did. I found the reports that prove when the Germans found out Patton was in Normandy and how, and I have tapped the telephone transcripts to put the reader in the command tent of the German army in France. Although we fought alongside our French allies during the latter half of the Second World War, I also located the diary of the man who commanded the French troops at Port Lyautey and who almost defeated Lucian Truscott and the left-most landing of Patton's Western Task Force in Morocco during the opening hours of Operation Torch in November 1942.

Who were the men who waged war against George S. Patton Jr.? What were the military experiences that shaped their methods of war, and how they would perceive their enemy, Patton? How did they interpret the quality of his actions on the battlefield? How much did they even know about what he was up to? This work answers these questions.

Although the thrust of this book is the enemy's perspective on Patton and his battles, Patton had the advantage of fighting most of them under conditions in which his side held the initiative. The narrative, therefore, often begins with the world as seen from the American perspective.

One runs into the problem of the "Patton myth," stories that have spread through the literature without much effort to ascertain their veracity, such as the tale of Adolf Hitler calling Patton that "crazy cowboy general." Of the major works on Patton, Ladislas Farago's *Patton: Ordeal and Triumph* strikes me as particularly riddled with idiosyncratic and hagiographic interpretations of Patton's achievements, such as a dramatic retelling of Patton advancing alone into the Hindenburg Line at St. Mihiel and depositing his silk tanker's flag there.[1] There is no way to prove a negative, but I do highlight incidents about which no authoritative source, who would have been present at the supposed events, has a thing to say or cases where timing renders the story improbable.

I intend this work in no way to detract from the achievements of the fighting men in the 1st Tank Brigade, the Western Task Force, II Corps, Seventh Army, and Third Army who fought under Patton and were justifiably proud of their achievements. They won. Their enemies lost. But the enemies' perspectives on the how and why of those outcomes, influenced as they may be by self-justification and missing information, completes the picture of the events and makes it whole. Readers may be surprised to discover how little they learn about the enemy if they peruse most works on George S. Patton Jr.

It may not be apparent to the casual reader, but it is darn hard to tell exactly what happened these many years ago. Contemporary reports written by separate participants in any given incident are likely to differ, sometimes substantially. Later accounts introduce additional flaws of memory and self-justification. One of Patton's enemies, *Generalfeldmarschall* Albert Kesselring, wrote after the war, "Distortion of military history begins the moment the battalion adjutant sharpens his pencil in the trenches. . . . [A]t this very moment, the objective opinion of the writer of the combat report is expressed and, consciously or unconsciously, for good or for questionable motives, the combat report is colored. . . ."[2] The reader should be aware that the tale offered here is merely as close as I can get.

I have taken small liberties with texts drawn from the military records and personal accounts, correcting grammatical errors and spelling mistakes and introducing consistency in references to unit designators, equipment, dates, and so on. I have generally used the local names for places, but I have used name variants familiar to English-speaking readers for features such as the Rhine and Moselle Rivers. Maps use standard NATO unit symbols where appropriate.

Harry Yeide
June 2010

Acknowledgments

I WOULD LIKE TO THANK my wife, Nancy, who is first in my book and makes me better in every endeavor, including this one. She helped ease me through a few trying moments.

Mark Reardon at the U.S. Army Center of Military History was, as always, generous with his assistance; he provided key information on the 10th Panzer Division, reviewed the manuscript, and offered helpful comments. Alexander Zeisberg went above and beyond the call to obtain a document from the Bundesarchiv. Thanks also to Mark Stout, who directed me to great material on Ultra and deception operations involving Patton. Likewise, Andy Rawlins opened my eyes to the rich resources of the George C. Marshall Foundation.

I would also like to thank the cheerful and efficient public servants at the U.S. National Archives and Records Administration's document, microfilm, still-photo, and moving-image reading rooms in College Park, Maryland, and Washington, D.C. The taxpayer is getting a good deal.

ONE

From Kid to Killer

GENERAL GEORGE S. PATTON JR. lost his life on 21 December 1945 as a legend, praised in retrospect as an armored commander even by a defeated enemy. Patton's daring and leadership had few equals among the Allied warlords, and some of his triumphs were magnificent. He earned his place in military history and popular lore. But was he really, as one of his most knowledgeable biographers, Martin Blumenson, suggested, a "hero even to professional German officers who respected him as the adversary they most feared in battle?"[1] Was it true, as Patton's World War II G-2, Col. Oscar Koch, asserted, that "where Patton was and what he was doing was of constant interest to the enemy high command?"[2] What did his mortal enemies really make of Patton and his skills as a combat commander?

How might an enemy come to know of and judge Patton as a military adversary? A man might meet him personally on the battlefield, close enough to look him in the eyes and see the sweat on his brow. Such meetings are rare in modern warfare, yet one antagonist briefly knew Patton in that way. Patton believed fervently in leading in combat from the front, and so an enemy might not see him as an individual on a faceless battlefield, yet know his hand from the tactical and moral performance of men under his command. To the extent that Patton could shape a plan executed by his subordinates, an enemy would learn his ways through the daring and conception of his schemes.

Asked about his views of American commanders after the war, Hitler's operations chief, *Generaloberst* Alfred Jodl, commented, "It is difficult, except through some very unusual stroke, to make oneself well known to the opponent." He praised Lt. Gen. Omar Bradley's strategic planning and execution of the

1

breakout from Normandy and First Army's bold seizure of the Remagen bridge. He doubtless knew who Gen. Dwight David "Ike" Eisenhower was, but Patton appeared to be the only other American general he could identify.[3]

Other, less direct considerations might come into play. The quality of soldiers and formations trained by Patton, compared with the quality of those shaped by other American officers of equivalent station, could say much. So, too, would the combat-leadership merits of the officers selected by Patton to be his chief subordinates. Patton's skill at extracting the best from his most competent subordinates and overcoming the weaknesses of those who needed corrective guidance would be particularly well understood by German opponents, because their principle of *Auftragstaktik* was nearly identical to Patton's philosophy of giving mission-type orders to subordinates. Both relied on the individual initiative of subordinates, on those subordinates' independent decision making, and on thinking leaders responding to their own tactical situations.[4] Patton had become familiar with German mission-type orders in 1935, when he read Adolf von Schell's *Battle Leadership*, though it was one part of the text where he made no marginal notes.[5] Patton believed, "a general should command one echelon down and know the position of units two echelons down."[6] By his own standard, an enemy could judge him by how he handled his immediate subordinate commanders.

Many soldiers who had experienced the fickle fortunes of war might consider Patton's luck—anathema, perhaps, to modern historians, but understood to be a decisive force in war by the likes of the ancient Romans and Napoleon Bonaparte (and, as we shall see, Eisenhower). In all these things, an enemy could consider whether Patton won or lost under odds that greatly favored or disfavored him, whether his battles were fierce crucibles of the military art or tests that any moderately competent commander could face and overcome.

We will examine the formative experiences of Patton's enemies to understand the context in which they interpreted his performance, in addition to the battle lessons and skills they brought to their fights against him. They almost invariably knew more of actual war than Patton did. Some of them were his full equals or better in the art of mobile warfare.

THE ENEMY'S ENEMY

This is not a biography of Patton, but no work about him can succeed without some picture of the man. Though it may seem odd, let us jump ahead to Patton's future to gain a sense of what he became as a man and military leader, and then let's return to a more chronological tour through his personal history, wherein his enemies appeared, one war after another.

Master of Battle, If Not Always Himself

Colonel Robert Allen, who served on Patton's staff at Third Army at the height of the general's military puissance and was able to observe his commander closely in good times and bad, concluded that to understand Patton, one had to grasp two primary characteristics: "His all-inclusive absorption in war coupled with his natural combativeness."

> Outstanding effectiveness in battle requires steel-hard ruthlessness and aggressiveness. Patton had these qualities in full measure. . . . A West Point classmate once summed up Patton as "purebred gamecock with brains. . . ."
>
> He did not become a soldier by accident or to earn a livelihood. He was five years old when he informed his parents he intended to become "a great general." When he learned to read, the first book he bought was a history of decisive battles. In school he was always organizing sham battles. On his honeymoon in France, he took his young bride to historic battlefields and fortresses. . . .
>
> Waging war was Patton's passion and avocation. All his life he consciously and purposely molded and trained himself to fight. Nothing else really mattered to him.[7]

Martin Blumenson, biographer and the organizer of Patton's papers, said of his personal character:

> He was, in fact, a complex, paradoxical, and many-faceted figure.
>
> He was unpredictable, capricious, at the same time dependable, loyal. He was brutal yet sensitive. He was gregarious and a loner. Enthusiastic and buoyant, he suffered from inner anguish. He displayed . . . an astonishing mixture of arrogance and humility.
>
> He was driven by ambition, tortured by self-doubt. . . .
>
> During his early years, even though he sought to epitomize violence, force, and drive, he was relatively stable, well-balanced, and usually mild-mannered. He played and worked hard, he was outspoken and could be blunt, but he tried to live by the code of the gentleman, the creed of the knight. . . .
>
> Part of the transformation was cultivated, self-willed. He undertook consciously to alter his image. . . . [H]e cultivated the ferocious face because he was probably concerned and worried about his voice, which was high-pitched, almost like a woman's, and because he believed that only he-men inspired troops to fight.[8]

Blumenson theorized that a head injury from a horse's kick had resulted in a subdural hematoma, which created a physiological predisposition to extreme mood swings.[9]

The result was a leader whom some adored and some loathed, at times simultaneously. General Omar Bradley, who served as Patton's subordinate and superior, recalled, "[W]hile he was profane, he was also reverent. And while he strutted imperiously as a commander, he knelt humbly before his God. . . . Patton believed that profanity was the most convincing medium of communication with his troops. But while some chuckled delightedly over the famed expletives he employed with startling originality, the majority, it seemed to me, were more often shocked and offended. . . . Patton chose to drive his subordinates by bombast and by threats. Those mannerisms achieved spectacular results."[10]

Blumenson argued that Patton's "battle proficiency flowed from his character and personality. Much of his martial ability was innate. . . ."[11]

A sketch of Patton's military qualities is best created by the prominent historians who have deeply considered his writings and deeds. Among the first was Douglass Southall Freeman, who in 1947 observed, "He was a man to win, to intrigue, and sometimes to enrage his fellow-commanders. Always he fulfilled the Napoleonic mandate of supplying by picturesque conduct the *causerie de bivouac* that makes soldiers swear at their commander and then swear by him. In the larger qualities of leadership, Patton's daring reminds one of 'Stonewall' Jackson. His determination to push straight to the Rhine of course recalls Sherman's march to the sea. Patton was cast in the mold of great American soldiers. . . ."[12]

Carlo D'Este concluded, "As a tactician, Patton ranged from superb to average in situations beyond his control. However, what separated him from his peers and cemented his reputation was his daring, freewheeling approach to modern warfare. His grasp of the capabilities of the weapons and equipment at his disposal was unexcelled."[13]

Blumenson summarized, "His exploits, there is no doubt, shortened the conflict. By his ardor and know-how, his seemingly reckless activity trans-formed campaigns, turning static, casualty-ridden warfare into exciting, mobile operations virtually free of losses. Many thought he moved instan-taneously, on the spur of the moment without deliberation. He preferred to be so regarded. In reality, he used his staff to study the options open to him, discussed with them the probable results beforehand—all this in private—then acted as though the decision was off-the-cuff. . . . No one dominated the field of battle like Patton."[14]

The Making of the Warrior

Patton was born in San Gabriel, California, on 11 November 1885, an auspicious date for a future soldier who would see his first real combat in the Great War. Patton's mother, Ruth Wilson, was the wealthy daughter of one of southern California's founding fathers. His father, George Smith Patton II, was a Virginian and an alumnus of the Virginia Military Institute (as was his grandfather, a Confederate colonel killed in action) who had made a comfortable life for himself in California as a lawyer and politician. Patton's step-grandfather, (Confederate) Col. George Smith (known to Patton as Papa), and a family friend, the great Confederate raider Col. John Singleton Mosby, imbued in the young Patton a worship of his Southern ancestors and fascination with military matters. His boyhood readings were the classics, the Bible, and military history. His games were of war, and he inscribed one toy sword with "Lt. Gen. G. S. Patton." As early as grammar school, his papers showed a grasp of tactics, troop concentration, and maneuvering. He became a fearless young horseman.

Suffering from dyslexia, which made academics exceptionally challenging, Patton enrolled in the Virginia Military Institute in 1903, which he hoped would be merely preparation for the U.S. Military Academy in West Point. His determined labors and lobbying by his father paid off, and in 1904 Patton was accepted into the cadet corps. Academics remained a challenge, and Patton had to repeat his plebe year. He excelled at the details of military life, however, and rose to become cadet adjutant. In 1909, Patton graduated 46th out of 103 in his class and received a commission as a second lieutenant in the cavalry. His classmates included William Simpson and Jacob Devers, and Courtney Hodges had dropped out of the class. These four men would form the majority of the top-level American ground-force chieftains in the European theater in World War II.

Patton reported to the 15th Cavalry Regiment at Fort Sheridan, Illinois. It was dull garrison duty, but Patton used his spare time to further his study of the military arts and to write the first of a years-long string of professional journal articles.

In 1910, Patton married Beatrice Ayer, a beautiful, smart, and musically talented debutante from an extremely wealthy Boston family. In 1911, the couple was blessed with the first of three children, a daughter named Beatrice. That year, Patton arranged a transfer to the 15th Cavalry's detachment quartered at Fort Myer, Virginia, which plugged him into the Washington social scene. The doors that opened for him there influenced the course of his professional career, starting with a chance horse-riding encounter with Secretary of War Henry Stimson that later blossomed into a lasting relationship.

Patton was a gifted polo player, and he built a competitive personal stable. In 1912, he participated in the Olympic Games in Stockholm, Sweden, where he placed fifth in the military pentathlon. The following year, Patton attended the French cavalry school in Saumur for lessons in swordsmanship. On his return, he became the army's first master of the sword and designed the M-1913 saber.

Patton graduated from the advanced course at the Cavalry School in Fort Riley, Kansas, in 1914. When war broke out in Europe in August, Patton sought permission to serve with the French cavalry as an observer, but was turned down by the U.S. War Department.

The 15th Cavalry shipped to the Philippines in 1915, and Patton used his influence in Washington to get an assignment with the 8th Cavalry, just returning from the islands, at Fort Bliss, Texas, near the Mexican border. There he came under the authority of Brig. Gen. John Pershing, who commanded the 8th Cavalry Brigade. Mexico was in the throes of civil conflict, and the self-styled revolutionary leader Francisco "Pancho" Villa was raiding American-owned properties on the Mexican side of the border. On 9 March, Villa's troops raided the town of Columbus, New Mexico, where they killed ten civilians and eight soldiers. Pershing received orders to mount an immediate punitive expedition into Mexico, and when Patton learned that his regiment would not accompany the expedition, he pulled every string he could—even appearing unannounced at Pershing's doorstep—to get assigned to Pershing's staff. As he did in so many things, Patton succeeded. By 15 March, he was in Mexico.[15]

PATTON'S FIRST MORTAL ENEMY

The last thing that passed through the mind of Col. Julio Cárdenas was a bullet fired by one of Lt. George Patton Jr's civilian scouts. Cárdenas, who may actually have been a captain or a general, sources being inconsistent on this point, led some of Villa's rough and ready personal bodyguards, *los Dorados* (the Golden Ones), so called because they wore distinctive shirts with gold sleeve fringes. Villa had formed *los Dorados* in the spring of 1913 in Ascension, Chihuahua, when he gathered the first elements of a 5,000-man army that came to be called *la Division del Norte* (the Division of the North) in order to fight the usurping Huerta regime after the murder of Mexican president Francisco Madero. Colonel Francisco Saenz, the first commander, organized and trained the disciplined cavalry force of some 600 men, who were armed with Colt .45 pistols and Mauser rifles.[16]

Having fought with Villa's *Division del Norte*, Cárdenas was the product of a culture of heroism and gallantry overlaid by one of brigandage that Patton might have appreciated. Unfortunately, as it turned out, Villa still used dashing cavalry charges against the machine-gun-equipped army of his civil war rival and head of the Constitutionalist Army, Venustiano Carranza. This method had resulted in heavy losses, but it was Pancho Villa's way. Carranza had defeated his civil war rivals and seized the Mexican presidency in 1915, and Villa had retreated to his northern stronghold.

Military gallantry was of a rough Mexican frontier type. Candelario Cervantes, who led one detachment during the Columbus raid, was heard shouting at one point, "Do not molest the women, but kill all the *gringos* [American men]!" Cervantes, at least, was a gentleman.

Cárdenas and *los Dorados* had participated in the horse-mounted raid on Columbus, launched at 0300 hours on 9 March 1916. The raid provoked the United States into launching the punitive expedition into Mexico, aimed at getting Villa and his men. The Columbus raid had ended in a *fracaso*, and Villa's men retreated across the border before 0600. Still, they had acquired arms and booty, and they retreated in good order. Once inside Mexico, Villa and his men headed south.[17]

Cárdenas remained close to Villa until his leader was shot in the leg by one of his own men during an attack on *Carrancista* forces in Guerrero on 27 March. His shinbone shattered, Villa had gone into hiding, and Cárdenas had joined a detachment of *los Dorados* commanded by Gen. Nicolas Fernandez. At this time, Col. George Dodd's 7th Cavalry Regiment was at least 150 miles to the north.[18]

Cárdenas had become impatient with Fernandez and one morning headed for home with his men.[19] The records of Pershing's intelligence office demonstrate that information collection was a haphazard affair in the expeditionary force, but somehow, in late April or on the first day of May, word reached the Americans that Cárdenas had arrived near Rubio, where Patton was billeted with the 13th Cavalry. Patton obtained permission from the regiment to hunt Cárdenas down.

On 2 May, Patton and Troop C headed for San Miguel, ten miles north of Rubio, where they found the uncle, wife, and baby of Julio Cárdenas. (In the shadow of the events at Abu Ghraib prison in Iraq in 2004, it is worth quoting Patton's letter to his father: "The uncle was a very brave man and nearly died before he would tell me anything.") Patton staked out the house in the hopes of bagging his quarry, but Cárdenas did not appear.

Patton's run of bad luck changed on the fourteenth. Patton was sent with three cars and fourteen men, four of them civilians, to buy corn. One of his guides, a former Villa soldier, spotted some men he had known in the ranks, so Patton decided to pay another visit to the uncle. Something about the man's

Key to Map Symbols
(for maps throughout)

◻️⟨O⟩	Armored/ Panzer
⊠	Infantry
⊠	Armored Infantry/ Panzergrenadier
⊠	Mountain
⊘	Mechanized Cavalry

X	Brigade/ Combat Command
XX	Divivion
XXX	Corps
XXXX	Army
——	River
▬▬	Road

behavior triggered Patton's suspicions, so he and his men headed six miles down the road to the wife's ranch at San Miguelito.

Cárdenas was home this time, enjoying the company of his family in a wood ranch house built around a courtyard that had one arched exit. Three men and a boy were skinning a cow in front of the house, doubtless for an evening *fiesta*. The group spotted Patton's team when it crested a hill less than a mile from the house and roared down the slope at full throttle. One man dashed to the house. Subsequent events suggest the following exchange took place.

"*Gringos!*"

"Get back out there and act natural!"

The man went back to the cow. Cárdenas presumably took a quick look and saw three cars and fifteen armed men. He had maybe three minutes to act. He had only two companions with him, and the rest of his men were at least fifteen minutes away. He had no idea how many more Americans might be coming. The mountains were close, offering shelter, and his horse could cover the rough ground in between while cars could not. Cárdenas ran to the still-saddled horses with his *compañeros* as the car bearing Patton whipped by the front door and slammed to a stop. Men piled out, guns drawn. The following cars stopped at prearranged spots; one group was positioned to assault the house with Patton's team and the other to provide covering fire.

Cárdenas and Patton were about to engage in a most primitive form of mortal combat. Movie heroics aside, relatively few soldiers, even among the infantry, are presented with the opportunity to engage their foes eye-to-eye.

The shootout at this rundown, dusty, Mexican ranch was a near perfect foreword to the story of Patton's fighting career. Cárdenas had much more battle experience than Patton, a man in his first fight, and most of Patton's enemies would be able to say the same. Patton outnumbered his enemy in manpower, had more firepower, and had more mechanization, as would almost always be the case in Patton's battles. Cárdenas was trying to get out of Patton's way, and that would be true in nearly every great triumph Patton was to win. When the enemy stood and fought, Patton fared less well. The drama flared like a fast fuse, and the speed of Patton's actions would surprise many an enemy. Then there is the matter of luck: Patton had it, and Cárdenas did not.

Cárdenas and his men rode through the courtyard archway, rifles and pistols in hand, and Cárdenas saw Patton, a rifle in his left hand, and an unarmed man only fifteen yards away. The Mexicans spun away and heard a shout in English: "Halt!" They probably did not know Patton had drawn his pistol, a new ivory-handled Colt .45 Model 1873 single-action revolver that he would carry until his death. Reaching the corner of the building, the men saw the second group of American troopers approaching.

The three horsemen spun back toward Patton and charged, firing their weapons. Patton returned fire with his pistol at twenty yards. Patton recalled, "Three of them [were] shooting at me about fifteen yards off. I kept wondering why they did not hit me. The guns seemed pointed right at me."

One of Patton's bullets struck Cárdenas in the arm and broke it, and he spun back toward the archway as Patton and the other man ducked behind the corner of the building, chased by bullets. The fugitive's horse had been hit, too, and Cárdenas was already thinking of a backup route. He raced through the house, leapt out a window, and ran along a wall. A bullet fired by a trooper penetrated one of his lungs and a second shot knocked him to the ground. A civilian scout, E. M. Holmdahl, approached Cárdenas, and the Mexican raised a hand as if to surrender. Then he whipped around his pistol and fired. He missed, and Holmdahl blew his brains out. The other two *Villistas* were also dead. The shootout had lasted fifteen minutes.

The Americans searched the house, but found no one other than the dead man's wife and baby and a few other women. Patton recovered Cárdenas's silver-inlaid saddle and saber as trophies, which he kept, and tossed two of the corpses onto the hoods of the cars, like game. Before the Americans could recover Cárdenas's body, they spotted a group of thirty armed men galloping toward them a thousand yards away. Patton decided it was time to go, and so his party did.[20]

The bloody ritual was complete. Patton had become a warrior in a way that probably seemed fit to a man who believed he had been reincarnated repeatedly and had, in a past life, fought in the age of the sword.

TWO

✳

All Violent on the Western Front

T HE GERMANS WOULD GET their first taste of Patton when he was a tank officer in World War I. But only a taste it would be, because Patton would be in actual combat against them for only four days.

The United States entered the Great War on 6 April 1917 and the following month implemented general conscription. On 26 May, Maj. Gen. John Pershing assumed command of the new American Expeditionary Forces (AEF) bound for war-torn France. One of the first men he tapped for his staff was Patton, who sailed for Europe with Pershing on the SS *Baltic* on 28 May. By scraping together most of the peacetime regular army plus a regiment of Marines, the United States was able to send a single division, the 1st Infantry, to France. The United States had to build the rest of a modern army from scratch.

Patton being Patton, he grew tired of staff work and put his name into consideration for the soon-to-be-organized Tank Corps. He argued that tank action was much like cavalry warfare and, referring to the incident at San Miguelito, pointed out that he was the only officer in the army who had conducted a vehicle-mounted attack. Pershing offered him command of an infantry battalion as a major, but after nearly accepting, Patton decided to go with the tanks when he heard that a school was being set up near Langres.[1]

World War I was a conventional enemy's first opportunity to observe Patton in battle. It was unique in that some of his German foes saw him personally at short ranges, while many others got their first taste of him in the form of the sword that Patton forged: the first American tank brigade to see combat.

Thereafter, Patton's enemies would almost always have to judge him on the basis of his will as applied through the men and equipment placed at his disposal.

Patton's force of will and his intellect shaped and formed the American 1st Tank Brigade, which initially consisted of the 1st and 2nd Tank Battalions (redesignated the 326th and 327th Tank Battalions in June 1918). The U.S. Army, which was the source of the Caterpillar-style track system that made tanks possible, played no role in the creation of early armored fighting vehicles.[2] The army first displayed serious interest in the new weapon when it dispatched Maj. Frank Parker to observe French tank operations in April 1917. The French fielded two vehicles, the St. Chaumond and the Schneider, that resembled armored artillery carriers rather than true tanks. Parker's report highlighted two problems that would trouble American armored and infantry forces through both world wars: the armored vehicles of the time easily caught fire when hit, and tank-infantry coordination was faulty. On several occasions, Allied tanks went ahead of the infantry, and many were destroyed.[3]

The British preferred to use heavy tanks alongside the infantry, while the French opted for light tanks. The British sent the two arms forward together, whereas the French preferred to hold tanks back with battalion-support elements until the riflemen got bogged down. Shortly after Pershing arrived in June 1917, he formed committees to study the British and French operations at the front and their equipment.[4] The tank board concluded in a report on 1 September that the tank was going to become an important element in the war.[5]

Americans often think big, and their plans for the Tank Corps were vast in scope. The army, as of September 1917, anticipated needing enough tanks to support twenty infantry divisions, and it decided to organize five heavy- and twenty light-tank battalions. Efforts started to launch American production of most of the 375 Mark VIII heavy tanks and 1,500 Renault light tanks that would be needed, but constant delays resulted in the completion of only ten Renaults by the armistice.[6]

As far as the AEF were concerned, any lingering debate about the usefulness of tanks evaporated following the battle of Cambrai, which started 20 November 1917. Though the British ended up losing more ground than they gained in their opening attack, tanks proved instrumental in achieving an initial penetration of 10,000 yards into the German line. The function of tanks, the U.S. Army decided, was to assist the infantry by making a path through the wire and to protect it from destructive loss by machine guns and rifle fire.[7]

It is difficult to put oneself in those times because the tank is so familiar now, but the weapon was new, hot, and stood to be the atomic bomb of its age when it came to trench warfare. Patton saw the promise, and in November 1917, he agreed to take command of the training school for light tanks to be established in Langres. On 10 November he became the first official American tanker.[8] Patton and Lt. Elgin Braine, appointed his assistant, reported to the French light-tank school, where they mastered the new French Renault FT17 tank and were enthusiastic about the vehicle. Indeed, they had ideas for improving the design. The AEF cabled the War Department and requested rapid action to begin construction of the FT17 in the United States.[9]

Stateside production could not crank up fast enough, so the French supplied Renault light tanks for American training use and, by August 1918, provided two battalions' worth (144 vehicles). Patton himself crafted both the organizational framework for tank battalions and the doctrine for using tanks with infantry that would still be in use in the next world war. He trained his men as realistically as he could and demanded perfect discipline. By August, the school in Langres had turned out 600 crewmen. Twelve more companies' worth of crews were beginning to arrive from the States, where a training center had been established in Raleigh, North Carolina. In mid-September, the British supplied a battalion of forty-seven Mark V heavy tanks. Eight hundred men had completed training on these heavy tanks in the United Kingdom by late August, and 1,200 tankers were in British schools.[10]

All U.S. Tank Corps troops were subordinated to Pershing's general headquarters to be allocated to the armies according to terrain and other circumstances of operations. Planners assumed that only two of the three armies would be able to use tanks at any one time. Each of those two armies was to be allocated a tank headquarters, five brigades (each with one light and two heavy battalions), and a training center. Tank brigades were to train and maneuver with the infantry divisions beside which they would fight. While this scheme was implemented, in reality, only the tank battalions equipped by the Allies ever went into combat.[11]

ST. MIHIEL: AMERICA'S FIRST OFFENSIVE, PATTON'S FIRST BATTLE

Things looked grim to Patton's enemies. The Central Powers were on the strategic defensive all along the western front following the failure in July 1918 of their general offensive in the second battle of the Marne. This set a pattern for all of Patton's dealings with the enemy: the other fellow would nearly always be on his back foot and fighting a defensive war. This meant that Patton never really had to prove himself capable as a commander in a major defensive battle.

Fate determined that Patton would fight across nearly the same patch of ground in Lorraine in two world wars. General John Pershing, in his final report on the war, explained how the Americans were allotted the St. Mihiel salient

and Meuse-Argonne sector for the first offensives by an American army in the European war:

> A further conference at the headquarters of [Supreme Allied Commander] Marshal [Ferdinand] Foch was held on 2 September, at which [commander-in-chief of the French Army] Gen. [Philippe] Pétain was present. After discussion the question of employing the American Army as a unit was conceded. The essentials of the strategical decision previously arrived at provided that the advantageous situation of the Allies should be exploited to the utmost by vigorously continuing the general battle and extending it eastward to the Meuse. All the Allied armies were to be employed in a converging action. The British armies, supported by the left of the French armies, were to pursue the attack in the direction of Cambrai; the center of the French armies, west of Rheims, would continue the actions, already begun, to drive the enemy beyond the Aisne; and the American Army, supported by the right of the French armies, would direct its attack on Sedan and Mezières. . .

The choice between the two sectors, that east of the Aisne including the Argonne Forest, or the Champagne sector, was left to me. In my opinion, no other Allied troops had the morale or the offensive spirit to overcome successfully the difficulties to be met in the Meuse Argonne sector and our plans and installations had been prepared for an expansion of operations in that direction. So the Meuse Argonne front was chosen. The entire sector of 150 kilometers of front, extending from Port-sur-Seille, east of the Moselle, west to include the Argonne Forest, was accordingly placed under my command, including all French divisions then in that zone. The First American Army was to proceed with the St. Mihiel operation, after which the operation between the Meuse and the western edge of the Argonne Forest was to be prepared and launched not later than September 25.

The [St. Mihiel] salient had been held by the Germans since September 1914. It covered the most sensitive section of the enemy's position on the Western Front; namely, the Mezières-Sedan-Metz Railroad and the Briey Iron Basin; it threatened the entire region between Verdun and Nancy, and interrupted the main rail line from Paris to the east. Its primary strength lay in the natural defensive features of the terrain itself. The western face of the salient extended along the rugged, heavily wooded eastern heights of the Meuse; the southern face followed the heights of the Meuse for eight kilometers to the east and then crossed the plain of the Woevre, including within the German lines the detached heights of Loupmont and Montsec which dominated the plain and afforded the enemy unusual facilities for observation. The enemy had reinforced the positions by every artificial means during a period of four years.[12]

On 15 August, Pershing wrote to Foch that he would need 150 heavy and 300 light tanks from the French to support his attack on the salient. Two days later, Foch replied that he would equip two American light-tank battalions and attach three French light battalions, and that he had asked the British to loan 150 heavy tanks. The British replied that all their heavy tanks were already committed.[13]

On 20 August, the American 304th Tank Brigade was attached to First Army for planned operations at St. Mihiel. (At this time, the formation was called the 1st Tank Brigade, and its two components were the 326th and 327th Tank Battalions. The designations were changed between the St. Mihiel and Meuse-Argonne operations in September, and this account uses the later numbers for clarity and consistency with the after-action reports.) Lieutenant Colonel George Patton, who took command of the new brigade that very day, reported to the commanding general of V Corps, which was to attack the western face of the salient. Patton conducted a complete survey of the area between Verdun, Haudimont, Ville-en-Woevre, and Tresauvaux along a five-kilometer front. The St. Mihiel salient was poor tank country. Trenches were wide and crumbling, and the water table was just below the surface, so that even a little rain created extensive bogs.[14]

Worse, definitive word arrived on 25 August that no heavy tanks, which could cross trenches and carve out routes for light tanks to follow, would arrive from the British. Their six-pounder (75mm) guns also would be absent, and the Renault carried only a 37mm (one-pounder) cannon or an 8mm Hotchkiss machine gun. The Renaults would be unable to reach the wire along most of the front, and engineers would have to prepare a route over any gap wider than six feet. A planned thirty-one-hour artillery barrage was likely to render much of the terrain impassable to the light tanks. Nevertheless, four French light-tank battalions, one more than promised, were added to support the offensive.[15]

It might have added up to a first American tank fiasco, but Patton was a lucky man. On 3 September, Patton's brigade was switched from V Corps to IV Corps, and Patton had to reconnoiter a new area of operations from Boucenville to Bois de Hazelleine. Here, at least, the Renaults could reach the wire and the trenches. The French provided thirty-three St. Chaumond and Schneider heavy tanks, but it was already known that they were incapable of leading the infantry. Early on 11 September, the French warned that the Renaults they were providing should not go into battle until they had been run for twelve days. That afternoon, a second warning arrived that due to rain, tanks would not be able to operate. To these messages, Patton replied that as long as there were fewer than two inches of mud, it would act as a lubricant, and the tanks would fight.[16]

First Army was to attack the St. Mihiel salient with a drive from south to north by I and IV Corps and another west to east by V Corps. IV Corps, consisting of the 1st and 42nd Infantry Divisions, was to attack on the front Limey-Rechicourt. The plan for the 304th Tank Brigade assigned twenty-four Schneiders of the French 14th and 17th Groups and the 345th (then 327th) Tank Battalion, less sixteen tanks, to the 42nd Infantry Division. The point of departure was the east edge of the Bois de Remieres. The 344th (then 326th) Tank Battalion was attached to the 1st Infantry Division, and its departure point was north of Xivray.[17]

Patton issued a special instruction to his tank battalions that read, in part:

> From a tactical point of view the present operation is easy. A complete success insures [sic] the future of the Tank Corps in which all have shown by their long and cheerful work that they are fully interested. . . . Remember that you are to make paths through the wire and put out machine gun nests for

the infantry; hence do not leave them. Never get more than a hundred and fifty yards ahead of them and never let them get ahead of you or, if they do, hurry to regain your place. No tank is to be surrendered or abandoned to the enemy. If you are left alone in the midst of the enemy keep shooting. If your gun is disabled use your pistol and squash the enemy with your tracks.[18]

The Enemy

Army Group Gallwitz, which consisted of Fifth Army and Army Detachment (*Armeeabteilung*) C, defended the Verdun sector, including the St. Mihiel salient.[19] *General der Artillerie* Max von Gallwitz commanded the army group that bore his name. The sector had been quiet for most of the year and had become a rest and reorganization area for worn-out divisions.[20] *Generalleutnant* Georg Fuchs commanded Army Detachment C, which had responsibility for the salient itself, the main defenses of which were part of the Hindenburg Line. All but one of the divisions at Fuchs's disposal were rated third class.[21] Group Gorz, named after the town southwest of Metz, appears to have functioned as a corps headquarters, and it held the zone opposite IV Corps with its 10th Infantry Division, flanked to the left by its 77th Reserve Division and to the right by Group Mihiel's 5th *Landwehr* (Territorial Guard) Division. The 31st Infantry Division constituted Group Gorz's reserve.[22]

Generalmajor Otto Adam *Freiherr* von Diepenbroick-Grüter (who fortunately signed his name simply Grüter), born 18 July 1860 in Düsseldorf, Germany, commanded the 10th Infantry Division. Grüter had commanded the 110th Grenadier Regiment Kaiser Wilhelm I, 28th Infantry Division, at the outbreak of the war, and within two months had stepped up to command the 58th Infantry Brigade, 29th Infantry Division. He had taken command of the 10th Infantry Division on 10 May 1917. On 13 June, Grüter had received the Pour le Mérite.[23]

The 10th Infantry Division had been in the St. Mihiel area for most of the time since it had gone into battle on 22 August 1914 near Virton, France. The division's recruiting area in Posen was inhabited mainly by Poles, and because there were many Poles in the ranks, the army had mixed in Prussian companies to improve reliability. In 1916, the 10th Division had suffered such a drubbing at French hands that it had been withdrawn to reorganize and refit. The division had been heavily engaged during 1918 in the battles of Picardy, the Aisne, and the Marne. Indeed, the American 3rd Infantry Division's successful defense against the 10th Division had earned it the nickname "Rock of the Marne." Rated first class, Grüter's division was at full authorized strength and equipment, despite heavy losses suffered along the Marne, because it had absorbed the 255th

Infantry Division on 7 August. But its drafts were of low quality, and its fighting value had declined.[24]

Grüter's commanders were about to place him in the worst possible circumstances to face a massive, tank-backed American offensive. Gallwitz offered this description of his operational posture on the eve of the American offensive:

> Our position between the Meuse and the well-known height of Combre, southeast of Verdun, looked like a [protruding] nose. It had taken this [shape] after the first battle in the summer of 1914, and had been retained, fortified, and honored as the field of many single combats.
>
> We had seven divisions that occupied this line [plus two in reserve], but they were reduced in number and among them were three of the militia [*Landwehr*] and one Austrian division. The peril of this faulty triangle had always been patent to us. It lent itself to attack on all sides. We had repeatedly discussed the question of giving up this triangle. The chief in command agreed with me that no big battle in this territory was permissible.
>
> But while we waited, the crisis came on apace. We never had time to carry off the materials we had gathered during an occupation of several years. On the other side lay the consideration that the yielding of a position held for years would be interpreted as a sign of weakness. Naturally we disregarded such considerations when the situation in other parts of the theater of war was difficult.
>
> There had been indications that something was brewing on the other side, but we were not certain as to which direction the attack might take. We were informed that the objective of the Americans was Metz and the territory east of that fortress, which would threaten our communication with the rear. . . .
>
> Then from foreign sources came the news that the American attack had been postponed—that the army was not yet ready for a big offensive movement.
>
> We were surprised, therefore, when, on September 12, a concentrated attack was launched against the triangle. It was soon demonstrated that this was not a partial attack, but the execution of a great concentrated drive. The order to retire, which I gave on my own responsibility, but too late, could not prevent the loss of many troops and much material, which had to be left behind.
>
> The first deep advance took place on the southern side and was directed against two of our divisions, extending some twenty-three kilometers. Against the front covered by this attack nine or ten American divisions were led into battle, six being held in reserve.

The two divisions that I had in reserve behind the southern front could not succeed in turning the tide.[25]

The 10th Infantry Division held the German line in the sector where Patton's tanks were to enter battle. By now, the German army had put a great deal of thinking into the problem of stopping tanks. The Germans recognized that passive antitank barriers could only slow enemy armor, not stop it entirely. Active measures, therefore, were to backstop antitank barriers.

By 1918, German doctrine considered the 77mm field gun the most effective element of their active antitank defense. The field gun n/A 96 (model 1896)—the rough equivalent of the French 75mm, but much lighter—firing brass cartridge casings could reliably kill Allied tanks at 1,500 meters with any type of round. The gun could be effective beyond that range when firing a soft-nosed shell. The field gun 16, also 77mm, was deemed to have too low a rate of fire to be useful.

Antitank rifles could penetrate armor only from less than 500 meters, and the German policy was to put several rifles in the hands of experienced, cool-headed soldiers. By 1918, a special soft-point round for trench mortars, capable of penetrating armor plate, was available. Bomb-throwers for close defense were assumed to be able to get, at best, a lucky kill.[26]

The defenders had done what they could to prepare for Patton and his tanks. The 10th Infantry Division controlled some number of antitank guns (*Tankgeschütze*).[27] Group Gorz, moreover, had obtained some German tanks to conduct displays for the line divisions of their capabilities against tank traps and obstacles at Xammes, not far from the front. The displays were to be as realistic as possible, so troops would have no false impressions about armor.[28] The real impressions were bad enough. Put yourself in the boots of a German rifleman, who has survived for months or years in disease-ridden, waterlogged trenches. The other side, when he attacks you, first rains shells on you, quite likely including poison gas, and then when the infantry closes with you, he has beside him lethal and strange steel monsters against which you have no weapon or protection.

As Gallwitz indicated, a retirement order reached the 10th Infantry Division at 1100 hours on 11 September, stipulating that as of 0400 hours the next morning, what was then the artillery protective position would become the new main line of resistance. (This account uses German time, which was one hour ahead of the clock used by the Allies, e.g., 0600 for the Germans is 0500 for the Allies.) *Generalleutnant* Fuchs, anticipating an imminent attack, had issued the implementation order on his own authority from Army Detachment C and obtained Gallwitz's approval shortly thereafter. Preliminary plans for a withdrawal had already been forwarded to units on 9 September. The horse-drawn German artillery limbered up and began pulling out at 2200 hours. Rain started to fall.[29]

Ground patrols and aerial reconnaissance had given no hint to the division that an American attack was imminent, though bad weather cut flights short on 11 September. Heavy truck traffic had been observed behind American lines, but Allied air activity had been light. American artillery had dropped only light harassing fire on German positions. Reports of heavy nighttime traffic that could be tanks were dismissed on 5 September, but then two reports of tanks in the vicinity of Noviant reached the division on 10 September. Then, the evening of 11 September, a priority message arrived from Group Gorz: a downed American pilot reported that First Army was about to attack near St. Mihiel with ten divisions, while French troops would strike near Les Eparges. The goal was to eliminate the St. Mihiel salient.[30]

The 10th Infantry Division's heart was *Oberst* Wild's 20th Infantry Brigade, which consisted of three regiments. *Oberstleutnant* Grussdorf's 6th Grenadier and *Oberstleutnant* Gerlach's 47th Infantry Regiments held the line in the zone assigned to the 42nd Infantry Division's tank-infantry team. Each regiment was spread out across a front of five kilometers, in a series of strong points. The 398th Infantry Regiment held Montsec against the 1st Infantry Division.[31]

The combat companies were, naturally, to be the last units to pull back, and they were left in the dark about the plan so that their determination to resist any encroachment would not be undermined. Behind them, work parties were still preparing the artillery protective line, which consisted of a continuous wire entanglement and abandoned trenches. There were no shelters or dugouts for the men.

The American artillery barrage beginning at 0200 hours caught much the 10th Infantry Division in the open as its units implemented the withdrawal order, accurately ripping into headquarters, communication centers, and crossroads as far back as the train station St. Benoit-Beney-Thiaucourt. Gas clouds floated onto Montsec and woods nearby. Shells crashed into the artillery protective line, tearing up wire and trenches and sending terrified work parties scrambling for whatever cover they could find. Almost immediately, German communications were reduced to visual signals (such as signal lights) and to foot and horse-mounted messengers. Only one telephone line running from an artillery battery in Beney to the division headquarters remained intact, which allowed the division to obtain some information about developments.

At 0230 hours, an ominous message reached the 10th Infantry Division headquarters: "Antitank guns appear to have withdrawn." Patton had just had

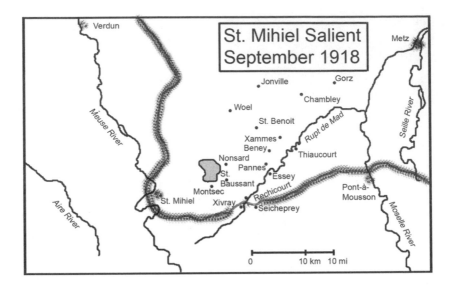

his first lucky break of the attack, and the artillery preparation had barely just begun.

By 0400, the 398th Infantry Regiment had generally completed its initial evacuations intact. The 2nd Battalion on its left wing, however, endured a shelling that caused heavy casualties. Officers desperately yelled orders to get the other two battalions in motion under covering fire from the construction companies, but the work crews had suffered heavy losses and were scattered in the jet-black night. Withdrawal of some artillery was delayed because horse teams could not move forward through the crushing artillery fire. An ordnance officer sent forward to establish contact with the front line reported that the road toward Essey was under heavy fire and covered with shattered limbers and wagons and dead and wounded horses.

By 0500, the shifting artillery explosions made it clear that the main attack would hit the center and left of the 10th Division line and the right wing of the 77th Reserve Division. *Generalmajor* Grüter ordered his own artillery to lay down waves of destructive fire (*Trommelfeuer*) in front of his lines in those areas. The general then went forward to command the fighting.[32]

At 0600 hours, forward positions reported seeing yellow and a few red lights appearing on the American side, an indication that Yank infantry was moving forward. The first American infantry attack struck at the Sonnard wood at 0630, and the 47th Infantry Regiment fell out of contact with the division. At 0715, the 398th Infantry Regiment reported that it was being smoked and could no longer see the American signal lights. Fifteen minutes later, Group Gorz passed along that the 77th Reserve Division had been under attack since 0700, and the 31st Infantry Division was already moving forward from reserve positions toward Xammes. Ten minutes after that, word arrived of strong American blows between Beney and Thiaucourt.[33]

The 345th Tank Battalion attacked with the 42nd Infantry Division that morning on the corps's right wing with two companies forward, each with two platoons forward and one in support. From a hill just behind the front line, Patton watched his tanks grind toward the enemy, and from that vantage point, he could see both of his battalions and the French heavies. After overcoming some initial qualms caused by artillery fire, he climbed from his trench and sat on the parapet, where the view was better. Because of the extensively entrenched terrain, the tanks followed the infantry until after they had crossed the Trenches d'Houblons. Progress was slow, and the tanks came under artillery fire while crossing the Trenches d'Houblons, two tanks taking direct hits. "I could see them coming along and getting stuck in the trenches," recorded Patton. "It was a most irritating sight."[34]

The men in the 10th Infantry Division watched the tanks approach with the American infantry, most of the vehicles led by the commanding officer on foot. The after-action report by the 2nd Battalion, 6th Grenadier Regiment, claims that it managed to immobilize several tanks, at least temporarily: "At 0600, the enemy attack began. It was carried out behind a line of tanks against the edge of the Sonnard woods. The assault was driven back with rifles, machine guns, and grenades. Tanks were taken under fire with S.m.K. [armor-piercing] munitions and destroyed or forced to turn back. *Unteroffizier* Krien of the 2d Machine-Gun Company at the Munich strong point succeeded in knocking out three tanks with his machine gun. One crashed, and the other two stopped. The crews of all three bailed out and were taken under fire. . . ."

The American attack drove through the defenses west of the 2nd Battalion and was into the trenches to the east. The battalion fell back by bounds, inflicting casualties on the enemy at each new position and finally stopping at the "green line" about half the distance back to Essey by 0800. *Vizefeldwebel* Hecke managed to down an American plane with his machine gun. The companies in the Sonnard woods, having never gotten a withdrawal order, held until 0820 hours and were never seen again; they had fulfilled their never-changed orders to defend the main line of resistance to the last man. The 2nd Battalion reported, "Before 1000, the enemy attack began again. A mass of tanks and infantry hit our line."[35]

In the zone defended by the 3rd Battalion, 47th Infantry Regiment, four light tanks and two heavy tanks, at 0715 hours tried to push down the road from

Seicheprey to St. Baussant, but artillery and mortars in St. Baussant were able to stop the advance. Word arrived that the 6th Grenadier Regiment's line to the left was giving way. An American infantry attack at 0800 carried St. Baussant, and the 3rd Battalion fell back to the "green line."[36]

Patton, about that time, moved forward two miles to within 800 yards of Montsec. When his telephone wire ran out, he left his adjutant with the phone and, accompanied by a lieutenant and four runners, went to find the tanks. "[T]he whole country was alive with them crawling over trenches and into woods," he recalled.[37]

At 0920 hours, a carrier pigeon arrived at the 10th Infantry Division headquarters with a message from the 1st Battalion, 47th Infantry Regiment: "Former main line of resistance in enemy's hands. . . . Hoppe." Twenty minutes later, word arrived by the artillery telephone line saying that the 6th Regiment could hold only if it got another battalion of artillery. Contact with the 77th Reserve Division had failed, and as a consequence, the 2nd *Landsturm* Battalion was made available to plug the hole on the division's left.[38]

Advised by a runner at about 1015 hours that the 345th Tank Battalion was delayed by bad ground, Patton headed west to find the stuck tanks.[39] Patton's tankers were already moving, however. Once past the great trench work, the American tanks moved ahead of the infantry toward Essey. Pressed by the tanks and infantry, the 2nd Battalion, 6th Grenadier Regiment, was flanked to both sides again and retreated to some high ground above the Madine Creek east of Essey. There, the exhausted men drove off four infantry probes supported by six tanks. The last attack receded just in time: machine-gun ammunition was exhausted.[40]

Patton arrived at the infantry's front line south of Essey, where he found all the riflemen hiding in shell holes except for their brigade commanding officer, Brig. Gen. Douglas MacArthur, whom Patton joined on a hill overlooking the scene. A desultory German barrage marched toward the two men, but neither chose to take cover.

For the first time, the Patton who would exploit fluidity on the battlefield for aggressive maneuver grasped the sword he had forged and acted. Patton could see the Germans streaming northward out of Essey, and he told a platoon of his tanks to drive into town. A French officer at the bridge over the Madine Creek forbade them from advancing because of shellfire, so an angry Patton led the Renaults forward on foot into the village. There, he prudently got behind the tanks and accepted the surrender of several Germans.

Patton asked MacArthur for permission to push into Pannes, some two miles away, and the general agreed. Patton and his five tanks set off.[41]

The left wing of the 47th Infantry Regiment's line was collapsing, and the regiment backpedaled toward Beney. The 3rd Battalion set up machine guns to cover the main road east of the town church in Pannes. At 1500 hours, *Leutnant* Dewald and his machine gunners watched a tall American officer with a walking stick approach along the road with four Renaults (one had run out of gas). Dewald's guns by now were out of armor-piercing ammunition, and his rifle support had failed to come up. The battalion's after-action report related, "When the tanks closed within 400 meters, Lt. Dewald withdrew, turning from time to time to present his front. The tanks caused heavy casualties." The battalion pulled back to a hill east of the road to Beney.

By the time Patton reached Pannes, three more tanks had run out of fuel. Patton told the sergeant commanding the last tank to roll into town and, because the sergeant seemed nervous, climbed aboard the rear deck to encourage him. A lieutenant and runner joined Patton. In Pannes, the tankers captured thirty Germans, and the tank passed through town and down the road toward Beney, Patton riding sidesaddle on top.

Soon, the 3rd Battalion opened up on the tank, and with paint chips flying about his legs, Patton jumped off into a shell hole. The tank, its commander unaware of what had happened, kept going. The closest American infantry were 200 yards to the rear. A runner near Patton was hit and went down, and the infantry showed no inclination to advance into the fire. Chased by machine-gun bullets, Patton advanced obliquely to the rear so it would not look like he was running. There, the major commanding the 1st Battalion, 167th Infantry, declined to advance to support the tank because his flank was exposed.

Patton, therefore, ran toward the receding tank, which was possible because it was clanking forward at the speed of a walking man. He rapped on the back door with his walking stick, and when the sergeant opened it to ask what Patton wanted, Patton told the disappointed man to turn around. Patton used the tank to shield himself from Dewald's machine guns during the return trip.

This was a missed opportunity, because at that moment the Germans in Beney were totally disorganized, with only one company under control of its officers. After supporting a renewed infantry drive to the Bois de Thiaucourt, seven Renaults preceded the infantry toward some woods northeast of Beney, where they drove out several machine guns and overran a battery of 77mm guns. *Oberst* Wild, who had arrived in Beney to sort things out, received a report on the American force, but by this time, he judged that if the attack continued toward town, he could easily deal with it.

Grüter moved his command post to a hill south of Beney and ordered the 47th Infantry Regiment to commit all its resources to stabilizing a line along a

J.R. 47
Lager 1º.π.
12/9.18

This German sketch map records the withdrawal of the 47th Infantry Regiment, through Essey and Pannes to Beney and the positioning of the machine guns (·|·) that fired on Patton on 12 September 1918.

ravine near Pannes. The Americans nevertheless poked a hole through the regiment's line, and the 6th Grenadier Regiment's left, exposed by the collapse of the 77th Reserve Division's right, was hit from the flank and rear. Grüter pulled the rest of his line back behind the Rupt de Mad River, and the arrival of a second reserve battalion from the 31st Infantry Division enabled him to stabilize his position for the remainder of the day. Orders arrived from Group Gorz at 2145 for the 10th Infantry Division to fall back to the area of Château Chembly, and it broke off contact with the Americans without incident.[42]

*

Oberstleutnant Zickhardt's 398th Infantry Regiment, on the 10th Infantry Division's right wing, confronted the left-most American tank-infantry attack. The 1st Battalion reported, "At daybreak we saw in the enemy's rear about seventy tanks in readiness positions and newly erected medical tents." The tanks rolled out about 0800 toward the zone to the battalion's left, and one company took them under long-distance fire. Those tanks hit the regiment's 2nd Battalion, which was deployed on the regiment's left wing along what the Germans called Cannon woods and the French Bois de Rate.[43]

The 344th Tank Battalion was able to precede the 1st Division infantry using the same tactical formation as its running mate, and the tanks cut through wire entanglements for the doughboys. Several tanks engaged German machine guns in the Bois de Rate.[44] The 2nd Battalion, 398th Regiment, reported:

> About 0700 twelve to fifteen thick infantry waves left the enemy's trenches at Xivray and east thereof. Shortly thereafter, twelve tanks drove up the road from Xivray toward Rechicourt. About 1600 [sic], eighty to ninety tanks followed. By noon, the two machine guns in the covering company, which was farthest forward, had expended all of their ammunition and had to withdraw.
>
> They had given the enemy a sharp reverse. About 1000, the enemy entered Cannon woods, having flanked them to the right under the protection of artillery and two tanks, where they were engaged by two machine guns of the 2d Machine-Gun Company from a distance of seventy-five meters. Unfortunately, the machine guns were attacked from three sides, defended themselves to the last cartridge, and fell into enemy hands.

The battalion committed its reserve and drove the Americans back, but the retreat of the neighboring 47th Infantry Regiment exposed the flank and rear to attack. The 2nd Battalion fell back. Meanwhile, the regiment's mortar company at Montsec, which had been given antitank defense as its primary task, could not see the tanks because of smoke and gas and fired at visible infantry instead.[45]

Many Renaults became hung up in the trench works, but twenty-five got through and reached Nonsard, one of the 1st Division's objectives. The 3rd Battalion, 398th Infantry Regiment, had just withdrawn to this area. It had been told, "Don't count on any support."

Oberstleutnant Makert, the 3rd Battalion commanding officer, reported, "About noon we received word from the machine guns on the high ground that the enemy was approaching Nonsard supported by tanks. As I myself can establish, the enemy advanced in thick lines with the tanks toward Nonsard. The follow-on lines enveloped the flank of Company 9, which reported this immediately."

A machine gunner in the steeple of the town's church opened fire on the tanks advancing into town ahead of the infantry. Before dying, the German gunner apparently had winged the nose of Maj. Sereno Brett, the tank battalion commander, who blasted the machine gun with his 37mm cannon. Several tanks laid down fire on machine guns and some 77mm guns situated along the edge of nearby woods.

Makert ordered his men to pull back. As they did, American tanks and machine guns took them under heavy fire. The battalion's withdrawal put the left flank of the 5th *Landwehr* Division in great jeopardy.

The tanks had used up fuel at three times the expected rate as they got through the mud and trenches, and all machines were dry by 1500 hours. This was doubtless a great relief to the defenders, who had spotted the tank concentration and concluded they faced a massive attack. Several tanks dragged fuel forward by sleds, but the Renaults were out of action for the day.

The Schneiders, meanwhile, had followed the infantry by such a distance that they never went into action. A 150mm shell struck one and killed fifteen men.[46] Patton, who was passing through St. Baussant at the same time as the town was being shelled, had just spoken with a French officer working on the tank and had gone barely twenty feet when the shell hit the vehicle.[47] He was a lucky man.

By 1430 hours, the 10th Infantry Division's 47th Infantry Regiment was a shambles, the 398th Infantry Regiment was out of contact with the division's headquarters, and the 6th Regiment was hanging on to some high ground north of Madine Creek with a few rifle companies. Group Gorz ordered the division to withdraw through the 5th *Landwehr* Division and reorganize as a reserve. The three infantry regiments had lost 4,150 men.[48]

The tanks were not used on 13 September, and the 344th Tank Battalion completely lost contact with the 1st Infantry Division. The next day, the tankers set off toward the sound of the guns in hope of finding the doughboys, and they did so at Kil, at about 0900. The infantry reported that the next village, Woel, had been taken by the French, and a patrol of three tanks and five dismounted men moved off to establish contact. The officer in command at 1330 reported that Woel was clear of the enemy and that he was returning.

Thirty minutes later, the tiny command crossed paths with an infantry battalion supported by 77mm guns and machine guns. The tankers say they were attacked, which may well describe the first contact; however, a captured

German report indicated that the battalion from the 65th *Landwehr* Infantry Regiment was intended to fill the gap, but instead was resting at the time the tanks appeared. A runner reached the tank battalion in Kil, and five Renaults roared off to help. The eight light tanks struck back, unsupported by infantry, and drove the Germans six miles to Jonville. The tankers attempted to tow several abandoned 77mm guns back with them, but after enemy fire wounded six men, they abandoned the effort.[49]

Pershing summed up in his final report, "The rapidity with which our divisions advanced overwhelmed the enemy, and all objectives were reached by the afternoon of September 13. The enemy had apparently started to withdraw some of his troops from the tip of the salient on the eve of our attack, but had been unable to carry it through. We captured nearly 16,000 prisoners, 443 guns, and large stores of material and supplies. The energy and swiftness with which the operation was carried out enabled us to smother opposition to such an extent that we suffered less than 7,000 casualties during the actual period of the advance."[50]

The 304th Tank Brigade was relieved from attachment to IV Corps on 16 September, and Patton for the first time basked in the praise of his superiors for his performance in battle. Major General Charles Summerall, commanding the 1st Infantry Division, wrote to Patton, "The operation of tanks in a most difficult country and under the most trying conditions of weather, mud, and swollen streams was carried out with the same vigor, skill, and devotion in which they were conceived. . . . The command feels that the tanks have saved many American lives and greatly contributed to this noteworthy success of American arms."[51]

Brigadier General Samuel Rockenbach, commanding the Tank Corps, which he had founded, congratulated Patton and his men on the dash of their attack: "Preceding our infantry, you not only saved them many losses, but by planting your red, yellow, and blue flag well in advance and on the Hindenburg Line, you had a very great, far-reaching, and disastrous effect on the enemy."[52]

German combat reports revealed how effectively the tank force created and led by Patton had influenced the course of battle at the tactical level. Crown Prince Wilhelm, the regional commander, credited Patton's tanks with making a key contribution to the American advance: "The American attacks were in themselves badly planned; they showed ignorance of warfare; the men advanced in columns and were mowed down by our remaining machine guns. No great danger lay there, but their tanks pierced our thin lines—one man every twenty meters—and fired on us from behind. Withal the Americans had at their disposal an incredible quantity of heavy and very heavy artillery. Their preliminary firing greatly exceeded in intensity and heaviness anything we had known at Verdun and on the Somme."[53]

But the Germans had been caught rolling back and off balance, and even Patton conceded in his official report that his brigade had enjoyed an easy go: "Owing to the fact of the enemy's failure at serious resistance, the full value of the tanks was not susceptible of demonstration."[54]

THE ENEMY WINGS PATTON IN THE ARGONNE

Patton's brigade shifted northwest to the Argonne, where it joined I Corps by the night of 25 September. The corps was to attack the next day, with V Corps to its right and French XXXVI Corps to the left. More French tanks than American were to fight beside the doughboys: one regiment, the 505th, with three battalions of light tanks; the 17th Battalion of the 506th Tank Regiment (light); plus two groups each of Schneider and St. Chaumont heavy tanks.

Dressed in a French uniform, Patton again reconnoitered the front and found that a three-kilometer front between the Argonne Forest and the Bois de Cheppy was "the least unfavorable" terrain in the sector. The tanks would fight here. The 344th and 345th Tank Battalions, each less one company, and the French heavies were attached to the 35th Infantry Division, which was to attack in a column of brigades on the corps's right wing. The two remaining companies were assigned to the 28th Infantry Division, which was to strike with two brigades abreast, in the corps's center; most of the division was to attack frontally into the Argonne Forest, where tanks could not go.[55] The Aire River divided the two divisions' zones, so tanks would not be able to switch back and forth. The 77th Infantry Division on the corps's left was to push through the heart of the Argonne Forest.

Pershing was wildly optimistic and expected his nine divisions with 250,000 men to plow nearly ten miles through two German defensive lines on the first day. The German Third Army had only five understrength divisions in the line; but the sector protected a key railway line, and several hundred thousand additional troops under Fifth Army were close by. Moreover, the twisted and wooded terrain of the Aire River valley was a natural fortress, which the Germans had augmented with pillboxes, trenches, wire entanglements, and machine guns.[56]

Group Argonne, a corps subordinated to *General der Kavallerie* Karl von Einem's Third Army, manned the sector opposite I Corps. Of its five divisions, only the 1st Guards Division was rated first class.[57] The division had only arrived in the Third Army sector on 8 September. Five days later, Third Army, on orders from Army Group German Crown Prince, restarted construction work on several areas of its defensive line, including that in the Argonne.

The division took up positions in the valley floor on 17 September, so its men were not all that familiar with the ground. By 22 September, after monitoring heavy enemy transport activity for several days, Third Army concluded that the other side was preparing an attack against its front, a suspicion confirmed the following day by prisoners.

There would be no surprise this time. Einem summoned his corps commanders and the commanding general of the 1st Guards Division, *Generalmajor* Prince Eitel, to a conference to discuss the looming battle. The officers erroneously expected the main American attack to occur at Verdun (III Corps), but correctly anticipated how operations in the Aire valley would unfold. Third Army alerted all divisions to full defensive readiness and ordered forward three reserve divisions.

"The enemy's modern attack," Third Army warned on 23 September, "is based on surprise and the use of tanks." Enemy tank attacks always miscarried, it added, when the field artillery could see the tanks, and "tank fear" took root only when infantrymen were scattered and could not see their comrades in neighboring units. Leaders needed to keep their men well in hand. The next day, air reconnaissance confirmed the presence of tanks.[58]

Wilhelm Eitel Friedrich Christian Karl Prinz von Preussen was the kaiser's second child, born on 7 July 1883 in Potsdam. He gained the nickname "the Hero of St. Quentin" in 1914 when, commanding the 1st Foot Guard Regiment, he had rallied his panicked men, grabbed a drum from a bandsman, and led his troops against the French to the beat of his own instrument. For this he had been awarded the Pour le Mérite and, later that year, the command of the 1st Guards Division. He had hated leaving his beloved regiment, with which he had been associated since his youth and with whose soldiers he had shared joy and misery, rain and sunshine.[59]

The 1st Guards Division was one of the best in the entire German army. It had entered Belgium on 13 August 1914, seen some of the worst along the Marne and in Flanders, and then fought in Alsace and Russia in 1915. The division had proved its worth again at various points along the western front, including the Battle of the Somme, before returning to Russia in 1917 for several months. Since then, the division had been in France. It had suffered tremendous losses in the Aisne offensive in June, however, and may have lost some of its old esprit de corps.[60]

Early on 25 September, Eitel ordered the 1st Battalion of his 4th Guards Regiment to stage a raid on the French lines to his front to gather prisoners. The four *Sturmtruppen* worked their way a kilometer into the French lines, well supported by artillery and mortars that knocked out troublesome French machine guns under direction of a radio-equipped observer, and returned with nine prisoners. However, *Sturmtrupp* I suffered numerous casualties when an artillery shell scored a direct hit while the men were returning to their own lines.

The prisoners had a story to tell. American forces had secretly moved into position behind the French lines and the following night would stage an attack from Verdun to the Argonne. The French had already removed the tank traps in their own lines to clear the way for the many tanks that would support the American attack. The men did not know whether French divisions to the west would attack simultaneously. Eitel concluded that there was no reason to think the Americans would show themselves before the onslaught and that he had to reckon with an imminent threat.

Eitel ordered his men to readiness and told his commanders that the 5th Guards Division had been ordered up in support, but that it had not yet arrived— although six batteries of its artillery had. Eitel ordered his three regiments—the 1st, 2nd, and 4th Guards, deployed in that order left to right and grouped under the 1st Guards Infantry Brigade—to withdraw all men from the outpost line to the first main line of resistance but for a single company each, which was to remain in the outpost line to ward off patrols. Each regiment by daylight was to man the main line of resistance; there was to be one battalion in the trenches, one in readiness, and one in reserve, and artillery units modified their fire plans to pull fire back to the area just in front of the trenches.

On 22 September, Eitel had received a two-page analysis of the American attack against the St. Mihiel salient; the analysis belittled the American infantry and said tanks had fought in small groups when mass would have brought success. Eitel planned rapidly and well to meet Patton and his tankers. Each artillery subgroup supporting an infantry regiment was to identify a battery of mobile guns that could deploy rapidly and to locate one of the guns on, or even in front of, the main line of resistance. The artillery commander was to survey the terrain to ensure the best possible antitank defense. Remaining batteries were to cease their fire and move to positions that had never been used before. Mortars were allocated to the ready, and reserve battalions were allocated for antitank defense. Eitel also positioned his seven antitank rifles in depth from the foremost companies to the reserves. He kept two of his eight antitank guns under his direct control near the reserves.[61]

Eitel had Patton's number. If his men could implement his plan, they would leave burning tank wrecks strewn across the battlefield.

At 2300 hours the night of 25 September, Allied artillery began to pound German lines east and west of the main point of attack to deceive the Germans and, with luck, convince them to shift parts of the 1st Guards Division. The first shells struck the 1st Guards Division's zone shortly after midnight. Third Army anticipated infantry assaults west of the Aisne River in the French Fourth Army zone at daybreak. As the sky lightened, a heavy fog cloaked the battlefield and deepened the fog of war. So did the fact that about 0400, artillery impacts destroyed all phone lines forward from the 1st Guards Infantry Brigade, and fog obscured blinker-light signals. The American doughboys moved out at 0630, but Third Army had no idea it was under attack. Indeed, by 0930, the army headquarters was beginning to suspect that an afternoon assault might be in the offing instead.

Major General Peter Traub's untested 35th Infantry Division attacked in a column of brigades, the 138th Infantry Regiment spearheading the advance toward Cheppy on the 69th Brigade's right in a column of battalions. The 2nd Guards Regiment, as well seasoned an outfit as any in the division, barred the way. Indeed, over four years earlier, on 4 August 1914, the storied Prussian regiment had marched wearing field gear before the eyes of thousands of Berliners from its barracks on the Friedrichstrasse across the Charlottenburg Chausee to the West End train station to board trains for the front.

A rolling barrage of 75mm shells plowed over the defenders' firing positions, a harbinger of the infantry following 100 yards behind. The three German companies along the outpost line pulled back without causing the oncoming mass of American infantry and tanks any trouble except at heavily fortified hill at Vauquois, and even there at least seventy unwounded defenders capitulated. The main German line was constructed around machine-gun strong points, but the gunners could see nothing because of the thick fog—visibility was between ten and forty yards. One by one, they were enveloped and fell to the Americans. These nests, unfortunately, had been issued most of the armor-piercing ammunition. Nor could the forward-most antitank gunners see a thing. Patton once again was a lucky man. It was little consolation that the Americans were suffering severe command and control problems and were navigating through the pea soup using compasses.

By 1000 hours, as the fog began to lift in the Aire valley, Third Army realized that American and French troops were striking along nearly the entire length of its front with tank and fighter support. The 2nd Battalion, 2nd Guards Regiment, defending the Vauquois heights, reported by carrier pigeon about that time, "The enemy is coming out of the fog from all sides and climbing the hill. It will be bitter and to the last man. Long live the Kaiser."[62] A company of Patton's tanks slipped by in the fog, but gunners on Vauquois were able to wound or kill at least two of the tank officers who were leading their vehicles across the boggy and shell-holed terrain near the hill.[63]

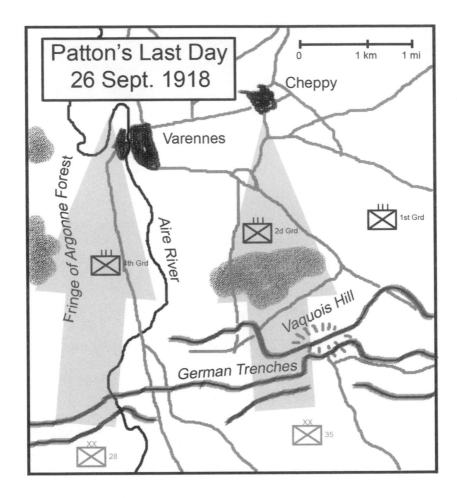

The Renaults of the American 344th Tank Battalion supported the advance, while those of the 355th Tank Battalion followed at a distance of 1,500 meters. The French heavies followed another 500 meters to the rear. The plan was that once the two American divisions reached their objectives, the trailing battalion would leap-frog ahead to support the advance from that line.[64] As things turned out, the tanks supporting the 28th Infantry Division became lost in the fog and played little role in the early morning fighting.[65]

The left wing of the 1st Battalion, 2nd Guards Regiment, held Cheppy. The first Americans to appear out of the thinning fog were runners from the 138th Infantry Regiment's headquarters detachment, who had gotten separated from their detachment in the fog and stumbled into the German line south of town.

Machine gunners, dug into some woods to the side of the road, opened fire, and the group stopped. The fog thickened again, and Company M was able to pass the same spot without harm. Prussian Guards manning pillboxes and dugouts south of town had no idea who was approaching until the Americans were on top of them, at which point they chose not to shoot because they could easily be taken from the rear. The Americans assumed the fortifications were empty and walked unmolested into Cheppy, where the fog was so dense as to resemble night.

The Prussian Guards south of Cheppy next saw emerging from the fog a group of men that turned out to be not combat troops but the 138th Infantry Regiment's headquarters section. Machine gunners opened up from the front and the rear, and an artillery spotter placed a barrage on the Americans that killed a dozen men. Some actual fighting troops eventually appeared (from Company I), and the Prussian gunners soon had them pinned down in a ditch. When Company I's captain, Alex Skinker, ran toward their emplacements, firing an automatic rifle from the hip and accompanied by two men, they casually mowed him down. (Skinker would be awarded a Medal of Honor for his bravery.)

Then things changed. Two of Patton's Renault tanks appeared and stopped near the infantry. The machine guns fell silent, as the gunners did not want to reveal their positions. Fortunately, a creek blocked the armor, preventing it from approaching the emplacements, and the paltry fire from two light tanks did little harm. A call to the artillery produced satisfying explosions around the vehicles, and they pulled to the rear. The gunners went back to working over the pinned-down infantry, as did the artillery.

Some of the lead tanks, however, bypassed resistance south of the village, probably thanks to the fog, and entered Cheppy's streets, where elements of Company 8 pulling back from Vauquois came under tank fire there about that time.[66]

Also about this time, machine gunners near the road junction south of Cheppy, apparently somewhat to the rear of the 138th Infantry Regiment's headquarters group and Company I, spotted through the slowly thinning fog Patton and about a dozen other men on the near side of a narrow-gauge railway. Patton had again become impatient because he could see nothing and had come forward to find his tanks, thinking that Cheppy had been secured. The Germans could finally see their targets well enough, and bullets whipped so close to the American party that the men scurried smartly away and over the crest of a nearby hill.

The Germans could also see that a French Schneider tank from the follow-on force had become stuck in a trench visible past the flank of the hill and had blocked the route. Machine-gun fire drove off the men trying to free it into the trench. From somewhere nearby, a friendly artillery battery also chimed in, and an observation plane appeared overhead to direct the fire. Soon, five American Renaults appeared and stopped at the obstruction.

The 1st Battalion men could plainly see the officer they had driven behind the hill stalk to the tanks and grab shovels and picks off the Renaults as bullets barely missed him and pinged off the steel plate. Soon, he had the crews out of their vehicles, digging away to create a path around the stuck Schneider. Some doughboys who had been hiding in the trench pitched in. The tall officer stood on the edge of the trench the entire time, gesticulating even as shells exploded and bullets whizzed by.

The American tanks negotiated the trench and disappeared, only to churn over the rise of the hill, followed by about a hundred infantrymen—rallied 35th Infantry Division stragglers, as it turned out—led by the officer, who was waving a walking stick in the air. Every gunner zeroed in, and the Americans dropped to the earth to avoid the grazing fire.

Whereas the Patton who had come under fire in the St. Mihiel salient had shown the good sense to get into a shell hole, the Patton who emerged now, when thwarted by the enemy, bull-headedly attacked even at the obvious and futile waste of soldiers' lives. German gunners watched across their sights as the officer and six men rose and came on. The 1st Battalion men knocked them down, one by one, until only the officer and another man were left. These two khaki-clad figures closed to within fifty meters of the closest machine-gun nest, where a round finally found Patton, and down he went, struck in the hip. The bullet passed through his body without hitting bone, nerve, or any vital organ. The last man standing dragged him to a shell hole. The Prussian gunners tried to kill them, but the bullets passed harmlessly over the depression. For a man who had just charged a machine-gun nest with nothing but a walking stick, Patton was again a very lucky fellow.

More tanks appeared over the hill, maneuvered into a line, and attacked, as the infantry huddled in their protective shadows. The 37mm cannons made short work of the field emplacements, and the 1st Battalion's Prussian Guards picked up their weapons and moved off toward the northeast. All German forces had evacuated Cheppy by early afternoon.[67]

Patton received the Distinguished Service Cross for his actions; the citation read, "Colonel Patton displayed conspicuous courage, coolness, energy, and intelligence in directing the advance of his brigade down the valley of the Aire. Later he rallied a force of disorganized infantry and led it forward, behind the tanks under heavy machine-gun fire until he was wounded. Unable to advance further, Colonel Patton continued to direct operations of his unit until all arrangements for turning over the command were completed."[68]

Patton's men supporting the 28th Infantry Division finally got into the action west of the Aire. But the fog was lifting, and Eitel's antitank artillery teams could now see the enemy. Gunners with the 4th Guards Regiment knocked out two tanks with direct hits during a tank attack on Varennes. Tanks entered the town at 1030 hours, but the regiment's machine guns were able to keep the doughboys out for four more hours. The 4th Guards Regiment abandoned Varennes when its troops there ran out of ammunition.[69]

Despite the fog that had disrupted his entire antitank plan, Eitel had knocked down Patton and many of his tanks besides. Throughout the morning, the 1st Guards Division fell back under pressure from doughboys who appeared out of the fog, falling back to the Giselher Line. Still, the terrain and 77mm guns claimed tank after tank, and by midday, two-thirds of them were out of action for one reason or another.[70]

"Due to the serious resistance of the enemy," recorded Brig. Gen. Samuel Rockenbach, "especially along the eastern edge of the [Argonne Forest] and in the vicinity of Cheppy and Varennes, and due also to the lack of support of the infantry, all the tanks had contrary to the plan entered the action before the evening of the first day."[71]

Third Army commanding general Einem, shortly after midday, exhorted his forward commanders to hold onto the second main line of resistance. Fortunately for him, U.S. I Corps had already mostly reached its day's objectives and stopped until the flanking corps caught up.[72]

At about 1530 hours, Group Argonne intercepted an American radio message: "We have been reinforced by tanks and will be able to move forward again." The American tankers and infantry reached Baulny during the afternoon, only to be ejected by a 1st Guards Division counterattack.[73] At day's end, so far as the 1st Guards Division could determine, the 1st Regiment had lost more than 500 officers and men killed, wounded, or missing; the 2nd Regiment nearly 800; and the 4th Regiment some 350.[74] Still, the 1st Guards Division had broken the back of the 35th Infantry Division.[75]

During his recovery, Patton was placed in command of the 302nd Center, Tank Corps, until he was reassigned as commanding officer of his old tank brigade on 11 October.[76]

The AEF, in judging the effectiveness of American tanks in the St. Mihiel salient and the Argonne from 11 September to 11 November 1918, concluded, "The most efficiently trained Tank Corps unit was unable to secure and hold its gain when operating with other arms, which had no training with the tanks. On the other hand, when operating with divisions that understood the operation and function of tanks, the results were highly satisfactory and gained the unstinted praise and commendation of brigade, division, and corps commanders."[77]

There is no indication that the Germans had taken any personal notice of Lieutenant Colonel Patton, a field-grade officer who had been in combat but four days. While he had forged his sword, his ability to wield it nearly evaporated once the infantry took charge of operations, and his inability to communicate with his tankers except in person meant he rarely directed the course of more than a platoon of Renaults once the shooting had begun.

The American press, however, made Patton a celebrity. He was written up and pictured riding astride a Renault in the St. Mihiel salient, and after he was wounded at Cheppy, the papers called him the "Hero of the Tanks." Might a growing public reputation expand into a living legend that would influence what Americans expected other armies to think about Patton?

PORTENTS OF THE FUTURE

Nearly all of the commanders who one day would confront Patton on the field of battle also fought in the "War to End All Wars," though all were more obscure and less marked by the chronicler's pen than Patton. Most of them, in fact, experienced much more of the war. None of them appear to have been involved in Germany's stunted tank program. We will encounter these men again, each in a crucial command position opposite Patton, so mark them well.

Of some surprise to readers may be the figure of Lt. Jean Petit, who arrived by train at the front on the Somme, south of Amiens, at 0300 hours on 10 January 1915. Born on 9 February 1894, Petit had entered the French Military Academy at St. Cyr in August 1914. The young officer had left his parents, sister, and newborn niece two days earlier and, wearing trench coat and pillbox hat, his pistol and binoculars on his belt, and carrying a walking stick in his hand, headed to war.

Petit reported to the 19th *Regiment Chasseurs à Pied* (19th BCP; literally, "Dismounted Hunters" or "Dismounted Light Cavalry"), 42nd Infantry Division. There he joined the 2nd Battalion's 6th Company in Berry-sur-Noye. There was a crying need for officers because most of their predecessors had been killed the preceding year. Three days later, Petit and his division traveled by train to the Argonne. Each man knew that the Verdun area had already been a grinding bloodbath against the crown prince's army. Several days later, the men moved into the trenches of the first line near La Harazée.

Only that morning, the Bosches had occupied the trench line left by the 3rd Battalion two days earlier and destined to be filled by the 2nd Battalion. Two companies of the 2nd Battalion, including Petit's, were ordered to recapture it. Events unfolded with vertiginous speed, and Petit acted on pure physical instinct. Bullets flying. Men going down. Can't even see the enemy. A German machine gun opens up. A bullet nicks his ear. Success.

Petit and his comrades suffered the typical life of men in freezing mud- and slush-filled trenches all along the dreary western front. He was evacuated with trench foot, but March found Petit back on the line near Mézières. Not much had changed. Unseen Germans fired their machine guns. The French wished they could see them and knock them out. Time passed, and one by one, friends died.

In September 1916, the French planned to attack at Verdun. Petit was now with the 102nd *Chasseurs*. At 2300 hours on the twenty-first, French troops penetrated Verdun, and Petit was there for some of the worst of it.

Wounded three times during the war, Petit was decorated on division or corps orders five times, made a chevalier of the Legion of Honor in 1916 and captain in 1917, and was awarded the Belgian Croix de Guerre with Palms. He was a soldier's soldier and had become an expert at high-intensity infantry combat.[78]

Alfredo Guzzoni saw nearly constant action with the Italian army and was perhaps the first of Patton's future enemies to have some experience with motorized warfare. Guzzoni was born in Mantova on 12 April 1877 and entered the military school in Modena in 1894. Two years later, he joined the 59th Infantry Regiment as a sublieutenant. By the outbreak of the war, Guzzoni was a captain assigned to the 2nd Mobile Battalion of the 52nd Infantry Regiment in Benghazi. He spent one year in the middle of this period as the chief of staff for the Cyrenaica military district.

Guzzoni transferred to Italy in 1915, where he joined the 51st Infantry Regiment. Assignments followed to staff positions with Fourth Army and the 7th Infantry Division. Assigned to the 11th Infantry Division in 1917, and now a lieutenant colonel, Guzzoni was awarded the Medal of Valor in gold for his personal intervention in the Battle of Vodice in August, on the slopes of San Gabriele, during the greatest Italian offensive of the war. Promoted to colonel, Guzzoni served with the *Commando Supremo* and then as the chief of staff for XXVII and III Corps. He was awarded a second Medal of Valor in gold and the Cavalry Cross in gold for his actions on the Montello and Piave Rivers and at Trentino in June 1918 during the last Austro-Hungarian offensive of the war, the failure of which shattered the imperial army.[79]

Fritz Kurt Hans *Freiherr* von Broich (he is generally referred to as Friedrich von Broich, but his German army personnel file gives his names as rendered here) was born on New Year's Day in 1896 in Strassburg (Strasbourg), which from the Franco-Prussian War until 1918 was a part of Germany. He had joined the German imperial army's 9th *Pommerisches Ulanen* (Pomeranian Lancers) Regiment as a *Fahnenjunker*, (officer candidate) on 2 July 1914 straight out of the *Gymnasium* (university preparatory school) he attended in Metz. The regiment was one of two in the 3rd Cavalry Brigade, which was the reconnaissance element of the 3rd Infantry Division. On 2 August 1914, the 3rd Cavalry Brigade became one of three brigades in the 4th Cavalry Division.

The 4th Cavalry Division saw action from the outbreak of the war in August 1914, first participating in the capture of Lüttich, then leading First Army's pivoting advance past Amiens toward Paris, and then screening the right flank of IV Reserve Corps as the front neared the French capital. On 6 September, the division, along with the IV Reserve Corps, fought a battle against overwhelming odds, but held on until the rest of II Cavalry Corps, commanded by the legendary *General der Kavallerie* Johannes Georg von der Marwitz, arrived and put the French to flight the following day. In mid-November, the division entrained to go east to the battlefields in Poland.

Broich was made lieutenant on 24 December 1914. Trained as a machine gunner in 1915, he was detached from May to September 1915 to the 7th *Kürassier-Regiment von Seydlitz*, part of the 2nd Cavalry Division's 8th Cavalry Brigade. The division was the 4th Cavalry Division's sister unit in *Korps Hollen*. The 3rd Cavalry Brigade became an independent unit on 30 September. Broich appears to have remained, except for training, assigned to the eastern front.

Both the *Ulanen* and *Kürassier* were classed as heavy cavalry units intended to attack the enemy en masse and create holes through which the infantry could advance. The *Ulanen*, nevertheless, was a specialized type of unit that combined the speed of light cavalry with the attacking power of the heavy cavalry. Patton, a romantic defender of the use of cold steel of sabers in his own army, would have loved the *Ulanen*, because they were the only German riders to still use the lance, in addition to the standard blade, carbine, and pistol. By the end of 1914, encounters with modern firearms and artillery had persuaded the German army that mass cavalry attacks were suicidal, though attacks in small groups were still possible; in large battles, the cavalrymen fought on foot.

After a period sick in the hospital, Broich returned to his old regiment in the field in January 1916. Broich achieved the rank of *Oberleutnant* and squadron chief by July 1918, and the war ended for him when he was wounded in October. By then, he had been awarded the Iron Cross first- and second-class. He had also learned a good bit about mobile warfare and, thanks to advanced machine-gun training, probably knew a thing or two about stopping an enemy from a defensive position.[80]

Hasso-Eccard von Manteuffel was another cavalryman in the Great War. Born to a retired captain of a distinguished military family and his wife on 14 January 1897 in Potsdam, Manteuffel grew up immersed in the sights and sounds of the nearby Potsdam garrison and imperial palace. A small lad, Manteuffel learned to compensate with aggressiveness. His chosen role model was *Generalfeldmarschall* Edwin *Freiherr* von Manteuffel, who, at the height of his career, had fought at Metz in the Franco-Prussian War and been the first military governor of Alsace-Lorraine.

After being educated as a cadet, when he learned English, Manteuffel joined the German imperial army as an ensign on 28 April 1916. He was assigned to the 5th Squadron, 3rd Brandenburg Hussars Regiment *von Zieten*, which was the divisional cavalry for the 6th Infantry Division. The 6th was a shock division and fought in the trenches where the horse had no role. Indeed, just as he joined his squadron in April 1916, the infantry regiments suffered 60 percent losses in a ferocious battle in the Douaumont-Caillette Wood near Verdun. When he arrived at Verdun, Manteuffel served as a forward observer for the division headquarters, which placed him in the front line with the infantry. He was wounded in the thigh by shrapnel in December 1916, and after he recovered, he was assigned to a divisional staff job.

The 6th Infantry Division was one of the best in the German army, a fact that probably instilled in Manteuffel a fierce pride. The division fought on the Somme in 1917 and at Cambrai in 1918.[81]

Kurt Wilhelm Gustav Erdmann von der Chevallerie, born 23 December 1891 in Berlin, entered the German imperial army as an officer candidate on 24 February 1910. The son of *Generalmajor* Hans von der Chevallerie, Kurt joined the elite 5th Guards Grenadier Regiment, where he was promoted to *leutnant* on 11 August 1911. On the outbreak of the war, he accompanied his regiment to the front as part of the 3rd Guards Division, one of two divisions in Second Army's Guards Reserve Corps, which captured Namur. On 27 August, following the Russian attack on East Prussia on the seventh, the division shifted to Silesia and participated in Ninth Army's counterattack through Poland, fighting battles against the Russians at Angerburg on Masurian Lakes, Goldap, Jendrzejow, Kielce, Bzin, Opatow, and Iwangorod, the last involving a particularly bitter struggle.

From 18 to 21 October, the Guards Reserve Corps sought to defend the link between German Ninth Army and Austrian First Army south of Warsaw against strong attacks across the Weichsel River by a much larger Russian force, execrable Austrian generalship having opened the door to the Russians. After a fierce, but fruitless, struggle and an Austrian withdrawal that the Germans learned of only by chance, a general withdrawal became necessary because of overwhelming Russian superiority in numbers, and the campaign ended in retreat. Chevallerie thus received an early education in the vicissitudes of war and the finer details of waging a coherent withdrawal.

In late November 1914, Chevallerie was transferred as a company commander to the 262nd Reserve Grenadier Regiment, which formed part of the newly raised 79th Reserve Division. The regiment and one of its two sister regiments, the 261st, recruited by selection from all of Prussia in the manner of the Guard. The division's first action was at Masurian Lakes in East Prussia in February 1915. Chevallerie then fought in northeastern Poland at Sejni, Krasnopol, and Krasne in March, continuing to fight across Poland until he was wounded during fighting near Wejwery in July. Chevallerie was promoted to *oberleutnant* while convalescing and returned to the 262nd Regiment in the fall. By year's end, he had been awarded both Iron Crosses.

Chevallerie served in various staff positions from 1916 to 1918, including as adjutant in the 34th *Landwehr* Brigade, 1st *Landwehr* Division, where he was promoted to *Hauptmann* in September 1918. After the armistice on the eastern front, the 1st Division was transferred to the west, where it conducted positional warfare in Lorraine, the very place Chevallerie would spend his last days in command of First Army fighting Patton.[82]

Otto Heinrich Ernst von Knobelsdorff, born 31 March 1886 in Berlin, was the scion of an old Prussian family. His father had been a major in the 12th Infantry Regiment, and his mother was born a von Manteuffel. After years being educated as a cadet, Knobelsdorff had joined the German imperial army's Infantry Regiment *Grossherzog von Sachsen* (5th *Thüringisches*), Nr. 94, in 1905 as an officer candidate. Knobelsdorff was nearly a head shorter than most of the men around him, but he made up for it with drive. He was endowed with boundless energy, clear judgment, and a good sense of humor. He was personally brave, friendly, and open.

Knobelsdorff was promoted to *leutnant* in 1908 and to *oberleutnant* in August 1914, having become the regimental adjutant in January. That year, he married Alexandria *Freiin* von Korff-Schmising, who bore him two sons and one daughter. His regiment, part of the 83rd Infantry Brigade, 38th Infantry Division, went to war on the western front, pushing through the Ardennes with XI Corps, and Knobelsdorff, too, reached Namur. The corps then entrained for the east after the Russian invasion of East Prussia in August and participated in Ninth Army's counterattack not far from Chevallerie and the Guards Reserve Corps. Knobelsdorff, too, fought at Masurian Lakes, Goldap, Opatow, and Iwangorod, and he experienced the retreat of his own army. In October, the corps joined the Austrian First Army to stiffen its fighting ability. Knobelsdorff remained on the eastern front until September 1915 and got to enjoy German arms' stunning return to success.

The 38th Division entrained for France on 25 September, where it absorbed new manpower and took up a quiet sector of the front at Tracy le Val until May 1916. On 22 March, Knobelsdorff received a promotion to *hauptmann* for his bravery. Between November 1915 and April 1916, Knobelsdorff commanded a company and, temporarily, first one then another battalion. In May, the division moved to the Verdun sector, where it fought for five months. After a brief rest recruiting for the division, Knobelsdorff took command of a separate infantry battalion that worked with the 94th and 95th Infantry Regiments from the summer of 1917 until October. The 94th Regiment waged an epic struggle for Hill 304 and "Dead Man's Hill," the last remaining German strong points at Verdun to fall to the French, and held them until 24 August. The 38th Division suffered heavy casualties, including 52 percent of the infantry, at Verdun. In October, the division moved to the Somme, where again it lost many of its men, but by then Knobelsdorff had stepped up to brigade adjutant and was no longer on the front line.

In November, Knobelsdorff set off to fill a string of staff jobs at Army Group B, VII Corps, the 200th Infantry and 1st Guards Infantry Divisions, the Bug Army, and the 242nd Infantry Division. It was during the last assignment that, while working as chief of supply, Knobelsdorff was seriously wounded, on 28 October 1918, less than two weeks before the end of the war.[83]

Knobelsdorff had seen some of the most horrid killing grounds of World War I, yet there was something in his makeup that caused him to stay in the army after the armistice. He had also proved himself to be extremely lucky.

Hans Erich Günther von Obstfelder served as a staff officer on the western front during the entire war. Born in Sternbach-Hallenberg on 6 September 1886, Obstfelder had received a *Gymnasium* education in Godesberg, picking up both English and French, before joining the imperial army's 2nd *Thüringisches Infanterie-Regiment* Nr. 32 as an officer candidate in March 1905. In 1912, by then a *leutnant*, Obstfelder married Greta Bürner, who bore him a daughter who died at the age of five. When the war broke out, *Oberleutnant* Obstfelder was serving as a regimental adjutant in the 71st Infantry Regiment, and as the war progressed, he filled staff jobs at the division, corps, and army levels. He served repeatedly in the Verdun area, so he was personally familiar with the area where he would first face Patton nearly three decades later. Somehow in the course of the war, he found himself awarded the Iron Cross.[84]

Many other future enemies of Patton participated as officers in the Great War, though their tracks are harder to trace. Hans-Jürgen von Arnim survived years of front-line combat and learned skills that would stand him in good stead nearly thirty years later in the North African desert. Hermann Balck fought as a machine gunner in an obscure battalion on the eastern front, which somehow did not imbue him with a defensive mindset. Erich Brandenberger served in the artillery in some of the greatest battles of the war, including those on the Somme and the Marne. Johannes Blaskowitz spent most of the war as a staff officer, which may account for his somewhat lackluster performance in the next war as a combat commander. Hans-Gustav Felber began the war in the infantry, but had the good fortune to rise to staff positions for most of the conflict. Paul Hausser also served through much of the war as a staff officer, but for a while commanded a rifle company in battle. Walter Hahm enlisted in the infantry in August 1914 and within a year had gained promotion to *leutnant* in the 12th Infantry Division's 23rd *von Winterfeldt* Regiment, which speaks highly of his soldier skills. Walter Hörnlein, by contrast, spent almost the entire conflict in a prisoner-of-war camp. Günther von Kluge served almost entirely in staff jobs, yet managed to get severely wounded at Verdun. Baptist Kniess fought with the 5th *Königlich Bayerisches Infanterie-Regiment Grossherzog Ernst Ludwig von Hessen*, where he earned both Iron Crosses. Smilo von Lüttwitz served throughout the war with the 2nd *Grossherzoglich Hessisches Leib-Dragoner-Regiment* Nr. 24, which shuttled back and forth between the two fronts. Gerd von Rundstedt held general staff assignments at the division and corps levels. Max Simon was a noncommissioned officer in the *Leib-Kürassier-Regiment Grosser Kurfürst* Nr. 1, part of the 5th Cavalry Division, which participated in the August 1914 offensive in the West, but thereafter fought mainly on the eastern front. The cavalrymen were retrained as infantry in early 1918, and Simon fought in bloody defensive battles in Champagne before the end of the war. Gustav von Vaerst was a cavalryman who saw action up and down both fronts, and he remained one until he took to the panzer arm just before the next great war began.[85]

THREE

✳

Between the Wars

A FTER THE ARMISTICE on 11 November 1918, Patton returned to the States and the peacetime army, reduced to his permanent rank of captain. When Congress in 1920 gave the infantry control over tanks, Patton returned to the horse-mounted arm and, promoted to major, took command of a cavalry squadron. There followed a string of standard peacetime assignments, including stints at the Command and General Staff College, office of the chief of cavalry, and Army War College.

Cavalrymen split over a big issue between the wars: whether the machine should replace the horse. Major General Herbert Crosby, chief of cavalry, in 1927 held maneuvers in Texas, in part to try out limited motorization of transport and artillery. Crosby believed that some degree of mechanization would increase cavalry's role, and after the exercises were completed, he created a new, trimmed-down cavalry division of some 5,000 men and that incorporated an armored car troop. He even considered adding a light-tank troop.[1] In February 1928, the forward-thinking Crosby established within the office of the chief of cavalry a "tactical development section," which was charged with watching developments at home and abroad that the U.S. Cavalry could exploit to make itself more effective. These included "developments in mechanization, particularly as to tanks, armored cars, and the mobility of artillery."[2]

Impressed by the lessons of British maneuvers in 1927, during which a mechanized force defeated a traditional one, the U.S. Army in 1928 issued its first clear statement endorsing large-scale mechanization. The secretary of war, Dwight Davis, who was concerned that the army would prepare itself to refight the last war, instructed the army to begin testing mechanized formations at Fort Leonard Wood—now Fort Meade—in Maryland.[3]

General Charles Summerall, as his last act as the army chief of staff, in October 1930 ordered the establishment of the army's first permanent mechanized force, to be stationed at Fort Eustis, Virginia. He still viewed the cavalry as a primarily horse-mounted arm—to be supported in its reconnaissance mission by mechanized elements.[4] Indeed, by then, the 1st Cavalry Division had been authorized one company of light tanks (infantry) and one squadron of armored cars (cavalry). No fast tanks were yet available, however, and even armored cars were in short supply.[5]

The new mechanized force, the command and support staff of which arrived at Camp Knox (soon renamed Fort Knox), Kentucky, in November 1931, absorbed the 1st Cavalry Regiment, which became the 1st Cavalry Regiment (Mechanized) in 1932. The War Department also in 1932 established the headquarters for the 7th Cavalry Brigade (Mechanized), which was to incorporate the 1st Cavalry Regiment (Mechanized) and a battalion (two batteries of 75mm howitzers) of the 68th Field Artillery. The 13th Cavalry was mechanized in 1936 and subordinated to the brigade, and two more batteries of artillery were added as well.[6]

For cavalrymen uncertain about the relative merits of the horse and the machine, the latter might not have looked like a good career bet because miserly defense budgets seemed to preclude creation of large mechanized formations. Major General Guy Henry lamented in 1931, "Had funds permitted the equipping of our units in accordance with our approved tables, we would now possess the most extensively mechanized cavalry in the world." There were fewer than 9,000 troopers in the small, 130,000-man peacetime army; a replacement armored car took nine months to acquire, whereas there were twenty million horses available in the United States.[7] As of February 1932, the cavalry arm had only four experimental Christie combat cars (light tanks) in hand.[8] That year, out of an army appropriation of $390 million, only $250,000 was set aside for tank purchases.[9] The first "modern" armored fighting vehicle, the machine-gun armed Combat Car M1/Light Tank M1A2, did not reach the cavalry and infantry until 1936, and then only in small numbers. (The Germans by then were prototyping the Mark III panzer with a 37mm main gun.) When planners at this time thought about the future battlefield environment, they concluded that given the high cost of mechanized formations—costs that seemed especially high in the mental context of Depression-era America—no army would be able to field more than a few such brigades.[10]

In May 1934, the German military attaché in Washington confidently reported to his German superiors on the state of U.S. cavalry mechanization: "In many cases, vehicles are still in use that long ago disappeared in Germany. Of the 8,309 trucks available as of 1 January 1934, 5,894 were from the [World] War, and 596 more were at least five years old. . . . With the exception of a dozen vehicles built in the last few years, every tank in the American Army is from the World War. These vehicles are completely obsolete and worthless in battle against armies with modern equipment." The attaché estimated that while the U.S. Army could quickly obtain modern trucks in a war situation, it would take a year for the United States to begin mass production of tanks. The Americans were hoping to mechanize no more than a cavalry brigade and two infantry regiments.[11] Indeed, by 1936, the sole mechanized cavalry brigade fielded only two mechanized regiments.

Patton kept abreast of evolving thinking about mechanized warfare at home and abroad, but the man who had been a pioneer of American armored warfare had, for practical purposes, reverted to the warfare of the nineteenth century. The beginning of 1939 found Patton commanding a horse regiment of the 1st Cavalry Division.

AN ENEMY REAWAKENS

Between 1920 and 1933, the German army, bound by the terms of the Treaty of Versailles, numbered 96,000 men and 4,000 officers. Both classes were professionals; enlisted ranks served for twelve years and officers for twenty-five. *Generaloberst* Hans von Seeckt, the first head of the *Reichswehr*, made the best of his limited numbers by emphasizing training to the highest level, plus obedience, performance, loyalty to the fatherland, and military submission to the then-democratic state. It recreated, under cover, a dispersed military academy (*Kriegsakademie*) and similarly resumed surreptitious training of general staff officers, both banned by the Treaty of Versailles. The army consisted of seven infantry and three cavalry divisions and had neither heavy artillery nor tanks. There was no air force, thanks to Versailles.[12]

Nevertheless, the seeds of a revolution in warfare were already being sowed. Military thinkers sloughed off the scabrous mold of never-wished-for trench warfare and returned to traditional Prussian thinking, in which war was about rapid movement at the level of armies and corps, and about surrounding and destroying enemy armies by envelopment and attacks against the flanks and rear. New weapons and technical possibilities made such dreams possible.

Hauptmann Heinz Guderian, assigned in 1922 to the Directorate of Transport Troops in the Defense Ministry, was having early thoughts about machine-based mobile warfare and participating in the first exercises with truck-mounted infantry that his genius eventually would transform into the theories that shaped the German panzer arm. Guderian drew inspiration mainly from the British and French experiences in the Great War and on the writings after the war by Capt. Basil Liddell Hart and J. F. C. Fuller, who conceived of using mechanized forces offensively to strike deeply into an enemy's rear. Guderian does not credit the writings of Patton as an influence, though Patton had written the book on American tank warfare in the Great War. Guderian also taught in while a staff officer of the 2nd Infantry Division in Stettin and emphasized Napoleon's campaign in Russia as a powerful example of mobile warfare, in addition to the German and French use of cavalry in 1914 before the beginning of trench warfare.

By 1928, Guderian had become involved in teaching panzer tactics—based on foreign reports and manuals—and carrying out the first tests of platoon-, company-, and battalion-sized formations using motorized dummies of sheet metal. He got his first hands-on experience with tanks in 1929 as an exchange officer in Sweden, which had a battalion of tanks of the last model Germany developed in the Great War, but never had an opportunity to field. That same year, he realized tanks would be unable to operate alone and would have to be part of a combined-arms team. Guderian's work laid the foundation of Blitzkrieg. By 1932, the army had the Panzer I, armed with a machine gun, ready for immediate production and the Panzer II, armed with a 20mm main gun, on the drawing board.[13]

Adolf Hitler became chancellor of Germany in 1933 and brought to the office a fascination for the potential of mechanized warfare. Hitler began to rearm the army and established the Luftwaffe (air force) in 1934. The army created the framework for twenty-four divisions and began tinkering with mechanization in the cavalry arm. On 16 March 1935, Hitler cast off the military restrictions imposed by the Versailles treaty and announced Germany's "freedom to arm." He reintroduced conscription and ordered the army to expand to thirty-six divisions. This declaration set off a frantic expansion that kept every officer busy trying to train not only new soldiers, but officers and noncommissioned officers as well. Quality gave way for several years to quantity.[14]

By 1936, Hitler's rearmament program had changed the picture dramatically. Germany formed three panzer divisions in October 1935, and Guderian took command of the 2nd Panzer Division. In 1936, the army created a panzer brigade to support the infantry, three light divisions with an organization similar to that of the later panzergrenadier divisions (two motorized infantry regiments, a reconnaissance regiment, an artillery regiment, and a tank battalion), and four motorized infantry divisions.[15]

By the autumn of 1939, the German army had grown to fifty-two divisions, including thirty-five infantry, three mountain, four motorized, five panzer, and four light divisions, plus a cavalry brigade. The plan for expansion of the army was to reach fruition in 1943.[16] Hitler was not that patient, as the world soon learned.

Most of Patton's future German enemies, like him, played no role in the mechanized march to the future, and all thus started from more or less the same limited base of expertise before the outbreak of World War II. But roughly three years of fresh wartime lessons would separate them by the time they met.

Fritz von Broich's career in many ways paralleled George Patton's: he was a cavalryman, had fought his first battles in World War I, remained a caval ryman between the wars, and became a master of mechanized warfare only after World War II was in full swing. A lean, brown-haired, blue-eyed man, five feet eleven inches tall, Broich in 1921 married *Freiin* Olegard von Lützow. A skilled horseman and dedicated athlete, much like Patton, he remained in the *Reichswehr* as a reserve cavalry officer, rising to *oberstleutnant* and command of a horse-mounted squadron of the 1st Cavalry Division in 1938.[17]

After a stint in the *Freikorps Hindenburg*, Kurt von der Chevallerie entered the *Reichswehr* in 1920, served briefly in the 102nd Infantry Regiment, and then took command of a company in the 4th (Prussian) Infantry Regiment. From 1928 to 1931, Chevallerie served in a squadron of the 3rd (Prussian) *Reiter-Regiment* (Mounted Regiment), which gave him his first taste of mobile military operations. A staff job and command of an infantry battalion followed, and when the army expanded in 1934, Chevallerie, by now an *Oberstleutnant*, was given command of the Infantry Regiment *Göttingen* and promotion to *oberst* the next year. Following two more regimental commands, Chevallerie moved on to the Army General Staff and the rank of *Generalmajor*.[18]

Otto von Knobelsdorff followed a similarly diverse and educational path. He returned to his 94th Regiment after the war and served as a company commander in several regiments, held staff jobs in two artillery groups, and took charge of a squadron of the 9th Mounted Regiment for a year in 1928. Knobelsdorff took command of the 102nd Infantry Regiment in 1935. A newly minted *Generalmajor*, he commanded the fortifications around Oppeln just before war broke out.[19]

Hans von Obstfelder was taken into the *Reichswehr* in 1920 and continued to fill staff jobs, with only a brief stint commanding an infantry battalion. Though he had never held a combat command, in October 1936, now a *Generalmajor*, he took over the 28th Infantry Division and was soon promoted to *generalleutnant*.[20]

Hans-Gustav Felber joined the Hessian *Freikorps* before being taken into the *Reichswehr*, where he rose from an infantry company commanding officer to *Oberstleutnant* through a series of staff jobs before taking command of an infantry regiment in 1933. In 1934, a promising *oberst*, he was named commander of the War Academy. He subsequently served as chief of staff for III Corps and Eighth Army, with which he participated in the Polish campaign.[21]

Hermann Priess was part of the new, dark wave in Germany. Born to a farming family on 24 May 1901 at Marnitz in Mecklenburg, Priess worked on the family farm and then for the local postmaster before deciding to seek more adventure. Priess volunteered for the army in 1919 and fought in the 18th Mounted Regiment with the *Freikorps von Brandis* in the Baltic theater, where he was wounded at Riga and earned both classes of the Iron Cross. In 1920, he became a twelve-year man in the *Reichswehr*, serving in the 14th Mounted Regiment *Ludwigslust*. He joined the Nazi Party in January 1933 and the *Schutzstaffel* (SS) two months later, listing his profession as "soldier." Priess was among the first to join the SS military wing in 1934, though he was still a reservist in the 14th Mounted Regiment and was said to be a skilled rider and instructor. Priess married and had two children. He won praise from his commanders in the SS for his calm and soldierly demeanor, and he proved an effective leader because of his character and long military service. Priess impressed Heinrich Himmler during an inspection so much in 1935 that the *Reichsführer SS* promoted him on the spot.[22]

Another member of this dark army was Max Simon. Simon had been born in Breslau on 6 January 1899. Towering over six feet in height and having steely, blue-gray eyes, Simon had the bespectacled, round face of a monk, but he became a monster. After his cavalry service in the Great War, which earned him the Iron Cross, Simon fought with the *Freikorps* in Silesia and then transferred to the *Reichswehr* in 1920. He once again became a noncommissioned officer in the 16th Cavalry Regiment.

Simon left the army in 1929 and held jobs in the civil service and as a salesman. Attracted by the Nazis, Simon joined the party in April 1932 and the SS in August 1933. Simon became an officer in the concentration-camp system until 1935, where he earned praise for his leadership and "restless reliability." At some point, he married but became a widower in 1933; he married again in 1935 to Edith Olscher, who bore him a son and to whom he was sufficiently devoted to elicit some criticism in his performance review for insufficient *Kameradschaft*. His Guard Group *Sachsen* was militarized and expanded into a regiment-sized formation, in which he took command of a battalion. His superior called Simon open and honorable, energetic, possesser of a decisive will and a smart head, a strong Nazi, and a man well suited for military duties. An American officer who interviewed him in August 1945 recorded, "Simon reminded me of a big, talkative, genial grocer." He was transferred in 1938 to command a battalion of the SS *Standart* (Regiment) *Oberbayern*. He soon received promotion to command the regiment.[23]

Paul Hausser joined the SS as a *Standartenführer* (colonel) in November 1934, and he was a very different sort than the usual SS recruit—a professional soldier of the first order. Born to a former imperial army officer in Brandenburg an der Havel on 7 October 1880, Hausser received his education in the cadet corps from the age of eleven and entered the imperial army in 1889 as a general staff officer assigned as a *leutnant* to the 155th Infantry Regiment, where he rose to become adjutant of first a battalion and then the regiment. Paul married a hometown girl in 1912, and the pair had a daughter. Hausser initially served with the Army General Staff and the staffs of an army, corps, and division in the Great War. He then commanded an infantry company on the western front, in Kurland, and in Romania, earning the Iron Cross first and second class.

After the armistice, Hausser joined the *Freikorps General Jütz*, where he remained until being accepted into the *Reichswehr* in 1919. He once again held several staff positions, followed by command of an infantry battalion and the 10th Infantry Regiment. By 1932, he had reached the rank of *generalleutnant* and retired from the service.

Hausser in 1933 signed on with the Nazi Party's bullyboys, the *Sturmabteilung* (SA, Storm Troops). SS chief Heinrich Himmler recruited him on 1 November 1934. The SS quickly made use of Hausser's military knowledge and assigned him to first reorganize the SS leadership school in Braunschweig and then to head the school. Hausser joined the Nazi Party in 1938 after three years of fruitless applications, despite a 1935 recommendation from the local party boss underscoring that his competence and political and world views that were "beyond any doubts."

Hausser, in 1936, became inspector of the *Verfügungs Truppe* (Reserve or Special Use Troops), the nascent *Waffen* SS (armed SS). Heinz Guderian considered him an excellent choice for the position and characterized Hausser as "a first-class officer, a brave and clever soldier, and a man of outstandingly upright and honorable character." Panzer general Fritz Bayerlein, who fought under Hausser six years later in Normandy, characterized him as "a sensible, approachable man. . . . [H]e was a good leader and always in front of his men." Himmler, in 1938, charged Hausser with organizing the 3rd SS Regiment, which he did using cadre troops from Hitler's bodyguard unit, the *Leibstandarte Adolf Hitler*.

Hitler, in November 1939, named Hausser to the command of the newly formed *Verfügungs Truppen Division*, the first of the SS infantry divisions. Hausser's command eventually would be renamed the 2nd SS Division *Das Reich*, because the *Leibstandarte Adolf Hitler* took the honor of 1st SS Division.[24]

A few of Patton's future enemies were taking part in creating Germany's panzer force. This early engagement probably contributed to them becoming superb panzer generals.

The son of a great World War I general, Hermann Balck was born on 7 December 1893 in Danzig, Prussia. Balck's father had instilled in him a facility for historical thinking and a deep appreciation for the welfare of the common soldier. Balck joined the military as an officer candidate in 1913, and as a young officer, he visited his father in Colmar, Alsace, where the latter was a brigade commander. Together, they toured the area as far north as Metz, considering the land in the context of a conviction that war with France was imminent. One day, Balck would face Patton on that very ground. Balck had fought on the western, eastern, Italian, and Balkan fronts in the First World War as a company-grade officer in a mountain infantry battalion. He was awarded the Iron Cross first class while still an ensign and was wounded seven times.

Balck remained in the army when the war ended, and in 1922, he obtained a transfer to the cavalry, with which he served for twelve years, including as a squadron commander in the 18th Mounted Regiment from 1928 to 1933. After a stint as a staff officer in the 3rd Infantry Division, Balck returned to semimobile warfare, commanding bicycle units from 1935 to 1938. Balck joined *Generalmajor* Heinz Guderian's Inspectorate of Mobile Troops in Berlin, where he was working when the war broke out.[25]

Hasso-Eccard von Manteuffel nearly left the military to go into industry, but his uncle convinced him he was a born soldier and should continue to serve. After a stint in *Freikorps von Oven* in Berlin, Manteuffel gained a slot in the *Reichswehr* and very quickly was given command of a squadron in his old 3rd Brandenburg Hussars Regiment. The cavalry, including his regiment, abandoned the lance and adopted the light machine gun. Manteuffel married in 1921 and fathered two children. By 1930, Manteuffel was regimental adjutant. He, like Patton, was a keen rider who kept his own stable and was successful in tournaments. Manteuffel thought Hitler's 1933 rise to power would be good for the army and the country.

In October 1934, Manteuffel saw the future and opted for the panzers, taking command of the motorcycle battalion in *Oberst* Heinz Guderian's 2nd Panzer Division. In 1937, now *Generalmajor* Guderian summoned Manteuffel to join him at the Inspectorate of Mobile Troops, where Manteuffel oversaw the motorization of four infantry divisions. In 1939, now an *oberstleutnant*, Manteuffel became an instructor at the panzer school in Berlin.[26]

After serving in the *Reichswehr*'s cavalry arm for most of the interwar period, *Major* Smilo *Freiherr* von Lüttwitz, in 1936, joined the new mechanized cavalry and took command of the 5th Reconnaissance Battalion (Motorized). In 1939, Lüttwitz became the adjutant of XV Corps. But mechanized warfare was now in his blood, and he would return to it during the campaign in France.[27]

Wend von Wietersheim followed a similar path. Born 18 April 1900 in Neuland, Wietersheim was another World War I veteran who rose to the rank of *leutnant* during the conflict. After serving in the cavalry between the wars, he transferred to the panzer arm in late 1938 as a *Hauptmann* and adjutant of the 3rd Panzer Division. He participated in the Polish campaign in this capacity.[28]

In France, Capt. Jean Petit also followed a peacetime track. France had moved far ahead of the Germans and Americans in the technological aspects of mechanization. In 1923, for example, the French army established within its cavalry arm fourteen battalions of armored cars carrying 37mm guns. Each cavalry division fielded a total of forty-two armored cars.[29] Yet, the army ignored the theories of mobile warfare offered by Gen. Charles De Gaulle and concentrated its resources on building the Maginot Line of fortifications facing Germany and training officers and men to fight a slow, carefully planned war much like the last one. Guderian, looking back, called French thinking a "mania for planned control."[30]

After serving occupation duty in Germany from 1920 to 1923, Petit became an instructor at French military schools, a task that kept him occupied until the outbreak of the next war. There is no indication, however, that he was particularly interested in developments in military mechanization. Instead, he was a respected mentor for junior officers and leader of young men. Happily, as things turned out, his leadership skills would be all that he needed.

Colonel Alfredo Guzzoni spent the early post-war years first as a member of the control commissions in occupied Austria and Hungary and then as the secretariat of the War Ministry. He returned to an infantry command in 1929, taking charge of the 58th Infantry Regiment. After a stint as the ordnance chief at the War Ministry, Guzzoni was promoted to brigadier general and took command of the 3rd Alpine Brigade. From there, he became, in 1931, the director of the Academy of Infantry and Cavalry in Modena and then of the Infantry School in Parma. Guzzoni moved to colonial affairs, became a *General di Divisione* (major general), and, in 1936, was appointed governor of the colony of Asmara. He played a key role in bringing the Ethiopian campaign to a successful conclusion, for which he was promoted to *General di Corpo* (lieutenant general).

In March 1939, Guzzoni was given command of the Italian force that occupied Albania. Despite annoying political interference, he competently executed that task in April, and he was appointed the military governor.[31]

DISTANT INTERACTION

Patton got a foretaste of his future enemies through the writings of some of their greatest thinkers, and to some extent, his view of war became much like theirs. In 1937, Erwin Rommel, Heinz Guderian, and Walter Warlimont published books and papers that sought to recast the art of war with their notions of autonomous, large-scale armored operations; increased mobility of infantry through cooperation with tanks; and a concept of "operations" lying above tactics and below strategy. These men became known in the United States, thanks to reports filed by the U.S. military attaché in Berlin and the accounts of an American major who attended the *Kriegsakademie*.

Patton, who had just transferred to the U.S. Cavalry School, seized on these writings with fascination. He himself had given lectures emphasizing the role that fast-moving armor could play on the future battlefield, though he still saw the horse-mounted cavalry as the primary mobile force.[32] Because modern German notions fit so closely with many of his theories in the old Tank Corps, he internalized the concepts quickly. After reading Guderian in 1939, he noted to himself: use tanks for firepower rather than shock; launch attacks on a wide front to disperse enemy fire; officers should lead from the front; a short battle results in fewer casualties, so tanks should advance rapidly, but not hastily.[33]

Patton, in 1938, had begun to conduct sand-table exercises drawing on descriptions of maneuvers in German military journals. By then, he had realized that if the horse cavalry was going to play any role in the next war, it was not going to be a large one.[34]

On 1 September 1939, the day the largest and most destructive war in history ignited, the United States possessed a small and obsolete armored force. The regular army's infantry branch had only the just-organized 66th Infantry (Light Tanks) and the 67th Infantry (Medium Tanks), based at Fort Benning, Georgia, plus one tank company in each of seven infantry divisions and eighteen National Guard infantry divisions. The 7th Cavalry Brigade was mechanized. But only two of its battalion-sized squadrons were equipped with light tanks, and they carried nothing more lethal than machine guns. Other than World War I–era tanks, the total American armored vehicle inventory amounted to some 240 machine-gun-armed M1 and M2 light tanks, plus a single M2 medium-tank prototype equipped with a 37mm gun. There were tentative budgetary plans to allocate $7 million for additional infantry tanks.[35] But the country had no tank in large-scale production.

Patton was still a horse soldier, commanding the 3rd Cavalry at Fort Myer, Virginia. He had not had a thing to do with the small-scale mechanization of the cavalry. He had commanded no troops in large-scale maneuvers.

✳

FOUR

The Enemy Goes to War

THINGS WERE QUITE DIFFERENT for Patton's future enemies in Europe. In Poland, the Wehrmacht used but a single cavalry brigade, which fought with Third Army, and all other cavalry regiments of the peacetime army had been allocated to the infantry divisions as reconnaissance elements.[1]

The German offensive on 1 September was a showpiece for Blitzkrieg and destroyed the Polish army in about two weeks. Fourteen mechanized or partially mechanized divisions, supported by an overwhelming Luftwaffe air arm, were decisive in the stunning success, though some forty regular infantry divisions also took part.

Oddly, few of Patton's future enemies held combat commands during the Polish campaign. *Generaloberst* Gerd von Rundstedt, just returned to the army after being dismissed for protesting the timing of the occupation of the Sudetenland in Czechoslovakia, commanded Army Group South. Rundstedt's army group included most of the mechanized formations in the German army and a total of thirty-six divisions. *Generalleutnant* Erich von Manstein, who would arguably mold the skills of some of Patton's most important enemies, was Rundstedt's chief of staff. *Generalleutnant* Johannes Blaskowitz commanded Eighth Army under Rundstedt. *General der Artillerie* Günther von Kluge led Fourth Army across the Danzig Corridor.[2]

Generalmajor Otto von Knobelsdorff had returned to the command of the 102nd Infantry Regiment, 24th Infantry Division. The division's records for that campaign were destroyed in a fire, so nothing is known about his performance in Poland—except that it was good enough to earn Knobelsdorff a divisional command for the campaign in France.

Generalleutnant Hans von Obstfelder led his 28th Infantry Division in the Polish campaign, and the seemingly terminal staff officer turned out to be a talented field commander. The division's war diary has disappeared, so we have no direct window into his tactical performance or leadership style. His commanding officer judged that he led his division with energy and tactical skill, that he was a fresh thinker, and that he exercised an excellent influence on his subordinates, who were fiercely loyal to him. He was a tough judge of his own performance. He was, however, a micromanager who needed to leave details behind.[3]

Hauptsturmführer Hermann Priess had risen to command a company in SS Regiment *Germania* before the war, but in 1939, he attended the Jüterborg artillery school and organized the first SS artillery battalion. Priess, now a *Sturmbannführer*, led his battalion during the campaign in Poland after it had been incorporated into the first SS field division, the *Verfügungsdivision* (Reserve Division), commanded by Paul Hausser. Priess received the Iron Cross of 1939 for his actions during the campaign.

Max Simon commanded his *Oberbayern Standart* in Poland, where it followed Tenth Army's advance, committing mass executions of Jews, political and religious leaders, and captured Polish soldiers.[4]

Just after the campaign ended, Priess's battalion became part of the *Totenkopf* (Death's Head) Division (which eventually became a panzergrenadier and then a panzer division) when it was activated at Dachau in October 1939, under the command of *Gruppenführer* Theodor Eicke. The division's core consisted of three regiments of *Totenkopfverbände* (Death's Head Units), whose members were recruited from concentration camp guards, including Simon's *Oberbayern*, whose atrocities—especially against Jews—in Poland had horrified some army commanders. Simon was transformed into the commanding officer of the 1st Infantry Regiment. Eicke, in his personnel rating, said that Simon was forthright; had a rough exterior balanced by an inner cordiality; was willing to pursue Nazi objectives without question; instilled trust in his men, who would go through fire for him; and was a true soldier.[5]

Distressingly for American planners, the Polish army that had crumbled before the Wehrmacht was similar to the U.S. Army in terms of size, reliance on cavalry, and incomplete mechanization. Brigadier General Adna Chaffee, who was in command of the 7th Cavalry Brigade (Mechanized) the day Hitler invaded Poland, led other mechanization advocates in calling for the establishment of "cavalry divisions, mechanized" built roughly along the lines of the German panzer divisions.[6] During Third Army maneuvers in May 1940, the 7th

Cavalry Brigade formed part of a provisional armored division, along with the 6th Infantry Regiment (Motorized) and the infantry's Provisional Tank Brigade, which included the two tank regiments from Fort Benning. The provisional division dominated the exercise.[7]

At the conclusion of the exercises, Brig. Gen. Frank Andrews, the War Department assistant chief of staff, G-3 (operations), met on 25 May in a high school basement in Alexandria, Louisiana, with now Maj. Gen. Adna Chaffee and other officers from cavalry and mechanized units, including George Patton. Their conversation would ultimately lead to the creation of the American armored divisions.[8] As the men talked, the German armed forces were just beginning the third week of their dazzling campaign to destroy the French army, as they had the Polish.

WAR IN EARNEST

The war in the West in the spring of 1940 taught German officers that they could fight and win even when outnumbered as long as they had an aggressive philosophy, good plans, first-rate commanders, some mobility, adequate troops, and air cover. The most senior general officers were surprised by their decisive victory against the Western Allies because they thought the British and French were too strong, and they opposed Hitler's intention to go on the offensive in the West. Following a plan crafted by *Generaloberst* Gerd von Rundstedt's chief of staff at Army Group B, *Generalleutnant* Erich von Manstein, Rundstedt's army group formed the *Schwerpunkt* (point of concentration, a key German concept on offense and defense), striking by surprise with three panzer corps through the heavily forested, but thinly defended Ardennes. Army Group A advanced into the Low Countries to pin down the British and French mobile forces that analysis and intelligence reporting indicated would advance from France to meet the army group's attack, thus allowing Rundstedt to cut them off. Army Group C was to pin the rest of the French army along the frontier south of the Ardennes.[9]

Manstein's vision was breathtaking in its audacity. And, as a successful plan to overwhelm with a few decisive strokes a numerically and in some ways technologically superior enemy in an entire theater of operations, it was never equaled by the Western Allies or Soviets. The original operational scheme had aimed merely to gain control over the length of the Channel coast to support U-Boat warfare against Britain. Manstein had aimed far higher and had conceived of a plan to take France out of the war.[10] Rundstedt called it a reverse Schlieffen Plan because the left wing wheeled northward rather than the right wing southward, as the Germans had tried in the Great War. "My Army Group A was to advance

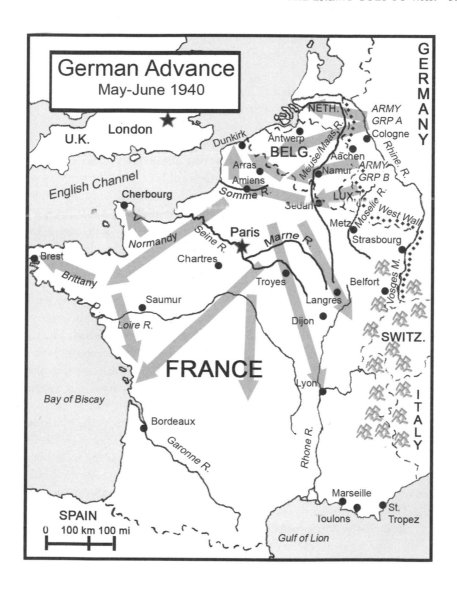

across the Meuse [Maas] as far as the Channel, then wheel against the enemy forces stationed in Belgium and annihilate them!" Rundstedt wrote. As a base of comparison for later Allied operations against Rundstedt, his army group controlled five armies (including Kluge's Fourth Army) and two panzer groups, a total of 86 divisions, for this offensive.[11]

When the Germans launched their offensive in the West on 10 May 1940, Patton was, as noted earlier, still a horse soldier, commanding the 3rd Cavalry at Fort Myer, Virginia. One of his future enemies, incredibly enough, was also still a cavalryman.

"Pferdebestand (horse inventory)," came the codeword, then *"Danzig."* These two words signaled the launch of the great offensive.

The German 1st Cavalry Division—the only horse-mounted division on the western front—crossed the German-Dutch border on the right wing of Eighteenth Army at 0535 hours on 10 May 1940. The division's order for the day ended, "Think forward, look forward, ride forward!"

The division in November 1939 had been constituted around the cavalry brigade that had fought in Poland, and additional squadrons had been pulled from the infantry division reconnaissance elements. Some 70 percent of the men were East Prussians, and the rest were drawn from the Rhineland and Westphalia. *Oberstleutnant* Fritz *Freiherr* von Broich, who on 5 December had taken command of the 21st Cavalry Regiment while the division engaged in intensive training, was aware that many would have been surprised to know that the German army still had a cavalry division, much less that it would be employed in the great offensive against the Western Allies. Broich had spent the Polish campaign in command of the 34th Infantry Division's reconnaissance battalion, waging the "Sitzkrieg" on the Western Front. Broich and the other men had been impatient for action as the spring months passed, one by one. Now it was time!

The division's mission was to occupy northern Holland, take the Ijseelmeer dike, establish a bridgehead west of the dike, and then attack "Festung Holland" from the northeast. The first stage for part of the division involved an amphibious operation across the Zuidersee. The attached navy component was to stay with the division and help it cross canals using confiscated boats until bridges could be built.

The division's bicycle battalion led the assault, clearing frontier bunkers with special assault groups and antitank guns, and rolled up prisoners. The cavalry moved through the gap and rode west, followed eventually by the division's tank platoons. The men could hear Dutch demolitions destroying bridges in the distance. Fierce Dutch resistance stopped the attack on the dike, however.

Moving all night, the division's main body deployed its armored car troop forward, which found a route free of enemy soldiers. Roadblocks erected by the civilian population posed the only occasional hindrance, which the engineers easily dismantled. In only forty hours, the division advanced 120 miles. Even the cavalry operation had shown the mark of German mechanization and combined-arms thinking, as artillery and mortars supported the squadrons.

Unfortunately for Broich, his regiment constituted part of the division reserve, and he saw no action during the brief period before the Dutch capitulation on 14 May. The division withdrew to Germany on the seventeenth.

Broich thought his big chance had come when the division's lead elements boarded a train at Aachen on 24 May and rolled toward France. Army Group B, however, did not seem to have a plan for the cavalrymen. The Ic (the German equivalent of G-2, intelligence) spotted the division commander and said, "Aha! My prisoner-of-war guards!" Great was the disappointment among the cavaliers. The commanding general got on the phone and called the high command. On the twenty-eighth, the decision was overturned, and the cavalrymen rejoiced.

The bulk of the division arrived by 5 June by road march, and impatience burned in the ranks. Would the fight be over before they could play a part? Fourth Army ordered the creation of an independent brigade using the division's bicycle troops and some of the artillery and engineers. This was good news and bad, as someone was going to fight, but it weakened the division. The rest of the division was to advance on the left of Manstein's XXXVIII Corps along the Amiens-Poix road and establish a bridgehead across the Poix River. It would be given elements of the 27th Infantry Division for the operation.

Subordinated to the strengthened 22nd Mounted Regiment, Broich set off with his men at 0530 hours on 7 June toward Amiens. The lead elements of the division crossed the Somme at 1000. The French were nowhere to be seen. After advancing forty miles, Broich's men got a two-hour break at Namps. The armored car troop, meanwhile, reconnoitered Fremontiers and reported it strongly garrisoned.

Broich climbed into an armored car and went to have a look. He found a good observation point and called forward the heavy-weapons commander. Broich decided he would act quickly and attack from the cover of woods about 2,000 yards from the town, which would allow his men to stay on the horses until almost the last moment. He thought he could storm the town without help and arranged that the 22nd Mounted Regiment advance on his flank to take the high ground across a brook.

At 1820 hours, Broich's antitank guns and machine guns opened fire on observed machine-gun nests and knocked several of them out. At 1845, the artillery opened fire on the high ground. The cavalrymen moved out on foot at 1900.

The French held their fire until the Germans were almost upon them and then cut loose. The cavalrymen plunged ahead, and suddenly the French broke and ran away. By the time Broich reached the village, his men reported it secured, with many French soldiers and machine guns taken. The 22nd Mounted Regiment had, meanwhile, captured the high ground as planned.

Broich's rapid attack had avoided a hard fight. The French were found to have dug in on the high ground with antitank guns and would have had a field day against a deliberate assault. The key had been that the Germans had arrived at the French line on the heels of the men fleeing the village, and the entrenched French soldiers could not shoot.

By 14 June, the division was only a dozen miles from Paris, and two days later the 21st Cavalry Regiment engaged French troops near Chartres. On the nineteenth, Broich's men took captive an entire battalion in Saumur, in the Loire valley, the home of the French cavalry school where Patton had studied the saber, having surprised most of the Frenchmen asleep in the houses. The French army was showing signs of gradual disintegration.

Broich now took command of a motorized advance battalion, which consisted of his own 5th Company, the antitank battalion, a company of soldiers in a bus, an artillery battery, and a platoon of engineers. Racing unopposed into Loudon, the command suddenly came upon nine French medium tanks in the marketplace. The antitank guns quickly knocked out two of them, and the rest disappeared.[12]

By the time the armistice took hold on 25 June, Broich had proved himself an aggressive and effective tactical leader and had fought with his men on horse, on foot as dragoons, and in motorized maneuvers.

Sedan was a perfect place to cross the Meuse and drive to the Somme estuary in the enemy's rear, a prospect that fired the imagination of *General der Panzertruppe* Heinz Guderian once he saw the objective of Manstein's plan for the offensive. Guderian was to command XIX Panzer Corps in this very drive, accompanied by XIV Panzer Corps as the main body of Panzer Group Kleist.[13]

Oberstleutnant Hermann Balck first displayed his tactical brilliance at the very point of Guderian's daring blitz, when he commanded the 1st *Schützenregiment* (Motorized Infantry Regiment), 1st Panzer Division. The regiment reached the Meuse at Donchery, a town located just west of Sedan, on 12 May, and Balck readied his troops to cross the river. The original plan had called for a pause while the infantry divisions caught up, but Guderian thought the opportunity for a crossing was there; *General der Kavallerie* Ewald von Kleist, commanding the panzer group, approved the idea. Unlike in his later battles, this time Balck had precise information on the French positions, and his officers and men had studied maps and photographs of the terrain for months and practiced the attack.

The following morning, however, French artillery fire drove German troops to cover and completely stymied Balck's plans. The German artillery was still stuck in traffic jams to the rear, and although rubber assault boats arrived, none of the engineers who were supposed to use them did. Balck knew he had to silence the French guns, and he sent a liaison officer to the headquarters of Panzer Corps Guderian (XIX Panzer Corps) to request maximum Luftwaffe support against the French artillery.

About noon, Stukas appeared over the battlefield and pounced on the French firing positions, sirens screaming as they descended. It appeared to Balck that the French crews abandoned their guns, and a sudden calm replaced the explosions and chaos of a few moments earlier.

Balck seized the moment. The reconnaissance battalion dragged the assault boats to the river under full view of the Frenchmen in their bunkers on the far bank and paddled across under the protection of plunging Luftwaffe bombers. The French resistance collapsed, and Balck consolidated a small bridgehead.

Balck had no tanks or antitank guns, but he decided to expand his bridgehead to make it more secure. By night march, he seized Chémery, six miles south of the Meuse. Balck's actions opened the way for the German swing past Amiens to the Channel coast and to victory in France.

Early on 14 May, a French armored brigade, supported by low-flying planes, counterattacked, and it briefly looked like Balck's gamble would turn up snake eyes. The beleaguered Germans were also struck by numerous low-level attacks from British and French bombers. In addition to their own light antiaircraft defenses, Balck received unexpected help from French Morane fighters, which downed four British light bombers of No. 142 Squadron.[14] Fortunately, the engineers had finally finished building a bridge across the Meuse, and the first panzers and antitank guns arrived in time to engage the French before the French completely deployed. The action was short and sharp, and the French left thirty of their forty tanks burning on the field. Balck's boldness had paid off handsomely.

Guderian considered Balck "efficient and brave." The panzer general described an encounter with Balck on the sixteenth that bears more than passing resemblance to Patton's charge with a walking stick in the Argonne, though Balck was luckier and did not get shot:

All that was known was that there had been heavy fighting during the night in the neighborhood of Bouvellmont. . . . In the main street of the burning village, I found the regimental commander, Lieutenant Colonel Balck, and let him describe the events of the previous night to me. The troops were over-tired, having had no real rest since the ninth of May. Ammunition was running low. The men in the front line were falling asleep in their slit trenches. Balck himself, with a wind jacket and a knotty stick in his hand, told me that the capture of the village had only succeeded because, when his officers complained against the continuation of the attack, he had replied: "In that case, I'll take the place on my own!" and had moved off. His men had thereupon followed him.

Balck was awarded the Knight's Cross for this action.

Balck showed early that he was willing to give up some ground in order to gain a bigger prize. On 20 May, Balck held a bridgehead across the Somme near Amiens but was supposed to participate in the attack on the city. When the relief force failed to appear on time, Balck simply abandoned the bridgehead because Amiens was the main objective. Confronted by an officer from the late-arriving 10th Panzer Division, Balck replied, "If we lose it, you can always take it again. I had to capture it in the first place, didn't I?"

Balck and the 1st Panzer Division reached the English Channel and very nearly Dunkirk on 24 May, the capture of which probably would have resulted in the loss of most of the British Expeditionary Force. Hitler, however, for reasons never fully explained, ordered Guderian to halt the advance on the port for forty-eight hours, which gave the British enough time to pull off the evacuation known as the "miracle of Dunkirk." For all that, Guderian's corps had accomplished one of the most stunning successes in military history.

On 28 May, Hitler directed Guderian to turn the Dunkirk operation over to an infantry corps and placed him in charge of a panzer group to drive south to the Swiss border. Balck, always at the spearhead, features prominently in Guderian's account of that operation. Launched on 9 June, the drive carried the panzer group west of the Argonne and across the Plateau de Langres to the Swiss border by the seventeenth, passing just west of the area where Balck would fight Patton in 1944. By the time it was over, Guderian—and Balck—had covered more French ground than Patton would four years later; and they'd covered that ground against a better-armed, larger, and hard-fighting enemy force (at least in the first weeks), whereas Patton would drive through a vacuum.

Balck later won laurels in Greece with the 2nd Panzer Division, where he commanded the 3rd Panzer Regiment and then replaced Gustav von Vaerst—another future Patton enemy—in command of the 2nd Motorized Infantry Brigade. He then served on the staff of the inspector of mobile troops from November 1941 to May 1942, when he developed the basic tactics used by the panzergrenadiers.[15]

*

SS Gruppenführer Paul Hausser's *Das Reich* division was employed on the right wing of Panzer Group Kleist for the invasion of the West. The division's first task was a difficult one, as many Canadian soldiers would learn in 1944: Hausser's men captured Walcheren Island in the Scheldt estuary in a fierce three-day battle, which led to the early capitulation of Antwerp. The division then took part in the envelopment of the British and French troops in Flanders. When Kleist's panzer group drove south in June, Hausser's division advanced all the way to the Plateau de Langres, capturing 20,000 French troops.

Guderian judged that Hausser had proved to be a superior field commander during these operations, being personally involved in his combat operations and the most dangerous points, self-confident and calm, and bitterly determined to master the most difficult situation himself.[16]

SS Sturmbannführer Hermann Priess saw his first mobile action performed by the masters of the art, albeit when he was still an artillery battalion commander rather than a panzer officer. Although the *Totenkopf* Division initially had received only requisitioned Czech equipment, it was one of the few fully motorized divisions the Germans had available. A month before Germany attacked in the West, the division had been fully reequipped with German vehicles and weapons. Combat training had improved dramatically.

After sitting in *Oberkommando des Heeres* (OKH, Army High Command) reserve on the Rhine in the opening stages of the Western campaign, the division was sent to Cambrai, where it arrived on 19 May. The panzers had achieved a stunning breakthrough and were headed for the English Channel coast. *Totenkopf* slid into the XV Panzer Corps front between *Generalmajor* Erwin Rommel's 7th and the 8th Panzer Divisions and advanced toward Dunkirk.

On 21 May, the division was caught up on the fringe of a British counterattack near Arras by two tank battalions supported by infantry, which were aimed mainly at Rommel's 7th Panzer Division. As luck would have it, British Matildas struck *Totenkopf* precisely where its antitank battalion was located. The German 37mm antitank guns proved helpless against the thick armor, and tanks rolled over several guns and crews. Other men fled. Only Priess's artillery, firing over open sights, brought the attack to a standstill.

The *Totenkopf* Division participated in the push to eliminate the Allied pocket from 27 to 30 May, earning a new reputation primarily through lackluster performance on the battlefield and the massacre of some hundred British prisoners at La Paradis.[17]

*

Given command of the newly raised 83rd Infantry Division in December 1939, Kurt von der Chevallerie participated in the campaign in the West the following year. His first order revealed a determined, take-charge officer. "The division is to be ready for deployment in the field by 10 February 1940. Should conditions demand readiness before then, the order must not find us unprepared." He intended, he announced, to train the division for mobile warfare. By the end of January, he considered his division capable of limited battlefield service, mainly due to missing equipment.

The 83rd Infantry Division entrained for the western front on 15 May, marched across the pacified Dutch frontier three days later, and entered France on the twenty-second. The division joined VIII Corps, which was trying to wipe out a French bridgehead at Bouchain on the Escault Canal, on 26 May. Chevallerie's men first tasted battle the next day, albeit only by conducting local attacks and preventing the enemy's movement through the line. Chevallerie went forward with his one regiment that was scheduled to attack that day. The following day, the division marched south and by 7 June joined XLIV Corps on the Aisne River near Soissons, where it was assigned to protect the corps's flank. It advanced southward with the corps to the Marne against virtually no resistance.

Finally, on 11 June, the division ran into well-trained and -led troops backed by artillery just before the Marne along the road to Paris. Attacking across the river the next day, the division, expecting heavy resistance, encountered none. The French had withdrawn to the defensive positions outside Paris. With *General der Kavallerie* Kleist's panzer group racing southward on the corps's right flank, the division crossed the Seine unmolested on the sixteenth. The advance rolled on, reaching the Loire at Orléans the next day. The French army had effectively collapsed, and air reconnaissance reported nothing but fleeing French troops and civilians on the roads. Crossing the Loire on the eighteenth, the division scooped up 5,000 prisoners. There would be no more battles.

The division's war diary was destroyed in a fire, so we know little about the general's leadership during the campaign. But the invasion had offered him few opportunities to show his promise. Still, it had taken him, from north to south, through the precise area where he would first face George Patton four years later.[18]

Generalmajor Otto von Knobelsdorff had taken command of the 19th Infantry Division on 4 February 1940. The division, part of XI Corps, was still in training on 9 May when the codeword "Hindenburg 10 05 35" arrived. *Generalleutnant* Joachim von Kortzfleisch, commanding the corps, briefly addressed his subordinate officers: "Germany will be victorious, because it must be victorious!" Knobelsdorff and the others responded with a hearty *Sieg Heil* to the führer and fatherland. (The fact that Knobelsdorff for a while sported a Hitler moustache suggests that he was a Nazi believer, and one personnel evaluation noted that he was a firm National Socialist.) In less than four hours, Knobelsdorff had his men on the march to their assembly area, straight from the maneuvers. Knobelsdorff was well pleased with the excellent organization and high morale that he saw among his troops.

By 0200 hours, Knobelsdorff's combat elements had closed in on the Dutch border. X-hour was 0535, XI Corps informed him. The invasion began on the dot.

The Dutch offered no resistance until the Germans reached Maasniel, where a Dutch motorcycle unit claimed the first casualties. The 2nd Battalion, 59th Infantry Regiment, supported by the 5th Panzer Platoon, reached the railroad bridge over the Maas, only to find it destroyed. As the panzers sat, Dutch gunners in bunkers on the far bank scored several direct hits on them and caused heavy casualties. By 0645, the rest of the division closed to the Maas, but every single span had been blown. Heavy fire stopped every attempt to cross.

Knobelsdorff was to show daring and aggressive instincts from the first hours of battle in this war. The general drove to the frontline at the bridge at Roermond about 0700 and surveyed the scene. The Dutch were brilliantly camouflaged, and they had made excellent use of invisible bunkers, set well back, and were placing raking fire on his flanks from them. Knobelsdorff ordered reconnaissance to identify the Dutch positions, so they could be shelled and a way forward opened. He personally oversaw the deployment of heavy antitank guns and pointed out to the commanding officer of the division's artillery regiment which targets he wanted blasted. He instructed his chief of engineers to hustle forward river-crossing gear to replace what had been destroyed.

Briefly returning to his headquarters to report the situation to XI Corps, Knobelsdorff made his way back to Roermond by 0900 to find that, under the cover of the heavy weapons, some of his reconnaissance troops were across the Maas. About 1000, an antitank gun knocked out the Dutch bunker at the west end of the damaged Roermond bridge, and infantry immediately clambered across the girders to find that the Dutch had largely disappeared. Elsewhere, the division's crossings succeeded under the cover of artillery fire. With Roermond secured and nearly 600 prisoners in hand, Knobelsdorff ordered two battalions to continue to the Belgian border and prepare to assault the bunkers there.

Knobelsdorff led from the front again the next day, directing his battalions toward objectives on the Albert Canal. Only individual Belgian soldiers were encountered, and they inevitably surrendered. The Belgians, however, were well entrenched on the far side of the Albert Canal. Knobelsdorff, late on 11 May, issued a special order of the day praising his men, who had created a break-through and advanced forty-five miles in only two days.

Kept on a leash by XI Corps while the divisions to the left and right crossed the Albert Canal, the 19th Division finally got its attack orders on the thirteenth and pushed across. Knobelsdorff reached the far bank on the heels of the assault troops and immediately took control of the battle.

By the seventeenth, the division was on the northern outskirts of Brussels, having fought the British for the preceding two days. The 14th Division, to the left, occupied the Belgian capital on the eighteenth. Brigadier A. J. Clifton's 2nd Armored Reconnaissance Brigade, covering the withdrawal of II British Corps southwest of Brussels, encountered Knobelsdorff's reconnaissance elements near Assche at about 1100 hours. The British were trying to link up with Belgian troops when they unexpectedly encountered the German forces. The British contingent, consisting of the 5th Inniskilling Dragoon Guards, 15th/19th The Kings Royal Hussars, 4th Gordon Highlanders (a machine-gun battalion), 32nd Army Field Regiment, and 14th Anti-tank Regiment, discovered the "enemy were round and between" them and their supporting artillery and machine guns.

Fighting raged throughout the morning. Antitank guns from the 19th *Panzerjäger Abteilung* (Antitank Battalion) had been positioned with fields of fire overlooking the routes utilized by the British, and Knobelsdorff rushed to the scene with a company of heavy antitank guns. A battalion each of infantry and artillery arrived, and in a wild melee, Knobelsdorff and his men engaged the British with cannons, pistols, hand grenades, antitank rifles, and antitank guns. The British reconnaissance vehicles became stuck in soft ground, and the Germans gunned down the fleeing crews. Several sections of the 15th/19th Hussars were completely wiped out during the fighting.

British orders to withdraw were issued at noon, but they failed to reach some units for several hours. By then, the Germans had surrounded them. When the shooting stopped about 1600, forty-eight British reconnaissance tanks, plus twenty-two Bren carriers, were accounted for. Knobelsdorff, on the field of battle, issued Iron Crosses to those men he had seen perform with outstanding courage.

Knobelsdorff obviously had a hand in the drafting of his division's *Kriegstagebuch* (war diary); not only did he sign the document, but his personal actions are also well covered and a bit of his personal viewpoint appears to creep in. An entry on 19 May refers to "the hated English before us," which suggests that he fought the war with passion rather than professional detachment.

Knobelsdorff had already proved himself an aggressive commander in the attack, even though he commanded an infantry division. At times, he rode with his leading reconnaissance troops so that he could survey the terrain. One British prisoner told his captors, "You are motorized troops with parachutists; otherwise, you could not possibly be here already!"

The race ended along the Scheldt River, where from 20 to 22 May, XI Corps launched fruitless and costly frontal attacks against a determined enemy well backed by artillery. Reconnaissance on the twenty-third revealed that the enemy had slipped away. Five days later, word reached Knobelsdorff's headquarters that a cease-fire with the Belgians had been declared. The British continued to fight, however, and the 19th Division did not cease combat operations until the thirtieth. Although the division moved to France in early June to join the reserve, its fighting days were over in the West.[19]

But Knobelsdorff's glory days were not. On 15 June came the surprising news that Paris had given up, and the 19th Division received orders to enter the city and secure it. Knobelsdorff became the conqueror of Paris, a city whose liberation destiny would deny Patton. Knobelsdorff's columns marched through Paris on the sixteenth, and he held regimental formations on the Place de la République and the Place des Nations. The 30th Infantry Division simultaneously entered from the west and remained in Paris as the occupation force.[20]

Knobelsdorff's performance review in late 1940 described him as an extremely energetic and forceful personality with tremendous influence on his troops. He had proved himself in the French campaign in a superior manner.[21]

Generalleutnant Hans von Obstfelder began the campaign in France at the head of his 28th Infantry Division and ended it commanding XXIX Corps. The 28th Infantry Division constituted part of VIII Corps, along with the 8th and 267th Infantry and 5th Panzer Divisions. As was the case in the Polish campaign, the division's war diary for the first ten days of the invasion of France, when Obstfelder was in command, is missing, so we lack a direct window into his performance.[22] Obstfelder's corps commander said of his performance as division commanding general that he led energetically, sure of his goals and with good tactical sense. His willingness to act had been a model for his men. That said, a later SS evaluation described Obstfelder as a distant figure who mixed uncomfortably with other officers and the troops.[23]

On 20 May, Obstfelder took command of the newly formed XXIX Corps, which was in OKH reserve. While a fire destroyed the original war diary for this period in 1942, reconstructed documents indicate the corps moved into Army Group A reserve from Germany on 11 June. On 15 June, the corps was ordered to advance to Paris, which it appears never to have actually reached. Obstfelder saw no combat prior to the armistice.[24]

PATTON SWAPS SADDLE FOR STEEL

In the summer of 1940, fortune intervened in the life of George Patton and set him upon a course that would shape the lives of many enemies to come—and end not a few of them. On 10 July, when the Armored Force came into being, Patton was still a horse soldier, commanding the 3rd Cavalry at Fort Myer, Virginia. His command lasted only forty-eight hours more. Army chief of staff Gen. George Marshall promoted Patton to the rank of brigadier general and personally saw to his assignment at Fort Benning, where he was to organize a brigade in the brand new 2nd Armored Division.[25]

This Patton did, learning in the process to be an effective leader in a formation so large that he could not know all of his men. In September, he became the acting division commander.

Although no records survive of the German military attaché reporting from this period, extant files from the 1930s show that these officers collected press clippings on the American military and sent them back to Berlin. The chief of military intelligence (*Oberquartiermeister* IV) in Germany at this time was future Patton enemy *Oberst* Kurt von Tippelskirch.[26] We can reasonably assume that they at least read the Washington papers and *New York Times*, which already were replicating the gushing press coverage of Patton seen in World War I. The Washington *Star*, for example, on 15 December 1940, published an article under the headline, "Gen. Patton of the Cavalry Sets Fast Pace for the Tank Corps—Army Knows His Name as Synonym for Daring Action." On 7 July 1941, Patton appeared on the cover of *Life* magazine. So far as one can tell, however, press clippings from Washington disappeared into the files of a German army engaged in combat against other European nations, and no notion of a possible war with the United States occupied its thoughts.

On 4 April 1941, Patton received a promotion to major general and command of his own division.

Patton Masters Tactical Maneuver

Patton's first opportunity to command armored troops against an "enemy" came in the corps- and army-level maneuvers in June 1941 and the interarmy maneuvers that followed. The exercises took place against a background of wide-ranging debate over the proper roles of tanks and antitank guns, all under the somber cloud of the army's realization that, so far, not even the well-respected French army had found a way to stop Hitler's Blitzkrieg.

The maneuvers were important in that they were the only large-scale exercises the U.S. Army had a chance to conduct before going to war. The scenarios in which Patton participated are noteworthy because each one anticipated one of his major battles; in half the cases, Patton tried out the role he would play in war, and in the other cases, he filled the place of his eventual enemy.

Brigadier General Leslie McNair, an artillery officer and chief of staff of the General Headquarters (GHQ), which was responsible for training the rapidly mobilizing ground forces, believed that antitank guns should bear the brunt of stopping enemy armor, while friendly tanks—an offensive weapon—should attack unprotected personnel and material. Tank-on-tank warfare, he argued, would result in heavy material losses on both sides, whereas a small, concealed antitank gun had an overwhelming advantage over a large, easily seen tank. The engagement would be analogous to one between a ship and shore batteries, in which the latter were clearly superior.[27]

McNair had overwhelming influence in drafting the rules for the maneuvers, and some of the rules he selected infuriated armor officers. Tanks, for example, could not destroy antitank guns by fire, but had to overrun them. Weapons as light as .50-caliber machine gun were ruled able to knock out light tanks—a notion ludicrous at the time, but one that anticipated the German development of small, light, and highly lethal short-range weapons, such as the panzerfaust, that gave infantry unsupported by guns a real antitank capability. McNair gave commanders two economical ways to destroy antitank guns—artillery and infantry assault.

It was during preparation for the Tennessee maneuvers that Patton first described his tactical approach as "Hold 'em by the nose and kick 'em in the pants," or pin the enemy by fire and maneuver to his rear. Patton's 2nd Armored Division joined VII Corps in Tennessee in June and ran riot, ending one day's maneuver after only three hours. Patton's "enemies" were befuddled by his speed of action. Observers noted, however, that he made poor use of his infantry and artillery against antitank guns.[28]

The Louisiana maneuvers, in September, McNair said, would test whether the U.S. Army could "crush" a major tank offensive. Patton's 2nd Armored Division was grouped with the 1st Armored Division under Maj. Gen. Charles Scott's I Armored Corps, which together with VII Corps constituted Lt. Gen. Ben Lear's Second Army. The opposition was none other than Third Army, commanded by German-born Lt. Gen. Walter Krueger, who had been assistant chief of staff in the World War I Tank Corps and, later during this war, led Sixth Army across the Pacific with great distinction. Krueger was well read and known in the service as a tough but fair officer. Krueger's chief of staff was Col. Dwight "Ike" Eisenhower.[29]

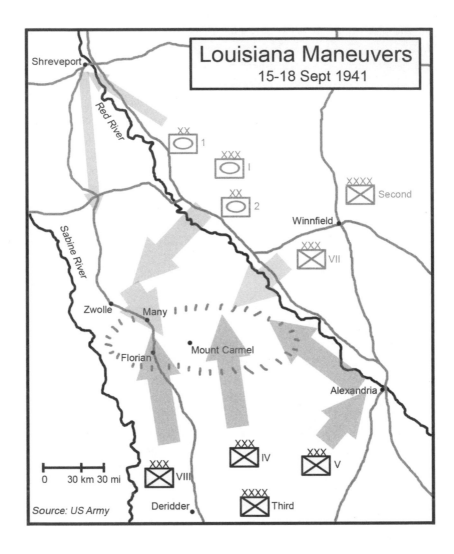

In the first phase of the maneuvers, a meeting engagement from 15 to 18 September, Krueger fought his army aggressively, while Lear kept his armor—his main strike force—in reserve for nearly three days while he tried to tee up a tank thrust onto open ground to destroy Second Army's left wing. Second Army's infantry took the high ground at Peason Ridge and Mount Carmel that Patton needed to stage his attack onto the plain below. Instead of advancing, the 2nd Armored Division found itself on the defensive, and when it did attack to recapture the high ground, Patton's failure to integrate infantry and artillery into his tank attacks led to heavy losses. Scott, meanwhile, scattered the 1st Armored Division all over the front, and it disappeared as an organized fighting force, an eerie harbinger of its fate in Tunisia some eighteen months later. After five days, Third Army had gained a clear victory.[30]

In the second phase, from 24 to 27 September, I Armored Corps—now consisting of the 2nd Armored and 2nd Infantry (motorized) Divisions joined Third Army to attack a defending Second Army, which still had the 1st Armored Division. The exercise opened under torrential rains. Second Army conducted a slow withdrawal, using demolitions and delaying forces to avoid pitched battle. Krueger again acted aggressively and sent the I Armored Corps around the enemy's right flank. Patton, who not only left the exercise area, but also purchased commercial gasoline with money from his own pocket while underway, eventually approached the objective, Shreveport, from the rear with reconnaissance elements and truck-mounted armored infantry, while his tanks struck the enemy south of the city. Lear waited patiently and did not commit his armored division or mobile antitank teams to deal with the threat, which was known to him from reconnaissance. The main threat was the rest of Third Army pushing up from the south, and he still had three uncommitted infantry divisions with which to defend Shreveport. Patton got some men into the outskirts, but he could not capture the town.

Eisenhower had reputedly concocted the plan, but Patton had executed the end-around. Armored enthusiasts praised the maneuver as putting Second Army in an untenable position; however, Lear still held the ground he had to, and the maneuver ended without a victor.[31] McNair rated all of the division and corps commanders after the exercises and concluded that Patton was "good," but "division [was] possibly his ceiling."[32]

The Carolina maneuvers in November pitted Lt. Gen. Hugh Drum's First Army, consisting of eight infantry divisions and three corps, against Maj. Gen. Oscar Griswold's IV Corps, controlling only the 31st and 43rd Infantry divisions, the 4th Motorized Division, and the 1st and 2nd Armored Divisions. The meeting engagement took place between the Pee Dee and Wateree Rivers, running north to south east and west of Monroe, North Carolina, respectively. The scenario was designed to test whether a small force possessing armor could defeat a much larger infantry force. Griswold also had slight superiority in the air, which meant he would be able to "destroy" existing bridges and disrupt First Army's bridging operations across the Pee Dee River. Looked at slightly differently, the maneuver tested whether a small, largely mobile force could eliminate a large infantry beachhead.

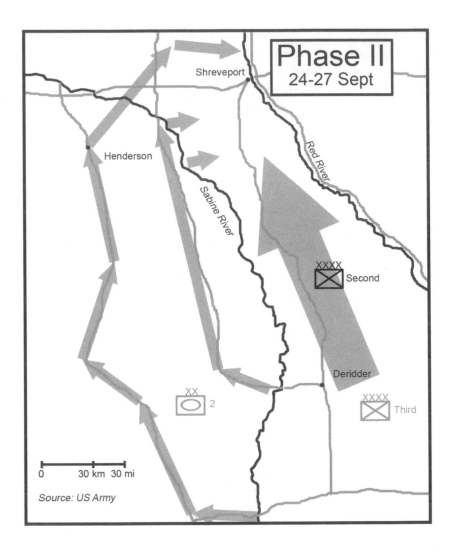

As the action began on 16 November, Griswold was allowed to cross the Wateree River and head east an hour before First Army crossed the Pee Dee toward the west, and he rushed his three mobile divisions forward to contain the enemy bridgeheads. Although the three divisions succeeded in the initial aim, they were in contact to such an extent that Griswold had great difficulty extracting tanks and replacing them with infantry to stage a decisive counterstroke. When he finally was able to push the 1st Armored Division into the enemy's rear on 18 November, its attack was conducted piecemeal in three columns, and active

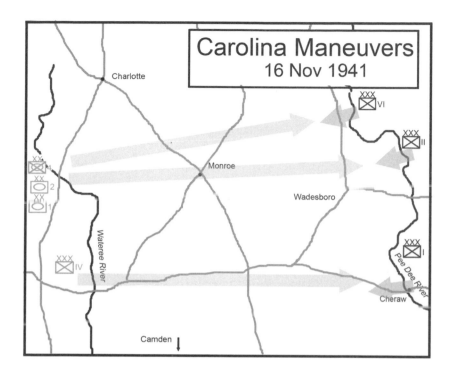

antitank defenses cut the division up to such an extent that it never recovered. By the sixth day, Drum's plodding, World War I–style advance had trapped IV Corps in a small pocket, with its back to a river.[33]

The first phases of the Louisiana and the Carolina maneuvers were the closest Patton ever came to fighting a defensive battle, other than a single day less than two years later in Tunisia, and even then using only one infantry division. Patton's side had failed to triumph in both of those simulated struggles, and history never provided an opportunity to see whether he would have done any better in a real war.

In the final phase, beginning 25 November, the numerically outmatched IV Corps sought to defend the town of Camden against Drum's First Army. The entire phase played out in a narrow band of territory along the line Monroe-Cheraw. Griswold initially confused Drum about his mission; he conducted spoiling attacks with his armored divisions and the 4th Motorized Division, concentrated on his left wing south of Monroe, to suggest a different task than the defensive one actually contained in his orders. Here, Patton was able to play offense in an overall defensive strategy. A copy of Griswold's plans fell into Drum's hands, however, and with perfect knowledge of the enemy's objective and strategy, Drum directed his corps to cut off the mobile divisions and capture Camden. On 27 November, the 1st Infantry Division punched through a thin line, and there was nothing between it and Camden. Drum could see another crushing victory in his grasp.

But then the armored divisions struck back, and Drum delayed the 1st Division's unhindered advance while he dealt with the threat. Griswold was able to extract his divisions and form a line to defend Camden. The maneuver ended with IV Corps holding on to what it had to.[34]

Patton took command of I Armored Corps on 15 January 1942. The real war was less than a year away.

CONFLAGRATION IN THE EAST

While Patton maneuvered his armor in June 1941, many of his future enemies were embarking on the most massive military conflict in history: Operation Barbarossa, the invasion of the Soviet Union. The führer had decided on 29 July 1940, only a month after subduing France, to conquer the Soviet Union by force. The decision had surprised some senior generals because Hitler had signed a nonaggression pact with the Soviets—a pact thus far respected by Josef Stalin—and had foresworn any repetition of the Great War's struggle on two fronts. (Great Britain, of course, was continuing to fight on the western front.) Hitler initially wished to strike that autumn, but was persuaded that the Russian winter would spell disaster for any invasion.[35]

The Italian invasion of Albania and Benito Mussolini's botched effort to conquer Greece in October caused further delay. Hitler decided he had to bail out the Italians to deny the British a foothold, recollecting the Great War's Salonika Front, where the Allies had defeated the Austro-Hungarian Empire. The British forced Hitler's hand when they landed troops in Greece in March 1941, which led to German intervention, mounted by forces that were to be part of the southern wing of the Barbarossa force. The Germans handily overran the Balkans, but Barbarossa was delayed for four weeks.[36]

Hitler's overweening ambition was to simultaneously capture Leningrad in the far north, Moscow in the center, and the Caucasus in the south in one huge blitz. Moscow lay 560 miles from the German frontier—a distance roughly equal to the greatest distance that would be covered by the Western Allies moving from the Normandy beaches into the heart of Germany by May 1945—and the far reaches of the Ukraine 700 miles from Germany. The German army high command, OKH, and the armed forces high command, *Oberkommando der Wehrmacht* (OKW), believed that the Wehrmacht could defeat the Soviet army in six to eight weeks, which meant that winter would not be a problem.

For all the fury of North Africa, Sicily, Italy, and Western Europe, the war against the Soviet Union was the decisive theater for the Wehrmacht. Germany launched the operation with some 150 divisions, including one cavalry, nineteen panzer, and fifteen motorized divisions, or most of the 205 divisions then available. Italian setbacks in North Africa, at British hands, had forced Hitler to divert a panzer division from Barbarossa to North Africa, so Mussolini had not only delayed, but also weakened the offensive. The Soviets began the conflagration with some 110 rifle divisions facing the Germans, plus fifty tank and twenty-five mechanized divisions. Although each divisions was smaller than the American equivalent, this total represented about twice the number of divisions Eisenhower ever commanded on the Western front.[37] As of June 1942, Germany had 171 divisions deployed on the eastern front and only three fighting the Allies in North Africa. In the decisive month of June 1944, Germany had 157 divisions on the eastern front; fifty-six in France, Belgium, and the Netherlands; and twenty-two in Italy.[38]

Three army groups—South (commanded by future Patton enemy *Generalfeldmarschall* Gerd von Rundstedt), Center, and North—each had one of Hitler's main objectives. They were of roughly equal strength, except that Army Group Center had two panzer groups while the other army groups had but one each. Hitler had defined no *Schwerpunkt*, or main point of effort. The army groups were to encircle and destroy Soviet forces near the border, while the panzer groups drove deeper into Soviet territory to prevent Stalin from constructing a defensive line.[39]

General der Infanterie Hans von Obstfelder's XXIX Corps was subordinated to Sixth Army, Army Group South, for the invasion. Obstfelder's three infantry divisions kicked off at 0315 hours, and their objective was Kiev. The corps easily established a bridgehead across the Bug River—the dividing line between the German and Soviet parts of occupied Poland. By 0630 *Generalfeldmarschall* Walter von Reichenau appeared at Obstfelder's headquarters to tell him that surprise had been achieved across the front, and he was considering moving a panzer division into the bridgehead to begin the 1st Panzer Group's exploitation. By 1800, Obstfelder's corps had made the deepest penetration in all of Sixth Army. Obstfelder made a bit of a pest of himself, so eager that he appealed in vain to one superior officer after another to commit the 1st Panzer Division in his sector. By 26 June, the corps was embroiled in fighting along its flank, from the foremost units all the way back to the Bug. The corps's *Kriegstagebuch* indicates that Obstfelder typically went to the forward division to oversee the battle at the most critical points, including the attack of Joseph "Sepp" Dietrich's

1st *Leibstandarte* SS Division—subordinated to XXIX Corps for the purpose—across the Olyka River on 2 July.

By 8 July, XXIX Corps, protecting 1st Panzer Group's northern flank, had fought its way through the Stalin Line and reached Zhitomir. Reichenau called Obstfelder, praised his corps's excellent performance, and then visited the corps to underscore his admiration. The corps subsequently participated in the reduction of the vast Kiev Pocket and then fought in the area just south of Kursk, where it remained into 1942. Obstfelder had taken much of the ground that the panzer generals who would face Patton later struggled so hard to retain.[40]

Promoted to *Generalleutnant* on 1 January 1941, Kurt von der Chevallerie commanded the 99th *Leichte Infanterie* (Light Infantry) Division during the invasion of the Soviet Union, where he was awarded the Knight's Cross for his performance in the south Ukraine. During the winter of 1940, Chevallerie had organized the division, which was a newly conceived type of infantry division intended to be able to retain its mobility under the worst conditions of weather and terrain. Instruction began in January amidst fearsome snow and ice storms, and Chevallerie spent his days in the open with his men. The soldiers received horse-mounted and mountain training. (The division would eventually be transformed into the 7th *Gebirgsdivision* [Mountain Division].)[41]

At the onset of Barbarossa, the division was subordinated to Sixth Army in Army Group South reserve. The division crossed the Bug River on 25 June and was ordered to clear Soviet troops from bunkers east of Krylow. Chevallerie personally reconnoitered the terrain the following day. The first attack failed: The bunkers had underground levels where Soviet troops could take shelter from 88mm gunfire. The division's pioneers (engineers) had no effective bunker-busting weapons. And the Soviets defended each bunker to the last man.

On 29 June, the division received orders more appropriate to its organization: to clear a forest at Bubniv, in the Ukraine, in cooperation with the *Germania* Regiment of the SS *Wiking* (Viking) Division. The Soviets had other ideas; some tried to break through the German ring around them on the thirtieth, while others fiercely defended the forest. Both sides were attacking and defending at the same time, and one of Chevallerie's battalions was badly shot up.

While the panzer spearheads grabbed the headlines, this was the war that Chevallerie would be fighting for the rest of the summer. Chevallerie realized that for men who had fought in France, a massive adjustment to a new enemy was necessary. These "partisans," survivors of shattered units, fought in battalion strength, had good ties to the civilian population, at times appeared in captured German uniforms, and took no prisoners. The campaign was but one week old.[42]

Oberst Fritz von Broich was actually still with his horse-mounted 1st Cavalry Division. The division, ironically, was part of *Generaloberst* Heinz Guderian's modern and motorized 2nd Panzer Group, part of Army Group Center, when it attacked across the Soviet frontier. By now, Broich commanded the 22nd Mounted Regiment.[43]

"The attack has begun!" recorded the 1st Cavalry Division's war diarist at 0315 on 22 June. The morning was cool, but the clear sky promised a hot day ahead. Broich led his men across the Bug River, arriving on the far bank by 0335 and meeting no real resistance. An hour later, the 22nd Mounted Regiment smashed the only resistance to flare up, at a customs house. Prisoners, who were from the Soviet 75th Infantry Division, said that most troops had pulled back eastward in haste the evening before. Off to the left flank, the 4th Panzer Division—*Oberst* Smilo *Freiherr* von Lüttwitz in command of the 12th Motorized Infantry Regiment—surged after them.

The cavalry's mission was to advance through the Pripet Marshes, which were impassable to vehicles, to screen the panzer group's right flank. The division first got caught up in a real battle at St. Dubica, where the 1st Mounted Regiment suffered heavy casualties. The Russians, it turned out, could fight after all.

Army Group Center thereafter used the cavalrymen as a mobile formation shifted from corps to corps to help where needed. The lot of a cavalry division was mainly working beside infantry and panzer divisions, conducting reconnaissance, battling partisans, assaulting small Soviet formations, and burning villages. The 1st Cavalry Division joined the XXXV Corps in late September, and while fighting with them, Broich was promoted to take command of the 1st Mounted Brigade on the twenty-ninth.

The division joined the LXVII Panzer Corps in October, which included the 17th Panzer Division and 29th Motorized Infantry Division. The first bite of winter was in the air, and snow made some roads impassable even for horses. Broich and his men suffered from the lack of winter clothing and gloves. The cavalrymen, in October, mopped up scattered Soviet troops in forests near Krapivna, which the panzer and motorized troops could not penetrate.

On 7 November, Broich and his division comrades had the great fortune of being taken to the rear by train. The weather had turned bitterly cold, and snow fell almost daily. The men would miss the Wehrmacht's disastrous first winter on the eastern front. Most of their 4,000 mounts, however, were left behind.[44]

Otto von Knobelsdorff had been promoted to *Generalleutnant* on 1 December 1940, shortly after his 19th Infantry Division converted into the 19th Panzer Division on 1 November.[45] The able general picked up the craft of armored warfare with remarkable speed.[46] The division was outfitted with Czech 38t tanks. The division's *Kriegstagebuch* for the period from the invasion of the Soviet Union through September 1942 was destroyed by enemy action. Fortunately, however, Knobelsdorff wrote a history of the division's operations.

Like the 1st Cavalry Division, Knobelsdorff's tanks formed part of Guderian's 2nd Panzer Group and attacked into the Soviet zone in Poland on 22 June. After following the 12th Panzer Division for several days, which meant fighting all the bypassed Soviet troops, the 19th Panzer Division was ordered by LVII Corps to advance to Minsk posthaste. Superior Soviet forces, however, were attempting to break out northward across his line of march, and most of Knobelsdorff's column became engulfed in a furious defensive battle lasting from 25 to 29 June, when an infantry division finally arrived to relieve the panzers. The corps headquarters offered no complaints, as it had been traveling in the center of Knobelsdorff's march column and had barely been saved from destruction by his panzers.[47] As events would demonstrate, it was fitting that Knobelsdorff's first action as a panzer general was a defensive fight against a superior enemy force.

This defensive warfare did not last long. After a week of fierce close-in fighting around Polotsk in Belarus, Knobelsdorff, on 13 July, began his first classic operation as a panzer general, attacking northeastward into Russia proper through Nevel to Velikiye Luki, a major rail center deep in the Soviet rear, and traveling a distance of nearly 100 miles as the crow flies. Fighting through sandy terrain that slowed vehicles, as did many lakes and swamps, Knobelsdorff, on the fifteenth took Nevel with a skillfully executed pincer attack. The capture of Nevel severed the Soviets' Kiev-Leningrad supply route. The Russians had destroyed a bridge there, and during the first night after its destruction, a stream of Soviet trucks, operating without headlights, drove off the span and crashed into the ravine below. Tanks probed the city from the east; the fighting ignited part of the city and, much to Knobelsdorff's dismay, burned down a vodka factory.

The next day, Knobelsdorff pushed on, moving so quickly that his troops captured bridge after bridge before the surprised Soviets could destroy them. Knobelsdorff's account of his time as division commander shows that he was a model panzer leader, nearly always advancing with his foremost elements so as to take control of the situation immediately when the unexpected occurred. On the seventeenth, the German spearhead encountered an antitank screen south of Velikiye Luki. Knobelsdorff smoothly brought his panzers forward and seized the dominant high ground south of the city. Then he pushed his infantry forward and took the city quarter by quarter. The Soviets counterattacked on the eighteenth and cut Knobelsdorff's only road to his rear. Faced with the threat of encirclement, he struck back furiously with an infantry regiment and tanks and restored the situation by midafternoon. As we shall see, it was a harbinger of events to come for other German generals in Velikiye Luki.

Because the town was a transfer point between the European-gauge and Soviet-gauge rail lines, many diplomats and businessmen had made layovers in Velikiye Luki. Consequently, the hotels were well stocked with caviar and champagne, and Knobelsdorff and his men were pleased.[48]

Having marched into Paris, Knobelsdorff now nearly reached Moscow. Joining Army Group Center's renewed offensive toward Moscow, the 19th Panzer Division was among the first to penetrate the concrete bunkers and antitank obstacles of the Soviet capital's outer defenses, maneuvering through seemingly impassable terrain to take the Soviet defenses from the rear near Ilinskoye on 16 October. Knobelsdorff was overseeing the elimination of heavy bunkers with direct artillery fire when the commanding general of Fourth Army, *Generalfeldmarschall* Günther von Kluge, appeared to personally praise the division's performance.

Riding with his panzer regiment, which advanced alone until other mobile elements could obtain their trucks and catch up, Knobelsdorff pressed on toward Moscow on the eighteenth and captured two bridges over the Protva River intact. Luftwaffe planes buzzed overhead, constantly in communication with ground troops and able to alert them to Soviet forces in their path. The lead company, blasting away, charged through antitank fire to seize the next bridge. Knobelsdorff thought it his panzer regiment's greatest day.

The division's own infantry caught up on the nineteenth, but the neighboring infantry divisions were still stuck forty miles to the rear at the Moscow defense line. The Soviets attacked the exposed panzer division from the front and flanks. Knobelsdorff reported that without panzer reinforcements, his division was too weakened to advance farther. The 98th Infantry Division finally worked its way forward, and Knobelsdorff's panzers crossed the Nara River. But that was it. The German drive had exhausted itself. Knobelsdorff was but forty miles southwest of Moscow. Winter arrived with a vengeance on 27 October, and the temperature dropped to forty degrees below zero centigrade.[49]

Oberstleutnant Hasso von Manteuffel had hardly taken command of the 2nd Battalion, 6th Motorized Infantry Regiment, 7th Panzer Division, when the division struck eastward as part of *Generaloberst* Hermann Hoth's 3rd Panzer Group and Army Group Center. The panzers slashed toward Minsk and on the very first day engaged Soviet forces in a ferocious battle, in which the Germans destroyed eighty-two of the enemy's tanks. Manteuffel recalled, "I experienced the first sharp battle in twenty-two years and watched the first men of my battalion fall, wounded or dead."

Following bitter fighting near Smolensk, Manteuffel, on 21 August, was named to the command of his regiment in place of his fallen predecessor. Every man thought the Russia campaign was going to end just like the others, and they would all be home by Christmas. Manteuffel took charge of the regiment the next day not far from the city of Belyi, a place about which we will hear more. His bywords were, "Lead from the front," and he thus began his journey to the ranks of great panzer generals.

On 23 August, OKH issued orders implementing a fateful decision by Hitler that, as many senior generals worried even as the order was being formulated, put the entire war effort at great risk. Hitler instructed Army Group Center to redirect its main effort from the drive on Moscow toward Kiev to speed the advance of Army Group South across the Ukraine. Guderian and other generals argued that Moscow was the solar plexus of the Soviet state and that its capture would ensure a strategic victory. Hitler believed that Ukraine's natural resources were essential to continuing the war effort. As the generals foresaw, by the time their forces got back on track toward Moscow, the Napoleon-destroying Russian winter was almost upon them.

Manteuffel and the 7th Panzer Division took part in the subsequent envelopment and reduction of Kiev in September. The Kiev Pocket, which yielded 665,000 prisoners, had closed when divisions commanded by two other future enemies of Patton—*Generalleutnant* Walter Model's 3rd Panzer Division, part of Guderian's panzer group in Army Group Center, and *Generaloberst* Hans Hube's 16th Panzer Division, the spearhead of Kleist's panzer group in Army Group South—met to the east of the city on 16 September. *Oberst* Heinrich "Heinz" Eberbach, another future antagonist, commanded the 5th Panzer Brigade in Model's division. It was a victory on the scale of Germany's later defeat in northern France at the hands of a British and an American army group.

Plans to reorient Army Group Center were under consideration the moment the Kiev Pocket was closed. Manteuffel, consequently, got about as close to Moscow as any other field commander in the German armed forces. Attacking north of the capital in November, *Kampfgruppe* Manteuffel— consisting of the remnants of two motorized regiments, some panzers, and some artillery—reached the frozen Moscow-Volga Canal at Yakhroma, only thirty-five miles due north of Red Square. Manteuffel planned a careful nighttime attack for 28 November across a bridge defended by Soviet troops who had not noticed the Germans in nearby woods. An all-volunteer storm company seized the bridge from the surprised defenders, and his panzers rolled across the span, guns blasting and tracks clattering. Manteuffel called for more divisions to enter the bridgehead and continue to Moscow, but there were no more divisions. The northern drive, too, had spent itself. Elite Siberian troops counterattacked, and Manteuffel had to give up his prize, pull his men back, and blow up the bridge. "[T]hat was the greatest disappointment of my military life," recalled Manteuffel.

On 5 December, the opening devastating barrage of the Soviet winter counteroffensive crashed into Manteuffel's lines, and at 1400 hours, the long and bitter retreat from Moscow began.

In March 1942, Manteuffel's last act on the eastern front before the division moved to France to rebuild was to order a halt to an infantry attack through two-meter-deep snow, where his dark-glad grenadiers were easy pickings for the entrenched Soviets. *Generalfeldmarschall* Walter Model, promoted and now commanding Ninth Army, had personally ordered the assault and told Manteuffel he would face a court martial for disobedience. Manteuffel's commanding general whisked him off to France before that could happen.[50]

SS Gruppenführer Paul Hausser led his 2nd SS Panzergrenadier Division *Das Reich* into the Soviet Union on 26 June as part of XLVI Panzer Corps, 2nd Panzer Group, Army Group Center. He had just participated with great success in the invasion of Yugoslavia and played a leading role in the capture of Belgrade.

Das Reich from the twenty-ninth cleared the area between the group's two main routes of advance. On 11 July, the division attacked across the Dniepr River to establish a bridgehead, and then followed the 10th Panzer Division in the direction of Smolensk, fighting a running battle to keep the flanks secure. Heinz Guderian, Hausser's corps commanding general, praised him for directing the tactical battle at the very front lines, destroying the elite Soviet 100th Infantry Division, and remaining in command after being wounded by shrapnel. By the twenty-first, the corps had reached Yelnya and, having outstripped the neighboring two corps and reached the end of its tether, had to go on the defensive. From the twenty-fourth to the twenty-seventh, the division dealt with attacks from three directions and artillery fire as crushing as the worst days on the western front in World War I. The troops learned that their 37mm antitank guns would not penetrate the armor of heavy Soviet tanks. The SS held on, using artillery as antitank guns while soldiers attacked tanks with captured Molotov cocktails. Hausser received the Knight's Cross for his actions.[51]

During the battle of the Kiev Pocket in September, Hausser led his division to one success after another. *Das Reich* protected the panzer group's flank against repeated counterattacks, while the spearhead conducted the envelopment of Kiev. Transferred to XL Panzer Corps in October, *Das Reich* struck toward Moscow.[52]

Hausser's personnel review in October recorded that he had a strong, hard personality; excellent tactical skills; and unusual physical abilities considering his age (sixty-one years that very month). He had proved himself and his division in both attack and defense.[53]

Hausser nearly reached Moscow and fought to break through the capital's defenses at Borodino, some seventy miles from the capital, where Napoleon had defeated the tsar's army in September 1812. Stalin had built an eight-mile-deep, layered defensive line, featuring, in order, automatic flame throwers, zigzag antitank trenches, a small river bordered by barbed wire entanglements, a large antitank ditch, steel antitank barriers, bunkers and field trenches, and heavy-gun batteries. The fresh 32nd Infantry Division from Siberia, backed by two brigades of T34 tanks, held the field.

Hausser's division reached the Soviet line on 13 October. Attacking under clouds and rain the next day, with his regiments *Der Führer* on the left and *Deutschland* on the right, Hausser became involved in a large tank battle. Standing beside a light-artillery battery on a hill overlooking the battlefield, like a Prussian commander on his *Feldherrnhügel*, Hausser received reports and issued fresh orders.

Soviet resistance was iron hard, and both regiments were decimated. Deciding to move farther forward, Hausser set off down the hill just as an artillery barrage struck the height. Hausser fell, badly wounded.

Der Führer Regiment captured Borodino on 15 October, but it would not get much closer to Moscow than that.[54] Snow and rain bathed the battle area for a month. The regiment would not follow Napoleon's *Grande Armée* into Moscow.

Army Group North's 4th Panzer Group, consisting of XLI Panzer Corps and Erich von Manstein's LVI Panzer Corps, drove toward Leningrad in parallel, arrayed on the left and right wings, respectively. Future Patton enemy *Generalmajor* Erich Brandenberger and his 8th Panzer Division constituted the main striking power of Manstein's corps, which also controlled the 3rd Motorized Infantry Division (which later fought Patton in Lorraine) and the 290th Infantry Division.[55]

Adolf Robert Erich Brandenberger was a surprise panzer commander. Born in Augsburg on 15 July 1892, he had entered the imperial army as a *leutnant* in October 1913. Brandenberger had displayed an unusual interest in the wider world, traveling between the wars to England, France, Switzerland, Italy, the Nordic countries, and North Africa as a tourist. Brandenberger had served in the artillery or in staff positions in the Great War, in the *Freikorps* and the *Reichswehr* between the wars, and during the first years of World War II. Why he was thought competent to command armored troops is unclear. He had entered the Führer reserve on 21 February 1941 with orders to become the head of the panzer school, having been chief of staff for XXIII Corps, but six days later he was instead given command of the 8th Panzer Division. He showed himself to be a brave soldier who was daily among his troops at the front, and he earned himself a name.[56] He would face Patton in the Ardennes.

Manstein's critical first objective was to capture the bridges across the Dvina River intact, which would cut off Soviet forces forward of the river and prevent the Soviets from forming a line behind the potentially daunting water barrier. Faced with the problem of a narrow initial front, Manstein attacked the Soviet frontier defenses along the Memel River at 0300 hours on 22 June with only Brandenberger's division and the 290th Infantry Division. The 8th Panzer Division broke through the pillboxes about noon, unhinging the Soviet defenses.

Manstein sent the 8th Panzer Division racing for the Airologa bridge, fifty miles distant. He had fought across this ground in the Great War, and he knew that if the bridge across the precipitous gorge were blown up, his corps would grind to a halt. Manstein spent most of the day with Brandenberger, whose reconnaissance troops successfully seized the bridge before dark.

The 8th Panzer Division led the way and by 24 June had reached the Dvinsk highway, 105 miles into enemy territory. Manstein had outstripped XLI Panzer Corps on his left and Sixteenth Army on his right and charged ahead with open flanks. The Soviets threw reserves against the advancing Germans, and in several fierce tank battles, the 8th Panzer and 3rd Motorized Divisions destroyed seventy Soviet tanks and surged ahead again. Brandenberger seized the critical Dvina bridges early on the twenty-eighth, and his troops battled the enemy in Dvinsk on the far bank. Manstein's panzer drive had achieved a great success.[57]

The SS *Totenkopf* Division also participated in Barbarossa as part of the 4th Panzer Group. On 14 June, Theodor Eicke had called his battalion and regimental commanders together. He told Max Simon, Hermann Priess, and the other officers that they would be attacking the Soviet Union. This war, he raged, had to be fought as an ideological battle, a death struggle between National Socialism and Jewish Bolshevism. This fight would demand the most ruthless and uncompromising conduct. The Soviet Union had not signed the Geneva Convention and could not be expected to wage a civilized war. On Hitler's orders, all captured commissars were to be executed. Thus was the stage set for the SS war in Russia.

The SS division was held in reserve for two days before receiving orders to fill a gap between the panzer group and Sixteenth Army on the right. Orders were soon changed, and the division was instructed to join Manstein's LVI Panzer Corps beyond the Dvina River. The division had to fight its way to the front through heavy resistance in central Lithuania to reach Dvinsk. This mission clearly was going to be no repeat of the campaign in France.

The panzer group had held Manstein's corps at the Dvina to consolidate its position and allow XLI Panzer Corps to come up alongside, a delay that Manstein judged gave the Soviets enough time to overcome their confusion and organize defenses that ultimately denied the Germans entry into Leningrad. LVI

Panzer Corps did not thrust forward again until 2 July and encountered very stubborn resistance.

Totenkopf fought hard and bled profusely up and down the army group front. Along with the 3rd Motorized Infantry Division, it played a leading role in a brilliant counterattack by Manstein at Dno in mid-August, an operation launched with complete surprise against the enemy's flank and crushing the Soviet Thirty-Fourth Army. Manstein viewed *Totenkopf* as the best SS division he ever worked with, but thought that inadequate leadership training caused excessive casualties and missed opportunities. By the end of August, nearly 5,000 of the division's men, about a quarter of its starting strength, had been killed. The Soviets had been able to strengthen Leningrad's defenses. In the north, the initiative was already shifting steadily to the Soviet side, whereas in the center and south, that shift would take two years more. *Totenkopf* would make its reputation as a division that was ruthless and unbreakable on the defensive.

A Soviet counterattack at Demjansk in September put LVI Panzer Corps on the defensive and opened a long, bitter struggle for Simon, Priess, and the rest of the division. By the end of November, the division had lost roughly half the ration strength it had at the beginning of Barbarossa, and only half of those men had been replaced.[58]

Times of Turmoil

Patton's future enemies had enjoyed stunning triumphs, but many of them were about to undergo trials that would prepare them psychologically and militarily for a time of disaster in France. It would be a side of war Patton would never have to face and overcome.

The first Soviet counteroffensive of the war blasted out of the ice and snow on 5 December along a 500-mile front, primarily against Army Group Center, which reeled back from the outskirts of Moscow. Knobelsdorff's history suggests that he began to lose his faith in his führer, who had continued to throw exhausted troops fruitlessly against Moscow's defenses during November, wasted irreplaceable manpower, and now issued stand-fast orders against the pleas of his senior generals. (After the war, Knobelsdorff's interrogators recorded that he was an outspoken critic of the Nazi Party.) Despite the orders from the high command, Fourth Army pulled back from its forward positions near Moscow in late December. Soviet cavalry had gotten into the rear areas and threatened to cut off XII Corps and future Patton enemy *General der Infanterie* Hans-Gustav Felber's XIII Corps. The much-weakened 19th Panzer Division attacked on 28 December through deep snow to clear an escape route for the two corps. Passing the battlefields where he had lost so many of his men, Knobelsdorff recorded,

"We were ashamed before them to have to retreat, those who had only known attack and success."

Generalfeldmarschall Günter von Kluge took command of the disintegrating Army Group Center on 19 December. Kluge had been born in Posen on 30 October 1882 and joined the imperial army as a lieutenant in 1901. He had held mainly staff jobs during World War I, but had been badly wounded at Verdun in 1918. Remaining in the *Reichswehr* between the wars, Kluge advanced from regimental command to commanding general of Fourth Army in only nine years during the 1930s, and he won laurels for his performance in the invasions of Poland, France, and the Soviet Union.

Hitler had just taken direct command of the army. Kluge wanted to pull back, but Hitler stiffened his spine and averted disaster.[59] In Hitler's view, according to Manstein, he had prevented a Napoleonic retreat. This was one of the occasions that seemed to confirm, in his mind, that he could overcome any difficulty by sheer force of will.[60]

Generalmajor Werner *Freiherr* von und zu Gilsa's 216th Infantry Division detrained from France into minus-thirty-five-degree weather on New Year's Day and formed a line on Knobelsdorff's flank as the Germans struggled to hold the Soviets at bay. By 4 January, Gilsa's division had been enveloped. Welcome to Russia![61] Gilsa and his division would pull through, and the general would one day return to France, there to briefly face George Patton. Knobelsdorff was evacuated due to illness on the sixth.

The night of January 7–8 1942, a massive blow struck the right wing of Army Group North. By 8 February, Soviet pincers had surrounded six divisions of Sixteenth Army in the Demjansk Pocket, including the *Totenkopf* Division.

Eicke formed two *Kampfgruppen* out of *Totenkopf* to hold the most imperiled parts of the line. The first, under his command, protected the western villages closest to German lines beyond the Soviet pincers. The second, commanded by *SS-Oberführer* Max Simon, faced northeast, where the rebuilt Thirty-Fourth Army was applying heavy pressure. The SS men stopped Soviet infantry attacks in a seemingly endless serious of vicious engagements into March. They at least had winter gear, which their army comrades lacked, to withstand the average temperatures of thirty degrees below zero centigrade. Eicke's *Kampfgruppen*, in February and March, battled the 7th Guards Division, four ski battalions and the 272nd Ski Regiment, and the 154th Naval Rifle Brigade.

On 13 March, the Soviets dropped two airborne brigades behind the lines of *Kampfgruppe* Simon. Simon personally led an attack by a force assembled from cooks, drivers, and other members of the trains. Fighting in the bitter cold,

Simon split the Soviet force into two groups, one of which he was able to annihilate. The second group tried to break out through the sector of the neighboring 12th "Wild Buffalos" Infantry Division, but was also destroyed.[62]

March brought better supplies and even some reinforcements delivered by air, and by 20 March, the exhausted Soviets stopped trying. The exhaustion was mutual. One *Totenkopf* battalion's doctor reported shortly before the siege ended that nearly a third of the men were no longer fit for combat, and that the others had lost an average of twenty pounds and were weak. The Germans, attacking into and out of the pocket, ended the siege on 22 April after seventy-three days.

Eicke had said of Priess's actions in the Demjansk Pocket—where despite his artillery job he was often at the point of a Russian breakthrough encouraging the troops—"If it wasn't for Priess, none of us would still be here."[63]

Simon took command of the division in June, when Eicke was summoned to Germany to report and to take leave. At this time, the paths of Simon and Priess crossed that of *Generalmajor* Otto von Knobelsdorff, who took command of II Corps on 1 June. Kept in the line to keep open the corridor into the pocket, the division dwindled away under constant Soviet hammering. On the twenty-second, after the heaviest artillery barrage the division had ever experienced, the Soviets attacked the corridor with T34 tanks and infantry. Simon personally led a counterattack against the flank of the Soviet penetration—an attack by headquarters personnel supported by a single howitzer, which destroyed five tanks. Back in Germany, organization of a new *Totenkopf* Panzergrenadier Division was underway. The remnants in Russia finally were released in mid-October and went to France to join the newly raised components and rebuild the division.[64]

Priess and Simon were now iron tough. They had seen the worst of war.

Return to Times of Triumph

The Tim and Chir Rivers (the latter known to the Germans as the Tschir) tie together many of Patton's enemies. After the setbacks of the grim winter of 1941, the Wehrmacht gathered its strength and prepared to resume the eastern front offensive in the summer of 1942.

During the winter of 1941, the 1st Cavalry Division had been reorganized in France into the 24th Panzer Division, and Fritz von Broich had taken command of the 24th *Schützen-Brigade* (Motorized Infantry Brigade), soon renamed the 24th Panzergrenadier Brigade. On 24 April 1942, the division had received orders to transfer to the eastern front.[65]

While getting their bearings near Kursk in June, the men received an order from the sector commander underscoring that proper treatment of the civilian

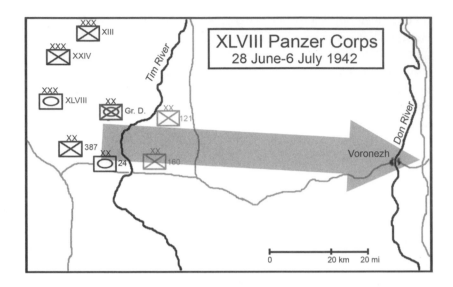

population was necessary to defeat Bolshevism. The battle experience shared by the 3rd Panzer Division was sobering: The Russian infantry fights to the last man. Russian tanks are good, and their men are well trained. The enemy is not very good at large-scale tank attacks, but he knows how to stop a breakthrough with two or three well-positioned T34s. German infantry and panzers have to stick close to one another at all times.

The division's first attack—part of an operation by *General der Panzertruppe* Werner Kempf's XLVIII Panzer Corps—was against Truchaschewka, not far east of Kursk, where the panzers would have to cross the Tim River once engineers could bridge it and attack eastward and uphill. The ultimate objective was Voronezh, on the Don River, 120 miles distant, where Fourth Panzer Army would wheel south and push along the river toward Stalingrad. The Soviets were thought to have only infantry divisions in the line, and the 160th "Gorki" Division was positioned opposite the 24th Panzer Division. Broich commanded the rightmost attack group, which consisted largely of his brigade's 26th Panzergrenadier Regiment supported by a battery of assault guns and some engineers, antitank guns, and artillery. The panzers, with a battalion of infantry, would attack en masse in the center of the division line, flanked on the far side by another infantry regiment. Once the high ground was secured, the corps was to continue its breakthrough eastward.

"G-Day" was 28 June, and the Soviets were caught completely by surprise, having expected the German summer offensive to take aim at Moscow. Broich's troops attacked up the slope and threw the Soviets off the high ground by afternoon. This was a formative experience in his career, and it would echo in his battle at El Guettar against George Patton. In ten days of hard fighting, the 24th Panzer Division played its part in creating the Voronezh bridgehead. The Soviets were reeling back along the entire front, and the division was ready to join the drive southward as the 16th Infantry Division took its place. (Patton would later nearly destroy the 16th Division in Lorraine.)

Broich took charge of *Kampfgruppe* Broich on 14 July, essentially his brigade's 21st Panzergrenadier Regiment strengthened by the motorcycle battalion and other elements. His mission was to advance in two columns on a wide front west of Morosovskaya to cut off the enemy escape route. This he accomplished by evening. The 29th Motorized Division (which Patton would face on Sicily) and *Grossdeutschland* Infantry Division, meanwhile, had cut the escape route north to the Don.[66]

Generalmajor Walter Hörnlein became the first commanding general of the *Grossdeutschland* Infantry Division, the 24th Panzer Division's running mate in LXVIII Panzer Corps in the June offensive, when it was activated on 1 April 1942 out of the *Grossdeutschland* Infantry Regiment (motorized). Hörnlein had already commanded the regiment, formed in 1939 from the Berlin watch regiment, for the prior eight months, mostly in fierce combat north of Kursk. The elite outfit's moniker, *Grossdeutschland*, meant "Greater Germany" and referred to the fact that its men came from every corner of the Reich. Recruits— preferably volunteers—had to be tall, have perfect eyesight, and possess no criminal record.

Hörnlein, born on 2 January 1893 in Blüthen bei Karstädt, had entered the imperial army as an officer candidate in January 1912. After his release from a prisoner-of-war camp in 1919, he served in a reserve infantry regiment between the wars until 1934, when he joined the 5th Infantry Regiment. Hörnlein married Erika Rarkow in 1927, and the couple had three children, one of whom died as a baby. Hörnlein took command of an infantry battalion in 1935, the 80th Infantry Regiment in 1939, and the *Grossdeutschland* Regiment in August 1941. Hörnlein's superiors found him to be capable and enthusiastic, a good man in a crisis, a father to his troops, and a dyed-in-the-wool National Socialist.

From the very start, the division was uniquely powerful for an army formation, possessing not only an assault-gun battalion, but a panzer battalion as well. As of June 1942, the division had twenty-two assault guns, eighteen self-propelled tank destroyers, twelve Panzer IIs, two Mark IIIs, eighteen Mark IVs with short 75mm guns, twelve Mark IVs with long 75mm guns, and four command tanks. Hörnlein had held his first commanding officers call not in a formal setting, but over dinner and drinks, to encourage a spirit of comradeship and teamwork.[67]

Hitler and OKW took particular interest in the division. *Generalfeldmarschall* Wilhelm Keitel, chief of the OKW, called Hörnlein some two months after the division's activation, as it was about to go into battle near Kursk, to instruct him that the division was never to permit itself to be split up into pieces for operations. The führer, he said, personally endorsed these instructions. If anybody tried to do that to the division, Hörnlein was to contact Keitel immediately. Joining Second Panzer Army's XLVIII Panzer Corps, Hörnlein found that commanders were "astounded and pleased" when they learned of the division's extraordinary order of battle.

As the time for action approached in June 1942, Hörnlein met with his commanders and gave them a series of general instructions for the coming attack that showed his concern for his troops. The first three were: Move the panzers forward as soon as possible and give them infantry support. Attack while it is still dark. Force the men to sleep during pauses.[68] Indeed, Hörnlein, a man with a good sense of humor, always had time for his troops, who called him "Papa" Hörnlein.[69]

By the time *Grossdeutschland* attacked across the Tim River beside the 24th Panzer Division on 28 June, XLVIII Panzer Corps had become part of Fourth Panzer Army. The division kicked off at 0215 hours under the cover of an artillery barrage. Stukas and other combat aircraft supported the advance. Hörnlein showed he grasped how a good commander should operate and was at the front with his leftmost *Kampfgruppe* to get a feel for the battlefield, while his operations officer held down the fort at the division's command post. He henceforth generally gave only verbal orders.

The division helped capture Voronezh and established a bridgehead across the Don on 6 July, and there it paused. It had destroyed 200 enemy tanks in reaching the corps's objective.[70]

On 24 July, Broich and the 24th Panzer Division shifted to the Chir River area a hundred miles northwest of Stalingrad, straggling because of fuel shortages. The next day, the division again attacked uphill onto high ground and smashed the Soviets who barred its way, including elements of the 219th and 229th Infantry Divisions. A night attack by panzers and half-track mounted panzergrenadiers broke through to the Don River.

For a time in August, *Kampfgruppe* Broich comprised most of the panzer division's striking power, including the 24th Panzer Regiment and the half-track-mounted panzergrenadiers of his own regiment's 1st Battalion. Operations at times received excellent close air support from the Luftwaffe, and the panzers were always victorious.[71]

Broich took temporary command of his division sometime around 20 August, when XLVIII Panzer Corps regrouped and launched a new, concentrated attack. The division had suffered roughly 30 percent casualties in the offensive, and Broich proudly reported that despite heavy losses and equipment shortages, the 24th Panzer Division had remained mobile and executed every attack order. A new general officer had arrived to take command of the division by the time of the drive to reach Stalingrad launched on 15 September. There the division, along with the rest of Sixth Army, was annihilated over the winter. Broich drops from the records in September, though why is not clear. By the time Broich was transferred to the *Führerreserve* (the high command leader reserve) on 31 October, a very lucky man for escaping doom in Stalingrad, he had been decorated repeatedly as commander of the 24th Panzergrenadier Brigade and of his armored assault group; his awards included the Knight's Cross, which he received in August.[72]

Broich had seen things in the Soviet Union that, by all accounts, gave him reason to loath the Nazis. In a conversation secretly taped by British intelligence at a camp in which Broich was a prisoner of war, *Generalmajor* Johannes Bruhn, who had commanded the 533rd Volksgrenadier Division, told Broich that Germany no longer deserved to win the war "after the amount of human blood we've shed knowingly and as a result of our delusions and blood lust. We've deserved our fate."

Broich replied, "We shot women as if they had been cattle. There was a large quarry where 10,000 men, women, and children were shot. They were still lying in the quarry. We drove out on purpose to see it. It was the most bestial thing I ever saw."[73]

Broich would soon share a friendship with another anti-Nazi German officer, Claus Schenk *Graf* von Stauffenberg, who would both fight Patton and attempt to kill Hitler.

Return to Times of Trial: Army Groups Center and B

Like a baleful air-raid siren, rising and slowly falling, only to rise and fall again, the German highs of the summer turned into the lows of another Russian winter. Observers along the entire front of *Generalfeldmarschall* Günther von Kluge's Army Group Center reported sudden action by small Soviet assault groups on 24 November 1942, accompanied by artillery fire. Enemy forces were spotted on the move south of Velikiye Luki, at the north end of the army group's extended

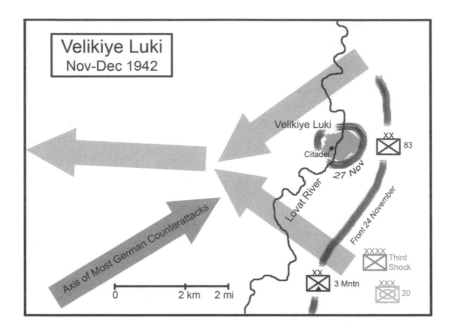

line. In the zone of *Generalleutnant* Maximilian *Freiherr* von Weichs's Army Group B, concern centered on the mess at Stalingrad, where the Soviet offensive that would surround Sixth Army in the city had begun on 19 November. But enemy forces were also spotted advancing on the Chir River valley northwest of Stalingrad.

As he considered the situation in the central sector the following day, Hitler was confident that Army Group B's Sixth Army, already surrounded in Stalingrad, could hold its own. The German chief of staff of Romanian Third Army, *Oberst* Walther Wenck, was building up a defensive line along the Chir River, and Fourth Panzer Army was just getting its first reserves from the rear. *Generaloberst* Walter Model, commanding Ninth Army in Army Group Center, was unworried about his own right wing, but he was concerned about his left, where his troops at Velikiye Luki were now under attack and his forces in the Rzhev salient might soon be.[74]

Patton's future enemies were to play a huge role in what happened next. At the peak of the crisis, the Soviets tore a 400-mile gap in the German front—a gap equal in size to the entire western front of World War I.[75]

Mini-Stalingrad at Velikiye Luki: Where some officers, such as Fritz von Broich, were shaped by the periods when Germany was on the offensive and rolling from triumph to triumph, Kurt von der Chevallerie experienced mainly times of travail. Indeed, he had become something of a master of the defense. Chevallerie had taken temporary command of LIX Corps, Army Group Center, at the end of December 1941. He was promoted to *General der Infanterie* in February 1942 and simultaneously made commanding general of LIX Corps.[76]

Chevallerie commanded a group named after him, essentially consisting of his corps at first, at Velikiye Luki, a city on the Lovat River west of Moscow. *Gruppe* Chevallerie sat roughly on the seam between Army Groups North and Center and protected the former's main supply line, a railroad a dozen miles to the rear. Chevallerie's troops, his old 83rd Infantry Division and the 3rd *Gebirgsjägerdivision* (Mountain Division), had been battered by constant fighting and were strung out over far too long a front. Dug-in companies were responsible for nearly two miles of frontage.[77]

Marshall Georgi Zhukov planned to attack Chevallerie with elements of the Kalinin Front as a supporting operation for his main assault on the Rzhev salient. Four Soviet Guards divisions belonging to Third Shock Army and supported by the 215 tanks of the 2nd Mechanized Corps and by ski troops, with more divisions to follow, punched through this weak line on 24 November and gradually encircled the German garrison in Velikiye Luki. An order from Chevallerie on the twenty-sixth reflects a steely spirit: "I expect commanders and units to show the necessary initiative. *Do not wait for orders! Act yourself!*" He acknowledged that the front-line troops faced extremely difficult conditions with extremely limited strength. But the fight had to be to the last man, he instructed, and at no time could security be sacrificed to concern for physical welfare.[78]

Despite some ten days of fierce struggle by Chevallerie's group to prevent the double envelopment of Velikiye Luki, the Soviets closed the ring. Spearheads pushed westward and briefly cut the vital rail line, but parts of Chevallerie's two divisions had regrouped and counterattacked, throwing the Soviets back.

Chevallerie now faced the challenge of penetrating the encirclement to evacuate the trapped men. Hitler would not permit an evacuation and ordered, "The battle in the Velikiye Luki area must develop in such a way that contact is established among the *Kampfgruppen* through offensive action. A breakout to the west is not an option."[79] Still, that order left open the option to break in, and Chevallerie tried.

Generalmajor Erich Brandenberger's 8th Panzer Division entered the battle from the northwest about 1 December, and tanks on both sides burned in the snow. The 291st Infantry and 3rd and 6th Luftwaffe Field Divisions joined Chevallerie's group, as did the 1st SS Infantry Brigade (motorized). It was not enough. By midmonth, the Germans held but a small bastion west of the Lovat and a pocket in the eastern part of the city; the garrison was in only sporadic radio communications and was being supplied entirely by air. One more entry in the interconnected fates of the eastern front generals who would fight Patton: on 12 December, Hitler and his commanders discussed whether to shift Balck's 11th Panzer Division, then bashing the Soviets along the Chir River under Knobelsdorff's panzer corps, to Velikiye Luki—originally captured by Knobelsdorff—to help Chevallerie.

On 23 December, the 20th Motorized Infantry Division, which had been given to Chevallerie at the beginning of the month, tried to break in from the southwest without success. In early January, the 205th Infantry Division tried to reach the citadel without success. Finally, a few troops reached the survivors at the citadel, some 150 of whom eventually broke free to safety, but rescuers could not contact the men trapped east of the Lovat. After three months of bitter fighting in the harsh Russian winter, the rescuers fell just short, and the last holdouts were taken captive on 14 January. *Gruppe* Chevallerie nevertheless had prevented a Soviet breakthrough that would have unhinged Army Group Center—commanded at the time by none other than Patton's future enemy Kluge—and he had done so with bare scraps of resources while the siege of Sixth Army at Stalingrad was drawing the attention of the high command.[80] Preventing a breakthrough while operating on a shoestring would be Chevallerie's task one day against George Patton.

Defending a Fortified Line with Mobile Reserves at Rzhev: Hörnlein's *Grossdeutschland* Division spent the last five months of 1942 south of Rzhev, where it had rushed in mid-August to deal with heavy Soviet pressure. The fragments of Hitler's military briefings show that the führer took a personal interest in the division's activities, and Hörnlein was sometimes mentioned by name. Hitler viewed the division as a strategic mobile reserve or, as the division's newspaper title captured it, the fire brigade. When the division arrived in the Rzhev area in late August 1942, it was considered an Army Group Center asset, and according to the division's *Kriegstagebuch*, Hitler's headquarters determined the timing of its commitment.

The division at that time was to attack toward Micheyevo to relieve tremendous pressure on the front of XXVII Corps from a bridgehead the Soviets had established across the Volga River. Ninth Army commanding general *Generaloberst* Walter Model personally visited Hörnlein at his command post before the assault. The division launched its attack on 10 September, striking as a powerful, concentrated force, its tanks and assault guns working closely with the infantry regiments. Nevertheless, the division suffered a bloody setback. Devastating artillery fire caused heavy losses in the panzer battalion, which left twenty-eight of its thirty-four tanks on the field. The Soviets had improved captured German field fortifications, and the infantry had to engage in a costly bunker-by-bunker close assault under a pounding by Soviet artillery, aircraft, and "Stalin's organs" rockets. The records suggest that Hörnlein was not out with his forward troops, but stayed at his forward command post, playing host to Model and the XXVII Corps commander.

Hörnlein consulted with Model and called a stop. He decided to shift the *Schwerpunkt* to his left wing and the 1st Infantry Regiment, which attacked midafternoon after a Stuka attack and supported by all the division and corps artillery. Again, the attack failed with heavy losses. Hörnlein chose to interpret the outcome as a success, because it stopped a breakthrough by Thirty-First Army and VI Tank Corps and forced them onto the defensive.

The division made no greater progress the next day. *Generalfeldmarschall* Günther von Kluge, commanding Army Group Center, visited Hörnlein at his forward command post, underscoring the high-level interest in the division, but also Hörnlein's absence from the battlefield.[81]

Model's use of *Grossdeutschland* had taken advantage of none of the division's strengths, especially its mobility against a maneuvering enemy. Instead, the division had been used as a battering ram. Despite having plenty of time to reconnoiter the Soviet positions and design a plan to address their strengths, Hörnlein had simply tried to smash forward with his regiments.

Grossdeutschland went onto the defensive and fought in the same area for a month before being withdrawn to rest and refit. At that time, its 1st Infantry Regiment was renamed the Grenadier Regiment and the 2nd Infantry Regiment the Fusilier Regiment.[82]

Marshall Georgi Zhukov, meanwhile, conceived of Operation Mars as a twin to Operation Uranus, the attack that was destined to successfully surround German Sixth Army in Stalingrad, to be launched against the German salient at Rzhev, the closest point the Germans still held to Moscow, only some 130 miles away. Model's Ninth Army had thoroughly fortified the salient, much as the Soviets did at Kursk the following year. Zhukov planned to attack the salient, which stretched north like an extended thumb from a fist, from the west, north, and east with an incredibly powerful force. The Kalinin and Western Fronts, supported by the Moscow Defense District, numbered 1.9 million men and 3,400 tanks—2,300 of which Zhukov had at hand for Mars, more than was available to the force opposite the Germans at Stalingrad. The Kalinin Front was to attack the western base of the salient south of Belyi (the Germans rendered it

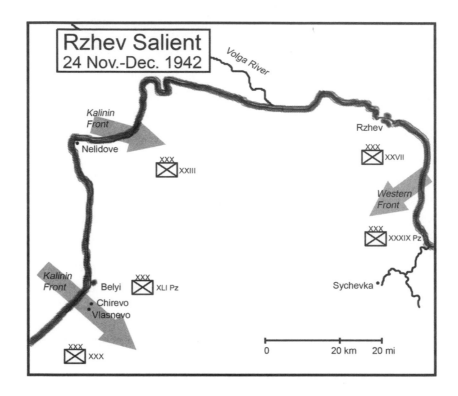

Bjeloi), the zone defended by *Generaloberst* Josef Harpe's XLI Panzer Corps. The Western Front's Twentieth and Thirty-First Armies were to attack the eastern face of the salient, defended by *Generaloberst* Hans-Jürgen von Arnim's XXXIX Panzer Corps, to meet up with the Kalinin Front. Arnim, whom Manteuffel called a "cavalier from head to toe," in just a few months' time would be fighting Patton in Tunisia.

XLI Panzer Corps (86th and 246th Infantry Divisions and 2nd Luftwaffe Field Division) learned of the looming Soviet offensive by 18 November. The Soviets aggressively probed the German front on 24 November, and the Germans realized it was the opening act in a major drama. Harpe inspected his defensive positions and concluded the work on them had not progressed far enough to stop a major offensive. Model, therefore, allocated the 41st Grenadier Regiment as a strong reserve, moved a *Kampfgruppe* from the *Grossdeutschland* Division (its Fusilier Regiment) and another from the 1st Panzer Division closer to the main line of resistance, and subordinated a battalion of *Grossdeutschland*'s artillery to the 246th Infantry Division. Harpe transferred antitank guns from the 2nd Luftwaffe Field Division's reserve to the 246th Infantry Division, where the probes had been heavy.

The Soviet Forty-First Army's 90,000 men and 300 tanks attacked through a driving snowstorm at 0900 on 25 November and made real progress in the first three days, in part because the reserves given by Model were still in transit on the twenty-fifth, and the Soviets threatened to break into the German rear. Forty-First Army had ordered I Mechanized Corps to avoid becoming entangled in the fortified city of Belyi, but the corps commander seemed drawn to it like a moth to a flame—perhaps because it was one of the few things the Soviets could find in the blinding snow. On the evening of the twenty-fifth, Harpe obtained release of the *Kampfgruppen* from the *Grossdeutschland* (less one battalion) and 1st Panzer Divisions to counterattack in the corps's zone at Belyi, where the Soviets had penetrated the seam between the 86th and 246th Divisions.

Harpe ordered that the counterstroke hit the Soviet flank. *Oberst* Wend von Wietersheim, who would later battle Patton with his 11th Panzer Division outside the fortified city of Metz, commanded the 1st Panzer Division's *Kampfgruppe*. He arrived at XLI Panzer Corps's headquarters in the late evening to personally discuss the situation with Harpe.

Hörnlein, meanwhile, had to commit *Grossdeutschland*'s Grenadier Regiment piecemeal by battalion in the neighboring XXIII Corps sector—the very fragmentation of the division that Keitel had ordered him never to permit. Division records again indicate that Hörnlein remained in his forward command post rather than joining his troops on the battlefield. The regiment provided just enough additional fighting power for XXIII Corps to hold its front, after some relatively minor tactical withdrawals.

Wietersheim was ready to strike early on the twenty-sixth, but the *Grossdeutschland* Fusilier Regiment had not arrived to support him. Wietersheim moved out alone—"and that is good," commented the corps *Kriegstagebuch*—and occupied Chirevo before the Soviets got there. The two battalions and the assault guns from *Grossdeutschland* straggled into the area, and one of the battalions moved quickly into a counterattack in the 86th Infantry Division zone. Wietersheim, at 1000 hours, ripped into the Soviet tank-infantry force at Vlasnevo. But *Grossdeutschland*'s elements had still not come up, and Wietersheim could not take the town alone. The 1st Panzer Division took charge of the sector, and the rest of the division was to come forward the next day. The *Grossdeutschland* battalion and assault guns finally appeared after dark, and the assault guns drove off twenty-five Soviet tanks and infantry that were staging a night attack.

On 27 November, *Grossdeutschland*'s Fusilier Regiment took the lead in the counterattack, while the 246th Infantry Division slaughtered Soviet troops making a direct assault on the fortifications at Belyi. XLI Panzer Corps success-fully closed the hole between its two divisions. The two battle groups continued to wage a successful, but extremely bloody defense of the city; Wietersheim held Chirevo against repeated assaults, and other elements counterattacked at the points of Soviet penetration and threw the enemy back. *Oberst* Smilo *Freiherr* von Lüttwitz and his 20th Panzer Division, part of XXX Corps, added its strength late on the twenty-eighth. *Grossdeutschland*'s motorcycle battalion, on the thirtieth cleared Soviets from a supply route where they had cut the delivery of ammunition to two divisions. That same day, the 12th Panzer Division arrived and put the Soviets to flight.

The opening of the offensive, meanwhile, caught Arnim's XXXIX Panzer Corps in the midst of rotating divisions. The northeastern face of the salient ran along the Vazuza River feeding the upper Volga, which bisects Rzhev, but that was of no help with the water frozen solid and able to bear the weight of tanks. Outnumbered five-to-one by 200,000 men and 500 tanks, Arnim managed to bring the Soviets to a cold stop over four days of chaotic fighting, despite confusion at the front, serious communications problems on the German side, and Zhukov's personnel guidance on the Soviet side. Arnim's first instinct, when tanks and infantry overran his forward positions on 25 November, was to lash back immediately with his reserve, two *Kampfgruppen* of the 9th Panzer Division (which would later face Patton in France). After some initial progress, one of his spearheads was attacked from all sides, and the other's attack shattered against the front of the massive Soviet force.

Arnim immediately realized he had to wage a defensive battle. The Germans, holding solid stone villages as strong points, slaughtered Soviet infantry advancing across wide-open ground, and Arnim used the 9th Panzer Division to firm up his sagging line.

Converging counterattacks by XXX Corps and *Grossdeutschland*'s Fusilier Regiment from 7 to 10 December cut off most of the Soviet Forty-First Army on the western face of the salient. By the fifteenth, Ninth Army had smashed every Soviet attack against its lines. Forty-First Army alone had lost 200 tanks and tens of thousands of infantrymen. Total Soviet tank losses in the operation amounted to 1,700, and the Red Army suffered half a million men killed, wounded, and missing. Oddly, the disastrous offensive merely cemented Zhukov's reputation with Stalin as a real fighter. German losses were heavy, too, and several months later, Model won permission to evacuate the salient.[83]

Although the defense of the Rzhev salient was largely forgotten thanks to the drama at Stalingrad, Model, Arnim, Hörnlein, Wietersheim, and Lüttwitz had taken part in one of the war's greatest defensive battles of a fortified front backed by mobile reserves. Most of them, one day, would put the knowledge gained from this experience to use against Patton.

Mobile Defense on the Chir: By December 1942, the situation along the Chir River looked much different than it had in the heady days of July. The Soviets were on the attack and well on their way to creating an unbreakable ring around Sixth Army at Stalingrad. Manstein's newly established Army Group Don had taken over the Chir River sector from Army Group B on 28 November, nine days after the Soviets launched their offensive. Friedrich-Wilhelm von Mellenthin was just arriving at XLVIII Panzer Corps, the stiffener for the Romanian Third Army, to take up duties as chief of staff. Looking at the situation map at the führer's headquarters on 27 November, while in transit to the front, Mellenthin recalled, "I tried to find the location of my XLVIII Panzer Corps, but there were so many arrows showing breakthroughs and encirclements that this was far from easy. In fact, on 27 November the XLVIII Panzer Corps was itself encircled in a so-called small cauldron to the northwest of Kalach." (The Germans referred to a surrounded pocket as a *Kessel*, or cauldron.)

By the time he arrived by *Storch* light plane, the corps had fought free and, along with the rest of the army, taken a line along the west bank of the Chir, which was assessed to be a tank obstacle except for several fords. *Generalmajor* Hans Cramer, an experienced panzer general who had fought beside Rommel in North Africa, took temporary command of the corps on 30 November. The corps, consisting of the 22nd Panzer, 1st Romanian Armored, and 7th Romanian Infantry Divisions, was just wrapping up a desperate and successful fight to stop the Soviet thrust through the Romanian front by attacking the Soviet forces' flanks with two *Kampfgruppen* from the 22nd Panzer Division. Cramer, on 3 December, was able to hand over his stretch of the line to II Romanian Corps. The XLVIII Panzer Corps was now to receive the 11th Panzer, 336th Infantry, and 7th Luftwaffe Field Divisions, with the idea that it would attack on Fourth Panzer Army's left in a planned operation to relieve Sixth Army in Stalingrad. Elements of all three divisions were already arriving. It had been snowing so heavily, though, that movement was difficult.

On 5 December, *General der Panzertruppe* Otto von Knobelsdorff arrived to replace Cramer. After leaving the 19th Panzer Division in January because of a severe illness, Knobelsdorff had served briefly over the past seven months as commanding general of II, X, and XXIV Panzer Corps. Knobelsdorff, Mellenthin found, "was a man of remarkable attainments, flexible and broad-minded, and highly esteemed by all members of his staff."

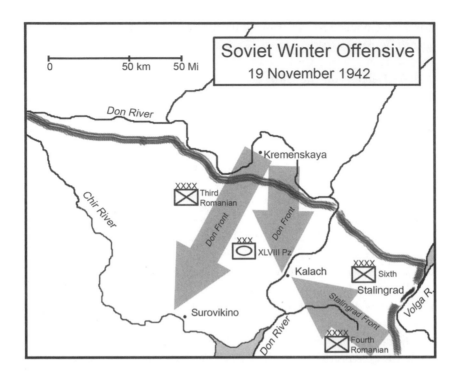

Knobelsdorff was just in time to meet the Fifth Tank Army, which was crossing the Chir in force. The corps's key strong point at Rytschov (unlocated) was just barely fending off tank-supported attacks and had lost two of its 88s.

Generalmajor Hermann Balck commanded the 11th Panzer Division, called the *Gespenster* (Ghost) Division, which had been fighting in the south. Each vehicle bore the division sign of a ghost bearing a sword and riding a half-track. *Oberst* Balck had taken command of the division near Smolensk on 24 May 1942 (officially as of 16 May), arriving from his position on the staff of the inspector of mobile troops. The division was just going into refitting, transferring its few remaining tanks to the 9th Panzer Division. Motorcycle losses had been 100 percent, and vehicles overall, 80 percent. Numerous replacements arrived, many of whom still needed training. Balck had had a chance to largely forge his own sword.

But quickly—by 5 June—the division was on the march back to the front at Krasnaya Slobodka, and on the twenty-sixth Balck received the start time and alert codeword for his first attack from XIII Corps. *Generaloberst* Wolfram von

Richthofen personally visited Balck's command post in the wee hours of the twenty-seventh to discuss the air support he would get. Balck had 124 panzers. This was the Wehrmacht at its peak.

Balck watched from a forward observation post as his men attacked across the Tim River at 0215 hours on the twenty-eighth. Once the attack got moving, Balck joined one of his forward *Kampfgruppen*. At 1605 hours, he informed his command post, "The enemy is fleeing." Moving quickly, the *Kampfgruppe* crushed an infantry battalion, overran the line of an infantry brigade, despite the presence of antitank guns, and tore into the enemy's rear area, destroying eight T34 and Mark II tanks in the process. It had not been a bad first day, and Balck and his 11th Panzer Division continued to perform in an outstanding fashion.[84]

Balck arrived on the Chir on 6 December, just as the Soviet I Tank Corps was knocking a hole in the XLVIII Panzer Corps's line of isolated *Kampfgruppen*, despite intervention by the newly arrived 336th Infantry Division. Balck went to get the lay of the land at corps headquarters about noon, and Knobelsdorff ordered him to seal the breach. Balck was to rush his antitank guns and a panzergrenadier battalion to Rytschov.

Balck called his commanders together at 0700 the next day: "The enemy has achieved a breakthrough of the Third and Fourth Romanian Armies. Sixth Army is surrounded in Stalingrad. Fourth Panzer Army has the mission of attacking from the south with XLVIII Panzer Corps to clear the enemy from the Don River bend."

Knobelsdorff's headquarters called at 0900 with the alarming news that fifty T34 tanks had burst through the line of a regiment of the 7th Luftwaffe Field Division where it tied into the 336th Infantry Division. The latter division was pushing its right wing forward and had its strength concentrated there, and it would be only a short time before the hole widened to three miles and the Soviets would reach the artillery positions. If the Soviets pivoted, they would take the 336th Infantry Division in the flank. Please send Balck's panzer regiment, begged the 336th Division's commanding general.

At 0915, Fourth Panzer Army approved the corps's request to counterattack with Balck's panzers, and ten minutes later, the orders reached Balck. The weather was improving slightly, and the Luftwaffe, which had been grounded all morning, ordered every available plane into the air. The 11th Panzer Division was rested and ready, having enjoyed a relatively quiet November near Smolensk, but nearly a third of its vehicles had fallen out during the march north. Although the precise number of tanks available on this date is unclear, on 12 December,

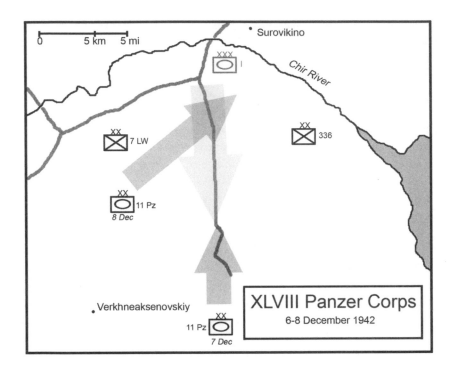

Hitler was told Balck had forty-five panzers, thirty of them Mark IIIs and five Mark IVs with long-barreled guns that could kill a T34 from the front.

Balck acted with incredible speed, and his 15th Panzer Regiment arrived at the Soviet breakthrough by 1045. Balck's order, which he could be certain his subordinates would interpret according to his wishes, was "Forward!" Throughout the operation, Balck controlled the battle only through verbal orders. The Soviets, meanwhile, were pushing more tanks, motorized infantry, and artillery—an estimated total of two infantry divisions and a tank brigade—into the hole. Knobelsdorff had lost contact with his infantry elements at the point of penetration, and at noon, he ordered the rest of the 11th Panzer Division to follow the panzer regiment. By 1700, the 110th and 111th Panzergrenadier Regiments and the motorcycle battalion arrived and sealed off the road to the south that led into the 336th Infantry Division's rear. The counterattack blocked the Soviet advance, but Knobelsdorff ordered the division to stop pushing forward until it could gather its strength.

Rather than make a frontal attack, Knobelsdorff wanted to attack the next morning against the enemy's flank and rear and issued his orders to that effect.

The 11th Panzer Division was to keep its forces tightly together. Mellenthin later implied this order had been Balck's idea, but XLVIII Panzer Corps records suggest that was not the case. Still, under the German practice of *Auftragstaktik* (mission-type orders), Balck had a free hand in deciding how to execute the orders.

Balck struck at 0430 hours and conducted a brilliant slashing panzer drive across the Soviet rear—he preferred to keep his tanks and grenadiers separated during attacks. The maneuver was all the more effective because the Soviets committed fifty of their tanks against the left wing of the 336th Infantry Division, where they could be cut off. At first, progress was slow against a strong tank-backed defense. The rolling hills were not tank friendly and offered the defenders good concealment. The panzers nevertheless caught the Soviet armor in the flank, destroyed many of the tanks, and pushed on. Then his 2nd Panzer Battalion caught a motorized infantry column in the open, and the Soviet defenses began to unravel. Stukas, meanwhile, crushed a Soviet break-through on the 336th Infantry Division's left, and the Luftwaffe conducted effective attacks across the corps's front. By 1430, the 11th Panzer Division had cut off the Soviet troops that had broken through. When the day was over, Balck had nearly destroyed the enemy corps, including most of forty-six tanks counted on the battlefield. His own losses had been slight. "With the coming of dark," Knobelsdorff's operations staff recorded, "the corps can look back on a great success."

Until 22 December, Balck, moving night and day, fell upon one Soviet penetration after another and destroyed nearly all of them. Working hand-in-glove with two infantry divisions, Balck gave a *Kriegsakademie*-perfect display of flexible defense. Balck's promotion to *Generalleutnant* followed on New Year's Day.[85] His experiences in late December were the first steps toward the his conception of the mobile defense he would mount in Lorraine against George Patton.

End of the Act: Germany faced a strategic disaster in the east in early 1943, and the panzer commanders who would later fight Patton in France, Belgium, and the Rhineland were a big reason catastrophe was averted. The *Schwerpunkt* of the Soviet winter offensive was aimed at the southern end of the German front. Army Group A's First Panzer Army was hurriedly withdrawing from the Caucasus through Rostov in late January while *Generalfeldmarschall* Erich von Manstein's battered Army Group Don struggled to keep the escape route open. In Stalingrad, Sixth Army, nominally part of the army group, capitulated on 1 February, releasing considerable Soviet forces that had been besieging the city. Army Group B was in tatters, which exposed the entire southern wing of

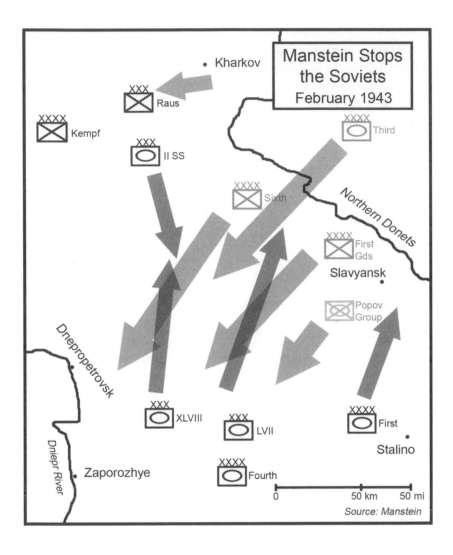

the German front to potential envelopment by forces driving through Kharkov and swinging down to the Sea of Azov. Army Group Don estimated that the Soviets on its front held a manpower advantage of eight to one.

Manstein, in a grueling argument with Hitler on 6 February, won permission to withdraw from the lower Don and eastern Donets basin to the Mius River line and to concentrate First and Fourth Panzer Armies on his left wing. Manstein's strategic shift was just in time: three Soviet armies took Kharkov, on Manstein's left wing, in mid-February.[86]

Obergruppenführer Paul Hausser's SS Panzer Corps, including the *Totenkopf* Division (with Hermann Priess and Max Simon), held Kharkov as the Soviets closed in. Manstein's Army Group Don was renamed Army Group South on 12 February and took over the southern end of Army Group B's front. On the thirteenth, Manstein ordered that Kharkov be held as long as possible, but he added that the forces there could not allow themselves to be surrounded. Hitler, through an intermediary by telephone, ordered Hausser to hold Kharkov at all costs; it was the fourth largest Soviet city, its capture was a matter of prestige in the führer's mind. But the wily SS general had his written orders and refused to sacrifice his troops. Hausser, on the fifteenth, ordered his divisions to break free to the southwest. The Soviets were already in the city when the last of his men slipped away.[87] Hausser had saved his corps to fight another day, and fortunately for him, that day would come soon enough that he would suffer no consequences from his defiance of the führer.

The Soviet offensive finally petered out in late February (Hitler had foreseen this, as he would accurately anticipate the Western Allies' supply difficulties in early September 1944), and the Germans were able to establish a line along the Dniepr capable of holding back the now-exhausted Soviet troops, who had advanced some 300 miles. The brilliant Manstein scripted the final scene in orders he issued on 19 February. He was aware that he had to act quickly to restore the situation, because some time in March, the spring thaw would turn the terrain to a sea of mud and prevent mobile warfare. First and Fourth Panzer Armies and Army Detachment Kempf (controlling the corps southwest of Kharkov), reinforced by refreshed panzer divisions, rushed forward by rail and attacked the Soviet Sixth Army, First Guards Army, and Popov's Mobile Group—commanded by Gen. Markian Popov, whom *General der Panzertruppe* Erhard Raus considered "the best Russian tank general"—from two directions southwest of Kharkov. They destroyed Sixth Army and Popov's group and savaged Third Tank Army, which also had entered the battle. Otto von Knobelsdorff's XLVIII Panzer Corps and Paul Hausser's SS Panzer Corps played the key roles in this crushing counterblow. As late as 25 February, Soviet troops were fighting fiercely and receiving reinforcements, but only two days later, *Generaloberst* Hoth's orders from Fourth Panzer Army to Knobelsdorff were, "Pursue the defeated enemy." Manstein had reclaimed the initiative.[88]

*

FIVE

French North Africa:
La Guerre des Trois Jours

PATTON'S FIRST MILITARY ENEMY as a commander in his own right was to be, oddly, his French allies of the Great War, whom he deeply admired. He would face them in what the French would call *la guerre de trois jours*, or the three-day war.

The Western Allies took the strategic offensive against Hitler on the periphery, in French North Africa, because, at that time, they lacked the wherewithal to challenge him at the walls of his "Fortress Europe." After somewhat acrimonious debate, the Americans and British agreed to seize the North African possessions of Vichy France. With luck, the French colonial administration would jump to the Allied camp, and a quick push eastward would secure Tunisia before the Germans could take control. Success would threaten the rear of Axis forces under the command of *Generalleutnant* Erwin Rommel, the Desert Fox, who was giving the British a hard time in Egypt.

After the Combined Chiefs of Staff agreed in July 1942 to occupy French North Africa, planners made every effort to package the operation as American one to deflect Vichy French hostility toward the British, though there would be substantial British participation. In July President Franklin Roosevelt decided to name Lt. Gen. Dwight "Ike" Eisenhower as commander in chief, Allied Expeditionary Force, for the newly named Operation Torch. Eisenhower did not receive a directive from the Combined Chiefs of Staff until 13 August, which meant that there would be two months available to pull together the largest and most complex amphibious operation ever attempted. Ike's mission was to, in conjunction with Allied forces in the Middle East, establish full control over North Africa from the Atlantic Ocean to the Red Sea. His first step was to establish lodgments at Algiers and Oran, Algeria, and then to gain control over all of French North Africa.[1]

The Americans and British debated whether to land only in the Mediterranean or on the Atlantic seaboard as well, and how far east to operate. As the main objective was Tunis, landings at Bizerte would be optimal, but Axis control of the air made that option too risky. Eisenhower initially favored the Mediterranean option, but U.S. Chief of Staff George Marshall and the U.S. Chiefs of Staff, for several reasons, strongly supported trying to put a force ashore at Casablanca, despite the strong possibility that the surf would, in the end, prove to be too heavy to permit the actual landing. They were concerned, above all, that fascist Spain, or a Spain rapidly occupied by Germany, would close the Strait of Gibraltar and cut off a Mediterranean-only operation. Casablanca was the western terminus of a rickety colonial rail line that ran across North Africa and could supply troops in Algeria and Tunisia if the strait was temporarily lost. Secondly, even Eisenhower calculated that any serious degree of French resistance would delay a ground advance into Tunisia long enough for the Germans to occupy it, and he wanted the most awe-inspiring invasion possible in the hope that the Vichy would throw in the towel quickly.[2]

Picked out by Marshall, Patton traveled to the War Department on 30 July, where he received his commission as commander of Western Task Force. He immediately visited Eisenhower and the planning staff in London. Eisenhower had hoped to get Patton for the job, but because Ike was junior to Patton in the regular army, he had been reluctant to ask. Eisenhower frequently told his naval aide, Lt. Cdr. Harry Butcher, that he wanted lucky generals, and Patton looked like one.

In his first meeting with Ike about Torch on 9 August, Patton was somewhat concerned that his troops would be outnumbered and about heavy sea swells, but he assured Eisenhower that he had a sixth sense and could divine the enemy's intentions better than any intelligence staff. On 17 August, Patton told Eisenhower he had already drafted a surrender ultimatum for Casablanca. Eisenhower, still thinking about the surf off Morocco, wrote to Patton on 3 September, "I am searching the Army to find the most capable chaplain to assure a fairly decent break in the weather when the big day comes." Patton would copy the idea later and spin it into another piece of his legend.[3]

In an age when the United States has the world's most powerful standing army, we should not lose a sense of wonder about the fact that a country that had only begun to mobilize in August 1940 planned to conduct the most difficult type of large-scale offensive (an amphibious one) just over two years later. The men in charge, though, had all served under Black Jack Pershing, who under similar conditions had demanded the right to conduct a large-scale offensive across the most difficult terrain on the western front as his first order of business.

The overall planning for Torch was done under Eisenhower's watchful eye in London, but Patton directed planning for his own piece in Washington.[4] Drawing on his staff from I Armored Corps, Patton set about designing an operation to capture Casablanca, an objective only firmly established on 5 September. Western Task Force's assault was to complement that of Center Task Force at Oran, and the two elements were to secure communications from the Atlantic to Algeria and build a force capable of overrunning Spanish Morocco, if that became necessary.

Casablanca was too strongly defended for a frontal assault, so planners decided to take it from the rear, after making landings above and below the city. Providing armored support for such an operations was a must.[5]

Technological limitations in sealift left few options for planners. The infant Allied amphibious force was capable of landing only light tanks aboard available tank lighters, as the medium tanks were too heavy. In the American fleet, the tanks had to be lifted from the holds of transports by cranes and lowered into the lighters waiting alongside.[6] The M5s available to the light-tank battalions assigned to Western Task Force were waterproofed, and hooded shrouds were attached over the air intake and exhaust, so the tanks could run through four-to-five-foot-deep water after leaving the lighters.[7] Medium tanks had to be offloaded dockside once the infantry and light tanks had secured port facilities.

Planners adopted a penny-packet approach similar in many ways to the initial plan for Sicily that Gen. Bernard Montgomery would later reject as unworkable because it violated the basic principle of concentration of force. Planners selected from among the small ports north and south of Casablanca two just big enough to handle medium tanks unloaded from transport ships—Port Lyautey and Safi, respectively. As Safi was 150 miles southwest of Casablanca and Port Lyautey was fifty miles to the northeast, infantry and light tanks—and Patton himself—were to land at Fédala, only eighteen miles northeast of Casablanca, and wait for the medium tanks to arrive.[8] This plan could only work if the French were taken by surprise and could not concentrate overwhelming force at some of the landings.

Patton and his planners do not appear to have considered how their opposite numbers would interpret operations as they unfolded. Patton committed a substantial force to the Port Lyautey landing—actually conducted across the beaches at Mehdia, a short distance to the west—in order to capture hard-surfaced airfields there and at Sale, three miles up the coast from Rabat, for aircraft that would support the attack on Casablanca (even though both towns lay on the far side of Rabat from Casablanca). Patton initially wanted to take Rabat, but he was induced to give up the idea because planners expected that city to be well defended; its port was too shallow; and combat might wound or kill the sultan, which could provoke a backlash among Arabs across North Africa.[9] The landings at Mehdia shaped French perceptions of American objectives— they thought Patton meant to attack Rabat—in ways that led to the bloodiest fighting of the operation.

Patton did not forge his sword for this operation, with one exception: the major elements of his assault force were the 3rd and 9th Infantry divisions (the latter less the 39th Infantry Regiment, which was assigned to Eastern Task Force), Patton's old 2nd Armored Division, and the 70th and 756th Tank Battalions.[10]

Nor did Patton frame his own operational plan. Brigadier General Lucian Truscott and a planning group in London, which Patton visited in September, put together the initial outline, which was delivered to Patton in late September or early October for further elaboration. Truscott had participated in the ill-fated Anglo-Canadian raid on Dieppe on 19 August—the only Allied experience with assaulting a defended shore—and according to then-Maj. Theodore Conway, who worked for Truscott and had participated in planning the Dieppe operation, "Truscott's experience in Dieppe had had a great deal of influence on the North African landings. . . ."[11]

VIEW FROM THE GERMAN HIGH COMMAND

Patton entered the war just as German fortunes, at the grand strategic level, were beginning to ebb, a fitting chapeau for the good fortune that smiled on his fate in so many instances. The view was grim from the perspective of OKW. In October 1942 the Germans found themselves facing another Russian winter, having failed to capture most of the objectives chosen for the summer offensive. Unlike the preceding year, the Soviets had managed to extract most of their forces from German encirclements, and the Wehrmacht manned a thin line over vast distances, its men exhausted and its equipment worn out, dangling at the end of long and tenuous supply lines. In eastern North Africa, Montgomery and his Eighth Army had driven the German-Italian Panzer Army into a long retreat at the Battle of El Alamein. An Allied invasion of Western Europe was expected as early as summer 1943, and construction of the "Atlantic Wall" was making only slow progress. Fearing landings along the 1,500-mile-long Norwegian coast, Hitler diverted material and equipment desperately needed elsewhere. Even the U-boat war in the Atlantic was turning against Germany.

All this had led to a crisis of confidence in the high command. Hitler and *Generaloberst* Alfred Jodl were barely speaking. Nevertheless, on 15 October, some discussion took place at Hitler's headquarters about reports, in ever-increasing numbers, that Anglo-American landings in West Africa were imminent. Hitler rejected a proposal to permit the French to send reinforcements from metropolitan France out of concern for Italian sensibilities.

There were voices in OKW, which was essentially Hitler's military staff, who, by the beginning of November, argued that French North Africa was the most likely place for an Allied amphibious operation. But they had few concrete indications to support their suspicions, and even these officers looked to early 1943 as the likely time for an Allied operation. The Germans had obtained indications from "obscure sources and round-about channels" that troops and ships were concentrating in western England. The types of equipment spotted suggested that this was an amphibious landing force. Similar, but even more vague, information was available concerning North American ports. American agents were reported to be increasingly active in French North Africa, but close monitoring of the Vichy French revealed no grounds for concern. *Generalfeldmarschall* Albert Kesselring, *Oberbefehlshaber Süd* (commander-in-chief south, *OB Süd*), claimed after the war that he, for one, had expected landings in North Africa. For Kesselring, however, it was almost academic, because in his view, Montgomery's defeat of Rommel had already sealed North Africa's fate, leaving him no better prospects than tying down the Allies there for as long as possible.

OKW paid little heed to these indications, but it forwarded warnings of imminent Allied action to *Generalfeldmarschall* Gerd von Rundstedt, *Oberbefehlshaber West* (*OB West*), and to the army command in Norway. Operation Torch would come as a strategic surprise to the high command and become the final push to the turn of the war against the Axis.[12]

DEFENDERS OF THE EMPIRE

Why would the French fight instead of welcoming the Americans with open arms? Morocco was the only place the colonial army and the French navy put up dogged resistance, so the answer appears to lie in the key officers in Morocco and what had brought them to that place.

General Charles Auguste Paul Noguès had been appointed the resident general of Morocco and commander of all armed forces in the colony in September 1936, at the age of sixty, and he was the perfect man for the job. Noguès was an artilleryman whose first assignment had been as a member of a survey team that mapped parts of eastern Morocco. He had been posted to Tunisia in 1908, and in 1909 had joined the Oran Division in Algeria for two years. In 1912, Noguès had taken a position in the office of Gen. Louis-Hubert Lyautey, then resident general for Morocco. The outbreak of war in 1914 led to Noguès's first assignment in metropolitan France in the cabinet of Minister of War Adolfe Messimy, after which he spent time at the front. In 1917, Noguès rejoined Lyautey. After serving in various positions in Paris, Noguès returned to the Maghreb in 1924, where he reached the rank of colonel that year, brigadier general in 1927, and general of the division (major general) in 1930. He took command of XIX Corps in 1933, and in July 1933 became inspector general for all troops in French North Africa.[13] By then, Noguès was probably deeply imbued with a sense that North Africa was his home and his responsibility.

Before the outbreak of war with Germany in September 1939, France had viewed its North Africa possessions as an integral part of the defense of metropolitan France. North Africa was both a source of manpower and a supply route for resources, particularly oil, from France's colonies. French planners had viewed fascist Italy as the primary menace, particularly as dictator Benito Mussolini increased Italian troop strength in Libya. Fascist Spain, with its military assets in Spanish Morocco, posed a threat to the links among France's North African colonies that greatly complicated planning. Recognizing the fragility of the transportation links between France and North Africa, the French devoted considerable resources to their Mediterranean fleet.[14]

Noguès, on 26 February 1938, became the theater commander for operations in French North Africa and was directly subordinated to the French command in Paris. In this capacity, Noguès, using his skills in the political and economic spheres, gained the confidence of the sultan in Rabat, for whom he acted as foreign minister, and ensured that Morocco's Berbers and Arabs were loyal to France. A month before the declaration of war in September 1939, Noguès mobilized his forces in anticipation of conflict with Italy. Mussolini, however, waited until the German Wehrmacht had clearly defeated the Allies in France before declaring war on 10 June. Military operations in North Africa were minimal. Italian planes bombed Bizerte, Tunisia, on 12 and 22 June, and Noguès's bombers struck back against the port facilities in Tripoli on 16 June. Italian and locally raised soldiers attacked a French border garrison on 13 June, but failed, over three days, to capture it. French troops destroyed an Italian border outpost at Pisidia on 19 June. The Spanish took advantage of the situation and, on 14 June, occupied Tangiers—an occupation to which France reluctantly acquiesced as a temporary measure.[15]

After Marshall Henri Pétain accepted the French presidency on 16 June and that night transmitted to Germany via Spain a request for a cease-fire, Noguès—encouraged by soldiers, airmen, sailors, the British governor of Gibraltar, and governors and commanders from throughout the French Empire—initially urged Pétain to continue the struggle in North Africa. The British put Brig. Gen. Charles de Gaulle on the BBC on 18 June to call on all Frenchmen to continue the fight. Noguès, however, turned aside direct attempts by de Gaulle to communicate with him, as well as entreaties from a British mission to fight on regardless of Pétain's decision. Metropolitan France could not supply his forces in North Africa, ammunition stocks there were low, and Noguès had little by way of air defense. Although some thousand modern combat aircraft flew to North Africa from France, they generally lacked armament, and there was enough oil for only fifteen days of operations. Pétain was determined to end hostilities, and Noguès accepted the decision of France's constitutional government, particularly because the armistice terms preserved French sovereignty over North Africa.[16]

The armistice with Germany, which went into force on 25 June, stipulated the demobilization of French troops regardless of their location in the metropolitan area or the colonies, but events quickly altered those plans. Hitler was focused on knocking Great Britain out of the war and displayed no interest in France's North Africa colonies, despite their ports and air bases. The British fleet attacked the French fleet in Mers el-Kébir on 3 July (and followed with an air strike on the sixth), which caused the Germans to suspend demobilization. French bombers hit back against British ships at Gibraltar on 4 July, which may have swayed German thinking about whether Vichy would fight the British. The French, furthermore, argued that they needed military resources to maintain internal stability in the colonies.

By August 1940, Germany had permitted France to rearm its coastal batteries in North Africa, deploy antitank guns along the coast, and more than double the number of machine guns to strengthen air defense. The Germans even permitted a delivery of ammunition to the battleship *Jean Bart* in Casablanca. In early 1941, the Axis powers decreed that France could maintain 100,000 soldiers (the cap Germany had faced under Versailles) and 20,000 unarmed workers (*mehallas*), 102 tanks, and 120 motorized machine guns in North Africa. General Maxime Weygand became the delegate general for all French colonies in Africa, and Noguès's position as theater commander was abolished, although he continued, from Morocco, to coordinate military affairs across North Africa. A Gaullist-British attempt to seize Dakar on 23 and 24 September provoked air attacks by French bombers against Gibraltar on the twenty-fifth and twenty-sixth.[17]

General Alphonse Juin, who replaced Weygand in his military capacities in November 1941, was much more resistant to collaborating with the Germans than his predecessor had been, and he secretly ordered French forces in North Africa to prepare to defend against whomever attacked. He expected that the Axis was the most likely threat, but he also drew up plans to fight the British.[18] This strategic posture was the basis for French reaction to Operation Torch.

Most senior French officers were, in fact, willing to fight the Allies, particularly after Mers el-Kébir and Dakar. Major General Ernest Harmon, who commanded the American 2nd Armored Division and came to know Noguès and other senior officers, offered this explanation:

> In the United States and Great Britain, professional military men are subject to civilian control. . . . The story in France was different. The officer caste came, in the main, from aristocratic families and patriotism was often an abstract ideal. Loyalty to France frequently did not include loyalty to a shabby Third Republic and its shabby political deals: in fact, the military caste's contempt for politics was often so unrealistic as to approach nihilism. . . . [My superiors] found it difficult to understand a "sense of honor" which obligated French commanders to observe pledges to Germany which had been forced upon a defeated nation by fiat and duress.[19]

There is a conventional wisdom among American historians that had Patton assaulted Rabat, Noguès would have folded like a weak reed. Ladislas Farago lacked Harmon's insight and held Noguès ("shifty," in his view) and French naval commander Francois "Frix" Michelier (a "knave" and a "fool") in evident contempt. Georges Lascroux, commander of the French army in Morocco, and other French commanders were "poker-faced henchmen."[20] Carlo D'Este claimed that, in retrospect, the French would have surrendered "at once" had Patton attacked Rabat.[21] As shall be seen, French commanders issued their orders to fight before they had any idea where the Americans were landing, and their strategy of defense in depth anticipated the eventual loss of the coastal cites.

At the time of the Anglo-American landings, actual Vichy military strength in North Africa was 109,584 officers and men. According to an agreement with the Axis control commissions, half the troops were French and half were indigenous. The French possessed 164 tanks, mainly obsolete Renault D1s and World War I–vintage Renault FT17s, like those Patton had used in the Great War; 167 armored cars; and 102 37mm antitank guns. Moreover, Noguès had been carefully "camouflaging" arms, equipment, and paramilitary manpower (mainly locally recruited troops, called *goumiers*, secreted in the *mehalla* labor organizations) not permitted under the terms of the armistice, with the aim of building an elite army that could serve as the core of a mass army if remobilization became possible and the fight against Germany could resume. He also implemented a program of clandestine arms manufacturing and, by November, had a dozen motorized 75mm antitank guns (later used in Tunisia), hidden in Casablanca and protected by *goumiers*, plus ten of a planned twenty-five motorized 37mm guns.[22]

The Americans fully expected the French in Morocco to fight, and in this they were right. But they largely misread the intentions of the French commander they would face. The Western Task Force G-2 anticipated that the French forces' center of mass would be dispersed in the area of Azemour, Kasbah Tadla, Meknès, and Port Lyautey, with the objective of defending Casablanca. French resistance was expected to be stubborn at Port Lyautey, Rabat-Fédala-Casablanca, Safi, and Agadir.[23]

The American grasp of French ground-force strength was weak, although estimates of air and naval strength were fairly accurate. The French, the G-2 estimated, would be able to reinforce the mobile garrison in the Rabat–Port Lyautey area with an infantry regiment upon word of a hostile fleet appearing, leaving three infantry regiments, a battalion of medium artillery, a cavalry squadron, and half a tank battalion in general reserve in the area of Meknès and Fès, east of Rabat. These elements could reach the Casablanca-Fédala area within two days by rail and four and a half days by road march. To the south, the Safi garrison could be reinforced by a motorized artillery battery within hours and by a mechanized cavalry group and a battalion of 75mm guns from Marrakech within a day. The G-2 estimated that the French had 200 armored vehicles: 80 in Rabat, and 40 each in Casablanca, Marrakech, and Meknès. The French air arm was assessed to have seventy-four fighters, thirteen reconnaissance aircraft, and eighty-one long-range bombers. The French navy was estimated to have at Casablanca one battleship (*Jean Bart*), two light cruisers, between eight and ten destroyers, around a dozen submarines, two torpedo boats, and thirteen navy fighter aircraft. Two squadrons of torpedo boats (twenty-four vessels) were in Port Lyautey.[24]

The French army in Morocco, commanded by Maj. Gen. Georges Lascroux, consisted of some 50,000 poorly equipped men. Lascroux, born in 1885, had commanded the 17th Infantry Division during the defeat in 1940, become commander of the Fès military region after the armistice, and advanced to commander-in-chief of Moroccan forces in 1942. The stocky Lascroux was to be Noguès's chief subordinate during the fighting in Morocco. Most of the army's best formations in Morocco, however, had been sent to metropolitan France, only to be caught up in the debacle of May and June.

Air force general Auguste Lahoulle had about 170 old planes, all of them inferior to the U.S. Navy's Grumman Wildcats that would soon be buzzing through the Moroccan skies from the deck of the USS *Ranger* and four escort carriers.

The French navy was the best outfitted of the services. The *Jean Bart*, which had been under construction in St. Nazaire and barely escaped capture by the Germans in June, was moored and unable to maneuver, but she still had four 15-inch guns mounted and ready in her forward turret. The 2nd Light Cruiser Squadron included one light cruiser, three large destroyer leaders, and seven smaller destroyers.[25]

Noguès had organized his forces into four defense sectors, including the ground, naval, and air components in each area, all commanded by a senior officer who reported to Noguès. These officers had a great deal of autonomy to act until events required the commitment of general reserves, at which point Noguès was to take command of the theater of operations. Major General André Dody commanded the Division of Meknès and the sector from Port Lyautey north. Vice Admiral Francois "Frix" Michelier commanded the navy of Morocco and all troops in the Casablanca sector. Major General Henri Martin, who had been tipped off by the Allies in general terms regarding Operation Torch, commanded the Division of Marrakech and the coast from Safi south to Mogador. The southernmost sector around Agadir was not affected by the invasion.[26] The French defensive plan anticipated some effort to hold onto coastal ports, but its focus was on a defense in depth up to fifty miles into the interior—with indigenous irregular forces expected to play a major role—and on the protection of Rabat.[27]

The American G-2 expected senior commanders, with the exceptions of Martin and Maj. Gen. Antoine Béthouart, commanding the Division of Casablanca, to be loyal to Vichy. Indeed, the peripatetic putsch-plotter cum envoy Robert Murphy, who achieved some success in Algeria, met Noguès as late as October and found him fiercely loyal to Vichy. Nevertheless, field-grade officers, including most regimental commanders, were believed to be overwhelmingly in favor of joining the Allies. Murphy fully expected the navy to fight because of bitterness over British attacks against it.

In its catalog of French leaders, the G-2 considered Noguès a political figure who was very correct and obeyed his superiors. He was judged to be able and intelligent, but indecisive. In this last judgment, the intelligence boys would prove completely wrong.[28]

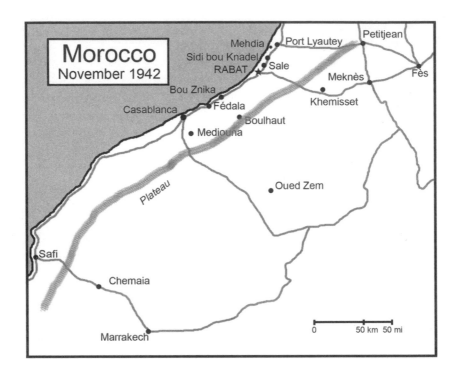

THE APPROACHING STORM

Task Force 34's 102 ships bore Patton's men from Hampton Roads, Virginia, and other East Coast ports toward the shores of Morocco the third week of October. Onboard ship, Patton and his staff were still working out some significant details of their plan. The first vessels carrying Center and Eastern task forces had departed from the United Kingdom on 22 October. The first ships bound for Algiers serenely passed Gibraltar the night of 5–6 November. The ships were to sail past the objectives and double-back at the last moment to deceive the Axis and French as to the true Allied intentions.

Reflecting the underlying goal of bringing Vichy French forces into the war on the side of the Allies, the guidelines for Torch stipulated that Allied elements were not to fire on the French unless they first demonstrated hostile intent. Patton had objected that this gave the enemy the same advantage as first draw in a gunfight, but Eisenhower was firm.[29] Ike signaled Western Task Force while it was under way to underscore his intention that every effort be taken to make the landings as peaceful as possible and to keep small incidents from escalating into generalized fighting. "We particularly desire to avoid heavy offensive action against Casablanca," he wrote.[30]

Patton, on 2 November, wrote to his wife, "From some messages we have, it seems that there is a good chance that the French Army and Air will join us. I hope not, for it would sort of pull the cork of the men—all steamed up to fight and not have to—also it would be better for me to have a battle. Well in six days we will know." Patton presumably thought he needed a battle because he had thus far accrued but four days of combat experience.

To his troops, Patton wrote, "It is not known whether the French African Army . . . will contest our landing. It is regrettable to contemplate the necessity of fighting the gallant French who are at heart sympathetic to us, but all resistance by whomever offered must be destroyed. However, when ever any of the French soldiers seek to surrender, you will accept it and treat them with the respect due a brave opponent and future ally."[31]

Just in case, Patton recorded, "Have been giving everyone a simplified directive of war. Use a steamroller strategy; that is, make up your mind on a course and direction of action, and stick to it. But in tactics, do not steamroller. Attack weakness. Hold them by the nose and kick them in the pants."[32]

Here was a pithy summary of Patton's philosophy. But would the enemy allow his nose to be held and his backside kicked? Or might he have a boot on his own foot?

The Allied convoys' deception maneuver completely took in French commanders in Morocco, who believed the ships were heading for Alexandria or Malta. With no threat in sight to coast watchers in Morocco, the fuel-short French air force put no reconnaissance flights into the air.

The maneuver also fooled the Germans. Hitler, who was riding to Munich on his special train, received a report from Jodl about Allied fleet movements derived from air reconnaissance that day. Jodl deemed a landing in French North Africa unlikely because it would push the Vichy French into Germany's arms. Hitler, that morning, declared the invasion would be aimed at Tripoli or Benghazi to cut off Rommel. Later in the day, he suspected a daring assault on Sicily, Corsica, or Sardinia, and—reflecting his appreciation of the Axis's precarious fortunes— said such an operation would drive Italy out of the war and spell defeat in the Mediterranean theater.

However, further calculations of convoy speeds during the evening led to the conclusion, at about 2000 hours, that French North Africa was, indeed, the Allies' destination. The train stopped for two hours in Thuringia (later occupied by Patton's Third Army), and orders went forth: contain Vichy France, prevent the French fleet from putting to sea, calm the Italians, establish a bridgehead in Tunisia, accelerate the delivery of reinforcements to Rommel.

The night of 7 November, the sea off Morocco was unusually calm, and the lights of neutral France's coastal cities blazed away.[33]

Unbeknownst to the military commanders of Western Task Force, Maj. Gen. Antoine Béthouart was at the center of a plot to paralyze Morocco, a plot that had been hatched by American Robert Murphy and pro-Allied French commanders in Algiers. As ordained by the law of unintended consequences, the attempted putsch caused French forces in Morocco to be on full alert when the American landings—an utter surprise to the rest of the French—began.[34]

At 2300 hours on 7 November, Rear Adm. Francois Missoffe awoke Admiral Michelier with incredible news: Béthouart had put his troops on alert and ordered the arrest of the Axis armistice commissions in Morocco. Indeed, Béthouart had marched a battalion of unwitting colonial troops to Rabat and detained Noguès, Lascroux, and Lahoulle. Michelier told Missoffe that Béthouart's act would give the Germans the excuse they needed to occupy Morocco, and they had to stop him. This suggests that Michelier had an outdated view of Axis strength and resources that may have contributed to his willingness to fight the Americans. Michelier immediately put all naval personnel on defensive footing, ordered all ships to implement measures for defense against attack from land, and converted his headquarters into a fortress. When the BBC broadcast President Franklin Roosevelt's message of goodwill toward French North Africa at 0130 hours, nobody of importance in Morocco heard it, because they were too busy. At 0300, one of Béthouart's subordinates appeared with a letter stating that Gen. Henri Giraud had taken command in Algeria (not yet true), that a massive American landing was imminent, and that Béthouart had taken command in Morocco. He urged Michelier to join him. The admiral and his staff dismissed the claims as ridiculous.

Radio operators monitoring friendly communications by 0315 delivered word that hostile landings were occurring at Algiers, however, and a quarter hour later, that foreign troops were coming ashore at Oran. At 0445, Michelier spoke by phone with Noguès, who raged that Béthouart had arrested him and locked him in his own office (but foolishly not cut off his phone!). Noguès ordered Michelier to annul Béthouart's orders, protect the Axis armistice commissions, and alert all military personnel and coastal defense posts. Noguès instructed Michelier to take command in his place if he became unable to exert authority over French forces in Morocco. Noguès also contacted the other defense-zone commanders and ordered them to put their men on alert. About the time the first American soldiers reached land, shortly after 0500, Béthouart's putsch had collapsed, and the general was himself under arrest.[35]

AGAINST WHOMEVER COMES

Unknown to the French, confusion also reigned off the coast in Task Force 34. At 0100, Patton contacted Maj. Gen. Jonathan Anderson, commanding Sub–Task Force Brushwood off Fédala, and informed him that radar on the flagship indicated that some transports were out of position by as much as 10,000 yards. Unloading transports went more slowly than expected, and Patton had to postpone H-Hour from 0400 to 0445 hours.[36] Similar confusion snarled operations off other landing zones.

Nevertheless, Patton had some incredibly good luck, too. The weather that morning was the calmest it had been on that date in sixty eight years.[37]

As the first reports of invasion reached Noguès, the general at first suspected he was being attacked by Gaullist forces and cabled Juin for instructions. The query was accidentally transmitted to Vichy instead, where Prime Minister Pierre Laval briefly considered firing Noguès and replacing him with Michelier before cabling back, "Your duty is clear. . . . Oppose the Americans."[38] At 0600, discerning from reports that an all-out attack was underway, Noguès implemented the defense plan and exerted his authority as commander-in-chief of the theater of operations.[39]

The following sections address the American suboperations to which Noguès and his subordinate commanders responded, starting with the operation at Safi, in the south, to that at Port Lyautey, in the north.

Safi: Fortune Favors the Bold

Noguès had only a small force defending Safi, a single company of the 2nd Battalion, 2nd Regiment of *Tirailleur Marocains* (Moroccan Infantry; RTM), but the riflemen were backed by the 104th Company, Shore Defense, 2nd RTM; the 3rd Porte [truck-carried] 75mm Battery of the 2nd Regiment *Etranger d'Infanterie* (Foreign Legion; REI); the 3rd Battery (155mm) *Grande Puissance Filloux* (GPF); a naval battery with two 75mm guns at the *Front de Mer* and two 130mm guns at La Railleuse; and a three-tank platoon of Renault FT17 light tanks.[40]

Major General Ernest Harmon, commanding the Americn 2nd Armored Division and Sub–Task Force Blackstone, had dreamed up the dramatic opening move for his attack on Safi after Task Force 34 had left Virginia. Believing that the French had laid a boom across the narrow entrance to the deep-water harbor, Harmon proposed to his naval opposite number, Rear Admiral Lyal Davidson, that two destroyers carrying infantry smash through the boom, storm the harbor, and secure the huge electric cranes needed to unload his medium tanks. Davidson approved the idea and diverted two World War I–vintage destroyers, the *Bernadou* and *Cole*, to Bermuda, where their stacks and superstructures were removed to make room for the infantry.[41]

Safi was the one place where the U.S. Navy delivered the army to exactly the right place. After disastrous confusion during exercises in the Chesapeake Bay, Harmon had every man briefed on the voyage over in wardrooms with the silhouettes of the coastline painted on wardroom walls, so landing craft crews knew their objectives by heart.[42]

On the face of things, the fight in Safi harbor was going to be on nearly equal terms. The *Bernadou* and *Cole* each carried but one rifle company of the 47th Infantry Regiment. The rest of the 47th Infantry, however, was to land on beaches just outside the harbor, and a company of light tanks from the 70th Tank Battalion was attached to the regiment.

At 0200 hours, fishing boats returning to Safi discovered the American fleet and notified the harbormaster. The lighthouse beacon was immediately extinguished.[43] Major Deuve, the Safi garrison commanding officer, received the message "Danger" from the navy a short while later, followed by an alert from the Division of Marrakech. Deuve ordered his garrison to arms and rushed to the *Front de Mer*, a building overlooking the harbor and the cliff just outside the harbor mouth. The battery at La Railleuse reported that a ship showing no lights was entering the harbor. Fearing the vessel might be French, Deuve had the signal light flash a query. There was no response.

Deuve recalled, "[F]inding myself next to the 75s of the *Front de Mer*, I saw a war vessel entering the port. . . . I ordered an immediate opening of fire. There was a quick and lively response from several ships (shells and machine guns), but not very accurate—one wounded at the 75 gun."

Soon, all the French guns, as well as machine guns and rifles, were firing into the harbor and its entrance. The battleship *New York* turned its fourteen-inchers on the guns at La Railleuse and managed to damage the fire-control center.

The American assault troops were soon ashore and bypassed most French points of resistance until light tanks appeared and persuaded the French to surrender or escape, as most had no antiarmor defense. The few antitank guns available were soon overrun, though one crew claimed to have immobilized an American tank.[44]

CASABLANCA: LARGEST ATLANTIC NAVAL ENGAGEMENT OF THE WAR

The equivalent of an infantry regiment with artillery and cavalry support defended Casablanca, augmented by most of the French navy in Morocco and combat aircraft at the nearby airfield. These elements included the 2nd Battalion,

Regiment d'Infanterie Coloniale du Maroc (Moroccan Colonial Infantry; RICM); the staff, regimental company, and 3rd Battalion, 6th RTM; the staff, service troop, and 2nd Squadron, 1st *Regiment de Spahis Marocains* (Moroccan Spahis, cavalry; RSM); staff, service battery, 2nd Battalion (105mm and 155mm), and 4th Battalion (75mm motor-drawn) of the *Regiment d'Artillerie Coloniale du Maroc* (Moroccan Colonial Artillery; RACM); and one platoon of Renault FT17 light tanks. The 3rd Battalion, 6th RTM, was barracked at Camp Mediouna, only nine miles southeast of Casablanca.[45]

The fight at Casablanca on 8 November was to be a naval battle and properly one between the French navy and Rear Adm. Henry Kent Hewitt, not Patton. Michelier was reputed to favor the Allies, but his sworn loyalty was to the legal government in Vichy.[46]

French antiaircraft guns and fighters engaged American aircraft circling above Casablanca shortly before 0700, and the *Jean Bart* and the coastal battery at El Hank opened up on cruisers of the Task Force 34 covering force at about the same time. The American vessels replied, and the USS *Massachusetts*, one of the most modern battleships in the fleet, trained her sixteen-inch guns on the *Jean Bart* and fired. Within twenty minutes, *Jean Bart*'s one working turret had been damaged to the point where she fell silent for the remainder of the day, while sailors worked furiously to put her guns back into action. Dogfights broke out in the skies above the city and its airfield, and the Americans quickly established control of the air.

From about 0830 until noon, French destroyers and the light cruiser made several sallies from the port to engage the covering force and try to reach the transports. Though the French damaged a pair of destroyers and at one point hit the *Massachusetts* with 5.5-inch shells, the cruiser and six destroyers were immobilized or sunk. By noon, the *Massachusetts* had expended 60 percent of her 16-inch shells, but the back of the French navy in Morocco was broken.[47]

Patton watched the show from the USS *Augusta*, and when the cruiser fired its first salvo at the French, the gun blast wrecked his landing craft and destroyed all his possessions except for his pistols, which he had sent an aide to get just in time.[48]

Fédala: Patton Goes to War

Once the landing craft headed for shore at Fédala, the U.S. Navy delivered some battalions to the wrong beaches. The first two waves of the 1st Battalion, 7th Infantry Regiment Landing Group, were ashore at Fédala before the French realized what was happening, and, helped by searchlights, the defenders thereafter aimed machine-gun and artillery fire at the sands.[49]

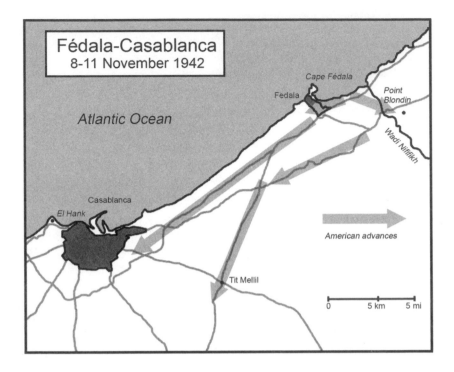

Coastal defense batteries at Point Blondin and Cape Fédala opened fire on the landing beaches as soon as gunners could identify their targets. French machine gunners on Point Blondin could not see the first wave of the 30th Infantry's 1st Battalion landing on Blue Beach. But searchlights lit the following waves, and the Frenchmen took full advantage of the visibility, raking the incoming craft with lead. They had just enough light in the brightening sky at 0600 to see and greet the 2nd Battalion's first wave northeast of Wadi Nififikh with heavy fire. As they sprayed the sand, they could see many craft capsizing and swamping, and men struggling toward shore in life vests. Only the 30th Infantry's 2nd Battalion reached Africa without experiencing much French fire.[50]

A single company of the 6th Regiment of *Tirailleurs Senegalese* defended Fédala against the 1st Battalion. Completely surprised by the overwhelming assault, the company surrendered quickly. Company A, 7th Infantry, at 0630 captured nine members of the German Armistice Commission who were fleeing the Miramar Hotel in cars and, with them, documents describing the dispositions of all French troops in Morocco, except for those Noguès had hidden from the Germans. The Germans had also created dossiers containing personal data on all French officers, including their political attitudes.[51]

At H plus one hour, a message was broadcast in French from the USS *Texas*: "Hello Morocco! Hello Morocco! This is the station of the American forces in the Morocco sector." There followed messages explaining the purposes of the American landings and repeating Roosevelt's words to the French.[52] Nobody ashore was paying the slightest attention.

Two 90mm antiaircraft guns on the outskirts of Fédala prevented Company C, 7th Infantry, from advancing, but the battery agreed to surrender after taking a pounding from the rifle company. Just as an officer and sergeant went forward to receive the surrender, naval gunfire dropped on the batteries, which resumed shooting and killed the two Americans. The crews surrendered by 1100 hours. The 100mm guns on Cape Fédala remained in action until noon, when they fell to a close assault by Company C and several M5 light tanks from the 756th Tank Battalion. Two 75mm guns and machine guns that continued an enfilading fire on the beach stayed in action until silenced by mortars and 75mm pack howitzers by 1500.[53]

Despite heavy naval gunfire aimed at French 138.6mm batteries on Point Blondin, the batteries' shelling harassed the landing beaches until about 0900. Rounds from the USS *Brooklyn* destroyed the fire-control tower, struck but did not explode the magazine, and dismounted one gun.

By midmorning, French aircraft from Casablanca arrived sporadically to strafe and bomb the beaches around Fédala. Nevertheless, by evening, the Americans had taken most of their D-day objectives.[54]

The directive covering chain of command in the Allied force stipulated that Patton did not command his own troops until such time as he could establish his headquarters on shore and signal his readiness to assume command. Until that time, Rear Adm. Henry Kent Hewitt, commanding Western Naval Task Force, had control over all sea, air, and land assets. Once Patton took charge, the offshore naval and air assets were to come under his authority.[55]

Patton expected to be engaged in hands-on battlefield command, like he had in the Great War. Two days before the landings, he wrote, "In forty hours I shall be in battle, with little information, and on the spur of the moment will have to make the most momentous decisions. . . ."[56] He was only half right.

The impatient general finally reached shore at 1320 hours, getting soaked in the surf. There was shooting in the vicinity, but no bullets came his way.[57]

Patton, as he had expected, had little information. News of the capture of Safi had taken seven hours to reach the *Augusta*, and communications were even more primitive ashore. Instead, Patton met with Anderson and a captured

French colonel, and then he inspected the town and port. He was in no position to make any momentous decisions.

That night, Patton slept in the damaged but luxurious Hotel Miramar, where he dined on cheese, fish, and champagne.[58]

Port Lyautey: The French Stand Firm

One of the strongest garrisons in Morocco defended Port Lyautey and Mehdia, the resort town on the Atlantic coast some nine miles to the west. Port Lyautey offered sheltered anchorage on the Sebou River, which, between the port and the ocean, formed a large loop to the north. The airfield was located within the loop, protected by extensive entrenchments and field emplacements. An ancient kasbah built by the Portuguese and home to a coastal battery guarded the river mouth at Mehdia.[59]

Colonel Jean Petit's entire 1st RTM, with three battalions, formed the core of the defense. The regiment had fought in all the major battles of the Great War, participated in the post-war pacification of Morocco, and served well in Belgium and at Dunkirk in 1940. It was reconstituted after the armistice at Port Lyautey, and Petit considered his young officers eager for war, confident of their strength, and loyal to Pétain, the hero of Verdun. The rankers were Arab men of the Atlas Mountains, sober and unpolished. Petit knew that his regiment was understrength due to various absences and was concerned that his 2nd Battalion was scattered, with companies posted to Mehdia and the airport, and another stripped of manpower to crew antiaircraft guns.

The regiment's machine guns and mortars all dated to the Great War or earlier. Supporting Petit's regiment were an antitank group armed with nine modern 25mm guns; a platoon of Renault FT17 light tanks; the 1st Porte Battery, 3rd REI (75mm); the static 1st Battery, 155mm GPF, positioned to fire only on the Sebou River; a battery of 75mm antiaircraft guns; and 1st Company, 31st Engineer Battalion, supported the infantry.[60]

Mobilized from the reserves in 1939, Petit had taken command of the regiment in April 1942. Petit would say of his experience in the coming battle that he had the certitude that the "duty of the soldier," who strictly obeyed the orders of his superiors without question, was the most admirable conduct in this world.

The colonel was awakened at 0130 by an officer from the division headquarters in Casablanca bearing an order signed by Béthouart. This order informed him that Tunisia was under attack by Axis forces, and that a large American force would land by sea and air at dawn. Béthouart instructed Petit to undertake a range of measures, from arresting members of the Axis armistice commissions

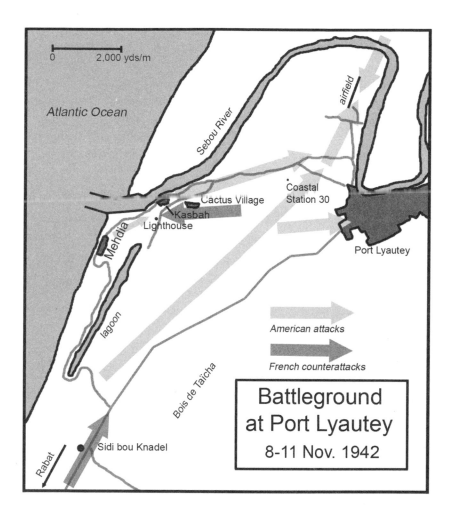

to ensuring that coastal batteries did not fire, combat aircraft remained on the ground, and ground forces remained in their stations until after the landings were complete. Petit immediately alerted civil and military authorities by phone. The reaction was surprise and an outburst of joy. France's American friends were coming, and the Army of Africa would go to war side-by-side with them! Petit made a special point of calling Lieutenant Durin's company, which garrisoned the kasbah, to make certain the coastal battery there was notified, and spoke with Durin's deputy, Lt. Ahmed Ben Hadj, an old Moroccan officer.

When Petit spoke with Captain Cadoret, the local naval commander, however, Cadoret told him that he had received absolutely contrary orders from

Michelier in Casablanca to implement the defense plan, and that Béthouart had launched a coup in Rabat and placed Noguès under siege at his headquarters. Petit was stupefied. Whom to believe? Whom to obey?

After calling various headquarters up his chain of command without anyone picking up the phone, Petit eventually reached Noguès, who told him to disregard Béthouart's orders and that the general was under arrest. "Implement the defense plan. Oppose any landing!" The senior civil and military authority in Morocco had spoken. The assignment was bitter, but Petit would comply. It was 0430 hours.

"Gentlemen," Petit told his assembled officers, "the orders I gave you earlier are annulled. Saddle up." The faces before him were somber, but not a man objected.

Colonel Petit had written orders: "In case of a landing from the sea in the region of Port Lyautey by foreign troops, no matter who they are, counterattack and drive the adversary into the sea." He had trained and exercised his men to fulfill these orders. Even before the first American boats touched sand, Petit had issued orders to prepare Commander Segond's 1st Battalion and a 75mm battery for a counterattack against the beach chosen by the enemy, whichever that might prove to be. Petit then set up his command post in Coastal Station 30, on the edge of Port Lyautey, from where one could see the entire defense area. For the next three days, Petit later recalled, he would engage in a gigantic chess game across ten kilometers of coast, mainly through the means of verbal orders.[61]

The 9th Infantry Division's 60th Infantry Regiment, commanded by Col. Frederick de Rohan, constituted the main element of Sub–Task Force Goalpost. It was augmented by the 2nd Armored Division's 3rd Armored Team; Company C, 70th Tank Battalion; the 60th Field Artillery Battalion; and various other components, including engineers and antiaircraft artillery. Major General Lucian Truscott, the veteran of the Dieppe raid, took command of the sub–task force at Patton's personal request. This battle would test Patton's quality indirectly by testing the quality of the men he handpicked as his subordinates, because Patton would have no influence over the course of events.

The landing plan dictated that the 3rd Battalion Landing Team was to go ashore five miles north of the Sebou River and immediately secure the high ground overlooking the stream. The 2nd Battalion was to silence shore batteries and other possible sources of fire at the kasbah, an old fort straight out of *Beau Geste* that guarded the mouth of the Sebou and the usable beaches at Mehdia. The 1st Battalion was to land south of a lagoon that paralleled the beach, move inland and then north, take the high ground to the rear of the kasbah, and in conjunction with the 2nd Battalion, capture the main objective— the hard-surfaced airfield.

The transports reached the rendezvous area at 0345, forty-five minutes late. Shortly thereafter, five French steamers, lights blazing, passed the lead vessel; one signaled by blinker, "Be warned. Alert on shore for 5 a.m."[62]

The first American troops from the 1st and 2nd Battalions reached the sand at Mehdia beach at 0540 hours. A spotlight illuminated a navy scout craft 700 yards from shore, and a red flare arced into the predawn sky. The coastal defense battery at the kasbah immediately opened fire at American destroyers loitering off shore, which replied in kind. The inexperienced landing craft crews delivered the 1st Battalion too far north and nearly on top of the 2nd Battalion, while the 3rd Battalion wound up five miles up the coast from its landing zone north of the Sebou River. Two French fighters roared along the beach, strafing the first Americans to reach shore, and several men were hit, but Lieutenant Durin's 7th Company at the kasbah could not place direct fire on the sand.[63]

Major John Dilley's 2nd Battalion almost immediately became somewhat scattered as it advanced toward the kasbah, in part because the navy was still dropping shells into the area. Roughly a platoon of French troops occupied trenches outside the kasbah, as well as a lighthouse nearby, all protected by barbed wire. The Frenchmen opened fire with machine guns and rifles when a force more than four times their number—Company E and a platoon of Company G—appeared and attacked under cover of mortar fire. The lighthouse was taken by a gallant rush, and the Frenchmen in the trenches were either shot or fell prisoner when assaulted by elements of Companies E and F. Some doughboys even got into the front gate of the kasbah; two men with Browning automatic rifles (BARs) climbed the wall and opened up on the Frenchmen inside, but the defenders threw them back out of the fort. During the battle, a machine-gun bullet struck Lieutenant Durin in the head, and Lt. Ahmed Ben Hadj was mortally wounded.

Petit was worried because his 1st Battalion was still assembling on the edge of Port Lyautey, and he thought he was a step behind the enemy. He had to hurry the preparations and send the battalion toward the kasbah, which he now deemed the invaders' main objective. Petit hurried on foot to the assembly point, where he found the men unready for battle and vulnerable to surprise. He ordered the 1st Company to take up arms and be ready. Then he took the horse of one of his captains and galloped on among the men until he found Segond. Here, too, the men were sitting ducks. Petit ordered Segond to transport the 1st Company to the kasbah using the trucks from the regimental trains and send the rest forward on foot. Petit also ordered his battery of 75mm guns forward to support the 1st Battalion. Naval gunfire targeted the 1st Company en route and five men were killed, but by 0815, the 1st Company had reached Mehdia and made contact with the 7th Company. Petit sent his 2nd Battalion to the forest east of Port Lyautey to form his reserve and protect the left flank and rear of the 1st Battalion's push toward the kasbah.

An air attack on the airfield at 0830 hours destroyed most of the French combat aircraft in Port Lyautey. From that time on, the Americans owned the skies. Lieutenant Guillaume's two 75mm guns, manned by Foreign Legionnaires, were firing over open sights at American infantry near the kasbah and lighthouse and were strafed by two American aircraft.

Petit rode by car toward the kasbah so that he could observe the 1st Battalion's counterattack. As it happens, he and a jeep in which two envoys from Truscott were traveling encountered one another—and both came under fire from the *tirailleurs*, who could not identify either vehicle. Colonel Demas Craw, U.S. Army, died in the incident, and Truscott's appeal for a cessation of hostilities—neatly inscribed in gothic lettering on a parchment—failed to persuade Petit to end the battle.

About noon (accounts differ somewhat), Petit, with deep dismay, observed the American 2nd Battalion—whom he overestimated to number 800 men—in the "cactus village" east of the kasbah, so called because of the cactus hedgerows among the reed huts. Just then, Commander Segond and the rest of the 1st Battalion arrived, having tramped without disturbance among the eucalyptus trees and along the ditches of the main road.

"Attack in the direction of the crest at the kasbah," Petit ordered. "Engage the enemy, destroy him, and throw him into the sea. Two companies of the 2nd Battalion of Commander Desjours will cover your left toward the lighthouse. Lieutenant Guillaume's 75mm section and the Mery Battery [64th RAA] will help you. Now, hurry, the situation is pressing!"

Officers deployed the men for battle as the first American shots rang out, and French artillery quickly got the range. The counterattack stopped the American advance in its tracks. It was the good fortune of the French that the 2nd Battalion's supporting artillery had been unable to land because of rising surf at Mehdia.

Joined by Petit's three tanks, which put the enemy to flight, the French pushed the 2nd Battalion back to the area of the lighthouse. Even Truscott's staff had to pitch in to hold the line against the French pressure. Two of the tanks fell prey to rifle grenades, and the third withdrew. The bodies of *tirailleurs* littered the open ground covered by the counterattack. Commander Segond—killed by a bomb aimed at the tanks—the adjutant of the 2nd Battalion, a company commander, and several junior officers were among the numerous casualties. Still, at dusk, the Americans were just holding their beachhead and sending every new man to the line while Truscott considered plans to attack again on the morrow.

To Petit, the situation looked precarious. Yet when he met with a group of officers that evening, their morale was sky high. He now had reports that American tanks were ashore, and he expected an overwhelming attack the next day. Two of his battalions were badly shot up, and he committed his only free reserve—the regimental company—to strengthen the 1st Battalion. The telephone system still worked perfectly, and Petit begged for reinforcement. Two battalions of the 7th RTM and a tabor (battalion) of *goumier* would arrive shortly, he was told.[64]

The 2nd Battalion, 60th Infantry, had been on its own the entire day because French machine guns hidden near the main highway east of the lagoon opened up on the bulk of the 1st Battalion after it had worked around the water and moved slowly northward. Petit, during the morning, had deployed his 3rd Battalion and three 25mm antitank guns along the road with orders to prevent any movement up the coast. Spahis scouted the American flank through a cork forest, the Bois de Taïcha, east of the highway, where the tall trees and lack of undergrowth gave the cavalry concealment. When American machine guns turned on the native horsemen, they melted away among the trees. This setup stopped the American troops for hours until mortars finally zeroed in on the machine guns, and the French had to pull back.

Returning to his command post around 1600, Petit found a message Noguès had sent around noon: "Throw the enemy into the sea!"

Meanwhile, American Company A, 1st Battalion, under the command of 2nd Lt. John Allers, oriented itself and worked around the south end of the lagoon, where it took position on a high ridge as the battalion reserve, watching the road north from Rabat.[65]

North of the Sebou, the American 3rd Battalion had come under attack by French aircraft as it neared shore at about 0630 hours, and bombs overturned two landing craft. The first troops ashore managed to get some machine guns into action before four more attackers appeared and sent two planes crashing into the sea. Despite landing five miles from its zone, by 1000, the battalion had taken its first objective, Hill 58, from which one could see the airfield south of the Sebou. Fire-control observers directed the guns of the battleship *Texas* and the USS *Kearney* onto French batteries that could be seen firing to the south. Incorrectly assuming the kasbah to have fallen by then, the battalion did not deploy its artillery to support the 2nd Battalion's attack, as planned.[66]

A Display of Skillful French Generalship

By 0800, Lascroux, in Rabat, was aware that American bombardment and air attacks were hitting airfields at Rabat, Casablanca, and Sale, and that fires were burning at the last. The port at Casablanca was also under attack. The French command judged that resistance at Safi had collapsed in the face of overwhelming enemy superiority. The news from Port Lyautey, where American troops were disembarking across the beach at Mehdia, was good, as French troops were reported holding under conditions anticipated by the defense plan.

Lascroux's first concern was the defense of Rabat, capital seat of the protectorate, and blocking any thrust into the interior toward Marrakech or other major towns. Not only had American landings straddled Rabat, but he had also received a false report that the Americans had advanced to Bou Znika, a third of the way from Fédala to Rabat. Lascroux, at 1005, ordered the Divisions of Meknès and Fès to send Mobile Groups A and B and the General Reserve to Petitjean (today's Sidi Kacem), an oil-producing area sixty-five miles east-northeast of Rabat, from where they could advance against American forces at Port Lyautey or defend against an attack into the hinterland. He ordered a light-armored brigade to concentrate near Boulhaut, though commitments of component elements during the day prevented that concentration from happening. His next step was to order three tabors (battalions) of *goumiers* to concentrate at Wadi Zem, halfway between Fès and Marrakech. He sent the XI Tabor toward Rabat and the XXII Tabor toward Boulhart, where it would be at the disposition of the Division of Casablanca.

Lascroux, at 1045, sent armored cars and motorcycles from Rabat south to check the report of Americans in Bou Znika, while he concentrated the 2nd Squadron, 1st Regiment of *Chasseurs d'Afrique* (literally Hunters of Africa, but essentially light cavalry), which was equipped with truck-transported tanks, in the suburbs south of Rabat to watch the road from Casablanca. He sent cavalry—the 1st Squadron, 1st RSM—to monitor the coastal area between Rabat and Sale. At noon, word arrived that the Americans at Port Lyautey had pushed south toward Rabat, and Lascroux ordered the commander of the subdivision of Rabat to reconnoiter toward Sidi bou Knadel, about halfway from the capital to Mehdia.

By 1300, Lascroux appears to have concluded that the American beachhead at Port Lyautey posed the greatest threat, and he took some risks to deal with it. He ordered a single armored-car troop from the 1st Regiment of *Chasseurs*

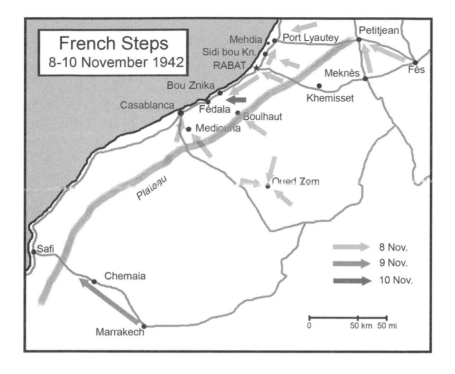

d'Afrique, accompanied by a cavalry troop from the 1st RTM, to protect the road north from Fédala, clearly intending these elements to be little but a delaying force. He ordered a second armored-car troop from the 1st Regiment of *Chasseurs d'Afrique* and the regiment's 2nd Squadron, equipped with truck-carried tanks, north toward Port Lyautey under the command of Colonel d'Oleon. His only reserve in Rabat was a troop of cavalry.[67]

Back in Vichy, Pétain had broadcast a reply to Roosevelt's radio message, and that reply was repeated periodically. His chief message was, "France and her honor are at stake. We are attacked, and we will defend ourselves. That is the order I give."[68]

Lascroux's reconnaissance troops spotted an American roadblock at Sidi bou Knadel, where a platoon of Company A, 60th Infantry, was protecting the right flank of the 1st Battalion as it tried to capture the airport and there the trucks unloaded the 2nd Squadron's tanks for the attack. About 1400, the French struck, the tanks churning dust into the dry air; amidst heavy shooting, American troops dropped like sacks, casualties in the first moments of their first battle. Fire struck an American crew manning a 37mm antitank gun, and French soldiers overran the piece and captured a wounded lieutenant. An American weapons carrier came careening down the road from Mehdia, and a French gunner laid the sights of his 37mm gun on the vehicle and fired. A puff of smoke ejected from the truck, and it burst into flames. It was 1450 hours.

The tanks pushed slowly northward past the burning truck, while others fanned out to the flank. Within twenty minutes, they approached a second American roadblock, defended by a platoon under the command of Lt. Jesse Scott. The tanks stopped several hundred yards away. An antitank grenade exploded on the road ahead of the foremost tank, causing no harm. Now the tanks opened fire with machine guns, spraying a line of foxholes dug along a slight crest. Men died where they lay.

Another few minutes passed, and four trucks arrived, bearing French infantry. The trucks stopped, and a company of riflemen piled out and deployed east of the highway. Now the tanks advanced again, accompanied by the infantry in squad columns. A flame blossomed from one American foxhole; a plume of smoke and a whoosh came next, and a bazooka round—perhaps the first time one was fired in anger—struck a tree next to the lead tank. Tanks, infantry, everyone opened fire, and the French charged forward in platoon rushes. An officer threw his hands in the air and went down, but his men pressed on, some of them falling, too.

The French overran the roadblock, and a half dozen Arab soldiers surrounded Scott. A French officer approached him and took away his Tommy gun. Nearby, tank fire destroyed a 37mm antitank gun, and the attackers took prisoner Second Lieutenant Allers, the Company A commander, who had put the gun into action. Two French tanks had been lost to American gunnery, however.

Two more French tanks pressed on toward the last row of sand dunes overlooking the beach, but the Americans by now had manhandled four 37mm antitank guns to the crest. Cannons blazed, and a tank erupted into flames. The other pulled back, and soon darkness blocked further action.[69]

While battle flared around Port Lyautey, Lascroux realized that his commanders in Casablanca could not control the action north of Fédala, so he placed Gen. Roger Leyer, commander of cavalry, in charge of the zone between Port Lyautey and Wadi Nififikh, and sent his deputy, Colonel Vernejoul, to Port Lyautey to take command of the forces operating in the area. At 1800 hours, Lascroux sent Brevet Colonel Lagarde south toward Fédala with the staff, regimental company, and the 1st Battalion, *Regiment d'Infanterie Coloniale du Maroc*, to join the armored cars and cavalry he had sent earlier. Rabat was secure for the day.

Lascroux, that evening, set forces in motion that would substantially strengthen his hand at Port Lyautey and Rabat, drawing in part on the resources Noguès had gathered in Mobile Groups A and B at Petitjean. The Mobile Group Meknès was to concentrate under Maj. Gen. Maurice Mathenet to be available to General Leyer. This group was to include the staff and 1st Battalion, 7th *Regiment Tirailleurs Marocains*; the 6th Motorcycle Troop of the Guard; Group C, with 25mm antitank guns; two batteries from the 2nd Battalion, 64th *Regiment d'Artillerie d'Afrique*; the staff, regimental company, and 3rd Battalion, 2nd *Regiment Tirailleurs Algeriens* (Algerian Rifle Regiment; RTA); the staff, service troop, and Horse Squadron, 1st *Regiment Etranger de Cavalerie* (Foreign Legion Cavalry; REC); and two Foreign Legion companies from the 3rd Battalion, 3rd REI. During the evening, Lascroux would change his instructions and order Mathenet to go to Port Lyautey to take charge of all forces engaged there—and to report directly to Lascroux.

Lascroux directed a second large and predominately cavalry group to concentrate at Chenes, east of Sale. This group was to include the 3rd Battalion, 7th RTM; the 10th Separate Squadron *Chasseurs d'Afrique*; the 2nd Squadron, 3rd RSM; and the staff, service troop, and 1st Squadron, 3rd RSM. Finally, Lascroux ordered two companies of the 2nd Battalion, 3rd REI, to move to Mediouna, where they would be available to the Division of Casablanca. This move created a force of nearly two battalions that could attack any enemy force from the rear that tried to encircle Casablanca to the east. Lascroux ordered the 2nd Battalion, 6th RTM; the 3rd Battalion (motor-drawn), 64th RAA; and the XXII Tabor to reinforce Casablanca's garrison in Casablanca itself.

As if that were not enough, Lascroux learned at 1915 hours that Noguès had been given responsibility for the delicate situation at Oran, whose garrison commander immediately requested reinforcements. Lascroux dispatched a battalion of infantry and two batteries of artillery from Oudja to help. Casting about for more resources for the battle north of Rabat, Lascroux, at 2330 hours, put on the road for Port Lyautey one half of the 2nd Battalion, 7th RTM, and ordered the 1st Battalion, 8th RTM, to join the force at Chenes. By midnight, he had also reinforced his command south of Rabat with the 10th Separate Squadron, *Chasseurs d'Afrique*, and one *goum* (company) of XI Tabor. The general toiled into the night arranging the deployment of *goums* along key roads into the interior.[70]

It had been a long and exhausting day.

Germany Reacts

Before the day was out, OB West *Generalfeldmarschall* Gerd von Rundstedt had put German units in motion to launch Operation Anton, the occupation of Vichy

France. The Italians had completed preparations to occupy Provence. But Hitler kept the Axis troops on their leash for the time being, waiting to see how the Vichy French fought the Allied invasion.[71]

Despite earlier ruminations about the possibility of Allied landings in North Africa, OKW had made no preparations to deal with such an eventuality. *Generalmajor* Walter Warlimont, then OKW deputy chief of operations, pinned the blame on Hitler because he had issued no preparation orders, and the military, by then, had been taught to take no initiatives on its own without the führer's say-so.[72]

The landings would have a fairly substantial impact on the eastern front, where many of Patton's future enemies would be scrambling to stop the Soviet winter offensive that began on 19 November. Concern over the western theater caused Hitler to hold in France his strategic reserves, including five fully equipped panzer divisions, that otherwise could have rushed to the east.[73]

The French command, early the afternoon of 8 November, received a message directly from the enemy as to his intent. On Patton's orders, Col. William Wilbur drove a French car decked with American and French flags to a French outpost and was conducted to Casablanca, where he was warmly received at the French army headquarters. There, Wilbur gave a letter containing American terms to Col. Jean Petite (not to be confused with Col. Jean Petit). Petite gently pointed out several errors in the French text. He told Wilbur that he would pass the substance of the letter to his superiors, but there was nothing he could do in response. According to Patton, Petite's staff officers quietly filled in Wilbur on Casablanca's defenses and suggested the city could be best taken from the rear. Wilbur then returned to Fédala.[74]

9 NOVEMBER: HOLDING PATTON AT BAY

Noguès, during the night, had received a query from Vichy asking whether he would accept a liaison officer from the Luftwaffe to plan the deployment of German aircraft to help in the defense of Morocco, a notion that he rejected. In the course of the day, the Germans offered ground troops, and again Noguès refused. When a cease-fire took hold around Algiers, Noguès command was expanded to include those elements in Algeria not covered by the cease-fire, and he moved his headquarters to Fès to better handle his eastern obligations. He cabled Vichy that all of his forces were heavily engaged. His men were fighting with courage and counterattacking, but the disparity in armaments was beginning to tell.[75] Reports reaching the führer indicated that the French were fighting hard, but the ultimate intentions of Vichy and Adm. Jean François

Darlan, the commander of all French forces who was in Allied detention in Algiers and under pressure to order a cease-fire, were unclear[76]

Both sides at Port Lyautey attacked on 9 November.

Petit had not slept at all that night. Commander Baudry had arrived just ahead of his 1st Battalion, 7th RTM, and Petit ordered him to relieve his own 1st Battalion at the kasbah and to attack the American left at dawn with two companies. By 0300, the first fresh troops had replaced Petit's exhausted men. But the new battalion was arriving too slowly to be in place in time, and Petit cancelled his order for a large-scale attack. At 0330, however, Captain de Beaumont arrived at the head of his VIII Tabor of *goumiers*, and Petit assigned him the job of launching an attack after daybreak.

The 1st RTM's 1st and 2nd Battalions went into defensive positions near Petit's command post. Petit joined his 3rd Battalion on the edge of the cork forest, where outposts had detected the sounds of tanks during the night. When the 2nd Battalion, 7th RTM, began arriving about 0630, Petit deployed it to buttress the 3rd Battalion along the road to Rabat. A battalion of the 3rd REI, arriving in trucks from Meknès, was strafed and the commander killed by American aircraft; Petit ordered it into reserve near the hospital. The leading elements of two horse squadrons, 1st REC, appeared as well, plus a motorcycle squadron from the 6th Motorcycle Troop of the Guard.[77]

It is unclear the extent to which Lascroux in Rabat and Colonel Petit in Port Lyautey coordinated their efforts, though Petit knew about Lascroux's plans, but the net result was pressure against the American bridgehead from both north and south. Elements of the VIII Tabor attacked the American 2nd Battalion's left flank at 0800 and caused some casualties. But the captain leading the attack was killed, and the *goumiers* fell back to French lines. At 1000, French artillery crashed into the American line near the lighthouse, and the Americans fell back. A second *goumiers* attack, by infiltration of the beach, netted nothing, and the commanding lieutenant fell into American hands; he escaped by pretending to be an emissary and was conducted back to French lines.

Almost simultaneously, the American 2nd Battalion attacked the kasbah four times, but each attack was driven back by the strengthened garrison. The French smashed each push with artillery and mortar fire, and answered each with a local counterattack that reclaimed all lost ground.

Late in the morning, Maj. Gen. Maurice Mathenet arrived and announced that he was taking command of the Group Port Lyautey. Petit became his adjutant. Lascroux had made his own personal choice for command of the key battle, and as events turned out, it may be that in replacing Petit—who had commanded aggressively from the front—he had made a fatal error.[78]

Now two battalions strong and joined by a battery from the 64th RAA after noon, the French defending the highway against the bulk of the 1st Battalion, 60th Infantry, handily defeated every attempt to advance, aided by well aimed mortar and artillery fire. When ten M5 light tanks and two assault guns from Company C, 70th Tank Battalion, appeared about 1600, artillery disrupted American attempts to launch a tank-infantry attack until darkness fell. The Americans had nonetheless inched forward far enough that reinforcing the kasbah would be difficult for the French.

The 1st *Chasseurs d'Afrique*, meanwhile, continued to hammer at the beleaguered Company A from the direction of Rabat, and it might well have carried the day had it enjoyed some artillery support. About 0600, French tank crews tangled with the seven light tanks from the 2nd Armored Division's landing team under Lt. Col. Harry Semmes, which had managed to get ashore and, just after dawn, rolled into French infantry positions along the Rabat road. French gunnery was good—several rounds embedded themselves in the turret armor of M5s—but the guns lacked the punch to kill from the front. The American 37s claimed four French tanks. The first French push occurred midmorning, but two American self-propelled 75mm guns had reached the high ground east of the lagoon about 0800. The 75s dispersed the French point. A dozen 70th Tank Battalion M5s, under Captain Edwards, arrived to reinforce Semmes, and the M5s counterattacked Renaults that had sought concealment in a cactus patch. French gunners knocked out two American tanks, and the rest fell back. French armored cars and motorcycles next sought a path northward, but again the 75s drove them back.[79]

Lascroux, during the afternoon, continued to reinforce the Rabat garrison with artillery and infantry from the general reserve, and he shifted the 10th Separate Squadron *Chasseurs d'Afrique* north of the city to strengthen the mechanized forces south of Port Lyautey.[80]

The 3rd Battalion had tried to reach the airport across the Sebou all day long, but Lt. Col. Peschaud du Rieu's 31st Engineer Battalion held the south bank with determination, and its fire disrupted every attempt to inflate rubber assault rafts. Du Rieu's supporting guns engaged in counterbattery fire against the 60th Field Artillery Battalion's guns. His machine guns dashed an American attempt to seize the one bridge across the river, despite support from a battery of field pieces and the USS *Kearny*. Although the French had held, Colonel Petit had to keep significant strength at Port Lyautey because of the threat from the north, just as the situation at the kasbah was about to become critical.

Night fell, rainy and dark, and the French succumbed to an American act of *élan*. A patrol worked its way across the bridge and, using grenades and bazookas, knocked out the two guns that covered the crossing. Company I got across the river at 2100 hours and dug in, waiting for daylight.[81]

Patton Plays Sergeant, and Casablanca Holds

Patton, by his own account, spent the morning of 9 November on the beach at Fédala, personally motivating men, who were supposed to be unloading supplies and reinforcements, to work harder. At 1300 hours, Patton returned to the USS *Augusta* and sent his deputy, Maj. Gen Geoffrey Keyes, and his staff ashore. He contemplated attacking Casablanca with the 3rd Infantry Division, supported by naval bombardment and air attacks.[82]

Except for a few delaying parties, the French garrison remained in the fixed defenses on the edge of Casablanca as the 3rd Infantry Division's 7th and 15th Infantry Regiments approached, and its guns lobbed some shells at the Americans. Noguès misinterpreted this movement as a withdrawal to get the American troops south of the city. To the rear of the advancing troops, the armored cars of the 1st *Chasseurs D'Afrique* arrived from Rabat and engaged the 30th Infantry Regiment along Wadi Nififikh, which was the stop line in the direction of Rabat for the landing force. Indeed, the Americans had prepared the bridge carrying Highway 1 across the wadi toward Rabat for demolition and could be seen laying mines. At about 1400 hours, the Americans pressing toward Casablanca ground to a halt—as it turned out, because of a lack of supplies.[83]

Protecting Marrakech

Lascroux, as of 0640 on 9 November, was little worried about the situation west of Marrakech. The American perimeter at Safi extended no more than five or six kilometers from town, except south along the coast road.[84]

Major General Henri Martin, commanding the Division of Marrakech, sent the motorized element of his mobile group toward Safi, presumably to give the impression that he was opposing the landings he secretly supported. The column consisted of some fifty trucks bearing a battalion of infantry, a field-artillery battalion, and a troop of truck-borne cavalry. Unfortunately, American naval aviation on its way to bomb the airfield at Marrakech spotted the column and machine-gunned it. The same aircraft strafed the column again on its return flight. The French troops did not proceed far enough to make contact with American ground forces.

Late in the day, however, an American column including thirty tanks and truck-mounted infantry appeared twenty-two kilometers east of Safi and engaged the mobile group's lead elements. The French destroyed two American tanks, but the 11th Separate Squadron *Chasseurs d'Afrique* lost almost all of its vehicles to American air attacks. The main body of the mobile group dug in on high ground some eight kilometers farther east, near Chemaia.[85]

10 NOVEMBER: PATTON'S MEN MAKE GAINS

Patton's personal selection of Truscott to command the operation now bore fruit, though French commanders were in no position to understand the act and its consequences. Truscott, who for the first of many times during the war showed tenacity in the attack, ordered Maj. Percy McCarley, commanding the 1st Battalion, to continue his advance during the night up the road from Rabat. In the dark, Companies C and D stumbled through the French lines, where the defenders could not see a thing through the heavy rain and probably were taking shelter, and into the outskirts of Port Lyautey. At daylight, the troops protecting Petit's headquarters were surprised to find Americans on their doorstep, and a short, sharp fight broke out. At this point, Petit surrendered with his staff and ordered his troops to cease resistance.

Meanwhile, Company B, after getting lost, returned to the line of departure, linked up with the tanks and assault guns from Company C, 70th Tank Battalion, and attacked toward the airport. The 1st Battalion, 1st RTM, concealed in an orange grove engaged the Americans, and a fast, hot fight ensued. When the French gave up, the Americans counted four antitank guns and twenty-eight machine guns.

After daybreak, a French colonel, accompanied by a troop of Foreign Legion cavalry, informed McCarley, who had become separated from his battalion in the dark, that an armistice was in effect. The colonel's news was, however, premature. This became apparent when firing erupted from the direction of the kasbah. Foreign Legion infantry took McCarley prisoner as he made his way toward the sound of the guns, though he escaped late that day while the legionnaires were eating dinner.[86]

The defenders of the kasbah, meanwhile, spotted two M7 Priest self-propelled 105mm guns, followed by infantry, attacking in the early morning light. The American 2nd Battalion was back. French troops outside the fort tried to disable the guns by throwing grenades at the crew compartments, but failed and had to surrender.

Those inside the kasbah drove back several assaults against the main gate. The American guns then blasted holes through several parts of the wall; then, ominously, the Americans pulled back. Soon the reason was clear. The 105s fired smoke shells to mark targets, and dive-bombers screamed down from the sky and dropped their loads into the kasbah. Before the smoke had cleared, American soldiers had charged through the gaps in the walls, led personally by Col. Frederick de Rohan.[87] Fierce hand-to-hand fighting raged through the fort, and the Americans had organized bazooka teams, made up of sailors, for use in the battle.[88] Finally, the kasbah fell.

French artillery had almost completely disorganized the American 3rd Battalion overnight, but another dashing operation led to success on the northern front, too. The destroyer USS *Dallas* raced through French gunfire up the Sebou River and deposited a raider detachment near the airfield, which the men secured by 0900 hours. By 1030, the first P40 fighters, catapult-launched from escort carriers off shore, roared over the runway, while foot troops repaired bomb damage so they could land.[89]

About 1000, the French knew they were licked, and Maj. Gen. Maurice Mathenet ordered a general withdrawal from Port Lyautey. When Lascroux had ordered Mathenet to take charge in Port Lyautey, he had authorized such a withdrawal to defend the road inland toward Meknès if the town could not be held.[90]

Lascroux's orders on 10 November indicated that he now judged the defense of Casablanca to be his chief priority, perhaps because no effort to take Rabat had become evident. Rabat and the road toward Meknès were his second concerns. At 1000 hours Lascroux decided to move his advanced command post from Rabat to Khemisset, where it was in operation by 1300, albeit with poor radio communications with subordinate elements. Noguès had already moved to Fès. With the fall of Port Lyautey, Lascroux confirmed his earlier orders to Mathenet: carry on the fight to protect strategic cities inland, including Petitjean, Meknès, and Fès.[91]

The French engaged the American 3rd Infantry Division continuously when the 7th and 15th Infantry Regiments resumed the advance toward Casablanca early on 10 November. Machine gunners and riflemen at dawn spotted the 2nd Battalion, 7th Infantry, along Highway 1 at daylight and, joined by artillery, swept the American ranks from front and flank. The Americans became disorganized when two company commanders became casualties. Nevertheless, the crew of one field piece was wiped out, and the gun taken by the Americans, while hostile fire drove two more crews from their guns. Two French destroyers operating just outside Casablanca harbor supported the ground troops with gunfire aimed at the 2nd Battalion and at the 3nd Battalion, which was advancing down the coast on the 7th Infantry's right wing.[92]

The French destroyers drew the cruiser USS *Augusta* and four destroyers in to chase them off, at which point the *Jean Bart*'s main battery came back to life, straddling *Augusta* and drenching Patton and Hewitt, on the bridge, with yellow-dyed water. The *Augusta* withdrew in haste, but the near triumph ended *Jean Bart*'s part in the battle. Dive-bombers from the carrier USS *Ranger* struck her at 1300 hours and caused enough damage that she settled in the shallow water.[93]

Inland from the action along the coast, French troops, during the night, had established a defensive position at Tit Mellil, positioned on high ground overlooking the coastal plain some eight miles southeast of Casablanca, and were ready when the American 15th Infantry, advancing beside the 7th Infantry, arrived before dawn. The French emplaced machine guns in concrete buildings to create ad hoc machine-gun nests, while a cavalry force was held in reserve. The hasty fortifications proved good enough to stop the American advance until the enemy manhandled forward several 37mm guns and opened fire on the structures. By noon, the Americans had enveloped Tit Mellil, and the cavalry was forced to withdraw.[94]

Small groups of mechanized cavalry using old Renault light tanks, meanwhile, launched repeated attacks against the 30th Infantry's outposts north of Wadi Nififikh. An armored column moving to join the engagement came under attack by American naval aviation at 1000 hours northeast of Boulhaut, and several vehicles were disabled.[95]

By dark, the defenders had mined all main bridges into the city and faced the Americans at the outskirts of Casablanca. They had blocked an American effort to advance along the railroad line into the industrial outskirts of the city. The garrison reported to Lascroux that it had so far suffered 1,800 casualties, though most of those were among the fleet's crews. Morale was reported to be excellent and the native population calm.[96]

Patton was so disconnected from the battle that he was unaware that the momentum had shifted in his favor. Patton wrote in his diary:

> Today has been bad. Could get no news from either Truscott or Harmon except that Truscott wanted help. I had none to give. Anderson closed in on Casa[blanca] and one battalion . . . broke badly under shell fire. Keyes, who was on the spot as usual, stopped them. I decided to take Casa[blanca]

anyway with only the 3d Division and an armored battalion. It took some doing, as we were outnumbered but I felt we should hold the initiative. . . .

At 2200 Admiral [John L.] Hall came in to arrange naval support [for the attack on Casablanca]. He brought fine news. The airport at Lyautey was taken and 42 P-40's were on it. Harmon had defeated the enemy column, destroying 19 trucks and 6 tanks. He is marching on Casa[blanca]. All this shows we should push in. "God favors the bold, victory is to the audacious."[97]

Eisenhower chided Patton, "Algiers has been ours for two days Oran defenses crumbling rapidly. . . . The only tough nut is left in your hands. Crack it open and ask for what you want."[98]

Victory or Draw?

Receiving word at 1000 hours of the defeat in Port Lyautey, Noguès sent a messenger to Vichy with a letter to Pétain. Noguès informed the marshal that it was useless to fight on, but he pledged he would accept orders to the end. About the time the plane left for Vichy, word arrived that Admiral Darlan had ordered French troops in Oran to stop firing. At 1600, Noguès received by phone word of an order from Darlan that hostilities were to end across North Africa. Unsure that the order was genuine, Noguès instructed Lascroux and Michelier not to counterattack, but to defend their current positions.[99]

Lascroux, at 1810 hours, instructed his ground forces to hold off on further defensive actions until further notice. This instruction was to be passed to naval forces as well. At 1930 hours, Lascroux transmitted a general order to immediately suspend hostilities and to send emissaries to inform American forces of the new French policy. Shortly thereafter, a formal order arrived from Admiral Darlan in Algiers, stating, "Our understandings have been fulfilled and the bloody fight become useless." Darlan declared he had taken command in North Africa and ordered French forces to stop fighting in Morocco and Algeria.[100]

At Port Lyautey, Mathenet's emissaries arrived at the airport at 2330 under a flag of truce and reached agreement that their commanding general would meet Truscott in front of the kasbah the next morning. There, before the battered walls, the generals agreed to a cease-fire.[101]

Shortly after midnight on 11 November, a French officer approached an outpost of the 30th Infantry Regiment under a flag of truce. He was carrying orders from Noguès for all French forces to cease firing.

Patton had organized a full-scale assault on Casablanca by the 7th and 15th Infantry Regiments, supported by tanks, naval gunnery, and naval dive-bombers. Patton ordered a halt to offensive action, and his command reached the navy's cruisers only fifteen minutes before they were to open fire.[102]

Patton ordered his assistant G-2, Col. John Ratay, to contact the French commanders in Casablanca to confirm cessation of hostilities. Ratay arrived at 0615 hours, having been fired on by American troops along the way and forced to detour around roadblocks and mined bridges. Brigadier General Raymond Desré, acting commanding general of the Division of Casablanca, received him immediately at his headquarters, in the company of Admiral Pierre Jean Ronarc'h, Michelier's chief of staff. Ratay asked Desré whether he wished hostilities to cease, to which the general replied that he had already given orders to troops that white flags should be displayed and American forces allowed to move unhindered. Ronarc'h added in English, "That goes for the navy, too."[103]

Germany had already decided to act, having discerned the end of effective resistance at Oran and Algiers on 10 November. At 0700 hours, Operation Anton began, and units of German First Army and Army Group Felber, commanded by future Patton enemy Hans-Gustav Felber, crossed the demarcation line into unoccupied France, encountering no resistance. SS *Obergruppenführer* Paul Hausser commanded the SS Corps, which included elements of the 10th Panzer Division destined for Tunisia, during the occupation of Toulon on 27 November. Two Italian divisions landed on Corsica, and the Italian Fourth Army marched into the French Riviera. The French did not resist, and Pétain initially remained in office in Vichy.[104]

Doubtless aware that the Axis powers were occupying the remaining parts of their homeland, Noguès, Lascroux, and Michelier met with Patton in Fédala at 1500 on 11 November. Patton told Noguès of his admiration for the courage, skill, and loyalty that French troops had displayed during the three days of fighting and expressed his hope that no more blood would be shed. Noguès replied that French forces had fulfilled their obligations and were now free of them.

That evening, Noguès's emissary returned from Vichy with word from Pétain. He authorized Noguès to do whatever was necessary to save France and the empire. The emissary related Pétain's words: "Morocco has saved the honor of France."[105]

Patton wrote in his diary, "I said I would take Casa[blanca] by D plus 3, and I did. A nice birthday present."[106]

*

The French had negotiated a cease-fire, not a surrender, and there is no indication that they viewed Patton as their conqueror. French troops retained their arms and honor. Patton had accomplished nothing that threatened the basic French strategy to defend Rabat and the hinterland. Noguès, Lascroux, Michelier, and their men, who had stopped shooting in response to orders from Algeria and whose defenses in Casablanca remained unbroken, might reasonably have differed in particular with Patton regarding his "capture" of Casablanca.

Patton's men had not even begun to crack Casablanca's defenses, and American troops' fierce battles to take defended cities in the Mediterranean, European, and Pacific theaters raise overwhelming doubts that Patton's planned bombardment and ground assault would have met with rapid success. By 11 November, Lascroux had four battalions of infantry, three battalions of artillery, a cavalry squadron, and numerous naval personnel to defend the streets. The bitter combat around Port Lyautey gave every indication that the French would have fought with commitment. Moreover, Lascroux had positioned nearly two more battalions of infantry and a tabor of *goumiers* outside Casablanca at Camp Mediouna, from where they could have harassed the American flank and rear.

Still, peace had come. On 14 November, Noguès agreed with Patton's representatives that he would cooperate fully with Patton to ensure there was no interference to the American use of Morocco as a base and line of communication to the east, that French forces in Morocco would oppose any Spanish invasion, that French forces would contribute to the antiaircraft and sea defense of Casablanca, and that Noguès would maintain order in Morocco. By the end of November, Noguès was addressing his letters to Patton, "My Dear General and Friend."[107]

Patton had exercised virtually no control over his battle, and probably for that reason his French opponents left no assessments of his quality as a commander. They spent far more time with Patton as a new ally than as an enemy.

Michelier, who became a friend of George Patton, had this to say of him:

> History willingly cultivates legends and fables. It will make of Patton an absurd idol of a warrior, a kind of giant called Blood and Guts, a mercenary of the type of Wallenstein, violent, strutting, blaspheming, brandishing his pistols, impetuous in hand-to-hand fighting, without fear of God or man, for all of which Eisenhower in his official reports and his *Crusade in Europe* will be partially responsible. I know how untrue is this popular picture. Patton was a very noble character whose alert mind instantly grasped the finest of distinctions. He was cultivated and refined, a model and

agreeable companion who spoke French with a pleasant accent. A great military leader, he was as generous as Hewitt and had in common with him enormous tact.[108]

Although the subject of this work is the enemy's view of Patton, the general's biographers have offered remarkably divergent views of Patton's performance in Morocco. Martin Blumenson opined, "The invasion of Morocco confirmed Patton's military brilliance. His zeal and unerring intuition had assured victory in the landings. His quick organization of a major attack on Casablanca was masterful." Perhaps more accurately, Blumenson noted that Patton's selection of key subordinates—Truscott and Harmon, in this case—was a key element of his generalship.[109]

Carlo D'Este more reasonably concluded, "The seventy-four-hour battle for Casablanca was hardly Patton's finest hour."[110] Likewise, Ladislas Farago observed, "The battle for Morocco lasted exactly 74 hours, but they were not George Patton's finest hours."[111]

SIX

Tunisia: Patton Tangles
With Hitler's Legions

P ATTON'S FIRST TEST in this war against a bitter and determined enemy, matching his own forces in equipment and still exceeding them in battle-honed skill and experience, raged with chaos, noise, and flames across central Tunisia. Patton understood that his new enemy would be tougher than his last, and he was not alone. Patton told observers from Washington that had the landings in Morocco been opposed by Germans, "[W]e never would have gotten ashore."[1] Major General Ernest Harmon wrote to a friend in December, "Really, I wonder how we will do against real opposition. I am greatly worried."[2]

The fact that there were Germans in Tunisia to fight Patton was almost an accident. The German high command had considered North Africa to be a secondary theater and the primary responsibility of Italy until it saw the possibilities of a drive by Rommel to link up with German forces pushing into the Caucasus. This realization caused Germany to pay greater attention, but it was the British success at El Alamein and the landings in French North Africa that convinced the high command to elevate North Africa to a main theater. A second front threatened to endanger the overall direction of the war by the Axis.

OKW's first reaction after the North Africa landings had been to hand over conduct of the fight against Eighth Army entirely to Italy's *commando supremo* and to take charge of the battle to the west, using mainly German troops. It initially hoped that France's colonial armies would rally to the Axis cause, an expectation dashed within the first days of Operation Torch.[3]

As the fighting wound down in French North Africa, the high command subordinated anticipated operations in Tunisia, and indeed the entire Mediterranean theater east and south of France, to *Oberbefehlshaber Süd* (Commander-in-Chief South, or *OB Süd*) *Generalfeldmarschall* Albert Kesselring in Rome. "Smiling Albert" Kesselring, an artilleryman who had switched to the Luftwaffe in 1936, was an odd choice. But he would prove to be one of the toughest and defensively brilliant German ground commanders the Western Allies would face. Commanders realized they were in a race with the Allies and dispatched the 10th Panzer, Hermann Göring, and 334th Infantry Divisions to build a wall of resistance and keep the Allies out of Tunisia.[4]

German combat aircraft and a handful of troops began landing at an airfield near Tunis on 9 November, the first of 15,500 reinforcements—including 130 tanks—that arrived by the end of the month. Nine thousand Italian troops also moved in, most having shifted west from Tripoli. British forces, meanwhile, advanced from Algiers by land and short seaborne and airborne hops. Thanks in part to the Axis incursion, the Allies persuaded the French in North Africa to join their cause formally as combatants on 13 November. On 17 November, a battalion of the German 5th Airborne Regiment encountered French holding forces and the British spearhead at Medjez el Bab. The bold German commander bluffed the Allied forces into pulling back.[5]

Generalleutnant Hans-Jürgen von Arnim arrived to take command of Fifth Panzer Army in Tunisia on 8 December. An officer of the old school, Arnim was a man of courtly manners.[6] Only three weeks earlier, he had been in command of a corps on the Volga River, engaged in furious defensive battles against the Soviets. Summoned to the führer's headquarters, he had flown by *Storch* and courier airplane to East Prussia. On 3 December, he walked past bunkers to a barrack building, where he found Hitler and field marshals Keitel and Jodl waiting in a situation room covered with maps from all fronts.

Hitler stood leaning over a map table. "Herr General, you will go to Africa immediately. As you know, the Allies have landed there," he said, pointing to the Northwest African coast. "Our first deployment of troops is too weak. I have therefore decided to create a new panzer army there from three panzer and three motorized divisions, of which you will take command. You will be under Italian command but will work directly with field marshals Kesselring and Jodl." *Generalleutnant* Heinz Ziegler, with whom Arnim had served when they were both captains, was assigned to be his deputy, and Arnim received immediate promotion to *Generaloberst*.

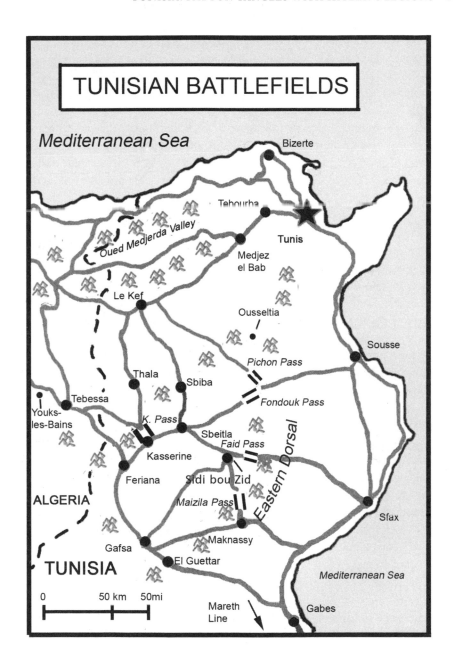

TUNISIAN BATTLEFIELDS

Mediterranean Sea

Bizerte

Tebourba

Oued Medjerda Valley

Tunis

Medjez el Bab

Le Kef

Ousseltia

Sousse

Pichon Pass

Thala

Sbiba

Fondouk Pass

Tebessa

Youks-les-Bains

K. Pass

Sbeitla

Faid Pass

Eastern Dorsal

Kasserine

Feriana

Sidi bou Zid

ALGERIA

Maizila Pass

Sfax

Maknassy

Gafsa

El Guettar

TUNISIA

Mediterranean Sea

0   50 km   50mi

Mareth Line

Gabes

The picture when he arrived in Tunisia was grim. To the east, Montgomery was driving Rommel back some 2,500 kilometers to the southern border of Tunisia, where his forces would rely on a single road and railway to bring supplies across 700 kilometers of empty land. To the west, weak elements of the 10th Panzer Division and airborne units had barely stopped an Allied attempt in late November and early December to seize the Tunisian ports. American reconnaissance troops had reached an extremely dangerous point near Faid Pass, the last barrier before Rommel's supply line. The French had gone over to the Allies, which added three to four divisions, albeit poorly equipped, to the enemy's ranks.[7]

Arnim's first task was to build a stable defensive line. One key element was going to be Division von Broich. On 11 November, in Italy, *Oberst* Lederer had been ordered by Kesselring's headquarters to form a *Kampfgruppe* to rush to Tunisia, with the mission of establishing and holding an Axis bridgehead. The priority was such that the very next day, elements of an infantry battalion and a panzer company were on the ground in Tunis. The day after that, the ad hoc formation was being called Division Lederer, and its mission had evolved into the specific task of defending the Tunisian border against the Anglo-Americans. By the fourteenth, the command had established control over all key points in Tunis and had taken command of a company of the 190th Panzer Battalion and a battery of the 190th Artillery Regiment. By the time *Oberst* Fritz von Broich arrived to take command on the eighteenth, his so-called division had established an outpost perimeter west of Bizerte and encountered the enemy at Djebel Abiod. His command mushroomed with the addition of a German infantry regiment, a mobile Italian *Bersaglieri* regiment, and a regiment of Italian marines for coastal defense. From 24 to 26 November, at Medjez el Bab, Broich, with the help of an airborne pioneer battalion, deftly used his single panzer company to defeat the first British attempt to reach Tunis. From the twenty-eighth, Broich had command over the entire 190th Panzer Battalion (three companies of Mark III and one of Mark IV panzers, plus a few Mark IIs), and from 3 December, he added some Tiger tanks. His command began to vaguely resemble a panzergrenadier division.

Arnim could rely on Division von Broich to defend his north wing. The experience commanding this defensive front was crucial for Broich; he got a quick schooling in waging defensive warfare against the Western enemy to add to the lessons he'd learned in mobile warfare on the eastern front. Broich quickly learned that he could not use Italian infantry in the attack unless there were Germans to stiffen their spine, but he also learned how to handle Italian officers. In February 1943, when Broich took command of the 10th Panzer

Division, the formation became the Division von Manteuffel, commanded by *Oberst* Hasso-Eccard von Manteuffel, whom Arnim said proved to be one of the best combat leaders and division commanders in North Africa. Manteuffel, who had been sent to Africa from France just after the Torch landings, claimed in his memoirs that he had organized the division, but this was patently untrue.

Arnim deployed the 10th Panzer Division, which began arriving in December, and an infantry regiment in the center of his front, facing west. He arrayed the Italian Superga Division and Brig. Gen. Giovanni Imperiali's 50th Special Brigade, stiffened by four German battalions, in the south [8] By 10 December, a combination of German resistance and horrifically wet weather had combined to stop the Allied advance toward Tunis.

On 14 February 1943, the Axis launched a crushing counterattack against American II Corps that came to be known as the Battle of Kasserine. In five days, mainly German forces sent American troops reeling back to the west side of Kasserine Pass and destroyed almost half of the 1st Armored Division's tanks. As American resistance stiffened, the threat posed to the German rear by Montgomery's Eighth Army forced an end to the Axis rampage.[9]

Still, the Axis forces had manhandled the inexperienced Americans. Many British officers concluded that the doughboy was just no good, and American morale nosedived. The need to restore American fighting spirit and prestige would soon open the door for Patton.

The need to restore Rommel's health, meanwhile, would close the door on Rommel and Patton ever meeting in battle, although that contest was once of Patton's fondest dreams. OKW, in the midst of the Kasserine fighting, was planning to reorganize Axis forces in North Africa. Hitler, on 18 February, personally ordered that Rommel was not to give up command of the German-Italian Panzer Army until the ongoing operations were finished. If he had to give it up, nonetheless, for health reasons, the führer instructed that the matter be kept secret and that Rommel's name continue to be used in order to mislead the enemy.[10] The Germans could use this tactic effectively because the Allies truly were obsessed with Rommel as an enemy commander, and the ruse, in fact, continued effectively until weeks after Rommel had returned to Germany.

The 10th Panzer Division, which would meet Patton in battle, played a prominent role in the Kasserine offensive, conducting the linchpin attack out of Faid Pass and through Sidi bou Zid to Sbeitla. And that was no surprise, for the division was one of the Wehrmacht's very best. The division had fought in Russia during the bitter winter of 1941, after which it had moved to Amiens, France, to rest and refit. The division then was instructed to draw "Tropical Equipment-East," which led to speculation that it was bound for the Caucasus. Part of *OB West*'s reserve, the division had participated in Operation Anton, driving south through the Rhône valley to take Marseilles. Its next orders were to head for Rome, and officers knew that could mean only one thing—service in North Africa. The division had moved to Tunisia by sea and air during November and December 1942.[11]

On 23 February, per the new organization, Rommel took command of the combined Axis forces in North Africa under Army Group Africa, consisting of the Fifth Panzer Army in western Tunisia and the Italian First Army, formerly Rommel's German-Italian Panzer Army, opposite British Eighth Army in the south. (German records continued to refer to the First Army's German element as the *Deutsches Akrika Korps*, or D.A.K.) Arnim remained in command of Fifth Panzer Army and the western front, where he had approximately thirty-five battalions and 175 guns to defend some 300 miles of front against an Allied force of around ninety-five battalions and 300 guns. Moreover, his 10th Panzer Division was not under his control, but seconded to Rommel. The total Axis front was some 400 miles long—about the same length as the western front in France in the First World War.[12]

Oberst Manteuffel displayed some of his flair when his division attacked the British at Djebel Abiod on 26 February. Personally leading from the front, Manteuffel ousted the British from the heights with his main body. On his right wing on the coast, Manteuffel had loaded infantry onto navy speedboats, which carried them around the British flank to capture Cap Serrat.[13] Patton would later use this tactic in Sicily.

On 1 March, Rommel informed Kesselring that because of the length of his front, the weak manning of the line, the lack of reserves, and the strength of the enemy, the next enemy offensive would break the front. The enemy could then defeat each Axis army in detail. Supplies reaching North Africa were entirely insufficient and less than expenditures. Rommel argued that it was necessary to reduce the front to 100 miles and dig into the mountainous terrain. This line, he said, he could hold for a long time.

Kesselring passed Rommel's message to OKW two days later, but recommended against the idea of shortening the line except in dire emergency. The Axis would have to abandon too many airfields, and the Luftwaffe would be swept from the sky. A planned strike against Eighth Army might soon produce results, and if not, Army Group Africa should establish a defense in depth. Reinforcements should be provided, because the only hope of beating the enemy was mobile warfare over open terrain.[14]

Rommel was suffering from heart problems and wanted to bring his pleas for more mobile formations and better logistics directly to Hitler, and he resolved to return to Germany.[15] Arnim took command of Army Group Africa on 5 March 1943, and Rommel departed for Germany on the ninth.

The boundary between the two armies was approximately at Gafsa. At that time, Fifth Panzer Army consisted of Division von Manteuffel, which was roughly 40 percent the strength of a motorized infantry division; the 334th Infantry Division, which was partially motorized and whose 3rd Infantry Regiment was a mountain regiment; much of the Hermann Göring Division, which amounted to roughly two-thirds of a motorized infantry division, but which lacked its organic artillery; the 10th Panzer Division, less sixty Mark IIIs and Mark IVs concentrated near Tunis, but available to Fifth Panzer Army; the 501st Heavy Tank Battalion, with about twenty Tiger tanks, plus fifteen Mark III and thirty Mark IV panzers; several separate infantry battalions without heavy weapons or artillery; and an Italian staff element. A group each of Stukas and fighters supported the army. Ammunition and fuel stocks were low, but not alarmingly so.

General der Panzertruppe Gustav von Vaerst knew when he took command of the Fifth Panzer Army in March that his ability to hold Tunisia depended on keeping an adequate flow of supplies across the Mediterranean Sea, and despite the problems with support experienced earlier by Rommel, the short distance from Tunisia to Italy left Vaerst mildly optimistic that maintaining the supply flow would be possible. Vaerst was now a seasoned panzer general. After being replaced by Hermann Balck in the 2nd Panzer Division in May 1941, Vaerst had commanded the panzer school at Krampnitz, where he was promoted to *Generalmajor*. In December 1941, he had arrived at the *Afrika Korps*, where he had taken command of the 15th Panzer Division. Twice wounded, Vaerst had risen to *General der Panzertruppe* by the time he took command of Fifth Panzer Army.

Vaerst estimated that the Allies outnumbered his forces already and would receive reinforcements faster than would he. The morale of his own troops was uniformly good, except among the Italians. He regarded the British as worthy opponents unlikely to undertake any rash ventures. As for the Americans, Vaerst judged that they were at full strength and were confident in their might, but he believed they were now aware of their lack of experience. The French, he doubted, had much zeal for the fight and were equipped with outmoded weapons.

Army Group Africa and Fifth Panzer Army concurred that the Allies were unlikely to attack along the coast or in the center until they had brought up additional forces. The main weight of the enemy's effort, therefore, was likely to be in the south, aimed at working through the eastern Dorsal Mountains to take First Army from the rear.

With his forces thinly spread along a 300-kilometer front, Vaerst calculated that he needed to accomplish several objectives to hold Tunisia. He had to destroy enemy forces where possible, control terrain that could be easily held by weak forces, create a reserve, and prepare fallback positions. In order to accomplish the first task, he planned to weaken portions of his front, concentrate his forces at a single point, and launch sudden, brief blows against the enemy.[16]

PATTON TAKES CHARGE

The very same day that Arnim took command of Army Group Africa, 5 March 1943, Patton flew from Rabat to Algiers in response to a summons from Eisenhower. Ike arrived on his converted B-17 bomber from Tebessa, where he had visited II Corps to weigh Maj. Gen. Lloyd Fredendall's leadership after the Kasserine disaster. Patton had loaned to Eisenhower Maj. Gen. Ernest Harmon from the 2nd Armored Division in late February to help straighten out the 1st Armored Division, and Harmon had told Ike, after a week at the front, that if he did not replace Fredendall with Patton, II Corps might disintegrate. Moreover, said Harmon, what II Corps faced was modern armored battle. Major General Omar Bradley, whom Ike had sent to II Corps to be his eyes and ears, reported that, to a man, the division commanders had lost faith in Fredendall.

Ike told his chief of staff, Maj. Gen. Walter Bedell "Beatle" Smith, to call Patton to the front, which he did at 2200 hours on 4 May. While the war had raged in Tunisia, Patton had sat in Morocco, attending soirées and viewing parades. Meeting Patton at the Maison Blanche airfield, Eisenhower explained that he would take over II Corps, which Gen. Sir Harold Alexander—commander of the 18th Army Group—planned to use to help British Eighth Army break through the Mareth Line by increasing pressure against Italian First Army's rear. Patton was to be on his best behavior with the British, Ike warned knowingly, and to restrain himself to the secondary role he and his corps had been assigned. Major General George Patton headed for Tunisia and, he hoped, a real fight against Rommel, the Desert Fox, and his legions. Only in the first part would fate disappoint him.[17]

Patton stopped in Constantine on his way and met with his new commander at 18th Army Group headquarters. Patton, who now had less than two weeks of accumulated battle experience, found "Alex's" experience—four years of service in the Great War, two years fighting the Bolsheviks in Russia, one year on the frontier in India, and three in World War II—impressive. Patton learned that in light of the crippling and confusing mixing of British, American, and French forces that had occurred before Kasserine, II Corps would be separated from British First Army and be subordinated directly to 18th Army Group. The American divisions would be consolidated under Patton's command.

Then he was off. Patton arrived at II Corps headquarters at 1000 on 6 May, handed Fredendall a hand-written relief order from Eisenhower (Fredendall was returned to the States with a promotion), and immediately imposed one of his most beloved military virtues—discipline, lacquered with spit and polish—on the admittedly scruffy and downcast corps. His requirements that all personnel wear helmets and all men wear neckties or face a fine or court martial are infamous and need not be elucidated here.[18]

II Corps certainly knew Patton had arrived. There is no evidence that the Germans did, however.

After the Kasserine offensive, the 10th and 21st Panzer Divisions had moved elsewhere, and the German Fifth Panzer Army held the front opposite II Corps, mainly at the passes through the Eastern Dorsal Mountains and mainly with static forces incapable of offensive operations. Their mobile reconnaissance forces were active probing the Americans, however.[19]

The German high command knew Eisenhower's forces were building up supplies and expected them to resume offensive operations soon. There was no mystery about the ultimate objective: to take Bizerte and Tunis. Nevertheless, Arnim thought he could repel Anglo-American attacks at the cost of surrendering some territory.[20] The battle at Rzhev, where Arnim had bested Zhukov, had presented a similar strategic challenge to the Germans, and they had succeeded in holding the salient against a massive Soviet offensive. Arnim might also have recalled, however, that Model had eventually had to abandon the salient.

The Axis line ran in the gaps along the Eastern Dorsal Mountains between stretches of impassable ground from Djebel Tebaga, near Maknassy, to the sea. The terrain, in effect, permitted the Germans to wage a defense by separated strong points, as on XXXIX Panzer Corps's front at Rzhev, rather than have to man a long, continuous line.

OB Süd Generalfeldmarschall Kesselring inspected the area on 10 and 11 March and correctly divined Allied plans. On the 12th, he reported to OKW that an attack near Gafsa, where the left wing of Fifth Panzer Army met the right wing of Italian First Army, seemed quite possible. He also expected an attack on the Mareth Line within days. As luck would have it, on 10 March, the 10th and 21st Panzer Divisions had pulled back from the relatively quiet Mareth Line to reserve positions, the former north of Khairoun and the later in the Schott, north of Gabès.[21]

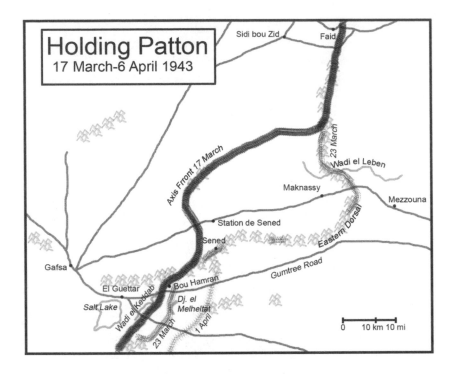

Eighteenth Army Group, on 15 March, warned II Corps that the 21st Panzer Division's reconnaissance unit, 580 Reconnaissance, was in Gafsa, which might indicate the division was in the vicinity and ready to strike along the Maknassy-Gafsa road. On the other hand, the German presence might be intended to buck up the Italian Centauro Division, which held the sector before II Corps and whose attempts to reconnoiter American positions from Gafsa had not prospered.[22] The Italian armored division had occupied El Guettar with its static elements and Gafsa with its mobile elements since the end of the Kasserine offensive.[23]

Then-*Oberst* Siegfried Westphal, who had been Rommel's operations officer in 1942 and seen Italian troops frequently in battle, later wrote:

> It would be superficial simply to dismiss the Italian soldier as a failure, because of his poor showing in the Second World War. The real causes lay much deeper, and some of them should be brought to light. Neither the armed forces nor the people had any inspiring war aim before their eyes. At home the soldier found no moral support. Nor was he equipped or prepared for war with a European opponent armed with all the weapons that modern

technique could supply. . . . The Italian Army's tank forces were particularly badly off in armor, fire-power, and the ability to traverse rough country. The penetrating power of its antitank weapons and the range, caliber, and sighting of its artillery, including anti-aircraft guns, were all inferior.[24]

The Italian general staff's assessment of its own men and equipment in North Africa was similar. Its soldiers were not motivated, it judged, and its equipment was generally inferior.[25]

The 131st *Divisione Corazzata* (Armored Division) "Centauro," commanded by Gen. C. G. Calvi di Bergolo, had been formed in 1937 from the 1st Armored Brigade. The division had participated in the invasion of Albania in 1939, the bungled campaign against Greece in 1941, and the somewhat more successful incursion into Yugoslavia that same year. Centauro had a three-battalion armored regiment, a three-battalion *Bersagliari* regiment (motorized infantry), an artillery regiment, and a reconnaissance and an engineer battalion. The division had shipped to North Africa in August 1942, but was too late for the battle at El Alamein. Centauro had been caught up in the panicked Axis retreat, and the fighting in Tunisia was the first real combat for the division. Still, it had participated in Rommel's exhilarating offensive against the Americans at Kasserine.[26]

Eisenhower's intelligence staff informed Patton on 16 March that the enemy appreciated the threat to Gafsa and that, despite the peril along the Mareth Line opposite Eighth Army, he would probably be willing to shift assets from First Army to deal with Patton—including the 21st Panzer Division with sixty tanks and nonarmored elements of the 15th Panzer Division. Elements of *Kampfstaffel* Rommel were already believed to be in the Gafsa area.[27] Patton's G-2 told him—incorrectly—that the enemy had effected a concentration of forces in the II Corps sector. In fact, there were very few Italian troops to Patton's front, and they were capable of offering little resistance.[28]

Patton, for the first time, surprised his enemies with the speed of his actions. After the Battle of Kasserine, German commanders believed they had delivered the Americans such a sharp reversal that the enemy would be incapable of action any time soon.[29] On the eve of battle, Patton was made lieutenant general. He had dreamed of reaching that rank as a boy.[30]

Patton's corps included four divisions, but he would attack with only the 1st Armored and 1st Infantry Divisions, while the 9th and 34th Infantry Divisions remained in reserve. He had not forged his sword and wrote to his wife, "I really have a hell of a job fighting with men I have not trained and with a staff

I don't know." He thought the 1st Infantry Division looked sound, but had his doubts about the 1st Armored Division. He was already considering relieving its commanding general, Maj. Gen. Orlando Ward.[31]

PATTON'S FIRST OFFENSIVE AS COMMANDING GENERAL

The weather had been bitterly cold and rainy for days. This was not the deep desert of the Sahara. Enough rain fell to dot the land with scrub among the cactus. When a lot of rain fell, the water turned to soil to muck.

The roughly two battalions of Centauro Division's 5th *Bersaglieri* Regiment in Gafsa had the support of between fifteen and thirty M13/40 tanks from the 31st Tank Regiment.[32] The first sign of trouble, on 17 March, was the loss of a security detachment north of town to a surprise night attack by the 1st Infantry Division's 18th Infantry Regiment. Soon, the Americans rolled into view and detrucked in the wan dawn light. For some reason, however, they did not attack. Several hours passed before American planes appeared overhead, about 1000, and dropped their bombs. This seemed to be what the enemy had been waiting for.[33]

In Gafsa, artillery fire crashed around the Italian troops and trucks. Vehicles loaded with men and equipment and the tanks pulled out and raced for El Guettar and safety even before the American ground attack struck. One tank company endured a barrage of 105mm shellfire as it rolled east. The German reconnaissance unit's sand-colored armored cars formed the rear guard.

With the enemy getting well out of his way, Patton signaled to 18th Army Group, "Infantry attack progressing [in] excellent style."[34] But that was it. Where Rommel almost certainly would have followed up his success aggressively, there came no pursuit.[35]

With the fall of Gafsa and reports from new reconnaissance of II Corps positions, the Germans concluded that II Corps intended to hit the rear of First Army from the west, just the impression that Alexander wanted to convey to draw resources away from the Mareth Line. Vaerst received orders to stop the Americans from plowing into First Army's rear.[36]

Riflemen from the 1st Infantry Division moved cautiously past abandoned positions outside El Guettar on 18 March and into the town, which they found abandoned by the enemy. Patton already was aware from intelligence reports that at least a battalion of the 7th Panzer Regiment, 10th Panzer Division, was within striking distance of the battlefield. But the 1st Infantry Division did not reestablish contact with the enemy until 2350 hours at Wadi el Keddab, east of El Guettar.

Here, the Americans halted, though the Axis had almost nothing with which to stop them had they pressed on. The key to the entire western Axis flank was in the hands of weak elements of the Centauro Division, augmented by Imperiali's

50th Special Brigade, some cavalry, and a few *Bersagliari* Regiment infantry battalions, deployed on the heights east of El Guettar and Station de Sened and screened by the German 580 Reconnaissance.[37]

Patton saw the opportunity to strike quickly through Gafsa and El Guettar and capture the heights beyond before the Germans could respond, but Alexander sent him explicit instructions on 19 March to take the heights east of Maknassy instead. From there, he was to stage an armored raid on the German airbase at Mezzouna. He was not to send large forces beyond the line Gafsa-Maknassy-Faid-Fondouk. Patton, not for the last time, ignored those instructions and ordered Maj. Gen. Orlando Ward to be ready to roll his 1st Armored Division all the way to Maharès.[38] He also told Maj. Gen. Terry de la Mesa Allen to push through El Guettar with his 1st Infantry Division.

Patton was attempting to do just what he had tried and failed to do in the first phase of the Louisiana maneuvers—take the high ground and sweep onto the plain below with his tanks. Could Arnim secure the high ground first and stop him, just as Krueger's Third Army had?

Alexander's headquarters, by 20 March, anticipated that the enemy would have to commit his entire mobile reserve to stop Patton.[39] However, up to this point, Army Group Africa had not been sufficiently impressed with Patton's offensive to even bother reporting it to OKW.

Montgomery attacked at the Mareth Line on 20 March, and Arnim's post-war account suggests this attack was his greatest concern. And well it might be: Montgomery had assembled 160,000 men, 610 tanks, and 1,410 guns against an Axis force of 80,000 men, 150 tanks, and 680 guns. Arnim flew to that front in a *Storch*, barely escaping an attack by Spitfires.[40] German eyes were focused in the opposite direction when Patton struck.

Blocking Patton's Blow

The 1st Armored Division, constituting Patton's left hook, rolled at 0900 hours on 20 March toward Maknassy, driving eastward parallel to the mountains separating it from the valley east of El Guettar. Combat Command C (CCC) and the attached 60th Regimental Combat Team undertook the main drive, while Combat Command A (CCA) pushed through mud toward Station de Sened. Faced with a large oncoming armored force, Italian tanks and armored cars bugged out of Station de Sened that evening under the eyes of American cavalry reconnaissance troopers, who the next day pushed on without resistance toward Sened.[41]

Bottlenecks slowed CCA, while rain and mud delayed CCC on 21 March. At about 1500 hours, Patton appeared at CCA's command post demanding to know where and when he could see Ward.[42] Things were going too slowly! Doubtless disgusted, Patton left Ward a written message to show more drive and to move his command post closer to the fighting.[43]

Reconnaissance elements gained sight of Maknassy by 1900 hours and reported that between one and two thousand enemy troops—mainly belonging to the 2nd Battalion, 92nd Infantry Regiment, and the 1st Battalion, 5th *Bersagliari* Regiment—were in town.[44]

The 1st Armored Regiment reported to the division G-3 at 2015, "The infantry of this unit has been moving since 0330 this morning. They have been under artillery fire since 1100 hours this morning. Their regular battalion commander is absent sick, and they don't feel any too well. Any night attack will meet with failure due to fatigue of the troops and heavy artillery present."

This activity was menacing enough that it was reported up the chain to OKW. Initial reports, however, expressed greater alarm regarding an attack against the northern end of the Mareth Line, beginning at 2200 hours on 20 March and creating a mile-plus-wide gap in the Axis front.[45]

At 0030 Ward ordered CCC to draft orders for an attack on Maknassy the morning of 22 March, using CCC plus one infantry battalion, a company of tank destroyers, and two battalions of field artillery. Patrols from the 6th Armored Infantry, however, entered Maknassy at 0415 and found no opposition.[46]

Patton now instructed Ward to take the heights with a night attack.[47] Ward, during the afternoon, ordered CCC and the 60th Infantry Regiment to attack that night at 2330 and to capture the high ground beyond Maknassy. The initial push put the Americans on their first objectives, hindered by little but artillery fire. The next objective was the pass through the Eastern Dorsal Mountains, and that attack kicked off at 0700 on 23 March.[48] The tempting plains lay just beyond the ridge.

Counterattacks by the Italian First Army by 23 March eliminated the breakthrough on the Mareth Line, and command attention turned to the threat posed by II Corps. The D.A.K. received orders to restore the situation opposite II Corps using the 10th Panzer and Centauro Divisions.[49]

The man who was going to thwart Patton at Maknassy, *Oberst* Rudolf Lang, 10th Panzer Division, at that moment was in command of a *Kampfgruppe* attached to the 334th Infantry Division opposite the British to the north, near Ksar Mezouar. Lang's command was a small but powerful force that included the regimental staff and 1st Battalion, 69th Panzergrenadier Regiment; the 1st Battalion, 86th Panzergrenadier Battalion; a battalion of the 21st Panzer Division's 104th Regiment; the 26th *Marsch-Battalion* [March Battalion,

Separate Infantry Battalion]; *Kampfstaffel* Rommel; an Italian infantry battalion and artillery battery; a 150mm field artillery battery from the 90th Panzer Artillery Regiment; a battery of 170mm guns; two batteries of 88s; an antitank company; and the Tiger tanks of the 501st and some from the 504th Heavy Tank Battalions.

Lang, a trim, bespectacled Bavarian, was born on 25 October 1898 in Neustadt an der Donau. He was a brave man, and he had been awarded the Knight's Cross in the Caucasus while commanding the 44th Antitank Battalion, part of the 1st Mountain Division. He probably became available for service elsewhere (namely Africa) because, try as it might, the mountain division had been unable to get its antitank guns through the mountain passes where it was fighting. The night of 22 March, Lang received orders to travel to the headquarters of Army Group Africa, south of Sousse, and to report to Arnim personally to receive a new assignment.[50] Arnim already knew Lang well and had personally witnessed the colonel's tactical brilliance in the fighting against British and American forces at Longstop Hill in December. After a bitter and complex seesaw battle across the strategic heights near Medjez el Bab, Lang had personally led the main strike force in a counterattack on Christmas Day that had firmly established German control over the feature.[51]

Arnim had summoned Lang because it appeared that the Italian defenses had collapsed before Patton's northern thrust that day near Sened. The deployment of German combat echelons from the headquarters of the Italian First Army could not stop the Americans, and the Axis line to the north of Sened, along with four Italian infantry battalions, was cut off and out of contact. Arnim was painfully aware that "mobile American elements"—the 1st Armored Division—had reached Maknassy on 22 March and were poised to achieve a breakthrough to the coastal plain.[52]

The very survival of the Italian First Army was at stake. Only thirty-four miles separated American troops from the sea.

The morning of 23 March, *Oberst* Lang reported to Arnim. The Americans were threatening the rear of First Army, the general told him, and Brigadier Imperiali, commanding the Italian troops cut off by the attack, had fallen out of communication. Lang was to head to the crucial pass through the Eastern Dorsal Mountains near Maknassy to deal with the situation. He was nominally under the command of Imperiali, but Arnim made clear that the responsibility was his.[53]

Lang set off, and his efforts to track down the Italian general proved fruitless. Italian troops were streaming to the rear in confusion. Lang found some energetic young officers from a German 88mm flak battalion and ordered them to see that not another additional man or vehicle fled eastward.

Lang proceeded toward the pass. American artillery crashed about his car, and he abandoned the vehicle and proceeded on foot, dripping with sweat, with only his adjutant. The pass was still in Axis hands, defended mainly by eighty men from *Kampfstaffel* Rommel's *Begleitkompanie* (bodyguard company) under the command of *Major* Franz Medicus. The major had one 88mm gun and one antitank gun with which to hold off the 1st Armored Division. The detachment had already been fiercely engaged. The American tanks, thankfully, had run into a minefield. The enemy infantry had overrun one position, and the pass had seemed lost until the reserve—a mere half platoon of engineers and a few communicators—had counterattacked and chased the Americans off. A second breakthrough was stopped only after hand-to-hand fighting, and a third when a sergeant had jumped to man the antitank gun after the crew had fallen and fired into the American ranks. Medicus and his band were exhausted.

Lang ordered the men to hold a while longer and assured them that help was on the way. A trained mountain fighter, who knew how to use high-velocity guns in such terrain and who had to hold a pass, Lang was in his element. He turned back, found the flak officers, who had rounded up a considerable number of Italians, and organized a straggler line. He ordered two batteries of 88s forward to provide antitank defense.[54]

Vaerst, meanwhile, sent toward the pass four infantry battalions supported by artillery, plus fifteen Tiger tanks and two battalions of 88mm guns—all but the last of which already belonged to Lang's own *Kampfgruppe*.[55]

The first troops to join Lang were his two battalions from the 69th and 86th Panzergrenadier Regiments. Both battalions had already proved themselves in offensive and defensive operations. Lang sent *Major* Friedrich-Wilhelm Buschhausen's 1st Battalion, 69th Panzergrenadiers, to join Medicus in the pass and ordered the 1st Battalion, 86th Panzergrenadiers, to form a line to the north of the pass as far as Wadi el Leben, a streambed that, when dry, provided a rough passage through the mountain chain. He radioed Arnim that the pass was still in friendly hands.[56] Judging by American reports of battalion-sized enemy reinforcements appearing, these reinforcements entered the battle about 1800 hours.[57]

Lang finally tracked down Imperiali, who, as it turned out had been at the front under fire, trying to rally his men. The arrival of two experienced German battalions stiffened the line, and by dusk, the Axis troops had repulsed five American attacks.[58]

Vaerst recalled:

[The arriving troops and] vigorous leadership of a regimental commander [Lang] stopped the enemy, who by this time was much superior in force. The fighting here developed along the lines of mobile warfare and was marked by frequent shifts in the tide of battle. In some places, the *Kampfgruppe* was attacking, but as a rule it was on the defensive, even with its tanks. Numerous enemy tanks were knocked out without our suffering any losses to speak of.

The enemy artillery fire was powerful and accurate. The *Stuka Staffel* intervened in the defensive action successfully—this probably being the last time aircraft took part in ground fighting in Africa. . . .

In constituting this *Kampfgruppe*, the Fifth Panzer Army used up its last reserves and weakened its western front by withdrawal of troops there. From this point on, Fifth Panzer Army had no freedom of maneuver.[59]

The arrival of additional Tigers from the 501st Heavy Tank Battalion and Lang's battery of 170mm guns, which could fire shells to a range of twenty-seven kilometers, greatly aided Lang's efforts. *Kampfstaffel* Rommel's reconnaissance battalion arrived and set up to protect the north flank at Wadi el Leben. A "Tunisia Battalion"—a march battalion with no supporting heavy weapons—settled in on Lang's left wing. As Vaerst indicated, a nearby airbase provided support from Stukas on request.[60]

Patton was so frustrated that on 24 March, he called Ward and told him to personally lead an attack to capture the heights. Ward did so, but after reaching the objective, the Americans could not dig into the stony terrain and were driven back. Ward was slightly wounded.[61]

Patton was back in the 1st Armored Division's sector before first light on 25 March, accompanied by Ward. The G-3 recorded, "Corps commander directs that the hill be taken; that he wants killing; that he expects to see losses among officers and particularly among staff officers. That will indicate that an all-out attack under proper leadership has been made to secure the objective." But this was not to be; the 1st Armored Division was digging in across its front to "contain the enemy," and its tanks were being scattered to back up the infantry.[62]

As of 26 March, Patton was still under the misimpression that he was fighting Rommel.[63] It was Broich's men, though, that had taken the initiative away from the 1st Armored Division, and tank battles flared along the front east of Maknassy as the Germans pressed the American line aggressively on 27 March.[64]

Lang's *Kampfgruppe* had become the centerpiece of the German effort to keep Patton trapped in front of the Eastern Dorsal mountain range. American attacks all but ceased on 29 March, just as German ammunition was running out and one last hard bash would have broken through. The Tigers were sent to help the hard-pressed Hermann Göring Division farther north, and some of the 10th Panzer Division's own tanks replaced them. Arnim transmitted his praise, and Vaerst personally congratulated Lang. Kesselring paid him the high honor of visiting his command post. "All the credit for making it possible for the troops on the southern sector to fight without being threatened from the flanks or rear belongs to *Oberst* Lang," recalled Kesselring. OKW noted Lang's deeds in its war diary. Even the enemy knew he was important: intelligence officers at 18th Army Group knew his name and the approximate location of his headquarters.[65]

Lang had this to say about his enemy:

> [D]espite the fact that in such a situation the pass, including the last hills separating the enemy forces from the valley extending as far as the ocean and lacking any natural obstacles whatever, must have had an outright magnetic force of attraction, the enemy followed up only hesitantly. If his advance had not been a kind of "approach march," if instead he had stormed ahead, he could have reached the pass almost without any fighting at the latest on the twentieth, and he would have stood in the rear of the [Italian] First Army still on the same or the following day, so that the First Army would have been cut off from its supply route. The fighting in the Tunisian area would have come to an end several weeks earlier.[66]

Patton's decision to shift most of his armor to the El Guettar area saved Lang's men to fight another day. Arnim noted, "One bright spot remained. The enemy had so far directed its main effort from Gafsa directly at the rear of Mareth and salt lake positions, and at the brink of success he moved his forces from Maknassy to the south. I would have been much more worried about the setbacks in the south if the enemy had carried through his attack against the overextended flank and broken through with strong forces at Fondouk-Khairoun at the same time as Montgomery's attack!"[67]

The Germans were not overly impressed with the 1st Armored Division's aggressiveness. Lang recorded, "Usually, [the enemy] covered one sector for hours and uninterruptedly with a true hell of shells of the most varied calibers. This fire then increased to heavy barrage with the addition of bombs and fire from aircraft weapons. Then the tanks pushed forward, and along side or right behind them the infantry. . . . Our defensive forces were not very strongly impressed by the tanks, since they knew that not far behind were their own Tigers with light accompanying tanks [Mark IIIs] and 88mm flak. . . ."[68]

*

Punch and Counterpunch

Patton's right hook, mounted by the 1st Infantry Division, southeast of El Guettar, ran into the heart of *Generalmajor* Fritz von Broich's 10th Panzer Division, which, along with several separate infantry battalions, had concentrated on the line between the two Axis armies.[69] By now, Broich was a vastly more experienced combat officer than Patton. Broich had taken command of the 10th Panzer Division on 3 February, after his predecessor had been killed when his car struck a mine, and been made *Generalmajor* on the fifteenth. His first action had been the devastating counterattack against the Americans at Faid Pass, and his troops reached the high watermark of the offensive near Thala. Broich's fitness reports in North Africa described him as being "of decorous, open, and honorable character and good natural demeanor, fully proven in the face of the enemy, possessed of foresight and a goal-oriented commander with good tactical understanding, spirited and physically fit." Arnim considered him decisive and of good judgment, said he had proved himself in battle, and rated him above average.[70]

The division's operations officer (Ia) had been badly wounded in the same explosion as Broich's predecessor, and on 14 February, a bitter and disillusioned member of an officers' cabal intending to assassinate Hitler, *Oberstleutnant* Graf von Stauffenberg, arrived to fill the position.[71] Stauffenberg had arrived just as the 10th Panzer Division launched attacks near Sidi bou Zid that marked the opening phase of Rommel's offensive against the American II Corps. These were heady times, as the Axis onslaught sent the Americans reeling back through Kasserine Pass—where Stauffenberg was forward with the 2nd Battalion, 86th Panzergrenadier Regiment, during the assault on the defenses in the pass itself—and handed the *Amis* (Americans) their first humiliating defeat of the war. With his uniform unfaded by the searing African sun, Stauffenberg looked like an outsider, but he quickly won the respect of the desert veterans, respectfully speaking his mind to superior officers and executing his duties cheerfully and with confidence and openness.

The Ia was the man who drafted battle orders and saw to their execution, and Stauffenberg controlled operations from the command post when Broich was in the field. Working out of a captured British armored command vehicle, Stauffenberg labored fourteen hours a day. He made a point of getting out to the division's components and got to know the company-level officers. Broich soon realized the young officer was anti-Nazi and trusted him enough to share his similar views.[72]

The 10th Panzer Division disengaged from Thala, where the British and Americans had succeeded in halting the German advance following the capture of Kasserine Pass, on the night of 22–23 February. Broich's troops were shifted to Rommel's D.A.K., where they fought against Eighth Army along the Mareth Line in early March. Hitler's inner circle was obviously following developments there with concern and was well aware of who was in charge on the other side. Nazi propaganda chief Joseph Goebbels, whose diary shows he had been monitoring Montgomery's public statements, lamented on 10 March, "Regarding Tunisia, the English claim that Rommel has now been defeated completely. [They say] Montgomery is now ready to make a final breakthrough. As a matter of fact, the situation in Tunisia has become somewhat critical, especially along the Mareth Line. We ought to make up our minds whether we can and want to hold Tunis or not."[73]

Pulled into reserve to refit, the division had been oriented toward the south, facing Eighth Army, until on 20 March it received orders to conduct a night march to Maharès and to be available there for employment by Army Group Africa for rapid movement toward Maknassy. Only a day earlier, the division had been told not to expect any replacement tanks.[74]

Showdown at El Guettar: Some tanks, possibly Italian, appeared to the 1st Infantry Division's front on 21 March. Unfortunately for the 10th Panzer Division, this activity persuaded II Corps to release the 601st Tank Destroyer Battalion, still using obsolete M3 half-tracked vehicles with 75mm guns, to the 1st Infantry Division for use, with the 899th Tank Destroyer Battalion, outfitted with new fully tracked M10s sporting the 3-inch gun, available if needed.[75]

Despite the arrival of a few tanks, the Italian troops were unable to stop the 1st Infantry Division's push onto the high ground east of El Guettar. Many of them surrendered. The 18th Infantry Regiment crossed Wadi el Keddab and reached the foothills of Djebel el Melhelat, and the 26th Infantry cleared Djebel el Ank except for a few machine-gun positions.[76]

With Italian defenses crumbling under Patton's assaults, the 10th Panzer Division, less *Oberst* Lang's *Kampfgruppe*, rolled forward to battle on 21 March. The 2nd Battalion, 69th Panzergrenadier Regiment, accompanied by panzers (American air reconnaissance reported "many light tanks" south of the road east of El Guettar between 0600 and 0700 on 22 March) reached the high ground east of El Guettar, but came under such strong pressure from the 1st Infantry Division that its line bent back. The 49th *Panzerpionier* (Armored Engineer) Battalion, meanwhile, secured Djebel el Meheltat and held it against increasingly strong attacks. The sector just to the south, defended by strong points of the Centauro Division, was close to collapse, and the *Kradschutzen* (Motorcycle) Battalion 10, commanded by *Major* Heinrich Drewes, had to contend with

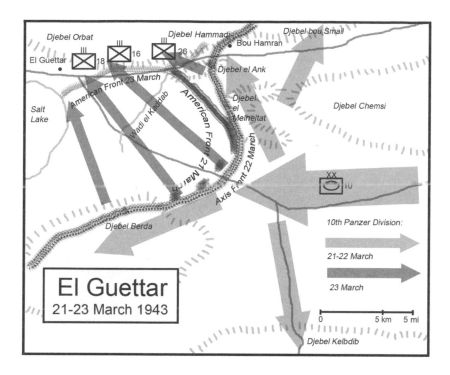

Djebel Orbat   Djebel Hammadi   Djebel bou Smail
                                        Bou Hamran
El Guettar   18   16   26
                                        Djebel el Ank
        American Front 23 March
Salt   Djebel   Djebel Chemsi
Lake   el
                                    Melheltat
                        American Front 21 March
                        Axis Front 22 March
                                                        10
Djebel Berda

El Guettar   10th Panzer Division:
21-23 March 1943
                                               21-22 March

                                               23 March

                                               0   5 km   5 mi
                                        Djebel Kelbdib

American attacks from that direction against the sand dunes of Draa Saada al Hamra and the rocky crest of Djebel Kelbdib.[77]

Kampfgruppe Reimann arrived at El Guettar on 22 March and established a defensive line at Djebel Hammadi and Djebel bou Smail, which secured the right flank. *Oberst* Hans Reimann commanded the 86th Panzergrenadier Regiment, and his battle group consisted of his regiment (less the 1st Battalion), an artillery battalion, a battery of 88mm guns, and a company of 76.2mm antitank guns mounted on the Skoda tank chassis, called "ducks" by the men because of their profile. Reimann's arrival definitively stopped the 1st Infantry Division's advance, and fighting flared here and there along the high ground as American battalions tried to press forward.[78] The 1st Infantry Division pulled back to Djebel Orbat, a strong position where the division's right end was anchored on a salt lake that was impassable for vehicles.

Surprised by the Germans' appearance, Patton's staff completely misread the 10th Panzer Division's intentions. It alerted the corps's divisions that the panzers were likely to attack at Maknassy gap. Patton expected Rommel—who was no longer in Africa—to strike him with everything he had no earlier than 24 March after "dealing with" with Eighth Army.[79] Patton, on 23 March, received some warning that the bulk of the 10th Panzer Division was going to attack the 1st Infantry Division instead, because II Corps, at 0410, alerted all divisions that there were indications that the panzers were on the move.[80]

According to Arnim's account, *Generalleutnant* Hans Cramer took command of the sector with the 10th Panzer Division's arrival and objected when Kesselring ordered that the panzers stage a frontal attack on the Americans. Cramer, an experienced panzer officer, wanted to take the Americans in the flank and thereby sidestep the enemy's overwhelming strength in artillery. Kesselring, however, stuck to his guns.[81] He may have underestimated the opposition and reckoned that the 10th Panzer Division had rolled over the Americans west of Faid Pass and virtually annihilated a tank battalion at the start of the Kasserine battle. But that day, two infantry battalions had been positioned on separate hills, with most of their supporting tanks piecemealed along a forward-outpost line, and this time, an entire American division occupied a mutually supportive position along a ridge with the 601st Tank Destroyer Battalion, which was arrayed along the crest, in hull-down fighting positions.

Broich probably thought the frontal attack made perfect sense because everything in his experience told him his tanks could attack enemy infantry entrenched on high ground with success. He had done it at Truchaschewka, on the Chir River, and at Kasserine Pass. But in all his battles, including at Kasserine, he had never encountered anything approaching the massed fires of an American infantry division.

A 10th Panzer Division situation map and division history indicate that the division, less the elements at Maknassy, attacked with the 7th Panzer Regiment in the center, flanked on the left by *Kampfgruppen* Kleinau and Reimann, apparently consisting of *Major* Drewes's motorcycle battalion and two platoons of engineers on the wing and two panzergrenadier or infantry battalions close to the panzers. Drewes's unit packed a particularly impressive punch, as it consisted of two motorcycle companies, a third company mounted in half-tracks, and a heavy weapons company with two infantry gun platoons and an antitank platoon. On the right, *Major* Paul Pommée's 2nd Battalion, 69th Panzergrenadier Regiment, advanced onto the Djebel el Ank ridge on the wing, accompanied by a few panzers and covered by flak guns. *Kampfgruppe* Pfeiffer, with one infantry battalion and most of *Major* Albert Krumsiek's 49th *Panzerpionier* Battalion, stayed with the panzers. This positioning indicates that additional formations, probably separate infantry battalions, had arrived over night.

By contrast, the 1st Infantry Division purported to have "positive information" that the attacking force consisted of the 7th Panzer Regiment's two battalions, the two battalions of the 86th Panzergrenadier Regiment, and two battalions of artillery. Sources differ on how many tanks participated in the attack. Arnim, in his post-war account, put the total number at fifty-five panzers. II Corps information, probably a radio intercept provided by 18th Army Group, as of 21 March, put the total number of 10th Panzer Division tanks at fifty-seven. American observers, however, claimed the total German force to be about 200 panzers. The actual number of serviceable panzers employed at El Guettar was approximately eighty. Each battalion in the 7th Panzer Regiment had three light companies equipped with Mark IIIs, which had long-barreled 50mm guns, and one medium company outfitted with Mark IVs carrying the short or long 75mm cannon.[82]

ME 109s, with yellow bellies and wingtips, and FW 190s buzzed protectively over the advancing troops, intercepting American aircraft and shooting down several Spitfires and P-39s, while Stukas pounced on American positions.[83] Fifteen Heinkel bombers in formation and JU88s bombed the enemy, too.[84]

At about 0500 hours, the Germans advanced slowly in a hollow-square formation of tanks and self-propelled guns interspersed with infantry carriers. Additional infantry followed in trucks. The panzers were close enough to American lines to be seen between 0600 and 0700 hours, and the grenadiers piled out of the trucks that had brought them this far. The 1st Infantry Division reported that six of the panzers were Tigers, although this is unlikely, as the 501st Heavy Tank Battalion, on 17 March, had been attached to the 504th Heavy Tank Battalion and was fighting at Maknassy.[85]

In the first attack, ten panzers and two companies of infantry met initial success when they struck the seam between the 16th and 18th Infantry Regiments. The Germans enveloped the left flank of the 3rd Battalion, 16th Infantry Division, and the regiment had to extricate itself by infiltration. When thirty panzers approached the 1st Battalion, 18th Infantry Division, at about 0700 hours, however, a crushing barrage by 155mm shells hit the Germans. M3 tank destroyers appeared suddenly over the crest, fired their 75mm guns, and disappeared backward in a cloud of dust, only to reemerge from some other spot a short while later. One tank destroyer hit two panzers before one of Broich's gunners pierced its thin armored skin with three shells, setting the half-track ablaze. The panzers and grenadiers got into American lines; but momentum ran out, and a half dozen of Broich's tanks were burning. Thwarted, the 10th Panzer Division pulled back by 0845.

A second push before 1100 hours split into three prongs, one of which drove a gap into the middle of the 18th Infantry Regiment's line and cut off one battery of the 5th Field Artillery Battalion. Four battalions of artillery concentrated their fire on the breakthrough, and again the 10th Panzer Division had to pull back. According to American claims, between thirty and forty panzers were disabled or destroyed by this time.[86]

A company of the 899th Tank Destroyer's M10s arrived from mobile reserve and pursued the Germans across the valley floor. The Germans' skillfully selected firing positions, combined with an American minefield, left the Americans little room for maneuver. Soon, half the M10s were disabled, and the rest withdrew.[87]

Broich's men made one last effort, at about 1700 hours, with thirty-eight tanks, but the Americans had somehow become aware of the plan and smeared the advancing troops with artillery. Though the panzers and grenadiers managed to reach the lines of Company K of the 3rd Battalion, 18th Infantry Division, the attackers took heavy losses. The Americans had deployed their antitank guns along the line and took a lethal toll of panzer steel.[88]

The panzer gunners had done some mighty good shooting, too. Twenty-four M3 tank destroyers had been knocked out, and all but two were beyond repair. The gunners had nailed another seven M10s, and five were destroyed for good.[89] Patton put German tank losses at thirty, half of which the Germans were able to tow away; American engineers destroyed the remainder.[90]

German wartime documents recorded the loss of forty-five tanks and two self-propelled guns. Only thirty-two tanks that began the attack remained operational when it ended. That evening, however, the Germans recovered thirty-six disabled armored vehicles, and many of these would be eventually returned to action. The 10th Panzer Division also suffered over 300 casualties that day. While one panzergrenadier battalion was considered to have had moderate casualties, the other was characterized as "completely exhausted." Consequently, a march battalion had to be diverted to the division to beef up its depleted infantry component.[91]

The 10th Panzer Division pulled most of its armor back on 24 March, leaving about one company of medium tanks east of El Guettar. It had already drained Patton's momentum, albeit at some cost. On 24 March, local counterattacks kept the 1st Division busy, and the next day, the Americans were "rectifying lines" and "consolidating positions."[92] Patton's G-2 speculated that the 10th Panzer Division had between fifty and sixty medium tanks still in action (the actual number was slightly lower), and he warned the 1st Armored Division that the Germans might attack in combat-command strength at Maknassy.[93] Infantry attacks on Djebel Berda, on the El Guettar front, continued all day, but panzers did not join the action. At Maknassy, Italian tanks appeared to strengthen the defenses, probably from the Centauro Division's 15th Battalion, 31st Tank Regiment, and about twenty German tanks probed the 1st Armored Division's positions. The situation was reported to be bad until tanks and tank destroyers knocked out six Mark IVs.

The 10th Panzer Division's attack had been costly, but it had stopped Patton from penetrating the last Axis line of defense protecting the communication routes from northern Tunisia to the Mareth Line. The 18th Army Group estimated that the 10th Panzer Division probably had, at most, forty running medium tanks. An intercepted ammunition report on 24 March indicated the 7th Panzer Regiment had ten Mark IVs and seventeen Mark IIIs, but it was thought that this figure might represent only one battalion.[94]

Kesselring may have felt he would be held responsible for the 10th Panzer Division's losses, as Arnim later charged that he was, because he told Arnim on the twenty-fourth that he was to cease sending copies of his reports simultaneously to OKW and transmit only to *OB Süd*, which would pass necessary information up the chain of command. Arnim simply shared these instructions with OKW, which tartly told Kesselring that he was not to interfere with reports going to the high command.[95]

East of El Guettar, pressure on the German line from the south increased on 26 March, when elements of the 2nd Battalion of the 9th Division's 47th Infantry attacked the motorcycle battalion's line along the dunes. Close-quarters fighting raged until *Oberleutnant* Wilhelm Reile led six men from Company 5 behind the Americans and opened fire. At first, forty rattled infantrymen gave up, then 140 did. When it was over, the Germans had taken 242 men prisoner, including the battalion's commanding officer, Lt. Col. E. G. Gershenow.[96]

Matching Patton in the Scrum: Stauffenberg, after tasting battle against Patton and his legions, wrote to his brother at the end of March, "Commander and senior staff officer are terrific!"[97] Perhaps Patton sensed his enemy's high spirits. He wrote his wife, "The Germans are very tough and well fed and cocky, especially the officers. . . ."[98]

The attention of Axis command at this point shifted quickly back to the First Army front, where Montgomery, after the failure of his frontal attack on the Mareth Line, had shifted his weight to the left wing and, on 26 March, had nearly turned the Axis right flank. German formations stopped the thrust at El Hamma long enough that all Axis forces were able to withdraw to a fallback line called the Wadi Akarit position.[99]

Kesselring visited Tunisia on 27 March, and his concern focused on the grave situation created by Eighth Army at El Hamma. He worried that within twenty-four hours the Commonwealth advance would take on the characteristics of another breakthrough.[100]

Alexander finally gave Patton the chance he wanted to attack toward Gabès, but the D.A.K. was well positioned to hold him off. Patton attacked on 28 March with the 1st and 9th Infantry Divisions and the 1st Armored Division's Task Force Benson, with much of the 1st Armored Division held in reserve to exploit any breakthrough. Initial progress was virtually nil.[101]

This was a fight at as close to even odds that the Germans would ever enjoy against Patton. Up to 25,000 German and Italian troops opposed II Corps, including more than 7,000 with the 10th Panzer Division and some 4,000 with the Centauro Division.[102]

Nevertheless, the Germans felt the II Corps pressure keenly. Army Group Africa, on 29 March, signaled Rommel in Germany, "D.A.K.: Hard fighting east of Maknassy; we hold our positions. 10th Panzer Division and Centauro Division hold on southeast of El Guettar against strong enemy pressure."[103] That day, some tanks belonging to the 21st Panzer Division arrived in the area, and the 7th Panzer Regiment shifted north to back Lang's troops in the pass east of Maknassy. Hitler himself was now following Lang's epic battle, and that day the determined *Oberst* lost the heights north of the pass only to recapture them in a desperate assault at 1500 hours. The leading tanks of the 7th Panzer Regiment appeared just in time to fend off an American tank attack.[104]

Patton's drive posed such a strategic threat that in the final days of March, additional scarce resources were shifted to reinforce Broich from the Mareth Line front. These included Panzergrenadier Regiment Afrika and a 21st Panzer Division light artillery battalion. At 1530 hours on 31 March, the entire 21st Panzer Division was subordinated to Broich.

Throwing II Corps back was now beyond the Axis's means, in part because the panzers lacked gas. The Italians were suffering terrible losses, and the Germans doubted their battle worthiness. Gradually, the heavily reinforced 10th Panzer and Centauro Divisions fell back some four miles, though never allowing a break in their line.[105]

Gabès and El Hamma fell to Montgomery on 30 March, and Commando Supremo instructed that a breakthrough was to be prevented by panzer counterattacks. With only the 15th Panzer Division still available, the idea was out of touch with reality. Eisenhower's brain trust, by the end of March, concluded that Eighth Army's pressure and II Corps's attack had weakened the Axis line and denuded it of mobile reserves. The time was ripe for a push along the Mediterranean coast.[106] The Axis retreat in southern Tunisia came off faster than that could be arranged.

Patton, on 1 April, was in a bleak mood and could see reasons everywhere, but not the real cause, namely the officers and men on the other side who were putting up a great fight. In his diary, Patton wrote:

> The plans of the Allied High Command are all about three days to a week too late, and too timid. When we took Gafsa we were told to halt at El Guettar. We waited there from the 19th to the 22d and gave the Bosches time to bring the 10th Panzer down from the north [sic]. At the same time they told me to take Maknassy and halt on the hills just east. . . . Here I failed by not personally backing the attack on the heights. Ward fooled around for three days and then he attacked with great personal courage but failed to take the ridge. However, I [had] asked to take the whole 9th Division in with the 1st Armored and was only allowed to take [part]. . . . Not enough. . . .

A day later, he was more situationally aware. "The action was very slow, due to strong enemy resistance, very difficult country, and the fatigue of our troops. . . . Our air cannot fly at night, nor in a wind, nor support troops. The Germans do all three, and do it as the result of three years' experience in war."[107]

Kampfgruppe Lang continued to hold the pass east of Maknassy, and Hill 350, Djebel bou Dousou, changed hands repeatedly in the first days of April. The 10th Panzer Division east of El Guettar held firm and even jabbed back at the attackers.[108]

The *Kampfgruppe* held the Maknassy sector successfully until 7 April against tentative American probes. On 4 April, it was subordinated to First Army and covered the right flank when First Army withdrew northward from the Mareth Line. As First Army pulled back, it took responsibility for each new sector and the troops from Fifth Panzer Army stationed there. Although many Italian troops surrendered during the period, German formations retained their cohesion. Vaerst attributed his success to the fact that the Allies had launched uncoordinated attacks from the west at different places and different times, each of which could be dealt with individually.[109]

By 5 April, hopes for a breakthrough were fading fast at II Corps.[110] Patton had sacked Orlando Ward the day before. But at the 10th Panzer Division headquarters, doubt was growing that the grenadiers could stop the Americans' grinding pressure for much longer, and Broich and Stauffenberg appealed urgently to Italian First Army headquarters for permission to withdraw.

The Axis was indeed shoveling sand with a spoon. Fifth Panzer Army, on 5 April, had but thirteen panzers, including six Tigers and eight Italian tanks in fighting order. The D.A.K. possessed only eighty-nine panzers, seven of them Tigers, that were running, plus twenty-four under repair. The Italian First Army fielded only twenty-one serviceable tanks, plus thirteen under repair. Ammunition was short in both D.A.K. and First Army.[111]

On 6 April, Montgomery punched through the Wadi Akarit line, and the 10th Panzer Division found itself in pressing danger of being cut off. Moreover, forty tanks from the 21st Panzer Division were ordered south to deal with the Commonwealth breakthrough, which badly weakened Broich's front. That day, *Kampfgruppe* Lang turned back two American attacks.

First Army finally approved the division's request to pull back. It was too late for an orderly withdrawal, and from his captured British operations center— under frequent shellfire in an olive grove west of Sidi Mansour—Stauffenberg told the desperate battalion commanders that they had to hold out until 2100 hours. Fortunately, the Americans spotted preparations for the withdrawal and misinterpreted them as the moves of a brewing counterattack—probably largely because Stauffenberg ordered the artillery to fire continually to drown out the sound of motors in vehicles pulling out. Instead of pressing their attack home, the Americans dug in to face the expected onslaught.

By 1800 hours, it was clear that there could be no more delay, and Stauffenberg authorized units to break contact in one hour and pull back through Mezzouna, taking their dead and wounded with them.

As the division struggled to worm through the El Hafay pass in the early light of 7 April, American reconnaissance planes spotted the bumper-to-bumper traffic, which soon received a rain of artillery fire and air strikes. Vehicles exploded, and men died to the left and right. At 0500 hours, Stauffenberg left the division command post on his Horch jeep to supervise the mess in the El Hafay pass, Broich's last warning still ringing in his ears: look out for fighter-bombers. Broich would follow in an hour after the last battalion was through.

East of the pass, Stauffenberg found a hellish scene: vehicles burned as American fighter-bombers roared up and down the road, strafing the retreating column. Stauffenberg, standing in his Horch, raced back and forth along the column shouting orders and trying to bring some organization to the chaos. Then his own vehicle came under fire, and Stauffenberg threw himself from the bullet-riddled Horch to the ground, face on his hands. Then a slug tore through his flesh. At a field hospital near Sfax, a surgeon removed Stauffenberg's left eye, right hand, and two fingers from his left hand.

Broich escaped two strafing attacks and made his way to safety.[112] Fortunately, as there were no German forces behind him, the American infantry was very slow to pursue him.[113] Broich ultimately became a prisoner of war when the Axis in North Africa surrendered in May.[114] *Oberst* Rudolf Lang, for his part, escaped the disaster and later became the interim commander of the 3rd Panzer Division from 5 January to 24 May 1944.[115]

At 1600 hours on 7 April, elements of the 899th Tank Destroyer Battalion, operating with the 1st Armored Division, established contact with Eighth Army.[116] There was now only one front in North Africa.

With the 10th Panzer Division out of his way, Patton was very nearly able to make the first of his classic dashing advances into a vacuum. At 1940 hours, he spoke with 18th Army Group and said he was sending a combat command of the 1st Armored Division to the coast. "Order them back," came the response. His troops would get in the way of Eighth Army. Angry and, finally, tired, Patton went to bed at 2200 hours.[117] The next day, D.A.K. was free to report, "Withdrawal carried out to the planned defensive line went without any enemy pressure so far. . . ."[118] This time, it was not Patton's fault.

Patton and Bradley decided to go look at the battlefield from the enemy's side. "After seeing how strong the position was, I don't wonder we took so long to take it," Patton concluded.[119]

With the German perimeter receding northward, Lt. Gen. Omar Bradley replaced Patton at the head of II Corps on 15 April so that the latter could return to overseeing the planning for Operation Husky, the invasion of Sicily. Pinched out of the line by the steady shrinkage of the Axis perimeter, II Corps shifted behind the British lines and took responsibility for the left flank along the coast. The new objective was Bizerte.[120]

After Axis resistance collapsed in Tunisia over three disastrous days, 10–13 May, two Italian-German armies went to the prisoner-of-war stockades. The total loss in manpower, 157,000 Germans and 86,700 Italians, was roughly the same as those taken at Stalingrad.[121]

A BLUR IN THE ENEMY'S EYES

There is no indication in the surviving records of *OB Süd* (then Army Group C), Fifth Panzer Army, D.A.K., or the 10th or 21st Panzer Divisions—which include the Ic (G-2) intelligence reports in the cases of *OB Süd*, Fifth Panzer Army, and the 10th Panzer Division—that Patton's enemies in Tunisia had any idea who he was, much less that they held him in some esteem as an opposing commander. They were aware through prisoner interrogations of the identities of officers at the division level and below. Likewise, the accounts of German commanders such as Kesselring and Arnim relate no cognizance of Patton, although they do of Eisenhower, Montgomery, and Alexander. The first observable mention of Patton in German documents comes in a mid-May report on American forces by OKH's *Abteilung Fremde Heere West* (Detachment Foreign Armies West), which noted that Patton at some point had replaced Fredendall as the commanding general of II Corps.[122] By then, of course, Patton had already left II Corps.

The Germans had collected more information by mid-June 1943, perhaps from Allied press reports. Detachment Foreign Armies West noted in a broad assessment of the Allied military posture that a strong, mainly American force had shown up in the Algiers-Oran area. These formations were gathered under the command of Patton, "known as an energetic and responsibility-loving command personality."[123]

Though they had been defeated in North Africa, the Germans were not overly impressed with Allied generalship in terms of dash and daring. A German assessment of American commanders in Tunisia noted that the Americans displayed uncertainty and based their battle leadership on careful and methodical plans built on absolute security. They steered away from bold attacks that could have exploited openings that suddenly emerged in the course of events. They held to a plan, even when it was not appropriate to the demands of the moment. They gained success on the basis of overwhelming materiel superiority.[124] Patton had done nothing at the head of II Corps to disturb this analysis.

The German view of British commanders about the same time was not much different. After their misadventures in the first eighteen months of combat, British generals had learned to gather all available strength at the point of decision, but they had been unable to free themselves from the methodical approach. Operations, from local actions to great battles, were meticulously prepared beforehand. British commanders avoided improvised battle leadership with the forces at hand. They never found the courage to send formations with open objectives deep into the Axis rear. (In his memoirs, Kesselring plausibly claims he realized after El Alamein that Montgomery "played for safety and was correspondingly methodical.") British success was attributed to the Axis inability to logistically sustain German and Italian forces in the field.[125]

SEVEN

Intermezzo:
The Brotherhood of Kursk

A LMOST EVERY SIGNIFICANT enemy commander that Patton was to face in France during 1944 played a part in Operation Citadel, the German attempt to eliminate a large Soviet salient at Kursk in July 1943. The Battle of Kursk was Germany's Gettysburg, the last time Hitler would launch a major offensive in the east. The scale was gargantuan, the largest tank fight of the war by most accounts, and it would live in the minds of the men who were there as a basis of comparison for their later conflicts, including the relatively small one they would face one day against George Patton's Third Army. Although the battle saw many German tactical successes, German commanders, in failing to achieve their objectives, lost the battle, and they probably recalled that combination of success and failure at the end of the late-autumn Lorraine campaign the following year.

In March, Army Group South's *Generalfeldmarschall* Erich von Manstein scored a victory at Kharkov that signaled Germany's recovery of the initiative after the Soviet winter offensive and allowed the Germans to reestablish a more or less continuous defensive line along the eastern front. Manstein struck northward toward Kharkov on 28 February with *Obergruppenführer* Paul Hausser's SS Panzer Corps (which had just abandoned Kharkov on Hausser's orders, in defiance of Hitler) on the left and *General der Panzertruppe* Otto von Knobelsdorff's XLVIII Panzer Corps on the right. *SS Oberführer,* Max Simon by now had taken command of the 3rd *Totenkopf* SS Panzergrenadier Division in Hausser's corps. Manstein's blow completely surprised the Soviets and took three corps opposite Army Detachment Kempf in the rear. The Luftwaffe's Fourth Air Fleet, under Richthofen, flew one thousand sorties per day and for the last time protected a major ground operation through complete dominance of the skies. Tiger tanks in Hausser's corps fought T34s in the first of many engagements, and the Tigers gave the Soviets a surprise similar to the one the Germans had received in the first encounters with T34s.

Manstein pressed on toward Kharkov, based on a plan proposed by Hoth, on 5 March; Hausser's corps was screened on its right by Knobelsdorff and on its left by Army Detachment Kempf's Corps Raus, the heart of which was Hörnlein's *Grossdeutschland* Panzergrenadier Division. Hausser's corps advanced in a wide arc north of Kharkov and enveloped the city, cutting off the enemy's retreat, while *Grossdeutschland* advanced on Belgorod. Hoth, on the eighth, authorized a quick grab of Kharkov if the opportunity presented itself, an instruction he repeated on the tenth.

Hausser almost certainly wanted to remove the stain from his earlier retreat, and he threw the 1st SS *Leibstandarte* Panzergrenadier Division into the city on the thirteenth with Hoth's full knowledge and approval. (Fourth Panzer Army records disprove allegations that Hausser ignored an order from Hoth to bypass the city.) The corps secured Kharkov after three days of costly street fighting, in which the Tigers played a key role. The bulk of the SS corps advanced to Belgorod starting 16 March, and the 2nd SS *Das Reich* Panzergrenadier Division linked up with the *Grossdeutschland* Division. This meeting created the launching pad for the next great German offensive.[1]

Sir Basil Liddell-Hart called the counterstroke at Kharkov "the most brilliant operational performance of Manstein's career, and one of the most masterly in the whole course of military history."[2] Four of Patton's future enemies were lieutenants under this exceptional commander during this extraordinary historical event. It is worth remembering what they were capable of when they had the means.

Following the victory at Kharkov, German divisions had a breather to refit, thanks to Soviet exhaustion and the spring rains that turned the Russian landscape into a sea of mud. Still, the panzer arm had been worn out, and Guderian, newly appointed the first inspector of panzer troops, hoped that he could restore the divisions merely to the point where they could stage limited-objective attacks. Refitting to enable strategic operations, he hoped, would occur in 1944.

OKH estimated that the Soviets would be unable to recover and launch their own offensive until late June. With the looming loss of Tunisia, Hitler and the German military commanders knew that this would be the last summer when they could attack in the east without facing pressure from a second front in the west. And Hitler wanted to regain the initiative on the eastern front completely.

MEXICAN PUNITIVE EXPEDITION

Patton's first mortal enemy was the commander of Francisco "Pancho" Villa's bodyguard during the Mexican Punitive Expedition. Left to right: General Álvaro Obregón, Villa, Brig. Gen. John Pershing, Capt. George Patton.

WORLD WAR I

Col. George Patton with one of his 1st Tank Brigade FT17s in France in 1918.

Otto *Freiherr* von Diepenbroick-Grüter, pictured as a cadet in 1872, commanded the 10th Infantry Division at St. Mihiel.

Prince Friedrich Eitel commanded the 1st Guards Division in the Argonnes.

General der Artillerie Max von Gallwitz's army group defended the St. Mihiel salient. *Library of Congress*

Crown Prince Wilhelm commanded the region opposite the Americans.

MOROCCO AND VICHY FRANCE

Patton and Rear Adm. Henry Kent Hewitt, commanding Western Naval Task Force, aboard the *Augusta* before invading Vichy-controlled Morocco in Operation Torch.

Arriving at Fedala to negotiate an armistice at 1400 hours on 11 November 1942, Gen. Charles Noguès (left) is met by Col. Hobart Gay. Major General Auguste Lahoulle, commander of French air forces in Morocco, is on the right. Major General Georges Lascroux, commander-in-chief of Moroccan troops, carries a briefcase.

Charles Noguès, was Vichy commander-in-chief in Morocco.

Jean Petit, commanded the garrison at Port Lyautey. *Courtesy of Stéphane Petit*

THE AXIS POWERS

Patton and his rival, Gen. Bernard Montgomery, greet each other on Sicily in July 1943. The two fought the Axis powers in Tunisia, Sicily, and the European theater.

Patton inspecting troops after he got back into action in France a month and a half following the Normandy invasion. Although at first the Germans didn't seem to pay much attention, that would change as Patton led the Third Army across France.

Some of Patton's enemies as prisoners of war. Front row, left to right: *Oberst* Hans Reimann, *Generalleutnant* Georg Neuffer, *Generalleutnant* Heinrich "Heinz" Eberbach, *Generalleutnant* Fritz von Broich.

Hans-Jürgen von Arnim commanded
Army Group Africa in Tunisia.

Rudolf Bacherer tried to stop Patton
at Avranches.

Hermann Balck brought eastern-front
strategy to Lorraine as commanding
general of Army Group G.

Franz Beyer commanded LXXX Corps
during the long battle west
of the Rhine.

Johannes Blaskowitz conducted Army Group G's retreat into Lorraine.

Erich Brandenberger led Seventh Army in the Battle of the Bulge.

Fritz von Broich and his 10th Panzer Division battled Patton in Tunisia.

Kurt von der Chevallerie commanded First Army in France.

Dietrich von Choltitz commanded
LXXXIV Corps in Normandy

Paul Conrath hit Patton hard with his
Hermann Göring Panzer Division on Sicily.

Hans Cramer commanded the sector
including El Guettar in Tunisia.

Hans-Gustav Felber commanded XIII
Corps and Seventh Army against Patton.

Edgar Feuchtinger led the 21st Panzer
Division in Lorraine.

Hermann Foertsch commanded First
Army in the Saar-Palatinate campaign.

Rudolf von Gersdorff participated in
the plot to kill Hitler and served as
chief of staff of Seventh Army.

Paul Hausser was a no-nonsense
commander of Seventh Army
and Army Group G.

Ludwig-Sebastian Heilmann and his
5th Airborne Division battled Patton
in the Ardennes.

Walter Hörnlein commanded the
Grossdeutschland Division in the east
and LXXXII Corps in Lorraine.

Hans-Valentin Hube led the XIV
Panzer Corps on Sicily.

Albert Kesselring opposed Patton in
Tunisia, Sicily, and east of the Rhine.

Günther von Kluge fought Patton in
France as commander of Army Group
B and Commander-in-Chief West.

Baptist Kniess battled Patton west
and east of the Rhine at the head of
LXXXV and XII Corps.

Otto von Knobelsdorff was a skilled panzer general who commanded First Army in Lorraine.

Walter Krueger commanded LVIII Panzer Corps in Normandy and Lorraine. *Bundesarchiv*

Smilo *Freiherr* von Lüttwitz was the last enemy commander to offer Patton a real fight at the head of LXXXV Corps.

Hasso-Eccard von Manteuffel commanded Fifth Panzer Army in Lorraine and the Ardennes.

Walter Model led Army Group B
after Kluge.

Hans von Obstfelder briefly
commanded First Army in Lorraine
and Seventh Army during the
collapse in the West.

Herbert Osterkamp commanded XII
Corps east of the Rhine.

Hermann Priess commanded XIII SS Corps in Lorraine and I SS Panzer Corps in the Ardennes.

Hermann-Bernhard Ramcke defied Patton as commander of Brest.

Eberhard Rodt led the 15th Panzergrenadier Division against Patton on Sicily.

Edwin *Graf* von Rothkirch und Trach led LIII Corps against Patton.

Edwin *Graf* von Rothkirch und Trach led LIII Corps against Patton.

Gerd von Rundstedt battled Patton as Commander-in-Chief West.

Max Simon was a bloodthirsty killer and seasoned panzer general who commanded XIII SS Corps in Lorraine.

Wend von Wietersheim fought Patton at the head of the 11th Panzer Division.

Late in the war Patton was promoted to four-star general. To his disappointment, he was not sent to fight the Japanese following victory in Europe.

Patton's original gravesite at the Luxembourg American Cemetery and Memorial in Hamm, near Luxembourg City.

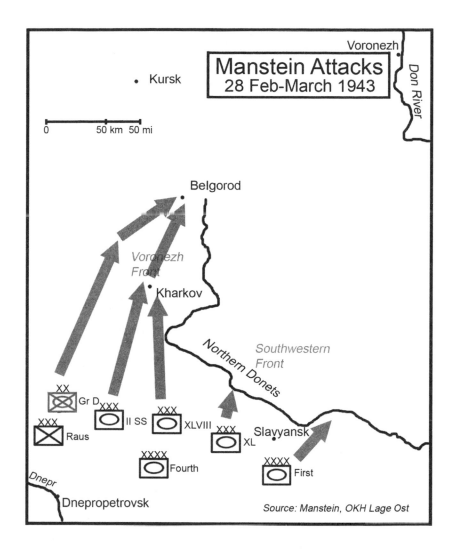

Hitler's first order for the operation, issued on 15 April, specified that "the best commanders" be assigned to the main effort.

German intelligence assessed that the Soviets would attack at the seam between Army Groups Center and South, where the large salient at Kursk happened to be located. *Generaloberst* Kurt Zeitzler, army chief of staff; *Generalfeldmarschalle* Günther von Kluge; and Manstein, the former commanding Army Group Center, argued that in view of Soviet materiel and manpower superiority, the Germans should let the Soviets attack, engage in an elastic defense, and then destroy them in mobile warfare, as Manstein had done at Kharkov. Others argued that the Germans should strike first and eliminate the possibility of a Soviet offensive, a view Hitler decided to back. He was afraid an elastic defense would turn into a rout that could not be stopped.

Once Hitler had spoken, Kursk was the natural objective, being a bite big enough to stall the Soviets and, it appeared, small enough for the Germans to chew. An early attack—initially set for 25 May—would give the Germans the element of surprise and catch the Soviets before they could fully recover. When delays in the delivery of tanks, especially the new Mark V Panther, led to postponement, OKH stressed that the offensive needed take place by mid-June to have any chance of success. The Soviets, meanwhile, were aware of German intentions and were busily building a triple band of fortifications on each shoulder of the salient. When *Generaloberst* Walter Model found out about the construction, he demanded further delay so that his Ninth Army—scheduled to attack the northern shoulder for Army Group Center—could obtain more divisions for the task.

On 20 June, Army Group South identified the Soviet First Tank Army in the area south of Kursk, and *Generaloberst* Hermann Hoth, commanding Fourth Panzer Army, concluded it could only have offensive purposes. In other words, it was very nearly too late for a German attack on Kursk, because it looked as though the Soviets would strike if the Germans did not. A week later, Manstein issued a written appraisal saying every passing day was a gain for the Soviets, and he doubted that he could succeed without more tanks. Hoth nevertheless believed success was still possible.

Hitler met with commanding generals at the corps, army, and army-group levels at his headquarters. The führer emphasized the military and political importance of the operation. Germany would show that its offensive spirit had not been broken! Hitler finally set the date for 5 July.

The plan was simple: Army Group Center was to attack southward with Ninth Army from Malo-arkhangel'sk, while Army Group South's Fourth Panzer Army and Army Detachment Kempf struck northward from Belgorod. They were to meet on the heights north of Kursk, shorten the line facing east, and destroy trapped Soviet forces to the west. The southern group fielded five corps with nine panzer and panzergrenadier divisions and eight infantry divisions. Army Group Center fielded five corps with six panzer and fifteen infantry divisions. The equipment, training, and morale of the units earmarked for the offensive were the highest they would ever be on the eastern front.

On the southern front, Fourth Panzer Army was to make the main thrust with II SS Panzer Corps (redesignated in April and consisting of the 1st

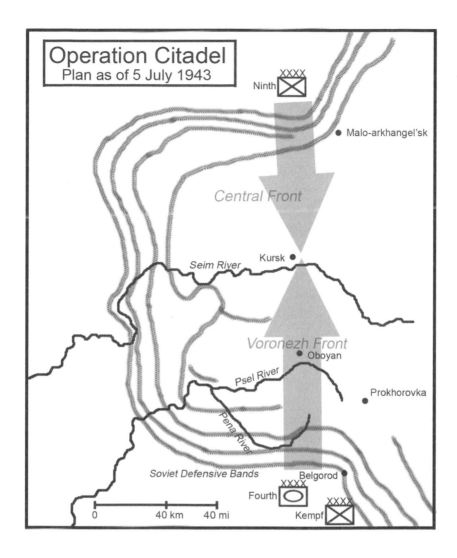

Operation Citadel
Plan as of 5 July 1943

Ninth

Malo-arkhangel'sk

Central Front

Seim River   Kursk

Voronezh Front
Oboyan

Psel River

Prokhorovka

Pena River

Soviet Defensive Bands   Belgorod

Fourth

Kempf

0   40 km   40 mi

Leibstandarte, 2nd *Das Reich*, and 3rd *Totenkopf* SS Panzergrenadier divisions)
on the right and XLVIII Panzer Corps on the left (3rd and 11th Panzer
Divisions; *Grossdeutschland*; the 10th Panzer Brigade—the 51st and 52nd
Panzer Battalions—with 188 factory-fresh Mark V Panthers; and elements of
the 167th and 332nd Infantry Divisions. Army Detachment Kempf (XI and III
Panzer Corps) was to screen the right flank and advance roughly parallel to
the main thrust with its panzers. LII Corps, with two infantry divisions, was
to screen the left flank. Commanders were still fiddling with the plan as late as

27 June, when Fourth Panzer Army decided to commit the 3rd Panzer Division to the first wave to cover *Grossdeutschland*'s left flank, which was a fairly substantial tweak to the original plan.[3]

General der Panzertruppe Otto von Knobelsdorff, who would lead First Army against Patton in Lorraine, still commanded XLVIII Panzer Corps and would be at the center of one of the deciding armored battles of the entire war. *Generalleutnant* Walter Hörnlein, who would command LXXXII Corps in Lorraine, led his famous *Grossdeutschland* Panzergrenadier Division. *Generalleutnant* Hermann Balck, who would battle Patton in Lorraine at the head of Army Group G, just missed being a full member of the brotherhood of Kursk, having commanded the *Grossdeutschland* Division temporarily from April through the last day of June; but he oversaw its transition from an infantry to a panzergrenadier division, and it is fair to say that he prepared the division for the battle.

SS Obergruppenführer Paul Hausser, who would lead Seventh Army in Normandy and Army Group G in the Saar-Palatinate, commanded II SS Panzer Corps. *SS Oberführer* Hermann Priess, who would fight Patton at the head of XIII SS Corps in Lorraine and I SS Panzer Corps in the Ardennes, had assumed command of SS *Totenkopf*.

The divisions of both corps had been pulled out of the line since April and had undergone extensive training, from the commanders down to rankers, in breaching fortified defenses, antitank ditches, and antitank strong points and in coordinating with the Luftwaffe. Knobelsdorff, who had been directed by Hoth to commit the 10th Panzer Brigade, with Hörnlein's *Grossdeutschland* division, at the *Schwerpunkt* of the corps's attack, knew the new Panthers were suffering severe mechanical teething problems and doubted they would live up to Hitler's high hopes. Still, between his own ninety-two tanks (including fourteen Tigers) and the panzer brigade, Hörnlein, on 5 July, controlled nearly as many tanks as all of II SS Panzer Corps, which as of 1 June had 228 panzers, including eighteen Tigers. Priess's *Totenkopf* Division had twenty-six Mark IVs with the long 75mm gun and seven Mark IVs with the short, forty-nine Mark IIIs with long guns, and ten Tigers—still a powerful force.

Ninth Army, on the northern front, was a sprawling affair. XLVII Panzer Corps (2nd, 9th, and 20th Panzer Divisions) was to deliver the main blow. XLVI Panzer Corps, with four infantry divisions, was to protect the right flank of the wedge. XLI Panzer Corps, controlling the 18th Panzer and 10th Panzergrenadier Divisions, as well as two infantry divisions, was to screen the left flank of the wedge. On Ninth Army's left wing, XXIII Corps was to capture Malo-arkhangel'sk, while on the right wing, XX Corps was to hold its position and follow up any Soviet withdrawal.[4]

The northern attack force included three more of Patton's future opposite numbers. Kluge and Model in turn would face Patton as Commander-in-Chief West in France. *Generalmajor* Werner *Freiherr* von und zu Gilsa, who commanded the 216th Infantry Division in XXIII Corps, would have a brush with Patton in Lorraine as the head of LXXXIX Corps.

General Konstantin Rokossovsky's Central Front defended the northern zone of the Kursk salient, while Gen. Nikolai Vatutin's Voronezh Front held the southern zone.[5] The overall balance of forces in the Kursk battle area, according to a statistical study completed for the U.S. Army by the ever-fascinating Dupuy Institute, was:

	Men	Artillery	Tanks and Assault Guns	Aircraft
Germany	900,000	10,000	2,700	2,500
USSR	1,337,000	20,220	3,306	2,650

David Glantz's and Jonathan House's more recent research, using formerly sealed Soviet records, indicates that the Soviet side had somewhat fewer men (1,272,219), but more tanks (4,206) than the Dupuy Institute found.

The tank figures for this single battle represented a more than 50 percent increase over *all* armor on the eastern front in December 1942. Data presented to Hitler in mid-December 1942 indicated that Germany had 1,300 tanks combat ready or under short-term repair, and the Soviets were estimated to have 2,400.[6]

According to the Dupuy study, the German force on the southern front comprised eight infantry divisions, five panzer divisions, and four panzergrenadier divisions. The Soviet force comprised thirty-five rifle divisions, eight tank corps, two mechanized corps, two airborne divisions, and one detachment. The average initial German unit personnel strength was 16,000 per infantry and panzer division, and 21,000 per panzergrenadier division. Average initial Soviet unit personnel strength was 8,500 per rifle division, 9,000 per tank corps, 15,000 per mechanized corps, and 8,500 per airborne division.[7]

Fourth Panzer Army, on which we shall focus, launched preliminary attacks on 4 July and captured observation points on both corps' fronts—points that were necessary for the direction of the artillery preparation the following day. The main attack, on the fifth, by Hausser's II SS Panzer Corps cracked with great difficulty through the first Soviet defensive line at many points, though the Russians held tenaciously to their positions until killed. Hausser was well forward and personally directed his panzers through the first minefields, following on the heels of his advancing infantry.

In the view of *Generalleutnant* Theodor Busse, Army Group South chief of staff, the inadequate number of assigned infantry divisions showed itself at this point. Nevertheless, Priess's *Totenkopf* Division, arrayed on the corps's right wing to protect the flank until an infantry division could move forward, made the most dramatic progress, blasting, with the help of its Tigers, through the first defensive belt; cutting the Belgorod-Oboyan road; and boring into the forward edge of the second belt. At about 0900, the entire corps effort benefited by Hoth's decision to direct all air support to II SS Corps, and the Stukas pounded artillery that had been causing problems. Indeed, Manstein viewed the Luftwaffe as the decisive element in the day's success.

After counterattacking with local reserves on the fifth, the Soviets struck back the following day with entire infantry divisions and tank brigades that had been held just behind the front.[8]

II SS Panzer Corps bore through the second belt of Soviet defenses on the sixth against what was, in light of the preceding day's gains, unexpectedly stiff resistance. Hausser again placed himself forward, just behind the assault troops, to keep the attack moving. Priess's division fought off an attack by II Tank Corps, with some 130 tanks, while the other two SS divisions continued to eradicate bunker after bunker full of determined Soviet soldiers. Army Detachment Kempf, to the right, had not made as much progress as planned, however, and the *Totenkopf* Division on 7–8 July became embroiled in defensive fighting against repeated attacks from the flank. The Luftwaffe virtually destroyed the II Guards Tank Corps as it rolled toward Priess on the eighth, which should have given him a real appreciation for the power of the air arm against armor in the open. Relieved by an infantry division, Priess brought his division into line on the corps's left on 9 July.

Knobelsdorff's XLVIII Panzer Corps battled thunderstorms on 4 July and on the fifth had to cross a seemingly bottomless sea of mud along a rain-swollen and heavily mined creek, under troublesome flanking fire and with little air support (aircraft having been concentrated that day on helping II SS Panzer Corps). Knobelsdorff, as usual, was well forward, visiting first the 3rd Panzer Division, then *Grossdeutschland*, and then the 11th Panzer Division.

Steven Newton, whose translations of several German sources constitute an important basis for this chapter, criticized Hörnlein for planning his attack with "tactical skills more closely resembling those of Sepp Dietrich than those of Hermann Balck." Hörnlein's earlier bull-charge tactics at Rzhev certainly established a precedent, though in this case, Hörnlein was not wholly responsible. Hörnlein was ordered to conduct a frontal assault; bad luck dictated that the commander of the assault battalion at the *Schwerpunkt* would be wounded the day before, and a company commander would lead the attack; and a Tiger broke down in the middle of the stream crossing and blocked the advance of the panzer regiment. The attack at the *Schwerpunkt*, moreover, occurred without tank support, possibly because of the incompetence of the 10th Panzer Brigade commanding officer (subsequently suspended by Knobelsdorff), though Knobelsdorff's account says he held his panzers back until *Grossdeutschland*'s own panzer regiment had crossed the water obstacle.

In addition, the attack by Hörnlein's second regiment was a textbook example, according to Newton.

Hörnlein's engineers simply could not build a bridge that would stay in place, and the planned mass tank attack by *Grossdeutschland* never did come off.

Still, Knobelsdorff broke through the first belt of Soviet defenses by 0700, according to the Fourth Panzer Army *Kriegstagebuch*. He finally got all his panzers across by evening. On 6 July, *Grossdeutschland*'s panzer regiment reported that it had penetrated the second belt at one spot. Finally, thought Knobelsdorff, the route north was free! Moreover, the Panthers were finally forward and doing some fighting. Knobelsdorff visited Hörnlein's command post, only to find the report was false and the division was still engaged in hard fighting in the middle of the defenses. Belatedly, at 2100 hours, the panzer regiment—now in control of the Panthers, too—really did break through the belt. But the Panthers were breaking down right and left.

The following day, Knobelsdorff ordered *Grossdeutschland* and the 11th Panzer Divisions to attack the Soviet flank forces hitting II SS Panzer Corps from Oboyan and then to advance in close parallel to the SS Panzer Corps. *Grossdeutschland* surged forward, but the 11th Panzer Division was still fighting its way free of the second belt and was under heavy air attacks. The 3rd Panzer Division, on the left, failed to cross the Pena because of swampy terrain and heavy enemy fire. Knobelsdorff, demonstrating his flexibility, decided to pass it forward behind *Grossdeutschland*.

Hoth told Knobelsdorff that he should expect a major fight with the Soviet tank reserves in the next few days. Indeed, Fourth Panzer Army's advance provoked furious counterattacks by the First Guards Tank Army, including II Guards and V "Stalingrad" Tank Corps, as well as by the lead elements of the fresh VI Guards Tank Corps. Air reconnaissance had failed to detect the Soviet concentration, which came as a surprise. "Thus came the panzer battle sooner than we had expected," Fourth Panzer Army recorded.

Hoth told Knobelsdorff he intended to smash the First Guards Tank Army from both its flanks. The aim was not to push the Soviet forces back, but to pin them and destroy them! Knobelsdorff got the upper hand that day and thrashed the Soviet tanks on his front, but neither corps gained noteworthy ground. Hörnlein, who had started with 300 panzers, now had only 80 combat ready, in large part because the Panthers were clogging his maintenance system with breakdowns. "It is to be hoped," recorded Knobelsdorff's Ia, "that tomorrow's envelopment succeeds, that after the annihilation of his panzer forces we push forward again, and that he [the enemy] has no stronger reserves north of the Psel."

General der Infanterie Friedrich Fangohr, Fourth Panzer Army's chief of staff, later recalled that, "7 July marked a complete victory for General Knobelsdorff's men. They had not only routed Soviet tank forces in a meeting engagement but—more critical from the overall perspective of the offensive—had succeeded in slogging their way close enough to Oboyan to bring the Psel River crossing, the last major barrier before Kursk, under artillery fire."

That same day, Hausser showed his nerves of steel. Elements of three Soviet tank brigades deeply penetrated the lines of *Das Reich* on his right wing, but Hausser fearlessly pressed ahead with a panzer attack on his left. Hausser personally went to the area of the Soviet breakthroughs and rallied his troops to destroy the enemy tanks in close-quarters battle.

Hoth's planned double envelopment of the Soviet tank forces on the eighth did not come off. XLVIII Panzer Corps's left flank was open and vulnerable, and when word reached Knobelsdorff that the main body of Soviet tanks was about to attack him from the north and northeast, *Grossdeutschland* and the 11th Panzer Divisions had to stop and throw out defensive screens. The corps held its line, just barely, under the combined assault of VI Guards Tank and III Mechanized Corps. The II SS Panzer Corps's maneuver to hit the Soviet left flank with the 1st and 2nd SS Panzergrenadier Divisions pushed even more Soviet forces against Knobelsdorff's front, but his divisions were able to destroy them. II SS Panzer Corps claimed it had been able to destroy some 250 Soviet tanks because they attacked in penny packets, which allowed the Germans to engage in mobile defense. Fourth Panzer Army reckoned actual tank kills as 95 opposite XLVIII Panzer Corps and 100 opposite II SS Panzer Corps.

On the northern face, meanwhile, Soviet counterattacks had stopped Model's Ninth Army by 9 July. On the 11th, the Soviets attacked Ninth Army's neighbor, Second Panzer Army, with such force at Orel that Model had to divert resources to stave off a collapse. The pincer operation had only one jaw left.

On the southern face, Soviet resistance suddenly eased, and air reconnaissance and reports from ground troops indicated the Soviets were falling back to the north. XLVIII Panzer Corps, finally supported again by the Luftwaffe, rolled ahead and reckoned that *Grossdeutschland* that day destroyed sixty-six enemy tanks and the 11th Panzer Division thirty-five, at virtually no cost to themselves. The lead battalion of Priess's *Totenkopf* Division cleared the last bunkers south of the Psel and forded the river. But Fourth Panzer Army was only halfway to Kursk.

On 10 July, II SS Panzer Corps readied to attack Soviet forces at Prokhorovka, while XLVIII Panzer Corps fought to clear a bend west of the Psel River. Even before Operation Citadel began, Hoth expected that the Soviets would throw their strategic reserve, including several tank corps, against his right flank when he reached Prokhorovka and while Fourth Panzer Army crossed the Psel and was unable to maneuver freely. Hoth's plans, therefore, included a fight with the Soviet tank reserves on terrain of his own choosing. Constant tank battles raged on Knobelsdorff's front, and the panzers won every engagement. *Grossdeutschland* alone claimed to have destroyed forty-nine Soviet tanks. Hausser's II SS Panzer Corps also fought large Soviet forces near Prokhorovka, which relieved some of the pressure on Knobelsdorff's flank. Hausser toured the fighting troops along the hard-pressed front, and at no point did the SS line give way.

Manstein met with Kempf and Hoth on 11 July and asked their advice on whether to discontinue the attack in light of Ninth Army's halt on the ninth. Kempf wanted to stop, but Hoth wanted to continue to the Psel River and destroy as many Soviet divisions on the south bank as possible. Manstein ultimately agreed with Hoth.

That day, *Totenkopf* tried but failed to expand its bridgehead across the Psel River, while Knobelsdorff's corps fought off more powerful counterattacks—the X Tank Corps had appeared on its front—and encircled and destroyed 100 Soviet tanks. The Fifth Guards Tank Army, the strategic Soviet tank reserve in the south, arrived in Prokhorovka, and the huge battle Hoth had foreseen erupted.

The Soviet attacks were so strong on 12 and 13 July that Fourth Panzer Army could only just hold its own. Fourth Panzer Army assessed that it was hit by at least parts of nine tank and mechanized corps and multiple rifle divisions. Waves of tanks with infantry perched on the deck—the fresh XVIII and XXIX Tank Corps—attacked Hausser's divisions, which reported to Fourth Panzer Army that it had destroyed some 120 Soviet tanks on the twelfth. By most accounts, the Soviets finally employed their armor en masse, and a furious and confused tank battle—the largest in history—raged across Hausser's front. Low German losses, however, strongly suggest that German gunners picked off tens of tanks charging headlong toward them rather than engaging in a cavalry-style, swirling engagement. Knobelsdorff, on his front, aggressively followed up each withdrawal of repulsed Soviet tank forces to strengthen his defensive positions, but he had to direct the weight of Hörnlein's division and the 3rd Panzer Division to the west, rather than the north, to deal with a Soviet breakthrough in the zone of the 332nd Infantry Division, which had taken charge of the corps's flank security.

The strain was beginning to show among commanders in II SS Corps. Hausser ordered Priess to attack eastward with his armor against the Soviets at Prokhorovka on 13 July. The panzers advanced as far as the road they were to use, but Priess evidently decided on his own to ignore the order and turn his panzers southwest to deal with a tank attack against his own lines. Hoth demanded to know what Hausser had to show that day for being the *Schwerpunkt* of the army's attack, and Hausser retorted with a list of explanations, including heavy losses among the infantry. When Hoth demanded casualty figures, Hausser responded that given the difficulties at the front, he was not up to date on personnel issues.

The drive northward had, in effect, stopped. Rain slowed movement everywhere, and Hoth worried that he would not be able to restore momentum. But the tank attacks from the northeast had been replaced by infantry attacks, and it seemed possible that the enemy had pulled back his armored reserve.

According to Manstein, Hitler summoned Manstein and Kluge to his headquarters on the thirteenth and told them that the Allies had landed on Sicily, the Italians were not fighting, and the island was likely to be lost. Because the next step would probably be an invasion of Italy or the Balkans, the führer had decided to stop Citadel in order to provide divisions to strengthen his armies in those areas. Kluge said Ninth Army was stuck and supported abandoning the effort. Manstein argued that the issue in Fourth Panzer Army's zone was still open and that stopping would mean throwing away a victory.

On 14 July, Hoth did reclaim the initiative, and Knobelsdorff's left wing seized high ground overlooking the Psel west of Oboyan. XLVIII Panzer Corps now faced human waves of infantry, which mortars and corps artillery mowed down. Losses were light. Morale in the corps was high. On the fifteenth, the 2nd SS Panzergrenadier Division punched through Soviet defenses and found freedom to maneuver. Army Detachment Kempf finally linked with II SS Corps and enveloped the Soviet forces that had stood between them. It appeared that Soviet resistance had been smashed, and Fourth Panzer Army believed itself to be on the brink of a major victory.

But the situation in Army Group Center had continued to deteriorate, forcing a decision to break off Army Group South's attack in order to transfer forces to the north. Fourth Panzer Army received word that it was to halt offensive operations northward on the fifteenth. The Soviets, on the seventeenth, added to the pressure to remove divisions from the Kursk battlefield by attacking Army Group South's Sixth Army. Operation Citadel was over.[9]

The outcome was very much like the one Patton would face in mid-December 1944 in Lorraine. After more than a month of bloody fighting, he thought his next attack would carry him to the Rhine. But the German stroke against U.S. First Army in the Ardennes forced a halt to his operations, and he had to send divisions to help.

The battle on the southern face of the salient had been extremely intensive, and the Germans had inflicted disproportionate losses on the enemy. According to the Dupuy study data, from 5 to 18 July, an average of 92 percent of the German manpower was in contact with enemy forces, versus an average 67 percent for the Soviets. Daily Soviet casualties were much higher than German. Relative to initial on-hand personnel, cumulative casualties amounted to 23 percent of the Soviet force and 12 percent of the German force. The largest differences were in killed in action and captured/missing in action (CMIA). Overall, the Soviets lost nearly five men killed for every German killed and twenty-four CMIA for every German CMIA. The fraction of force wounded was similar for both combatants. The number of German tanks available on 18 July was about half the starting number, while numbers of artillery and other weapons were about the same. Soviet tank strength, by contrast, was down by 60 percent and infantry support weapons by a third.[10]

Nevertheless, *General der Infanterie* Busse, in his summary of Citadel, observed that the battle consumed most of Germany's reserves on the eastern front, but remarkably not its troops' morale. He concluded, "Operation Citadel did not produce the results desired by Hitler. The battle neither denied the Soviets a base of operations around Kursk nor destroyed sizable enemy forces, nor even eliminated the *Stavka*'s [Soviet high command] intention to conduct a major offensive in 1943."[11]

Again, the situation was analogous to the one in Lorraine in autumn of 1944, which helped determine whether Hitler would be able to launch a major offensive in December. The German failure in the conflagration at Kursk was the fight the brotherhood of commanders would remember when they considered who won in Lorraine. So might we all.

Hörnlein would be in Lorraine in part because Hoth had concluded that while Hörnlein was a brave commander worshipped by his troops, his complete lack of schooling in panzer operations made him unsuitable to continue at the head of *Grossdeutschland*. Hörnlein, Hoth believed, did not grasp how to use all the parts of his division in mobile offensive war. The division needed a real panzer officer, not a man trained as an infantryman, and such a commander would produce better results with lower losses. Hörnlein would be kicked upstairs to command an infantry corps.[12]

EPILOGUE

Kurt von der Chevallerie was not at Kursk, but he and some of Patton's other future enemies were caught up in the aftermath. After the winter battle at Velikiye Luki, Chevallerie received the Oak Leaves to his Knight's Cross for his corps's further defensive achievements at Kiev in November 1943.[13] LIX Corps by then was part of Fourth Panzer Army and was falling back north of Kiev, where the 1st Ukrainian Front pressed its part of a broad-front Soviet offensive that had forced the German line westward along most of the eastern front following the Battle of Kursk.

The 1st Ukrainian Front—with thirty infantry divisions, twenty-four tank brigades, and ten motorized brigades—burst out of the Liutezh bridgehead on the west bank of the Dniepr on 3 November and captured Kiev three days later. Chevallerie pulled his corps back, from one improvised defensive line to another. His LIX Corps—the equivalent of a mere two divisions—held a fifty-mile front, "no longer a main line of resistance, but a security line," noted the corps's *Kriegstagebuch*. His flanks hung loose, and he faced eleven or twelve Soviet infantry divisions and a few tanks. Fortunately, he at least had assault guns to support his infantry and blast the Soviet armor. Drop behind the next river and man the bank with strong points, or hold a bridgehead for a bit longer, had been the drill. When the enemy cracked his thin line, Chevallerie pulled back again, always in good order. He traded territory for survival. His instructions to his officers were, "Reconnoiter, fight, give clear orders, and report!"

On 12 November, he ordered his corps to hold the current line for a while, to give the men a chance to rest, but also to bare his teeth and show the enemy that his strength was not spent. But within two days, the Soviets created several holes, and the withdrawal began again. At Korosten, Chevallerie stopped backpedaling. Ammunition and a security division arrived, and when Army Group Center said he had to hold Korosten under all circumstances, he did just that, his men battling the Soviets to a standstill amid the burning buildings over several days beginning 16 November. The Soviets claimed the city taken, and history has recorded that claim as fact. But it was not so. Chavallerie's counterattacks destroyed every Soviet breakthrough, and the enemy suffered bloody losses. The Soviets nevertheless were able to surround Chevallerie's command in the city. The OKW *Kriegstagebuch* records the continuing battle between Chevallerie's men and the Soviets in Korosten on 19 November.

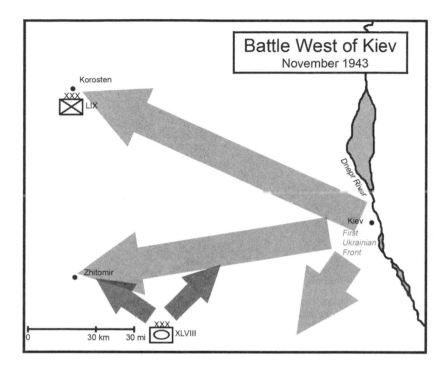

Fortunately, newly promoted *General der Panzertruppe* Hermann Balck had just taken command of XLVIII Panzer Corps from Otto von Knobelsdorff, and the corps had been ordered to gather strong panzer forces south of the Kiev salient to attack the long left flank of the 1st Ukrainian Front. The Soviets, if not stopped, could swing south and cut the lines of communication of Army Groups South and A; Manstein viewed this as the greatest danger facing the southern wing of the front and persuaded Hitler to let him commit fresh panzer divisions the führer had intended to use in the Dniepr bend. Balck wanted to boldly drive straight to Kiev, but *General der Panzertruppe* Erhard Raus, commanding Army Group South's Fourth Panzer Army, thought that goal overly ambitious and ordered the corps to first recapture Zhitomir, which lies south of Korosten.

The corps attacked on 15 November with future Patton enemy *Generalleutnant* Walter Krüger's 1st Panzer and the 1st SS Panzer Divisions in the center; *Generalmajor* Hasso von Manteuffel's 7th Panzer Division and the 68th Infantry Division on the left; and the 2nd SS and 25th Panzer Divisions guarding the right flank. The attack reached Zhitomir on the eighteenth, and Manteuffel, on foot, led six panzers and a hundred grenadiers through the night to surprise the Zhitomir headquarters and capture the city. The Soviets had to concentrate to deal with this new threat, which relieved the pressure at Korosten. Chevallerie's men enjoyed their first peaceful days in many long weeks. Meanwhile, a substantial tank battle ensued between XLVIII Panzer Corps and the V and VIII Guards Tank corps, and Balck won that battle just before a thaw on the twenty-sixth turned the earth to mud and temporarily ended the fighting.[14]

Chevallerie's fight had well prepared him for a day when he would have to stage a retreat across France against overwhelming odds. Balck, on a grander scale than on the Chir River, and Manteuffel, for the first time, each had been able to stop a vastly superior and onrushing enemy by attacking his extended flank. Their experience, too, would become relevant in France.

*

EIGHT

Sicily: Empty Glory

"WELL, MY FÜHRER," said *Sonderführer* von Neurath, a civilian expert with temporary military rank who had just returned from Italy, "the Italians say 'when the war is over'—that's a very frequent expression; at another moment they say, 'You never know what is going to happen.'"

Hitler listened intently, as did Keitel, Rommel, and members of the headquarters staff. It was the afternoon of 20 May 1943, and a stenographer tapped quietly away, recording the conversation for posterity.

"The German troops in Sicily have undoubtedly become pretty unpopular. It's easy to see why; the Sicilians consider that we have brought the war to their country and that we've snapped up more or less everything they have. Now we're going to be the reason for the arrival of the English which however—and I must emphasize this—the Sicilian peasant would be quite pleased about. . . . Once they arrive, it's the end of the war."[1]

A week after the Axis collapse in Tunisia, men at *Führerhauptquartier* were worried that the British were going to invade Sicily. The Americans were an afterthought.

A few moments later, Rommel spoke. "Would it be possible, my führer, for the Italians to send more troops to Sicily and hold it instead of us?"

"Anything's possible," Hitler replied, "The question is whether they *want* to defend it. What worries me is that it can't be defended. . . ."[2]

*

Siegfried Westphal, who by June 1943 had been promoted to *Generalmajor* and, after a stint as German section chief at Commando Supremo, been named chief of staff to *OB Süd* Kesselring, wrote:

> What was the condition of the Italian armed forces in the early part of 1943? The Army had lost its best troops in Africa and Russia. Of what remained, more than thirty divisions were tied down in Greece, Yugoslavia, and Southern France. Only twenty serviceable divisions were left for the defense of the motherland, and of these, eight were stationed in Sicily, Sardinia, and Corsica. . . . One thing was quite certain: that the Italian troops would not be able to stand up unaided to the further onslaught of the enemy. German help would be necessary. . . . As early as the summer of 1943, therefore, eight high-grade German divisions were moved into the Italian theater.[3]

Some of these divisions, however, were short of equipment, insufficiently trained, and not fit for battle. The formations that OKW had intended to form the mobile reserve for the Mediterranean theater were on the eastern front, waiting to participate in Operation Citadel at Kursk.[4]

The Axis command structure on Sicily was complex. Italy's Commando Supremo in theory held sway in all areas that were under Italian sovereignty, but in practice could make decisions regarding large-sized German formations only with the agreement of Kesselring. Count Cavallero, the chief of Commando Supremo, always tried to play a mediating role between Kesselring and the Italian chief of defense, Gen. Vittorio Ambrosio. Kesselring found that Mussolini almost always supported him, but that by spring 1943, his influence was fading.[5]

Italian military intelligence during the first half of 1943 indicates that the Commando Supremo was not at all interested in the whereabouts of Allied generals or in establishing where the Allies would attack first in the Mediterranean. So does a Commando Supremo study of a possible Allied invasion of Sicily produced in June. The Italians looked to strategic statements by Churchill and Roosevelt, rumors scrounged in capitals around Europe and elsewhere, troop dispositions, and logical arguments (Sicily would be too costly an objective, argued one attaché). In the end, Commando Supremo did not appear to know for certain where the Allied invasion would come.[6]

Generalfeldmarschall Albert Kesselring, however, had a good idea, and the Germans were keeping track of Allied generals. *OB Süd*, on 30 June, signaled OKW that one should expect simultaneous landings on Sicily and Sardinia in the near future. The Americans could field ten divisions and the British eight divisions, he estimated, and their immense shipping capacity would permit the

Allies to supply them all.[7] On 21 May, Kesselring's intelligence staff had received a report that Patton supposedly had been named the commander of American ground forces in the western Mediterranean. Ten days later, the existence of his headquarters had been confirmed. The intelligence staff was also keeping tabs on many other American, British, and French generals, including Montgomery and Mark Clark, commanding Fifth Army, and Patton was not mentioned again.[8]

Defending the island of Sicily posed real problems. There were 1,115 kilometers (some 700 miles) of coastline and numerous suitable landing areas, including Marsala, Mazara del Vallo, Sciacca, Porte Empedoele, the Gulf of Gela, Pozzallo, the Gulf of Catania, the Gulf of Milazzo, Termini Imerese, the Gulf of Castellammare (for an attack on Palermo), and Trapani.[9] In early July, *Generale d'Armata* (General of the Army) Alfredo Guzzoni and Kesselring agreed that an assault on the south coast, particularly the eastern part, was most likely. Kesselring did not give much importance to the western part of the island, though he thought the Allies might take advantage of the weakness of Axis defenses there to conduct a landing and advance on Palermo.[10]

Guzzoni commanded both the Italian Sixth Army and the island of Sicily. After his assignment in Albania, Guzzoni had commanded Fourth Army when it occupied southern France in 1940, and he had then become deputy chief of staff of the army. He had been promoted to *generale di armata* in 1941 and taken command of Sixth Army in June 1943. Kesselring considered Guzzoni a weak leader, though a responsible commander.[11] Nevertheless, Guzzoni exercised full authority over German formations on the island, which were subordinated to a German liaison staff at Sixth Army for administrative purposes only. Kesselring had no direct authority over the German units and had to exert influence through Commando Supremo.[12]

Two Italian corps defended the island, *Generale di Corpo D'Armata* (Lt. Gen.) Mario Arisio's XII Corps in the west and *Generale di Corpo D'Armata* Carlo Rossi's XVI Corps in the east. XII Corps included General Romano's 28th Aosta Division and *Generale di Divisione* (Maj. Gen.) Francesco Scotti's 26th Assietta Infantry Division. XVI Corps included *Generale di Divisione* Gotti Porcinari's 54th Napoli Infantry Division. Guzzoni directly controlled the mechanized Livorno Division. All divisions were mobile, were rated "efficient," and were at full strength. Several static coastal-defense divisions and brigades, most of them subordinated to XII Corps, occupied the shoreline. (These are not displayed on the map because they were irrelevant to the battle.)[13]

Kesselring—responsible for German forces in southern Italy, while *Generalfeldmarschall* Erwin Rommel commanded those in the north—had

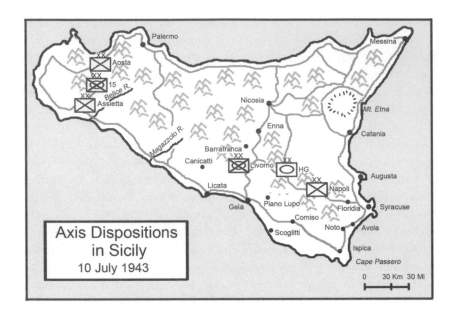

Axis Dispositions
in Sicily
10 July 1943

buttressed the Italians with the Hermann Göring Panzer Division assigned to
XII Corps and the 15th Panzergrenadier Division attached to XVI Corps, though
he would change his mind about their deployments repeatedly. Guzzoni, not the
corps commanders, exercised direct authority over the German divisions. At
Kesselring's insistence, the two German divisions were positioned close to likely
landing areas on the west and south coasts, so that they could counterattack
quickly to drive invaders back into the sea. Guzzoni had wanted to keep them
together as a powerful reserve in the east. The Germans instead were imbedded
among the Italian divisions to such an extent that Kesselring thought it would
encourage the Italians to fight.[14]

Kesselring, who had known some fine commanders in North Africa, considered the German division commanding generals on Sicily to be above average.[15]

The 15th Panzergrenadier Division, commanded by *Generalleutnant*
Eberhard Rodt and originally called the Sicily Division, was fully trained and
intimately familiar with Sicily's terrain.[16] The division had three panzergrenadier regiments, the 104th, 115th, and 129th, each consisting of three battalions,
and the 215th Panzer Battalion. It was rich in artillery, with one self-propelled
battalion, a light and a heavy field-artillery battalion, and one battalion of
massive 170mm guns. However, its training was inadequate, as were its motor
vehicles. At the insistence of Hermann Göring and Kesselring, most of the

division shifted to the western part of the island on 9 July, while the Hermann Göring Division deployed south of Mount Etna in the east with one regiment of the 15th Division and a Tiger company recently transferred from the 215th Panzer Battalion.[17]

The Hermann Göring Panzer Division, which had responsibility for the area where the Americans were going to land, would earn a fearsome reputation, but as of early July 1943, the division was green, as few of its soldiers who had fought in Africa had been rescued. It had just organized as a panzer division and had few seasoned tank officers. Most of the division's components first got to know one another on Sicily, and there had been little combined-arms training. Division commander Generalmajor Paul Conrath had experience as the Hermann Göring Regiment's commander and, with his regiment, had fought beside panzer divisions in France and Russia early in the war. The division, at full strength in terms of manpower and outfitted with about thirty-five Panzer IIIs and Panzer IVs, had attached to it the company of Army Tiger tanks.[18]

The division's personnel would not be much more familiar with the home field than the visitors. The bulk of the division had only arrived in Sicily in the last ten days of June, and elements of a panzer and a panzergrenadier battalion were still in transit.[19]

Kesselring told commanders in May that the coast was to be the main line of resistance, which meant that mobile reserves would have to attack right away. Guzzoni, however, as of June, planned to abandon the coast and fight in the mountains.[20] Commando Supremo viewed the Hermann Göring Division as the key to its initial defense against an Allied landing because that division could move speedily to invest a beachhead. This view presumed that the division could be properly placed near the most likely landing area. It is noteworthy that, as of June, Commando Supremo did not conceive of the division eradicating a beachhead.[21] The Germans, however, expected the counterstroke to destroy the landing force.[22]

In either case, the Axis formations were going to attempt, for the first time, to defend against a major seaborne assault. This attempt would replicate in the real world the task that had been faced by Maj. Gen. Oscar Griswold's IV Corps— including Patton's 2nd Armored Division—in the Carolina maneuvers. Then, a mechanized force had failed to eradicate or contain a strong bridgehead/beachhead.

Kesselring and Guzzoni met in early July with all unit commanders to lay down plans to react to any landing contingency. Kesselring drummed into their heads one point: "It makes no difference whether or not you get orders from the Italian army at Enna. You must go into immediate action against the enemy the moment you ascertain the objective of the invasion fleet."

Conrath, commanding the Hermann Göring Division, replied in a growl, "If you mean go for them, field marshal, then I'm your man." Still, Conrath judged that he received no specific orders, and his coordination with the Italian coastal defenses and the Livorno and Napoli Divisions was poor. Conrath took matters into his own hands and stationed panzer reconnaissance troops along the southern coast from Gela to Augusta. Kesselring returned to Italy feeling fairly confident.[23]

Patton and the other Allied generals, however, would be attacking an island that most German commanders fully expected they would have to give up. Hitler was not the only one with this expectation. Keitel told *Generalleutnant* Fridolin von Senger und Etterlin, who in late June was headed to Sicily as the liaison officer to Italian Sixth Army and nominal "commander" of German forces on the island, that defense of the island was "hopeless." Westphal told him privately that in the event of a major Allied landing, he would do best by moving his troops to the Italian mainland.[24]

THE FIRST INVASION

The Axis powers had never before had to defend against an invasion. The war in North Africa had been one between colonial powers, and it was already under way when Hitler injected a relatively modest German force into it. Only the French had confronted Operation Torch. This, the first major test in the West, was to take place, in the Allies' eyes, on the periphery of enemy territorry. For the Axis, North Africa had been the periphery, and now the enemy was attacking the Italian homeland. The upcoming battle would, thus, pit the German panzers against an Allied amphibious invasion for the first time.

The Allies in January had decided to follow up the victory in North Africa by invading Sicily in the hope of driving Italy out of the war, which would force the Germans to occupy Italy and pick up Italian military commitments in the Balkans. President Roosevelt also wanted to keep American troops active in the European war during the remainder of 1943 to placate Stalin. The plan for Operation Husky ultimately called for two corps to land under the British Eighth Army on the southeastern corner of the island. The U.S. Seventh Army's II Corps, under Lt. Gen. Omar Bradley, controlled the 1st and 45th Infantry Divisions and assaulted beaches somewhat farther west, around Gela. Patton, who commanded Seventh Army, retained personal control over the 3rd Infantry Division, which landed on the left at Licata. The landings on 10 July 1943 constituted the largest amphibious assault of the war and put seven divisions ashore.

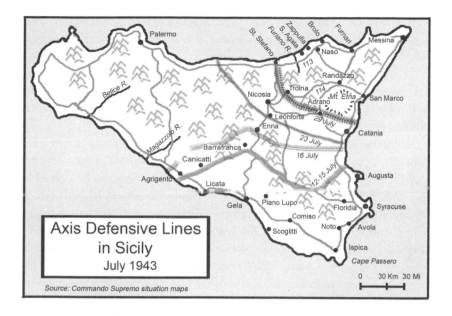

Axis Defensive Lines in Sicily
July 1943

Source: Commando Supremo situation maps

0   30 Km   30 Mi

Once on land, Montgomery's Eighth Army was to push up the east coast to capture the main objective, Messina. Seventh Army was to advance on its left, its mission being to protect Montgomery's flank. Patton had no more specific objective.[25]

On 27 June, Kesselring's intelligence staff had warned that all Allied divisions expected to participate in landing operations were moving into assembly areas.[26] In the wee hours of 9 July, the Axis began tracking a fleet that was on a course from Malta to Sicily. Hitler responded to the news by ordering that the 1st *Fallschirmjäger Division* (Airborne Division) prepare immediately to move by air to Sicily.[27] By 1630 hours, air patrols had spotted between 150 and 180 landing-craft tanks (LCTs) plowing through the sea from North Africa. Naval bombardment of Syracuse commenced at 2230 that night, and one by one, reports came in overnight of incoming shells or air attacks— Taormina (0330), Trapani (0400), Augusta (0700). From 0200 hours, the first landings were reported along an arc of coastline from Licata in the west to Capo Passero and then Augusta. Parachute landings also occurred near Gela and other towns. Air reconnaissance confirmed the worst as the sky lightened enough for the pilots to see: 300 ships off Augusta and Cape Passero, as many as 400 off Licata.[28]

In the American zone, the naval bombardment began only fifteen minutes before the assault boats reached the sand because Patton wanted to achieve tactical surprise.[29] Indeed, even though the Italian coastal defenses had an hour's warning because of airborne drops inland, the 1st and 3rd Infantry Divisions rolled ashore against virtually no opposition.

The 45th Division landed three regiments abreast as destroyers provided the close support against targets on the beach. Resistance on the beaches in the 45th Division's zone ranged from spirited in the 180th Infantry's area to nothing elsewhere.

Conrath's scout cars near the south coast informed him immediately that the Americans were coming to shore at Gela. Conrath, good to his promise, did not wait for orders but launched a counterattack with his division and the attached *Kampfgruppe* Schmalz. Conrath attacked on his right at Gela with his panzer regiment, reconnaissance battalion, and two battalions of artillery, and on his left with a panzergrenadier regiment, the Tiger company, and a battalion of artillery. Guzzoni committed the Livorno Division to the attack, as well. Conrath sent *Kampfgruppe* Schmalz toward the British landing beaches. Fortunately for the Americans, German sources say that only the leading elements of the attacking force were able to reach the beachhead on D-day.[30]

That was bad enough, because Conrath was able to exploit a decision that must be pinned on George Patton. Except for the 3rd Infantry Division, Patton had assigned his assault force grossly inadequate tank support, particularly in light of his foreknowledge about the presence of the Herman Göring and 15th Panzergrenadier Divisions. Tank destroyers had gotten a bad reputation in North Africa with some senior officers, including Patton. Seventh Army had assigned no tank-destroyer battalions to the Sicily operation, which meant that Patton was relying on tanks to fight panzers in situations of maneuver.

At Gela, one column of the Italian Mobile Group E and a battalion of the Livorno Division attacked two Ranger battalions, which were attached to the 1st Infantry Division and had no armor support. The Axis for the first time experienced the crushing power of naval gunnery, which broke up two groups consisting of French-built Renault R-35 tanks and riflemen. Ten tanks managed to penetrate Gela, but several fell prey to TNT blocks, hand grenades, and bazookas, and the surviving vehicles withdrew.[31]

At Piano Lupo crossroads, 82nd Airborne Division paratroopers and the first advancing GIs from the 1st Division's 16th Infantry needed naval gunfire to beat back first Italian tanks and then much of the Hermann Göring Panzer Division. A second column of Mobile Group E, at about 0900, ran into the paratroopers and the Big Red One, 1st Division, near Piano Lupo and might have pushed through the lightly armed troops but for naval gunnery that knocked out several tanks and convinced the Italians to pull back. An assault at 1400 by much of Conrath's panzer regiment also ground to a stop under a battering by five- and six-inch naval shells.[32]

It is unclear how far behind the 45th Division's assault wave the 753rd Tank Battalion landed (the tank battalion's records for Husky are missing), but it went ashore with the 157th Infantry. As of midnight on D-day, the division G-3 was unaware of any action involving the tanks, and the tanks' presence is first reflected in 45th Division message traffic about combat operations on D plus 1.[33]

Once the 45th Division's regiments moved toward their objectives inland, a combat group from the Hermann Göring Panzer Division—consisting of Mark IVs and fearsome Mark VI Tigers, infantry, and artillery—badly mauled the 1st Battalion, 180th Infantry, pushed the regiment back, and created a potentially dangerous gap between it and the 179th Infantry, which was advancing on the Comiso airfield. When Conrath's green troops ran into the II Corps reserve—the 3rd Battalion of the 180th Infantry—however, they panicked, broke, and ran.[34]

The Axis understanding of the forces arrayed against Guzzoni had improved by 11 July. The American II Corps had been identified at Licata-Gela and British 13 Corps at Cape Passero–Augusta, and situation maps indicate Axis leaders knew Patton and Montgomery were in command of their respective national forces.[35] The struggle in the American sector looked hopeful to Commando Supremo on 11 July. A combat group had stopped the American advance at Licata, and counterattacking troops had regained some ground. The garrison at Gela airfield was putting up stiff resistance, and the bulk of the Livorno Division had arrived in the area. The Hermann Göring Division was three miles east of Gela. Still, Commando Supremo conceded, the enemy had taken Vittoria, just west of Comiso, and Scoglitti. (Conrath had a more dire view: to him, the battle for Sicily had already been lost because the Italians were fighting so poorly, and his main concern was to prevent his flanks from being enveloped.)

In the British sector, however, towns were falling like dominoes—Syracuse, Floridia, Avola, Noto. Italian troops in Ispica were still resisting, and the Napoli Division and *Kampfgruppe* Körner were trying to establish a line outside Syracuse. From the German perspective, however, the Napoli Division was simply disintegrating.[36]

Guzzoni, late on 10 July, had ordered the Hermann Göring and Livorno Divisions to conduct a coordinated attack against the Americans at Gela. Conrath met *Generale di Divisione* Domenico Chirieleison, commanding general of the Livorno Division, at XVI Corps headquarters, where they received their orders.

The German division was to attack from the northeast in three columns, while the Italian division struck from the northwest in three columns.

Conrath and Chirieleison nearly became the first and only commanders to deliver Patton a good whipping with an attacking force. Early on the eleventh, the Hermann Göring Division thrust forward, paced on its right flank by a column of the Livorno Division. German and Italian aircraft bombed the beachhead and ships off shore—the one time an enemy would fight Patton with one of the advantages he usually enjoyed. Conrath personally commanded the force driving down the road through Piano Lupo, and the panzers rolled through and around elements of the 16th Infantry Regiment to the Gela plain. Conrath ordered most of his panzer regiment to cross the plain to the beaches, and Chirieleison threw most of the Livorno Division at the same objectives.

Chirieleison's troops nearly reached Patton, who had joined a group of Rangers on the 1st Infantry Division front.[37] Little did the Italians know that Patton was watching them from a house on the edge of Gela. Patton ordered a naval ensign, who happened to be nearby, to place some fleet fire on the enemy. Minutes later, shells from the cruiser *Boise* thundered overhead and crashed into the Italians. Tanks caught fire, and the bodies of riflemen were hurled into trees; the survivors staggered around, shell shocked, and the attack collapsed.

Conrath's panzers and grenadiers, meanwhile, were pushing in the 1st Infantry Division's right wing. Panzers were only a mile from the water and foot soldiers were within 700 yards of the 26th Infantry Regiment's supply dumps. Then they ran into four howitzer batteries of the 32nd and 33rd Field Artillery, which were emplaced in the dunes and firing at them over open sights. These were the same guns that had savaged the 10th Panzer Division during its attack at El Guettar. The first platoon of Sherman tanks to reach the division also joined the carnage. Then the *Boise* chimed in, sending fifteen six-inch shells every six seconds, and was soon joined by another cruiser and several destroyers. Panzers began to burn, and grenadiers were cut to pieces. At 1400, Conrath gave up.[38]

Conrath and Chirieleison had very nearly turned Patton's mistakes into a devastating blow to the Allied invasion. Patton had been very, very lucky that the navy had been there to bail him out.

Retreat to the Hinterland

Guzzoni decided that after the failures at Gela, he would move the Hermann Göring Division to Syracuse to fight the British and use the Livorno Division at Licata to block the Americans there.[39] He judged that his forces were too weak to eliminate the Allied beachheads and, according to Senger und Etterlin, already was thinking about the need to evacuate the island and planning a withdrawal to the "Etna Position" on the northeast corner of the island. Kesselring was still far more optimistic, but had no control over Guzzoni's decisions.[40]

Guzzoni ordered the 15th Panzergrenadier Division to cover the movement of the Hermann Göring and Livorno Divisions by shifting from Salemi in the west to the area east and southeast of Enna. This meant returning the division to an area it had left just days before at Kesselring's insistence. It also meant that the most powerful Axis division on the western part of the island was moving off Patton's road to Palermo. On the other hand, the 129th Panzergrenadier Regiment ended up at Canicatti, and the 104th Panzergrenadier Regiment moved south of Barrafranca, blocking II Corps's route due north.[41]

Hitler, despite his earlier doubts that Sicily could be held, decided to double down against the Allies. He ordered the 1st Airborne Division to Sicily, and its 3rd Regiment to proceed there immediately by air. *Generalmajor* Walter Fries's 29th Panzergrenadier Division, just arriving in southern Italy, and the XIV Panzer Corps headquarters were to ship to the island as well.[42] Guzzoni strongly objected to the transfer of more German divisions to the island. Already anticipating evacuation, he thought they would only make that task more difficult.[43]

Because neither a rigid nor mobile defense was possible in Sicily's mountainous terrain, and because the Germans estimated the Allied predominance in ground strength to be about eight to one, German forces initially would favor a defense by delaying action, which the small interwar *Reichswehr* had trained in extensively. Units always reconnoitered fallback positions, had at least a small mobile reserve available, and pulled back at the first sign of attack by a superior enemy force. German formations would, during the campaign, execute their game plan in almost every case.[44]

The night of 11–12 July, Guzzoni returned to his plan to shift the Hermann Goring Division to Syracuse. He would reinforce the Licata area with elements of Arisio's XII Corps, which were to cooperate with the Livorno Division. The 15th Panzergrenadier Division would operate between Licata and Syracuse, ready to help to the east if it was not needed against the Americans. At this point, Commando Supremo's knowledge of the enemy was vague and inaccurate: the Americans had three divisions near Licata, while two British and one French division were thought to be at Vittoria.[45] Kesselring, by contrast, had received a fairly accurate report of the Allied order of battle by evening of the day of the landings.[46]

The Hermann Göring Division pulled out of the American sector on the twelfth. The division's panzer reconnaissance battalion staged a screening attack against the 16th Infantry Regiment at Piano Lupo, spooking the Americans so thoroughly that they interpreted it as another attempt to push into Gela.[47] The most lethal Axis division on the island would be Monty's problem now, not Patton's. And it would indeed prove to be a problem.

Guzzoni had to abandon his plan to move the Hermann Göring Division all the way to the east coast and ordered it to defend the Caltagirone-Grammichele-Vizzini line. Its running mates in XVI Corps were deployed as follows: Napoli Division at Palazzo Acreide, *Kampfgruppe* Körner in Sortino, and the Livorno Division north of Licata. (See map, defensive line of 2–15 July.) XII Corps was to move the Assietta Division, up to this point concentrated about halfway between Seventh Army and Palermo, eastward to the area of Troina. *Kampfgruppe* Schreiber, commanded by *Generale di Brigata* Ottorino Schreiber, commander of the 207th Coastal Division, was to take over the defense of Canicatti, where the enemy was pressing forward with tank-supported attacks, with all available Italian and German forces, including the 129th Panzergrenadier Regiment.

As the weight of the Axis defenses shifted eastward, the situation was becoming dire opposite the American left. At Agrigento, the 10th *Bersaglieri* Regiment was under heavy attack, and the enemy had achieved penetrations in the area. North of Licata, the Livorno Division was also under heavy pressure. Still the best Italian formation, it was hurting on 12 July, having suffered heavy casualties from air attacks and naval gunfire. The Napoli Division was holding on against the British, but Guzzoni was again desperately hoping to send the Hermann Göring Division to its aid.[48]

In Kesselring's view, the Italian defense had gone off the rails everywhere.[49] Then-*Oberst* Max Ulich, who would soon arrive with the 29th Panzergrenadier Division, observed, "From the very beginning of combat action, the attitude of Italian units proved that morale had disintegrated. Even though a few commanders still wanted to fight, and even though some units (the Italian artillery, for example) still gave a fair account of themselves, nothing was left of coordinated leadership and combat effectiveness. The Italian soldier was tired, aimless, and undisciplined. Consequently, Italian units only rarely constituted an asset in combat, and for the most part only proved to be a liability."[50]

By 13 July, the Livorno Division was in retreat northward through the mountains. Guzzoni had to commit motorized elements of the 15th Panzergrenadier Division to the fight in the hills north of Licata. The Napoli Division was falling back, too.[51] Guzzoni ordered XVI Corps to send part of the Hermann Göring Division to Catania to improve defenses against any possible additional landing.[52]

The Italians had neglected to harden Guzzoni's headquarters in Enna, and consequently he and his staff were bombed out. Temporarily deprived of all means of communication, Guzzoni lost any ability to control his forces for the rest of the day.[53]

For once dropping his optimism, Kesselring signaled OKW that the Italian coastal defense had failed totally and that German troops alone could not hold the island. The Luftwaffe had been reduced to impotence, and a mobile counterattack was no longer possible. The Germans, he said, probably could not reinforce as quickly as the Allies could. Nevertheless, Kesselring argued, it would pay to fight for time, because a rapid loss of Sicily would undermine Italy's continued will to resist.

General der Panzertruppe Hans-Valentin Hube and his XIV Panzer Corps staff arrived on Sicily several days after the landings, though German sources differ on precisely when. Hube was of middle size, but extremely strong, and he did not let the loss of his left arm in the Great War stand in the way of his capabilities in the field. Born on 29 October 1890 in Naumburg an der Saale, Hube had entered the imperial army in February 1909. He had married and had two sons and one daughter. Between the wars, Hube had served as a tactics instructor at the infantry school. His rating officers described Hube as an open, straightforward, reliable man, an officer of the front the way one is supposed to be. A skilled horseman like Patton, he was energetic and a model soldier.[54]

Hube's arrival marked a real improvement from the perspective of German combat elements. Conrath recalled that Senger und Etterlin had tried to improve communications within the chain of command, but been ineffective because he lacked a staff. Radio instructions arriving from Kesselring in Italy could not be carried out because they were totally out of touch with conditions on the ground. Hube brought with him the power to issue the clear orders that Conrath craved.[55]

Hitler decreed that the new objective would be to halt the enemy forward of Mount Etna. XIV Panzer Corps was to take charge of this operation on 14 July, and OKW dispatched an officer to instruct Hube to take control over all Italian forces on the island and direct the defense himself. Hitler ordered that additional air squadrons be sent from the Balkans and from France.[56] Kesselring sent a message saying it was of "decisive importance" to send additional reinforcements to the left wing, opposite Montgomery, which should be accomplished by detaching troops from the center.[57] This order was a clear indication that Montgomery was the enemy commander who worried him the most.

Likewise, the führer's decision to anchor his fallback line forward of Mount Etna indicated that his eye was on Montgomery. Indeed, by 15 July, the Germans had concluded that Eighth Army represented the Allied

Schwerpunkt.[58] Axis commanders had concluded that they did not have to worry that Patton was going to pivot eastward and slam into the unprotected flank of the German-Italian forces fighting Montgomery.[59] Commando Supremo situation maps show that by 15 July, plans were in place to withdraw to a defensive arc running from the east coast south of Mount Etna to the north coast at Sant' Agata di Militello.

Guzzoni, at this stage, was still in overall command, but Hube got on well with him and began to wield strong influence over operational decisions.[60] Kesselring, too, was able to influence events to a great extent.[61]

Jodl, at OKW, produced a rare written assessment that said, "As far as can be foreseen, Sicily cannot be held." He advocated purging untrustworthy officers from the Italian military command and putting German officers in all key positions in the Mediterranean, though Mussolini would remain nominally in charge in Italy. Jodl wanted to give Rommel overall military command in Italy under the assumption that Italians would gladly serve under him. Hitler was not yet willing to offend Mussolini and go that far.[62]

On 16 July, Guzzoni was firming up a redoubt in northeastern Sicily, while Hube offered guidance aimed at establishing a common front for the two German divisions. All counterattacks had been called off, and the aim was now purely defensive. The Hermann Göring Division and *Kampfgruppe* Schmalz had taken positions on the edge of the Catania plain at Bicocca–Stazione Gerbini–Catenanuova, but were under pressure along the coast from tank attacks supported by naval gunfire. The Livorno Division had tied into the Hermann Göring Division south of Leonforte. Guzzoni planned to deploy the 15th Panzergrenadier Division in positions between Leonforte and Nicosia. Plans were in place to move the Aosta Division east from the coast southwest of Palermo and the Assietta Division from its spot between Seventh Army and Palermo to the western edge of the pocket Guzzoni was forming on the northeastern tip of the island. The 15th Panzergrenadier Division would pivot back to complete the perimeter.

The Livorno Division had suffered 50 percent losses in less than a week. The Hermann Göring Division reported losses of 600 men and an unknown number of panzers, and casualties in the 15th Panzergrenadier Division were unknown.

The lead elements of the 29th Panzergrenadier Division, meanwhile, had already crossed the Straits of Messina, and parts of the 1st Airborne Division had arrived by air. The 29th Division included the 129th Panzer Battalion, with forty-three Sturmgeschütz III assault guns.[63]

THE OTHER FELLOW GETS OUT OF THE WAY

The next day, 17 July, Commando Supremo wrote off the last serious resistance in western Sicily. The defense at Agrigento had collapsed under the estimated pressure of one armored and two motorized divisions. Guzzoni ordered the defenders to resist furiously. Meanwhile, he instructed elements of XII Corps and the Aosta and Assietta Divisions to begin their redeployment eastward. The other fellow was just about to step out of Patton's way.

Commando Supremo appealed to OKW for more help, underscoring the insufficiency of German air support and an alleged suspension of moving more German ground units to Sicily.[64] OKW, however, ruled that a gradual evacuation of Sicily was unavoidable, and that it was time to prepare the defense of the mainland.

When one of II Corps's key north-south roads was taken away and given to Montgomery, who was bogged down on the east coast, Patton cast about for a way to get back into the game and settled on a drive to Palermo, Sicily's capital, which at least bore a patina of prestige. He first wangled authorization for a "reconnaissance" led by the 3rd Infantry Division, starting 15 July. He then added the 2nd Armored and 82nd Airborne Divisions on the 3rd Division's left to create a "provisional corps," which had orders to dash the hundred miles into Palermo.[65]

The night of 17–18 July, Axis forces disengaged along Seventh Army's entire front. Kesselring's staff judged that the Axis withdrawal from Seventh Army's front had surprised the Allies. His Ic expected Seventh Army to attack into the void because it needed a major port to supply itself.[66]

On 18 July, the two Italian divisions in western Sicily scampered out of the path that Seventh Army would take and moved to the eastern defensive perimeter. The German command dismissed the American pursuit of the withdrawing right wing as "hesitant." With Hube's XIV Panzer Corps taking formal authority from Senger und Etterlin over all German formations in Sicily on 17 July, Kesselring considered the military situation to have stabilized. Guzzoni remained nominally in command, but no longer attempted to issue or modify orders to German formations.[67]

Hube took operational command over the Livorno, Hermann Göring, and 15th Panzergrenadier Divisions on 19 July. The Aosta Division began arriving in the Nicosia area. Italian XVI Corps was given responsibility for defending the coast.[68]

Mussolini, knowing that he and his losing war were deeply unpopular in Italy, informed the king secretly on 20 July that he intended to end his alliance with Germany by mid-September. Hitler, who had just met with *Il Duce*, mistakenly thought he had succeeded in shoring up the Axis.[69]

Patton was well aware that the Axis forces were withdrawing to the northeast, so when he made his decision to race for Palermo, there was nothing bold about it. Patton's provisional corps pushed off on 20 July. Major General Geoffrey Keyes, who was to command the provisional corps, on 21 July moved the Seventh Army advance headquarters to Agrigento and signaled Patton that if given the ball, he could make a touchdown. Patton told him he had the ball and to call the signals.[70] It was time for the end-around, just like in the Louisiana maneuvers. Keyes's men entered Palermo a day later, after encountering no resistance beyond a few roadblocks. Bradley's II Corps, meanwhile, reached the northern coast east of Palermo.

One source quotes Kesselring as saying that in the Sicily campaign, "Patton just marched and captured unimportant terrain." *Generalmajor* Fries recalled that Patton's move did not bother Axis commanders the least bit.[71] This was about to change.

BACK TO THE LINE PLAY

Having taken Palermo and gained his headlines, Patton now faced a task not unlike the one that had frustrated him in Tunisia: pushing eastward through mountainous terrain against a well-trained, mobile German command. General Sir Harold Alexander, on 23 July, ordered Patton to attack along the coast toward Messina. Eighth Army was stuck in Catania, and Alexander had realized Montgomery would be unable to take Messina on his own. Alexander gave each army two roads toward Messina. In addition to the coast road, Highway 113, Patton got Route 114, which ran through the mountains north of Mount Etna via Nicosia, Troina, and Randazzo. During the first phase, the 45th Infantry Division pushed along the coast, while the 1st Infantry Division struggled through the interior.[72]

The bull-headed Patton that demanded a smashing attack when confronted by a sound static defense emerged again. He told Bradley, "I want you to get into Messina as fast as you can. I don't want you to waste time on these maneuvers, even if you've got to spend men to do it."[73]

The Italian XII Corps, at the western end of the perimeter, began to experience serious pressure from the Americans again on 23 July. At that time, XII Corps held a line running roughly north to south from the northern coast to Nicosia; the 15th Panzergrenadier was up front and somewhat west of the line, backed by the two Italian infantry divisions. The German XIV Panzer Corps defended a line running east from Nicosia to the coast south of Mount Etna. The Italian XVI Corps occupied the northeastern corner of the island.[74] Hube, with Guzzoni's consent, had taken day-to-day control over the battlefield and was now Patton's chief enemy.[75] (Hube would be killed on the eastern front in April 1944, so he penned no personal account of his fight against Patton.)

What a match-up Hube faced! He battled the two Western generals many would come to view as the best. Montgomery and his vaunted Eighth Army, who had overcome Rommel, pounded his perimeter from the south. Patton bashed at him from the west. If his line caved in at any point, the panzer general would lack the mobile resources and the open terrain to respond.

By 24 July, the German command realized that the Allied *Schwerpunkt* had shifted to the American sector.[76] Under strong pressure, the 15th Panzergrenadier Division withdrew to a position on XII Corps's left wing, while the 29th Panzergrenadier Division moved onto the right wing—and set up astride the coast road.[77]

The next day, the 29th Panzergrenadier Division took over the entire Italian corps's front, and the two Italian divisions pulled back to man a reserve line some five miles to the east. Other than a small sector held by the Livorno Division in the center of the perimeter, the Allies now faced a solid front of German steel.[78] The 15th Panzergrenadier Division, meanwhile, lost Leonforte to the Canadians and was beset by the Americans at Sperlinga and plagued by the defections of Italian infantry to the Allies.

Hube had now consolidated his German divisions and a sprinkling of more or less reliable Italian ones in a coherent arc. Nevertheless, outmanned by an estimated ratio of ten to one and suffering under the pressure of now total Allied control of the air, Hube knew he could not hold his present line. XIV Panzer Corps had already received orders to construct a shorter line running from Sant' Agata to west of Troina-Adrano and south of Mount Etna—a line the U.S. Army history refers as the "Etna line."[79]

Mussolini's personal views of Italy's alliance with Germany, as it turned out, mattered little: the Fascist Grand Council stripped him of power on the twenty-fifth. On hearing the news, Hitler ordered that existing plans to take control in Italy and Rome be set in motion, though he thought better of that idea in the next few days and limited the action to securing the Alpine passes. Hitler ordered that German formations be extracted from Sicily, especially the Hermann Göring Division, even if they had to destroy all their heavy equipment and save only the personnel.[80] Thus, it was Italian politics and the threat they posed to the lines of communication, and not Allied military pressure, that persuaded Hitler to order the evacuation of the island.

The next day, Hitler was hopeful that he could get his tanks from Sicily to the mainland, too. At last word, there were still 160 panzers in action. Hitler had just received a report on the Hermann Göring Division's performance that fired his spirit. "These young men are fighting like fanatics because they come from the Hitler Youth. They're young German kids, mostly sixteen-year-olds," the führer enthused. "Eighteen years," corrected Heinrich Himmler.[81]

On 28 July, the Livorno Division pulled back from the front, but the next day, the two other Italian infantry divisions moved forward, so that XII Corps was briefly arrayed, from north to south: Assietta Division on the coast, elements of the 29th Panzergrenadier Division, Aosta Division, the remainder of the 29th Division, 15th Panzergrenadier Division.[82] The reason for Hube's decision remains obscure, though he may have been relieving German elements to fall back to the next defensive line.

Kesselring informed OKW on 29 July that he could evacuate Sicily in three days. Intermediate positions were ready for troops falling back. All preparations had been completed to receive withdrawing formations in Calabria.[83]

The staged withdrawal of the 15th Panzergrenadier and 29th Panzergrenadier Divisions began without any difficulties.[84] Patton was regrouping and, on the thirtieth substituted the 3rd Infantry Division for the 45th Infantry Division on the coast road.[85] The 29th Panzergrenadier Division, on 31 July, concentrated its defensive strength on the coast, deploying the northmost battalion and most of the artillery across a two-mile front, and the leftmost battalion across a ten-mile front.[86] When the division withdrew through San Stefano on 1 August, the Americans again did not follow up.[87] In fact, *Generalmajor* Fries's main problem was naval gunfire, which was able to hit his division along the length of its main line of communications.[88] After frustrating the 1st Infantry's Division's best efforts to capture Nicosia for several days, Rodt's 15th Panzergrenadier Division pulled back to Troina the night of 27–28 July and was left untroubled by Patton's legions on the twenty-ninth, mired in rain and mud, to settle into the prepared positions there.[89]

Guzzoni, on 1 August, on orders from Rome, transferred command over all Italian troops to XIV Panzer Corps, effective 2 August.[90] Hube took responsibility for landward defenses at 1200 hours.[91]

The Walls of Troina

The 15th Panzergrenadier Division and elements of the Aosta Division were well dug in at the hilltop town of Troina, the highest village in Sicily, and on 31 July began a bloody, weeklong battle against the 1st Infantry Division and the attached 39th Regiment of the 9th Infantry Division.[92] Rodt had employed a special staff for nearly a week preparing his positions at Troina, where, like Hector of Troy, he would gather his warriors and hope to stop the invaders from the sea. He deployed his 129th Panzergrenadier Regiment on his right and his 104th Panzergrenadier Regiment on his left, at Adrano. An outpost line west of the town was to spot and delay the enemy's advance. Rodt's forward command post sheltered amid the walls of Troina's stone buildings.[93]

The 15th Division was now considered "fought out," but still it held on.[94] Rodt's outpost line delayed the 39th Infantry Regiment for three days before the men had to fall back to the main line of resistance. Rodt executed an effective defense, repeatedly counterattacking with infantry and panzers, and throughout the battle, he visited his forward units to keep up morale. This weak screening force, well supported by artillery with ample ammunition, finally convinced the Americans that they faced a truly tough nut, and Maj. Gen. Terry Allen committed two regiments of the 1st Division to an enveloping attack on 4 August. The Germans endured barrages of white phosphorous and the carpet-bombing of Troina. Rodt, watching the battlefield from his forward command post and reading the reports from his embattled troops, recognized the envelopment plan and positioned his panzers for an attack eastward out of Troina.[95]

On 5 August, German resistance remained fierce across the front opposite Patton, despite rising casualties, especially in the 15th Panzergrenadier Division. The Germans informed Commando Supremo that while they appreciated the support of Italian artillery, the infantry were of much less use in the intensive combat because of insufficient weapons. Because of weak resistance, XVI Corps pulled the Aosta Division from the line, leaving the Assietta Division the only Italian formation on the front. Guzzoni sketched out plans for a new fallback line, codenamed Tortorici and running from Zappulla to Mount Etna.[96] It was his last contribution to the battle, because Hube took command over Italian Sixth Army from Guzzoni on 6 August.[97]

The 15th Panzergrenadier Division had lost 1,600 men at Troina, about 40 percent of its fighting strength, but its panzers counterattacked when the Americans broke through north and south of Troina on 6 August. This success kept the division's escape route open, and the panzergrenadiers pulled back to the next prepared line. The Americans did not realize the advantage they held, recalled Rodt, and again failed to pursue.[98]

The rest of XIV Panzer Corps also initiated its withdrawal to the Tortorici line on 7 August, nearly untroubled by the enemy. Once more, the Germans found the Allied pursuit "hesitant," and they were largely left in peace again on the eighth.[99]

✷

Fighting with One Flank Open

The 29th Panzergrenadier Division was comfortably settled in strong fortifications, holding the 3rd Infantry Division at bay along the Furiano River where it fed into the sea. For *Generalmajor* Fries, though, the sea represented an open right flank that stretched all the way back to Messina. The Germans intercepted Patton's orders to move to Palermo equipment for loading vehicles onto ships, so they had some inkling that he was planning an amphibious operation. Fortunately for Fries, the U.S. Navy's Task Force 88 supporting Patton had only enough landing craft to move one reinforced infantry battalion at one time.

Fries began a step-by-step pullback when it became apparent that the 15th Panzergrenadier Division was going to retreat from Troina and expose his left flank.[100] The 29th Panzergrenadier Division found itself embroiled in serious fighting again on 9 August, when the Americans attacked just as it was engaged in its phased withdrawal for the day. The division had to deal with an amphibious landing by the 2nd Battalion, 30th Infantry Regiment, supported by two batteries of artillery, a tank company, and engineers at Sant' Agata. Almost all of the division's forward elements had already withdrawn past Sant' Agata, though, and the Americans snared only a thousand men.[101]

Commando Supremo judged the situation to be "confused" on the 29th Panzergrenadier Division's right and in the center of the 15th Panzergrenadier Division's zone as of 1600 on 10 August. Fortunately, the Allies inexplicably gave the Axis another day nearly free of pressure to get its house in order. XIV Panzer Corps reported that it anticipated pulling back to the final planned line of resistance running from San Marco to Furnari.[102]

Hube doubted he would be able to ferry all Axis elements to the mainland because of fierce Allied air attacks. He anticipated that he would have to evacuate only personnel and automatic weapons and destroy the heavy equipment.[103]

Patton had left Allen and his 1st Infantry Division to their own devices at Troina, but he was breathing down the neck of Maj. Gen. Lucian Truscott and his 3rd Infantry Division. Patton badly wanted to beat Montgomery to Messina, and Truscott's division was the only force that could do it. When the 29th Division's 71st Panzergrenadier Regiment occupied a ridge at Naso and again brought Truscott to a stop at the Zappulla River on the tenth, Patton ordered Bradley to conduct another amphibious end-run to land at Brolo, which lies on the coast a bit more than a mile from the village of Naso. Truscott's 15th Infantry Regiment, attacking toward Naso and Castell Umberto while the 7th Infantry pushed along the coast highway, had not gained enough ground, in Truscott's view, and he wanted to postpone the amphibious hop until 12 August. Patton rammed an immediate operation down his throat.

Fries had Patton figured out by now and had placed a fairly strong force just east of Brolo to defend against precisely the kind of amphibious landing Patton had ordered. The battalion landing force came ashore in the dark and achieved tactical surprise, cut the highway, and threatened much of the panzergrenadier division's line of withdrawal. Soon, gunplay in the dark alerted the Germans, and Fries counterattacked with a like-sized force. At daylight, the 7th Infantry attacked up the highway to link with the landing force, while the division's other two regiments assaulted the Naso ridge defenses. The going was extremely slow, and over the course of a day of bitter fighting, the 71st Panzergrenadier Regiment cleared its escape route and slipped away.[104]

Patton's risky and bloody operation had been totally unnecessary. The amphibious landing at Brolo on 11 August was a setback for XIV Panzer Corps, but Fries had to pull back his left wing anyway because of the success of the 3rd Infantry Division's attack in the direction of Naso and Castell Umberto—and he was already scheduled to pull the entire division back the next day. The 29th Division fell back to the line Brolo–Sant' Angelo di Brole-Ucria, stopped again, and turned to challenge Truscott.

Even though pressure against the 15th Panzergrenadier and Hermann Göring Divisions eased, Hube decided to withdraw that night to the final line of resistance from San Marco to Furnari. The corps headquarters would cross the Straits of Messina to Calabria. The Luftwaffe, meanwhile, escalated attacks against all Allied naval units along Sicily's east coast to protect the evacuation, while Allied aircraft struck both sides of the straits.[105]

Once again, the German withdrawal continued on 13 and 14 August with little Allied interference. XIV Panzer Corps completed its retreat to the final line on the fourteenth.[106]

While the 29th Panzergrenadier and Hermann Göring Divisions held off the enemy on 15 August, the 15th Panzergrenadier Division pulled back to Messina and ferried to the mainland. Rodt ascribed the ease of the operation to the Allies' passive behavior. The entire Italian XVI Corps, with 70,000 men, 300 vehicles, and some eighty guns, also escaped by sea. The screening force dropped back slowly, blowing up bridges behind it.[107]

Unable to wring a clear decision out of Hitler, Keitel and Kesselring took it upon themselves to order the final evacuation of Sicily without so much as informing Commando Supremo.[108]

The bulk of the 29th Panzergrenadier and Hermann Göring Divisions left Sicily on 16 August behind a thin rearguard screen. The last men pulled out that night. The evacuation was completed at 0630 hours on 17 August. The Germans had succeeded in withdrawing 60,000 men—with all their heavy weapons.[109]

Available evidence indicates that they considered themselves to have waged a successful defensive battle. *Generalmajor* Ulich commented, "Command and troops can be proud of their successes in the defensive battle, which was conducted in a fair manner by both opponents."[110]

PATTON COMES INTO FOCUS

Unlike in Tunisia, in the Sicily campaign, the Axis commanders knew that they had been fighting Patton, as well as Montgomery. They had been unimpressed by Patton's race to Palermo through country they had already abandoned. Their assessment of the American performance once the smash-mouthed fighting erupted along the northeastern perimeter suggests that he did not much impress them then, either.

A German assessment of American military leadership on Sicily noted an improvement over Tunisia in that the enemy quickly absorbed battle lessons. Still, the American soldier had not matured into fully developed enemy.[111]

Rodt, who had almost always faced Patton's men, concluded, "The [German] troops realized early on that the enemy very often conducted his movements systematically, and that he only attacked after a heavy artillery preparation when he believed he had broken our resistance. This kept him regularly from exploiting the weakness of our situation and gave me the opportunity to consolidate dangerous situations. The old Africa veterans were familiar with the enemy's style, and we behaved ourselves accordingly."[112]

German observers would repeat this refrain, already heard in Tunisia, regarding troops under Patton's command in the European theater as well. Patton was hesitant in the clinch. The Germans were developing a sense that Patton exhibited certain flaws in the use of his sword.

———*———

NINE

Bait and Wait

T HE ALLIED WARLORDS assembled in the United Kingdom from
  the corners of the Mediterranean theater in January 1944. Lieutenant
General Omar Bradley had been there since October in command of U.S.
First Army. Montgomery took charge of 21st Army Group in early January,
and Eisenhower arrived in London on the fourteenth to take up his duties as
supreme commander.[1] Patton arrived in London on 26 January. Eisenhower
kept Patton's selection to command Third Army under wraps because Patton
was still the subject of a political firestorm in the States over the two infamous
slapping incidents in Sicily.[2]

One of the great elements of the Patton myth is that after his campaign
in Sicily, as admiring biographer Ladislas Farago put it, the American general
"inspired respect and fear in the enemy, who came to regard him as their most
dangerous adversary in the field, the Allies' counterpart of Rommel in his
halcyon days. . . . For a while the Germans watched the comings and goings of
Patton like rubbernecked spectators following a tennis ball at Wimbleton. . . ."[3]

There does not appear to be an iota of fact behind this claim.

The notion that Patton could be used to deceive the Germans appears
to have arisen from a presumption about German thinking in Washington
rather than any evidence that the Germans had a particular interest in the
general's activities. On 21 October 1943 Gen. George Marshall had written
to Eisenhower about the importance of not letting the Germans know that
Seventh Army's divisions were shifting from Sicily to the United Kingdom,
stating that "it seems evident to us that Patton's movements are of great importance to German reactions and therefore should be carefully considered. I had

thought and spoke to [Bedell] Smith about Patton being given a trip to Cairo and Cyprus but the Corsican visit appeals to me as carrying much more of a threat [to the Germans in northern Italy]."[4]

Eisenhower replied, "As it is I am quite sure that we must do everything possible to keep him confused and the point you have suggested concerning Patton's movements appeals to me as having a great deal of merit. This possibility had not previously occurred to me."

On 28 October, Patton and four of his staff officers visited Corsica.[5] Soon, he was off to Malta and reached Cairo on 12 December.[6] There is no indication, however, that the Germans paid any attention to Patton's peregrinations.

Why the Americans thought that Patton would draw German attention was simple: the United States had no other seasoned and widely known general other than Eisenhower. Months later, in the wake of the furor in the States caused by press accounts of a speech by Patton to a group of British ladies in April 1944, in which he said it was the destiny of Britain, America, and Russia to rule the world, Marshall signaled Eisenhower that "Patton is the only available Army Commander for his present assignment who has had actual experience in fighting Rommel and in extensive landing operations followed by a rapid campaign of exploitation."[7] Marshall's misimpression that Patton had fought Rommel only went to show how far Patton's reputation had been inflated in his own country.

But unbeknownst to the Germans, Patton, with his bouts of shaky self-control, had already undermined Eisenhower's confidence in him to the point that, on 29 December 1943, Ike had signaled to Marshall, "In no repeat no event will I ever advance Patton beyond army command."[8]

From the German perspective, Patton was simply one blip in a noisy pattern of very dangerous enemy commanders, many of whom, such as Montgomery and Soviet marshall Georgi Zhukov, probably loomed much larger than Patton in their thinking. Montgomery had defeated Germany's most celebrated panzer commander and hurled the Germans back from the gates of Egypt. Zhukov had kept the German spearheads out of Moscow in 1941. Patton, by contrast, had romped around an undefended part of Sicily, and relatively weak delaying forces had held him at bay until the Axis evacuation had been completed in an orderly fashion.

Had the Germans been paying any attention to the American media and been caught up in Patton fever, they would have noticed an Associated Press item in April 1944 that revealed, "News of the [slapping] incident [in Sicily] involving Lieutenant General George S. Patton, Jr., was delayed because 'that General was to be used in a cover plan following his operations in Sicily. In view of that, the Theater Commander was extremely desirous that his reputation should not be impaired by a wide discussion of the soldier-slapping incident.'"[9]

In reality, Patton was in the doghouse, and he had killed time rather than Germans while in command of a steadily dwindling Seventh Army on Sicily for five months before he learned his next assignment. Six more months followed until he was back in combat.[10] Collectively, that pause was more than three times his lifetime combat experience to date.

THE GREAT FAKE

On 3 November 1943, OKW, had issued *Weisung* 51, which declared, "The danger in the east remains, but an even greater shows itself in the west: the Anglo-Saxon landing!" Indeed, OKW expected the decisive battle of the war to take place on the Western front. There was plenty of room on the eastern front to deal with setbacks, but a successful cracking of the defenses in the West, OKW worried, would quickly lead to unforeseeable consequences. It would weaken forces in the West no longer and would significantly build them up, instead.[11]

Allied "deceivers," as early as May 1943, had launched an operation to convince the Germans, through double agents, of a false order of battle and an exaggeration of the number of American and British divisions in the United Kingdom. This operation was a precondition for other deception operations that were intended to sell to German intelligence notional threatened operations from Norway to Brittany by establishing an apparent capability beforehand. By October 1943, the German high command's Detachment Foreign Armies West, responsible for assessing Western armies, significantly overestimated the number of Allied divisions at forty-three, although it is unclear to what degree the deception operations contributed to the error. OKW appears to have believed there were fifty divisions in the United Kingdom as of April 1943, before the deception operation even began, so the German estimate initially declined. By 23 May 1944, however, *OB West* put the number at between seventy and eighty. Despite detecting false and genuine operational preparations for the mythical operations, the Germans took none of the response measures—including holding divisions in France needed on other fronts—for which the Allies had hoped. The one exception was Operation Tindall, a suggested invasion of Norway that Hitler already took seriously and that tied down twelve divisions.[12]

After considering and rejecting several plans to persuade the Germans that the main landings in France would occur in July 1944, the Allies in February decided to try to convince the Germans that the main landings would take place at the Pas de Calais, a short hop across the English Channel, to be followed by a drive through Antwerp and Brussels to the Ruhr industrial basin with a force ultimately involving some fifty divisions. Operation Fortitude South was the Allied deception operation aimed at convincing the Germans that First U.S. Army Group (FUSAG) would conduct landings along the Pas de Calais in France during July, and that the invasion of Normandy was nothing but a feint to draw German forces away from the real main assault. The Germans would be fed a false order of battle based mainly on real, existing corps and divisions. Dummy equipment and fake radio nets would be employed to provide sporadic German reconnaissance flights and radio-intercept teams information to support the cover story, as would double-agent reports. Increased Allied air activity over the Pas de Calais would feed the ruse.[13]

Allied planners could be confident that the Germans smelled the bait. Great Britain's Ultra code-breaking program, which since the Battle of France in 1940 had been cracking German Enigma ciphers, indicated on 9 January 1944 that the Germans were aware of FUSAG's existence.[14] Indeed, on the sixteenth, Foreign Armies West reported to German commanders, "According to a report by a reliable source, the 1st American Army Group is in Great Britain. This is probably the command staff of American forces in Great Britain, and the same source reports the existence of a First American Army."[15]

The Germans were known to have respected Patton's abilities, emphasize a number of prominent historians, an assessment seemingly constructed mainly on a single entry in the OKW *Kriegstagebuch*, on 20 March, indicating that Patton, "who was formerly employed in Africa and is highly regarded for his proficiency," had arrived in England.[16] The entry, of course, reflects no German awe at Patton's role in Sicily, and in context it suggests that it was the Allies who highly regarded his proficiency and hence moved him to the United Kingdom. The brief mention is also one small bit in a broader discussion of enemy preparations, which devoted more space to a single two-hour speech by Montgomery than it did to Patton's arrival.

Farago amplifies the argument and claims that the Germans assumed that Patton would lead the American component of the invasion force, and that, therefore, the main effort would be wherever Patton appeared. Indeed, he elevates an obscure paper, "*Invasionsgenerale*" ("Invasion Generals"), evidently produced by the Luftwaffe's *Luftkriegsakademie* (Air War Academy), to the status of a key indicator that the Germans were gripped with tracking Patton.[17] Oddly, considering the supposed German obsession, in a copy originally disseminated in February 1944 and available at the German federal archives, Patton is the only senior Allied general in Britain and the Mediterranean *not* profiled with a brief, one-paragraph summary; perhaps a later edition of the paper, lost to the archives, included Patton. Bradley was included, as was Montgomery.[18]

Surviving Luftwaffe documents show that the Germans collected biographical data on hundreds of senior American and British air commanders, and the same was doubtless true for ground-force generals, although those records have perished. Jodl told interrogators that he routinely received lists of enemy commanders that included the leaders' ages and experience.[19]

It is true that by 23 March, the Germans had associated Patton with FUSAG, as they had been fed information to that effect, but they did not believe he was the commanding general.[20] On 1 April, Foreign Armies West assessed, "The arrival of Ninth U.S. Army in Great Britain was reported in mid-March by reliable sources. The presence of two American armies (First and Ninth) in Great Britain is thereby established, and they are suspected to be subordinated to the 1st Army Group. In this connection, a believable report from *Abwehr* [military intelligence] indicates that the former commander of Seventh Army, Lt. Gen. Patton, has arrived in England with part of his staff. It seems possible that Lt. Gen. Patton, who commanded Seventh Army in the Sicily landings, has taken command of the First or Ninth Army in England."[21]

There is no evidence that the Germans paid any particular attention to Patton's whereabouts. By contrast, during the months before D-Day, *Abwehr* bombarded its (double) agents in the United Kingdom with questions about Gen. Bernard Montgomery's travels.[22] Patton, though, apparently believed the Germans viewed him as a dangerous commander. He told some troops, "Don't forget, you don't know that I'm here at all. . . . Let the first bastards to find out be the goddam Germans. Some day I want them to raise up on their hind legs and howl, 'Jesus Christ, it's that goddam Third Army and that son-of-a-bitch Patton again!'"[23]

Patton's notional role appears to have been incidental to the strategic conclusions the Germans reached on the basis of false order-of-battle and other information. The Germans did not decide until mid-May that Patton had become commanding general of FUSAG, which *OB West* began referring to as "Army Group Patton," months after OKW had wrongly decided that the most likely invasion area was the Pas de Calais or Belgium, so his fictional command of FUSAG did not contribute to that analysis.[24] In none of the surviving documents from the preinvasion period at OKW, Army Group B—responsible for northwestern France—or lower echelons, is there any mention of Patton outside of the deception-driven intelligence linking his name to FUSAG. The memoirs of key participants reflect no interest at the time in Patton.

When Hitler changed his mind in April and decided that the Allied landings would take place at Normandy and Brittany—he expected the enemy to try to capture Cherbourg and Brest—it was his famous intuition speaking and not consideration of Patton's whereabouts. Indeed, then-*General der Artillerie* Walter Warlimont, Jodl's deputy, described Hitler's decision as being "for no apparent reason," though Hitler once referred to increasingly detailed information on Allied concentrations in southern England. On 6 May, OKW declared that the Cotentin Peninsula would be the enemy's primary objective; it ordered that the 2nd *Fallschirmjäger* (Airborne) and 243rd Infantry Divisions reinforce the sector and instructed that all troops there be dug in.[25] This was an eerily accurate forecast, and Patton had nothing to do with it.

Patton was only one small piece in the deception operation, a fact underscored by the continued German treatment of FUSAG as real and a potential threat even after Patton appeared at the head of Third Army in Normandy.[26] *Generalfeldmarschall* Gerd von Rundstedt, *OB West* himself, told B. H. Liddell Hart at the end of the war, in a forthright description of his own errors regarding Allied intentions, that it was the overestimation of the number of American divisions in the United Kingdom that "had an indirect effect of important consequence, by making us the more inclined to expect a second landing, in the Calais area."[27]

Hitler and Keitel, on 12 April, agreed that Allied landings on the Channel coast and southern France could be expected at any time. Rundstedt, on the eighteenth, informed the high command that the Allies were ready to attack somewhere between the Scheldt and the Seine Rivers, and the only explanation why they were not doing so was that they were waiting for good and steady weather and perhaps an optimum moment politically. Four panzer and panzer-grenadier divisions resting in France were nearing full strength, and three more were starting to organize or rebuild (most of these divisions having been worn out on the eastern front). Plans were afoot to shift the Panzer Lehr Division to France from Hungary.[28] By 23 May, Rundstedt had expanded his concept of the "danger front" to include Normandy and northern Brittany. The Germans grasped that the fighting in Italy was intended to tie their forces down there.[29]

But the Germans were in the dark about a key fact. The German high command's map depicting American troop deployments globally on 1 June placed Third Army in the United States.[30]

A GENERAL AT THE FORGE

Patton learned on 26 January that he was to command Third Army, an organization with no combat experience. This gave Patton the opportunity to forge his own sword—but only the hilt. The blade was supplied by the huge Army Ground Forces mobilization and training system in the States. Divisions were expected to arrive "fully schooled in their tasks," according to the official U.S.

Army history.[31] Lieutenant Generals Walter Krueger and Courtney Hodges, both infantrymen, had run Third Army during its stateside training. The army's staff, when it arrived in the United Kingdom, was largely drawn from the infantry.

Key experienced staff officers accompanied Patton from Seventh Army, which rapidly transformed the staff into a primarily cavalry and armor team. These were men who thought in terms of sweeping movement. If the Germans were later impressed by Third Army's dashing maneuver and unimpressed with its conduct of grueling positional warfare, Patton's staff selection would be one reason. Patton told his staff, "If you don't like to fight, I don't want you around."

Colonel Oscar Koch, the G-2, set up an elaborate war room that was under constant armed guard. Here, Patton planned, received briefings, and met with his corps and division commanders. He encouraged free and open discussion of his plans, up to the point where he made a final decision. Patton personally selected *Lucky* as Third Army's code name.[32]

Patton was simply assigned four corps: VIII, XII, XV, and XX.[33] The corps actually under his command would come and go, as would the divisions within each corps. The fighting end of Third Army was the same stuff as that of First, Ninth, and the other armies: general issue—GI.

A review of thousands of pages of German records, post-war reports, and memoirs gives no indication that the enemy thought Third Army was any better trained than other American armies. After all, First Army received intensive on-the-job training after D-Day and knew its business. Seventh Army came ashore with battle-hardened VI Corps and infantry divisions from Italy. These men, too, knew their business. The only possible nod to Third Army's reputation occurred when a group of 20,000 German troops trapped south of the Loire surrendered in early September 1944; they reputedly wanted it known that they were giving up to Third Army rather than the fresh-faced Ninth.[34]

Patton tried to imbue his officers down to the tactical level with his own fiercely offensive view of war. In April, he issued a general order that told his men how he wanted them to fight. Nevertheless, his diary and private letters offer a sharp contrast to his public praise and reveal that he never thought much of the offensive spirit and initiative of most of his own troops. We shall review the contents of this general order at the point a copy fell into German hands.

The Operation Neptune package for the assault on the French coast gave Third Army no role in the drama and was passing vague about what Patton was supposed to do with his army after it joined the fight and captured the most important ports in Brittany. So Patton set about creating his own scheme within the general framework. Patton thought Operation Overlord's objective—to seize a lodgment for subsequent advance eastward—was too timid. He expected the cautious Montgomery to stall before Caen, his D-Day objective.[35] Patton's first idea, which he proposed to Bradley, was that when things bogged down, Third Army should land at the Pas de Calais, precisely as the Germans were being led to expect.

The Germans could not know that Patton would be drawn to their fortified baubles, big and hard-to-capture fortress cities from Brittany to the German border. But his imagination was already fired. The only specific task he gave his G-2, Col. Oscar Koch, was to devote all his long-range planning to reaching the fortress city of Metz, far off in Lorraine.[36]

As of mid-May, only VIII Corps was fully equipped. The other corps were still waiting for their major equipment items.[37]

SITTING OUT D-DAY

The D-Day story is well known and need not be repeated at any length. Preceded by airborne drops and a massive naval and air bombardment, the main Allied invasion force landed on the coast of Normandy in the early hours of 6 June 1944. British 1 and 30 Corps stormed Gold, Juno, and Sword Beaches, while U.S. VII Corps landed at Utah and V Corps at Omaha Beaches. It was one of the decisive days of the entire war.

Patton sat in England. When the news that the Allies were ashore came in over the wireless, he summoned his staff to listen and proposed a toast to an early and speedy victory.[38]

Third Army went on an operational basis on D-Day. Koch issued his first daily periodic report, and the first daily briefing took place. Patton told his staff, "The war is finally on. We aren't in it yet, but we will be very soon."[39]

The night of 30 June–1 July, Patton had his second idea for how to fix Operation Overlord. He crafted a draft proposing an armored thrust southward out of Normandy down a narrow corridor. This proposal may well have been the inspiration for Bradley's later plan for Operation Cobra, which led to the great Allied breakout from the Norman hedgerows.[40]

---
*

TEN

Normandy:
Patton Returns to War

PATTON AND OTHER ALLIED COMMANDERS would be fighting some of the cream of Germany's eastern armies, which on the one hand brought to the German cause men who had learned hard lessons about fighting on the strategic defensive, but on the other hand brought expectations about enemy capabilities and behavior shaped by a very different opponent on the eastern front. Rommel was the only one among the German commanders in the West who had fought the British since 1940 or the Americans since 1918—or to have witnessed the devastating impact of Allied airpower.[1]

The Germans met the Allies with a force that was larger, but widely spread out and, to a great extent, static. *OB West Generalfeldmarschall* Gerd von Rundstedt commanded *Generalfeldmarschall* Erwin Rommel's Army Group B in northern France and *Generalfeldmarschall* Johannes Blaskowitz's Army Group G in southern France, a total of some fifty-eight divisions. Rommel had charge of Fifteenth Army, arrayed along the Pas de Calais to just south of the mouth of the Seine, and Seventh Army, covering the Normandy beaches. Fifteenth Army had nineteen divisions, five of them panzer, and Seventh Army thirteen, only one of them panzer. Panzer Group West, constituting the armored reserve, was situated near Paris.[2]

The first two weeks of battle in Normandy met the expectations of neither side. The Allies had expected the Germans to retreat beyond the Seine and were utterly unprepared for the fierce battle they faced in the *bocage*, as the Norman hedgerow country was known. The hedgerows divided the region into tiny fields, each a miniature fortress that had to be cleared, and canalized movement. Rundstedt had planned to strike the landing force hard with his panzer reserves, but Allied control of the air and devastating naval gunnery prevented large-scale armor operations. Indeed, on 17 June, Rundstedt asked permission to withdraw from range of the naval guns before conducting any further attacks against the British flank. Hitler, recalling the success of his stand-fast orders before the gates of Moscow, refused.[3]

Rundstedt and his chief of staff, *General der Infanterie* Günther Blumentritt, by about 20 June, decided that a second landing at Calais was not in the cards. Hitler's headquarters still believed the threat was real, however.[4]

By late June, Hitler began to think he needed a new commander-in-chief in the West. Rundstedt by then had concluded that he would not be able to destroy the Allied beachhead and begged Hitler to come to France and talk. Joined by Rommel, the führer and old Prussian warhorse met on the seventeenth in the *Wolfsschanze II* (Wolf's Lair II) in Margival, near Soissons, where—according to Blumentritt in his post-war account given to Capt. Basil Liddell Hart—Rundstedt and Rommel proposed that they withdraw to the Orne River, hold that line with infantry divisions, and extract the panzer divisions to refit them for a counterstroke against the Americans. Rundstedt allegedly told Hitler that he could not carry on unless he had a free hand.

Blumentritt claimed later that Hitler believed he could still throw the Allies into the sea and would countenance no retreat. This is an unlikely claim if for no other reason than that by the eighteenth, VII Corps had driven west across the Cotentin Peninsula and isolated Cherbourg, which the Americans stormed a week later. Indeed, the OKW *Kriegstagebuch* indicates that Hitler had much more realistic aims at the June meeting and ordered measures to defend Cherbourg and pull the line back a bit on the Cotentin Peninsula. It also suggests that the proposed withdrawal to the Orne and Rundstedt's call for a free hand actually came in a message to OKW at 0700 hours on 1 July. OKW interpreted that report as Rundstedt's declaration that he would be unable to destroy the bridgehead and a hint that German forces must either evacuate France, perhaps as far as the West Wall fortifications along the frontier, or risk everything in one, last, all-out battle.[5]

In light of Rundstedt's attitude and increasing pessimism, Hitler sacked the field marshal on 2 July (effective the following day) after one final affront.[6] *Generalfeldmarschall* Wilhelm Keitel, chief of OKW, queried Rundstedt by phone about options. "End the war," Rundstedt had replied. "What else can you do?"

"Thank God that I won't be in command during the coming catastrophe!" Rundstedt told Rommel.

On 1 July, the Allies had more than 900,000 men in Normandy, roughly three times the total German strength. OKW estimated the Allied manpower level to be only between 225,000 and 250,000 and the number of vehicles at 43,000—one quarter the actual figure. The Germans were badly overmatched and did not yet know it.[7] Moreover, after capturing Cherbourg, Bradley had turned First Army southward and was driving slowly and at the cost of hideously high casualties through the *bocage* toward St. Lô.

Rundstedt's challenge to the high command raised the question of whether to continue a hard defense, which left the initiative to the enemy and was burning out the mobile divisions, or adopt a flexible defense, as the field commanders seemed to want. Hitler had concluded that a flexible defense was impossible because of Allied air superiority. Only a hard defense would do, and he could see that the Allies were striving to break into the open and engage in mobile warfare as they thrust toward Paris. The bridgehead must be contained![8]

Hitler's strong aversion to retreat was not the product of mindless fanaticism, but of a steely eyed appreciation for the military costs involved. From the first setbacks in Russia, he had been sensitive to the inevitable loss of heavy equipment that would be difficult or impossible to replace. And then there would be the casualties. Observing Rommel's thousand-mile retreat after El Alamein, Hitler had observed, "Of the men we've lost, I bet 50 percent were lost during the retreat. . . . It's miles easier to go crashing forward with an army and win victories than to bring one back in good order after a setback or a defeat. Perhaps the greatest feat of 1914 was that they managed to get the German army back after making fools of themselves on the Marne and to get it to stand and reorganize on a definite line."[9]

Generalfeldmarschall Günter von Kluge happened to be at Hitler's headquarters speaking with the führer when Keitel appeared to report Rundstedt's words about ending the war. Kluge had spent the past nine months recovering from severe head wounds suffered in an automobile crash on the eastern front. Hitler had intended to put him back in command of Army Group Center, but decided on the spot to send him West to replace Rundstedt instead.

General der Panzertruppe Adolf Kuntzen, a longtime friend of Kluge's, said of him, "He was active, buoyant, had great ideas." *General der Infanterie* Blumentritt, who had served with Kluge on the eastern front, described him as "a very energetic and active commander who liked to be up among the fighting troops." When Kluge arrived at headquarters *OB West*, he was full of optimism and vigor. Within a few days, however, visits to the front had convinced him that his men were hanging on by their fingernails.[10]

As July began, Army Group B was referring to Allied forces in Normandy as "Army Group Montgomery," and intelligence officers expected it to drive toward Paris. The American FUSAG was still believed to be in the United Kingdom, and an uncorroborated agent report said it would conduct landings between the Scheldt and Calais.[11] The army group's assessments made no mention of Patton. Rommel told *General der Panzertruppe* Heinrich "Heinz" Eberbach on the tenth that a second landing was unlikely because of materiel constraints and dispersion of forces; Rommel clearly was not concerned about Patton's whereabouts.[12]

Third Army began moving to Normandy on 29 June. Patton and his staff crossed the Channel on the Fourth of July and debarked the following day. Patton's men quietly reached their camouflaged assembly areas.[13] Major General Troy Middleton's VIII Corps had already been in Normandy since mid-June, fighting under Bradley and his First Army, not Patton.

By mid-July, the Germans realized that divisions supposedly subordinated to FUSAG were showing up in the Normandy bridgehead. Those who still believed a second landing was in the cards apparently bought into a deception story claiming that Eisenhower had decided he had to reinforce the Allied army group in Normandy because the battle was not going well.[14]

The Germans by now knew they faced a competent enemy in Normandy. Army Group B's intelligence section reported on 10 July, "The enemy begins attacks with a systematic and mathematically exact destruction of the defenders through artillery barrages and carpet bombing. When despite this attacks fail, they are broken off, only to be launched again with more troops and material. . . . In the defense, the English infantry have proven especially tenacious. The American infantry is not so tough, but it will fight tenaciously as long as it has sufficient fire support. . . . Cooperation among ground, air, and naval forces is good."[15]

Rommel saw what was coming and begged for more resources. On 15 July, he wrote in a report to Kluge:

> The situation on the front in Normandy becomes more difficult every day and is nearing a crisis.
>
> Our own losses in the hard fighting, the incredibly strong material resources of the enemy, above all in artillery and tanks, and the unchallenged enemy control of the air, mean that the battle strength of the divisions quickly sinks. Replacements from the homeland come only in spurts. . . .
>
> Material losses of committed troops are also extremely high and up 'til now have barely been replaced, such as seventeen of 225 panzers.

The newly supplied infantry divisions are untested in battle and ill supplied with artillery, lacking antitank weapons, and in no shape to withstand hours-long artillery and air attacks in a large enemy offensive....

Under these conditions it must be reckoned that the enemy in the foreseeable future will manage to break through the thin front, especially that of Seventh Army, and strike into the vast interior of France. . . . [T]here are no mobile reserves to stop a breakthrough of Seventh Army's front.[16]

Kluge sat on Rommel's report for nearly a week. Rommel attempted to withdraw his mobile divisions from the line and replace them with infantry divisions. Kluge reported on 17 July, however, "The replacement of panzer units with infantry units has not yielded the desired results because of combat conditions. The infantry divisions are so overmatched by modern Anglo-American formations in arms and manpower on the front that assault groups from the panzer units generally have to be sent back into action."[17]

Back in Germany, Hitler was trying to improve the supply of infantry divisions by organizing a new type of formation with fewer troops but increased firepower to spread scarce manpower resources further. On 13 July, he summoned to his headquarters the commanders and immediate subordinates of fifteen infantry divisions and told them they would be the first of what was at first called "defense divisions," but became more famous as volksgrenadier divisions. Organization of the divisions began on the thirtieth, with the goal of having field-ready formations on 1 September.[18]

Blows to the German Battle Leadership

Allied air superiority arguably delivered a telling blow on 17 July, when a Royal Air Force fighter-bomber machine gunned Rommel's car and seriously wounded the field marshal. On the front, the Americans were creating the preconditions for Bradley's breakout plan in the zone defended by LXXXIV Corps. Near St. Lô, two regimental headquarters of the 352nd Infantry Division were under close assault. Farther west, the right wing of the 17th SS Panzergrenadier Division's line was bending back.[19]

With Rommel's loss, Kluge took direct command over Army Group B. He decided to make the 10th SS Panzer Division available to LXXXIV Corps, and Hitler did not object. This change could have meant Patton would be confronted with a much tougher opponent when he first entered battle ten days later, but because the situation around Caen was so uncertain, Kluge was unable to carry out the transfer.[20]

On 18 July, Kluge told the high command that the Normandy fighting had all the hallmarks of a large-scale war of attrition. German losses since D-Day, which were not being made good, amounted to some 2,360 officers and 100,000 men. By 24 July, Kluge counted the loss of nearly 400 more officers and 10,000 noncommissioned officers and men. Only 10,078 replacements had arrived since D-Day.[21]

The catastrophic situation in the east largely accounted for the shortfall in infantry replacements. The Soviets on 22 June attacked Army Group Center with 146 rifle and 43 tank formations, advanced without pause, and in July expanded the offensive to the front of Army Groups North and A. The Soviets destroyed Army Group Center and twenty-five German divisions. The high command was rushing every available resource to the east, where *Generalfeldmarschall* Walter Model had taken command of the army group remnants and was well on his way to reestablishing a front.[22]

The eastern front also drew away all panzer replacements. As of 29 July, Army Group B had lost 393 panzers—the equivalent of roughly three panzer divisions—including 12 38(t), 224 Mark IV, 131 Mark V, and 23 Tigers, plus 60 assault guns and 132 armored half-tracks.[23] The Germans, interestingly enough, had not included the French tanks equipping two independent battalions that had been virtually wiped out in the early phase of the Normandy invasion. "[T] hese losses could not now be made good," noted Inspector of Panzer Troops Guderian in his memoirs, "since after 22 June the whole eastern front threatened to collapse, and all available replacements had to go there instead of to the previously favored western front."[24]

On 20 July, just ten days before Patton took command of Third Army and five days before the launch of the American breakout from Normandy, a bomb exploded in Hitler's bunker, placed there by a group of army conspirators, including senior general officers. Hitler was wounded by the blast, but lived. The bomber was none other than Claus Schenk *Graf* von Stauffenberg, who had nearly been killed in Tunisia when he was with the 10th Panzer Division. The event set off a metaphorical bomb in the German officer corps, much as if a military cabal had nearly killed President Franklin Roosevelt and Eisenhower ten days before the beginning of the Battle of the Bulge, for Hitler was not only the sole political leader that German military commanders had served for more than a decade, but he was the commander of the field armies, too.

A message was circulated to troops in the West on the twenty-first: "A small circle of deposed officers have undertaken an assassination attempt against our führer. The führer lives! He spoke this night to the German people and his soldiers. . . . For us soldiers in the West there is only one slogan: to hold firm on the front against the enemy with unshaken determination and unconditional loyalty to the führer. Long live the führer! Long live Germany!"[25]

After the assassination attempt, Hitler's trust in his Wehrmacht commanders, never very great, turned into outright paranoia and even hatred.[26] The situation must have seemed menacingly familiar to Kluge, who had risen to command Army Group Center in 1941 as the result of Hitler's sweeping purge of general officers whom he deemed disloyal. Combat generals would fight with one eye looking over their shoulder, seeking any sign that the Gestapo had uncovered a hint, true or false, that they had been involved in the conspiracy.

Nevertheless, Kluge had fully realized the perilous state of his front, and on 21 July, he finally forwarded Rommel's assessment to Hitler and added: "My führer! I have been here about fourteen days and after conversations with the most important commanders on this hot front, particularly those from the SS, have come to the conviction that the field marshal regrettably sees things correctly." He went on to underscore most of Rommel's points. "Despite heated efforts," he concluded, "the moment is near when the overloaded front will break. And if the enemy gets into open country, orderly control will hardly be possible in light of the insufficient mobility of our troops."[27]

One result of the assassination was that Hitler on 21 July named Guderian as his new army chief of staff. Guderian was no friend of Kluge's and immediately suggested that Hitler replace him because he had lacked a "lucky touch" commanding large armored formations. According to Guiderian, Hitler responded, "And furthermore, he [Kluge] had foreknowledge of the assassination attempt."[28]

Regarding the enemy, Kluge evidently was beginning to smell the same "Army Group Patton" rat in England that Rundstedt had sniffed out a month earlier. Foreign Armies West at OKH still believed in mid-July that FUSAG controlled between thirty-two and thirty-five American and British divisions, and as late as 21 July, Kluge's headquarters believed that "Army Group Patton" posed a real threat in the form of new amphibious landings along the French coast.[29] Nevertheless, Kluge believed that every meter the Allies gained to the south in Normandy made a second landing less likely. He had pressured Hitler to give him the 116th Panzer Division—the last panzer division in reserve along the Pas de Calais—to use in Normandy, and the führer agreed on 19 July.[30] OKW had supported Kluge's assessment, and the combination for once sufficed to sway Hitler.[31]

The first report that Patton had arrived in Normandy reached the Germans on 22 July, when the 17th SS Panzergrenadier Division *Götz von Berlichingen* reported that prisoners taken from the 83rd Infantry Division's 331st Infantry were saying that Patton was rumored to be in the area and Third Army was behind the front. The prisoners described Patton as "*the* great tank commander" who had met with success in Africa. Documents captured on the 21st appeared to confirm the presence of Third Army, providing the codenames for First and Third Armies, all of their subordinate corps, and the Third Army's divisions. Identification of elements of the 4th Armored Division along a road strengthened the case. The SS division warned that the calm along the front should be interpreted as a regrouping by the enemy and that an attack by strong armored elements should be expected. The captured documents were passed through LXXXIV Corps, which concurred with the 17th SS Division's belief that a large attack was imminent, shared verbally with Seventh Army that day, and reached Seventh Army on 24 July. The information was shared with other divisions in the corps.

Yet Patton's name did not electrify the Germans, and the matter was handled routinely. Perhaps *Oberstgruppenführer* Paul Hausser, who had taken command of Seventh Army on 28 June and from 1940 until that month had fought exclusively on the eastern front, had never heard of Patton before. It is clear that even though II Airborne Corps had, on 19 July, reported capturing a sergeant's notebook indicating that some units in the bridgehead had been subordinated to Third Army, the intelligence chief at Seventh Army did not recognize the importance of the information. The courier schedule meant that the captured documents were not sent until the following day to Army Group B, where they arrived on 26 July.[32] Army Group B's intelligence staff recorded the existence of Third Army under General Patton on the twenty-seventh, though Third Army and Patton's name—followed by a question mark—didn't first appear on the army group's enemy situation map until 30 July.[33] There is no evidence that the information went farther up the chain at this time.

It was by then too late to prevent the Operation Cobra breakout, which was underway. Kluge's weekly report issued on 24 July reflected no anticipation of a large-scale American offensive.[34] Another twelve days would pass until the admittedly distracted Germans put two and two together and conclusively concluded that Patton was commanding Third Army in the field.

COBRA: PATTON LEADS THIRD ARMY TO FAME

The scheme for the Allied escape from the clinging hell of Normandy was almost, though not quite, Mansteinian in its conception. General Bernard Montgomery, by his own account, formulated the strategy well before D-Day. The British and Canadians were to draw German armored reserves to the eastern wing around

Caen, which would allow Bradley to shove forward at the western wing. Where Manstein imagined goals such as "drive France out of the war," however, the Allied strategy focused much more on the breaking free part and posited relatively modest objectives for the movement phase—"a wide sweep to the Seine about Paris," according to Montgomery.[35] Of course, Manstein had not been constrained by having to ship all of his supplies across the English Channel and move them forward over a transportation system ground to dust by air attacks.

Lieutenant General Omar Bradley's operational plan to break out of the Normandy stalemate with his First Army was dubbed Operation Cobra. Major General J. Lawton Collins's VII Corps was to make the main effort in the American center immediately west of St. Lô, with the 83rd and 9th Infantry divisions on the left, the 30th Infantry Division in the center, and the 29th Infantry Division on the right to protect the flank. Once a penetration had been achieved, the motorized 1st Infantry Division, with Combat Command B from the 3rd Armored Division attached, was to exploit it and move four miles southward to Marigny, then turn west ten miles to Coutances, on the coast, to cut off the German left wing. The remainder of the 3rd Armored Division, with a 1st Infantry Division rifle battalion attached, was to secure the southern exits from Coutances. The 2nd Armored Division, with the motorized 22nd Infantry attached, was to drive through the gap and establish more blocking positions. XIX and V Corps were to launch smaller attacks to pin the Germans in place along their fronts east of VII Corps, while VIII Corps pushed southward down the coast to the west to destroy the German left wing, after delaying just long enough for VII Corps to cut off the enemy's retreat.[36]

Kluge accurately anticipated that the main Allied thrust, when it came, would occur in the American sector aimed at taking the area from the Orne River south to Avranches.[37] But Montgomery's Operation Goodwood around Caen, initiated on 18 July, had drawn off most of the German armored strength to face the Commonwealth troops, leaving only a much-weakened Panzer Lehr Division facing VII Corps and the 2nd SS Panzer and 17th SS Panzergrenadier Divisions opposite VIII Corps.

During mid-July, mobile operations by those two panzer divisions had consumed fuel faster than it could be replaced, mainly because of the aggressive disruption of rail lines by Allied fighter-bombers. Only six Army trains per day were able to get from the German border even to Paris.[38]

General der Infanterie Dietrich Choltitz's LXXXIV Corps held the front against VIII Corps across the base of the Cotentin Peninsula, although its rightmost division—Panzer Lehr with one regiment of the 5th Airborne Division attached—opposed the right wing of VII Corps. The corps's other divisions, from right to left, were the 17th SS Panzergrenadier Division with a regiment of the 5th Airborne Division attached; the 2nd SS Panzer Division with the 6th Regiment of the 2nd Airborne Division attached; the 91st Air Landing Division; the 353rd Infantry Division; and the 243rd Infantry Division abutting the coast. The II Airborne Corps, also part of Seventh Army, held the sector to the right.

Panzer Lehr was no longer capable of attacking, but it appeared to be fit enough to defend its line. The 17th SS Panzergrenadier had suffered tremendous casualties in early July and worried Choltitz. One regiment of the 91st Division had been destroyed and was being rebuilt.[39]

As early as late June, Choltitz had foreseen the worst and prepared accordingly. He had defined a series of coded fallback lines, which supply troops were to improve with some field fortifications. He kept knowledge of his preparations restricted to his closest circle, knowing full well the higher authorities would object to them. Indeed, when Kluge stumbled upon the existence of his first fallback line, the Mahlmann Line, he had accused Choltitz of lacking the will to resist. Choltitz's left wing by now rested on his second fallback line, the "water line."[40]

Cobra experienced an inauspicious false start on 24 July. Bad weather forced commanders to cancel the air operation, but the word did not reach some of the heavy bombers already in flight. American troops had withdrawn 1,200 yards from the bomb zone, but some bombers released their loads early and hit soldiers of the 30th Infantry Division some 2,000 yards north of the Périers–St. Lô highway "no-bomb" line. Twenty-five American soldiers were killed and 131 wounded. Cobra was postponed for twenty-four hours.[41]

The day's events were enough to convince *Generalleutnant* Fritz Bayerlein, commanding Panzer Lehr, that this was the real deal. He told Seventh Army that the Americans were about to launch their expected great offensive toward St. Gilles and Coutances. Seventh Army concurred and expected the American main effort to be against the right wing of LXXXIV Corps's line. It incorrectly believed it had beaten off the attack that day, not grasping that the Americans had pulled up short.[42]

VII Corps kicked into gear the next day, disregarding additional "friendly" bombings of its line. Fifteen hundred B-17 and B-24 heavy bombers from the U.S. Eighth Air Force dropped more than 3,300 tons of bombs in a 2,500-yard by 6,000-yard box in front of VII Corps. More than 550 fighter-bombers from the IX Tactical Air Command dropped more than 200 tons of bombs and a large amount of napalm, while 396 B-26 medium bombers unloaded more than 650 tons of high explosive and fragmentation bombs.[43]

Carpet-bombing had a devastating impact on the Panzer Lehr Division. Bayerlein, recalled, "The digging in of the infantry was useless and did not

protect against bombing as the bombed area had been turned into a terrain pitted with craters. Dugouts and foxholes were smashed, the men buried, and we were unable to save them. The same happened to guns and tanks. . . . For me, who during this war was in every theater committed at the points of the main effort, this was the worst I ever saw."[44]

Despite the fact that most of the carpet-bombing hit its intended targets, the Germans fought stubbornly, and for the first day and a half progress, seemed glacially slow to the Americans. Seventh Army, however, by 2100 hours, acknowledged that, "various small breakthroughs in the zone of Panzer Lehr and to the left have grown together into a comprehensive breakthrough." The Ia believed that a general withdrawal to a line running through Coutances might be necessary because there was no place farther north where an effective line could be anchored; the staff began packing materials in preparation for a move to Mortain. Kluge opined that Panzer Lehr was near the end of its strength and said he wanted the division extracted from the line.[45] Army Group B assessed that Seventh Army's front on the first day had "broken" along five miles of its length to a depth of more than a mile.[46] Choltitz apparently acted on his own and ordered all of its divisions to fall back to the "yellow line" that night.[47]

From the German perspective, the launch of Cobra was just more bad news. Montgomery's troops attacked again on the twenty-fifth along a four-mile front and drove the Germans back more than two miles before the I SS Panzer Corps could stop them. Still, Kluge was worried about the new American pressure and asked Hitler's permission to pull back his left wing to free up the 2nd SS Panzer Division *Das Reich* to form a mobile reserve.[48]

Collins decided on 26 July to commit his mobile forces, despite the failure to capture objectives that he had originally deemed necessary to permit use of his exploitation force. His timing was impeccable, because the German fabric had begun to tear.[49]

Collins sent two armored columns driving south into the guts of the disintegrating German defenses on the afternoon of 26 July. On the right, Maj. Gen. Clarence Huebner's 1st Infantry Division (motorized) with Combat Command B (CCB), 3rd Armored Division, attached, passed through the 9th Infantry Division and pushed toward Marigny. Major General Edward "Ted" Brooks's 2nd Armored Division, with the 4th Infantry Division's 22nd Infantry Regiment attached, drove south and east on the left, passing through the 30th Infantry Division to seize St. Gilles.[50]

Brigadier General Maurice Rose's Combat Command A (CCA) led the 2nd Armored Division advance as the second column punched south toward St. Gilles against sporadic resistance. The combat command rolled through St. Gilles by midafternoon, and therewith the breakout from Normandy was guaranteed.[51]

Seventh Army reported that it was counterattacking these penetrations, but that was pure bluster.[52] Without even consulting Hitler this time, on 26 July, Kluge, on his own authority, ordered the 2nd Panzer Division to shift from Panzer Group West opposite the British to stem the tide. Orders for the 116th Panzer Division and XLVII Panzer Corps followed the next day.[53] The 2nd Panzer Division moved out on the twenty-seventh, but would never reach the point of the breakout.[54]

On 26 July, *Generalleutnant* Otto Elfeldt, commanding the 47th Infantry Division, was summoned to the Army Group B headquarters, where Kluge told him he was to take command of LXXXIV Corps. He was to hold his line until the promised panzer counterattack occurred the following day.[55]

Faced with what was obviously a great offensive, Kluge stopped worrying about the possibility of an additional Allied landing on the channel coast. On 27 July, Kluge told OKW that the best available information indicated that all positively identified staff elements of combat echelons were in Normandy, as were the majority of available American and British combat troops. Any landings in the near future by the FUSAG were unlikely.[56] Kluge was clearly more interested in where the Allies' combat divisions were than in any putative role of George Patton.

The breach in Seventh Army's front had grown quickly to ten miles wide and up to ten miles deep. Kluge by now knew that he would soon have to grapple with Third Army, not just First Army.[57] Kluge asked Hitler that the 9th Panzer Division be sent to him from German First Army in southwestern France, and the worried führer agreed, even though that left but one panzer division in the south of France. Convinced that a landing in southern France was likely, Hitler forbade weakening Nineteenth Army, which protected the Mediterranean coast, any further. OB West that evening received a message from Bayerlein that his Panzer Lehr Division had been annihilated, and the Allies were pouring south—a message Kluge forwarded to Hitler shortly after midnight. At 2200 hours, Hitler ordered the 708th Infantry Division, also part of First Army, and Fifteenth Army's 84th and 331st Infantry Divisions to rush to Kluge's aid, decisions approved by Hitler even before Bayerlein's shocking message arrived from OB West.[58]

Elfeldt finally reached Seventh Army headquarters at 1700 hours, having been delayed by three attacks by jabos (Jagdbombers, fighter-bombers) on the way. There, Oberstgruppenführer Hausser denied having played any role in sacking his predecessor, Generalleutnant Choltitz, and made it clear he was far more pessimistic about the situation than Kluge was. He did not even know where the main line of resistance ran along the front of Elfeldt's LXXXIV Corps. The armored counterattack had not come off, and the steely eyed Hausser doubted it would the next day, either, because of Allied control of the air. Driving on to his new headquarters, Elfeldt met Choltitz and his staff, and he found that they, too, were uncertain where the front was at the moment.[59]

Kluge's overall logistical situation, meanwhile, was becoming chaotic, which meant that even the troops he had were fighting ever less effectively. "As a consequence of new large battles, both attacked armies are consuming ammunition at higher levels," noted the Army Group B quartermaster. "Supplies from depots have been completely inadequate for days. Not a single train has arrived in ten days. All remaining reserves will be sent forward to partially cover demand." That day, a single supply train reached Seventh Army. The situation was all the worse because the army group had lost 1,866 trucks and more than a thousand other transport vehicles since the landings.[60]

Appointed Bradley's deputy, with responsibility for the right wing, Patton on 27 July began to oversee VIII Corps operations, as Middleton's corps was to become part of Third Army upon the latter's activation. Let us review the many aspects of Patton's good luck the day he became an active player in the European war. Nearly seven weeks of hard fighting by the British, the Canadians, and the Americans of First Army had worn the German army in Normandy to tatters. The enemy's front ahead of Patton had already crumbled, and the opposing commanders did not even know where their forward lines were. His enemies' mobile divisions were all heavily engaged elsewhere. Allied control of the air had nearly broken the opposition's logistic chain, was interfering with the movement of panzers, and would deny enemy commanders aerial reconnaissance of his operations. The German command was also shuddering with the aftershocks of the attempt on Hitler's life.

Patton, whom the Germans were not supposed to know was in Normandy, remained in the background, but as the official U.S. Army history observed, "[H]is presence was unmistakable, and his imprint on the operations that developed was as visible as his shadow on the wall of the operations tent." That evening, Patton showed his hand and ordered that the corps's two armored divisions, the 4th and the 6th, to replace the infantry divisions at the point of the attack the next day.[61]

On 28 July, Maj. Gen. John Wood's 4th Armored Division passed through the 90th Infantry Division on the corps's left, while Maj. Gen. Robert Grow's 6th Armored passed through the 79th Infantry Division on the right. Both struck southward toward Avranches, the strategic town at the base of the Cotentin Peninsula. The capture of Avranches would open the door to Brittany and the interior of France.

The inexperience of the armored divisions, more than any resistance, determined the relatively slow pace of Patton's initial advance—some fifteen miles per day—because for practical purposes, except for scattered remnants, both LXXXIV Corps and Seventh Army were out of contact with VIII Corps from 27 through 30 July, when the 4th Armored Division took Avranches without much fighting, but encountered resistance for the first time in the environs.[62]

Indeed, Elfeldt toured the left wing of his front the morning of 28 July and found that three exhausted divisions, each with but 300 to 400 riflemen still in the field, held an incoherent front from the seacoast to the Percy area. He concluded that his corps could not withstand another attack. He returned to his headquarters, where he found Choltitz and Hausser. Choltitz told him, "You are arriving at an historic moment. The enemy has made a breakthrough. The first enemy tanks are probably moving into Avranches at this moment."[63]

According to Elfeldt, Hausser at first ordered him to stand fast, but at some point—with American tanks nearing the corps command post, according to Hausser—the army commander told LXXXIV Corps to break out toward the southeast, a move that threatened to create a gap between the left flank and the coast.[64] Kluge, unaware of the order, again begged for and was promised the 116th Panzer Division in order to finally get a counterattack under way.[65] He was, however, aware that Seventh Army had concluded the front on the coast to be lost and had ordered formations around Coutances to break out of the developing encirclement.[66]

The German priority was now to prevent VII Corps from slashing to the coast and cutting off LXXXIV Corps—not stopping Patton, which had clearly become impossible. On 28 and 29 July, the Germans succeeded in building a masterful ad hoc defensive line running north to south parallel to the coast with elements of the 243rd and 353rd infantry and 91st Air Landing Divisions. Kluge intended to hold these positions until the 116th Panzer Division could arrive and launch a counterattack beside the 2nd Panzer Division (both under XLVII Panzer Corps).[67] Allied fighter-bombers had imposed significant delays on the panzer columns, ensuring that the panzers would not arrive in time.[68]

The line nevertheless denied the 1st Infantry and 3rd Armored Divisions their objective at Coutances, allowing the bulk of the units north of the town to slip the noose and escape to man a ramshackle east-west line that had been thrown together about ten miles to the south.[69]

While this was unfolding, on the night of 28–29 July, the high command intervened to countermand Seventh Army's retreat order and instructed LXXXIV Corps to maintain its front abutting the sea under all circumstances. Kluge already had leapt into action to change Hausser's orders. *Oberst* Rudolf *Freiherr* von Gersdorff, who had supplied Stauffenberg with the fuse and explosives for the attack on Hitler, arrived at Army Group B's headquarters on the twenty-eighth to become Seventh Army's new chief of staff. He recalled, "Kluge lost his temper, called up. . . Hausser, and ordered him to revoke the orders immediately and to keep close contact between the left wing of the army and the west coast. The communication was bad, and [Hausser] observed that it might be too late for counterorders."

Meanwhile, OKW contemplated a possible fallback position, using the Seine as a temporary line while a line along the Somme-Marne and running down to the Vosges Mountains was fortified. Hitler had reacted favorably to Keitel's presentation on the possibility on 23 July, even before the Cobra storm had broken. On the twenty-eighth, orders went to *OB West* to begin construction of the fortifications and to place mines in front of the West Wall, Metz, and the Vosges.[70]

Rather than counterattacking on 29 July, the 2nd Panzer Division fell back under heavy pressure and suffered numerous losses. Only the reconnaissance battalion of the 116th Panzer Division managed to arrive in the threatened sector, and its arrival had no impact on the battle. Kluge's orders to stop LXXXIV Corps's withdrawal had no effect, as Hausser had forewarned, and the 2nd SS Panzer and Panzer Lehr Divisions had withdrawn farther than ordered, leaving only the 91st Air Landing Division fighting on. American tanks passed within 100 yards of Seventh Army's headquarters, which immediately decamped to Mortain.[71]

Kluge spent 30 July personally opposite Patton and VIII Corps, trying to keep his left wing from caving in. The 91st Air Landing Division was shredding, however, under tank attacks supported by fighter-bombers. The 116th Panzer Division was entangled with VII Corps and having the worst of it, and elements of the 2nd Panzer and 17th SS Panzer Divisions were surrounded south of Percy and fighting to break free. No armor was going to arrive to save the day. The road to Avranches was open.[72]

Oberst Eugen Koenig's 91st Air Landing Division had already been "badly decimated" in the fighting before Operation Cobra exploded. Koenig had been a junior officer in the Great War and then returned to civilian life. The army had recalled him to active duty in 1936, and he rose from company to division commander with extreme speed because of his excellent performance (and the death of his immediate predecessor in battle on D-Day). Koenig had been awarded the Knight's Cross with Oak Leaves, and Choltitz considered him a young and fresh personality who had a tremendously positive influence on his troops. Koenig recalled the collapse of his exhausted division under Patton's blows:

> The enemy situation was at first completely obscure. Our aerial reconnaissance had ceased to function. . . . On 30 July, *Oberst* Klosterkämper, commander of the remnants of the 243rd Infantry Division, arrived at my command post and reported that his units had been almost completely annihilated. . . . Simultaneously, reports came in that the enemy was pursuing the remnants of the 243rd Infantry Division with strong forces and tanks. . . .
>
> The situation on our front became critical. The strength of the grenadier regiment was scarcely 200 men. It was possible to occupy the main line of resistance only with individual strong points. . . . Reports of the appearance of tanks came from everywhere. Early on 30 July, the division still had two assault guns, but these were put out of action. . . .
>
> The available supply of ammunition and fuel began to diminish rapidly. More and more elements on the front were put out of action, were cut off, or

were taken prisoner. The enemy advanced closer to the division command post. The division ordered all available forces to assemble on a small hill north of the command post. . . . Isolated elements were ordered to fight through to the southeast at dawn. . . .

[W]e were able to disengage from the enemy at dawn and withdraw to the south. We were unable to carry out our plan to occupy the high ground north of Avranches on both sides of the Avranches road; the enemy had already captured Avranches and the high ground. Attempts to break through to the south failed. Therefore, we decided to cross the inlet at Avranches with the remnants of the division. . . at night at low tide.[73]

Kluge reported on 30 July, "After an artillery preparation and carpet-bombing of never before seen intensity, the enemy succeeded in days-long fighting in breaking through between Vire and the sea. Our losses in men and material were so high because of the enemy's superiority in artillery and the air that the quick reestablishment of a defensive front was not possible. . . . The situation between the line St. Hilaire-Percy and the sea is unclear. . . ."[74] Seventh Army was trying to stitch together a string of strong points running from Percy to south of Avranches, which was now held by the enemy.[75]

NO BETTER FORTUNE

Just as Patton strode onto the stage of the European theater, the other fellow in Normandy was reeling backward and out of Patton's way; off balance; running out of men, equipment, and supplies; and looking for a way to extricate himself from an *already* losing fight. The large German army group to Patton's south was pinned in place by the threat of more Allied landings on the Mediterranean shore.

The headquarters of Army Group B appears by 31 July to have been out of touch with reality. At 0100 hours, *Generalleutnant* Hans Speidel, Kluge's chief of staff, called Seventh Army to order LXXXIV Corps to withdraw to the line Avranches-Villedieu, a line already lost to the enemy. He was told it was questionable whether the order would get through. Moreover, the left wing had collapsed. Less than an hour later Seventh Army reiterated: Speidel's orders will not work, because LXXXIV Corps was in such a state that one could hardly expect it to mount any further resistance.[76]

Kluge reported to the high command at 1040 on 31 July that the Allied advance beyond Avranches could not be stopped.[77] Army Group B had identified three armored divisions under U.S. First Army that appeared ready to push to the southeast. American troops arrived at the LXXXIV Corps headquarters and forced the staff to flee. XLVII Panzer Corps now controlled but remnants of its mobile divisions, and U.S. VII Corps stood solidly between it and the Avranches breakthrough.[78] Fuel was so short that panzers were being abandoned on the battlefield, as were many invaluable trucks.[79]

Eberbach's panzer group was waging a desperate battle against the British, but Eberbach was now looking over his left shoulder with alarm. The veteran panzer general contacted Army Group B and proposed that he conduct a general withdrawal to the Seine before it was too late to avoid disaster.[80]

Eisenhower, on 31 July, signaled Marshall that Third Army under Patton would become operational the next day, but that there would be no public announcement in order to maintain the Pas de Calais deception plan.[81] Ike had concocted a story to leak to the Germans about Patton having been demoted to command of an army because of various indiscretions, though there is no sign that the Germans picked up this tale.[82]

Hitler met with Jodl on the thirty-first to discuss the grand strategic situation. Hitler said he was most worried that day about the situation in the east, where Army Groups North and Center had been mauled, and Soviet troops were nearing the Prussian frontier. The führer nevertheless was confident that his countermeasures would stabilize the situation. In Italy, the war was tying down enemy forces that could be used elsewhere, and Germany had to hope it could cling to a line in the Apennines because after that, there would be no stopping until the Alps.

Then Hitler dropped a bombshell: France, he said, could not be held, even though losing it would undermine the U-boat war. Hitler's analysis was remarkably dispassionate, if not unclouded, and he was already thinking clearly about what had to be done.[83]

"[It is] clear that an operation in France—and I believe we must be fully aware of this at all times—is totally impossible in so-called open field of battle under today's circumstances," he said. "We can't do that. We can move some of our troops, but only in a limited manner. With the other ones we can't move, not because we don't possess air superiority, but because we can't move the troops themselves: the units are not suitable for mobile battle—neither their weapons nor their other equipment."[84]

During the spring debate about whether the panzer reserves should be held back in central France or kept very close to the coast, Rommel had perceptively argued that it would be impossible to move the panzers forward quickly enough because of the Allies' control of the air. He had wanted to place as many divisions forward as possible to repulse a landing and to deal with any airborne operations. But, according to Jodl's diary, Rommel had also asserted something far more dire and fundamental: "Mobile battle with panzer units is a thing of the past." Movement was possible only at night or during the day with 150 meters between vehicles. The führer, however, had sided in early April with Rundstedt, who had wanted to hold most panzer divisions in reserve to stage an open-field counterattack.[85] By the end of July, Hitler appears to have developed a synthesis of those two opinions.

Hitler reasoned that he barely had had enough strength to hold the short line in Normandy and that the small fraction of divisions mobile enough to withdraw to a fallback line would be far short of the manpower needed to hold it. Germany could fight in France only if it could reestablish control of the air, but since that was not possible, Hitler and Jodl considered and dismissed trying to stand along the Seine River. The Somme offered possibilities for a delaying line because some preparation of field fortifications was already underway along the river. That might work if the Allies concentrated their effort in the north for a drive toward the Ruhr industrial basin. Eisenhower's broad-front strategy would crush this notion.

But Hitler fully grasped the logical conclusion. "A proper defense can only be established where we have either the West Wall or at least ground conditions to permit this—and that would be the Vosges [Mountains]. There we can organize resistance."

The West Wall, known to the Allies as the Siegfried Line, ran nearly 400 miles from north of Aachen along the German frontier to the Swiss border. The Germans had neglected the defenses after 1940, and Hitler on 23 July, in another sign of strategic realism, had authorized renovating the defenses.

"[Y]ou can see that a breakthrough . . . can happen quickly!" he said.

Hitler issued his orders. First, OKW, working with the navy, was to identify which ports the Allies would need the most—the only evident bottleneck to a seemingly unlimited supply of reinforcements—and then those ports were to be held. "[W]e should be able to hold the harbor for six, eight, or ten weeks—and those six, eight, or ten weeks will mean a lot in the months of August, September, and October." Hitler's grasp of the supply problems the Allies would face was unerring and better than that of most commanders on the opposing side.

The second point was to get combat units out safely to the east. "[N]ow we have to demand from *OB West* that units which are not intended for fixed positions be made mobile—temporarily mobile—and that he report all of this," Hitler said. He also sketched out his plan to withdraw Army Group G from southern France, orders he would be forced to issue in only six more weeks.

Hitler, however, told Jodl that he was not to share the big picture with the army group commanders. Moreover, Hitler was aware that the Allies had excellent intelligence on his intentions, which he blamed on the coup plotters at his headquarters and in Paris rather than Ultra. Jodl was not to transmit the führer's desires through the chain of command, but rather, tell Kluge only what specifics he needed to answer questions and act.

Finally, Hitler and Jodl talked about setting up a central staff to control the western front because Kluge was too stretched acting as both chief of Army Group B and *OB West*. "He's not in Paris at all," said Jodl. "He's leading the army group. They never see him anymore. . . . They want to have Rundstedt back, because Kluge is hardly accessible to them."[86]

Jodl contacted Blumentritt at *OB West* and using indirect language told him to expect a withdrawal order and to immediately begin planning and preparations, including sending work crews to assist the Todt Organization (a civil and military engineering group in the Third Reich) in constructing a line along the Somme and Marne Rivers.[87]

Near Avranches, meanwhile, Kluge cast about for some means—any means—to stem the breakthrough. He ordered XXV Corps to strike back with whatever troops it could gather from northern Brittany.[88] One could have heard a pin drop, it was said, at the headquarters of the 77th Infantry Division, located near a crucial bridge across the Sélune at Pontaubault, four miles from Avranches, the evening of 30 July when the Ia read out a signal from the field marshal. *Oberst* Rudolf Bacherer, whose division had been shredded in the Normandy fighting and was just refitting, was to take and hold Avranches at all costs: "It is the keystone of our defense. On it hangs the decision in the West," Kluge told him.[89]

Bacherer may have thought the idea to be crazy, because he was soon on the phone with Seventh Army headquarters, which told him, "You are to occupy the bridge with at least one *Sturmgeschütz* [assault gun], prepare it for demolition, advance toward Avranches, and take the city."

Bacherer was a reserve officer who had been thrust into command upon the death of the regular commander in June, and his corps commander, Choltitz, had considered him a "determined and completely fearless leader" who enjoyed the deep confidence of his men. It was Bacherer who had held the division together long enough to get it out of Normandy. Bacherer scraped together what resources he could, including his own troops, fourteen assault guns, a battalion of the 5th Airborne Division, and stragglers from collecting points, and attacked Avranches at dawn on 31 July.[90]

Bacherer ordered a demolition party to destroy the valuable bridge across the Sélune, but the first group of pioneers ran into American fire and was cut down. A second team was ambushed, and all the men were taken captive. American tanks were soon crossing the span, and some appeared outside Bacherer's command post. Bacherer and his staff narrowly escaped capture by scurrying away along a sunken lane, just out of sight of the Americans.[91]

Kluge called Speidel at 0920 hours to say that the enemy occupied Avranches, his own assault guns had been driven back, and the results of 77th Division's attack were unknown. Fighter-bombers, he said, were making all planned movement impossible. The two generals admitted they had no real idea what was going on in the Avranches-Villedieu area. But it was obvious that the western front had been torn open. This had to be made clear to OKW. Kluge was particularly concerned about Villedieu, a road hub whose capture would allow the enemy freedom to operate to the east and south.

A short while later, Kluge told Warlimont at OKW that he still hoped to stem the tide at Avranches by bringing everything available from St. Malo. But he described the desperate battle situation in the strongest terms: "With the forces available, we cannot rebuild the front." OKW had to send him formations from Fifteenth Army immediately. He told Warlimont that the French in the Great War had used the public buses of Paris to rush reinforcements to the front. But even with more men, Kluge concluded, it wasn't clear if he could stop the enemy.[92]

The morning of 1 August must have been one of the most thrilling in Patton's life, for that day he would take the sword of Third Army in his hand and wage war as he had longed to wage it. The omens were good: it was a warm day, and early morning clouds that grounded fighter-bombers were to give way to bright, clear skies in the afternoon. XIX Tactical Air Command became operational the same day under the command of Brig. Gen. O. P. Weyland, whose headquarters was adjacent to Patton's, so Patton would have his own air force to sweep through those heavens to wreak destruction on the enemy. Supplies of fuel and ammunition were brimming full.[93]

Lieutenant General Courtney Hodges and his First Army were just finishing with irrevocably opening the exit door from Normandy. That day, V Corps's 4th Infantry Division captured Villedieu, the inland doorjamb with hinges matching those of the outer doorjamb on the coast at Avranches, and Kluge's worst fears were realized.[94] Kluge signaled OKW from Seventh Army headquarters, "As a result of the breakthrough of the enemy armored spearheads, the whole Western front has been ripped open. . . . The left flank has collapsed."[95] He could move nothing from his right wing, and, in fact, that day, Panzer Group West had been forced to pull I SS Panzer Corps away from the critical sector at Caen to prevent a second strategic breakthrough by the British at Coulvain.[96]

The Army Group B daily report observed, "Montgomery appears to be striving for the meeting of the English and American [armies] at Falaise. . . ."

Enemy tanks had, nevertheless, appeared at Rennes, in Brittany. The Germans, however, had only a first idea that the enemy was George Patton and his Third Army.[97]

BRITTANY: A STRATEGIC CUL-DE-SAC

Third Army became active at high noon on 1 August. In addition to Middleton's VIII Corps, Patton had in his charge XII Corps, commanded by Maj. Gen. Gilbert Cook; XV Corps, commanded by Maj. Gen. Wade Haislip; and XX Corps, commanded by Maj. Gen. Walton Walker, the latter three corps being located in rear areas.[98]

Because the Germans had continued to believe in the threat to Pas de Calais until well into July, they had shifted formations from Brittany to reinforce the Normandy front rather than denude Fifteenth Army. That meant that once Third Army broke into the peninsula, Brittany "could be plucked like an overripe fruit," as Col. Robert Allen, Patton's deputy G-2, put it.[99] Third Army had only a vague picture of German capabilities in Brittany, but assessed the enemy capable only of delay and local counterattacks and likely to either evacuate by sea or withdraw into the coastal fortresses.[100]

Three of the five German divisions assigned to Brittany as of D-Day were static and composed of older men only conditionally fit for active duty. By the time Third Army arrived, XXV Corps, responsible for the peninsula's defense, had two static divisions—the 265th and 266th Infantry—and the 2nd Airborne Division, which was still rebuilding after fighting in the east and was short of arms. To these were added the shards of the 77th and 91st Divisions retreating from Avranches.[101]

Patton now ordered VIII Corps to make a sharp right turn into the Brittany peninsula in accordance with Operation Overlord plans that anticipated using captured Breton ports to supply the Allied armies. Under the plan, Third Army's mission was to capture the peninsula and "hold open" the ports, and at the same time keep the corridor out of Normandy free from enemy interference. It was also to be prepared for further operations to the east.[102] Patton intended first to drive through Rennes to Quiberon Bay, on the south coast, to cut the peninsula at its base, then to drive westward up the central plateau and pen German forces into coastal fortresses along both coasts. VIII Corps's wide-open left flank was to be screened by patrols from the 106th Cavalry Group.

A three-pronged mechanized force, trailed by infantry divisions as quickly as they could move, surged into the peninsula. The 4th Armored Division led the advance on Rennes, the 6th Armored Division slashed up the middle toward Brest, and the provisional Task Force A rolled toward Brest along the rail line

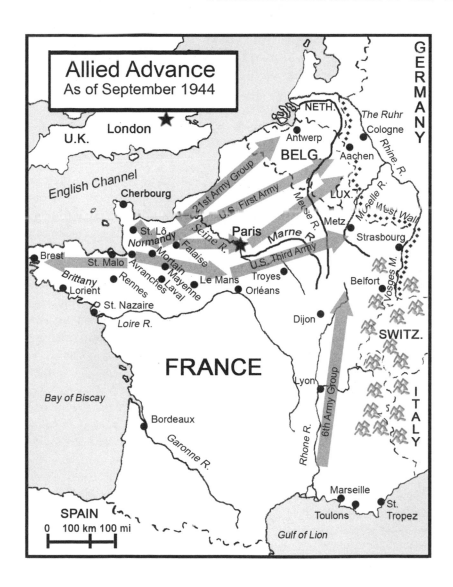

Allied Advance
As of September 1944

that generally follows the north coast. Major General Wade Haislip's XV Corps, activated on 31 July, followed through the Avranches chokepoint, ready to strike eastward toward the Seine River.[103]

As noted earlier, Hitler wanted to hold onto key ports in large measure to constrict the flow of supplies and men to the Allied armies. Hitler, in January 1944, had declared the most important harbors on the Atlantic and Channel coasts to be "fortresses" and provided them with resources to construct fortifications in the landward side. Then-*Generalleutnant* Walter Warlimont, Jodl's deputy, described the idea as Hitler's own, inspired by the success of strong points on the eastern front. The führer underscored the importance he gave this plan by summoning all the fortress commanders to his headquarters to personally explain their duties to them.[104]

Seventh Army followed reports from Brittany as the Americans advanced, but there was nothing it could do about the situation there.[105]

Phosphorus and Brimstone at St. Malo

Although the Germans would use old fortifications in modern war without any specific thought that Patton would be their enemy, they hit upon a temptation that would reliably sucker the American general into bloody and expensive operations to take them. Bradley's directive to Patton stipulated that VIII Corps could bypass St. Malo if taking it would demand too much time and too large a force.[106] *General der Infanterie* Wilhelm Farmbacher, commanding XXV Corps, had ordered *Oberst* Bacherer and his 77th Division remnants to delay the American advance toward St. Malo, a mission well beyond Bacherer's capabilities. He also instructed that efforts be made to mount a defense in Rennes. By 3 August, however, Farmbacher was aware that American tanks were racing through Brittany and could not be stopped, and he ordered all formations to withdraw into the nearest coastal fortress.[107]

Any man could see that the collapse in the West was general, that no relief would be forthcoming, and that soldiers who locked themselves in coastal fortresses faced probable death—and at best capture. *Oberst* Bacherer, leading the 700 men still surviving after the 77th Division's defeat near Avranches, summoned his *Landsers* into formation upon reaching the St. Malo fortress. "Family men, two paces forward!" he bellowed. These men, Bacherer sent toward the Americans to be taken prisoner and kept safe.[108]

While the 6th Armored Division did bypass St. Malo on its race to Brest, Task Force A did not. The garrison commanding officer, *Oberst* Andreas von Aulock, waged the battle for the fortress on his own, with no guidance from XXV Corps. Bacherer took charge of the forces west of the Rance estuary. On 4 August, the task force, joined by the 330th Infantry Regiment, 83rd Infantry Division, attacked the city from the south. Resistance was fierce, and the next day, the 83rd Division took over the siege and released Task Force A to continue along the coast road toward Brest. The garrison at St. Malo constituted the only cohesive resistance that day in all of Third Army's zone.[109]

All Army Group B knew about the situation in Brittany on 6 August could be summed up in its report: "*Kampfgruppen* of XXV Corps are fighting around

St. Malo, Dinan, and St. Brieuec . . . against a superior enemy, who already holds many of the road centers with the help of the terrorists."[110]

On 7 August, Hitler ordered Kluge to hold St. Malo to the last man.[111] Fighting there, XXV Corps reported, was in full swing. The 265th Infantry Division reported numerous enemy tanks between Redon and Vannes, and the 4th Armored Division had cut off Lorient on the landward side. The 6th Armored Division turned up at the walls of Brest, the second-largest port in France. XXV Corps promptly ordered that all harbor facilities in Brittany be destroyed.[112] Brittany no longer held any strategic importance, yet Hitler's fortresses would tie up the valuable 6th Armored Division for weeks, much to Patton's ultimate disgust.[113]

In the weapon pits of the 86th Chemical Mortar Battalion, men dropped huge rounds into their 4.2-inch tubes and sent payloads of Willie Pete—white phosphorus, or WP—arcing toward the fortress. White phosphorus was employed mainly to create smoke screens to shield the movement of ground troops, but the stuff clung to clothing, skin, or pretty much anything else and burned with a hellish intensity. For a week, the mortar men delivered Aulock's and Bacherer's men a daily shower of fresh brimstone.[114]

On 8 August, the Americans reached St. Malo's harbor, just after two last boats slipped away bearing German wounded to the Jersey islands. The harbor had been thoroughly destroyed. Attacker and defender grappled in bitter house-to-house fighting. Hard fighting swirled around Josefsberg, and the defenders' assault guns ran out of ammunition. The 83rd Infantry Division pushed the Germans under Aulock's command into the citadel on 9 August.[115]

Early on 15 August, Bacherer picked up the telephone ringing in his underground headquarters on Paulus Hill, west of the estuary, and was shocked to hear the voice on the other end say, "This is Major General Macon." Through an interpreter, Maj. Gen. Robert C. Macon, commander of the 83rd Infantry, pointed out that his men had penetrated the Germans' strong points, and he invited Bacherer to surrender. The colonel declined, but asked if the Americans would accept his wounded, and a brief cease-fire was agreed upon so the casualties could be transferred.

Then came the final battle, Armageddon for the Germans. White-phosphorus shells rained down again. The ammunition dump exploded, and straw in the unventilated dormitories caught fire. Men staggered, coughing, through smoke and gloom. Bacherer saw further resistance was useless and raised the white flag. The 350 men he had left put their hands on their heads and marched into captivity.[116]

Aulock had told his men on 12 August, "We have sworn allegiance to the führer unto death." He apparently had second thoughts, and the day before he surrendered, Aulock commented to another officer that he had never been a National Socialist. The defenders of the citadel capitulated the seventeenth.[117]

Lorient Ignored

Farmbacher and his XXV Corps staff were located in Lorient, and it was the only battle the general could control. The city and wharfs had already been badly damaged by bombing aimed at the U-boat pens. The pens themselves had never been penetrated, and Farmbacher had his command post there.[118]

The garrison of 25,000 men—two infantry battalions and two or three fortress companies, plus battalions in the outer defenses—lacked mobile antitank weapons, assault guns, and other antitank weapons, and additional "thrown-together" units, including naval and other personnel, had neither the weapons nor training for the fight they faced. The garrison also had some *Osttruppen*, former Soviet soldiers recruited into the Wehrmacht, and these men proved completely unreliable. Nevertheless, the garrison possessed three artillery battalions plus a dozen other batteries, as well as heavy and light flak.[119]

Farmbacher expected an American attack almost immediately, but when nothing but probes ensued, he realized the enemy had his sights set on Brest. The Americans surrounded the landward side with much of the 94th Infantry Division, giving Farmbacher a month to organize and strengthen his defenses. He had time to give infantry training to the naval and other personnel who had none and organize five infantry regiments, a *pionier* battalion, and two separate battalions.

No assault ever developed, and eventually the Americans were able to free up their combat troops by replacing them with a weak division of French volunteers.[120]

The Americans likewise never tried to assault St. Nazaire, which was garrisoned by only two battalions and two or three fortress companies, though it was well stocked with artillery in its fortifications. The Germans reckoned the defenses tied down one and a half divisions for nine months.[121]

Brest Defies Patton

Brest was going to be a tough nut to crack. The old French fortifications overlooked a spectacular natural harbor, as did terrain well suited to the defense. Any approach by sea would be extremely difficult because of the narrow inlet. Farmbacher had concentrated in the city the 343rd Infantry Division, the 2nd Airborne Division, and elements of the 266th Division, most of which had arrived just ahead of the posse on 5 and 6 August. On direct orders from OKW, *General der Fallschirmtruppe* (General of the Airborne Troops) Hermann-Bernhard Ramcke, commanding general of the 2nd Airborne Division, took charge of the defenses on 13 August. Ramcke, who had fought in the naval infantry in the Great War, had participated in the invasion of Crete and fought in Africa, Italy, and Russia. His greatest moment had been during the beginning of Rommel's retreat from El Alamein, when his brigade had been cut off and thought lost for good. Instead, he led 600 paratroopers back to Rommel. "They had been equipped with very few vehicles," recalled Rommel, "but had ambushed some British lorries and made themselves mobile. Ramcke must have led them extremely well."

Naval and alarm units filled out the garrison of some 15,000 men. The artillery was fairly weak, with only two batteries of coastal artillery available. But the defensive works were of the latest construction and were proof against the heaviest bombs and shells.[122]

Middleton's VIII Corps, on 26 August, began the assault on Brest with more than three divisions, an operation that would drag on until after Patton turned control over Brittany to Ninth Army. Bradley and Patton both had fallen into Hitler's trap. Patton recorded, "[Bradley] said to me, with reference to the Brest operation, 'I would not say this to anyone but you, and have given different excuses to my staff and higher echelons, but we must take Brest in order to maintain the illusion of the fact that the U.S. Army cannot be beaten.' More emotion than I thought he had. I fully concur in this view. Any time we put our hand to a job we must finish it."[123]

As of 2 September, the Brest garrison had suffered 619 men killed in action, 1,965 wounded, and 2,799 gone missing. Sixty-three of 193 artillery pieces had been destroyed and another nineteen damaged.

On 4 September, the Ramcke reported, "Continuing and strong artillery and mortar fire as well as high- and low-altitude air strikes hit the entire fortress area, the Crozon peninsula, and the La Conquet sector. Strong enemy attacks on the west part of the fortress in combination with heavy artillery and mortar fire, as well as tank and close air support, were stopped by our troops with heavy casualties on both sides; penetrations in the north and at La Trinité were turned back. . . . Destruction of all militarily significant facilities in Brest (train station, electrical station) as well as destruction of the port have been completed."[124]

The defenders at Brest tied up VIII Corps until 19 September in the fortress proper and 22 September on the Crozon peninsula. The entire struggle for the city lasted six weeks.[125]

PATTON'S RACE TO GLORY

As far as the route to Paris and the Third Reich was concerned, the other fellow was out of Patton's way. Kluge contacted OKW by telephone late in the morning of 1 August to report that American tanks had breached the line at Pontaubault.[126] "The area east of Avranches is wide open," Kluge reported. Asked later by interrogators when he had concluded the war was lost, Jodl replied, "The war was already lost in the West at the time of the breakthrough at Avranches and the beginning of the war of movement in France."[127] In other words, the struggle in gross terms was over before Patton had really done a thing.

The führer told Kluge he could use any and all resources in Brittany and Normandy to seal the breach the Americans had created, but at the point of decision or anywhere nearby, no such resources existed. The problem was particularly acute regarding mobile divisions, which were out of position and badly shot up. OKW reckoned that of the 1,347 Panzer IV-VI and 337 assault guns available in Normandy since D-Day, as of 31 July, 406 panzers and 75 assault guns had been completely destroyed, and another 353 panzers and 117 assault guns were damaged and out of action. A tally five days later indicated that fourteen generals and 201 lower-level commanders had been killed in action.[128]

Nevertheless, Hitler ordered Kluge to mount an armored counterattack to the coast at Avranches to seal the breach. Infantry divisions were to replace mobile formations between the Vire and the Orne, and some pullback and shortening of the line was acceptable. Kluge was to gather at least four panzer divisions for the counterattack.[129]

In principle, Hitler's idea was sensible, and such counterstrokes time and again had rectified disastrous situations on the eastern front. It made perfect sense in the context to apply proven methods from the only war of maneuver the Wehrmacht had been fighting since the Kasserine offensive in February 1943. But the enemy was not the Red Army, with a meat cleaver ground force and no air superiority.[130] And the Americans had stopped every large armored counterattack they had faced since Kasserine Pass, including those at El Guettar, Gela, Salerno, and Anzio.

Several probably apocryphal stories arise from this period. David Irving, offering no source for his story, asserts that before issuing those orders, Hitler had said at a war conference, "Obviously, they are trying for an all-out major decision here, because otherwise they wouldn't have sent their best general, Patton."[131] Although one cannot prove a negative, hard evidence suggests that Hitler and OKW did not know Patton was in command until after this conversation would have taken place. After the war, Jodl told interrogators flatly that OKW did not know Patton was in Normandy as of 1 August, and as we shall see, Patton first appears as confirmed in the German assessment of the Allied order of battle five days later.[132]

An oft-repeated canard lacking any apparent authoritative parentage holds that Hitler told his commanders, "Just look at that crazy cowboy general, driving down to the south and into Brittany along a single road and over a single bridge with an entire army. He doesn't care about the risk and acts as if he owned the world! It doesn't seem possible!"[133] Accounts by officers present at the daily war briefings relate no such tale, and again, there is no documentary evidence that Hitler could have been aware that Patton was in command of the breakout force at this time. In fact, *Major* Percy Schramm's notes from the OKW war diary make clear that OKW (and Hitler), as will be seen, had no idea that something so large as an army had squeezed through at Avranches.[134] Moreover, VIII Corps, by 1 August, had captured three bridges across the Sée River and four across the Sélune, although the main artery was vulnerable to the loss of the bridge at Avranches. Third Army, by 4 August, deemed that it had "solved" the problem of bottlenecks by separating arterial roads where they joined and building a wooden trestle bridge across the Sélune. A dense net of antiaircraft guns protected the key bridges.[135]

Hans von Luck, in his memoir, says that on 31 July he received word that George Patton had broken through at Avranches.[136] He may have heard of a breakout that day, but as a mere *major* leading a 21st Panzer Division *Kampfgruppe* thickly engaged in battle against the British and under a chain of command that was just learning that Patton was in command, Luck almost certainly did not hear that day that *Patton* had broken through. We must consider his claim to be post hoc knowledge retrofitted to his account.

Patton's Third Army men were no longer the only ones sprinting into the German secondary. On 2 August, VII Corps captured Mortain, ten miles east of Avranches, which was to be the pivot point for a sweep by the American right wing through northern France. As the town was also destined to become the epicenter of the German counterattack toward Avranches, VII Corps, which had created the breakthrough in the first place, would bear the defensive burden of keeping Third Army's supply route open.

Bradley, who had taken charge of the newly activated 12th Army Group on 1 August, ordered Patton on 3 August to leave the minimum necessary force in Brittany and to throw the weight of Third Army toward Le Mans. Montgomery, who still commanded all Allied ground forces in France, issued a bold order the next day: "Once a gap appears in the enemy front, we must press into it and beyond it into the enemy's rear areas. Everyone must go all out all day and every day. The broad strategy of the Allied forces is to swing the right flank towards Paris and to force the enemy back to the Seine."[137]

What had happened to the divisions that had crumbled before Bradley's hammer blow? Seventh Army summarized:

> As a consequence of the breakthrough by enemy armor on the left wing of the army's front, most of the divisions (77th, 91st, 243rd, 275th, parts of the 265th, parts of the 352nd, parts of the 353rd, 5th Airborne Division, 2nd SS Panzer Division, and 17th SS Panzergrenadier Division), which since the beginning of the invasion were constantly in action without rest or large-scale provision of replacements, have shattered into groups. These are slipping individually through the enemy's cordon. Some are responding to appropriate rally orders, others under no control, for the most part without officers and NCOs, wander aimlessly in an easterly or southeasterly direction. The gathering points are Bagnoles and Le Mans.

These groups carried little more than small arms. Their clothing was in tatters, and many men were barefoot. There were no rations. The men had to avoid the increasingly hateful citizenry and members of the French Resistance. Morale, for the most part, had collapsed. The only bright spot was that most of the soldiers aimed to reunite with their units.[138]

Kluge, on 2 August, summoned *General der Panzertruppe* Adolf-Friedrich Kuntzen, commanding LXXXI Corps on the Channel coast, and told him that his corps was to take charge of organizing a counterattack by panzer divisions toward Avranches. He confessed to Kuntzen, long a close friend, his doubts that even a successful counterblow would restore the situation, but he thought it would help facilitate a withdrawal. By the time Kuntzen reached Seventh Army's headquarters, the project had been turned over to XLVII Panzer Corps.[139]

Kluge, on 3 August, issued orders that set in motion the concentration of panzer divisions for his counterattack. The main striking power of *General der Panzertruppe* Heinrich Eberbach's Panzer Group West, four panzer divisions, would shift from the area opposite the British to the left wing of Seventh Army, and Kluge would add the 116th Panzer Division and *Kampfgruppen* of the 2nd SS Panzer and 17th SS Panzergrenadier Divisions to what Hitler hoped would be a steel fist. Kluge worried the shift of panzer forces would leave his right wing in just as critical danger as his left wing. Eberbach, from the start, viewed the plan as hopeless without reinforcement on the ground and in the air and urged Warlimont, who visited Eberbach's headquarters on the third and who held a realistic view of the situation, to have OKW authorize a withdrawal to the Seine.[140]

Still, there was optimism at Seventh Army regarding the operation's success because, lacking information about Third Army's activities, it was thought the American forces south of Avranches were weak. Moreover, a captured situation map indicated that the forces approaching Le Mans were to continue in the direction of Paris—there was no hint of a hook into Seventh Army's rear—which added to the confidence.[141]

In the meantime, the Luftwaffe tried unsuccessfully to bomb out the main bridge at Avranches. Undetected by Ultra, Montgomery was unaware of the looming counterstroke when on 4 August he ordered 12th Army Group to make for Paris.[142]

Patton was already thinking more or less the same thing as Montgomery and, the night of 3–4 August, ordered Haislip's XV Corps to race to Mayenne and establish a bridgehead across the Mayenne River. From there, the corps was to be ready to move north or northeast on army order. XX Corps was to slide in on the right and secure crossings of the Mayenne between Château Gontier and the Loire.[143] This order indicates that Patton already foresaw the possibility of slashing northward to cut off Seventh and Fifth Panzer Armies, and it triggered one of the greatest operations of maneuver warfare in history, whatever the Germans thought of it.

Conditions for exploitation were perfect: Seventh Army had prepared no security measures in its rear areas, which were covered by understrength guard troops of the Military Commander Southwestern France. Static battalions, consisting mainly of overaged personnel, protected bridges, headquarters, and communications centers. Remnants of Panzer Lehr had pulled back to the area east of Mayenne for a rehabilitation, which was prevented by events; otherwise, a few "Ostbattalions," manned by Soviet turncoats and positioned near Mayenne, and the 13th Flak Division, spread from Mortain to Domfront, posed the only speed bumps in the road. The 9th Panzer and 708th Infantry Divisions, the latter reinforced by the 1st *Sicherheitsregiment* (Security Regiment) from Paris, were allocated to cover Seventh Army's southern wing, but were still en route to the area. Kuntzen's LXXXI Corps's staff had only just arrived in Alencon to take control over those two divisions—the assignment Kuntzen had received instead of the Avranches counterattack.

Other than a few telephone calls, no reports on American actions in Third Army's zone outside Brittany were reaching the Germans on 3 August. LXXXI Corps had no ground or air reconnaissance assets. "[The conduct of battle] was actually a blind one," recalled Kuntzen, "and had to be carried out by intuition or on the basis of local reports which, perforce, were only sparse and contradictory."

The next day, Seventh Army had no communication whatsoever with LXXXIV Corps. In Brittany, XXV Corps was able to provide news of armored spearheads arriving at Rennes, Chauteaubriand, and the road to Nantes. As late as 4 August, German commanders misinterpreted XV Corps's role as being to screen operations in Brittany. The Americans would not drive eastward, Seventh Army believed, until the British broke through on the north flank, and then the two forces would operate in conjunction.[144]

This misreading of American intentions had fateful consequences, because a counterattack toward Avranches looked as eminently feasible as a strike against the flank of an enemy presumed to be committed to an operation westward into Brittany. Seventh Army, on the fourth, proposed that armored forces, at least two or three divisions, be gathered immediately for just such an attack, but warned that something would have to be done about Allied control of the air if there was going to be any chance of success. After cutting the American supply line, mobile forces could clean out Brittany.[145]

While the Germans were pursuing this line of thought, the 106th Cavalry Group, which had been screening VIII Corps's left flank until attached to XV Corps on 3 August, peeled off on 5 August to lead the XV Corps advance. That day, Patton learned from Bradley's staff that XV Corps was to continue its drive past Mayenne to Le Mans, the main supply center for Seventh Army.[146]

The staff at *OB West*, on 5 August, had confirmed that Patton commanded Third Army, having left his position, it was thought, as commanding general of FUSAG in England. Third Army, *OB West* now grasped, controlled VIII and XV Corps. The Germans suspected that Bradley had taken command of 12th Army Group, and assessed that Montgomery was still in overall command of the ground war.[147] Army Group B's enemy order of battle, however, remained confused and inaccurate through August, dropping Third Army entirely at one point.[148]

Nearly ignorant of Third Army's activities, Kluge and his staff fought the battle they could see, against First Army and 21st Army Group.[149] German commanders began to realize how powerful a force the Americans had squeezed through the gap only when, on 5 August, XV Corps's 90th Division was in Mayenne and the 79th Division appeared at Laval, which was held by two reinforced infantry battalions and a battalion of 88s, and probable mechanized cavalry units were spotted near the Loire. The high command had been under the impression that fighting had been fairly light on the left wing on the fourth and fifth—which it had been, because there was nothing in Third Army's path.[150] Seventh Army observed, "All reconnaissance confirms that the enemy is driving into the army's deep flank with strong forces on the line Mayenne-Laval. The earlier conclusion that he is only screening to the east must be abandoned." LXXXI Corps was to engage the enemy on the south flank.[151]

Even then, however, U.S. First Army's breakthrough at Vire was the topic of Kluge's evening conversation with Hausser at Seventh Army, not events in the vaguely perceived vacuum on the German left. Seventh Army viewed the reports from Mayenne as "exaggerated," judging that there was, at most, an American division there, and it saw no threat to plans for the counterattack toward Avranches.[152]

But by 6 August, Kluge saw the writing on the wall. Kluge, who evidently credited Bradley with orchestrating the offensive against him, reported,

> The operations in northern France reveal that the enemy command remains determined to drive to Paris. We can expect that the American army group [commander] will commit everything to his southern wing, where he has won operational freedom of movement, before German countermeasures well known to the enemy can be implemented, and will push as far east as possible. The southern attack group will be deployed through Laval and Le Mans. . . . Eight large formations [divisions] are available to assist the force identified there (two divisions?). We must assume the enemy commander will avoid allowing himself to be pinned frontally but will exploit the great mobility of his formations at all times.[153]

In this last reference to the enemy commander, we *may* see a first indication that Kluge was aware that he faced Patton and recognized Patton's enthusiasm for maneuver warfare.

At Laval that day, fighter-bomber attacks panicked German troops, who fled eastward. An SS assault-gun unit also tore eastward with the explanation that it lacked fuel for a counterattack, and the enemy was likely to capture the bridge at Laval and cut off the guns.[154]

That evening, Allied commanders, thanks to Ultra, were only ninety minutes behind their German counterparts in receiving Kluge's orders that XLVII Panzer Corps was to attack at 1830 hours from the Sourdeval-Mortain line with 1st SS, 2nd SS, 2nd, and 116th Panzer Divisions.[155] These were all the divisions Kluge had been able to scrape together, but he was convinced that he had to strike with what he had in order to achieve surprise and before Allied fighter-bombers could destroy the panzers in their assembly areas. Hitler wanted to wait until all the anticipated forces had gathered, and though the führer did not stop Kluge, he sent *Generalleutnant* Walter Buhle to deliver the message personally.[156]

LXXXI Corps, that day (6 August), took responsibility for the "unclear situation" east of Mayenne, where six battalions of the 708th Infantry Division had arrived.[157] Seventh Army was aware of an unconfirmed report that American tanks were rolling from Mayenne toward Le Mans. The next day, Seventh Army's chief of staff, *Oberst* Rudolf *Freiherr* von Gersdorff, opined, "There's only one way to set that right, and that is if our counterattack [at Mortain] substantially eases the pressure."[158]

Gersdorff would get no joy from that quarter. At Mortain, Allied fighter-bombers (in the German view) brought the attack to a halt, just as Kluge feared. In point of fact, the dogged resistance mounted by the 30th Infantry Division and its supporting tank and tank-destroyer battalions had a great deal to do with it, too. Kluge told OKW that he had decided to risk all in the north and to add the 9th, 10th, and 12th SS Panzer Divisions and the bulk of the 9th Panzer Division to the offensive and to strike again on 10 August. Buhle's arrival with Hitler's message favoring further concentration of forces formally put *OB West* and the high command on the same page.[159]

By the afternoon of 7 August, Seventh Army believed that the Americans had three or four divisions between it and the Loire River. Gersdorff observed, "We have to be clear that the forces with which we can oppose them are not strong enough to stop them." He could see only three options: stand and be destroyed; withdraw to Le Mans and the Sarthe River, at the risk of creating a hole through which the enemy could strike; or withdraw to the northeast and write off Le Mans. Seventh Army favored the last option, but because the question was decisive for the entire army group, the decision would be left to Kluge.[160]

Kluge did not respond immediately when consulted by phone. Nevertheless, quite likely in response to this portentous information, Kluge in his operations report for the week informed the high command that he was now concerned that his attack toward Avranches would result in the encirclement of Seventh Army.[161] He saw one silver lining in the cloud: the breakout meant that he did not have to worry any longer about a second landing in northwestern France. He misjudged Eisenhower, as he deemed a landing in southern France to be less likely, too.[162]

The net effect of Kluge's indecision was that the Germans would stand in Patton's path and be, if not destroyed, badly knocked about. The newly arrived 708th Infantry Division came under attack north of Mayenne, and some of its elements were surrounded. The division reported almost too many enemy spearheads to count, including one only five miles southwest of Le Mans. The

9th Panzer Division joined LXXXI Corps and assembled at Alencon, from which it was supposed to move to Mortain.[163]

Kluge was starting to think about a plan B for the Mortain venture. When Kluge phoned Hausser for an evening update, he was told, "About the same. Monstrous fighter-bomber attacks. Heavy losses among the panzers."

Referring to the attack at Mortain, and despite his announced grand plan to expand the offensive, Kluge said, "If we are not a lot farther along tonight or tomorrow morning, the entire thing will be set aside. Alencon must remain open, or else the troops can't be supplied any longer. The resistance west of Alencon must be enough that the enemy cannot get any farther. I'm giving you what's left of the 33 *Leibstandarte* [1st SS Panzer Division]."[164] As it happened, Hitler, for now, would give Kluge no choice but to press the counteroffensive, but the field marshal was already looking over his shoulder.

The Falaise Cauldron

Bradley gripped his First and Third Armies like a shield and sword. The shield on his left arm absorbed the blow of the counterattack at Mortain, while the sword in his right hand remained free to swing. Patton's only concession to the counterstroke on 7 August had been to order XV Corps's French 2nd *Division Blindé* (Armored Division, 2nd DB) and 35th and 80th Infantry Divisions, plus XX Corps's 5th Infantry Division, to be ready to attack northward if needed. The rest of XV Corps had pressed on toward Le Mans, and by the next day, Patton was fairly confident that the danger at Mortain had receded—though the 35th Infantry Division pitched in to help VII Corps's counterattack in the Mortain area.[165]

In response to orders from Bradley, Patton, on 8 August, told Haislip to advance along the route Le Mans-Alencon-Sée to the line Sée-Carrouges and there prepare for further operations against the enemy's flank and rear. XX Corps was to occupy Angers and protect the army's southern flank.[166]

At Seventh Army headquarters, *Oberst* Helmdach, the Ia, and Gersdorff, the chief of staff, lacking any firm intelligence information, could only discuss a gut feeling that the forces at Le Mans intended to advance again in division strength. Gersdorff told Hausser that if those forces turned northward toward Alencon, it would mean a "death stroke" for not just the army, but for all forces in the West. Just after noon on 8 August, LXXXI Corps reported the sounds of fighting northwest of Le Mans. The Germans had nothing but an airmobile security battalion and some company remnants in the city itself, plus a storm battalion east of the city. Enemy tanks and infantry were entering the city, and communications with the defenders had broken down. The enemy was also bypassing Le Mans to the north and south.[167]

Beyond what was happening on their doorstep, German commanders had almost no grasp on the situation in the Third Army zone. The Army Group B situation maps show the lines facing First Army and 21st Army Group in sharp detail, but offer only vaguely placed symbols for Third Army's corps and divisions; many of the symbols have small question marks beside them, and equally imprecise arrows and arcs depict supposed advances and battle lines. The appearance of American tanks in Le Mans, captured by the 79th Infantry Division on 8 August, and Tours, due south of Le Mans, left the situation "obscure," and attempts were underway to scrape together elements of Panzer Lehr and the 9th Panzer Division's Panther battalion to block them, as well as to patch together another defensive line east of Mortain.[168] The potential threat from the south to key supply dumps at Alencon kept most of the 9th Panzer Division in that area and thereby weakened the attack at Mortain. Kluge could see the consequences, but he also saw no alternative.[169]

Hitler, far from being interested in what Patton was up to, saw British pressure on the northern front as the main threat in France. A British breakthrough—Falaise seemed to be the most likely spot—would prevent the renewal of the attack to the sea.[170] And, right on cue, the British—supported by an estimated 600 tanks—broke through the German front on the eighth and advanced toward Falaise.[171] Neither Hitler nor Kluge had yet focused on the menace to their plans posed by the little understood American presence to the south. And, so far, those American divisions appeared to be heading generally eastward.

Kluge could find no way to interpose German units from northwestern France in front of Third Army, so on 9 August, he won Hitler's approval to move the First Army headquarters from the Bay of Biscay to take charge of a "powerful force" to stop the Americans.[172] Kluge also ordered Eberbach to assemble a staff for "Panzer Group Eberbach," leave Fifth Panzer Army (the renamed Panzer Group West) to take charge of the renewed attack toward Avranches, and report to Hausser at Seventh Army by dark. Newly promoted SS *Oberstgruppenführer* Sepp Dietrich was to take command of Fifth Panzer Army. Eberbach objected and asked that someone else be assigned the task, but Kluge told him to obey his orders.[173] Hitler, meanwhile, had concocted a fantastic plan to fill out LXXXI Corps with infantry divisions from Fifteenth Army to create a new strike force that would echelon to the left of the panzers at Mortain or, in an emergency, attack the north flank of the Americans to the south.[174]

Eberbach, who had taken command of Panzer Group West on 3 July, was a seasoned eastern-front panzer general. Born 24 November 1895 in Stuttgart, Eberbach had entered the imperial army in February 1915 as a lieutenant. Eberbach had fought in the infantry during the Great War and risen to

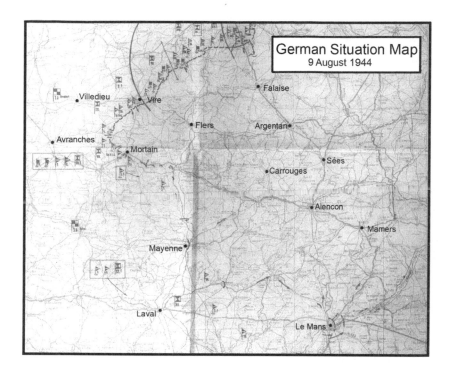

the rank of *Oberleutnant*. Between the wars, he had settled down, served in the police, married, and had three children. Eberbach transferred to the army as a major in 1935. After leading the 5th Panzer Brigade in the 3rd Panzer Division and earning the Knight's Cross with Oak Leaves, he had commanded the 4th Panzer Division through most of 1942 and briefly stepped up to take charge of XLVIII Panzer Corps and then Army Group Nikopol before being sent to the reserve for medical reasons. Taken on by the inspector of panzer troops in 1943, he had filled in as temporary commanding general of the XLVII, XLVIII, and then XL Panzer Corps during the autumn.

In June 1944, Eberbach had joined Army Group Center to command a group of three panzer corps that was to launch a limited-objective attack at Rast. Upon arriving, he learned of the landings in Normandy. The invasion caused an indefinite delay of the planned attack, and soon one of the three corps—II SS Panzer—was rushed to the west. Eberbach was sent back to the inspectorate, but almost immediately received orders to report to Kluge in the west. He was just the man Kluge needed: Eberbach's superiors viewed him as a fresh, open officer who instilled trust, as energetic and clear-headed, and as a brave and unyielding commander in the toughest situations—"one of our best." One factor clearly contributed to his selection: Eberbach had impressed his superiors as being a hard-core Nazi in "deed and word."[175]

On 10 August, the Ia section of First Army traveled to the headquarters of Army Group B, where it received orders to block the Loire River from Orléans to Nantes and maintain bridgeheads on the north bank for as long as possible. In other words, its initial assignment was to keep Third Army from turning south, not from continuing to the northeast. But almost immediately, the instructions were changed to create a line from Alencon, where it would tie into Seventh Army, to the Loire.[176]

German ignorance of Third Army's actions remained deep. At 0930 hours, LXXXI Corps reported, "The enemy shows a tendency to storm eastward. Where his spearheads are is hard to say." This ignorance was shared with Kluge in a telephone briefing at 1030.[177] Seventh Army's daily report, however, noted a potentially ominous development: the enemy appeared to have stopped pressing eastward at Le Mans and was directing some of his strength to the northeast.[178]

On 10 August, Ultra intercepted orders from Kluge to renew the attack at Mortain toward Avranches the next day, which showed that the Germans would not extricate themselves from the noose that Bradley was drawing around their necks. Bradley could be confident that he had as much time as he needed to envelop Seventh Army from the south. The renewed attack at Mortain would include *General der Panzertruppe* Hans *Freiherr* von Funck's XLVII Panzer Corps and Walter Krueger's LVIII Panzer Corps, which now controlled between them the 1st SS, 2nd SS, 2nd, 10th SS, and 116th Panzer Divisions and part of the 9th Panzer Division.[179] Patton, therefore, knew that most of the German armor in Western Europe was to his left and behind his spearheads and tightly engaged against U.S. First Army. Indeed, two days earlier, Kluge had conceded that he was unable to mount any military operations south of Mortain.

General der Panzertruppe Kuntzen, commanding LXXXI Corps, spoke at 0910 hours on 10 August with the Seventh Army chief of staff Gersdorff: "I would like to report that with my forces, four battalions, no advance by the enemy can be stopped. We have to expect that the enemy will hold Alencon by tomorrow morning."

"Does Herr General have the impression that the enemy is attacking toward the north or northeast?"

"*Jawohl*, there can be no doubt."

By afternoon, the Germans knew that the 5th Armored Division was driving northward toward Alencon. Elements of the 9th Panzer Division were engaged.

When word reached Kluge, he recognized the intention of Patton's stroke and his army group's mortal peril. For the moment, though, he had no reserves to respond with. Seventh Army begged Kluge for reinforcements from opposite the British. "That's out of the question!" snapped Kluge. "How you will help yourselves I don't know. . . . At the moment, I have no forces available."[180]

The strategic implications of Patton's advance were alarming. Commenting on this period after the war ended, Gersdorff offered, "The American break-through at St. Lô Avranches, led by General Patton, was carried out with opera-tional genius and unprecedented dash. It developed into a deep thrust into the flank and rear of [Army Group B], which gave the German High Command the choice of either crossing the Seine as quickly as possible, or facing the danger of utter annihilation of the bulk of the German army in the West."[181]

At 2115 hours, Kluge reported to the high command that the enemy had pivoted northward and seemed to be attempting a two-pronged envelopment of Fifth Panzer and Seventh Armies in connection with the British attack toward Falaise. Now he realized he needed panzers to stop the thrust northward, or he would lose control over the Alencon-Flers road—and the battle. The only place he could get panzers was to pull them from Mortain, where, he concluded, the attack could not possibly resume until 20 August. Kluge begged OKW for a decision.

The following day, 11 August, Kluge received Hitler's refusal. XLVII Panzer Corps was to attack at Mortain again. Furthermore, the führer demanded to know why no attack could begin until the twentieth. Yet he also revealed a hint of doubt: if it were true that no attack could begin until the twentieth, Hitler reluctantly conceded, then, yes, an attack before then against the American XV Corps was necessary. He had already, the day before, granted blanket permis-sion for tactical withdrawals wherever necessary.[182]

Kluge responded that the attack at Mortain could be renewed only after reorganization, because the troops were exhausted. Meanwhile, the 9th Panzer Division at Alencon was fighting with its back to critical supply depots, but it failed to stop the 5th Armored Division's advance, which reached a point only eight miles from Alencon. As if that were not enough, unconfirmed (and false) reports indicated that the French 2nd DB had appeared near Mamers. Kluge reiterated that he needed armor to save his collapsing south wing. The 116th Panzer Division could get there by the morning of 12 August, and two more panzer divisions by the next day. He conceded that such redeployment would end prospects for a breakthrough to the sea.

Patton exacerbated Kluge's problems by strengthening Third Army's advance into the Army Group B rear. He now directed XV Corps north through

Argentan to Falaise, there to halt and await further orders. Patton gave XX Corps the objective of reaching the Sées-Carrouges line, except for the 5th Infantry Division, which was to continue northeastward, clearing the north bank of the Loire River. As it turned out, the 2nd DB took Carrouges during the day, while the 5th Armored Division seized Sées. Both divisions pelted toward Argentan, followed by the 79th and 90th Infantry Divisions. Patton told XX Corps to stop and await further orders once it contacted XV Corps at Alencon.

That evening, the 9th Panzer Division lost its hold on Alencon. Its remnants— a half dozen panzers, about a battalion of infantry, and an artillery battalion— rallied in the woods north of town. The loss of the supply dumps there would start to hurt Seventh Army almost immediately.

Eberbach was cut off at LXXXI Corps's headquarters, where he had been meeting with Kuntzen to discuss Kluge's proposed attack against XV Corps. Kuntzen ordered an immediate evacuation and breakout east of Argentan. "But immediately from nearby tank fire was heard, and enemy flyers made every movement impossible," recalled Eberbach. "Enemy shells struck us. We were surrounded by smoke clouds from burning vehicles." All managed to slip away in the evening.[183] But these were the straights to which two panzer generals had been reduced.

Hitler finally gave in. A *Führerbefehl* (a "Führer Order," or a personal order from Hitler) arrived, instructing that the panzers assigned to the counterattack toward Avranches turn about and stop XV Corps, supported by the 9th Panzer Division. As the führer's order explicitly mentioned XV Corps, Haislip could be said to have come to Hitler's attention, at least to some degree. Of great future relevance to Patton, Hitler ordered First Army to build up an infantry force to include the 338th and 48th Infantry Divisions and eventually the 18th Luftwaffe Field Division to protect Paris and the rear of Army Group B.

Kluge jumped on his new authorization and on 12 August ordered that the XV Corps attack be stopped. Eberbach's panzers were to hit the Americans in the flank, joined by the 9th Panzer Division attacking from the north when possible. The panzer divisions at Mortain were to be replaced by infantry divisions from Seventh Army. Seventh Army protested that it had only four exhausted divisions available, and that unless they were reinforced by more infantry and antitank weapons, it would be better to abandon the Mortain position, which now resembled a salient.

Some of Kluge's plans were simply unrealistic. He still hoped that Mortain would represent the *Schwerpunkt* in his defense on the south wing, while Falaise filled that role against Montgomery. Looking to his rear, Kluge directed the 48th and 338th Infantry Divisions to First Army in compliance with Hitler's instructions, and he hoped to bring forward those divisions toward Le Mans at some point. One idea was shear fantasy: after defeating XV Corps, another drive to the sea would commence, from Mayenne if necessary.[184]

The 116th Panzer Division, having been forced to leave its reconnaissance battalion and nearly all of its tanks and artillery behind at Mortain to support other divisions, ran into the French 2nd DB on 12 August at Sées and, after a bloody battle, had to withdraw northward. The 156th Panzergrenadier Regiment was all but destroyed, as was much of the available artillery.[185] Eberbach had made it to the headquarters of XLVII Panzer Corps, where fighting could be heard in Sées, but nobody knew who held the town. Again, the *jabos* stopped both Eberbach and the headquarters from moving. Enemy tanks appeared in Le Bourg, east of Argentan, and turned west toward the latter town.[186] Seventh Army lost all contact with LXXXI Corps.[187]

The 1st SS Panzer Division had made its way through heavy air attacks to the crisis point and XV Corps on 13 August, followed by the 2nd Panzer Division. They were by now so weak that Hitler ordered the 9th, 10th SS, and 21st Panzer Divisions to move rapidly to the decision point. Hitler, considering the impending landings in Nineteenth Army's zone in southern France, was aware that his problems were probably about to grow worse.[188]

Kluge, on 13 August, judged that XV Corps was turning west to strike against Fifth Panzer and Seventh Armies from the rear and, thus, block the Eberbach's armored units moving toward the area—a move the enemy evidently had detected.[189] Army Group B's situation map shows that the headquarters had some idea of where Americans were attacking, but still an unfocused grasp on who was fighting where. Kluge had lost radio contact with Panzer Group Eberbach, located somewhere southwest of Argentan, and the 9th Panzer Division and a *Kampfgruppe* from Panzer Lehr were fighting a stronger enemy in the area of Carrouges. The 9th Panzer Division now had fifteen tanks, 120 panzergrenadiers, and no artillery. At least the lead elements of the 1st SS Panzer Division had reached the area and entered the fight. German forces in Argentan turned back the first armored probes, but Fifth Panzer and Seventh Armies now shared but a single supply road to the east. Moreover, the Canadians had driven the German main line of resistance back by some three miles northwest of Falaise.[190]

The morning of 13 August, Patton stood on the brink of one of the greatest victories of the war. Third Army was well aware that the Germans were slipping eastward through the Falaise gap as quickly as they could and that many of their armored remnants were being thrown at XV Corps to keep the escape route open. The Americans were confident that they could brush that resistance aside and close the gap, and Kluge probably would have agreed.[191] Moreover,

Patton's thirst for publicity was about to get a good quenching. A German news service, Transocean, the previous morning had broadcast news of his presence in Normandy and described him as a "proponent of mobile warfare," a report that was picked up by the American press. Two days hence, Patton would hear the "news" on the BBC.[192]

But then, at 1130 hours, Patton had one of the worst breaks of his life. A call came from 12th Army Group: the interarmy group boundary in the Argentan-Falaise area was sacrosanct, Bradley instructed, and XV Corps was not to advance beyond Argentan.[193] It was up to Montgomery to reach the Americans. The Germans never grasped by what means a looming Armageddon was reduced to an outright disaster, and in their immediate post-war writings they offered a range of theories, none of which pinpointed the strange, incredible truth.

Montgomery renewed his attack toward Falaise on 14 August with a huge artillery barrage and carpet-bombing, and the First Canadian Army tore a hole in the German line on a front of ten miles to a depth of some six miles. Kluge understood full well that the Britsh aimed to link up with the Americans at Argentan, and he threw his few remaining reserves into the struggle. If the Americans attacked to meet Montgomery's troops, Fifth Panzer and Seventh Armies would be surrounded. Munitions and fuel shortages already were becoming debilitating.

"14 August was the most critical day," recalled Seventh Army chief of staff *Oberst* Gersdorff. "The specter of imminent encirclement became more and more distinguishable." Kluge ordered Fifth Panzer Army to clear up the situation at Alencon with armored reconnaissance units, an idea that suggests that strain was affecting his reason.

Kluge did not realize that Bradley had leashed Third Army. He could only hope that Eberbach's panzer group had the wherewithal to drive into XV Corps's flank. Little was certain there, other than that the 116th Panzer Division (reinforced by the shanghaied Panther battalion of the 9th Panzer Division that had just turned up) held a line that still included the southern edge of Argentan.[194]

Hitler, on the fourteenth, berated Kluge for bungling the counterattack against XV Corps and directed that he renew it farther north so as to take the Americans in the flank. All further decisions would await the outcome at Alencon, said Hitler. Herein the führer erred, for Montgomery's drive was in the process of creating such a crisis that troops intended for the fight at Alencon had to be diverted to the collapsing northern front instead.[195]

The 12th SS Panzer Division, with a last-ditch counterattack, managed to stop Montgomery's breakthrough on 15 August. American tanks, however, probed northward from Argentan toward Falaise. The gap between the Allied

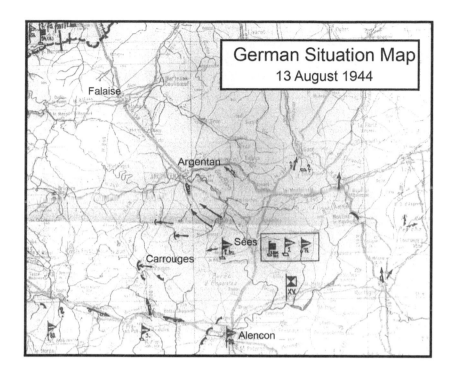

spearheads was only twelve miles.[196] Kluge told OKW that a British break-through was imminent, and he misinterpreted the Allied stop-line decision. The American forces to the south, he concluded, were now engaged in a screening operation, presumably for the divisions pushing eastward farther south. Kluge ordered First Army to build a blocking line from Chartres to Orléans, with its main effort at the latter city.[197]

Kluge's instructions were very nearly too late, for in the meantime, reports indicated that American troops advancing north of the Loire had reached Chartres and Orléans, which lay a hundred miles southeast of Argentan. Kluge was unaware that Patton on 13 August had deployed XII Corps to take on the role of protecting his south flank as Third Army plowed forward, and that it was Cook's corps that had arrived at Orléans. The only relief for Kluge was that First Army reported it had just taken control over Chartres-Orléans sector, as ordered.[198]

Kluge discussed the situation with Eberbach and Hausser, and the three agreed it was time to break out to the northeast. Kluge was out of contact with OKW most of the day, driving across the pocket with Kuntzen. Kluge told his friend that he had done everything possible to convince Hitler of the need to end the war. He believed that Hitler was no longer in possession of his mental capacities. Kluge said he owed the troops his best effort and would call OKW that evening to make this position clear. As the two generals drove, Hitler summoned *Generalfeldmarschalle* Walter Model and Albert Kesselring to his headquarters to select one as his new *OB West*. Hausser was given temporary command of Army Group B. Kluge would kill himself the following day after being sacked in favor of Model.[199]

A Thin Gray Line

General der Infanterie Kurt von der Chevallerie, commanding First Army, had made use of the time Third Army was focused on trying to close the sack at Falaise to do what he could to create a defense to fight Patton, although it is highly unlikely he harbored any fantasy of stopping the Americans. From 10 to 14 August, only reconnaissance elements probed his front because Third Army had pivoted northward. First Army's only corps, LXIV, was still guarding the Atlantic coast in southwestern France. The headquarters had arrived with only an assault battalion of the First Army's Service School, the escort company (motorized), an armored reconnaissance company outfitted with French equipment, and a signal regiment. From Seventh Army's rear area, Chevallerie grabbed the 1st Security Regiment with two battalions and the 1010th Security Regiment with three. With these, First Army created a string of battle positions of little combat value. Two antitank companies arrived and were dispatched to Fontainebleau. Finally, the lead elements of an infantry battalion from the 48th Infantry Division appeared and took up residence in Chartres. OKW privately acknowledged that Chevallerie had "weak and not fully combat worthy" forces at his disposal.[200]

Chevallerie could well understand the danger Fifth Panzer and Seventh Armies now faced in France because just five months earlier, he and his corps had become trapped in the Kamenets-Poldoskiy Pocket along with the rest of First Panzer Army commanded by *Generaloberst* Hans-Valentin Hube, who had fought Patton on Sicily. The Soviets had cut the army off on the Dniestr River in western Ukraine in March. Hitler had forbidden any retreat as the pocket was forming and rejected Hube's wish to go over to a flexible defense. The winter weather had still been horrid, and First Panzer Army had 125 miles to cross when Hitler finally gave it authority to break out toward the west. The Germans, barely supplied by air, had successfully pierced the Russian ring in a drive lasting from 27 March to 6 April.[201] Hitler, saying the time for grand operations was over, had relieved Manstein from his command of Army Group South (now called Army Group North Ukraine) because of their disagreements over the situation and replaced him with Model, a man he believed would "cling stubbornly" to what the Germans still held.[202]

After a brief period in the *Führerreserve*, Chevallerie had taken command of First Panzer Army on 21 April 1944 upon Hube's death in an airplane crash (somewhat ironically on a return flight after receiving the Diamonds to his Knight's Cross). Only weeks later, however, he was transferred to France and given temporary command of First Army on 2 June 1944.[203] Now he faced a new struggle that, in terms of the resources available, the odds against him, and the strategic implications of failure, was eerily similar to the worst days in Russia. Like an American football cornerback, he had to backpedal and stay between the other team and the goal line—and avoid being trapped in his own pocket as he did so.

"Of all operations of war," observed Mellenthin in his memoirs, "a withdrawal under heavy enemy pressure is probably the most difficult and perilous. Indeed, it is recorded of the great [Helmuth von] Moltke that when he was being praised for his generalship in the Franco-Prussian War, and was told by an admirer that his reputation would rank with such great captains as Napoleon, Frederick, or Turenne, he answered, 'No, for I have never conducted a retreat.'"[204]

Nearly the first combat operation resembled a Velikiye Luki in miniature. American activity escalated again on 14 August—the same day that that U.S. Seventh Army landed on the southern coast of France—and the 7th Armored Division's Combat Command B rolled into Chartres on the sixteenth. The rifle battalion from the 48th Infantry Division had combined forces with local elements, which the American account estimated to total 3,000 troops, including one flak battalion and scattered antitank strong points estimated to number fifty guns ranging in size from 20mm to 80mm. The defenders had laid scattered minefields. The Germans stopped the initial attack with heavy antitank fire, and the enemy's M4 medium tanks, which the Germans called by their British nickname "Sherman," were unable to maneuver in the narrow streets.

The defenders were deployed in a circled-wagon manner, facing outward in depth. Combat Command B surrounded the center of resistance on 17 August and attacked it from all sides. Chevallerie threw First Army's assault battalion and fresh elements of the 48th Infantry Division into the street fighting to open an escape route, but the attempt failed and cost many casualties. The defenders held out one more day. "Heavy antitank, mortar, machine gun, and scattered artillery pieces and rifle fire and bazooka strong points were encountered in the three-day battle," recorded CCB. German losses amounted to 1,800 men killed, wounded, and captured.[205]

*

Seventh Army fell out of communication with First Army on 18 August as the ring closed around Seventh Army and part of Fifth Panzer Army. First Army had to take control of remnants of the 352nd Infantry Division, which had claimed so much blood at Omaha Beach, and fight west of Paris and of the Paris military district itself. OKW instructed Model that Chevallerie had been ordered to hold before the Seine, but the situation was hopeless, as the Americans had already reached the Seine just below Paris. Total First Army strength, including elements in Paris, amounted to twenty-six infantry battalions, twelve artillery batteries, fifteen panzers, and thirty 75mm antitank guns.

As if that were not enough, the American landings in southern France had caused OKW to divert the 18th Luftwaffe Field and 338th Infantry Divisions— less a reinforced regiment—which were to constitute most of First Army's fighting force. Even the 48th Infantry Division had not completely assembled.

OKW viewed this day as the most perilous in the battle of France. II SS Panzer Corps, which was outside the ring, attacked toward Trun to reopen an escape route, while elements inside the pocket tried to punch through to meet it. II SS Panzer Corps made progress, but only on the second try did Seventh Army reestablish a fleeting bolt-hole. OKW reckoned that perhaps half the troops inside the pocket were able to slip away, most without any heavy equipment. Of the two army, four corps, and thirteen divisional staffs in the pocket, only one corps and two or three divisional staffs were destroyed; the rest were ready for immediate commitment. Thanks to Bradley's decision to stop Patton, these divisions and corps would rebuild and fight again along the German border, claiming more lives than had been spent thus far. Hausser was badly wounded during the breakout, but was evacuated safely. He received the Swords to his Knight's Cross for his leadership during the crisis. Model dubbed Hausser a "model of courage and decisive leadership."[206]

Patton had been denied the chance to take Paris, however, and so German First Army's struggle against U.S. Third Army played out farther south. U.S. First Army would win the prestige of liberating the French capital.

Chevallerie's assets were questionable. The 48th Division—thrust into the role of lion of the First Army—had just been formed in Belgium. The outfit had inadequate training, equipment, and armament. The artillery battalions had prime movers, but no guns. The 1010th Security Regiment was made up of older men armed with French weapons. They had no antitank guns, steel helmets, or entrenching tools. The regiment of the 338th Infantry Division did have an artillery battalion and an antitank company attached to it; however, it had been trained for coastal defense, and its vehicles were scrounged from the French countryside.[207] These unfortunate men, young and old, were nearly all that stood in the path of the by now battle-hardened Third Army.

Fortunately, OKW relieved Chevallerie of responsibility for defending Paris. Realization was dawning that Seventh Army was going to have to retreat across the Seine merely to survive.[208]

Hitler, on 20 August, ordered Model to prevent the enemy located between the Seine and Loire—in other words, Third Army—from pressing southeast to Dijon, which would cut off Army Group G in southern France. Heretofore, OKW had assumed that the Overlord force would continue in a compact mass and that its southernmost wing would sweep through Paris. Hitler instructed Fifth Panzer Army to protect Seventh Army's retreat across the Seine, but insisted that bridgeheads be retained west of the Seine at Paris and southwest of the city. Army Group B was to link up with the retreating Army Group G forces when they reached the area northwest of Dijon. In a subsequent order, Hitler mandated that the 15th Panzergrenadier Division, then in Italy, be sent to the area of Troyes to join First Army, a movement totally overcome by the pace of events.[209]

As the 79th Infantry Division approached the Seine at Mantes, German infantry and engineer units shifted northward out of the way—leaving a foot-bridge intact in Mantes—because Kluge expected Third Army to turn sharply left to cut off Fifth Panzer and Seventh Armies from the route to the east on 21 August. Engineers mined the main road to Paris, while infantry deployed to stop an attack that never came.[210]

That same day, *Kampfgruppe* commanding officer *Major* Hans von Luck was able to reach *Generalmajor* Edgar Feuchtinger, commanding general of the 21st Panzer Division. "The situation is completely out of hand," Feuchtinger told him. All that was known for certain was that Patton had reached Chartres on 18 August and the Seine at Fontainebleau that very day. "From Chartres, Patton has turned north with part of his army and is advancing on the Rouen area. No one seems able to stop him," Feuchtinger said.[211]

This is the earliest first-person citation of a conversation among enemies in which Patton is clearly identified, though, as we shall see, Luck appears to be only sporadically reliable as a raconteur of conversations. Patton, for example, was not advancing on Rouen—on 14 August, he had ordered XV Corps to advance eastward toward Dreux—though that idea was consistent with Army Group B's understanding of the overall situation that day. Nor was Patton yet in Fontainebleau.[212]

Fifth Panzer Army gathered everything it could near Evreux to stop the anticipated Third Army drive toward Rouen. In addition to a 17th SS

Panzergrenadier Division *Kampfgruppe* in Evreux, the 1st SS Panzer Division had some infantry, but no tanks or artillery; the 2nd Panzer Division had one panzergrenadier battalion and no tanks or artillery; the 12th SS Panzer Division had 300 men and ten tanks; the 116th Panzer Division had two panzergrenadier battalions, twelve tanks, and two artillery batteries; and the 21st Panzer Division had four panzergrenadier battalions and ten tanks. The Germans believed that they managed to stop Third Army north of Evreux on the twenty-third, but Patton had merely moved off in another direction.

The 21st Panzer Division headquarters was ordered to transfer to the region west of the Vosges Mountains to establish a defensive line and receive the units retreating from southern France. Luck was to get the remaining combat elements out. "From now on, you are on your own," Feuchtinger told him. "I can't tell you where you will get fuel, ammunition, or food. Help yourself. . . . Bring me back lots of men from our division."[213]

Hitler scraped together everything he could to reinforce the western front, and for the heretofore great military power, the pickings were slim. Having already stripped the 15th Panzergrenadier Division from Italy, he ordered the 3rd Panzergrenadier Division to move north of the Alps, too, and the 105th and 106th Panzer Brigades to deploy from their training areas in Germany. Three infantry divisions then in training would become available on 1 September, and two more skeleton divisions would be transferred soon. The führer sent individual static "fortress" infantry battalions, separate infantry march battalions, and machine-gun battalions to man the West Wall. To these formations Hitler added 416 field pieces. In all of the Third Reich, he had for replacements only 144 Mark IV and 20 Mark V panzers and some hundred assault guns.[214]

A strange upwelling from the ranks of the SS completed Chevallerie's motley "army." The so-called 26th and 27th SS Panzer Divisions, made up of personnel from schools, arrived in the Nangis-Provin area on 22 August. These formations were referred to in SS communications as the 49th and 51st SS Brigades. The first consisted of an infantry regiment supported by an artillery battalion and an antitank company. The latter included an infantry regiment and single artillery battery and possessed only 20mm antiaircraft guns with armor-piercing rounds and panzerfaust rockets for antitank defense. The divisional staff of the 17th SS Panzergrenadier Division, which had arrived from Normandy on the eighteenth, was given charge of this assemblage, apparently on the twenty-sixth.[215]

The 4th Armored Division ran into the 51st Brigade in Troyes, founded as the Roman city of Augustobona Tricassium and once conquered by Joan of Arc, and it put up a stiff fight. The Americans attacked on 25 August with some fifty tanks and infantry mounted in half-tracks and rolled over the SS infantry line. Once the Americans got into the city and its half-timbered houses, the brigade's 2nd Battery was able to stop the attack firing over open sights. But the situation was hopeless, and the SS pulled out, losing all of its artillery either to tank fire or *jabos*. OKW fretted that, from Troyes, American tanks would turn toward Dijon and cut off the forces retreating from southern France.[216]

First Army's left wing, if it could be dignified with such a description, fell back toward the Marne River on 22 August. First Army was receiving no messages from the reinforced regiment of the 338th Infantry Division, but the latter heard a broadcast order from Chevallerie to pull back to Troyes from Montargis, near Orléans. Unfortunately, the regiment was annihilated over the next twenty-four hours. Attacked from the front by the 35th Infantry Division, the Germans suddenly found that Combat Command B of the 4th Armored Division had moved around their flank and was attacking from the rear. They died well— Third Army characterized the fighting as heavy. Other First Army elements, which now included a replacement transfer battalion, three artillery battalions from the 708th Infantry Division, and First Army's armored reconnaissance battalion, were able to slip back toward Troyes. Third Army detected all this activity and misinterpreted it as possible preparation for a counterattack.[217]

Chevallerie expected the enemy to press on toward Châlons-sur-Marne but hoped that he would pause first to prepare his next effort. The general could see no way of stopping such a thrust, though he sent the 17th SS Panzergrenadier Division to the sector. He also deployed newly arrived remnants of the 9th Panzer Division, consisting of a battalion of panzergrenadiers, four or five tanks and assault guns, and an artillery battery.

Chevallerie otherwise devoted all his energies to the area southeast of Paris and protecting the withdrawal of Army Group B across the lower Seine. There he placed his 48th Infantry Division, the only coherent force at his disposal, as well as remnant panzer divisions grouped under Krueger's LVIII Panzer Corps east of Paris.[218] U.S. First Army's advance on the capital, not Patton's charge, was his main problem.

U.S. First Army's 2nd DB and 4th Infantry Division entered Paris on 23 August. Patton was philosophical: "On the twenty-fourth, the British Broadcasting Company announced that Patton's Third Army had taken Paris. This seemed to me poetic justice, as I could have taken it had I not been told not to."[219]

Army Group B, on 23 August, assessed that the enemy clearly intended to destroy Fifth Panzer Army and the remnants of Seventh Army west of the Seine. Meanwhile, a thrust by six divisions passing to the south of Paris had to be reckoned with. The intelligence officers incorrectly guessed, however, that the aim of this operation would be to cut off German forces withdrawing from southern France, although a thrust toward the Marne and Somme was possible. The next day, they suggested that the Allied airborne divisions in the United Kingdom might be dropped in the Nancy-Dijon area.[220]

As of the twenty-fourth, *OB West* Model told subordinate commands that the positions being built along the Somme-Marne line were not yet battle ready. His plan was to man the Seine line upstream from Paris with four corps (LXXXVI, LXXIV, LXXXI, and XLVII Panzer) controlling twelve divisions, although Model doubted he could hold there for very long. A panzer group consisting of six remnant panzer divisions that could be quickly refreshed would form a mobile reserve between the Seine and Somme. Model also proposed to OKW that seven or eight panzer divisions be concentrated on the south wing of First Army to protect the flank of the retreating Nineteenth Army—the first in a series of German steps that would give rise to the myth that Hitler was obsessed with counterattacking Patton.[221] Some units from Fifteenth Army were stopped to form a rally line along the Seine for Seventh and Fifth Panzer Army troops, and OKW hoped that Chevallerie could hold along the Seine briefly before retreating to the Somme-Marne line.[222]

First Army was lucky to get the elements of the 48th Infantry Division, assault battalion, and 1010th Security Regiment back across the Seine before Combat Command A, 4th Armored Division, closed to the south bank on 24 August. Chevallerie's headquarters evacuated Fontainebleau, which lies southeast of Paris, that same day, just ahead of the 5th Infantry Division.[223]

While Paris was falling and Chevallerie was preoccupied with consolidating remnant divisions in LXIII Panzer Corps east of Paris, First Army's right wing disintegrated over the next few days. The 48th Infantry and 17th SS Panzergrenadier Divisions fragmented into scattered *Kampfgruppen*, and First Army's headquarters had no real idea what was going on. Chevallerie believed in moving his command post only when it came under direct threat, as a morale booster for frontline soldiers, and as a consequence, an armored spearhead passed less than a mile from the army headquarters near Fontenay on 26 August.[224]

The next day brought a miracle: American forces passed to both flanks, and what was left of First Army was able to pull back to the Marne. Chevallerie and his staff had another narrow escape on 27 August in Montmirail, when American tanks approached from Sezanne and fighter-bombers attacked the headquarters. All escaped after the escort company knocked out several tanks.

Arriving at the Marne, Chevallerie took control of LXXX Corps, which was organized for coastal defense and had been constructing fortifications between Soisson and Châlons. By default, he suddenly had a coherent line once again, albeit almost no actual troops.[225]

That lasted one day. On the twenty-eighth, XII Corps forced a crossing of the Marne near Châlons and XX Corps forced a crossing at Epernay. Major General Manton Eddy had taken command of XII Corps on 19 August because Cook had been in poor health and could no longer continue.[226] Third Army judged that First Army was capable only of delaying actions and small-scale counterattacks spearheaded by tanks, which exaggerated Chevallerie's actual capabilities.[227]

FROM PURSUIT TO BATTLE

The German high command was beginning to think about fighting back, and its initial schemes were drawn straight from the eastern front. Indeed, they were Mansteinian in scope and sweep of maneuver. As had been true in the east since 1943, however, the thoughts exceeded the resources.

First Army handed off the LVIII Panzer Corps, with its remnant divisions, to Fifth Panzer Army on 28 August, bringing the center of gravity in its defensive battle back to the south and Third Army.[228] This move doubtless was for the best, because the American spearheads were fast approaching the Meuse and would be across that river by 1 September.[229]

OKW signaled Model on 28 August that it was clear he was so busy trying to save Army Group B that he was overwhelmed with the simultaneous duties of *OB West*. Hitler was considering renaming Rundstedt to command the western front with his earlier staff.[230]

A series of signals intercepted by Ultra in late August and early September revealed that Hitler and Model were most concerned about three areas on the western front—the Low Countries, Aachen, and the Moselle valley from Metz to Trier—and that they viewed the last as their greatest point of weakness. Model's chief of staff informed Jodl that unless the gap south of Trier could be filled, an American thrust could rip through the West Wall before it could be prepared for defense. An American army in the Moselle valley also would threaten the escape route for First and Nineteenth Armies, the latter withdrawing from southern France.[231]

Patton's assistant G-2, Col. Robert Allen, had this to say about Chevallerie's performance so far: "XII and XX Corps were battering toward the German frontier against a constantly withdrawing but still doggedly defending and delaying enemy. His continued tactical control, despite the tremendous difficulties under which he operated, was a remarkable military feat. In the face of shattered communications, tremendous losses, constant retreating, and practically no air support, the enemy still maintained overall control of his tactical situation. He constantly fell back, but there was no mass collapse. At every critical point, he stubbornly defended and delayed."[232] Here were the fruits of Chevallerie's battles on the eastern front.

As of 29 August, First Army had tenuous contact with Fifth Panzer Army to its right, but to its left, there was nobody from Verdun to the Saar. Accordingly, orders arrived that the army was to stop withdrawing to the northeast and move behind the Moselle River to fill the space between the two army groups from Luxembourg to Nancy.[233]

Model, on the twenty-ninth, took stock of what he thought he had rescued from the Normandy disaster. From eleven SS and army panzer divisions, each with between five and ten tanks and only individual artillery batteries, he thought he could, with available replacements, build eleven regiment-size *Kampfgruppen*. Eleven remnant infantry divisions, if reinforced with personnel from five fought-out divisions in the Reich, might give him the equivalent of four divisions, albeit lacking key equipment.[234]

With the exception of Kluge's single reference to the American army-group commander, at no point to this time had German assessments of Allied intentions mentioned a commanding officer or suggested that individual generals exercised any particular influence over likely avenues of advance or tactical and operational behavior. Indeed, German assessments made no mention of individual Allied officers. Asked specifically about Patton, Jodl after the war said that consideration of Patton as a person was never a decisive factor in decisions such as deployment of forces, which were driven by the military situation.[235]

As if to illustrate that point, Hitler, in a *Führerbefehl* on 29 August, ordered that all available mobile formations—then thought to include the 3rd and 15th Panzergrenadier Divisions, Nineteenth Army's 11th Panzer Division, and the 105th and 106th Panzer Brigades—were to concentrate in the area of the Langres Plateau and attack the extended southern flank of the "American army group" because its drive into *Belgium* threatened to unhinge all German defenses along the coast. This second step toward the eventual counterpunch against Third Army's spearheads, therefore, was conceived as a way to "threaten the enemy attack [by Hodges's First Army] from the rear," according to Hitler's order.[236] Jodl confirmed after the war that Belgium had been the planned objective.[237] Here was the Mansteinian conception of maneuver over vast spaces, an operation aimed at restoring the situation across nearly an entire front.

Some historians, Third Army memoirs writers, and even, to a degree, Mellenthin (who was not present when Hitler issued his order) have attributed the counterattack that eventually occurred in mid-September to Hitler's desire to hit and stop Patton, the vaunted enemy commanding general, but German records indicate this was not the führer's thought or intent.[238] The story is a piece of the Patton myth. Only the unfavorable tide of military events eventually forced the German command to launch a much smaller counterstroke aimed only at Third Army.

Chevallerie was to take charge of this operation against the 12th Army Group's flank and of XLVII Panzer Corps, which was en route from Fifth Panzer Army to direct the mobile divisions. The two panzergrenadier divisions were still moving north from Italy by rail and scheduled to reach assembly areas on 1 September.[239]

The entire plan came unglued because of Patton's speedy approach to the Reich. The Americans had already overrun the 15th Panzergrenadier Division's detraining stations, so the division was carried via Luxembourg to Stenay and unloaded. The 15th Division was up to strength and a battle-seasoned formation, but its panzer battalion had not yet arrived. Meanwhile, Chevallerie's weak defenses astride the Argonne collapsed, and Chevallerie, on instructions from OKW, ordered the newly arrived division to counterattack late on 31 August southward to Verdun. Even that plan went awry, and the 7th Armored Division, which had liberated most of the area where Patton had fought in the last world war, noted only that enemy artillery at Verdun was "active."

Chevallerie ordered the rest of XLVII Panzer Corps, whatever he imagined that to be, to attack simultaneously to cut off the American spearheads. But communications had broken down, and the message did not get through. The panzer corps had to pull back behind the Meuse on both sides of St. Mihiel, and Model fatuously expected to hold the Meuse line until at least 15 September. Model's chief of staff, however, told OKW that the panzer corps's attack was not possible because it had no battle-ready formations available.

Things could have been worse. The British that day overran Seventh Army's headquarters in Amiens and took the staff and commanding general, *General der Panzertruppe* Eberbach, prisoner.[240]

THE BIG STOP

Chevallerie was perplexed: from 29 August to 6 September, Third Army kept its forces hunkered down in the Argonne west of the Moselle River.[241] In light of continuing Allied advances in Belgium and the Netherlands, OKW wondered whether the enemy even intended to advance farther along the Metz axis.[242] The reason for the stop was that Eisenhower had, on 29 August, issued a directive designating Montgomery's advance along the coast as the Allies' main axis, and he had ordered Bradley to support that drive with most of U.S. First Army. Otherwise, 12th Army Group was to "build up" east of Paris in preparation for a drive into the Saarland. In other words, Patton was to regroup! By the 31st, these strategic priorities resulted in a near total cutoff in the delivery of scarce fuel supplies to Third Army, and Patton's mechanized warriors ground to a halt.[243]

Patton was convinced that had he been given the fuel, he could have smashed through against no resistance, a view endorsed by some prominent historians, but there was not enough fuel getting to the front to sustain *any* drive deep into Germany, even had Third Army been favored over U.S. First Army. On 9 September, First Army—which was guzzling an average of 571,000 gallons of gasoline daily (compared with some 400,000 gallons per day in Third Army's drive across France)—was living hand-to-mouth. Despite yeoman efforts using every truck available (including the famous Red Ball Express, which itself consumed 300,000 gallons a day moving supplies to the front) and even air delivery in bombers, the army's three corps were 1.3 million gallons short of their basic gasoline load on 19 September. With German resistance reappearing, supply worries shifted suddenly to ammunition. First Army, on 18 September, for the first time requested that the Red Ball Express deliver some ammunition in place of fuel.[244]

Furthermore, the lost window of opportunity was, at most, less than forty-eight hours during which it is just possible the Germans could have interposed no coherent military formations in Patton's way. As of 1 September, total First Army strength amounted to nine infantry battalions, two artillery batteries, ten panzers, and ten 75mm antitank guns.[245] German forces were consolidating and fresh divisions were arriving, however, and Chevallerie most probably would have been able to impede an ammunition- and maintenance-short Third Army before it reached the West Wall. As of 1 September, the 17th SS Panzergrenadier Division's 49th Brigade was between Verdun and Metz with orders to establish bridgeheads at Metz and St. Mihiel and to defend Metz to the last man. The fresh 559th Volksgrenadier Division was detraining in Metz, the 553rd Volksgrenadier Division in Saarbrücken, and the 106th Panzer Brigade in Trier.[246]

Even Patton may have had a sneaking feeling he was overblowing the "lost opportunity." On 7 September, he told war correspondents that with adequate fuel he would have reached the Moselle four days earlier. Patton added, "We are over now, so it doesn't make much difference."[247]

The stage was set for the battle of Lorraine. No German commander had expected to fight such a battle, but Patton had been thinking about it since England. Patton was following an invasion path that the Romans had blazed in the first century BC and that many a general had followed since. From Chevallerie's perspective, once he had backpedalled halfway from Verdun to Metz, he would be defending German territory. The modern reader will think of the battle has having flared in France, but during the century leading up to the fight, Lorraine had been part of Germany—which had existed as a unified state since only 1871—for just over half the time and had been a constituent territory (as part of Alsace-Lorraine, or *Elsass-Lothringen*) of the new state. France had taken control of Alsace-Lorraine in the Treaty of Versailles that ended the Great War, the onerous terms of which had helped propel Hitler to power.

Hitler, on 2 September, issued a general instruction for combat operations on the western front. Formations were to fight for every foot of ground, but they had permission to pull back to avoid being encircled.[248] This was no fanatical stand-fast order.

From the German perspective, First Army on 2 September was, for the first time in over a month, close to establishing a coherent defensive line to face Third Army. On its right wing, opposite U.S. First Army's V Corps, *General der Infanterie* Franz Beyer's LXXX Corps, controlling most of the 48th Infantry and Panzer Lehr Divisions, the 17th SS Panzergrenadier Division, and elements of the 15th Panzergrenadier Division, was falling back under overwhelming pressure, but elements of the 48th Infantry Division had secured Longwy in time to fend off American reconnaissance forces. LXXXII Corps, commanded from 1 September by *Generalleutnant* Walter Hörnlein, had established a security line west of Metz, with the 559th Volksgrenadier Division on the right, which tied into LXXX Corps, and parts of the 48th Infantry Division on the left. The 559th Division was part of the first wave of volksgrenadier divisions and was comparatively well manned. Its officers were young, but nearly all had experience on the eastern front—where it had been intended to fight—as did about 70 percent of the noncommissioned officers (NCOs) and most of the troops. Artillery and antitank guns (apparently only one company of the latter) were of the latest design.

Generalleutnant Walter Wissmath's 19th Volksgrenadier Division, moreover, pulled into Esch from Holland and was available to plug any hole in the main First Army line from Sedan to Metz. The 19th Division was newly transformed from a Luftwaffe field division, and while it included two battalions each of light and medium artillery—and, oddly, a company of panzergrenadiers—its assault-gun battalion was missing. It had not completed unit-level training, and its NCOs and enlisted ranks were about 25 percent below establishment. Its arrival allowed Chevallerie, in turn, to move a regiment of the 15th

Panzergrenadier Division into army reserve, a benchmark of stabilization. The 36th Volksgrenadier Division was also on the way. All the newly arriving volks-grenadier divisions, except the 19th Division, moved up to the Moselle River, where they were to complete their training on the job and absorb wrecked units withdrawing from France.

Hörnlein had spent the preceding month commanding the LXIV Corps during its withdrawal along with the rest of Army Group G, having arrived at his command barely a week before Chevallerie and his First Army headquarters had been sent north to stem the tide. In the crisis, Hörnlein made a much better commander for LXXXII Corps than did the artillery general he replaced. His long command of the "fire brigade" *Grossdeutschland* Division in the east made him a man who understood the nature of the fight, and he would already know personally other members of the east-front panzer mafia that was about to fill the command ranks opposite Patton.

XLVII Panzer Corps was fighting back along the Moselle near Pont-à-Mousson with parts of the 15th Panzergrenadier and the arriving 3rd Panzergrenadier Divisions, and it had moved elements of the 553rd Volksgrenadier Division to cover the Moselle River crossings. A regiment-sized airborne element also happened to be in the area of Nancy, which lay just west of the 1944 border between Lorraine and Germany.[249]

On 4 September, *General der Panzertruppe* Heinrich *Freiherr* von Lüttwitz took command of XLVII Panzer Corps from the irascible Hans *Freiherr* von Funck. Lüttwitz had commanded the 2nd Panzer Division in Normandy and was the only senior commander in the Lorraine battle who had not served beside the others at some point in the Soviet Union.[250]

The staff of XIII SS Corps arrived at the front on 1 September and would soon be available for action.[251] Its new commanding general was rushing from the eastern front to meet it.

The forested and increasingly rough terrain, sloping upward from west to east and cut by rivers across the American route of advance, for the first time favored the defender. By the time Third Army threw back the screening forces on 4 September, First Army judged its plan and the coherent line—except for a gap at Briey between the Metz defenses and the rest of the army—to be a major success.[252] Colonel Robert Allen conceded of this patchwork line, "[The enemy] defended and delayed tenaciously. Counterattacks were numerous and aggressive."[253]

On 1 September, the *New York Times* reported that efforts to encourage German worries about an attack on Pas de Calais by Patton's FUSAG had made a major contribution to the victory in Normandy. There is no sign that the Germans paid any attention to the report.[254]

While First Army had been transitioning from flight to fight, Hitler's concept for an attack on the "extended eastern flank and rear" of the Americans by 1 September had evolved in response to his straightened circumstances. Now the operation's first goal was to protect the withdrawal of Nineteenth Army and LXIV Corps from southern France, which would entail an attack on the American XII Corps. The force was then to drive farther into the American flank and rear, leaving its effect on Hodges's First Army merely implied and contingent. Still, the plan was not conceived around Patton or intended to stop his advance per se, particularly as Patton at the time had stopped advancing.

Once Seventh Army could stand on its own north of First Army, Fifth Panzer Army was to take control of the attacking force. Hitler now ordered the concentration of the 3rd, 15th, and 17th SS Panzergrenadier Divisions; the 11th, 21st, and, if possible, Panzer Lehr Panzer Divisions; and the 106th, 107th, 108th, 112th, and 113th Panzer Brigades. These formations were not to be committed piecemeal, the führer insisted, doubtless recollecting the failure at Mortain.[255]

Model's concern about Third Army relative to the rest of the western front appears to have grown in the first days of September. On 4 September, he concluded incorrectly that while 12th Army Group was likely to push in an easterly and northeasterly direction in support of 21st Army Group's drive against Fifteenth Army along the Scheldt, its main effort was likely to be on its southern wing.[256] Model's changing calculus may have reflected the fact that his staff was getting more information about the enemy, as a firming defense allowed better reconnaissance and radio-intercept collection. The daily enemy situation reports by now had gained more granularity, as the Germans developed a much firmer idea of who was doing what, and a clear distinction between the mass of 12th Army Group and Third Army emerged in German discussion for the first time.

Third Army was expected to attack at any time toward the area between Luxembourg and Metz. The lack of pressure from this quarter since 29 August had let First Army make meaningful strides in building its defenses, and it was now in the best condition of any army on the western front, judged Model.[257] The weakest sector had become the strongest.

ELEVEN

Lorraine: Patton Faces Germany's Best

PATTON FINALLY HAD some gas again. On 4 September, Third Army received 240,265 gallons, and 1,396,710 gallons arrived over the next three days. The critical shortage eased by 10 September, but rationing and shortfalls continued into late October. On 10 September, Bradley gave VIII Corps in Brittany to the newly activated Ninth Army, though its 83rd Infantry and 6th Armored Divisions were to return to Patton.[1]

Patton also was getting too little ammunition, which was a very big deal because the American style of warfare relied far more on crushing artillery fire than the German style. Third Army's shortage was, in part, a consequence of so much ammunition being fired for prestige purposes during the pointless siege of Brest. As of 10 September, Third Army's batteries were getting only one-third of a unit of fire per day.[2]

Simultaneously with Patton regaining his power to maneuver on 4 September, Hitler reinstated the old Prussian warhorse *Generalfeldmarschall* Gerd von Rundstedt as *OB West*. U.S. First Army's interpretation of Rundstedt's renewed appointment was that "the moment called for a real soldier."[3] Model took on his duties as commanding general of Army Group B full time.

Manstein wrote of Rundstedt, "As an exponent of grand tactics he was brilliant—a talented soldier who grasped the essentials of any problem in an instant.... The General had a charm about him to which even Hitler succumbed."[4] Jodl described the late-war Rundstedt who finally came to blows with Patton in these terms: "He was an intellectually superior, well-trained officer. He did

280

not waste time on details. . . . Because of his age, however, he was not so well fitted to spur men to superhuman efforts in an adverse situation. . . . Rundstedt always enjoyed complete authority and had an excellent head for operations. He had studied in the old school."[5] Kesselring said of him, "He commanded from his headquarters by issuing instructions which clearly showed adaptability to the situation; almost never did he visit the front, and he made telephone calls only rarely. Vertical communications were almost exclusively in the hands of the chief and the assistant chiefs of the general staff. This procedure had some undisputable advantages; the [commanding general] had peace and quiet, and he was not exposed to the pressures caused by personal observation at the front. He was the prototype of the distinguished leader, far removed, whose name was mentioned only with a certain amount of awe."[6]

Rundstedt, scion of an old Prussian-Saxon military family, had entered the imperial army in 1891. He received general staff training before the Great War and served in that capacity along most of the eastern and western fronts during the conflict. Between the wars, he had served as chief of staff and commanding general in both cavalry and infantry divisions, so he had had some taste of mobile warfare. As we have seen, he had commanded army groups in the invasions of Poland, France, and the Soviet Union.[7]

Third Army knew that the Germans had constructed a defensive line along the east bank of the Moselle, but Patton had no idea that Chevallerie had made so much progress when he ordered XII and XX Corps to cross the Moselle on 5 September. Patton had grown used to throwing the long passes into the opponent's secondary during the romp across France. His G-2, Brig. Gen. Oscar Koch, however, had recognized on 28 August that Chevallerie's preventative defense had been skillfully executed. The enemy had "been able to maintain a sufficiently cohesive front to exercise overall control of his tactical situation. . . . [T]he German armies will continue to fight until destroyed or captured." Koch recognized that fresh German formations were arriving at the front, even from other fronts, and he probably had knowledge of the transfer of two panzergrenadier divisions from Italy.[8]

Patton's operational directive of 5 September instructed XX Corps to seize Metz, advance rapidly to Mainz, establish a bridgehead across the Rhine, and there prepare to advance on Frankfurt. XII Corps was to capture Nancy, guard the flank until relieved by elements of XV Corps, and prepare to advance rapidly to the northeast to capture Mannheim and establish a bridgehead across the Rhine. XV Corps was to take up responsibility for guarding the flank, but also prepare to advance toward Karlsruhe and establish a bridgehead across the Rhine. The 6th Armored Division was to move from Brittany to Troyes and

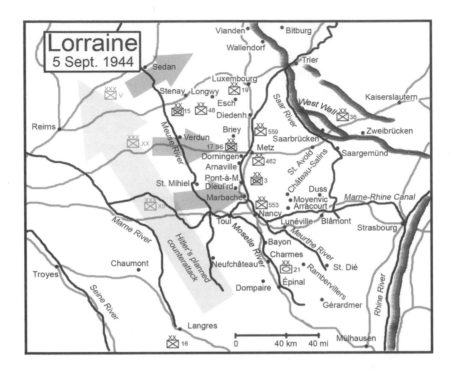

would constitute the army reserve.[9] American security was so porous that *OB West* knew by the next day that Third Army had just issued orders to attack eastward, with XX Corps to reach the Rhine.[10]

Here, then, was the first, strategic-level standard by which one might judge who triumphed in Lorraine: Patton aimed to reach the Rhine, and Rundstedt intended to stop him.

When Maj. Gen. Manton Eddy's XII Corps kicked off on 5 September, Eddy, according to his diary, was of a mind that "[n]one of the Germans in this sector have any fight left in them." Patton wrote that he would soon "have a chance to do some open field running."

But Chevallerie's defenders stuffed Patton at the line. The 317th Infantry Regiment, 80th Infantry Division, crossed the Moselle at Pont-à-Mousson only to run into *Generalmajor* Hans Hecker's 3rd Panzergrenadier Division, which threw the Americans back with the loss of 300 officers and men. The 318th Infantry's attempt to cross at Marbache failed to even secure the west bank. Only at Toul, which sits above a wide loop in the Moselle west of Nancy, was the 319th Infantry able to establish a small bridgehead on the heavily forested east bank.[11] Patton conceded he'd been given a "bloody nose."[12]

For once, the *jabos* stayed away. Eisenhower had ordered XIX Tactical Air Command to concentrate its operations against Brest—yet one more unanticipated advantage of Hitler's fortress strategy. Indeed, XIX TAC would fly a majority of its missions against Brest every day but three through 18 September.[13]

Chevallerie was now thinking in terms of a mobile defense in the style of the eastern front, but Third Army's attack disrupted a pincer attack he had ordered for the fifth. Chevallerie had instructed the 15th Panzergrenadier Division and 106th Panzer Brigade, followed by the 48th Infantry Division, to strike southward around Briey under Chevallerie's direct command, while *Generalleutnant* Werner-Albrecht von und zu Gilsa's LXXXIX Corps strengthened by the 17th SS Panzergrenadier Division was to push northward out of the bridgehead west of Metz to meet them.[14]

The setback seemed to stun Eddy, who did not come on aggressively again for five more days. Chevallerie felt confident enough to formally release the rest of the 15th Panzergrenadier Division to XLVII Panzer Corps in the Lunéville area, where it partially filled the gap between the two German army groups.[15]

Despite Chevallerie's success in holding together what had been an army in name only during the chaotic retreat through France, Hitler evidently had not been impressed with his performance. On 6 September, Chevallerie was relieved and sent to the *Führerreserve* again, from which he did not return to active duty.[16]

On 7 September, after speaking with Model and others, Rundstedt filed his first report to OKW appreciating the situation of *OB West*. He was most concerned about the situation of Fifteenth Army on the coast and the defenses around Aachen, which, if they gave way, opened the door to the Ruhr industrial basin. He needed five, or better ten, more divisions in the north, he said, and he was shifting the weak 9th Panzer Division to the Aachen area along with the available assault-gun units. Rundstedt appeared little concerned with the situation opposite Third Army.[17] According to Jodl, Rundstedt had a mere 70,000 to 80,000 ground troops along the entire western front at about this time.[18]

Nevertheless, Rundstedt's chief of staff, then-*Generalleutnant* Siegfried Westphal, commenting on those desperate times, wrote after the war, "[H]eadquarters of *OB West* was located in the vicinity of Koblenz. Whenever after sunset we could the rattling of [tank tracks] in the street where the Field Marshal had his quarters, he would ask, 'Can this be Patton?'"[19]

As Liddell Hart observed, Rundstedt had a sense of humor, and Westphal concedes that Rundstedt spoke in jest. But the field marshal at least by now knew who Patton was.[20]

Bringing in the A-Team

Hitler, over the summer months, had been shifting battle-hardened commanders from the eastern to the western front, and he placed some of his best Russian-front talent opposite Patton. Generals no longer physically fit for the east had been assigned to the west since early 1942 to transfer their experience to the occupation army, but this wave consisted of generally physically fit men. Chevallerie's appointment to First Army had been one of the first of such assignments, but the pace accelerated as the situation deteriorated. *General der Panzertruppe* Erich Brandenberger was put at the head of Seventh Army on 1 August, and *General der Infanterie* Gustav von Zangen in command of Fifteenth Army about 20 August. In general, these officers were young and had not been deeply imprinted by the imperial army; they had held field-grade ranks at the beginning of the war and had risen through the ranks extremely quickly because of ability. Most were deemed more reliable National Socialists than the members of the old guard, who continued to dominate command positions on the eastern front.[21] Hitler had increasingly emphasized Nazi fealty in making appointments down to division level since early 1944, evidently believing that faith would win as setbacks mounted in the east.[22] All key members of the command team that took charge of the Lorraine fighting during September knew each other well and formed a cohesive group.

On 7 August, XIII SS Corps took charge of the Metz sector. *SS Brigadeführer* Hermann Priess, the new corps commanding general, and his staff, dismayed by the weak units at their disposal, expected heavy fighting in the immediate future, and they were not wrong. U.S. XX Corps on 5 September had reached the lines of the 559th Volksgrenadier Division holding a bridgehead west of the Moselle at Diedenhofen (Thionville). The Americans launched their first serious attacks near Metz the very day that Priess and his team arrived.[23]

Priess had just arrived after more than a year in command of the 3rd SS Panzer (*Totenkopf*) Division on the eastern front. He had replaced Max Simon in that job in May 1943 when Simon was moved over to command the 16th SS Panzergrenadier (*Reichsführer*) Division in Italy. (Simon had been thrust back into temporary command of *Totenkopf* on 26 February 1943, when long-time commanding general Theodor Eicke had been shot down in an observation plane over the battle lines.) Under Priess, *Totenkopf* had fought up and down the front, rushing to wherever the situation was darkest.

Priess had established himself as a brave commander. He earned the Knight's Cross for his actions during the destruction of the Third Tank Army southeast of Wlassovka in 1943; participated in Operation Citadel, as we have seen; and received the Oak Leaves and Swords for his performance during defensive campaigns in 1943 and early 1944. His commanding general in Eighth Army, *General der Infanterie* Otto Wöhler, in April 1944, judged that Priess had consistently proved to be a calm man in a crisis. When Priess had temporarily left the eastern front in July 1944, suffering from a relapse of dysentery, *Generaloberst* Ferdinand Schörner, the commanding general of Army Group South Ukraine, wrote several letters to Heinrich Himmler praising Priess's high achievements in battle and in the military arts and characterized him as a decisive man of "strong nerves"—just the kind of man he needed. Yet Schörner also candidly noted that Priess was a "difficult subordinate"; needed to be more obedient to orders, especially when they caught him by surprise; and still had room to learn to employ his division tactically to its greatest effect.

Priess had just finished his eastern-front service fighting with *Gruppe von Knobelsdorff*, commanded by *General der Panzertruppe* Otto von Knobelsdorff. Knobelsdorff had recommended Priess for the Swords to his Knight's Cross, praising his clear leadership and self-reliance during the preceding months and for making the group's withdrawal possible.[24] Neither the XIII SS Corps records nor a personal account survive of Priess's command in Lorraine, and tracks of his personal influence on the battle against Patton are, therefore, few.

Major General Walton Walker's XX Corps pushed off on 7 September in what was to have been the second swing of a one-two punch. Two days earlier, freshly emplaced antitank guns on high ground east of the Moselle and shellfire from Fort Jean D'Arc had driven off five task forces from the 3rd Cavalry Group probing toward Metz and Arnaville.

On the seventh, excellent troops from the officer-candidate school in Metz, who had been attached to *Generalmajor* Heinrich Kittel's 462nd Infantry Division (essentially the Metz garrison), waited in prepared positions and stopped cold most of the four advancing columns of the 7th Armored Division, supported by the 5th Infantry Division, which Walker had ordered to conduct a frontal assault. The three 100mm guns of Battery Moselle, part of Fort Kronprinz (Fort Driant), laid down a terrible and costly flanking fire. Only two battalions of the 11th Infantry Regiment reached the Moselle at Dorningen (Dornot).

A weak German defensive force greeted a crossing by forty men of the 23rd Armored Infantry Battalion with heavy fire and pinned them down. Only artillery fire harassed the 2nd Battalion, 11th Infantry, when it joined the small band the following afternoon and pushed forward across open ground and up hill to the outer entanglements of the *Feste Graf Häseler* (Fort Verdun

Group), a turn-of-the-century fortification with ten turreted artillery pieces, sixteen armored observation cupolas, and a 500-man garrison. The 17th SS Panzergrenadier Division was just arriving, and the SS took full advantage of the moment. They infiltrated behind the Americans while pasting them with mortar and artillery fire. Machine-gun teams interdicted the American route to the river.

SS tank-infantry teams struck the perimeter on the riverbank thirty-six times, and the infantry followed the panzers into the forward positions with what American observers characterized as desperate courage. One group advanced while shouting, "Yanks kaput!" German losses were heavy in each attack, but the company holding the shore was rapidly dwindling, too.

The Americans at the fortress, realizing their predicament, crawled back to the Moselle, leaving scores of dead and wounded men on the slope. Under cover of darkness, the Americans formed a compact horseshoe defense of their small bridgehead.[25] Patton's G-2, Col. Oscar Koch, said that the 17th SS Panzergrenadier Division "by October [had] become one of Third Army's 'favorites.' Whenever it appeared, things were bound to happen. . . . It was a fighting outfit."[26]

It is likely that the sudden aggressiveness displayed by the SS division was the result of Priess's arrival at the front. Priess had demonstrated just such tenacity in his actions on the eastern front. The orders that arrived at the division head-quarters on 8 September instructed the division to counterattack "and throw the enemy back across the Moselle." This was vintage Priess. Moreover, a division order on 25 September indicates that from the engagement at Dorningen through the stabilization of the front on that day, the division was engaged in a "mobile defense," just as Priess had employed in the east.[27]

Panzer generals worked best when they had panzers, and Hörnlein's LXXXII Corps was about to get some. Unfortunately, on 8 September, First Army suffered one of those flukes in the fortunes of war when about half of its fresh 106th *Feldheernhalle* Panzer Brigade—its only real mobile reserve—got lost on the way to Briey, took a wrong turn in the dark, and stumbled into the 90th Infantry Division's command post and the 712th Tank Battalion. In a confused battle lasting from the predawn hours through the course of the day, the brigade lost forty Panthers, more than one hundred half-tracks, and 764 soldiers, by American count.[28]

This incident appears to have been an accident and not a planned attack. Model had wanted to use the panzer brigade and 15th Panzergrenadier Division to attack in this very spot on 6 and 7 September to straighten the line. Hitler, however, had agreed only on the condition that the operation be completed by the evening of the seventh, which had not been possible.[29]

It would not be unreasonable to suppose that Hörnlein looked back at the disintegration of 10th Panzer Brigade during Operation Citadel and wondered whether he bore some curse when it came to Panther brigades.

General der Panzertruppe Otto von Knobelsdorff took command of First Army on 10 September. His sprawling army at this point faced U.S. First Army's right wing in Luxembourg and Third Army in Lorraine. His first orders to XIII SS and XLVII Panzer Corps were to throw the Americans back across the Moselle with their reserves.[30] This was vintage Knobelsdorff, and he was thinking just like Priess.

Knobelsdorff had literally just arrived from the eastern front, where from 26 February until 4 September he had commanded the XL Panzer Corps, also labeled *Gruppe von Knobelsdorff* and *Panzergruppe von Knobelsdorff* at various times, in the Ukraine. *Generalleutnant* Hasso von Manteuffel, as it happened, had arrived in the sector just before him to take command of the *Grossdeutschland* Panzergrenadier Division in the neighboring XLVII Panzer Corps. On transferring Manteuffel from the 7th Panzer to the *Grossdeutschland* Division, Hitler had told him, "You should build this division to be the strongest in the army, Manteuffel." Manteuffel and his division were subordinated to XL Panzer Corps on 11 March.

The two panzer corps, fighting along the Bug and Dniestr Rivers, were just beginning a withdrawal movement in anticipation of a major Soviet offensive, dropping back overnight to a "B Line," with further phased night withdrawals to follow. On 10 March, after weeks of quiet, the Soviets launched a ferocious attack on the *Grossdeutschland* Division—part of a general offensive aimed at the Romanian oil fields—that broke through the line and was stopped only after the most heroic efforts by the infantry. The Soviets aggressively followed each of the corps' steps backward, knocking small holes in the XL Panzer Corps line with tanks and infantry, but counterattacks resolved many problems, and further retreats the others. Knobelsdorff and Manteuffel had, therefore, gotten to know one another under conditions not all that dissimilar from those prevailing on First Army's front.

A survey of Knobelsdorff's orders to his officers and men in XL Panzer Corps reveals a commander with a fine sense of frontline combat. In one, he demanded that units stop exaggerating the size of the enemy forces attacking them, as he said he knows they were, because he would make mistaken decisions on the basis of false information. In another, he instructed panzer unit commanders that they were not to pull back their tanks and assault guns to rearm and refuel and leave the infantry stranded. Supplies were to be brought forward, and it was the duty of every *Panzermann* to be the steadfast backstop for the infantry in attack and defense. He underlined, "That is why we are the Black Hussars," a reference to the black panzer uniform. In a third, he urged his commanders to keep in mind that their troops had been in constant battle against overwhelming odds. Patton would have appreciated that he also ordered that all men from battalion command posts forward had to wear their steel helmets when outside a bunker.[31] Knobelsdorff was decorated again for his command of the corps during its skillful withdrawal into East Prussia during August.[32]

Knobelsdorff's performance appraisal for his command of the corps noted that he was a mobile combat soldier, decisive, and a doer. He exercised wide personal influence across the front and over all subordinates. He was firm in a crisis, unyielding, and a dedicated optimist. The only criticism was that at times he followed impulse rather than thinking through all the tactical possibilities. The commanding general of Third Panzer Army judged him suitable for command above the corps level.[33]

With Knobelsdorff's arrival, the First Army team was in place. The men at army and corps level had known far more of war than Patton did. They had commanded men in more critical and far bigger battles than Patton had. They had fought defensive campaigns against overwhelming odds before, and each had been in Patton's shoes as the commander of a modern, mechanized force supported by superior air power. They had been through more grueling times than Patton had. Arguably, they were just plain tougher than Patton. Knobelsdorff, in particular, had proved to be one of the best corps-commanding generals in the entire Wehrmacht.

Patton, however, had an edge himself, besides his lopsided materiel advantage. Patton had commanded an army since Sicily. Each of his opponents was brand new (or nearly so) to his level of command, and the jump from division to corps or from corps to army brought entirely new stresses and strains, as well as more complex considerations regarding operations and tactics. Any errors reverberated far more widely.

Knobelsdorff found his new staff at First Army to be men over forty years of age who had spent much of the past year on garrison duty and were "not suitable for mobile warfare [or] fit for service." They were not going to help him much in his adjustment to army-level command. His communication regiment was really only a battalion, had lost most of its vehicles and equipment, and was mainly trained to manage telephone lines. The supply system was in chaos, and moving up ammunition, fuel, and other supplies was a "constant headache." Two of his corps headquarters, LXXX and LXXXII, were trained only for coastal defense and had no signal or supply units. XIII SS Corps, although commanded by his familiar subordinate Priess, had been organized only three weeks earlier and was not up to full strength, and it had but a single communications platoon.[34] Neither LXXXII nor XIII SS Corps staffs were going to be of much help in their new commanders' adjustment, either. Knobelsdorff shuffled his army's organization, transferring the 559th Volksgrenadier Division from XIII SS Corps to LXXXII Corps, and giving Priess control over the 3rd Panzergrenadier and 553rd Volksgrenadier divisions on his left wing.[35]

The moment was one of psychological recovery after weeks of unending disaster. From the Germans' perspective, they had stopped Third Army's attempt to smash through their tentative line around Metz. All the Americans had succeeded in doing was to establish a few small bridgeheads across the Moselle River.

This moment of relief was just about to end. *Oberst* Albert Emmerich, First Army operations officer (Ia) from late 1944, recorded, "While the German First Army had succeeded in setting up a more or less coherent defensive front behind the Sauer [Sûre, in Luxembourg] and Moselle rivers with bridgeheads near Metz and Nancy by 10 September after its successful escape from France, where it was able to withstand the main pressure of the enemy attacks that were carried out after 7 September, the situation on both wings of the army was becoming extremely critical between 10 and 15 September."[36]

Oberst Willy Mantey, Knobelsdorff's operations officer, recalled that at the handover, First Army was tightly tied into Seventh Army on its right, on the line Vianden-Bitburg, but that its link to Nineteenth Army on its left, on the line Bayon-Blâmont, consisted of a string of strong points. First Army still held a bridgehead west of the Moselle at Metz, mainly due to the high morale and fierce resistance offered by the officer candidates and NCO trainees attached to the 462nd Infantry Division. To the south, the Americans already had several small bridgeheads of their own on the east bank. First Army was holding its own west of Nancy, primarily because the Americans had not yet arrived there in force. Knobelsdorff's total reserves consisted of remnants of the 48th Infantry Division, the 106th Panzer Brigade (already nearly burned out), and the army's weapons-training school.

How important were the officer candidates? *Generalmajor* Friedrich-Wilhelm von Mellenthin, who was soon to become the army group chief of staff, related, "As a result of their high morale, the defenders of Metz dominated the situation and repeatedly confused the enemy in rear areas by spirited counterattacks. For example, on 10 September 1944, a reconnaissance patrol composed of one officer and seven officer candidates was ordered to conduct a night reconnaissance in the vicinity of Amanvillers. At dawn, they surprised an American company, which had just been lined up in a town. By opening surprise fire with their machine pistols, the patrol overpowered the company and returned with their prisoners—two officers and ninety-six men."

First Army's missions were, first and foremost, to hold Metz and Nancy. Secondarily, it was to reduce the enemy bridgeheads east of the Moselle, strengthen its line to repel future attacks, and establish a perimeter defense in the Metz-Diedenhofen area. The Germans had developed the fortresses at Metz and Diedenhofen, which consisted of fortified groups integrated into the surrounding terrain (a precursor to the Maginot Line), between 1871 and 1916. Few of the forts now had guns, fire control, or ammunition. Only Fort Kronprinz had functioning guns on 6 September. XIII SS Corps, responsible for the defense of Metz, viewed the city, in the words of the corps chief of staff *Oberst* Karl von Einem, as "completely obsolete as a fortress and without military value." In case of an American breakthrough, troops within the Metz perimeter were ordered to allow themselves to be surrounded in order to tie down enemy divisions—an idea soon abandoned, which meant resources were not wasted on building fortifications east of Metz. First Army accurately expected Third Army to attack above and below Metz in the direction of Saarbrücken and Saargemünd.[37]

This, then, was a third, tactical-level standard by which to judge who won in Lorraine. Knobelsdorff was to hold Nancy and Metz, and Patton's plans demanded that he take those cities. Hitler had not yet formulated and revealed to his commanders the second, intermediate-level standard—to hold the West Wall running northwest-to-southeast between Metz and the Rhine until a major counteroffensive, versus Patton's firm intention to penetrate the fortifications.

Knobelsdorff had sufficient intelligence information to know that Third Army aimed to cross the Rhine between Mannheim and Koblenz. Knobelsdorff recalled, "[I]t was also completely clear to the Army that everything had to be done to prevent the Americans from achieving this and that [it] would have to deal with the task which was now [its] responsibility, cost what it might." Knobelsdorff interpreted Third Army's recent inactivity as a building up for a major thrust against his front.

The commanding general of Third Panzer Army had suggested that Knobelsdorff was no towering tactician, but Knobelsdorff did not need to be a Manstein to know how to fight a defensive struggle at this place, because he had rich experience in just this sort of problem. After surveying the battlefield, Knobelsdorff concluded that he lacked the strength to hold the length of the high eastern bank of the Moselle, where the Americans could pound his positions with artillery and where his own artillery support against the enemy below would be difficult because of the sharp slope. The Americans had already gotten across at two spots, anyway. He decided instead to establish his defenses on the reverse slope of the eastern bank and carry out a mobile defense, just as he always had in the east. Army Group G, however, transferred XLVII Panzer Corps to Nineteenth Army almost immediately after Knobelsdorff's arrival, which left him with little to execute a mobile defense.[38]

Almost at the same time that a brand new commanding general took charge of First Army, on 9 September, Army Group G took control over First Army, grouping under it LXXX Corps in Luxembourg, LXXXII Corps, XIII SS Corps, XLVII Panzer Corps, and XXV Corps, holed up in Normandy.[39]

Generaloberst Johannes Blaskowitz, who prior to the Allied landings in southern France had last seen battle in Poland in 1939, commanded Army Group G. Mellenthin described Blaskowitz as an officer of the old school, "with all the staunch virtues associated with his native province of East Prussia."[40] His American interrogators later found him to be reticent by nature.

Blaskowitz almost certainly viewed his new responsibilities for defending Metz and fighting Patton as but one small piece in his desperate need to stabilize a defensive line along the Vosges with the troops he had extricated from southern France. Blaskowitz viewed Metz as just one anchor in the line he was expected to form and later said, "Of course, we were fully conscious of the weakness of the Metz forts, but they furnished an opportunity to delay."[41]

Blaskowitz was juggling many balls already as Nineteenth Army rushed to beat 6th Army Group to the Belfort Gap through the Vosges. During Nineteenth Army's withdrawal up the Rhône valley from southern France, it had lost 1,316 of its 1,480 guns.[42] The last two divisions to slip free were badly mauled: The 198th Infantry Division was reduced to 350 to 400 men per regiment, but had escaped with much of its heavy equipment. The 338th Infantry Division had escaped with a total strength of only 1,100 combatants and ten artillery pieces.[43] Still, the retreat had been masterful and orderly compared to the flight from northwestern France, and most divisions still had solid skeletons on which to layer muscle and flesh. On 3 September, Blaskowitz received authorization from Hitler to rebuild his divisions with all Wehrmacht personnel he could get his hands on as they retreated.

Blaskowitz, on 4 September, acting on instructions from Hitler, issued orders that Army Group G was to link up with Army Group B's First Army to the north, hold the area west of the Vosges Mountains to Dijon as a staging area for a counterattack against "the rear and flank of the American forces," and protect the routes to the Belfort Gap.[44]

By 5 September, Blaskowitz had turned over command of the battle in the Dijon area to Nineteenth Army and moved his headquarters to Gérardmer, at the edge of the Vosges Mountains. He saw his main task as overseeing preparation of a defensive line exploiting the high ground, construction of which had begun only on 1 September. Blaskowitz had spent time in those hills in the days before World War I and knew them intimately. Here, he thought, one might stop even a modern mechanized army.[45]

A *Kampfgruppe* of the 21st Panzer Division, which the army group appears to have attached to itself, had been fending off reconnaissance elements from Seventh Army since 5 September. On the sixth, north of Chaumont, LXVI Corps on the army group's right wing also encountered American armor, which threatened to drive a wedge between the two army groups. Blaskowitz's staff reached First Army's headquarters by telephone to arrange a linkup between LXVI Corps's newly arrived 16th Infantry Division and First Army's 553rd Volksgrenadier Division south of Nancy.[46]

A few new resources were trickling in. Blaskowitz received the 112th and 113th Panzer Brigades as mobile reserves on 7 and 8 September, with the latter earmarked to participate in the planned attack against Third Army's flank.[47]

The action was hot and heavy on Blaskowitz's new right wing the day he took over First Army on the ninth, and he probably was largely in the dark about what was going on. The fact that Knobelsdorff was brand new in his command cannot have helped one bit. The first sketchy account of First Army's dispositions and contacts with the enemy appeared in the Army Group G *Kriegstagebuch* on 9 September, and the First Army chief of staff did not arrive to brief the army-group staff until the evening of the 10th. Blaskowitz's LXVI Corps south of Nancy beat off the first probes by U.S. XV Corps—which had returned to Third Army on 6 September—that could be characterized as attacks rather than reconnaissance north of Charmes, on the west bank of the Moselle. This was bad news, because the salient at Nancy was now under pressure from the northwest and southwest, and Blaskowitz had to hold onto the ground west of Nancy to screen the assembling armored group for the counterattack Hitler wanted to mount.

Blaskowitz ordered First Army to hang on there at all costs. In the zone opposite XX Corps, XIII SS Corps had two divisions available at Nancy. The 3rd Panzergrenadier Division was incomplete, but it was battle tested, at roughly 50 percent fighting strength, and capable of limited offensive operations. The 553rd Volksgrenadier Division was newly formed, and the men had undergone no unit training. The division had but one medium and two light artillery battalions and a single antitank company; its assault gun company had not yet appeared. First Army reinforced the division with its replacement and training battalions and naval personnel, amounting to some 3,000 men.

The seeming house of cards that was Blaskowitz's Moselle front extended all the way into Luxembourg, and the fate of his defenses was inextricably linked with events beyond his ability to control. Hodges's 5th Armored and 28th Infantry Divisions, on 9 September, penetrated the north wing in the LXXX Corps zone. The corps committed its last reserve—an infantry battalion and a few assault guns—but failed to stem the tide. Briefed on the scale of the breakthrough by First Army's chief of staff on 10 September, Army Group G consulted OB West, which authorized a withdrawal to the Moselle Line and gave the 36th Volksgrenadier Division, then in reserve in the Saar Heights (Saar-Höhenstellung) position west of the Saar, to First Army. First Army was to leave a substantial delaying force behind as it withdrew. By 15 September, Hodges's penetration had expanded to the point that it threatened to roll up the Moselle defenses from the north.[48]

Hitler, the evening of 9 September, instructed Jodl to order the Fifth Panzer Army to strike the flank of the advancing enemy. He forbade any frontal attack because of the enemy's strength.[49] Rundstedt, in turn, ordered Blaskowitz to mount a counterattack against XII Corps, specifically named, using the 111th and 112th Panzer Brigades and Kampfgruppen of the 21st Panzer Division, while other elements of the armored group assembled. Blaskowitz was to exercise direct control over those formations until the arrival of the Fifth Panzer Army headquarters. Once Manteuffel arrived to take command of Fifth Panzer Army, he was to come directly under OB West. Blaskowitz reported that the 111th, 112th, and 113th Brigades had all started to arrive; that the 15th Panzergrenadier Division was available, but stuck by lack of fuel near Metz; and that XLVII Panzer Corps and the 3rd Panzergrenadier and 17th SS Panzergrenadier Divisions, as well as the 106th Panzer Brigade, were all still engaged with the enemy.[50]

The reason that First Army's plans to eliminate the American bridge-heads across the Moselle never came to pass was because resources were not available, and American pressure was growing at the left end of First Army's line, where XIII SS Corps had nothing but some roadblocks and air between it and Nineteenth Army's 16th Infantry Division. The 17th SS Panzergrenadier Division was being well stocked with replacements by Himmler, but the SS declined to share information on the division's status with First Army. Events would show that the combat effectiveness of the replacements—ethnic

Germans from the east—was so low that the division never performed very well again in German eyes even when it was rebuilt. The panzer battalions of the 3rd and 15th Panzergrenadier Divisions were still on their way from Italy. Not only had the 106th Panzer Brigade suffered heavy tank losses, but its inadequate maintenance section was having trouble keeping any panzers running at all.[51]

Yet the Germans thought Patton had let them off the hook. "I was lucky when I took over the First Army," recalled Knobelsdorff, "that I had time to build a new defensive front and to reorganize the troops. Reinforcements could be brought up. . . . Only the comparative passivity of the enemy saved First Army from threatened disaster."[52] *Oberst* Maney, First Army Ia, recalled, "At Nancy, the enemy moved forward cautiously with strong forces against the bridgehead."[53] *Generalmajor* Kurt von Mühlen, commanding the 559th Volksgrenadier Division west of Diedenhofen, recalled, "Until 18 September 1944 the enemy felt his way cautiously forward with but weak detachments—reconnaissance troops—against the positions of the division . . . [No] combat activity of special significance took place."

The German interpretation of caution within the American command, including by Patton, was accurate, in part because of the discomfort with bold action on the part of Major General Eddy. As Patton indirectly earned respect among the enemy for his selection of Truscott to command the Port Lyautey landings, his decision to put Eddy in command of XII Corps must count against him. Patton recognized that Eddy, an infantry officer, was leery of the risks Patton was willing to run and had not absorbed Patton's own notions of speed. Patton's diary is replete with references to Eddy's lack of drive and skittishness about rapid action. Yet Patton left Eddy in charge. John Nelson Rickard, in his analysis of Patton's Lorraine campaign, furthermore argues that Patton had a loose grip on the corps-level operations along the Moselle.[54]

The Germans Seek to Claim the Initiative

On 5 September, *Generalleutnant* Hasso von Manteuffel, who had been in command of the *Grossdeutschland* Panzergrenadier Division on the eastern front, was summoned to Hitler's headquarters, where he had been a frequent visitor and was obviously a Hitler favorite. Hitler told the surprised Manteuffel that he would take command of the Fifth Panzer Army. Along with the job came an immediate promotion to *General der Panzertruppe*. Hitler was still planning a major attack to the northwest from Plateau de Langres, but by the next day, it was already clear that the Americans were going to overrun the assembly areas before Fifth Panzer Army could gather.[55]

Major Hans von Luck, who arrived in the Vosges about 10 September with his *Kampfgruppe* of the 21st Panzer Division, encountered Manteuffel, his former comrade in arms in Russia with the 7th Panzer Division, just as Manteuffel reached the front. According to Luck, Manteuffel told him, "The situation, my dear Luck, is bloody awful. . . . Before I left Belgium, Montgomery had taken the offensive with his army group and, against weak resistance, had reached Brussels on 3 September and Antwerp on the fourth. Far more dangerous, however, was the thrust of the Americans, General Patton, and his Third Army. . . . I would almost call him the American Rommel." As Manteuffel had been on the eastern front rather than in Belgium, Luck's account is again highly suspect.

Luck asserts that Manteuffel quoted Hitler as saying that he wanted Manteuffel to attack and "seize Patton in the flank, cut his lines of communication, and destroy him." As we have seen, however, neither Hitler's nor Rundstedt's implementing orders had made any mention of Patton.

Manteuffel's own account rendered just after the war says that Hitler at first wanted him to eliminate the enemy (i.e., 6th Army Group's) threat to Belfort and to assist the First and Nineteenth Armies in joining their lines. When Hitler sometime between 6 and 10 September realized that events were outpacing his plans, he changed his orders to move "against the southern flank of the enemy forces that were advancing in the direction of Metz, since this enemy thrust threatened to disrupt the cohesion of the front." In his immediate post-war account of the meeting, Manteuffel gave no indication that Hitler had mentioned Patton. In his later memoirs, however, Manteuffel says that Hitler told him that "it seems that the Americans want to attack in the Vosges [Mountains] with Patton's Third Army." This seems an improbable statement, because Seventh Army, not Third Army, was attacking into the Vosges. We are, nevertheless, left with the possibility that Hitler, by early September, thought of Patton in personal terms as an enemy.

Manteuffel, according to Luck, believed the mission reflected a complete misjudgment of the situation and the possibilities open to the Germans. Manteuffel's own account confirms, "I found the situation for an attack by an army yet to be formed, as I had been ordered, to be beyond all hope."

Manteuffel had last fought the Americans west of Bizerte in Tunisia during the last gasp of Axis resistance. He spoke with the frontline troops to get some sense for the fighting style of the enemy now, with which he was in no way familiar, but he found that after their long flight across France, they could give him no coherent picture. He did learn that when the weather was good, the movement of tanks by day was nearly impossible because of American fighter-bombers. At the führer's headquarters, he had been assured that there was only an atmosphere of "plane fright" akin to tank panic on the Western front in World War I.

Indeed, the situation must have shocked Manteuffel. On the eastern front, *Grossdeutschland* had only really begun to face pervasive interference from Soviet fighter-bombers in late summer. Indeed, as of August, his division—the most powerful in the entire army—had been fully up to strength. Less than four weeks earlier, Knobelsdorff's XL Panzer Corps, including Manteuffel's *Grossdeutschland* Division and the 7th and 14th Panzer Divisions, had been capable of conducting successful offensive mobile warfare against the Soviets around Kursenai during a momentarily successful drive to reestablish contact between Army Group Center and Army Group North, which had been cut off in Kurland. The Luftwaffe had still been able to provide effective close air support.[56]

Like First Army, Fifth Panzer Army now had a team on which two key members had no experience whatsoever at their level of command. Manteuffel had jumped from division to army without even the experience of being a corps commander. Lüttwitz, at XLVII Panzer Corps, had been a division commander less than two weeks earlier. Yet both had considerably more experience than Patton commanding men in battle.

General der Panzertruppe Walter Krueger, whose LVIII Panzer Corps was about to join Fifth Panzer Army, had been in his position since the beginning of the year. Born on 23 March 1892 in Zeitz, Krueger had received a *Gymnasium* education in Berlin and Chemnitz and spoke French. He was smart, a clear thinker, and personally courageous. Krueger entered the imperial army in March 1910 as an officer candidate and had risen to *leutnant* by the time the war broke out in 1914, when he was serving as an ordnance officer in the 24th Reserve Division. During the war, he received general-staff training and joined an artillery regiment only in the final months. Krueger entered the *Reichswehr* and joined the cavalry, where he showed a real flair for cavalry tactics. In 1927, Krueger had wed Charlott-Benita *Freiin* von Hammerstein, the daughter of a senior general, who bore him one daughter. When the next war broke out, Krueger, much like Patton, was in charge of a cavalry regiment, the 10th.

Krueger had served with distinction as commander of the 1st Panzer Division's 1st Motorized Infantry Brigade in France and Russia and won plaudits as a tactician and leader in battle, including as acting division commander. Model had thought highly of him as a subordinate in Ninth Army during the horrid winter of 1942–1943, though he judged that Krueger could improve as a National Socialist. Krueger as commanding general of the 1st Panzer Division, the reader may recall, had fought under Hermann Balck in XLVIII Panzer Corps near Zhitomir in December 1943, where Krueger probably also had come to know Manteuffel. By 1944, he held the Knight's Cross with Oak Leaves, among his many decorations.[57]

Fighting a Tar Baby: As Blaskowitz had pointed out, some of his key mobile formations were so deeply engaged against Third Army that he could not extricate them for a counterattack. This was not due to any particular strategy on Patton's part to pin down mobile divisions, but rather to the simple shortage of German formations.

XX Corps obtained its first durable bridgehead across the Moselle at Arnaville on 10 September, with the objective of capturing Metz from the south, and opened the five-day period of renewed crisis highlighted by *Oberst* Emmerich. The 5th Division's 10th Infantry Regiment crossed in the predawn darkness under Third Army's first-ever large smokescreen and caught the defenders, who were concentrating on the bridgehead at Dorningen, by surprise. The 17th SS Panzergrenadier Division counterattacked immediately with armor and infantry and pushed the Americans back toward the river, but thirteen battalions of supporting artillery, tank destroyers firing directly across the river, and the reappearance of P47 *jabos* broke up the assault. That evening, the Americans evacuated their tattered companies—three of which had no surviving officers—from the Dorningen bridgehead, chased by an SS panzer, which sank the last boat to cross.

Panzer-led counterattacks resumed on the eleventh only to break down under well-directed American artillery fire. German artillery raked the bridgehead and prevented construction of a bridge, and only a few 57mm antitank guns had been ferried across. It was the heaviest and best-directed fire the 5th Division had yet encountered in France.

By the time Priess, thinking like a panzer general, could gather elements of the 17th SS, 3rd, and 15th Panzergrenadier Divisions for a concerted counterattack on 12 September, the Americans had managed to get tanks and tank destroyers, via a ford, and additional infantry battalions into the bridgehead. The Germans struck from all directions behind a rolling artillery barrage at 0330 hours. The attackers at some points got into the Americans lines, but the infantry suffered heavy casualties. By 0800, the last serious attempt to erase the bridgehead was over.[58]

Attacks against the 3rd Panzergrenadier Division by XII Corps, meanwhile, had been so heavy on 10 September that it pulled its last elements back across the Moselle. There it fought to keep the Americans off the east bank. But on

11 September, the Americans forced crossings south of Nancy at Crevechamps against the 553rd Volksgrenadier Division and at Bayon against the 15th Panzergrenadier Division and severed First Army's connection to Nineteenth Army. Knobelsdorff tried to organize a counterattack by the 15th Panzergrenadier Division, and he found he could not communicate with formations south of the American breach.[59] A battalion-sized attack by the panzergrenadiers to destroy the bridge at Bayon failed, with the loss of most of the attacking force, and the 104th Panzergrenadier Regiment had to withdraw behind the Meurthe River.[60]

As if that were not enough, the French 2nd DB, part of XV Corps, on 11 September appeared out of the west quite unexpectedly—almost no air reconnaissance was available to the Germans—and plowed into the rear area of the 16th Infantry Division, which was now deployed west of the Moselle between Charmes and Neufchâteau. If XLVII Panzer Corps could not clear the division's rear, further operations west of the Moselle would be nearly impossible and the division would be cut off. Blaskowitz told Rundstedt that he had no choice but to commit the 21st Panzer Division and 112th Panzer Brigade to a flank attack against the 2nd DB spearhead south of Chaumont. The 111th Panzer Brigade would have to stop the 4th Armored Division spearhead near Lunéville on its own. He expected he might have to send the 113th Panzer Brigade to stiffen Nineteenth Army's LXVI Corps.

Hitler sounded off again, underscoring that Fifth Panzer Army was to attack the enemy's flank, not stage a frontal assault. He again demanded that the 3rd and 15th Panzergrenadier Divisions be transferred to the armored group.

Rundstedt, on 11 September, subordinated XLVII and LVIII Panzer Corps and available armored formations in Army Group G to Fifth Panzer Army. He instructed Blaskowitz to attack with Fifth Panzer Army as soon as possible in a northwesterly direction between the Argonne and the Marne against the flank and rear of Third Army, the first time Third Army had been mentioned in an operational order regarding the counterattack. Rundstedt said it might be necessary to strike southward first (against U.S. Seventh Army) in order to secure Fifth Panzer Army's rear area, which seems to have been a synthesis of Hitler's two sets of instructions to Manteuffel.

Blaskowitz argued back with Rundstedt about Hitler's orders to accelerate the shift of the 3rd and 15th Panzergrenadier Divisions to the armored group. He could only hold his line on the Moselle, he stormed, if he had those divisions available as a mobile reserve. Otherwise, a large attack would take the enemy all the way to the West Wall. No official record exists of Rundstedt's decision, but two days later the divisions had not moved, and Hitler was still railing about it.

*

Priess continued to slash away at Patton. Attempts from 13 to 16 September to destroy a new 80th Infantry Division bridgehead at Dieulouard, established on the 12th, not only failed, but also collapsed—although in the first counterattack panzers, assault guns, and troops from the 3rd Panzergrenadier Division's 29th Panzergrenadier Regiment very nearly reached the bridges before being stopped by tank fire. Each day, the Germans succeeded in pushing tank-infantry teams down the valleys and cutting off nearly entire regiments on the hilltops, but the panzergrenadiers lacked the strength to deliver a deathblow.[61]

Stopping Patton's Final Spurt: Priess, appropriately enough, underwent his first real crisis in Lorraine at the hands of Patton's favorite division. American spearheads from CCA, 4th Armored Division, took off like a rocket from the Dieulouard bridgehead on 13 September, penetrated twenty miles, and reached a point only three miles from Château-Salins, held only by a screening force from the 3rd Panzergrenadier Division's armored reconnaissance battalion. At XIII SS Corps headquarters, Priess scraped up every resource he could find to reinforce the sector, which included three battalions from Nancy. Priess had to abandon the Nancy area except for a delaying force in the western part of the city.[62]

When the 4th Armored Division's CCA bypassed Château-Salins and reached the area of Arracourt-Lunéville the following day, smashing a column of the 15th Panzergrenadier Division (evidently redeploying southward to join the armored strike force) on the way, from Knobelsdorff's perspective the tanks had broken his front completely. To the German rear, the portions of the West Wall around Saarbrücken were unoccupied and unrepaired. Moreover, the 4th Armored Division was now behind First Army's left flank, and a huge gap existed between First and Nineteenth Armies.

"An immediate enemy thrust in the general direction of Saarbrücken (direction indicated on a captured enemy map)," recalled Knobelsdorff's Ia, *Oberst* Mantey, "would have been bound to lead to a breakdown of the Moselle front and the destruction of strong portions of First Army. In addition, the enemy would have succeeded in breaking through the West Wall on either side of Saarbrücken almost without having to fight. However, he did not take advantage of this most favorable situation."[63]

Army Group G's chief of staff *Oberst* Heinz von Gyldenfeldt concurred and added that Third Army could have cut off all of Nineteenth Army had it plunged through the hole and turned south. But Third Army, he observed, did not even send reconnaissance elements through the gap.[64]

Indeed, the enemy commanding general did not take advantage. Eddy opted to tidy up his bridgeheads and told Patton he could not attack again until 19 September. Patton was not happy, but he did not force Eddy to act earlier than that. The pause, once again, gave the Germans a chance to regroup—and even to take the initiative.[65]

On 14 September, Blaskowitz flatly told Rundstedt that a major counterattack launched from west of the Vosges against the deep flank was no longer possible because too much ground had been lost west of the Vosges. XV Corps's 2nd DB was threatening the northern tip of the concentration area. In a twist of fate, any chance the Germans still had of hitting Patton where he was most vulnerable was being taken away by Maj. Gen. Lucian Truscott, Patton's old reliable warhorse from Port Lyautey and Sicily, who, with his VI Corps, was pushing up against most of the concentration area from the southwest. Blaskowitz told Rundstedt that Seventh Army's advance had left a gap of less than thirty miles between its own and Third Army's spearheads. Indeed, a discussion had occurred at OKW the day before about using the still largely notional concentration of armor against VI Corps's advance on Épinal and Rambervillers, and not Third Army at all!

Blaskowitz suggested using Fifth Panzer Army instead in a much more tactical operation to hit the flank of American forces at Lunéville and then Château-Salins. He was, therefore, the intellectual author of the operation that eventually took place. Rundstedt proposed to OKW that the 15th Panzergrenadier Division attack at Lunéville while Krueger's LVIII Panzer Corps, with three brigades and the 11th Panzer Division, hit VI Corps at Vesoul. Hitler approved the idea so long as LVIII Panzer Corps was strengthened sufficiently to offer some chance of success. All of these proposals and counterproposals serve to illustrate the indecision reigning in German command ranks over what to do in the south (there was a clear line of march in the north) and the fact that these men were by no means concerned only with Patton's drive to Metz or the West Wall.[66]

At the moment of crisis, unaware that Manton Eddy was about to pull his fat from the fire, Rundstedt, at 0100 hours on 15 September, approved Blaskowitz's proposal of the preceding day to strike at Lunéville, and ten minutes later Blaskowitz's chief of staff, Gyldenfeldt, issued orders to Fifth Panzer Army to put *Generalleutnant* Heinrich *Freiherr* von Lüttwitz's XLVII Panzer Corps on the road to a concentration area in the Rambervillers-Épinal-St. Dié area, from which it would attack toward the northwest. Men were already scrambling when, at 0535, a telex arrived indicating that the führer had agreed to the plan. Hitler attached the 11th Panzer Division—still far away in Nineteenth Army's zone—and 113th Panzer Brigade to the strike group and indicated he was holding the 107th and 108th Panzer Brigades until further decision. VI Corps's continuing pressure at Épinal kept elements of the 21st Panzer Division tied up there.[67]

But first, on 16 September, clearly on orders from Blaskowitz, Lüttwitz told the 112th Panzer Brigade to attack the French 2nd DB at Dompaire and throw it back toward the west. Elements of the 21st Panzer Division were to follow. Manteuffel, who did not formally take command of Fifth Panzer Army until 14 September, was unable to influence the decision or the tactics, which were determined by Nineteenth Army. He criticized the attack as "premature" in his memoirs. Manteuffel was well aware of the risk of disaster when tanks and infantry attacked without artillery support because he had lost eighty-two tanks in a single day in August when compelled by a *Führerbefehl* to assault a strong Soviet force before any of his artillery had arrived. (That *Führerbefehl*, it turned out, had been an OKW misinterpretation of Hitler's words.)

The 112th Panzer Brigade fought without artillery support, and the promised help from the 21st Panzer Division never arrived. Engaged by French tanks and American fighter-bombers, the brigade suffered such heavy losses, including nearly all of its Panthers and 30 percent of its Mark IVs, that it never recovered. Most of the 16th Division was destroyed despite the counterstroke, and *Generalmajor* Ernst Häckel narrowly escaped capture. The strategic lesson drawn by German commanders was that combat operations were no longer practical west of the Moselle.

These new panzer brigades were, in Manteuffel's words, "improvisations" designed for mobile combat on the eastern front. They lacked internal cohesion, and two of the commanders had first met their troops when they had detrained at the front. They had no artillery, no common staff for their two tank battalions (forty-five each of Mark IVs and Mark V Panthers), and inadequate communications equipment, engineers, and vehicle-recovery support. The panzergrenadier regiment and tanks, moreover, had never trained together.

Despite these dire developments, Knobelsdorff considered the northern penetration by Hodges on the border with Luxembourg more dangerous than Third Army's thrust, because LXXX Corps controlled only shattered remnants from France—it had but a single artillery battery in the entire area—plus the 36th Volksgrenadier Division in the Saar Heights position well south of the breakthrough. Knobelsdorff thought incorrectly that the enemy here was Third Army and was astonished that the Americans did not energetically pursue this opportunity, which he thought could take them quickly to Koblenz. Jodl, after the war, agreed that this had been the weakest portion of the entire German front and argued that two well-supplied divisions would have reached the Rhine.

Bits of the Panzer Lehr, 2nd Panzer, and the 5th Airborne Divisions had been rushed to the sector on 13 September, but they were burned out and unable to restore the situation. On the fourteenth, the American V Corps took a stretch of the West Wall at Wallendorf before any German troops could man the fortifications. Knobelsdorff sent his only reserve to reinforce the sector, the battered 106th Panzer Brigade with a regiment of the 19th Volksgrenadier Division attached to it.

A hastily organized counterattack failed, and the enemy had a clear run to Bitburg over open country. Rundstedt criticized Knobelsdorff's performance for being insufficiently determined and told Blaskowitz that the failure might make it impossible to stop the breakthrough. This failure seems to have soured Rundstedt on Knobelsdorff, a feeling that would grow stronger.

"To our great surprise," *Oberst* Albert Emmerich, the First Army operations officer from November 1944 until the end of the war, later recalled, "the enemy was stalled by the antiaircraft defense cordon around Bitburg. This gave LXXX Corps, transferred to Seventh Army in Army Group B on 18 September, time to organize a counterattack that convinced the Americans to pull back on 21 September." The West Wall was in German hands once again.[68]

On 16 September, Patton again ordered XX Corps to capture Frankfurt and tightened up his anticipated army front somewhat. XII Corps now was to drive to the Rhine at Darmstadt and to establish a bridgehead, and XV Corps was to seize Mannheim and cross the Rhine or, depending on circumstances, cross into XII Corps's presumptive bridgehead.[69] Mellenthin, looking back with knowledge of Patton's instructions, commented, "This was the order of a commander who could think on big lines, and who thoroughly understood the character of armored warfare; it could not possibly be misunderstood or misconstrued."[70] Patton recorded that, "at this time, I was certainly very full of hopes . . . and saw myself crossing the Rhine."[71]

Eddy was consolidating his bridgehead, though, so actual implementation of Patton's scheme was limited to local activity that was, nevertheless, troubling to the defenders. The Americans attacked the 15th Panzergrenadier Division in Lunéville on 16 September, and the town was largely in the enemy's hands by the next evening. A few panzergrenadiers nevertheless held out through the seventeenth.

Hitler issued a *Führerbefehl* on 17 September that began, "The battle in the West has largely moved onto German soil; German cities and villages will be battlegrounds. This fact must make our fighting more fanatical and harden every available man in the battle zone to turn every bunker, every apartment block in a German city, every German village into a fortress. . . ."[72] According to the OKW *Kriegstagebuch*, Hitler decided to remove Blaskowitz from command of Army Group G because he was dissatisfied with the performance of Nineteenth Army. Rundstedt took responsibility for the setbacks in the south, but that did not satisfy Hitler. He already had a replacement in mind—one of his best eastern-front panzer generals.[73]

Rundstedt ordered that the 21st Panzer Division and 111th Panzer Brigade were to counterattack at Lunéville no later than 18 September. After defeating the enemy there (a heroic assumption), they were to strike the Americans east of Pont-à-Mousson. Nineteenth Army was to accelerate its withdrawal to the Moselle River line in order to free the 11th Panzer Division to join the assault group. XLVII Panzer Corps was just beginning to assemble, and the 111th and 112th Panzer Brigades, the remnants of the latter subordinated to the 21st Panzer Division, occupied Châtel sur Moselle.[74]

Nineteenth Army released XLVII Panzer Corps to Fifth Panzer Army, and it gathered north of Rambervillers. *General der Panzertruppe* Walter Krueger's LVIII Panzer Corps, meanwhile, assembled northeast of Blâmont. Manteuffel described his resources to Blaskowitz: "Very weak."[75] After having a face-to-face chat with Knobelsdorff in Duss (Dieuze), Manteuffel realized that if the gap between First and Nineteenth Armies was to be filled, his men would have to do it because First Army was stretched to the breaking point.[76]

Indeed, Knobelsdorff had almost nothing available to plug the hole on his south wing. At the First Army headquarters at St. Avold, the only thing standing in Third Army's way was the *Begleitkompanie* (escort company) and an antitank company. Priess sent more elements of the 3rd Panzergrenadier Division's reconnaissance battalion toward Château-Salins and barricaded crossroads, occupying each with ten to twenty infantrymen. Two battalions of antiaircraft guns shifted from Diedenhofen to the area. Knobelsdorff ordered Priess to defend the heights northeast of Nancy at all costs with his 553rd Volksgrenadier Division and to attack the American north flank at the Dieulouard bridgehead with the 106th Panzer Brigade (before it had to race to LXXX Corps at Wallendorf).

If the XLVII Panzer Corps attack failed, First Army faced catastrophe. Knobelsdorff hoped his simultaneous thrust could link with Fifth Panzer Army and cut off the tip of the American spearhead. He would thus gain time to bring more forces to bear, including a regiment of the 559th Volksgrenadier Division and most of the division's artillery from the Diedenhofen sector.[77]

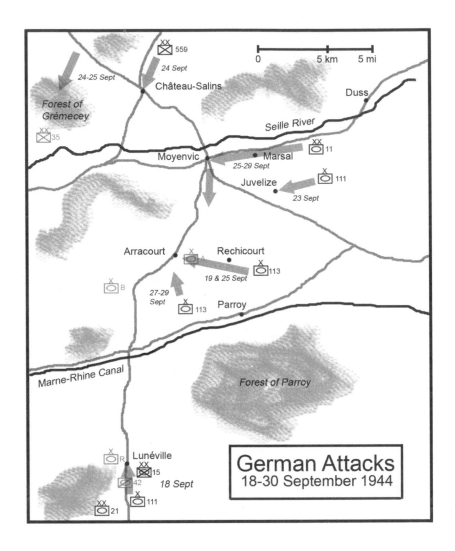

Panzers at Lunéville: LVIII and XLVII Panzer Corps launched the dim shadow of Hitler's dream of an offensive against the rear of Hodges's First Army on 18 September. Seventeen tanks and the panzergrenadiers from the 111th Panzer Brigade advanced northward toward Lunéville. Men of the 42nd Cavalry Squadron and Combat Command Reserve, 4th Armored Division, held most of the town, but were still battling elements of the 15th Panzergrenadier Division in the streets. The panzers swept the cavalry aside and, attacking in concert with the panzergrenadiers already in Lunéville, pushed the Americans back into the north part of the city.

Combat Command A, 4th Armored Division, had to direct a rescue force away from the main route of advance to help the defenders, thus meeting, in part, the German objective.[78] But an unanticipated interloper was about to throw all German calculations into a cocked hat. The 603rd Tank Destroyer Battalion's Company C—preceding the main body of CCB, 6th Armored Division, which was hustling east from Brittany—clanked up to the southeastern edge of Lunéville during the day.[79]

The 21st Panzer Division and 112th Panzer Brigade, meanwhile, pushed toward Lunéville from the southwest, but never quite made it because *Generalmajor* Edgar Feuchtinger had to divert assets from the forward drive to protect his left flank against "lively" American pressure from the 6th Armored Division. "The resistance increased every hour," recalled Feuchtinger.[80]

The 113th Panzer Brigade struck the rest of the 4th Armored Division's CCA near Arracourt at daybreak on 19 September. Fifth Panzer Army had requested additional artillery support from Army Group G, but there was none to give. Luftwaffe support was promised, but it is doubtful that Manteuffel put any stock in that offer.[81]

A thick fog masked the gray panzers as they probed toward the American positions. Sudden, surprising fire fights erupted as they encountered Sherman tanks and M18 Hellcat tank destroyers in the dim light and at short ranges. The fog protected the panzers from American air attack, but the close combat eliminated the advantages the Panthers enjoyed in long-range gunnery due to their superior optics and powerful long-barreled 75mm guns.

The fog lifted at about noon, and the 113th Panzer Brigade suffered an astoundingly bad break in the fortunes of war. Some forty panzers found themselves arrayed under the guns of the 704th Tank Battalion Hellcats sitting on high ground just before Arracourt. The tank destroyers were well concealed in defilade and repositioned after firing, so the Germans never had good targets and returned little fire. The 113th Panzer Brigade withdrew. Combat Command A physically counted forty-three knocked-out panzers, most of them Panthers— some with only between fifteen and ninety miles on their odometers.

Observing the wreckage that evening, Patton said, "This is the kind of thing that's going to end the war quicker than anybody had hoped." He stuck with his plan and ordered CCA to advance to Saargemünd in the West Wall.[82] Patton, nevertheless, conceded in his memoirs, "The nineteenth, instead of being the day I hoped it would be, was bad."[83]

*

Battle also raged in Lunéville on 19 September. The Americans seized the initiative and struck southwest of Lunéville and penetrated the 21st Panzer Division's security line protecting the XLVII Panzer Corps's flank—a move the Germans had clearly not anticipated. This threat to its own flank caused XLVII Panzer Corps to go over to the defensive on the twentieth and withdraw behind the Meurthe.[84]

Little had been accomplished, and the American spearheads pressed eastward to Duss. By the end of 22 September, CCA, 4th Armored Division, and the 704th Tank Destroyer Battalion claimed to have accounted for a total to date of seventy-nine panzers in exchange for fourteen Shermans, seven M5s, and one M18 damaged beyond repair.[85] Manteuffel told army group headquarters that there was no hope of success because of the balance of forces; the Americans had 200 tanks, and he had but forty-five.[86]

A Flexible Defense

Generalleutnant Hermann Balck, who arrived on 20 September at army group headquarters with his chief of staff, *Oberst* Friedrich-Wilhelm von Mellenthin, immediately realized that with the forces available, they would not even reach the Moselle River.[87] The situation must have struck both men as eerily similar to the one they and Fourth Panzer Army had faced at Zhitomir near Kiev in 1943, though there were differences. That time, they had sufficient panzers to strike a powerful blow against the enemy's extended left flank. Then, Chevallerie had held the enemy at Korosten, and Knobelsdorff had just departed. Now, Chevallerie was gone, and Knobelsdorff was holding back the horde. Then, Manteuffel had commanded one of Balck's counterattacking panzer divisions. Now, he commanded the Fifth Panzer Army counterattack. Balck's XLVIII Corps had stopped the 1st Ukrainian Front's imminent breakthrough. Could Balck now stop Third Army?

Balck's hard-charging presence is immediately visible in the *Kriegstagebuch* that day, which suddenly reflects a crackling energy that had not been seen before: "From the day's events, it is clearly necessary to issue clear instructions to the leadership of Fifth Panzer Army, which is showing a strong tendency to limit itself to the defense, to activate the required offensive spirit." Balck had put his finger on Manteuffel's seemingly diffident attitude toward Patton, though Manteuffel had never even commanded a corps before, and he had no well functioning army staff to ease his transition to command at that level. Blaskowitz, probably with Balck standing at his shoulder, three times during the course of the day ordered Fifth Panzer Army to continue its attack against the American flank with whatever it had. Balck, still commanding

XLVIII Panzer Corps in December 1943 after the battle at Zhitomir, had stopped the Soviet Christmas offensive with deft shifts and lightning counterattacks; his three panzer divisions, with only 200 panzers in the field, had stopped each and every breakthrough in Fourth Panzer Army's zone by six Soviet armies with 1,200 tanks. In the last conversation of the day, Blaskowitz told Manteuffel he had to attack to draw the American tanks to him and thereby deny the enemy operational freedom. He had to prevent the hole from widening further.[88]

Balck's challenge of stopping Third Army, unbeknownst to him, was just becoming somewhat simpler. Patton definitively decided not to waste resources capturing Metz, but to contain the city and to focus on pushing to the Rhine.[89] The only battle that mattered now was the one Manteuffel and Knobelsdorff were fighting south of Metz.

Balck formally took over Army Group G from Blaskowitz on 21 September, a position he was to hold until 22 December, thus roughly overlapping with Patton's engagement in Lorraine. Rundstedt doubted the wisdom of Balck's selection because he lacked experience against the Western Allies.[90] But Balck was coming off a big success that Hitler clearly hoped he would now repeat. In August, Balck, commanding Fourth Panzer Army, had staged a counterattack that stopped the Soviet summer offensive at the Vistula, for which Hitler awarded him the Diamonds to his Knight's Cross.[91] Army chief of staff Guderian recalled, "It was thanks to the inexhaustible energy and skill of General Balck that a major disaster was finally avoided." Guderian lamented Balck's transfer from the eastern front because with his departure, the energetic efforts to destroy all Soviet bridgeheads west of the Vistula came to an end.[92]

Balck was a thoughtful man of few words who exuded an aura of confidence that reflected an inner iron will.[93] He never hesitated to express his views forcefully when he did speak. Friedrich von Mellenthin served with Balck in France and through much of the war. Mellenthin said of Balck, "He was one of our most brilliant leaders of armor; indeed, if Manstein was Germany's greatest strategist during World War II, I think Balck has strong claims to be regarded as our finest field commander. He had a superb grasp of tactics and great qualities of leadership. . . ."[94]

Balck was in spirit a commander much like Patton. After the war, Balck summarized his philosophy in Pattonesque terms:

It's quite remarkable that most people believe that the attack costs more casualties. Don't even think about it; the attack is the least costly operation. . . . The matter is, after all, mainly psychological. In the attack, there are only three or four men in the division who carry the attack; all the others just follow behind. In the defense, every man must hold his position alone. He doesn't see his neighbors; he just sees whether something costly is advancing towards him. He's often not equal to the task. That's why he's easily uprooted. Nothing incurs higher casualties than an unsuccessful defense. Therefore, attack wherever it is possible. . . .

First and foremost, never follow a rigid scheme. Every situation is different—no two are the same. Even if they appear to be the same, in one case the troops will be fresh while in another they'll be fatigued. That difference will lead to completely different decisions. I'm against the school approach that says, "In accordance with the ideas of the General Staff, in this situation you must do thus and such." On the contrary, you must proceed as dictated by the personalities involved and the particulars of the situation. . . .

Another principle that follows from this is: Never do the same thing twice. Even if something works well for you once, by the second time the enemy will have adapted. So you have to think up something new.[95]

Unlike Patton, Balck concluded that the need to consider every military contingency with a fresh eye made the study of military history dangerous.[96]

Mellenthin had a gentler manner than Balck and was thoughtful, bright, and articulate. He was a thorough professional and a classic product of the German general-staff system. Balck viewed Mellenthin as his deputy commander and stand-in. Like Balck, he knew the area of Alsace-Lorraine from an earlier time, having been the operations officer for the 197th Infantry Division when it breached the vaunted Maginot Line in May 1940, pushed by forced marches to Château-Salins, and then turned into the Vosges before the French capitulation.[97]

When Balck arrived at his headquarters, he found that he had stepped into another world from the eastern front. Troops were pulling back to refit, traffic control was a mess, and no one seemed to accept responsibility.[98] Balck recalled, "My army group headquarters was first near Strasbourg. But I soon moved because, after every air attack on Strasbourg, my communications wires would be cut. The next location was further north near the old Reich boundary. Although the Allies were constantly searching for that headquarters, they never found it because I scattered my radios so widely."[99]

Balck set to work and issued his orders. To Fifth Panzer Army: prevent the enemy from advancing toward the east or northeast from Château-Salins or Duss. To First Army: force the enemy as far south as possible; really push him—fight an active battle.[100] At age fifty, Balck labored from 0300 until 2200 hours each day. He caught most of his sleep in moving cars. Each day, he visited the front. Each evening, he shared his simple meal with combat troops.[101]

Knobelsdorff reported that the enemy already was advancing northeastward from Château-Salins and was pressing him hard out of Nancy toward the north. XIII SS Corps had been required to give up control over the 3rd Panzergrenadier Division, presumably because the division was supposed to move south to join the armored strike group (though it never did), and the 553rd Division was in danger of being cut off. Knobelsdorff had, the day before, ordered the 559th Volksgrenadier Division to shift from Hörnlein's LXXXII Corps sector to Priess's XIII SS Corps south of Metz, giving its sector to the 19th Volksgrenadier Division, now commanded by *Generalmajor* Karl Britzelmayr, which was just returning from Wallendorf. The 559th Division, though, was no real substitute for the mobile division. Balck summoned Knobelsdorff, his former boss, to his headquarters.

"You simply have to move enough forces to hold at Château-Salins and reach Moyenvic," Balck told him. Moyenvic lay just east of the Franco-German border. "Fifth Panzer Army will attack to meet you at Moyenvic, and the 11th Panzer Division is on the way to help," just as the 11th Panzer Division had been in the dark days along the Chir River. Knobelsdorff knew the current 11th Panzer Division commander, *Generalmajor* Wend von Wietersheim, well, because his division had been a key element in his XL Panzer Corps during the spring until it had been ordered to France in May for rebuilding. To shorten the line, Balck added, Knobelsdorff was to abandon all bridgeheads west of the Moselle, except the one at Metz.[102]

The German jabs, though they had not stopped Third Army, had rattled Patton. On 21 September, he recorded in a letter, "For the last three days we have had as bitter and protracted fighting as I have ever encountered. The Huns are desperate and are attacking in half a dozen places. Once or twice we gave ground but in all but one case got it back. . . . I won't be able to do any broken-field running till I cross the next river. . . ."[103]

Rundstedt sent OKW an appreciation on the twenty-first in which he said that all the forces available on the western front amounted to the strength of only twenty-one full-strength volksgrenadier and between six and seven panzer divisions. He planned to fight for time, but only until he could build a reserve and go over to the offensive himself.[104] Perhaps coincidentally, Hitler at this very time conceived of launching a great counteroffensive in the West during the late autumn, when bad weather would ground the *jabos*. The seventy-odd Allied divisions were insufficient to fully man a 400-mile front, and Hitler concluded he could mass forces somewhere along the line and overpower the enemy. His first thoughts were of Alsace and the Netherlands.[105] His mind would soon turn to the plan crafted in 1940 by Erich von Manstein.

While Balck worked to mend the hole in his front, Hitler weighed in again on 22 September with another demand that all available armor concentrate for an attack northwestward toward Nancy. But the führer's goal had become yet more modest: to link up with First Army's 553rd Volksgrenadier Division and destroy the enemy in between. XLVII Panzer Corps's jabs that day were thrown back, however, and the Americans forced back the right wing of the 21st Panzer Division two miles southeast of Lunéville. The next day was even worse, and the Americans rolled over the German line southeast of Lunéville. XLVII Panzer Corps scrambled to shorten its front, and the 15th Panzergrenadier Division deployed along the western edge of the Forest of Parroy to block any breakthrough there by XV Corps, which within days would become part of U.S. Seventh Army.[106]

The 111th Panzer Brigade mounted a last tank-infantry assault toward Arracourt on 23 September. East of Moyenvic, American tanks maneuvered onto high ground near Juvelize and picked off the panzers as they came in. When German infantry moved into Marsal on the Moyenvic-Duss road, fighter-bombers wreaked havoc on them.[107] Mellenthin recalled:

> The morning . . . was shrouded in fog and so our tanks were protected against the dreaded fighter-bombers . . . . At first the attack. . . went well, but as soon as the skies cleared, the *jabos* swarmed down on the panzers. American artillery kept up a heavy fire, and their tanks put in a vigorous counterattack. The result was that the 111th Panzer Brigade was virtually destroyed and at the end of the day was left with seven tanks and eighty men. . . . [I]t was clear that American air power put our panzers at a hopeless disadvantage, and that the normal principles of armored warfare did not apply in this theater.[108]

Rommel had known months earlier that the normal warfare rules didn't apply in the west, but the knowledge had not reached the men coming from the east.

So much for "plane fear." The eastern-front commanders had been dealt a harsh lesson in how the American enemy differed from the Soviet. They had known the power of air superiority once themselves from having employed it against the Poles, French, and Russians. But years had passed, and the air war on the eastern front was still a more even affair.

Yet it was Patton who recorded, "The 23rd was one of the bad days of my military career." He learned that he would lose XV Corps to Seventh Army, give up the 6th Armored Division, and go onto the defensive.[109]

Rundstedt was, therefore, quite lucky. As of 24 September, he was more worried about the Allied pressure of Army Group B's right wing than he was the state of defenses around Metz, and he was already planning to shift XLVII Panzer Corps with the three panzer brigades north. He explained to OKW that he would have to strip from Army Group G practically all the resources he would need to shore up the front of Fifteenth and First Parachute Armies, which were battling Montgomery's 21st Amy Group.[110]

Fortunately, all had been quiet on First Army's right wing for days. XIII SS Corps, on the left wing, could not redeploy its assets quickly in response to Balck's orders, and its opening attack southward to meet Fifth Panzer Army on the twenty-fourth was a popgun affair: one regiment of Mühlen's 559th Volksgrenadier Division supported by five or six tanks from the 17th SS Panzergrenadier Division. Nevertheless, attacking down the Mörchingen (Morhange)-Château-Salins road, the Germans cleared the path and reestablished contact with troops in the latter town.[111]

Balck concluded that he lacked the wherewithal to cut off the American spearheads and would be fortunate merely to stop them. Fifth Panzer Army, on 24 September, barely deserved the name. It had but twenty-nine Mark IV tanks, twenty Panthers, and ten assault guns that were battle ready. Nevertheless, it was now tying down considerable enemy forces.

The XIII SS Corps's surprising progress showed that the Americans were extremely weak around Château-Salins, so Balck contacted Manteuffel and ordered him to advance immediately to Moyenvic from the south. Lüttwitz's XLVII Panzer Corps attacked the next day against "hard-headed resistance" and American tank-infantry attacks in the opposite direction, but the corps gained more than a mile of ground.[112]

Balck had finally been able to set the 11th Panzer Division in motion from its assembly area near Sarrebourg to strengthen Krueger's LVIII Panzer Corps. He intended to use the division to stage another counterattack in the Arracourt area against the 4th Armored Division. He ordered that what was left of the panzer brigades be incorporated into the 11th and 21st Panzer and 15th Panzergrenadier Divisions. Delayed by Allied air attacks, the division, less a *Kampfgruppe* left at Belfort, took a week to arrive, and the combat elements reached their assembly areas on the twenty-fourth. The division had twenty Panthers, ten Mark IVs, most of its two panzergrenadier regiments, an armored artillery regiment (less its self-propelled battalion), and an armored engineer battalion—about 70 percent of the division's strength. Morale was good, despite the long retreat with Nineteenth Army from southern France.[113]

Generalmajor Wend von Wietersheim and his commanders were able to reconnoiter the terrain over which they would attack, a reflection of the lack of any American pressure against the scattered strong points of the 111th and 113th Panzer Brigades. On 23 September, the division absorbed the thirty Panthers (only 10 percent of which were battle ready) of the 111th Panzer Brigade.

On the twenty-fifth Wietersheim went after the 4th Armored Division with his 11th Panzer Division and the remnants of the 113th Panzer Brigade north and east of Rechicourt, a village just east of Arracourt, recapturing Moyenvic and thereby reestablishing contact with First Army and XIII SS Corps. Manteuffel had gained surprise by committing the 11th Panzer Division north of Arracourt, where reconnaissance had shown the American line was weakly held. Rain kept the dreaded *jabos*, away until midday, when air strikes brought the panzers to a stop. Back at *Führerhauptquartier*, Hitler, on the twenty-fifth, told the generals that Balck was to continue to wage a mobile defense in the Lunéville area, and that he was to be given all panzer and panzergrenadier divisions and panzer brigades to make that possible. Balck had already reclaimed half the ground lost east of the Moselle and north of the Marne-Rhine canal, as measured by the American spearheads that had reached Duss.

The 11th Panzer Division made slow, but good progress against the 4th Armored Division until the skies cleared on the twenty-ninth. Smacked again by American fighter-bombers—Wietersheim lost eighteen tanks—Fifth Panzer Army stopped the counterattack on 30 September. Plans to reinforce this thrust with another panzer brigade were thwarted when that brigade was rerouted to Arnhem to join the fight against the British airborne forces there.[114]

Don Fox's history of the 4th Armored Division, *Patton's Vanguard*, is replete with references to Tiger tanks battling the Americans during mid-September. German records make clear, however, that no Tigers were in the Lorraine fight and that the defenders made do with medium tanks and assault guns.

On the northern flank of the American salient, meanwhile, Priess had attacked with his 559th Volksgrenadier Division and the 106th Panzer Brigade (now only some eight tanks) on 24 September west of Château-Salins into the Forest of Grémecey. The troops encountered elements of the 4th Armored and 35th Infantry Divisions in the forest on the twenty-fifth and were brought to a complete standstill.[115] Though the assault failed to achieve its objective, it did contribute to establishing a firm link between First and Fifth Panzer Armies and firmly sealed the hole in the Moselle line.[116]

An Interim Assessment

Manteuffel summed up, "The attack by [Fifth Panzer Army] had shown that, contrary to the assumption of the High Command, no open flank could be found in the enemy advance toward the Moselle."[117] Army chief of staff Guderian, harking back to Hitler's original hope to strike deeply into First Army's rear, observed, "While our panzer units still existed, our leaders had chosen to fight a static battle in Normandy. Now that our motorized forces had been squandered and destroyed, they were compelled to fight the mobile battle they had hitherto refused to face. Favorable chances that the boldness of the American command [an oblique reference to Patton] occasionally offered us we were no longer in a position to exploit. The original intention— to counterattack the southern wing of the advancing American armies—had to be given up."[118]

The German success in sealing the hole had a great deal to do with the fact that Third Army was no longer pressing forward. At 2255 hours on 27 September, Balck had received surprising news. Signals intelligence indicated that the Americans planned to pull their most advanced units east of Lunéville back across the Meurthe River. The next day, the Americans were dropping back in some parts of the Pont-à-Mousson bridgehead.[119]

The enemy had become inactive, and the Germans believed that they had forced the Americans to pull back their forwardmost tank spearheads.[120] Knobelsdorff considered the threat to his southern wing to be eliminated. "The enemy," recalled *Oberst* Emmerich, "shifted the center of gravity of his attacks to the area of Metz. . . ."[121]

"We now know that Patton was compelled to halt by Eisenhower's orders of 22 September," wrote Mellenthin in his memoir. "The Supreme Allied commander had decided to accept Montgomery's proposal to make the main effort on the northern flank, clear the approaches to Antwerp, and try to capture the Ruhr before winter."[122] On 25 September, Patton informed his corps commanders that, because of the tight supply situation, the Supreme Commander had ordered Third and Ninth Armies to go onto the defensive. They were to conduct only the limited-objective attacks necessary to secure launching points for the next offensive.[123] That very day, Hitler issued guidance that the *Schwerpunkt* of the German defensive effort was the northern end of the front.[124]

Major General Wade Haislip's XV Corps, consisting of the 79th Infantry Division, French 2nd DB, and the 106th Cavalry Group was transferred to 6th

Army Group effective 29 September, and Eisenhower established a new interarmy-group boundary running roughly Chaumont-Lunéville-Saarburg-Heidelberg.[125] With that change, Fifth Panzer Army no longer faced Third Army.

The outcome of the September fighting in Lorraine should have been familiar to Patton. The Germans had done to him what he and the rest of IV Corps had done to Drum's First Army back before Camden in the Carolina maneuvers of November 1941. They had aggressively used their armor against a superior enemy to prevent him from capturing his objective until operations were called to a halt.

It has been suggested that Patton performed a role in Lorraine analogous to Montgomery's in Normandy in terms of drawing German divisions away from what was to be the main thrust, but this is not true.[126] The Germans did not shift divisions from the right wing to oppose Patton, and Hitler backed off from even sending the small 108th Panzer Brigade south to Lorraine. It is true that the Fifth Panzer Army and XLVII Panzer Corps staffs were moved to face Patton, and that the panzer brigades and volksgrenadier divisions sent to Army Group G *could* have gone north instead, but Germany was sending a stream of reinforcements to fight Montgomery and U.S. First Army at the same time—enough to stop them just as the Germans had stopped Patton.

Indeed, the German high command had judged that the West Wall would hold at Aachen—which Brandenberger's Seventh Army had been ordered to defend to the last man—if the Americans failed to break through immediately. The generals had anticipated a concentrated American thrust through the line at Aachen in mid-September. By 25 September, the high command concluded the immediate crisis had passed.[127]

During September, the Germans had managed to throw an estimated 230,000 men into the defense of the West Wall. Of these, some 100,000 formed fresh divisions. Another 50,000 came from fortress battalions, which U.S. First Army termed the "hidden reserve of the German Army."[128]

On 25 September, Hitler ordered Rundstedt to concentrate on striking back at the British in Holland, where he expected the Allies to shift their main effort for a while. He ordered most of the available panzer units in Army Group B to that sector.[129]

On 27 September, British Ultra codebreakers deciphered a message sent several days earlier directing that all SS formations—beginning with one panzergrenadier and four panzer divisions and three Tiger battalions—be withdrawn for rest and refitting.[130] First Army detected the departure of the 1st, 2nd, and 12th SS Panzer Divisions, and the 9th and 116th Panzer Divisions from its front. The Americans conceded that "the enemy had been able to stabilize his line."[131] Model and Rundstedt had accomplished a "miracle in the West," and the withdrawal of the panzer divisions was the first physical step toward the Ardennes offensive.[132]

The argument that Patton weakened forces in the north is compelling only when judged against a counterfactual case in which Patton posed no threat whatsoever in the south, and Germany were free to use all its resources elsewhere. Developments in October illustrate the case, as Patton's stand-down allowed Rundstedt to shift more combat formations to the north. The U.S. First Army's drive to crack the Siegfried Line around Aachen came to dominate German thinking as the most critical problem on the Western Front, and on 6 October, the 3rd Panzergrenadier Division was transferred to Army Group B, to be followed in midmonth by Fifth Panzer Army's staff.[133]

METZ: ABSORBING THE PUNISHMENT

Oberst Emmerich was quite correct: Patton, about 25 September, shifted his attention and priority to XX Corps and the capture of Metz. He appears to have drawn no lessons from the difficult operation to capture Brest and was overly enthused by the idea that air power could reduce the fortifications to rubble.[134] It could not. If Balck and Knobelsdorff could have wished one thing from the enemy commanding general, it would have been that he would expend his resources against fortifications that had no strategic value to the Germans. If Patton had been thinking in American football terms, he was about to get a dose of boxing instead, and Knobelsdorff was willing to keep his gloves up and absorb the punishment.

When Knobelsdorff had arrived on 10 September, panic had reigned in Metz. The German civilian population and local administration were evacuating, and local military authorities were burning precious stores without orders.[135]

Hitler, on 15 September, ordered that strenuous measures be taken to defend Metz, though he left until later the decision as to whether, in case of a breakthrough, to fight to the last or withdraw the garrison. Metz, as of mid-September, was the most strongly manned section of Army Group G's entire front. Rundstedt, on the sixteenth, instructed that First Army was to retain two bridgeheads west of the Moselle opposite Metz and Diedenhofen to maximize its defensive perimeter.[136]

German forces, fighting in the infantry positions associated with each fort and counterattacking vigorously, brought the 5th and 90th Infantry Divisions to a sharp stop during mid-September at Metz and Diedenhofen. Knobelsdorff had managed to create a stalemate.[137]

Hörnlein's LXXXII Corps took responsibility for the defense of Metz from Priess's XIII SS Corps on 3 October. The corps staff had been trained for coastal defense, so there was some logic to the selection. Until the Americans arrived, the staff of *Wehrkreiskommando* (Military District Command) XII and chief of the Replacement Training Army and *Reichsführer SS* Heinrich Himmler had been in charge of defensive preparations.[138]

The 462nd Division manned the defenses. The division absorbed local anti-aircraft units, the Metz officer-candidate and NCO training schools, the local replacement unit, and the tired 1010th Security Regiment, whose "old men" had made good their escape from France. The officer candidates and NCOs formed two regiments, which were well equipped and had high morale. The division's artillery was a mixed bag consisting of captured Soviet pieces and old, immobile fortress guns. The one bright spot for the defenders was that American counter-battery fire would find it very difficult to silence the latter. There were also two battalions of the 14th SS Division.

Knobelsdorff viewed *Generalmajor* Heinrich Kittel, the division commanding general, as mediocre, but the regimental commanders were all combat veterans and performed superbly. Kittel was a slow-speaking, dignified, meticulous Bavarian with combat experience on the eastern front. He was tired, old, and ironic, a man who carried out his orders with little hope of success.

The 17th SS Panzergrenadier Division was brought back up to strength, reequipped, and stationed east of Metz. The replacements, however, generally lacked combat experience, and many were *Volksdeutsche*—ethnic Germans from outside the Reich—who were deemed less dependable.[139]

Patton's plan for taking Metz was to capture Fort Kronprinz (Fort Dilaim), which would open the door to an armored drive from the west into the heart of the city.[140] Patton, apparently having learned nothing at St. Malo and Brest, approved the 5th Infantry Division's proposal to attack Kronprinz beginning 27 September. The main works stood on a hill 360 meters tall and consisted of four casemates with reinforced-concrete walls seven feet thick and a central fort shaped like a pentagon. All the elements were connected by tunnels. Each casemate mounted a three-gun battery of either 100mm or 150mm, and the southern side received additional cover from a detached fort mounting three 100mm gun turrets. The central fort was surrounded by a dry moat running up to thirty feet deep. Barbed wire surrounded the fortification and wove among its individual elements. The gun turrets, as it turned out, could shrug off repeated hits by American 8-inch guns.[141]

The first battalion-sized infantry attack received artillery, air, and tank-destroyer support, all of which proved ineffective against the walls. The Germans pinned down the infantry with small-arms, machine-gun, and mortar fire, and the effort was called off after about four hours.[142]

After the failure of the first operation, the 735th Tank Battalion was brought into the fight as part of a carefully constructed assault plan. For the special operation, on 30 September, the battalion assembled a composite company consisting of its eleven tanks with 76mm guns, four 105mm assault guns, and a single 75mm Sherman for an artillery observer. They trained in the use of the explosive "snake," designed to blow a path through barbed wire much like the bangalore torpedo would, and the use of concrete-piercing ammunition.[143] From 5 to 8 October, tanks tried to work in the confined space of the complex with the GIs, subject to repeated close assaults by men from the officers-candidate school. The tanks made absolutely no difference to the outcome, which was failure.

On 9 October, Patton decided that the attack—which thus far had cost twenty-one officers and 485 men killed, wounded, or missing in action—was too costly to continue. This decision ushered in a period of relative quiet in most of the Third Army zone.[144]

DECEIVING AND ENSNARING PATTON

Patton entered the autumn battles ignorant of the point of the struggle in the view of the German high command, a perspective that was to shape the German actions for nearly four months. During the last two weeks of September, Hitler had outlined to his senior generals his plan for a massive counterstroke against the Western Allies through the Ardennes Forest, to be launched as early as November if conditions permitted. The goal was to crack the Western alliance just enough for Berlin to extract a separate peace and then turn to stave off the Soviet avalanche in the east. Hitler ordered Rundstedt to defend as long as possible in front of the West Wall fortifications that guarded the German frontier.[145]

Hitler reiterated that order to Balck—who, along with *Generalmajor* Mellenthin, was briefed on the planned offensive—when the latter was on his way to take command of Army Group G. Balck was to hold Alsace-Lorraine ("I would greatly appreciate it if you could," said Hitler), and under no circumstances could he allow developments to require the diversion of forces from the Ardennes offensive. Hitler accurately anticipated that supply difficulties would bring the Allies to a stop on a line running from the Sheldt estuary in the Netherlands along the West Wall to Metz and then to the Vosges Mountains. "[O]ur whole strategy in Alsace-Lorraine," recalled Mellenthin, "was based on the principle of gaining time for the Ardennes offensive." Now, Balck thought, we must fight like cornered rats to buy time.[146]

On the one hand, this meant that German commanders would have the luxury of trading space for time so long as they held the West Wall. Nevertheless, the need to keep the defense industry along the Saar working as long as possible meant that Balck would have to try to hold as far from the West Wall as he could. Balck issued orders for his corps to construct fortifications to support a defense that would "delay and wear down" the enemy.[147]

A Mobile Defense

Balck was used to fighting a defensive war in wide-open spaces with mobile divisions. In a mobile, elastic, or flexible defense (one sees the Germans use all three terms for roughly the same idea), the commander would sacrifice territory and preserve his fighting strength to the extent possible, stopping breakthroughs with mobile reserves rather than holding a line and suffering grinding attrition. Balck was highly critical of the tactics employed by *Generalfeldmarschall* Walter

Model, a proven defensive genius who in mid-September was taking the first steps toward accomplishing what became known as the "miracle in the west."

"Do you know that I had a meeting with Model where I asked him to change because his command techniques were wrong?" said Balck after the war. "Of course, he was a very energetic man and had some notable successes. However, his approach was mainly to pump up people to stand fast and to build fortifications wherever he thought someone might attack. His position defense approach was completely opposed to my views on mobile defense."[148]

Hitler's *Führerbefehl* endorsing Balck's plan to wage an elastic defense arrived on 29 September and decreed that Army Group G would concentrate its panzer divisions and brigades and panzergrenadier divisions in the area Duss-Lunéville.[149] Balck instructed First Army to fight in front of the West Wall and forbade any withdrawal into the fortifications.[150] Higher command *Saarpfalz* (Saar-Palatinate), meanwhile, took charge of rehabilitating the West Wall in coordination with First Army.[151]

But Balck did not have available the mobile formations on which his elastic-defense strategy depended. Fortunately, as things turned out, he would be able to exploit the respite the Americans gave him in October to gather them.[152] His first step, on 29 September, was to order XLVII Panzer Corps to extract the 11th Panzer Division from the line by 2 October to form a mobile reserve. He also ordered that the 3rd Panzergrenadier Division leave the front to form a reserve near Metz.[153]

When Balck received orders on 5 October to send the 3rd Panzergrenadier Division to the Aachen area, he ordered Fifth Panzer Army to halt offensive operations and to shorten and secure its line in order to make this possible.[154] In the ten days preceding 5 October, fighting in the Metz bridgehead had cost 700 casualties and, in the Pont-à-Mousson bridgehead, 3,100 men. All Balck could replace the departing division with was a regimental group from the 19th Volksgrenadier Division that he placed east of Metz. He ordered all sectors to form a local reserve. On the ninth, First Army conducted one local counterattack to eliminate an American salient at Delm (Delme) ridge. A regiment of the 553rd Volksgrenadier Division, supported by twenty-five tanks supplied by Fifth Panzer Army, hit the Americans in their flank. The attack succeeded, but most of the infantry were killed, including, it appears, the regimental and battalion commanders and staffs.[155]

The American pressure at the seam between First and Nineteenth Armies appeared to pose the greatest threat, so Balck decided on 10 October to gather his mobile formations at the point of danger to be ready to counterattack. These formations by now consisted only of *Kampfgruppen* from the 11th Panzer and

15th Panzergrenadier Divisions, which took up stations behind the right wing of the latter division.[156]

That same day, Rundstedt told Balck that he understood Army Group G was operating on a shoestring with low manpower, but the threat posed by the British in the Netherlands and the Americans at Aachen was so dire that most of the reinforcements had to go there. If determined defensive fighting gave the Reich time to rebuild some divisions, then in a few weeks time, some of those would come to Balck. Yet two days later, Rundstedt ordered Balck to turn over the 15th Panzergrenadier Division for the theater reserve and to send Fifth Panzer Army and XLVII Panzer Corps staffs to Army Group B. Rundstedt promised to give him a corps headquarters and one volksgrenadier division in exchange, and Jodl, on the fourteenth, pledged to send all new fortress battalions to Army Group G for the remainder of the month.[157]

First and Nineteenth Armies took responsibility for Fifth Panzer Army's front, and First Army took control of Krueger's LVIII Panzer Corps (21st Panzer and 15th Panzergrenadier Divisions). The Germans reconnoitered aggressively; patrols remained for days up to a dozen miles behind American lines.[158]

Balck understood that every spare man, shell, and liter of fuel would be needed to build the strategic reserve, so German forces in the south would have to wring the most out of their tight resources. Balck and his staff expected Patton's Third Army, not 6th Army Group, to be the main threat along Army Group G's front and, therefore, gave First Army in Lorraine priority over Nineteenth Army for replacements and supplies.[159] Replacements were often Luftwaffe or navy personnel who, reassigned to the infantry, required basic training on arrival. Reinforcements were few: during October, Army Group G received some twenty additional but poorly equipped infantry battalions, mostly made up of older men grouped into "stomach" and "ear" battalions (units in which the troops shared the same chronic ailment). The static machine-gun battalions that arrived, by contrast, consisted mostly of well-trained eastern-front veterans. Most of these were distributed as security garrisons in the Vosges positions opposite U.S. 6th Army Group, in the West Wall, and in the Maginot Line. Balck wanted to ensure that the West Wall fortifications were manned should the worst case occur, and he forbade the armies from bringing these troops forward to the front without his express permission; he ordered a particular concentration of men at the heretofore vulnerable Saarbrücken portion of the West Wall.[160]

American air superiority was a major problem for the Germans because when the weather was clear, they could not move during the day across open countryside. Having faced strong American tactical air power at Salerno, Balck learned to have a bombing map drawn up every day. He found the results more useful than any other form of intelligence at revealing where the enemy's main effort was aimed. Tactical intercepts of American war correspondents, who often talked twenty-four hours too early, was another valuable source of intelligence.[161]

"October brought us a break," observed Balck. "Completely unexpected."[162] Army Group G assumed that Third Army was resting and refitting its troops and believed it would take the Americans three to four weeks to restart offensive operations.[163] First Army judged Third Army's attacks during the month to be limited-objective operations intended to set the stage for a future offensive.[164] Almost all of the action in early October took place around the German bridgehead at Metz, the Americans sometimes gaining a bit of ground, and the Germans likewise on other days.[165] Two battles that loom large in histories of Third Army—the 5th Infantry Division's fruitless and bloody weeklong effort to capture Fort Kronprinz (Fort Driant) and the 90th Infantry Division's successful, but bloody, house-to-house fight to capture Maizières-lès-Metz—barely receive mention in German accounts, as neither action demanded great resources or proved operationally significant. The situation in Nineteenth Army's zone to the south was much different during the month; there 6th Army Group—despite its own shortages of fuel and ammunition—pressed its drive into the Vosges foothills.

Balck at this time did not think highly of Patton and the other opposing commanders. On 10 October, Balck wrote a letter to Rundstedt in which he said, "I have never been in command of such irregularly assembled and ill-equipped troops. The fact that we have been able to straighten out the situation again and release the 3rd Panzergrenadier Division for the northern front can only be attributed to the bad and hesitating command of the Americans and the French, [and that] the troops, inclusive of the irregular hordes, have fought beyond praise."[166] Looking back on his battles against Patton throughout the autumn, Balck commented, "Within my zone, the Americans never once exploited a success. Often Mellenthin, my chief of staff, and I would stand in front of the map and say, 'Patton is helping us; he failed to exploit another success.'"[167]

Balck used the break to the fullest. He dissolved shattered units, including those from the *Volksturm* (militia) sent forward by Himmler. Good soldiers were sent to other units. Untrained men joined specially organized training units. Underage boys from the Hitler Youth, supplied to fill noncombat jobs in the rear, were sent home.[168] The assault guns belonging to the volksgrenadier divisions finally appeared, which added considerably to their defensive strength.

Generalmajor Kurt Pflieger's 416th Infantry Division arrived between 5 and 8 October from Denmark to reinforce the Moselle position south of Trier after the 559th Volksgrenadier Division had shifted south, and it took charge of the so-called Saar-Moselle triangle and the Orscholz Switch extension of the West Wall across its base. The division had six rifle battalions—to which was added one airborne battalion, one fortress battalion, two fortress artillery battalions, and a communications and an engineer company. The average age of the men was thirty-eight years, and almost none of them had combat experience. Morale was good, and the division was rated fit for limited offensive operations. Pflieger, an artilleryman in the Great War and policeman between the wars, had combat experience as commanding general of 31st Infantry Division on the eastern front in 1942 and 1943.

Army Group G judged that the concentration of XX Corps west of Diedenhofen and of XII Corps northeast of Nancy indicated that Third Army still planned to attack north and south of Metz to encircle the city, capture it, and push on to Saarbrücken. Indeed, Rundstedt, apparently on the basis of hard intelligence information, informed Army Group G on 25 October that the American offensive would hit north and south of Metz with, it was thought at the time, two armored and three infantry divisions. Rundstedt believed that the 11th Panzer Division alone would not constitute a sufficient mobile reserve, and he told Balck that he would take steps to free the 21st Panzer Division from the front line. The 11th Panzer Division, with its dispersed artillery battalions assembled again, was to move by rail to the area east of Delm ridge.

Rundstedt asked OKW to guarantee fighter support once the Americans launched their offensive and was assured that the Luftwaffe high command would see to it. Balck ordered that all troop movements and supply operations take place during storms and at night to prevent losses to American *jabos*.[169]

Balck also implemented some of the same defensive measures that he had frowned on when Model had employed them. Balck's former commanding general in Fourth Panzer Army, Erhard Raus, had developed these "zone defense" tactics in early 1944 when commanding First Panzer Army and explained them thusly:

> After weeks of [Soviet] logistical buildup and moving up the enormous quantities of ammunition that would be required, our front would be breached after several hours of concentrated artillery, mortar, and rocket fire. This was followed by the breakthrough of massed infantry forces and deep thrusts of tank units attempting to gain freedom of maneuver. In 1944, the employment of massed armor somewhat altered this sequence of events, as large numbers of tanks led off the assault, followed by infantry in deep wedges. . . .

There were two ways to prevent the annihilation of our front-line troops, either by constructing bombproof and shellproof positions, or by withdrawing the forward units in time to evade the devastating barrages. . . . Such evasive tactics had already been employed during the last stages of World War I. . . . The loss of some ground that was necessarily involved in the application of these tactics was a well considered sacrifice, but achieving any permanent gain required that the new positions be held without fail. . . .

Past experience indicated to us that the Russians fired their concentrations only on the main battle line and preselected strong points. . . . [I]t was usually sufficient to withdraw the forward-most troops only 900 to 2,200 meters. Here was where we would organize the real forward defensive line, taking advantage of all favorable terrain features. Numerous strong points and sizeable local reserves were distributed throughout these positions, which extended back to the artillery emplacements and even beyond.[170]

First Army's frontline positions were hardened, especially along the Delm ridge, where a major thrust was expected. XIII SS Corps, which held that zone, flooded the lower reaches of the Seille and Nied Rivers. The Germans busily laid minefields, particularly around Metz and on the east bank of the Moselle. Construction began of a second line of defenses, which would shelter the main body of troops so the men would not be annihilated in the front line by artillery in the initial assault. Fallback positions sprang up all the way back to the Maginot Line, and engineers prepared bridges and roads for demolition. Even though the Maginot fortifications faced the wrong way, some effort went into improving them, including the Falkenberg switch position of the Maginot Line, which thrust southeastward from Falkenberg athwart XII Corps's route of advance. Improved positions on the Saar Heights appeared farther east. The West Wall was cleaned up and improved. Artillery was echeloned in depth so that at maximum range for each caliber gun, the batteries could just lay down a curtain of fire in front of the main line of resistance. All flak batteries were woven into the ground defenses.

Balck maintained the West Wall garrisons at full strength so if the worst should happen, the Americans would not be able to roll through. He believed that the West Wall fortifications along the Saar would be strong enough to stop the Americans come what may. Nevertheless, Rundstedt organized commands to hold bridgeheads on the west bank of the Rhine should even the West Wall not live up to Balck's expectations.

The threat posed by Hodges's First Army at Aachen continued to draw resources intended for Balck's army group. Rundstedt, on 20 October, told Balck that the appearance of U.S. Ninth Army on the right wing of Army Group B would likely only make matters worse.

By late October, the Germans had discerned that Third Army was aiming its small-scale attacks at the seams between divisions and corps and having some success at it. Balck ordered that strong points be built at all such seams and that neighboring units establish clear agreements on who was responsible for what.

By the end of October, Knobelsdorff's army was in barely acceptable shape to face whatever was to come. It had seven of its eight infantry divisions strung out along a front of seventy-five miles. In late October, the 553rd Volksgrenadier Division relieved the 11th Panzer Division as planned, and the latter moved into Army Group G reserve at Falkenberg, from where it could support either Hörnlein's LXXXII Corps or Priess's XIII SS Corps. First Army's total manpower was some 86,000 officers and men. It confronted six infantry and three armored divisions, plus two mechanized cavalry groups, totaling some quarter of a million men. Patton, moreover, would be able to concentrate his strength at the points of attack.[171]

LXXXII Corps, in the Metz area, controlled three infantry divisions, from south to north: the 462nd Infantry Division in Metz, the 19th Volksgrenadier Division in the center, and the 416th Infantry Division in the Saar-Moselle triangle.[172] Knobelsdorff was concerned about the corps because he thought that Hörnlein, while still a brave and reliable man, was physically no longer up to the demands of the job. Already a thin man, Hörnlein had shed weight and could offer Knobelsdorff no explanation. He seemed listless.[173]

The 462nd Division had had to release its officer candidates and NCO trainees, who had formed the backbone of the division. Balck replaced them with two "sick battalions," men with ear and stomach problems, whom he viewed as useless at the front, and with a replacement battalion and a machine-gun battalion.[174] The 19th Volksgrenadier Division was a battle-tested outfit with its personnel and equipment at 80 percent or better strength. It fielded one medium and two light artillery battalions. The 416th Division, which came to be known as the "whipped cream division" for its lack of toughness, had two full-strength infantry regiments, but only one light-artillery battalion. Hörnlein had organized the second into an antitank battalion.

XIII SS Corps, holding First Army's center, had the rebuilt 17th SS Panzergrenadier Division just south of Metz, and both of its regiments were up to strength. The replacements, however, were mostly without combat experience, and 100 seasoned officers and men had been transferred as cadre to other formations. The division had only six tanks, and it was fit only for defense. The 48th Infantry Division, in the corps's center, had returned to the line in mid-October after rebuilding. One regiment consisted of trained replacements, but the other was formed from Luftwaffe personnel who had received only two weeks of infantry training.

The 559th Volksgrenadier Division, on Priess's left, had suffered some combat losses; but it had performed well in battle, and its artillery was in good order. The division was stretched over a nearly twenty-mile front and had few antitank defenses.

General der Infanterie Werner *Freiherr* von und zu Gilsa's LXXXIX Corps held the left of First Army's front opposite Third Army. Gilsa, a World War I veteran, had languished in obscurity in this war, his only prominent position having been commanding general of the 216th Infantry Division in the east from 1941 to 1943. The 361st Volksgrenadier Division, on the corps's right wing, consisted of three regiments, each of two battalions. The manpower was drawn mainly from the navy and Luftwaffe, and up to half the officers and NCOs lacked combat experience. Still, it was fully equipped, including its artillery, and its men had undergone training as assault troops. The 553rd Volksgrenadier Division, on the left wing, had been badly shot up fighting at Nancy and had lost one entire regimental staff. It was reinforced with several static infantry units and flak batteries, which the regiments absorbed.[175]

Nineteenth Army had the 21st Panzer Division positioned on the right end of its line, which provided Balck with one more resource that in *extremis* he could shift opposite Third Army. Balck was still waiting for a promised volksgrenadier division that could replace Feuchtinger's panzers on the front so that he could withdraw them into reserve as authorized by Rundstedt. Since its retreat from France as mere remnants, the division had been brought back up to strength except in tanks, of which it had at most thirty. Once the 21st Panzer Division became available, Balck estimated that he would have about 100 panzers on First Army's front versus about 2,000 on the American side (in truth, closer to a thousand).[176]

Balck ordered each infantry division to hold in reserve one regiment with an assault-gun battalion, one artillery battalion, and one antitank company. The artillery could remain in position, but other elements had to be ready to move immediately against any breakthrough. These orders met with protest from nearly all divisions, whose commanders wanted as much to hand as possible. Balck insisted that this approach meant one was always weak at the point of decision and too strong where nothing was happening. Balck personally visited each division commander to explain his orders. Balck ordered that all reserves receive intensive training in night attacks to permit offensive operations free of interference by the *jabos*, having clearly learned his lesson in September.

Balck later observed, "Up 'til then, I had conducted all of my defensive battles offensively. Defensive arms are hopelessly outclassed, and nothing is as costly as a failed defensive battle. . . . [But] an offensive approach was just not possible. The balance of forces was too unequal. The troops were not up to form, and the enemy's air superiority was overwhelming. . . ." Still, the command to hold the West Wall allowed for an elastic defense, and Balck could anticipate counterattacking at some points. Balck knew his defenses were a house built on sand, but he reckoned that the Americans would again fail to fully exploit any great success.

Balck wanted to abandon Metz, but he knew he would never win the führer's permission to do so. He therefore had to reckon on gaining some time with its defense and console himself with the knowledge that the men who would be captured there would not suffer the same grim fate as those at Stalingrad.[177]

The high command took several final steps to ensure that if all of Balck's and Knobelsdorff's plans failed, Germany could still prevent Third Army from achieving a strategic success. In early November, OKW provided the 401st *Volksartillerie* Corps, which Balck could employ only with its permission. OKW also moved the 25th Panzergrenadier Division, then just reorganizing, from the training ground at Grafenwöhr to the one at Baumholder, just behind the front. The division remained in OKW reserve, however. OKW informed Balck that, on 11 November, the 276th Volksgrenadier Division would move to his sector and also remain in OKW reserve.[178]

While all this was going on, Patton, on 18 October, issued his first instructions for resumption of offensive operations. His aims were to surround and capture Metz, and then to advance to the Rhine and capture Mainz, Frankfurt, and Darmstadt. His corps were then to prepare for a continued advance to the northeast.[179]

As the plan gelled in early November, Patton instructed XII Corps, consisting of the 26th, 35th, and 80th Infantry and 4th and 6th Armored Divisions to advance from Pont-à-Mousson to Falkenberg, destroy enemy forces withdrawing from Metz, hand off the 80th Infantry Division to XX Corps, and advance to the Rhine and establish a bridgehead. XX Corps, initially controlling the 5th, 83rd, and 90th Infantry and 10th Armored Divisions, was to cross the Moselle in the vicinity of Fort Königsmachern, destroy enemy forces withdrawing from Metz, cross the Saar, and advance to the Rhine. III Corps was just arriving and would follow when appropriate.[180] Patton, despite the lessons of Brittany, apparently expected the Germans not to fight for Metz and had ordered no one to capture the city.

PATTON'S NOVEMBER OFFENSIVE

The events of November and December were overdetermined. Patton had such a huge advantage in materiel that he was certain to break First Army's front. The Germans had built so many fallbacks and reserves that they were certain to stop Third Army from crossing the Rhine. The open question was whether Balck could stop Patton from penetrating the West Wall, which ran along the (old) German border roughly forty miles ahead at the most distant point, before the Ardennes offensive began.

The Germans knew Third Army would attack soon. They watched the buildup of troops and spotted bridging equipment. Their intelligence knew of the arrival of the 10th Armored and 95th Infantry Divisions in the area, despite clever efforts to cloak the infantry division's arrival. They recorded a substantial increase in American reconnaissance activity. OKW noted that the American forces near Metz were receiving more additional divisions than those at Aachen and expected the southern group to strike first. OKW was correct.

Balck grasped Patton's intentions full well, though he ever so slightly, yet nearly fatally, underestimated Patton's speed. Army Group G assessed on 29 October that the great offensive would not begin before 11 November because some American divisions had suffered heavy casualties and needed to be refreshed. Perhaps for this reason, Knobelsdorff was able to go on leave, and *General der Infanterie* Kurt von Tippelskirch took over temporary command of First Army on 30 October. Nevertheless, the Germans fully expected the attack to strike to the north and south of Metz and estimated that three fresh armored and two or three infantry divisions had arrived. The attack force at Diedenhofen would consist of two or three infantry divisions and two armored divisions, while that between the Forest of Parroy and Pont-à-Mousson would include four infantry and two armored divisions. The two attack groups would pursue a double envelopment of Metz in order to take it from the rear. The ultimate goal would be to penetrate the Saarland. The assessment concluded soberly, "In light of the enemy's known material superiority, we must anticipate that the enemy will break through our positions with [all] attack groups."

Hitler ordered that an artillery perimeter in depth be constructed in front of both concentrations. He supplied Rundstedt with extra resources—apparently one more *Volksartillerie* corps and several fortress artillery battalions—to make that possible.

Balck's solution was to rely on a strong-point-based defense in depth backed by regiment-sized reserves for counterattacks to force the Americans to waste prodigious quantities of ammunition and to channel their movements. The 19th Volksgrenadier Division alone had laid 40,000 mines. Two defensive lines had

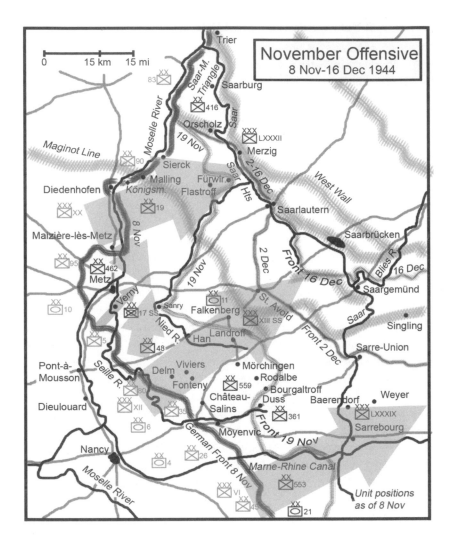

been finished north of Metz, both anchored on the Königsmachern fortress at their right end.

Balck's sole strategic reserve was the 11th Panzer Division, located in area west of Falkenberg. That division possessed forty Panthers, twenty Mark IVs, and ten Jagdpanzer IV tank destroyers. Wietersheim, now well aware that massed use of tanks would prove costly against the Americans, formed mixed companies consisting of one platoon of tanks and two of panzergrenadiers. Additional teams including one tank, a half-track, and an artillery observer were organized to cover gaps. Balck asked Rundstedt to make the 21st Panzer Division available by 12 November, to use as a reserve to parry attacks north and south of Metz. He warned that should the enemy break through on both sides of the city, a quick decision would be necessary as to whether to allow the garrison to be surrounded. If that were permitted, he argued, it would be too weak to tie down many American formations—a clear hint that he wanted to abandon the city when the time came.[181]

North of Metz, the 416th Infantry Division occupied its forward positions with only security forces, withdrawing the main body and concentrating its strength on its left wing. Two of its artillery battalions and three from the 19th Volksgrenadier Division concentrated behind the seam between the two divisions. LXXXII Corps deployed its tank destroyer battalion, consisting of three companies, each with fifty heavy *Panzerschreck* bazookas, in the area south of Sierck. Over 20,000 mines had been laid from this area southwest to Diedenhofen.

Balck also ordered that a regimental strike group, supported by a mobile antitank company and a mobile artillery battalion, be quickly organized and withdrawn from the Metz bridgehead. He added a machine-gun battalion from Nineteenth Army to the mix and authorized Knobelsdorff to shorten his lines in the bridgehead to make the troops available. Balck also moved a machine-gun battalion into the West Wall on both sides of Saarburg in case the Americans made it that far. For Metz, he ordered that the various battalions in the fortifications be melded into a "fortress division," which was to release the 462nd Infantry Division into reserve. This was another sign that he hoped to write off Metz at the lowest possible price.[182]

Hörnlein's LXXXII Corps had no tanks, which was a major shortfall for a general whose main experience was commanding a mobile fire brigade. The 19th Volksgrenadier Division had but eleven assault guns. These had been teamed with infantry under orders never to leave the armor for whatever reason, and the arrangement allowed the crews and riflemen to get to know and trust one another. At first, the corps would have to rely heavily on the Moselle as an antitank barrier along most of its front.

The Seille River, in the XIII SS Corps's, zone was not an adequate antitank barrier along its entire length, and once the Americans were across, the terrain greatly favored the attacker. The 17th SS Panzergrenadier Division had just received fourteen assault guns, but otherwise Priess could count on only two towed antitank battalions with captured Soviet guns and some 88mm flak deployed back with the artillery. This lack of equipment would prove a serious problem, and Balck probably expected as much, because he had learned on the eastern front to hold his antitank guns back and rush them to the enemy's *Schwerpunkt* when it became clear to him. Balck hoped that the defense in depth, with the main line of resistance along the line Verny-Delm ridge, would slow the enemy long enough to bring forward the 11th Panzer Division. *Oberst* Kurt von Einem, the corps chief of staff, after the war asserted that Priess received orders to hold every meter of ground, but there is no documentary evidence to that effect.[183]

As of 1 November, Army Group G's total manpower, with which it had to defend a zone stretching from north of Metz to the Swiss border against the U.S. Third and Seventh and French First Armies, amounted to 136,161 officers and men. Of the total number of troops, 86,622 belonged to First Army.[184] Third Army's strength on that same day was about 252,000 men.[185]

The Storm Breaks

Patton's attack on 8 November caught Balck's troops by surprise, despite the many warning indicators they had seen. Ground reconnaissance had detected no signs of an immediately impending attack, and the absence of air reconnaissance left the Germans ignorant about a buildup of armor directly behind the front. Torrential rains began on 5 November, and the mud became as deep as it ever was on the eastern front. Seven inches of rain fell during November, the most recorded in thirty-five years. An offensive seemed out of the question under those conditions.[186]

Balck's planned large-scale withdrawal of the main force to the second line prior to the offensive's preparatory fires, therefore, did not take place. When more than 700 American guns opened fire at 0515, they caught the infantry in forward positions, and casualties were heavy.[187] By contrast, when the U.S. First and Ninth Armies attacked in the Aachen sector a week later, the Germans accurately anticipated the timing, and the zone-defense tactics worked flawlessly and effectively.

Patton had consoled himself during the rain-swept night by reading from Erwin Rommel's book *Infantry Attacks*, in which Rommel described a successful assault in a downpour. Patton's luck was good, and the skies cleared just in time for American aircraft to fly and pound the Germans. Patton, fearing another stop order, had not let Bradley know the offensive had begun. After all the rain, Bradley, in turn, had worried that Patton would delay his attack and called him to check. Eisenhower got on the phone and told Patton, "I expect you to carry the ball all the way."

The American onslaught mainly hit XIII SS Corps, aiming, it appeared to the Germans, at Saargemünd (Sarreguemines) and Zweibrücken. A heavy raid by four-engine bombers hit positions on the Delm ridge between the Pont-à-Mousson–Han-sur-Nied road and Moyenvic; *Oberst* Einem, corps chief of staff, recalled that the bombing largely missed the troops, but hit the 17th SS Panzergrenadier Division's headquarters. The troops suffered under the heavy artillery barrage for nearly three hours, and the pelting rain filled trenches and foxholes, caused the edges to collapse, and filled the depressions with mud. Despite substantial losses, the troops fended off most ground assaults on the first day.

The American nevertheless managed to cross the Seille River at Moyenvic. The heavy presence of *jabos* interfered with early attempts to counterattack with local reserves across the front. Priess found out about the push fairly late in the day and at first believed it to be a holding attack because of its limited scope. Balck, however, viewed the action on his front as the long-awaited great offensive; he decided that the penetration at Moyenvic was so threatening that he ordered the 11th Panzer Division to attack in that direction. When the division appeared to be dawdling, Balck called Tippelskirch and told him to get the panzers moving. Knobelsdorff would not have needed that reminder.

Tippelskirch should not have been stunned by the vast American onslaught. Born on 9 October 1891 in Berlin-Charlottenburg, Tippelskirch had entered the imperial army in March 1910 as an officer candidate. When the Great War broke out, he almost immediately had fallen into French captivity. He had served in the infantry between the wars, but his first combat command had been that of the 30th Infantry Division in 1941. He had taken charge of XII Corps in February 1943 and Fourth Army in June 1944, departing the front the next month after suffering injuries in a plane crash. Tippelskirch had fought against huge Soviet offensives and been decorated for his leadership. By comparison, Patton's offensive was a smallish affair.[188]

Balck asked Rundstedt to send a *Kampfgruppe* from the 25th Panzergrenadier Division to replace the 11th Panzer Division near Falkenberg, but Rundstedt refused on grounds that the division was not yet ready for battle. Fortunately, the 708th Volksgrenadier Division had reached the area of the front, and Balck ordered it to relieve the 21st Panzer Division "train by train." Balck instructed the 21st Division to send a *Kampfgruppe* to the battle zone immediately and also alerted Nineteenth Army to send the 951st Grenadier Regiment to First Army. Balck placed the 401st *Volksartillerie* Corps on alert, and Rundstedt gave him permission to use it. Balck told Rundstedt he intended to pull XIII SS Corps back to the intermediate defense line.

Rundstedt immediately grasped the signs of a major offensive and requested permission to use divisions from the OKW reserve in a crisis. Hitler, hoarding the divisions he was rebuilding for the Ardennes offensive, refused except in the event of a large-scale airborne assault.

The main line of resistance started to crumble in several spots on 9 November, in part because of the loss of antitank guns. The 48th Infantry Division was back-pedaling and had lost its positions on the Delm ridge entirely, as well as much of its manpower. The 17th SS Panzergrenadier Division maintained an intact front only by shifting a regiment from an area that had not been attacked—a move that created a risky vulnerable spot for the future, but was a model of improvisation. It was clear that Combat Command A, 6th Armored Division, was driving toward the Nied River and tearing the seam between XIII SS and LXXXII Corps.

The 559th Volksgrenadier Division retreated from Château-Salins after a bitter fight, but held the high ground beyond. *Generalmajor* Mühlen recalled, "[T]he enemy succeeded in making a breach in the left flank of the division, which, however, we succeeded in sealing off. In the days following, the battle raged back and forth within our main defense line; the will to resist of the troops was strong and tough." Tippelskirch lauded the division's "stiff-necked" resistance.

Initiating Mobile Defense

Balck concluded that the American *Schwerpunkt* was at the Delm ridge and that he must commit Wietersheim's 11th Panzer Division there instead of at Moyenvic. As a substitute, he ordered the 106th Panzer Brigade up from Nineteenth Army to strengthen Priess's left wing. Priess had operational control over Wietersheim's panzers by 1600 hours on 9 November and ordered them to attack at the Delm ridge the next morning at 0500 hours. XIII SS Corps's line was stretching very thin, and commitment of lead elements of the 21st Panzer Division—a small armored group and a battalion of panzergrenadiers—and the 106th Panzer Brigade with some twenty to twenty-five tanks all told did little to help.

The 90th Infantry Division north of Metz, meanwhile, forced two crossings against the 19th Volksgrenadier Division at Malling and Fort Königsmachern, between Sierck and Metz, and was able to unify the bridgeheads. The rising Moselle waters inundated the extensive mine fields, but they also prevented construction of a bridge for tanks to cross. Once again, the *jabos* disrupted attempts by the 19th Division to counterattack with local reserves. Fort Königsmachern held out, but a two-battalion counterattack at Malling, supported by ten assault guns, failed to eliminate the bridgehead and resulted in fairly heavy casualties.

The situation here was clearly more worrisome than had been expected, and Hörnlein had no armored mobile reserve of his own to deal with the threat. Rundstedt, for the first time, expressed a willingness to consider providing a *Kampfgruppe* from the 25th Panzergrenadier Division. He also said he might make the 2nd Panzer Division—intended for use in the Ardennes—available to clear up the breach south of Sierck, including at Königsmachern. OKW refused to release the 2nd Panzer Division but approved committing elements of the 25th Panzergrenadier Division.

Balck ordered all reserves and available parts of the 25th Division to eliminate the northern bridgehead through a flank attack from the south the next day. Tippelskirch was to draw as needed on troops in the German bridgehead west of the Moselle at Metz for reserves to use in the attack sectors, an improvisation that would badly weaken the still peaceful front there. South of Metz, the 11th Panzer Division, supported by the 401st *Volksartillerie* Corps, was to conduct a flank attack against the Americans on the Delm ridge. The 559th Volksgrenadier Division and 106th Panzer Brigade were to hold near Château-Salins until the 11th Panzer Division cleared the ridge and could come to their aid.

Rundstedt issued orders that Metz was to be held as a fortress and be provisioned to hold out for some time if surrounded. The 17th Panzergrenadier Division, however, could not be allowed to be pinned in Metz, he instructed.[189] Tippelskirch was disgusted by this order. He had witnessed the establishment of such fortified places at Orscha and Mogilev while commanding Fourth Army on the eastern front, and each time the only result had been the loss of a precious division after but a few days of resistance.[190]

Fort Metrich fell on 10 November, and American infantry penetrated Königsmachern, though the garrison continued to defend the interior and the guns were still in action.[191] Tippelskirch reluctantly committed his reserve regiment of the 416th Division to the fight. He was most worried about the situation south of Metz, but wanted to prevent the situation north of the city from reaching crisis proportions.[192] A counterattack against the 90th Infantry Division's bridgehead reduced it slightly, but that was all.[193]

By 11 November, the Americans were expanding their bridgeheads, and Balck reported to Rundstedt that the Americans were into Diedenhofen and had captured the train station. All three regiments of the 90th Infantry Division were across the Moselle, though no tanks had made it yet. Signals intelligence indicated that the 83rd Infantry Division and the 10th Armored Division would soon reinforce the bridgehead, so if it were not eliminated immediately, it would be too late. This was true, though Bradley was just then denying Patton the use of the 83rd Division, which he had initially promised to loan Patton from U.S. First Army to clear the Saar-Moselle triangle north of the Orscholz Switch defensive line.

This disarray in the American chain of command would prove a boon to Hörnlein's LXXXII Corps.[194] Pflieger, facing no threat to his rear from the 83rd Infantry Division, was able to refuse the 416th Division's left flank and extend the new line with the 59th Grenadier Regiment from the crumbling 19th Volksgrenadier Division.[195] This enabled Hörnlein to hold the triangle, which remained in German hands for months more to come.

Hitler signed the operations order for the Ardennes offensive on 10 November. It was clear that four of the fifteen panzer and panzergrenadier divisions—a respectable 25 percent of those designated for the operation—and one of the twenty-three infantry divisions that OKW had allotted for the attack were going to be tied up fighting Third Army, and the high command could not count on their timely transfer to Army Group B. The operations staff scrambled to find other divisions to fill the gap created by Patton's offensive.[196]

The American *Schwerpunkt* still appeared to be south of Metz, where four infantry divisions and two armored divisions had been identified. Indeed, the 4th and 6th Armored Divisions were now in action against First Army's south wing, though the deep mud kept American tanks bound to the roads—what American tankers called "a front one tank wide." The 4th Armored Division attacked with its CCA through the lines of the 26th Infantry Division on 10 November, after CCB's attempt to advance through the 35th Infantry Division encountered heavy resistance and bad terrain. The 6th Armored Division struck with both combat commands through the lines of the 80th Infantry Division and became the main assault formation on XII Corps's left wing. The western wing of the 17th SS Panzergrenadier Division fell back under this bashing, though the Americans characterized its resistance as "bitter." This allowed the 6th Armored Division to capture two bridges at Han-sur-Nied and Sanry-sur-Nied intact, the latter after a brave engineer cut the demolition wires before being shot and killed.

Recapture of the Delm ridge was by now out of the question, but the 11th Panzer Division fought a delaying action to allow the battered infantry to retreat behind the Nied River. Screened by rain and snow from the *jabos*, the 11th Panzer Division, on 10 November, fought a seesaw action against CCB, 4th Armored Division, which was attacking toward Mörchingen, and by dusk, one *Kampfgruppe* had briefly recaptured Viviers. The Ghost Division thereby cut off Task Force Churchill (8th Tank Battalion), and the small village became the battlefield for survival of the combat command. Mellenthin claims that the panzer men knocked out thirty American tanks (he is probably actually referring to the simultaneous fight at Fonteny against Task Force Maybach, which lost an entire company of tanks to German fire and to mud), and Wietersheim recalled that one man destroyed four Shermans with a bazooka. CCB's after-action report glosses over the fight, though it concedes the Germans "infiltrated" Viviers with panzers and infantry, and the army's combat interviewers chose not to pry into the matter. A postwar account by the 8th Tank Battalion commander noted the impasse had been broken by dispatching a tank platoon to the rear, where it linked up with soldiers of the 35th Infantry Division. The panzer division's second *Kampfgruppe* faced continuous attacks near Château-Salins and fended off the last American assault of the day only after Wietersheim's personal intervention in the fighting.

Wietersheim had stopped the center of the American attack, but the 4th Armored Division also was making gains against First Army's left wing south of Mörchingen. The 48th Infantry and 559th Volksgrenadier Divisions fell back behind the Nied, and the 11th Panzer Division counterattacked the 4th Armored Division's columns to cover the withdrawal. Wietersheim's men that day captured a map showing the planned routes of advance by the 4th and 6th Armored Divisions to Zweibrücken.

XIII SS Corps chief of staff, *Oberst* Einem, recalled that the corps's "withdrawal was only made possible by the clever tactics with which the battle was conducted by the 11th Panzer Division, which supported the worn out infantry on a broad front." The corps lost contact with friendly elements to its left as it withdrew.

Balck planned to pull the 17th SS Panzergrenadier Division back yet farther and to commit the bulk of the 21st Panzer Division, which was to be available by noon the next day, along the Nied. The 347th Infantry Division was on the way from Holland and intended to relieve the 17th SS Division. The 17th SS, 48th, and 559th Divisions had all suffered heavy losses to Patton's violent assaults, and Balck had issued orders parceling out an engineer battalion, a machine-gun battalion, and a regiment shifted from LXXXIX Corps's 361st Volksgrenadier Division to fill the ranks.

At Mörchingen, panzer fire from dominating ground forced CCA's spearhead to pull back on 11 November, while panzers and antitank guns slowed CCB near Château-Salins and brought forward movement to a halt before dark. A night attack at Rodalbe by a *Kampfgruppe* of the 111th Panzergrenadier Regiment riding ten Panthers netted 400 prisoners.[197]

As of 12 November, according to Balck, he had in action thirty tanks and assault guns in Lorraine (only a slight exaggeration) as against some 700 in Third Army. The Americans conducted an estimated 1,200 air attacks that day, compared with none by the Luftwaffe.[198] The 19th Volksgrenadier Division, supported by the *Kampfgruppe* from the 25th Panzergrenadier Division, was able to reduce the size of the Malling bridgehead, but could not eliminate it.[199] Recognizing the futility of his counterattacks north of Metz, Balck ordered a stop to assaults against the Malling-Königsmachern bridgehead. He had been promised the 276th Volksgrenadier Division and would use it here to obliterate the bridgehead—or so he thought.[200]

The 11th Panzer Division's attacks against the 4th Armored Division, meanwhile, continued to stymie the American advance. Wietersheim's panzers and infantry hit CCA's flank on the twelfth and stopped one penetration entirely near Château-Voue, halfway between Rodalbe and Château-Salins, in the morning. A second battalion-sized panzer-infantry thrust, well supported by artillery and prepositioned antitank guns, forced a second American column backwards during the afternoon. A concentration of invaluable antitank guns, however, fell prey to CCB's 8th Tank Battalion, which spotted them on high ground, flanked the position, and took them from the rear.[201] Twenty-one antitank guns, including ten 88mm pieces, along with six mortars, seven half-tracks, and three trucks, were destroyed.[202] The 17th SS Panzergrenadier Division did not display the same verve as Wietersheim's division and used its panzers and antitank guns defensively as it tried to slow the advance of the 6th Armored and 5th Infantry Divisions.[203]

Situated between the two divisions and out of contact with the 11th Panzer Division on his left, Feuchtinger used small attacks by storm troops and a few panzers to mask his weakness from the Americans until the rest of his 21st Panzer Division could arrive.[204] Feuchtinger had learned the tricks of improvisation and deception. Born in Metz on 9 November 1894, Feuchtinger had entered the imperial army as an officer candidate in August 1914, joining the 14th Artillery Regiment. He served as an artillery officer between the wars and during this war until January 1943, when he was assigned to France to organize the Mobile Brigade West—dubbed a model of improvisation by his superior officer, as it was equipped with customized captured French vehicles and weapons. The brigade, in June, expanded into a motorized division, which, in turn, became the reborn 21st Panzer Division, and Feuchtinger was promoted to *Generalmajor*. He had been promoted again to *Generalleutnant* in August 1944. Feuchtinger's records indicate he was a dedicated National Socialist, and he had worked side-by-side with members of the Nazi Party before the war.

Nevertheless, his talent at improvisation had also led him into the world of black marketeering, and he would be court-martialed, stripped of rank and honors, and barely escape the executioner in early 1945.[205]

Knobelsdorff, who had scurried back from his leave on the 11th, realized by 12 November that the enemy did indeed intend to encircle Metz. Over the next forty-eight hours, the American drive across the Nied River toward Falkenberg ripped a hole in the center of XIII SS Corps's line that he could not fill. Yet the Americans stopped, evidently not recognizing their opportunity. Seizing the grace period, Knobelsdorff rushed the regiment of the 361st Volksgrenadier Division by truck from LXXXIX Corps to the area and sent forward elements of the 36th Volksgrenadier Division.[206]

So far, Balck had succeeded in using flexible defensive tactics to prevent a full-blown American breakthrough. It was his good fortune that when an opportunity for a breakthrough occurred, Patton did not exploit it.

Balck's Troubles Multiply: Monday, 13 November, began a period of near disaster for Army Group G. That day, Haislip's XV Corps in Seventh Army began an offensive that would, with remarkable speed—a mere ten days—unhinge the Vosges defenses and capture Strasbourg on the Rhine. The 44th Infantry Division struck up the road to Sarrebourg (Saarburg) with two regiments abreast and carved out rapid gains until encountering heavy artillery, mortar, and machine-gun fire across its entire front at about 0800, courtesy of the 553rd Volksgrenadier Division, the southernmost formation in First Army.

Just to the south, the 79th Infantry Division's attack struck the seam between the First and Nineteenth Armies. Here, the untried 708th Volksgrenadier Division, just formed in Slovakia around remnants of the 708th Infantry Division, had begun to take over the 21st Panzer Division's zone during the night of 9–10 November and had not fully consolidated its positions.[207]

Mellenthin's post-war study written for the U.S. Army's Historical Division makes clear that Balck viewed Third and Seventh Armies' offensives as parts of an integrated whole. That was not the case beyond their places in Eisenhower's overall strategy to attack along the entire western front in November and pledges by Lt. Gen. Jacob Devers at 6th Army Group that he would watch Patton's right flank. Balck initially tried to divide his battlefield into two zones separated by the line between First and Nineteenth Armies. Army Group G transferred command over the 553rd Volksgrenadier Division from First Army to Nineteenth Army's LXIV Corps during the afternoon of 13 November in order to allow the former to concentrate on fighting around Metz.[208] Nevertheless, U.S. Seventh Army's rapid gains over the coming days and the combined threat to First Army's flank posed by XV Corps and Third Army's right wing would draw to that area some of the mobile formations Balck needed to conduct his elastic defense around Metz against Third Army.

American attacks and German counterattacks surged back and forth on 14 November, but the Germans were so weakened that many small breakthroughs occurred both north and south of Metz. OKW insisted on holding the 276th Infantry Division, which was still in transit, in its reserve, which spiked Balck's plan to use the division to restore the situation north of Metz. All mobile divisions were too hotly engaged to pull back into Balck's reserve or move elsewhere.

That said, the panzer generals' mobile defense accomplished what it could. Wietersheim's remarkable 11th Panzer Division managed to restore the line by concentrating its remaining forces and attacking southwest of Bourgaltroff.[209] The panzers and grenadiers caught the 4th Armored Division's powerful Task Force Oden-West hunkered down for the night in Guebling and, backed by crushing artillery support, wreaked havoc on the Americans and forced them to retreat westward.[210]

Knobelsdorff's army was stretched to its limits. The 11th Panzer and 17th SS Panzergrenadier Divisions were tied up launching counterjabs against the Americans south of Metz, while the 21st Panzer Division backpedaled because it was being outflanked on both wings. The 48th Infantry Division had been so badly chewed up that Knobelsdorff decided to fold the remnants into the 559th Volksgrenadier Division, which became known as *Kampfgruppe* Mühlen, after the 559th Division commanding general.

The 36th Volksgrenadier Division arrived in XIII SS Corps's sector on 13 and 14 November with three fresh regiments to relieve elements of *Kampfgruppe* Mühlen in the Mörchingen-Falkenberg zone. Committed to stopping an American thrust toward St. Avold, important to the war effort because coal-fired plants there supplied critical electricity to defense factories, the division was nearly destroyed in two days of fighting. Priess exercised fairly direct control over the division, mandating a counterattack against the 6th Armored Division at Landroff and ordering other elements to defend their line to the last man. The division tried, but *jabos* and artillery destroyed its few 88s and handful of assault guns. The fourth and last attack captured most of Landroff in the dark, but the Americans—the tankers fighting as infantry because they could see nothing through the gun sights—drove the Germans out after terrific hand-to-hand fighting. Fortunately, the Americans, who could have easily severed the forward battalions' lines to the rear on the 16th, hesitated and thereby lost the chance to annihilate the division. Interviews with American troops suggest that Priess's aggressive action had convinced the Americans that the Germans were much stronger than they actually were.[211]

North of Metz, the Germans, on 14 November, identified elements of the 10th Armored Division entering both the Malling and Königsmachern bridgeheads. This spelled real trouble, because there were almost no mobile antitank resources available.[212] Knobelsdorff asked for an assault-gun brigade and two heavy antitank battalions, but Rundstedt had none to give. Rundstedt, in fact, was already considering falling back to the Maginot Line along the entire front, but that position would have a frontage just as long and would not allow him to extract any units to form a reserve.[213]

On the fifteenth, the 10th Armored and 90th Infantry Divisions achieved a large breakthrough, and American troops also appeared on the heights north of Metz. Simultaneously, a surprise attack caved in the northern face of the weakened Metz bridgehead. South of the city, after a fierce struggle, Mörchingen fell to the 4th Armored Division's CCB.

Balck sought permission from Rundstedt to withdraw to the Maginot Line, or if necessary, the Saar Heights position west of the Saar River, and leave the Metz garrison to fend for itself. Rundstedt agreed at 1700 hours. Balck ordered reinforcements into the West Wall to his rear, just in case the withdrawal turned to a rout.[214]

The Abandonment of Metz and Retreat to the Maginot Line: Army Group G considered the fortifications at Metz to be obsolete and incapable of sustaining a defense for very long. Most of the heavy guns had been moved to the Atlantic Wall, and only some thirty were still in place. Balck intended to use Metz as merely a strongpoint in a broader defense, but after the American offensive began, Hitler had ordered the fortress complex held to the last cartridge. Hurried attempts ensued to deliver a stock of food and ammunition sufficient for several months, but on the fourteenth a train arrived with rations for only three or four weeks. Even these supplies were unevenly distributed among the various forts, and Knobelsdorff assessed that ammunition stocks were insufficient to allow the garrison to hold out for very long, despite Balck's repetition of the order to defend every strongpoint to the last cartridge. The total garrison amounted to some 10,000 men.[215]

The Americans linked their bridgeheads east of Metz on 16 November and the next day got into the suburbs. The capture of Metz was a big deal in Third Army's view of the world, but the battle there from the German side was nothing but a welcome distraction for the Americans while Knobelsdorff tried to build a new defensive line to the east. The greatest cost was that, at the last moment, Balck had to order the 38th Panzergrenadier Regiment, 17th SS Panzergrenadier Division, to join the doomed garrison.[216] At this critical time, at Sepp Dietrich's request, Priess departed to take command of I SS Panzer Corps, which unknown to him had a role to play in the Ardennes offensive. Indeed, he would be convicted for war crimes as the corps commander responsible for the Malmédy Massacre.

SS Gruppenführer Max Simon arrived to replace him. His welcome to the western front and first day's task was to disengage his right wing from Metz. Simon brought with him an intimate knowledge of the American enemy, whom he had faced in Italy while commanding the 16th SS Panzergrenadier Division. There, in late June 1944, his division had played a key role in stopping Fifth Army's continued advance northward after the fall of Rome. He had gained a particular respect for American artillery, which had cost his division high casualties.[217] He was fortunate that Priess took none of his now seasoned corps staff with him.[218]

Since we last saw Simon in Russia, he had added to his count of crimes against humanity committed during his time in Poland. In November 1943, a Soviet military tribunal had condemned Simon to death in abstentia for killing 10,000 civilians in Kharkov that spring, when the *Totenkopf* Division had played a central role in Manstein's counterattack to capture that city. A British military tribunal condemned him to death after the war for complicity in the murder of up to 2,000 civilians at Marzabotta, Italy, in September 1944, as a reprisal for partisan attacks against his division, though the sentence was commuted in 1954.[219]

Meeting near Falkenberg, Priess explained the huge imbalance Simon would face in weaponry, quality and freshness of manpower, and air power. The corps had no reserve other than battalions it could take from the already weak divisions. Antitank weapons were generally lacking. The 11th Panzer Division was, at present, subordinated to LXXXIX Corps on the left. Only the terrain favored the defenders.

Priess told Simon, "To me, it is clear as daylight that under these conditions, in the long run, it is out of the question to fulfill the assigned mission of staving off the enemy attacks [before] the West Wall. I believe we will have to limit our activity to maintaining continuity of the front and preventing an enemy breakthrough. During the first week of the enemy offensive, I have succeeded in doing this, but I doubt whether it can still be done."[220] Priess, as things turned out, was overly pessimistic.

"I pursued [Priess's] methods," Simon recalled later. "I had no alternative as I was still a stranger in this theater of war." Asked about the quality of

Third Army's tactics, Simon replied, "In general, the tactics were good. I got the impression you were very cautious and systematic."[221] Here was yet another German commander who viewed Patton and his subordinates as cautious in smash-mouthed line fighting.

Simon later recorded the status of his divisions at the time he took command, which provides an excellent window into the losses they had suffered during the offensive thus far. The 11th Panzer Division was still trustworthy, but stood at between 50 and 70 percent of its manpower and had between thirty and forty tanks in running order. The 17th SS Panzergrenadier Division was still in moderately good shape, with between 60 and 70 percent of its authorized strength. The 21st Panzer Division was badly battered and at less than 50 percent strength. The 36th Volksgrenadier Division was "worn out," but well led. The 347th Infantry Division (just arriving) was poorly trained and equipped and at roughly 70 percent strength. The 559th Volksgrenadier Division had suffered extremely heavy losses, but it was gallantly led and a good combat formation.[222]

Knobelsdorff, on 17 November, made plans to get out of Patton's way on orders from Balck. With the Americans focused on Metz, Knobelsdorff told Balck that fighting along most of his line amounted to isolated skirmishes, and that it was an excellent moment to pull back. Balck saw an opportunity to create a reserve where Rundstedt had not. Balck told Knobelsdorff to withdraw his right wing, LXXXII Corps, in stages to the Maginot Line during the nights of the seventeenth, eighteenth, and ninteenth and to extract either the 17th SS Panzergrenadier or 21st Panzer Division into reserve; Knobelsdorff selected Feuchtinger's panzer division because the SS had left a regiment in Metz, and he pledged to create a second reserve from an armored group of the 11th Panzer Division. Late on the eighteenth, he ordered Feuchtinger to withdraw his division from the line and subordinated it to Hörnlein.

Balck had already told Knobelsdorff that when the retreat began, he was to offer bitter resistance as he fell back and to inflict the highest possible losses on the enemy. First Army was to destroy anything that could be of use to the enemy. While concentrated American armor made gains east of Diedenhofen, the XIII SS Corps front at Mörchingen was strangely quiet, which Balck interpreted as the result of heavy American losses the preceding day. Balck had signals intercepts indicating that part of the 4th Armored Division had lost so many men and tanks that it was going to pull back to reorganize.[223]

Simon commented on the American use of tanks:

At first, their formations were like ours in the 1940 Blitzkrieg and on the eastern front: a formation of three echelons—tanks, motorized infantry, and artillery (threefold division of tanks, three alongside each other). The tactics were the same. We saw these independent commitments had an advantage. Had we the necessary countermeasures—antitank guns, airplanes, and gasoline—many local penetrations would not have succeeded. The tactics of the Americans were based on the idea of breaking down a wall by taking out one brick at a time. They did this with tanks, against which we had nothing to employ. . . . Had you made such attacks . . . on the eastern front, where our antitank guns were echeloned in depth, all your tanks would have been destroyed.[224]

XIII SS Corps dropped back east of Metz and began a step-by-step withdrawal of its salientlike front, tracking the course of the Nied toward the Maginot Line, much like slowly releasing the air from a balloon. Each step backward shortened the corps's frontage. The rain was so heavy that German infantry could not fight from their water-filled trenches and foxholes that had been prepared behind them, and they had to seek cover above ground. Nevertheless, recalled Max Simon, "We retreated purposefully." The Maginot Line pillboxes offered no alternative to field fortifications because they faced the wrong way.

The arrival of the 347th Infantry Division from Holland provided a resource to fill the gap left by the abandonment of the Metz garrison. The division had been a static formation and had been hurriedly equipped for mobile warfare. The troops were from older age groups, antitank weapons and artillery were insufficient, and the division had no assault guns. The 21st Panzer Division successfully pulled out from the front, and Balck again had a mobile reserve for his elastic defense. Balck, on 18 November, ordered First Army's right wing to pull back all the way into the Orscholz Switch position of the West Wall and to reinforce that front.

The First Army front appeared to be well in hand for the moment, although signals intelligence indicated that a combined attack by the 4th and 6th Armored Divisions at Mörchingen was in the offing. The defenders in Metz were tying down strong American forces. North of Metz, the Americans had made gains at Flastroff on the seam between XIII SS and LXXXII Corps, but the 21st Panzer Division was now available to clean up the mess. Knobelsdorff thought the Americans were trying to reach Merzig, east of the Saar in the West Wall, and Balck told him to shift what he could to the area east of Merzig so he could defend the Saar crossings in depth.

The situation on Army Group G's left was far more worrisome. Balck's attention turned to Nineteenth Army, against which 6th Army Group had launched its part of the November offensive. The skies had temporarily cleared, and the *jabos* were giving the Americans and French an edge again.

Then, for a span of a few days, it looked like Balck was going to have good use for the extra troops he had sent into the West Wall. Hörnlein and his LXXXII Corps retreated all the way to the Saar Heights position west of the Saar River, which was honeycombed with fire trenches, prepared antitank positions, and antitank traps. The 19th Volksgrenadier Division was still arriving when American troops reached the heights at Fürweiler on 18 November. The American attacks penetrated in many places, and Hörnlein had no reserves nearby. Nor did Knobelsdorff. The road to the West Wall was wide open.[225] Patton recalled, "Things looked so good that I could almost picture myself going through the Siegfried Line any day."[226]

"Surprisingly enough, however," recalled *Oberst* Emmerich, "the enemy did not take advantage of the situation. He regrouped his forces and extended his breakthrough toward the flanks, thereby losing valuable time."[227] Emmerich had accused Patton of behaving like Montgomery.

Indeed, Third Army had suffered so many casualties and received so few replacements that Patton had decided to narrow the front of each corps before pushing on. III Corps, meanwhile, was to take over the troops reducing Metz.[228]

XIII SS Corps, which regained control over the 11th Panzer Division on 18 November, experienced almost no pressure against the right and center of its line for five days, from 19 to 24 November. In Simon's view, had Hörnlein been able to hold at the Maginot Line, Simon's own corps could have held its part of the Maginot Line for between seven and ten days.

Knobelsdorff used the pause to pull the 17th SS Panzergrenadier Division into reserve in exchange for the 347th Infantry Division. He concentrated the SS troops behind *Kampfgruppe* Mühlen.[229] This achievement was short lived. Seeing a need to strengthen LXXXII Corps, Knobelsdorff shifted *Kampfgruppe* Mühlen (once again called the 559th Volksgrenadier Division) north, and the 17th SS Division had to replace it in the line.[230]

The rejiggering of the front left a string of mostly infantry divisions holding the north end of his line from the Orscholz Switch to St. Avold: from north to south, the 416th Infantry, 25th Panzergrenadier, 19th Volksgrenadier (Merzig), 559th Volksgrenadier (Saarlautern), 347th Infantry, and 36th Volksgrenadier (St. Avold). Knobelsdorff had concentrated most of his mobile divisions just to the south opposite the 6th Armored Division, with the 17th SS Panzergrenadier and 11th Panzer Divisions at the left end of First Army's line southwest of Saargemünd. As we shall see, within days, Balck would move the Panzer Lehr and 25th Panzergrenadier Divisions to the adjoining right end of Nineteenth Army's zone.[231]

The Panzer Generals Act Again

Knobelsdorff's hand now appears in control of a series of three classic mobile-defensive maneuvers, a display of skill with threadbare resources that resembled his better days in the east and brought XX Corps to a temporary standstill. The main evidence for attributing the moves to Knobelsdorff, in the absence of First Army records, which were destroyed, is that Balck was preoccupied with the unfolding disaster in Nineteenth Army; Army Group G records and Mellenthin's accounts provide no evidence of decisions or hands-on control by Balck; the tactics were far too sophisticated to be attributed to Hörnlein; and *Oberst* Karl Redmer's account directly attributes the final blow to Knobelsdorff.

In the first move, on 20 November, Knobelsdorff's mobile reserve—Feuchtinger's 21st Panzer Division—attacked the Americans in the 19th Volksgrenadier Division's zone and restored a stable line at Flastroff, rescuing an encircled *Kampfgruppe* south of that town at Filstroff and closing the door to Merzig in the process.

Just as Emmerich had observed, on 21 and 22 November, the 90th Infantry and 10th Armored Divisions directed their efforts northward against the Orscholz Switch line at a right angle to the axis of advance that might have carried XX Corps through the West Wall. Knobelsdorff took advantage of the slackening pressure toward the Saar and attached the 21st Panzer Division to the 25th Panzergrenadier Division. Counterattacking part of CCB, 10th Armored Division, in the Saar Heights on the twenty-first, Feuchtinger's men rescued two artillery batteries that had been cut off and several Panther tanks that had been left behind when the 25th Division had been forced back. (The official U.S. Army history attributes the attack decision to Balck and cites one of Mellenthin's accounts as the source. But Mellenthin, in the cited report, says only that Balck released the 21st Panzer Division for use by Knobelsdorff and that a *Kampfgruppe* of the 25th Panzergrenadier Division conducted the counterattack.)

Job done, Knobelsdorff, on 23 November, sent Feuchtinger and his fire brigade north to act as a mobile reserve for the weak 416th Infantry Division, which he judged to be of little remaining combat value, in the Orscholz Switch. Indeed, the division's combat strength had sunk to 30 to 40 percent, and its heavy artillery batteries had completely run out of ammunition and withdrawn. The Americans had captured several bunkers, and nothing stood between their tanks and Saarburg—and beyond that, Trier and the left flank of the sorely beset German Seventh Army. Knobelsdorff met with Hörnlein, Feuchtinger, and

Pflieger at the 416th Division headquarters and instructed that the bulk of the 21st Panzer Division was to remain in reserve, and Feuchtinger was to use only what he needed to recapture the lost fortifications. Hörnlein supplied additional heavy artillery to support the attack.

The Americans advanced in the early morning of the twenty-fourth under a thick smokescreen, and guns in bunkers engaged American tanks along an antitank ditch. The German fire was heavy enough to pin down the infantry, who were unable to cross the ditch. The two sides were so closely engaged that neither army's artillery could fire. Now the 21st Panzer Division struck near the "Great Star" fortification. Feuchtinger paid no heed to the injunction to keep the bulk of his division in reserve. Leading with his panzergrenadier regiments supported by tanks, Feuchtinger recaptured most of the bunkers between 24 and 26 November. The Americans were still attacking the 416th Division at some places simultaneously. "It was ferocious hand-to-hand fighting involving casualties and prisoners on both sides," recalled Feuchtinger.

While the Americans had bashed their heads against the Orscholz Switch, Pflieger had pulled all his good troops out of the West Wall north of Merzig. Only a fortress battalion and some *Volksturm* militia manned the line. The Americans could almost have strolled through, but did not spot the opening.[232]

Hörnlein was relieved of command of LXXXII Corps on or about 25 November. Knobelsdorff, shortly before the offensive, had begun had recommended that Hörnlein, on health grounds, be moved to a quiet front. Balck had sealed his fate on the twenty-second. Observing that no quiet fronts existed any longer, he recommended that "this proven and brave general" be transferred to a military district command, and Rundstedt had concurred.[233]

While Knobelsdorff's mobile defense was checking Patton in the north, Balck judged that Third Army was shifting the *Schwerpunkt* of its offensive farther south, where the 4th Armored Division's CCB, as of 23 November, was making steady gains northeast of Duss along the seam between First and Nineteenth Armies. Here, the rightmost elements of the 4th Armored Division overlapped with the 361st Volksgrenadier Division's and, hence, *Generalleutnant* Werner-Albrecht *Freiherr* von und zu Gilsa's LXXXIX Corps zone, the corps otherwise facing U.S. Seventh Army. Balck expected that the enemy was likely to take advantage of XV Corps's gains in Seventh Army's zone to strike northward into First Army's flank. He pondered shifting the center of the 361st Volksgrenadier Division's defenses to Finstingen, just east of Duss and right in the seam, and sending the 25th Panzergrenadier Division to help it face the 4th Armored Division. Balck's impression of the shift in American effort probably was, in part, the result of the painfully slow progress being made by the 6th Armored and 35th Infantry Divisions—progress that was, in fact, partly slowed simply by mud.

U.S. Seventh Army's drive to Strasbourg, not the activities of Third Army, was Balck's main worry. *General der Infanterie* Gustav Hoehne, as of 23 November the brand new commanding general of LXXXIX Corps, had barely escaped capture on the twenty-second when Seventh Army troops had liberated Zabern (Saverne), location of his command post. Balck planned to attack Seventh Army's north flank with the Panzer Lehr Division, supported by the 25th Panzergrenadier Division rushing south from LXXXII Corps's zone, to close the hole emerging between First and Nineteenth Armies. His order to Panzer Lehr's commanding general *Generalmajor* Fritz Bayerlein observed, "The fate of Alsace depends on your decisive thrust to the objective."[234]

Panzer Lehr had required two days to move into position because air attacks confined its movement to the hours of darkness, and even the lead elements were not into position to attack until late on 23 November. The division had been in reserve and rebuilding, and its panzer regiment—nominally thirty-four each of Mark IVs and Panthers—had been combined into a mixed battalion of Panthers and Panzer IVs. Only two of its four panzergrenadier battalions had half-tracks, and the antitank battalion consisted of two short-handed companies of Jagdpanzer IVs and a third with towed 75mm antitank guns. None of the three artillery battalions had any self-propelled pieces, and one battalion even lacked towing vehicles. On a positive note, the division's armored reconnaissance battalion possessed four well-equipped companies mounted in half-tracks.

The panzers caught troopers from the 106th Cavalry Group, which was screening the area between Third and Seventh Armies, eating a turkey dinner for Thanksgiving in Weyer, and Panzer Lehr easily recaptured Baerendorf and several other towns by dark. Almost out of fuel, the Germans settled in to await the arrival of their trains, but Balck demanded immediate forward movement. Running on fumes, Panzer Lehr pushed on and took Hirschland, halfway between Baerendorf and Weyer, before halting in the face of heavy artillery and tank fire early the next morning.

Unknown to Bayerlein, the 361st Volksgrenadier Division just to his west was collapsing, and on 24 November, elements of the 4th Armored Division's CCB overran Panzer Lehr's artillery positions and entered Baerendorf. Panzer Lehr had to redirect its attention to fighting this new threat, although part of the division continued to push south in accordance with the original mission. Rundstedt and Hitler acknowledged that the counterattack had no hope and ordered the division to break it off late on 25 November.[235] By the twenty-sixth, the 25th Panzergrenadier had entered the line on Nineteenth Army's extreme right northeast of Duss and tied into the 11th Panzer Division on its right and the 361st Volksgrenadier Division on its left.[236]

Yet, while a secondary concern to the Germans, Eddy's XII Corps from 24 to 26 November made progress cracking the XIII SS Corps front southwest of St. Avold, where it still bulged forward well before the Maginot Line. Intercepts revealed that one reason was the arrival of the 95th Infantry Division from Metz. The 416th Infantry Division was still holding XX Corps at bay along the Orscholz Switch, and Balck sent the 404th *Volksartillerie* Corps to strengthen its defenses further.[237]

The Weight of Numbers

As Napoleon observed, God is usually on the side with the big battalions.

First Army on 25 November reported the status of some of its divisions. In LXXXII Corps, the 416th Infantry and 19th Volksgrenadier Divisions were rated category IV (suitable for static defense), and the 21st Panzer Division, which had only seven tanks and not much transport, was rated category III (mobile defense). In XIII SS Corps, the 347th Infantry Division was rated category IV; the 36th Volksgrenadier and 17th SS Panzergrenadier Divisions, the latter only 40 percent motorized, category III; and the 11th Panzer Division, with only four operational tanks, but 90 percent mobile, category II (limited offensive operations). LXXXIX Corps's 25th Panzergrenadier and 256th Volksgrenadier Divisions were rated category III, as was the Panzer Lehr Division, with thirteen tanks, and the 361st Volksgrenadier Division was rated category IV. The 553rd Volksgrenadier Division had been smashed by Seventh Army at Zabern, and the 462nd Infantry Division was surrounded in Metz.[238]

Army Group G estimated XIII SS Corps at this time was outnumbered 570 to 60 in tanks and assault guns, 26,000 to 5,318 in infantry, 468 to 267 in artillery, 580 to 268 in medium and heavy mortars, and a lot to nothing in aircraft.[239]

On 25 November, Third Army attacked Simon's corps along its entire front, with strong support by *jabos* and tanks. By the evening of the 26th, Knobelsdorff reported that the Americans had penetrated XIII SS Corps's front at many points, although nowhere by more than two miles, and that he lacked sufficient forces to plug the gaps. That night, joined by the 25th Panzergrenadier Division on its left wing, the corps conducted an orderly withdrawal to a shorter fallback line.[240]

Balck and Knobelsdorff had an excellent grasp of Patton's intentions. By the twenty-seventh, signals intelligence revealed that XII Corps's immediate objective was Saarbrücken. Army Group G also had detected that XX Corps was concentrating its divisions opposite the Merzig-Saarlautern area and concluded that a major attack in that sector could be expected soon. Knobelsdorff had made good progress building a reserve at Merzig. With the pressure off along the Orscholz Switch, Balck ordered that the 21st Panzer Division be released to go into reserve at a more threatened point, assigning it to XIII SS Corps. Balck forcefully reminded Knobelsdorff that he had to protect the war industries in the Saarland and that he had to use every means to hold his present main line of resistance.[241]

Exhortations could not overcome the balance of forces, however. XX Corps, on 28 November, attacked the LXXXII Corps line and rolled over the worn-out 19th Volksgrenadier Division in the Saar Heights position. Where XIII SS Corps still held ground before the Saar Heights, after a day's fighting, Knobelsdorff told Balck that the strength of the 559th Volksgrenadier and 347th Infantry Divisions had sunk so low that he could not maintain a continuous main line of resistance. He asked permission to pull his line back into the Saar Heights position. Balck, at about 1730, approved Knobelsdorff's request—for the last time, he said. Simon ordered Feuchtinger to move his panzer division to support the hard-pressed infantry. The 719th Volksgrenadier Division was reported to be underway from Holland by rail to reinforce the sector.[242]

With the Americans again driving against the seam between XIII SS and LXXXII Corps, the weak 559th Volksgrenadier Division gained little respite on 29 November from holding prepared positions on the Saar Heights, and numerous small breakthroughs took place. The 21st Panzer Division counter-attacked the American spearheads across flat ground visible from American positions on the Saar Heights, but with only a few local successes. Balck sensed that his men were looking over their shoulders toward the bunkers to their rear and urged Knobelsdorff to do everything he could to counter "West Wall psychosis." There could be no further retreat: Balck's armies had to "entangle the enemy and win time!"

Nevertheless, the next day, west of Merzig, in some spots the exhausted troopers in the 19th Volksgrenadier Division crossed the Saar and stumbled into the welcoming shelter of the West Wall. The 559th Division, however, this day held firm on the Saar Heights west of Saarlautern. Knobelsdorff directed the 404th *Volksartillerie* Corps to shift from the Orscholz Switch to positions on both sides of the seam between LXXXII and XIII SS Corps.[243]

Simon recalled that during this period up to 2 December, "the enemy cut slice after slice out of the corps front. The troops of the corps, who had been fighting heavily for months without rest, without adequate ammunition, with little or in many cases without any kind of antitank weapons, defended themselves desperately against the superior enemy, who was attacking with strong air forces."[244]

Knobelsdorff was relieved of command on 30 November. Knobelsdorff's old comrade Balck wrote in his performance review in early December that as First Army commanding general, he had continued to be an active leader and a man of clear decisions and firm will. But, assessed Balck, the previously observed fact that he was not an outstanding tactician had shown itself during the fighting in Lorraine. Knobelsdorff, said Balck, had not come up with fresh ideas. Rundstedt in his comments nailed the coffin closed: "[D]espite laudable personal enthusiasm for action, he did not fully meet the challenges that I had to put before him as commanding general of First Army, because he did not always find the improvisations necessary for waging this defensive battle. His demanding physical activities in the East may play a roll." Rundstedt suggested he was fit to be a deputy army commander or the commander of a fortress installation on some other front.[245]

Knobelsdorff had failed to hold Nancy and Metz, which were impossible tasks in light of the balance of forces, and in this he had given Patton a tactical victory. His fatal mistake, however, had probably been failing to *improvise* a way to stand for a time on the Maginot Line. His experiences, vast though they were, had not prepared him for that. Ironically, Chevallerie, whom he replaced, probably would have been better suited to such a task. Knobelsdorff did not receive another combat command through the end of the war. It was a lamentable fate for one of Germany's truly talented operational commanders.

DECEMBER: DEFENSE OF THE SAAR

On 1 December, Balck pulled the 19th Volksgrenadier entirely back behind the Saar north and south of Merzig in order to avoid its destruction on the west bank. He ordered the division to prevent an American crossing with all means. With its flank exposed, the 21st Panzer Division also pulled back into the fortifications that night. Once again, the Americans did not pursue either division. "The enemy followed hesitantly to the Saar River on 2 December," recalled Feuchtinger.

First Army shifted the corps boundaries, subordinating the 559th Volksgrenadier Division to LXXXII Corps and formally subordinating the 25th Panzergrenadier Division to XIII SS Corps. Simon placed the SS panzergrenadiers under Wietersheim's command.

Rundstedt broke the bad news that Army Group G would have to give up the Panzer Lehr and 11th Panzer Divisions, plus its two *volksartillerie* corps, to Army Group B by 4 December, as they had roles to play in the Ardennes offensive. Balck pleaded to keep the two panzer divisions. First Army had suffered much too heavy losses to hold its line without them.

Rundstedt replied with a blast aimed nominally at Knobelsdorff, but by implication also at Balck. Since the beginning of the American offensive in Lorraine, Rundstedt scolded, he had watched the leadership of First Army with worry. He had the impression that Knobelsdorff had not countered the enemy attacks—even though the enemy had outnumbered First Army twice over—with sufficient skill, which had prevented success. One reason had been Knobelsdorff's propensity to scatter his formations, including the *volksartillerie* corps. There were no grounds for the rapid withdrawal of the front, such had just happened with LXXXII Corps. Rundstedt could not permit this practice to continue. The field marshal observed that his other armies had successfully resisted equally overwhelming odds.

It is unclear who was in control at First Army when Balck spoke with the headquarters a short while later. First Army said that it could not hold its front, and perhaps not even the West Wall, without the panzer divisions. The acting commander, handed a bag of dung, foreswore any responsibility if the divisions departed. Balck authorized further pull backs across the Saar as far south as Dillingen. After ruminating another two hours, Balck ordered a withdrawal into the West Wall all the way to Saarlautern, and of XIII SS Corps's right wing to tie in.[246] "Screw you," he seemed to be saying to Rundstedt.

Balck's other army—the Nineteenth—had just lost most of Alsace, and Balck had ordered the withdrawal of First Army's right wing. The message from Rundstedt was clear: he, too, had fallen from favor at *OB West*. Balck apparently had decided his days were numbered and that he would do the sane thing, come what may.

Generalleutnant Walter Hahm took charge of LXXXII Corps on 1 December.[247] Hahm was born on 21 December 1894 in Neudorf Sulau. Hahm had remained in the infantry between the wars and risen slowly to the rank of *oberstleutnant* by 1939. When the war broke out, Hahm was an instructor of infantry tactics at the War School in Munich. In December 1940, he had taken command of the 480th Infantry Regiment, in which position he rose to *Oberst* and, in May 1942, to *Generalmajor*. That same month, he took command of the 260th Infantry Division and won plaudits for his performance on the eastern front. Hahm gained the rank of *Generalleutnant* quickly, in January 1943. One month later, he entered the führer reserve. Later that year, he briefly commanded the 389th Infantry Division. Hahm's superiors judged him an outspoken personality, an excellent leader, and so much a loner that he was sometimes hard to handle. He disguised a weak constitution with ferocious energy. He was personally courageous, a wearer of the Knight's Cross, and an uncompromising National Socialist (called by one commander a "fanatic"). Hahm had been assigned to *OB West* in November 1944 before taking command of LXXXII Corps.[248]

American planes bombed settlements all along the Saar on 2 December, and heavy artillery and rocket preparations against the West Wall announced an impending assault. The consequence of Balck's decision to pull back across the Saar was that the Americans penetrated the western half of Saarlautern, where the soldiers tore at each other in fierce and bloody house-to-house fighting. XIII SS Corps managed to stop attacks at St. Avold, but the Americans penetrated the line at the intercorps boundary.

Rundstedt, to his credit, had raised the objections to removing the two panzer divisions with the high command, and he told Balck that the order came from "the highest quarters." He held out the possibility that, in case of disaster, he personally would hold one division in place. The 719th Volksgrenadier Division was arriving to take up positions in the West Wall near Saarlautern, which offered the possibility of again extricating the 21st Panzer Division into reserve.[249]

The 95th Infantry Division entered the center of Saarlautern on 3 December, reached the citadel, and captured intact the old bridge across the Saar. The 559th Volksgrenadier Division, which was defending the city, lost contact with XIII SS Corps on its left, and because the bulk of the division had been destroyed on the west bank of the Saar, most of the bunkers in the West Wall around Dillingen, Fraulautern, and Ensdorf were manned by local *Volksturm* militia. These communities constituted the eastern half of Saarlautern, which had been combined with Saarlouis on the west side in 1936 under the new name. American troops were now only yards from fulfilling Patton's goal of penetrating the West Wall and, conceivably, pressing on to the Rhine.

With the Americans on the east bank, Balck was able to get Rundstedt's approval to counterattack using a *Kampfgruppe* of Panzer Lehr (a counterattack that, for some reason, never occurred), though the field marshal insisted that the division still had to go to Army Group B the next day. Rundstedt was furious that First Army had failed to destroy the bridge in Saarlautern. First Army, he instructed, was to destroy that bridge at all costs. Feuchtinger's 21st Panzer Division was to restore the link between LXXXII and XIII SS Corps.[250]

The counterattack in Saarlautern took the battle to its crescendo, and in the end, it was Feuchtinger and his fire brigade that had to do the job. The leading elements entered Saarlautern on 4 December and were surprised to find the

Americans there, because nobody had thought to inform Feuchtinger that the enemy had crossed the Saar. City fighting requires reserves of manpower that the division no longer had in its line companies, and Feuchtinger had to form two scratch battalions with men from the trains and workshops. Assault troops struck north toward the bridge. American tanks prevented German engineers from blowing up the span, and all the pioneers who tried were killed in action. "Both sides fought to the bitter end," recalled Feuchtinger.[251]

Army Group G provided a strength report for First Army on 4 December. In the format Total (Infantry), the divisions reported their declining frontline strength: 416th Volksgrenadier: 2,400 (1,550); 19th Volksgrenadier: 1,780 (630); 559th Volksgrenadier: 360 (80); 347th Volksgrenadier: 2,600 (800); 36th Volksgrenadier: 3,400 (1,300); 17th SS Panzergrenadier: 4,000 (1,100); 11th Panzer: 3,500 (800); 21st Panzer: 2,180 (200); 25th Panzergrenadier: 2,500 (400); Panzer Lehr: 2,400 (560); An OKH report on ration strength, or total of assigned personnel regardless of military-occupation specialty, for these units listed much higher numbers. Panzer Lehr, for example, counted 12,887 officers and men on its rolls as of 1 December. The daily strength for some of the other divisions on that date included 7,913 for the 416th, 8,054 for the 19th, 8,516 for the 559th, and 10,446 for the 21st Panzer Division. The disparity reflected both the complicated manner in which the Germans reported their divisional strengths (daily/battle/combat) and the disproportionately heavier casualties suffered by frontline troops in comparison to supporting units.

Rundstedt that day dropped the boom. The panzer divisions and artillery corps had to move north as ordered. He did promise to move a heavy-tank destroyer battalion immediately to Saarlautern, however. He also told Balck he would understand any decisions to shorten the front. Balck, however, told First Army that it would fight wherever possible before the West Wall, not in it.[252]

Patton was still tied down in Metz and on 4 December formally ordered III Corps to take over responsibility for containing the remaining forts. The 87th Infantry Division was to relieve the fifth Division.[253] On the fifth, Patton wrote in a letter, "I believe the enemy has nearly reached his breaking point. As a matter of fact, we are stretched pretty thin ourselves. . . ."[254]

The Americans crossed the Saar in battalion strength north and south of Saarlautern on 5 December, and the GIs were able to capture a few bunkers in the West Wall. Strong enemy infantry and tank forces from the 6th Armored and 35th Infantry Divisions struck toward Saargemünd and achieved some break-throughs of the main line of resistance. An unconfirmed report indicated that the 10th Armored and 90th Infantry Divisions were on their way to Saarlautern, and Balck seized on the information to point out to Rundstedt that a break-through there would threaten the flank not only of his army group, but Army Group B as well. It appeared that Third Army intended to penetrate the West Wall at these two points, link up, and push on toward Kaiserslautern. Rundstedt caved, and he authorized that the 11th Panzer Division and one *volksartillerie* corps remain, demanding a daily report as to whether conditions had changed to allow their transfer. The 404th *Volksartillerie* Corps was ordered to replace its sister corps at the seam between LXXXII and XIII SS Corps. Rundstedt reiter-ated his orders that First Army hold fast and criticized First Army for submitting reports that were much more pessimistic than those arriving from hard pressed Nineteenth Army.

Nevertheless, First Army reported that the Americans captured several more bunkers, and Balck threatened to court-martial whomever was respon-sible for letting that happen. He issued an order to his troops: "The West Wall is the final line."

Balck angrily told the 17th SS Panzergrenadier Division that it had fought poorly and that it had plenty of men in the trains to make up its losses. He asked Rundstedt to tell Himmler to bring the division up to snuff or replace it with a division capable of fighting. Simon had a different view and thought that the SS division was defending its ground tenaciously. Balck also got his first look at the 719th Volksgrenadier Division and reported the next day that the men were overage and the artillery was a "museum."

In the midst of all this, *General der Infanterie* Hans von Obstfelder took command of First Army on 5 December.[255] Although Obstfelder had not fought with the panzer generals he was joining in Lorraine, he had earned high marks and numerous decorations on the eastern front for his command of XXIX Corps, particularly during the difficult retreat from the Caucasus in 1943. There, his superiors rated him personally brave, by temperament a soldier, an experienced leader of troops, and a man who stuck to his opinions and decisions. The only criticism offered was that he tended to pay too much attention to minor details.

Obstfelder had just come from command of LXXXVI Corps, which he had held since August 1943. His corps had held the line against Montgomery at Caen, and its unyielding defensive struggle had been one reason Montgomery had spent so long "pivoting on Caen," or "Cane" as the Americans liked to pronounce it. Obstfelder had won high marks for his leadership during the disastrous retreat from Normandy. During October, fighting the British and U.S. 7th Armored Division along the Maas River as part of First Parachute Army, Obstfelder's leadership skills were displayed, as *General der Infanterie*

Günther Blumentritt recalled, "adjusting in accordance with the ever changing situation, withdrawing forces from one place in order to reinforce other points or vice versa. This was a continuous fight with makeshift possibilities and material shortages."[256] He was, it seemed, the perfect general for the occasion.

Obstfelder's evaluation report for December 1944 characterized him as a battle-proven commanding general with fresh ideas, just the characteristics Rundstedt and Balck had found lacking in Knobelsdorff, yet with Knobelsdorff's enthusiasm for action. An earlier review described him as having a direct personality and as a man who spoke his mind. Model, who commanded him during the retreat across France, judged him to have led his corps with certainty and decision, to have set an excellent personal example, and to be a strong man in a crisis. He was assessed repeatedly to be a convinced Nazi.[257]

Obstfelder was the first of a different breed of enemies that would fight Patton in 1945—mainly infantry and artillery generals in place of the panzer generals who had jousted with him thus far. Obstfelder was probably the best of that lot, but he was not to have enough time to make a firm mark on the battle in Lorraine. He would get his chance in the new year, when his resources would make the his current tattered army look positively robust.

The enemy crossed the Saar in LXXXII Corps's zone north of Roden on 6 December and captured Dillingen and Pachten despite the 19th Volksgrenadier Division's best efforts.[258] But perhaps Obstfelder's invigorating leadership had some effect, because for several days his troops held back the Americans and recaptured bunkers lost in the West Wall. On 10 December, Obstfelder had First Army counterattacking to restore the main line of resistance at Dillingen and gained some ground in the zone defended by the 11th Panzer and 25th Panzergrenadier Divisions. Obstfelder also took steps to free up the 21st Panzer Division and 404th *Volksartillerie* Corps. Nineteenth Army provided to First Army *General der Flieger* Erich Petersen's XC Corps headquarters, which took charge of the sector between XIII SS and LXXXIX Corps, including the 11th Panzer and 25th Panzergrenadier Divisions.[259]

Bashing by Patton's armored fist was easing off just as German defenses reached the brink of collapse. The 6th Armored Division suspended operations after 5 December, when its lead elements reached Saargemünd. The 4th Armored Division's attacks on Singling and Bining on 6 December were the division's last in Lorraine.[260] Hahm's Ia, *Oberst* Ludwig *Graf* von Ingelheim, recalled that as of the sixth, the Americans had consolidated their bridgeheads at Dillingen, Saarlautern, Roden, and Ensdorf: "There was an acute danger, both for the corps and for the front of the entire army, that from his extended bridgeheads, the American might launch a thrust to roll up the entire West Wall or to reach Saarbrücken. The enemy would undoubtedly have been successful in an operation of this nature, particularly as no reserves were available and as the 21st Panzer Division, after its unsuccessful attack [in Saarlautern], had been detached and as of 10 December had been transferred to the plains of the Rhine [opposite U.S. Seventh Army]."

First Army was no longer capable of mounting a mobile defense against Third Army, but Patton did not seize the opening. Obstfelder's ability to mount a static defense, however, improved as the 719th Volksgrenadier Division's lead elements arrived and took over the Saarlautern-Roden-Fraulautern sector.[261]

Whatever Rundstedt expected from substituting Obstfelder for Knobelsdorff, by 11 December, the new commanding general sounded just as pessimistic as his predecessor. Ordered to drive home attacks to eliminate the Dillingen bridgehead, Obstfelder objected that it was pointless to set any but the most limited objectives because his forces were inadequate and were too embroiled fighting off constant American attacks to break loose.[262]

Balck thought that the enemy had begun his final "great offensive" to reach the Rhine on the eleventh when at least five infantry regiments and 120 tanks hit the front defended by XC Corps's 11th Panzer and 25th Panzergrenadier Divisions. "The 11th Panzer Division, which reports the hardest day of fighting since its deployment on the western front, is now mainly an infantry formation and is near the end of its strength," recorded the army-group war diary. "It is only holding its front through unrelenting counterattacks with its [few] panzers." The Americans, however, suffered heavily, too, and the attacks the next day were less forceful.[263]

While fighting raged along the West Wall from Saarlautern to Saargemünd, Balck's left wing opposite Seventh Army, where the Americans were driving north parallel to the Rhine to reach the West Wall where it ran from the Rhine along the Lauter River west toward Saarbrücken, became his main problem. Balck personally spent most of his time visiting his units on that front for the next several days.[264]

The Big Issue Is Decided

On 12 December, the struggle that Patton did not even know he was waging—over whether the preconditions would hold for Hitler to launch his Ardennes offensive—ended, and Patton had lost. Hitler that day ended his hour-long address to the German generals, from division upward, who would command his legions in the Battle of the Bulge with the statement, "I am determined to carry through the operation, taking into account the great risks, even if the enemy attacks on both sides of Metz and the looming attack toward the Ruhr lead to the loss of significant land and defensive positions."[265] OKW had little concern that Patton could do much more harm. Jodl expected him to be drawn to the Ardennes, and if he persisted in attacking the West Wall, reserves being accumulated for Operation North Wind in Alsace were available to stop him.[266]

The panzer generals, even the dismissed Knobelsdorff, had done their job. Now it was up to others to determine whether Germany still had hope of any outcome other than unconditional surrender.

The campaign continued for the span of another week, the matter of control over the West Wall remaining at issue. Himmler took command of a new Army Group Upper Rhine, which left Army Group G with only First Army and a corps in Alsace.[267]

By 14 December, XIII SS Corps had been thrown back across the Blies, and the next day the enemy followed.

On the fifteenth, Balck faced the real prospect that Third Army was going to puncture the West Wall after all. First Army reported that the Americans had gotten all the way through the bunker line near Saarlautern at three spots. Local reserves were containing the penetrations, but Obstfelder worried that the Americans would reinforce the sector. Balck firmly agreed and told Rundstedt as much.

Rundstedt had good reason to doubt the Americans were going to still care very much about Saarlautern in the near future. He told Balck to make preparations to pull the 11th Panzer Division into reserve near Saarlautern in the event of a withdrawal into the West Wall. He also was to regroup the 21st Panzer Division, for which some fifty tanks were on the way from the Reich, and return all detached pieces of the 25th Panzergrenadier Division to it so that it could effectively cover the withdrawal of the 11th Panzer Division. Finally, Balck understood that he was to pull his entire left wing back to the West Wall the next day, though Rundstedt later complained that he had meant on 18 December.[268]

And, on the battlefield, events did not turn out as badly as they might have. Sheltering in excellent positions amid the hills behind the Blies, the 17th SS Panzergrenadier Division held XIII SS Corps's line until Third Army abandoned the attack on 16 December.

At first, 16 December looked very much the same as the day before on LXXXII Corps's front. The Americans at Dillingen were threatening to crack through the West Wall, and at Saarlautern they were attempting to expand the small holes they already had created. Obstfelder, however, was counterattacking with the 19th Volksgrenadier Division, which had managed to rebuild somewhat during a few days of quiet along its front, supported by the 719th Volksgrenadier Division and the massed artillery of LXXXII Corps. Balck's left wing withdrew into the West Wall. With the first news of the Ardennes offensive came a *Führerbefehl* that Balck was to send the 11th Panzer Division north as soon as it withdrew from the line.[269]

Balck on 16 December issued an order to his troops: Army Group B had gone on the offensive that morning in the Ardennes! The mission of his army group was to ensure there was no penetration of First Army's front that would endanger the rear of Army Group B, to tie down as many divisions as possible, and to report immediately any sign that American divisions were heading north. "The West Wall is the last line. We will die here. There is no more retreat."[270]

The phone rang at Patton's headquarters that night, and Bradley's chief of staff ordered Third Army to rush the 10th Armored Division to the Ardennes. Patton, who had been planning a massive assault on the West Wall in a few days' time, protested that loss of the division would preclude XX Corps's attack and disrupt the entire offensive. Bradley got on the horn. Patton had no choice. The 10th Armored Division was desperately needed by VIII Corps.[271]

The American threat to the West Wall in Lorraine had just evaporated.

GERMAN CONCLUSIONS

Balck attributed First Army's success in stopping Third Army's best efforts to breach the West Wall to several factors: His men had fought with skill and courage. He had been allowed to wage a mobile battle free of orders to stand in place and hold. The ancient fortresses of Metz had bought him five days' grace. Finally, the American commanders had never exploited their successes. Balck and his staff concluded that the Americans intended instead to use their overwhelming material superiority to literally destroy the German field units.[272]

Emmerich held the same opinion. "The front remained intact, and the enemy was unable to gain a decisive victory. He was unable to use any of the numerous critical situations for decisive blows. His hesitant advance after a forceful penetration helped considerably in giving [First Army] the chance to effect timely countermeasures, although its forces were stretched to the limits."[273]

Max Simon concluded, "XIII SS Corps did carry out its mission. . . . The American offensive started on 8 November 1944. At that time, the corps held a front on the general line Corny on the Mosel-Château-Salins, seventy kilometers from Saarbrücken as the crow flies. On 16 November, when I assumed command, the front had been pressed back about twenty kilometers. . . . Five weeks later, on 15 December 1944, the U.S. divisions in general still were ten kilometers from the West Wall."[274]

To the many veterans of the Battle of Kursk, the defense of Rzhev, the defensive struggle along the Chir, or a host of other battles similar to or larger in scope than the Lorraine campaign, the result almost certainly looked like a win for German arms against overwhelming odds. As the Soviets had managed at Kursk, the German panzer generals had prevented the enemy from disrupting Germany's planned strategic offensive and denied him his operational and strategic objectives, penetrating the West Wall and reaching the Rhine. They doubtless believed, with good reason, that they had beaten Patton.

Patton might even have agreed. He recalled that "while my attack was going forward by short leaps, it was not very brilliant. . . ."[275]

Balck later wrote, "When the Ardennes offensive broke out, the Americans stopped their attacks and pulled back to the Maginot Line, and we could release our breath. We had held for four weeks longer than anticipated [because of the delay in launching the Ardennes offensive], and we felt that we had done the impossible."[276]

Hitler evidently judged that Balck had commanded as well as conditions allowed, though some sources allude darkly to a plot by Himmler to have Balck removed. With the crisis over in Lorraine, Balck on 23 December left Army Group G and went back east, where he took command of Army Group Balck, consisting of Sixth Army and two Hungarian armies at Budapest. No accounts by officers who were at the high command, nor the OKW war diary, suggest that Hitler was angry with Balck over the loss of Alsace, and Balck would not have received such a sensitive command without Hitler's support.[277]

TWELVE

Battle of the Bulge: Patton's Greatest Moment

JODL HAD HELD a highly secret meeting at Model's Army Group B headquarters on 3 November to give commanders a briefing on Hitler's plan for a counteroffensive through the thin American line in the Ardennes, aimed at driving to Antwerp and splitting the Western Allies. In the north, the SS-heavy Sixth Panzer Army (later renamed Sixth SS Panzer Army) was to strike toward the Meuse River and Antwerp. In the center, the Fifth Panzer Army was to attack toward Brussels. The Seventh Army was to push forward in the south to reel out a line of infantry divisions to protect the flank of the operation.

Manteuffel, still commanding Fifth Panzer Army on the Aachen front, had learned a thing or two about Patton's speed. "I don't think we need anticipate strong reaction coming from the north on the east bank of the Meuse," he observed. "But I am rather worried by the possibility of strong enemy counteraction from the south." Rundstedt, who expected that four infantry and five or six armored divisions would at some point attack from the south and southwest, would have agreed, though he also anticipated a strong reaction from the north.

"General Brandenberger will have six infantry divisions and a panzer division in his Seventh Army to cover the southern and southwestern flanks," Jodl reassured him.

"Yes, I know, but I have to anticipate strong enemy forces—maybe even the bulk of his forces—in action in the Bastogne area by the evening of the third day of our attack."[1]

Manteuffel did not mention Patton, but it was clear of whom he was thinking. For once, a German commander overestimated Patton—but not by much.

Unlike the team of commanding generals who had long known one another before battling Patton in Lorraine, the German commanders he would face in the Ardennes in most cases were scarcely acquainted. They were a mix of panzer and infantry generals who, to a near certainty, did not instinctively share a common view of how to wage battle. It is likely that these factors exerted a certain unseen friction on the German execution of the struggle.

General der Panzertruppe Erich Brandenberger held a rank that did not really reflect the course of his career, which had mainly been in the artillery and infantry. His only panzer command had been that of the 8th Panzer Division, which he led on the eastern front from February 1941 until January 1943. His personnel reviews had been positive, but lacked the "walks on water" verbiage that many successful panzer generals received. He was, however, rated a firm National Socialist. Brandenberger had fought under Kurt von der Chevallerie's command as part of LIX Corps, including at Velikiye Luki, and had filled in for Chevallerie for two months in early 1943. Coincidentally, he then replaced Hans von Obstfelder in command of XXIX Corps in May 1943. Even the military hierarchy was perplexed: his promotion from *Generalleutnant* in August 1943 had mistakenly been to the rank of *General der Artillerie*, an error quickly corrected.

It was at the helm of XXIX Corps that Brandenberger probably caught Hitler's eye. *Generaloberst* Karl-Adolf Hollidt said in his November 1943 evaluation, "General Brandenberger commanded XXIX Corps since the end of May in the position warfare on the Mius and then the defensive battles back to the Dniepr. Gifted militarily, full of foresight, and very active, he filled his divisions with action and passion. A very experienced combat leader, even in the worst circumstances he always improvised and mastered the situation. Excellent National Socialist behavior. . . ."

As noted earlier, that was the type of general Hitler had wanted on the western front as the disastrous summer of 1944 unfolded. Brandenberger had taken charge of Seventh Army on 31 August.[2] With shell-rimmed glasses and graying hair tending toward baldness, Brandenberger had the air of a steady, careful worker, rather than a flashy or brilliant one.[3]

Brandenberger's Seventh Army began the Battle of the Bulge with three corps. Instead of the panzer division—actually the 25th Panzergrenadier Division, as things turned out—Jodl had promised, Brandenberger was to receive the Führer Grenadier Brigade after the beginning of the offensive.[4] Patton had influenced

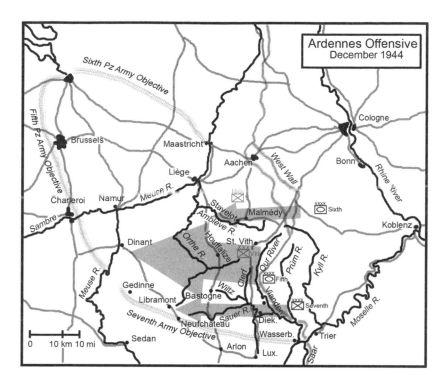

his own fate by tying the 25th Division down near Metz, and he would not have to face it in the Ardennes in a timely fashion.

General der Infanterie Baptist Kniess's LXXXV Corps included *Oberst* Ludwig-Sebastian Heilmann's 5th Airborne Division, which was to make Seventh Army's main effort adjacent to Fifth Panzer Army, and *Oberst* Erich Schmidt's 352nd Volksgrenadier Division.

Kniess, born 14 April 1885 in Grünstadt, had entered the imperial army as an officer candidate in July 1906. He had joined the Bavarian 5th Infantry Regiment, with which he served throughout the Great War, rising to the rank of *Hauptmann*. Kniess had married but been childless. He remained with the Reichswehr between the wars and by 1935 commanded the 63rd Infantry Regiment. Kniess took command of the 215th Infantry Division in August 1939 and led it in the western campaign and the initial onslaught against the Soviet Union, where he had proved a superb division commander in the defense, but been judged to lack the "big picture" he needed in the attack. Kniess had the good fortune to be named commanding general of the LXVI Reserve Corps in southern France just before the horrible winter of 1942. He had remained on occupation duty until the Dragoon landings, and he had been judged superior for his command of LXXXV Corps (from July 1944) during the long fighting retreat from the Riviera to the Vosges Mountains. His superiors rated him an optimistic, active, energetic, and passionate officer with a solid military education and good grasp of tactics. He was also deemed a committed Nazi. Kniess reminded an American interviewer the summer after the war of "the traditional absentminded professor."[5]

LXXXV Corps's headquarters had shifted to the Ardennes from the Belfort area opposite French First Army only in late November, so Kniess and his staff had little experience fighting Americans, even though they had been on the western front. Kniess had never met his division commanders before.[6]

The 5th Airborne Division mostly consisted of recently converted Luftwaffe ground personnel with no infantry experience at all, and it suffered from inadequate training, inexperienced officers, and inadequate motor transport. It had only just reorganized from September to late November after being smashed in France, and Heilmann considered his division to be only category IV—suitable for limited defensive operations. Only the 15th Airborne Regiment, pioneer battalion, and assault-gun brigade were manned by trained troops, and they, therefore, constituted Heilmann's striking power. The division was twice the size of a comparable volksgrenadier unit, with some 20,000 men and thirty assault guns, as compared with the 10,000 men and twelve assault guns. The only advantage held by the latter was in the number of field-artillery pieces: fifty-four compared to thirty-six for Heilmann's division. When Heilmann complained about the division's training shortcomings to Model, the field marshal had replied that the airborne would get by on "audacity."

Heilmann, born on 9 August 1903 in Würzburg, had joined the Reichswehr's 21st Infantry Regiment in 1921 as a twelve-year enlisted man. He had participated in the Poland and western campaigns with the 27th Infantry Division and then volunteered for the airborne. Promoted to *major*, he had taken command of a battalion of the 3rd Airborne Regiment in November 1940. He had been part of the large airborne operation on Crete in May 1941 and then led his regiment on the front near Leningrad. In July 1943, he and his regiment had flown to Sicily, but they had fought Montgomery and not Patton. There, he had been known to his troops as "King Ludwig" and shown himself to be courageous, but also arrogant, stubborn, and opinionated. He had fought in the bloody battle of Cassino in Italy, by which time he had earned the Knight's Cross with Oak Leaves and Swords.[7]

Heilmann was a seasoned veteran, but he had never commanded at the division level before. Heilmann had attended one of the briefings given by Hitler before the offensive and come away skeptical. "As I personally did enough fighting while continuously employed at the Italian front," he recalled, "I started the work with the purpose to save blood by using my experience gained in fights."

Schmidt's 352nd Volksgrenadier Division had rebuilt after its battles from Omaha Beach back across France to the West Wall. Its poorly trained replacements were drawn from the navy and Luftwaffe. The division had fewer assault guns than prescribed, so Brandenberger attached to it a towed antitank battalion.[8]

General der Infanterie Franz Beyer's LXXX Corps included *Generalmajor* Kurt Möhring's 276th Volksgrenadier Division. *Generalleutnant* Franz Sensfuss's 212th Volksgrenadier Division was to arrive after the start of the offensive. The former had no assault guns and the latter had but four.[9]

Beyer, born on 27 May 1892 in Bautzen, had joined the imperial navy in 1911, and he served on battleships during the Great War. Beyer, an easy man to like, had entered the army from the police, where he had served between the wars, in 1935. Beyer had commanded the 331st Infantry Division in the east, including during the fierce winter fighting around Velikiye Luki, from early 1942 through January 1943, where he had served in Brandenberger's LIX Corps and earned his commander's praise. He had then taken charge of the 44th Reich's Grenadier Division *Hoch- und Deutschmeister* in Italy through January 1944, fighting in the Cassino sector prior to the epic battles to defend the town. Beyer had been awarded the Iron and Knight's Crosses and was considered personally courageous by his commanders. Most of his superiors, however, had found him unimpressive as a leader, albeit well educated in the military arts, and best suited to division command. He had not been involved in a major battle while in Italy, though he had filled in as commander for four separate corps on the eastern front over several months before taking command of LXXX Corps in August. Now, perhaps because he was considered a convinced National Socialist, he was expected to lead a corps in an offensive.[10]

General der Kavallerie Edwin *Graf* von Rothkirch und Trach's LIII Corps headquarters, just activated in November, was held in reserve near Trier. It was to be used when Seventh Army's line became overextended past Bastogne.[11]

Seventh Army's mission was to protect the left flank of the panzer armies, and the initial orders Brandenberger had received on 6 November anticipated that this flank would extend in an arc westward from Bastogne through Namur to Brussels and Antwerp.[12] Brandenberger assessed that he had about half the manpower necessary to execute his mission successfully. Replacements and reserves would be scarce.[13] Guderian agreed that "this army lacked the mobile strength necessary for carrying out its difficult assignment."[14]

The German military leadership clearly was not all that concerned with Patton in the big scheme of things. Hitler and the high command, according to Brandenberger's account, believed, based on past American behavior, that the enemy would deploy reinforcements along the Meuse to block any further advance rather than attack the German flank. Army Group B's plan was that Seventh Army would establish a blocking line from Gedinne through Libramont to Wasserbillig.

Brandenberger disagreed. At some point, as Manteuffel had so baldly said, Brandenberger had to expect an American counterattack from the south. Brandenberger recalled, "The fact that these forces would probably be commanded by General Patton (who, in the Battle of France, had given proof of his extraordinary skill in armored warfare, which he conducted according to the fundamental German conception) made it quite likely that the enemy would direct a heavy punch against the deep flank of the German forces scheduled to be in the vicinity of Bastogne." All available troops in Alsace-Lorraine were likely to participate in the operation, which Brandenberger expected to begin no earlier than 20 December. Brandenberger asked that he be given more mobile forces—and large amounts of ammunition—so that he would be able to mount a flexible defense, but the only answer he received was that some mobile divisions would be available in OKW reserve for temporary use if necessary.[15]

Patton's G-2, Col. Oscar Koch, and his staff were the only Allied intelligence officers who correctly anticipated Hitler's Ardennes offensive in scope and rough timing, albeit not the exact date. Koch had been carefully watching information about the growing German strategic reserve opposite U.S. First Army largely because Patton was planning another attack to break through the West Wall for 20 December, and the large forces concentrating to the north—some as close as the interarmy boundary between Third and First Armies—posed a potential threat to the left flank of any penetration by Patton's men.

Koch formally briefed Patton on his assessment on 9 December. Patton listened and then rose to his feet. "We'll be in a position to meet whatever happens," he told his staff. And thus, Third Army became the only Allied headquarters to begin planning for its eventual role in the Battle of the Bulge.[16]

THROWING THE DICE

Hitler's last great offensive opened at 0530 hours on 16 December with a ninety-minute artillery barrage by Sixth Panzer Army, soon joined by similar preparatory fires in the zones of the two other attacking armies. The leading infantry attacked out of the snow and fog a short while later. The divisions attacking along the boundary between Sixth and Fifth Panzer Armies drove up the seam between V and VIII Corps, the most successful initial thrust and one that, by 18 December, led to the envelopment of two regiments of the 106th Infantry Division and a breakthrough in the Losheim gap. Hermann Priess commanded the I SS Panzer Corps, part of Sixth Panzer Army, which was to conduct the main penetration of the entire offensive with the 1st and 12th SS Panzer Divisions, once the three infantry divisions temporarily assigned to his corps broke through the American line. Elements of Priess's corps racked up the biggest initial gains, *Kampfgruppe* Peiper reaching Stavelot halfway to the Meuse, and the 1st SS *Leibstandarte* Panzer Division breaking through north of St Vith.[17]

Other than making relatively small jabs at Third Army in Lorraine and First Army in the Netherlands, the German commanding generals in the Ardennes had not conducted an offensive against the Americans before. To some extent, the eastern-front panzer generals tried to apply lessons from the east. Priess recalled, "It was believed that that the tactic of cutting off enemy strong points and continuing our advance—which had proved so successful in the east—would be relatively unknown to the Americans, and that therefore these strongpoints would not resist for very long. That the course of the offensive proved the contrary to be the case is true."[18] Jodl confirmed that standing orders were to bypass strongpoints, though he did not make specific allusion to the east-front experience.[19]

Bradley, on 18 December, asked Patton to come to Luxembourg to discuss something Patton wasn't going to like. When Patton arrived, he was surprised to see how large the German penetration was. Bradley asked what he could do. Patton had already discussed with Maj. Gen. John Millikin turning his III Corps northward if it became necessary. Patton told Bradley he could have the 4th Armored Division concentrating in Longwy by midnight, the 80th Infantry Division on the road to Luxembourg the next morning, and the 26th Infantry Division under way within twenty-four hours.[20]

German signals intelligence on 19 December detected two American divisions being withdrawn from the Metz-Longwy sector and suggested that they might be headed toward Bastogne.[21] Patton, meanwhile, met with Eisenhower and senior Allied commanders at Verdun, where Eisenhower told him to take over the battle in Luxembourg and to make a strong attack with six divisions. Patton replied that he would attack strongly with three divisions on the twenty-second, because to wait longer would cost him the element of surprise. Ike agreed, and he arranged for Sixth Army Group to take over Patton's front as far north as Saarlautern.[22]

It was Patton's finest hour.

Let us consider the remarkable good luck enjoyed by George Patton. His superb G-2, almost alone among Allied intelligence officers, had prepared him to respond at the moment of crisis. While First Army had battled the huge armored weight of Fifth and Sixth Panzer Armies for a week, Patton would initially face the weak Seventh Army, which had not even a panzergrenadier division to oppose him. As we shall see, by the time Patton gained real contact with the enemy in the Ardennes, most German commanders had concluded that the offensive was *already* spent. Patton once again would attack his enemy when the other fellow was shifting to his back foot.

Patton was with Bradley on the nineteenth when Eisenhower called to say that he was giving Montgomery operational control over U.S. First and Ninth Armies north of the growing bulge because Bradley's telephone links with them were tenuous. Though that meant that Patton was Bradley's only horse in the race, according to Patton, Bradley never meddled in decisions regarding Third Army. Whatever the enemy commanders were going to face from the south, it would be formulated in Patton's mind.

Patton doubted that the Germans knew Third Army was on the move, and he expected to achieve surprise with Millikin's III Corps (4th Armored and 26th and 80th Infantry Divisions). VIII Corps, of course, was in the thick of the fight already on what would be Patton's left.[23]

PATTON HOLDS, BUT DOES NOT CONQUER

Bastogne, Bastogne. Of all the fierce American defenses in the course of the Battle of the Bulge, the one at Bastogne was probably the most crucial. It was Patton's arrival that turned Bastogne into a critical battle, however, because before he came, the Germans viewed the town as a mere irritant that they had bypassed without great difficulty.[24]

Brandenberger's mission was to bypass the strategic road hub to the south, while Lüttwitz's XLVII Panzer Corps captured Bastogne. The Fifth Panzer Army's advance had been held up by a tenacious American defense of St. Vith and Seventh Army's by difficult river crossings, but the 5th Airborne Division, on 19 December, reached Harlange, some distance to the southeast of Bastogne. The reinforced pioneer battalion hooked northward and surrounded a group from the 28th Infantry and 9th Armored Divisions, netting the paratroopers several hundred prisoners and some Sherman tanks, several of which the engineers were able to put into service. Crewmen from the assault guns manned the M4s, and though they were not capable of coordinated mobile operations, they strengthened the German spearhead.

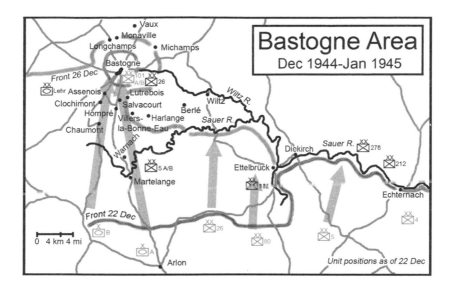

American resistance south of Bastogne appeared to have been smashed, though the 352nd Volksgrenadier Division faced local American counterattacks farther east in the heights around Diekirch, where the Americans still held a bridgehead north of the Sauer River. The only disappointment for Brandenberger was that Beyer's LXXX Corps, on his left, though it had progressed steadily southward against the 4th Infantry Division, had not gained its assigned objectives, leaving a very thin cushion for Fifth Panzer Army's flank.[25] Indeed, Beyer concluded that his corps had achieved only its first day's objectives by the nineteenth. The advance was, therefore, inadequate to enable him to defend effectively against a counterattack from the south, and losses had been too heavy for him to continue offensive operations. And an American counterstroke was imminent.[26]

The Führer Grenadier Brigade, Brandenberger's only mobile formation, arrived in the Eschdorf area on 20 December. The brigade was a complete mess. The panzers, assault guns, and panzergrenadiers had apparently never worked together before. On the twenty-first, it declared itself unfit to enter battle. Brandenberger would get little effective use out of it until 8 January, after putting a new commander in place.[27]

The paratroopers south of Bastogne had a peaceful day on the twentieth and advanced westward without hindrance. The division "was moving fast and just kept on going," recalled corps commanding general Kniess. Its speed was stretching his south-facing line very thin. The 352nd Volksgrenadier Division captured Diekirch, where a damaged bridge was still able to support the transfer of heavy weapons to support infantry that crossed to the south bank of the Sauer. Kniess was already impressing Brandenberger and Model with his skillful leadership and ability to improvise, wiping away the weak reputation he had earned in the east as an offensive commander.

While the situation looked bright for Kniess's corps on the twentieth, XLVII Panzer Corps's attack on Bastogne was not going well. The 101st Airborne Division had taken up residence, and American tanks and tank destroyers were holding up the advance at several villages north and east of the town.

Brandenberger had no support from reconnaissance aircraft, but ground probes revealed no evidence of fresh enemy forces approaching Bastogne from the south. There were, however, indications that tanks and elements of the 5th Infantry Division were arriving in the zone of the 4th Infantry Division, opposite LXXX Corps at the eastern end of his line, which was unexpected.

Brandenberger was uncertain what the appearance of the first American forces from the south against his left wing meant. It suggested that Patton planned to cut into the German salient at its base. But where were the 4th and 6th Armored Divisions, the enemy's main tank reserve? They might still be heading for Bastogne.[28]

This same day, Sepp Dietrich, commanding the Sixth Panzer Army, which had been jammed to a stop on the northern shoulder of the Bulge, privately concluded that the Ardennes offensive had failed.[29] Jodl, too, viewed the day as critical, because fresh American divisions were arriving from First Army's VII Corps: "We had to turn north, meet the Allied attack, and try to take the Elsenborn Ridge to avoid being crushed." It was Hodges who first forced the Germans to shift their forward momentum to a flank battle.[30]

ENTER PATTON

The 5th Airborne Division continued its advance on 21 December and turned one regiment to face south to protect the Sauer crossings. Brandenberger met Lüttwitz in Berlé, where Lüttwitz informed him that Bastogne was surrounded. He had demanded that the garrison surrender, and he expected the Americans to capitulate soon. It was true that the panzer corps was well behind schedule on its drive to the Meuse, but the enemy to the west appeared defeated. Lüttwitz was optimistic that he could make up time once Bastogne fell.

American pressure against LXXX Corps was so heavy, though, that Brandenberger had no doubt that Third Army was arriving. The day marked the turning point for Beyer's corps. The Germans fell back slowly over the next four days, launching counterattacks where necessary to maintain the integrity of the front. Its mission was simply to fix the enemy in place through constant battle.[31]

Back near Bastogne, Brandenberger brought his third corps headquarters into the line for the first time on 22 December, when he placed the right wing of the overextended LXXXV Corps under the control of *General der Kavallerie* Rothkirch's LIII Corps. This meant that Rothkirch commanded the 5th Airborne Division and the Führer Grenadier Brigade, while only the 352nd Volksgrenadier Division remained under LXXXV Corps.[32]

A trim five feet eleven inches tall, with brown eyes and steely gray hair, Rothkirch had been born on 1 November 1888 in Militsch, Silesia, and joined the imperial army's 17th Dragoon Regiment in March 1908. He served with his regiment in the Great War until becoming an ordnance officer in June 1917. Rothkirch in 1922 married Albertine *Gräfin* von Schaumburg. Rothkirch had served with the cavalry between the wars, rising to command a mounted regiment, and competed internationally with Germany's equestrian team. In 1939, as an *Oberst*, he became the commanding officer of the fortress at Breslau, an odd turn of events that took him far from the path of mobile warfare. One month later, Rothkirch was named commanding officer of the 442nd Infantry Division and promoted to *Generalmajor*. In November 1940, he had moved to command the 365th Field High Command in Krakow, followed the next year by command of the 330th Infantry Division, which fought on the eastern front. In October 1943, Rothkirch had become military governor of White Ruthenia. He had succeeded in all his assignments and in December 1943 had risen to his present rank. But Rothkirch had never before commanded a corps in battle.[33]

Rothkirch knew full well that monstrous nature of the regime he served. He was caught on tape by British intelligence while a prisoner of war, talking about what he had seen in the east. "Let me tell you, the gassings are by no means the worst," he said. "To start with, people dug their own graves, then the firing squad arrived with Tommy-guns and shot them down. Many of them weren't dead, and a layer of earth was shoveled in between. They had packers there who packed the bodies in, because they fell in too soon. The SS did that. I knew an SS leader there quite well, and he said: 'Would you like to photograph a shooting? They are always shot in the morning—but if you like, we still have some and we can shoot them in the afternoon sometime.'"[34]

Brandenberger recalled, "[22 December] represented from a tactical and organizational point of view the turning point in the conduct of the offensive by Seventh Army. On this day, the last offensive successes occurred on the one hand;

on the other, a striking change occurred in the enemy situation. The flank attack of Third American Army, under General Patton, began to make itself felt."[35] It was also the day that the skies cleared enough that the besiegers of Bastogne suffered under an increased number of attacks by the dreaded *jabos*.[36]

The day started well when the 5th Airborne Division captured Martelange, on the Sauer. *Oberst* Heilmann met with Rothkirch, his new corps commander, and told him that he planned to send his reconnaissance elements westward to Libramont and then to advance in that direction. Rothkirch fully expected an attack from the south at any time, and he told Heilmann to be careful. Heilmann decided to heed Rothkirch's words and ordered his men to build a defensive line instead of pressing on. The paratroopers started constructing strongpoints along the north bank of the river, precisely where they had to be to deal with Third Army when it arrived.

Behind them, the Panzer Lehr Division rolled westward as it bypassed Bastogne and drove toward St. Hubert. Heilmann encountered Panzer Lehr's commanding general Fritz Bayerlein, who told him he thought everything was developing just fine. *General der Panzertruppe* Heinrich *Freiherr* von Lüttwitz, commanding XLVII Panzer Corps, expected Bayerlein and the 2nd Panzer Division to reach the Meuse by Christmas Eve. This day, he had no worries about his southern flank, but was concerned that the slow progress of LVIII Panzer Corps to his right would leave his spearhead vulnerable on that flank. *Generalmajor* Heinz Kokott's 26th Volksgrenadier Division—one of the best new-type divisions, with seasoned eastern front officers and NCOs, and trained as an assault division—had taken charge of the siege of Bastogne, though Lüttwitz was skeptical it was strong enough to capture the town.

That evening, word arrived that unidentified enemy troops were advancing toward Martelange from the south.

The 352nd Volksgrenadier Division, meanwhile, was pushing southward and was almost on its objectives. Then the grenadiers ran into the 80th Infantry Division and parts of the 10th Armored Division. The Americans flanked and surrounded the 915th Regiment, and the rest of the division reeled back to a bridgehead at Ettelbrück. The 915th Regiment received orders to fight its way out to the northeast, but most of the regiment never escaped the trap.[37]

The first American blow to the 352nd Volksgrenadier Division had ended its move southward and caused numerous casualties and loss of materiel. Nevertheless, LXXXV Corps, using a regiment of the just arriving 79th Volksgrenadier Division and elements of the Führer Grenadier Brigade, managed to hold onto the Sauer River line.[38]

III Corps had advanced an average of seven miles during the day, which was less than Patton had expected. He consoled himself by thinking that it is always difficult to get an offensive rolling and anticipated greater progress the next day. The Germans, he thought, would need at least thirty-six hours to react.[39] Patton was underestimating the opposing commanders.

Holding the Barricade

The 5th Airborne Division had the job of stopping Patton's drive to Bastogne, which Brandenberger calculated was his opponent's only plausible objective. The division had suffered few casualties thus far, morale was high, and the men exhibited clear enthusiasm. Heilmann's career had been dominated by operations involving fast-moving advances (Poland, France) or taking a key point and holding it against all comers (Crete, Russia, Cassino). He had rapidly advanced to this place, and now he had to hold it. If that were possible, Heilmann was just the man for the job.

Brandenberger judged that any chance of success hinged on his artillery and antitank assets. He already had reinforced the division with *Volksartillerie* battalions and shifted more guns from LXXXV Corps to LIII Corps. He concentrated his assault guns and antitank guns on the division's right wing, where the most probable route of American attack was to be found.

The icy blast of the approaching storm first stung the 5th Airborne Division on 22 December, when the leading task force of the 4th Armored Division's CCA arrived at Martelange. Heilmann's 13th Regiment was still mopping up somewhere back near Wiltz, and he faced the prospect of trying to block an armored thrust on a fifteen-mile front with but two regiments and fifteen operational assault guns. His experience in Italy told him such a defense would be unsuccessful. His joy was, therefore, probably bounded when a message arrived informing him that he had been promoted to *Generalmajor*.

A lone company of paratroopers from the 15th Airborne Regiment held Martelange and offered determined resistance. Overmatched, the paratroopers finally slipped away at 0300 on 23 December. While they stalled the enemy, Heilmann set up strongpoints on both sides of the highway to Bastogne to prevent a breakthrough. He concentrated his assault guns in the 15th Airborne Regiment's zone.

When the American armor crossed the Sauer at Martelange on a newly laid Bailey bridge later on the twenty-third, the paratroopers—whom the Americans admiringly called "fanatical, tenacious, and daring"—and the concentration of antitank fire power frustrated every advance. When the Americans finally cleared Warnach after a heavy artillery bombardment and pressed on into the woods to the north, the paratroopers reoccupied Warnach behind them.

The 26th Volksgrenadier Division got its first word of trouble at Chaumont, when some paratroopers who had broken and run showed up in Hompré, where Kokott had his headquarters. Kokott's staff got the stragglers under control, turned several artillery batteries located there around to fire southward, organized a defensive line out of his replacement battalion and other odds and ends, and attached to the battle group four Jagdtiger heavy tank destroyers that happened to be in the area. Kokott ordered the paratroopers back to Chaumont and sent the four Jagdtigers with them.

As things turned out, German paratroopers in Chaumont gave CCB an even harder time than at Warnach. They greeted the Americans one mile south of town with a counterattack organized in depth and supported by twenty-two panzers, artillery, and antitank guns. The panzers appear to have been the assault guns and the four Jagdtigers that Kokott had sent. The attack brought the Americans to a stop a thousand yards short of town. Panzers worked down the column's flanks, and the paratroopers poured fire into their ranks from the buildings and the woods on both flanks. About 1700, the Americans retreated to high ground south of town. The commanding officer of the 8th Tank Battalion reported that he had faced the heaviest fire in his experience. That night, Kokott deployed mines, panzers, and antitank guns from the 901st Panzergrenadier Regiment—attached from the Panzer Lehr Division—south of Bastogne to slow the 4th Armored Division's advance into his rear should Heilmann be unable to hold out.

"The advances for the day were not impressive," recalled Patton. Rather than accelerating his advance, the Germans had held his divisions to gains of between two and five miles.

Nevertheless, army chief of staff Guderian concluded on the twenty-third that the offensive no longer had any chance of achieving a great success. The next day, he would propose that Hitler extract as many resources as possible and send them to the eastern front (making such suggestions was his responsibility as army chief of staff), where German estimates indicated they were outnumbered eleven to one in infantry and seven to one in tanks. Hitler would refuse Guderin's proposal.

The climactic battle for Patton and Brandenberger in the Bulge commenced on 24 December. The 5th Airborne Division in general held its front, withdrawing in good order. To Brandenberger, it looked like the 4th Armored Division was still closing up its ranks from the rear, in part because CCB stood pat following its beating the day before at Chaumont. Patton viewed the day as "very discouraging."

Father Christmas delivered to the paratroopers a full-blown attack by 120 American tanks, well supported by artillery and infantry. The skies had cleared, and *jabos* roamed over the battlefield, pouncing on columns of German vehicles. The Americans captured Chaumont and advanced to Hompré. In general, the defenses held; however, losses in men and equipment were heavy, and the 5th Airborne Division's replacement battalions had great difficulty moving men forward over the snow-cloaked and forested hills. The 26th Volksgrenadier Division at Bastogne was still engaged in fruitless efforts to capture the town and, after suffering monstrous casualties in a final, all-out assault, was, in Kokott's eyes, completely burned out. Lüttwitz, who had been extremely worried for days about his right flank, suddenly faced a potential crisis on his left.

The American 2nd Armored Division engaged Panzer Lehr at the exposed tip of XLVII Panzer Corps's salient on Christmas Day. Lüttwitz joined the ranks of senior generals who had concluded that the great gamble had failed. This would be the high-water mark of the offensive, and Patton had not yet substantially influenced the battle. That was about to change, and Patton would have the advantage of working with the reversed momentum of a receding tide.

Brandenberger begged for the 9th Volksgrenadier Division to be sent up from OKW reserve to reinforce his collapsing front, but was disappointed. He was unsurprised to learn, therefore, that the 4th Armored Division's Combat Command Reserve, on 26 December, punched through the 5th Airborne Division and Kokott's encircling ring to link up with the hard-fighting American paratroopers in Bastogne. American tanks and infantry had overrun the headquarters of two battalions of the 15th Airborne Regiment and captured both commanding officers, and Heilmann considered his 14th Regiment to be nearly destroyed. Kokott's account indicates that the paratroopers' line gave way, and the first word the 26th Division or higher command had of the penetration was when the Americans brushed aside Kokott's small security force in Clochimont. The commanding officer of the 39th Fusilier Regiment called Kokott with the news and concluded, "Some ten to twelve tanks in a thick bunch—all guns firing—ran through and over the blocking line at Assenois and broke through to Bastogne!" The American spearhead also penetrated into the rear area of the 26th Volksgrenadier Division's 39th Fusilier Regiment and chanced upon artillery positions at Salvacourt and La Lune. The gunners fired at the approaching Shermans over open sights and destroyed enough to discourage further advances. Two or three guns were lost to direct hits, and one battery had to displace.

Kokott knew more tanks would follow. Lüttwitz had little help to offer from the rest of XLVII Panzer Corps. The situation of the 2nd Panzer and Panzer

Lehr spearheads had taken a turn for the worst, despite the arrival of the first elements of the 9th Panzer Division to help out. The 15th Panzergrenadier Division, which had been committed to the last effort to capture Bastogne, was in ruins. Hold what positions you now have, ordered Lüttwitz, and he would send the Führer Escort Brigade.[40]

Patton wrote on 26 December, "The speed of our movements is amazing, even to me, and must be a constant source of surprise to the Germans."[41]

Brandenberger, the night of 26–27 December, pulled LXXX Corps back from his left wing into the West Wall fortifications, ending its ability to pin American forces and handing the initiative to the Americans. The divisions had lost a third of their manpower, however, and were no longer strong enough to fight in the open field.

Brandenberger now benefited from Patton's failure to follow through, just as First Army had repeatedly in Lorraine. Brandenberger expected that the Americans would pursue LXXX Corps, which was weakened by casualties and plummeting morale. They had every prospect of smashing right through the West Wall, which would create a strategic crisis for the high command. "Surprisingly enough," he recalled, "the enemy pressure now relaxed completely." This ease of pressure allowed him to withdraw the 276th Volksgrenadier Division in early January, refresh it, and shift it to his embattled right wing.[42]

Lüttwitz, on 27 December, received orders to turn his attention to his left flank and capture Bastogne. The 1st SS Panzer Division was being shifted to him from Sixth Panzer Army. The 3rd Panzergrenadier Division arrived and entered the line, and Lüttwitz was given the staff of XXXIX Panzer Corps, arriving directly from the eastern front the next day, to take charge of the 1st SS Panzer and 5th Airborne Divisions north and east of Bastogne. Manteuffel instructed that "Army Group Lüttwitz," controlling XLVII and XXXIX Panzer Corps, should stand up on the thirtieth with the limited mandate to close the corridor into Bastogne.[43]

The SS drive westward had burned out by 28 December, when the 1st SS Panzer Division, which had already lost an entire tank battalion, plus half-tracks and sixty self-propelled artillery pieces with *Kampfgruppe* Peiper, assembled east of Vielsalm, harassed by *jabos* the entire day. The division was to attack the Americans at Bastogne, though fuel shortages prevented the division's attack from getting under way until the twenty-ninth.[44]

Much as Patton had before the gates of Lorraine, Manteuffel and his Fifth Panzer Army were finding their mobile operations badly constrained by a lack of gasoline. The fuel reserves were held east of the Rhine, where they were deemed to be safer; Manteuffel had told Hitler that he would need five units of gasoline (a unit was enough to cover 100 kilometers) with the vehicles for each formation, but he was given only one and a half. Clogged roads and, eventually, the *jabos* made getting fuel forward to the spearheads extremely difficult. "All our attacks on Bastogne were made by small groups," Manteuffel recounted shortly after the war, "because of this gasoline shortage."[45] Priess recorded that I SS Panzer Corps, despite being the *Schwerpunkt* of the offensive, had slightly less fuel for each division than in Fifth Panzer Army as the attack began and faced the same difficulties moving supplies forward.[46] Both generals observed that because of the rough terrain, a fuel unit actually permitted far less movement than calculated by OKW, more on the order of sixty to seventy kilometers.

Lüttwitz, on 29 December, consulted with *General der Panzertruppe* Karl Decker, commanding XXXIX Panzer Corps. The attack to capture Bastogne, he instructed, was to begin the following day on the line along Lutrebois-Villers-la-Bonne-Eau-Assenois, with the objective of cutting the American corridor into Bastogne.[47] The following day, Patton later calculated, was the biggest coordinated attack against troops under his command that he ever faced.[48]

The 1st SS Panzer Division's attack on 30 December against CCA, 4th Armored Division, and the 35th Infantry Division on the east shoulder of the Arlon-Bastogne highway corridor consisted of thirty panzers, about ten self-propelled guns, and Heilmann's battalion-sized 14th Airborne Regiment. The Germans threw a battalion of the 134th Infantry from out of the woods at Lutrebois, got within 400 yards of the highway, and took under fire the battalion command post, as well as that of the 51st Armored Infantry Regiment. About 1100, however, six American tanks, fighter-bombers, and artillery engaged a group of thirteen panzers and destroyed eleven of them. This took the fire out of the advance, and the counterattack ended by 1600. It was the last German attempt to cut the corridor.[49]

Lüttwitz, meanwhile, ran afoul of the fresh American 11th Armored and 87th Infantry Divisions attacking northward to the west of Bastogne. He had just begun an attack toward Bastogne, using 3rd and 15th Panzergrenadier Divisions, and it ran head-on into the 11th Armored Division's advance. By New Year's Eve, the Americans were also pressuring the 9th and 2nd Panzer Divisions and Panzer Lehr, the foremost divisions in the corps. Lüttwitz hoped only to hold his line and prevent a breakthrough to Houffalize, and the short-lived Army Group Lüttwitz was dissolved. The inexperienced 11th Armored Division, however, had lost numerous tanks and was in no condition to break through to anywhere.[50]

By New Year's Day, LIII Corps, in Seventh Army's zone, had established a fairly coherent line east and north of Bastogne. Elements of the 9th Volksgrenadier

Division held the left wing, the 5th Airborne Division the center, and the 167th Volksgrenadier Division the right wing. During the first week of January, the 276th Volksgrenadier Division arrived from LXXX Corps to strengthen the left wing. The Führer Grenadier Brigade constituted the corps reserve.[51]

Under Hitler's plan, Priess was never to have been anywhere near Patton and Third Army. Nevertheless, on orders from Model, Priess and his staff arrived near Bastogne on New Year's Day to take charge of the 1st SS Panzer, Panzer Lehr, and 12th SS Panzer Divisions, the last just then arriving from the north. The corps squeezed into the line to the left of XLVII Panzer Corps, which now was to merely hold its line. Indeed, I SS Panzer Corps would be the epicenter of a violent struggle over the next week, while Lüttwitz would record of XLVII Panzer Corps, "During the time from 2 until 9 January 1945, there was no fighting of special importance along the entire corps front."

Priess once again faced Patton, and this time he had the tools to attack, which was his natural inclination. Priess met with Manteuffel, who told him that Lüttwitz's attacks on Bastogne had failed, and that the arrival of the 6th Armored Division in the sector had put tremendous pressure on Kokott's 26th Volksgrenadier Division. Manteuffel expected immediate breakout attempts north and east of Bastogne, and Priess's corps was to take over Kokott's sector the following day. Amusingly enough, Patton's intuition that night told him Manteuffel was just about to stage an attack against him.

A major American attack did not occur (nor did a German one), however, and Model visited Priess and Manteuffel on 3 January to discuss plans to regain the initiative at Bastogne. Elements of the battered 340th Volksgrenadier and 9th SS Panzer Divisions were arriving, in a trickle because of fuel shortages, and joined I SS Panzer Corps.[52]

The 9th SS Panzer Division, which had only about twenty-five tanks and assault guns, finally attacked toward Monaville at 0800 on 4 January with scarcely any artillery support. Exposed on flat ground, the Germans were driven off by heavy fire. Priess had foreseen this exact outcome and objected to the proposed attack, but Manteuffel had insisted that it be carried through. The 9th SS Panzer Division did manage to get into Longchamps, where the fighting continued into the night. A weak regiment of the 340th Volksgrenadier Division and the 12th SS Panzer Division joined the battle at noon, but gained little more than a mile of ground southwest of Michamps.[53] Other attacks supported by company-sized groups of panzers lashed the VIII Corps front at half a dozen points.[54]

Priess had rattled Patton. The American wrote in his diary, "We can still lose this war," which, Patton later observed, was the only occasion during the war that he expressed such sentiment. "[T]he Germans are colder and hungrier than we are, but they fight better."[55]

The next day, however, Manteuffel told Priess he would soon have to send the 12th SS Panzer Division back to Sixth Panzer Army. Priess continued his assault with all three divisions, but, as he recalled, "The 101st Airborne Division was made up of very good troops, who fought hard and tenaciously." Casualties were heavy, and gains were tactical and insignificant.[56]

Priess halted his drive the evening of 6 January, when the 12th SS Panzer Division received orders to withdraw into corps reserve. The 340th Volksgrenadier Division had to extend its line to fill the gap.[57]

Patton was spinning up an attack with three corps abreast: VIII, III, and XII. He was managing his corps commanders, too. "I had to use the whip on both Middleton and Millikin today," he wrote on the sixth. "They are too cautious."[58]

The events of 8 January marked the initial shift in momentum from Manteuffel to Patton. American troops pushed the 26th Volksgrenadier Division back in fierce house-to-house fighting. A regimental staff and weak elements of the 12th SS Panzer Division had to be committed near Vaux to stop the Americans. It was the last day that groups with up to twenty panzers attacked American positions.[59] Lüttwitz received orders to withdraw from his most advanced positions, and the night of 9–10 January, he pulled back elements of the 2nd and 9th Panzer Divisions.[60]

Patton attacked across his front on 9 January with nine divisions. Despite his high hopes, no division gained more than two miles, and German accounts barely mention the event.[61]

Patton did not know it, but the Ardennes were about to drop from the main German theater to a secondary concern. The OKW *Kriegstagebuch* recorded on the ninth, "Enemy attack intentions across the entire eastern front." The tsunami hit four days later.[62]

Priess's men were not yet licked. The 4th Armored Division attacked toward Houffalize on 10 January. When CCA pushed off, German gunners on dominating ground pounded the Americans with direct fire from antitank guns and artillery, inflicting heavy casualties. Three of Priess's self-propelled guns finally fell victim to tank fire from the neighboring CCB zone, but the American attack did not resume that day. Supreme Headquarters Allied Expeditionary Force (SHAEF) had ordered Patton to pull a division out to form a reserve, and the 4th Armored Division the next day pulled back to rest and refit.[63]

The 5th Airborne Division, in LIII Corps, meanwhile, had faced growing pressure at Wiltz beginning 8 January. Some men panicked and fled eastward across the

Wiltz River, while others fought desperately. The 5th Airborne Division was thrown into confusion by the 90th Infantry Division's attack into its rear area on 11 January. The American division's well-concealed arrival in the sector from XX Corps had caught the Germans completely by surprise. Elements of Fifth Panzer Army retreated across the airborne division's rear, which added to the chaos. The division disintegrated, and two regiments were wiped out. The confusion and losses were such that Brandenberger considered the division to be destroyed.

Fortunately, its artillery was still safe, and Heilmann, now subordinated to Fifth Panzer Army, was able to reestablish an oblique defensive line. Manteuffel ordered Heilmann to take strenuous efforts to gather the paratrooper stragglers in the rear area and restore his division to fighting shape.[64]

There followed weeks of strategically and even tactically senseless bloodletting in the snow and ice—senseless because the high command had already decided to pull back, and only the speed, a week or two one way or the other, was at issue. Army Group B, on 10 January, ordered that the 1st and 12th SS Panzer Divisions withdraw into army group reserve, the first sign that Hitler was giving up any hope of further progress. The next day, Priess was instructed to turn his sector over to LIII Corps.[65] Lüttwitz pulled back his entire corps line and surrendered the 2nd Panzer Division into Fifth Panzer Army reserve.[66]

On 12 January, Brandenberger received orders that Army Group B would evacuate the Bulge, gradually and only when under enemy pressure. Brandenberger now had a mission similar to the one Knobelsdorff and Obstfelder had faced in Lorraine: screen the retreat and keep Patton from penetrating the West Wall. Manteuffel extracted all of his divisions before U.S. Third and First Armies joined hands at Houffalize on 16 January, thereby officially eliminating the Bulge. Rothkirch's LIII Corps, now consisting of only the weak 9th and 276th Volksgrenadier Divisions, pivoted its right wing back and withdrew from one temporary defense line to the next, keeping pace with Fifth Panzer Army on the right. It managed to hold each of these lines without breaking, which is probably a tribute to Rothkirch's leadership and to the lack of energy in Patton's pursuit. Patton was trying, but he conceded his divisions were worn out, and the weather was vicious. Hitler, on the twenty-second, decided to transfer the now formally labeled Sixth SS Panzer Army to Hungary to deal with Soviet advances there, and Sepp Dietrich turned his frontage over to Manteuffel. Brandenberger pulled his last men behind the Our River on 31 January, and LIII Corps occupied the Vianden section of the West Wall.[67]

Lüttwitz commented that the withdrawal of his corps unfolded according to plan and without harassment by a pursuing enemy except in a few isolated cases. "During the withdrawal, no fighting of special significance took place," he summarized.[68]

Patton's crystal ball failed him. On 24 January, Patton told his diary, "Personally, I am convinced the Germans are pulling out, probably as far as the Rhine. . . ."[69]

GERMAN VIEWS OF PATTON

Though Patton's ability to pivot and thrust against the southern flank of the Bulge represented his finest hour, his enemies did not view his intervention as decisive in destroying the offensive. He had arrived just about when they had expected him to. Speaking of Third Army's operations against Fifth Panzer Army at Bastogne, Manteuffel in his memoirs aims a dismissive indirect critique at Patton: the Americans, he said of Third Army's attack, did not "strike with full élan." He praised Eisenhower, without naming him, for halting all offensive operations on the western front to permit concentration of forces, and for moving the reserve 101st Airborne Division into Bastogne faster than the Germans had ever thought possible. He viewed Ike's decision to put the northern forces in Montgomery's hands as decisive and credited Montgomery with bringing coherence to what had been a string of isolated battles along the north flank.[70] The OKW *Kriegstagebuch* paid careful attention to Bradley's status and tracked Montgomery's control over American formations during this period, but mentioned Patton not a single time.

On 4 February 1945, the *Luftwaffenfuhrungsstab* Ic circulated within OKH a translation of a letter of instructions written by Patton on 17 April 1944 and recently captured from V Corps, which, it assessed, was "characteristic" of Patton. Patton's letter began with a section strongly emphasizing discipline. There followed extensive remarks on tactical principles in general and specifically as related to infantry, artillery, armor, reconnaissance, antiaircraft and antitank weapons, and troop welfare.

Patton's first tactical principle was, "There are no approved solutions for any tactical situation." There was only one basic principle: to employ available means in such a way as to cause the enemy in the shortest possible time the greatest possible quantity of casualties through wounds, death, and destruction. One's own casualties depended on the amount of time spent under enemy fire, and speed of the attack minimizes that time. "A pint of sweat," the translators conveyed in German from the original, "saves a gallon of blood."

Battles are won, wrote Patton, by instilling fear in the enemy. Fire from his rear is three times more effective than from the front. "Catch the enemy by the nose with fire, and kick him in the pants with fire emplaced through movement," the translators offered in German. Hit the enemy fast and hard—two battalions up in a regiment, two divisions up in a corps.

On and on the document flowed, laying out Patton's battle philosophy.[71] But by now, practically everyone who mattered on the western front probably knew it already.

✳

THIRTEEN

Patton Flattens
Germany's Remnants

I N STRATEGIC TERMS, the war in the West was over by February 1945, after Hitler's offensive against Seventh Army in Alsace—Operation *Nordwind* (North Wind)—had burned itself out in January. "The psychological and physical strength were used up and at an end after the obvious failure of the [Ardennes] offensive," recalled Manteuffel. The panzer general was called to Hitler's headquarters on 28 February, where he was awarded the Diamonds to his Knight's Cross. Then, like Balck and Priess, he was sent back to the east, where he took command of Third Panzer Army. The German soldier, he believed, now fought only because he feared enslavement to the Western powers under "unconditional surrender," or being crushed by the Bolsheviks.[1]

From the German perspective, Patton's Third Army represented a front of tertiary importance, and defensive forces there were not going to get even the parsimonious support Army Group G had enjoyed in late 1944. The most likely *Schwerpunkt* for renewed Allied attacks in the west appeared to be the area west of the Rhine between Düsseldorf and Cologne, because the Ruhr industrial basin remained the primary strategic prize. Allied bombers, meanwhile, in mid-January had destroyed most of Germany's synthetic oil plants, which left the Wehrmacht largely dependent on oil wells in Austria and Hungary on the eastern front. Fuel shortages had delayed the Sixth SS Panzer Army on its deployment to Hungary to defend those very wells. By late January, the Soviets had captured nearly all of the industrial area in upper Silesia, which had become the center of Germany's remaining war industry as Allied bombers ground the Ruhr to rubble. Factories had replenished the ammunition expended in the Battle of the Bulge, but now a production crisis set in. Armaments Minister Albert Speer penned a memorandum to Hitler that began, "The war is lost."[2]

A decision emerged from the *Führerbunker* under the ruins of Berlin during February 1945 that underscored the de-emphasis of the western front: 1,675 tanks and assault guns (new or repaired) were sent to the eastern front, while only sixty-seven went west. The führer was more worried about the Soviet threat to Berlin and Hungary than the danger that the Western Allies would leap the Rhine.[3] The panzer assets still available were concentrated opposite Montgomery's command, where the main thrust was expected.

"The entire western front had been so weakened after the Ardennes offensive that a defense was no longer possible, only a delaying battle to buy time," recalled *Generalmajor* Carl Wagener, Army Group B's chief of staff. There were not enough forces at the front, reserves, fuel, or ammunition. The most sensible idea was to pull back across the Rhine; however, not only was that notion out of the question at OKW, but until February there also was a ban in place on even constructing defensive positions on the east bank of the river.[4]

The state of German weakness is impossible to exaggerate. As of 1 February, the Third Reich had less than three and a half months left, less than the time First Army had held Patton at bay between the Moselle and the West Wall. Casualties would be high, the destruction of material and civilian infrastructure monstrous, but from henceforth, German commanders could view Patton as nothing other than one of the many Allied commanders who were crushing the remnants of the Wehrmacht in the West.

Patton, on the other hand, was enjoying the best replacement and supply situation ever. His divisions were nearly up to strength and armed to the teeth.[5]

PRELUDE TO DISASTER: LOSS OF THE MOSELLE GATE

The Germans referred to Trier and its surrounding West Wall defenses as the Moselle Gate, or *Moselpforte*, because if opened by an enemy, it provided a path straight down the Moselle valley to the Rhine.

The German assessment of Allied strategic intentions was quite correct, and Trier was not even in American sights as of late January. Eisenhower had ordered Bradley to support Montgomery's drive toward the Rhine opposite the Ruhr with most of First Army (Montgomery still controlled U.S. Ninth Army). The 12th Army Group could unleash its own drive to the Rhine only once Monty was settled on the west bank. Eisenhower told Patton to wait on the defensive until then.

This directive sat well with neither Bradley nor Patton. Bradley, after quietly winning Ike's approval, instructed Patton to attack through the Eifel highlands along the German border. Patton's drive was "was to be strong enough to keep the enemy from shifting his strength [northward against the main offensive] but not so strong as to arouse the objections of Monty." He was to "quietly" advance across the Kyll River to establish a springboard for the big push to the Rhine. Patton called his approach "aggressive defense."[6]

As February began, Third Army's VIII Corps, on its left wing, was just finishing the phase of slow, painful gains as the Bulge became a slowly growing mirror penetration of the German frontier in the opposite direction. The corps was nearing Prüm, and on the sixth, Patton awoke with a plan for a break-through by VIII Corps and its neighbor XII Corps fully formulated in his head. Despite the wink he had received from above, Patton kept his "Bitburg offensive" secret so that nobody could order him not to do it. He was convinced that when the break came, he would be able to throw two or three armored divisions into a Brest-style campaign in the opposite direction.[7]

Seventh Army and the right wing of First Army, subordinated respectively to Army Groups B and G, stood in Third Army's way. Model still commanded Army Group B, and Paul Hausser had returned from his convalescence in late January to take charge of Army Group G. Blaskowitz had again led the army group after Balck's departure, but now headed north to take charge of Army Group H.[8] The interarmy-group boundary was set at Grevenmacher, southwest of Trier, and First Army's LXXXII Corps still defended the Saar-Moselle triangle against Third Army's right wing, XX Corps. The remainder of First Army held the West Wall and northern Alsace, from Merzig to the Rhine, against the U.S. Seventh Army.[9]

Seventh Army deployed a nearly all-infantry force that reflected the zone's new backwater status. *General der Infanterie* Hans-Gustav Felber's XIII Corps (167th and 340th Volksgrenadier Divisions, plus, from 8 February, the 5th Airborne and 326th Volksgrenadier Divisions) was on its right wing abutting Fifth Panzer Army; Rothkirch's LIII Corps (9th and 276th Volksgrenadier Divisions) was in the center; and Beyer's LXXX Corps (79th, 212th, and 352nd Volksgrenadier Divisions) was on the left. All divisions except the 212th had been reduced to roughly regimental strength, insufficient to man most West Wall bunkers in combat strength. Brandenberger's only mobile reserve was the partially rebuilt 2nd Panzer Division. Fuel was so short that damaged armored vehicles could not be moved to repair facilities, and supply in general was spotty. Morale was terrible.[10]

Of First Army's five corps, two would become embroiled with Third Army west of the Rhine. *General der Infanterie* Walter Hahm's LXXXII Corps

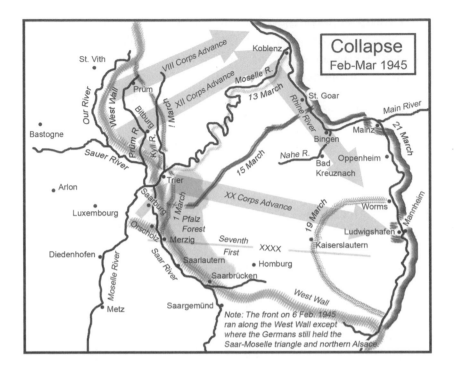

Note: The front on 6 Feb. 1945 ran along the West Wall except where the Germans still held the Saar-Moselle triangle and northern Alsace.

controlled the 256th and 416th Volksgrenadier Divisions in the Orsholz Switch position. *General der Infanterie* Baptist Kniess's LXXXV Corps (719th, 559th, and 347th Volksgrenadier Divisions) had moved from the Ardennes to take charge of First Army's front between Merzig and Saarlautern on 25 January. Unusual for this time, Kniess's divisions were near full strength, but they lacked transport. They held one of the strongest stretches of the West Wall. *General der Infanterie* Gustav Hoehne and his LXXXIX Corps staff would also briefly fight Patton, but would do so commanding divisions in a sector other than those that he defended at the beginning of the campaign.[11]

Army Group G had no reserves other than a handful of volksgrenadier divisions being rebuilt behind Nineteenth Army on its left wing, and those would not be ready until late March.[12]

From roughly Trier north in the zone opposite Third Army, the Germans benefited from three north-south rivers—the Prüm, Kyll, and Selm—that offered excellent terrain for organizing a well-anchored line. If they could not stop the Americans there, the enemy would sweep onto the Rhine plain, which offered excellent tank country for operations along the west bank that could cut off all German forces along the border.

Rundstedt expected the main American thrust to occur farther north, toward the Ruhr. Brandenberger's chief of staff, Rudolf *Freiherr* von Gersdorff, recalled, however, "The mere fact that Patton's American Third Army stood opposite us indicated that the Allied command would also seek a breakthrough here." An "armor commander" like Patton, thought Gersdorff, would want to attack straightaway with the momentum achieved during the destruction of the Bulge, and he appeared to have his main strength on his left wing.[13]

Felber, commanding XIII Corps, observed increased *jabo* activity despite bad weather on 3 and 4 February. American artillery activity also increased, particularly against headquarters and supply routes. The past ten days had been relatively calm, but a new attack was obviously coming.[14]

General der Infanterie Hans-Gustav Felber was an old hand, already a *Generalleutnant* only ten days after the war had begun. Born on 8 July 1889 in Wiesbaden, Felber had entered the imperial army as an officer candidate in March 1908 and had served in staff jobs throughout the Great War. He had commanded XIII Corps in 1941. He had been proposed for an army command in December 1941, but Kluge—his commander in Army Group Center—had judged that his toughness and energy in a crisis fell short and showed no interest in having Felber return after he reported sick in March 1942. Kluge thought Felber, at best, qualified to command a corps on a quiet front. After a brief exile at a military district command, Felber returned to the field at the head of XLV Corps, then Army Group Felber in occupied France—where, after Operation Anton, he was photographed with SS police during the deportation of the Jews from Marseille—and then LXXXIII Corps the Balkans. He had briefly commanded the fortresses in the Vosges before Nineteenth Army was booted out of Alsace and led the reestablished XIII Corps in the Ardennes battle. His personnel folder held one key fact that recommended him for higher command late in the war: he was a reliable National Socialist.[15] Kesselring, who would eventually sack Felber, characterized him as being of calm judgment and great tactical knowledge as an army commanding general—but insufficiently ruthless in executing his operations.

Third Army's Left Hook

General der Infanterie Franz Beyer, still commanding LXXX Corps on Seventh Army's left wing, pinpointed the beginning of the end of the war west of the Rhine:

On 5 and 6 February 1945, the pursuing movements of the Third U.S. Army [VIII Corps] developed into a breakthrough at the junction between

the Fifth German Panzer Army and the Seventh Army. . . . Its direction
was toward Prüm, and it first began in the Brandscheid and Habscheid
area. From the very start, the tendency of this attack was evident—to roll
up the West Wall to the south. Therefore, when on 8 February, U.S. XII
Corps with the 5th and 80th Infantry Divisions began its breakthrough
in the Echternach sector [on the seventh], the breakthrough was viewed
as a prong . . . aiming at the same objective. . . . Behind was the U.S. 4th
Armored Division, for the strategic exploitation of the breakthrough.

German intelligence had believed that the American armored divisions
had departed VIII Corps's front, but it now became apparent that the 6th and
11th Armored Divisions were behind VIII Corps's attacking infantry divisions.
The strategic danger was becoming apparent to Seventh Army. Felber's XIII
Corps was given charge of the defense of Prüm, and Felber established a special
command controlling all available reserves.

Felber's infantry divisions were so badly stretched that the general judged
that if the Americans had committed an armored division against him on 6
February, they would have smashed through, and with two armored divisions
they could have reached the Rhine. "Fortunately, the enemy did not recognize
his favorable situation and halted his advance at dark as usual," he later said.
Felber was mystified. "The commander of the Third Army opposite us was no
man of hesitation. [His operations in March] proved that General Patton was
fully aware of the decisive value of armored divisions."[16] Here was a familiar
refrain from a German commander: Patton was failing to seize opportunities
for long gains opened up by the fierce struggle along the line.

The opportunity passed quickly. In light of the armored divisions identified in VIII Corps, Brandenberger, with a heavy heart, pulled *Kampfgruppen*
from LIII Corps to strengthen Felber—a move that would have dire consequences later. He also placed the 2nd Panzer Division, the 506th Heavy Tank
Battalion (Royal Tigers), and additional assault guns—a total of between sixty
and eighty tanks—under Felber's control. Felber committed the 2nd Panzer
Division—which had only ten running panzers after the debacle in the
Bulge—at Prüm on 7 February, beginning with a counterattack that brought
the 90th Infantry Division to a stop. This defensive *Schwerpunkt* succeeded,
at the cost of high losses, in holding VIII Corps west of the Prüm, though
the rubble of the town fell on the thirteenth. Felber, on the ninth, managed
to win Model's approval to stop all counterattacks in order to conserve
infantry strength, doubtless the sort of act that Kesselring later thought
lacked ruthlessness.[17]

Opposite XII Corps, meanwhile, troops from the 212th Volksgrenadier Division, the 320th Infantry Regiment, the army weapons school, and the LXXX Corps combat school gave the 5th Infantry Division in particular a good fight when the Americans crossed the Sauer River. Beyer had placed forward-artillery observers behind American lines, and shelling destroyed bridge after bridge as they were built by engineers. "Their success," recalled Beyer, "was evident in the numerous pontoon debris and corpses drifting ashore in the Sauer loop at Steinheim."[18]

Brandenberger could provide Beyer no help at all because of the need to reinforce Felber, and he counted on the fighting strength of the 212th Volksgrenadier Division and of the West Wall fortifications to enable Beyer to hold. Model supplied the 560th Volksgrenadier Division, which had been filled out with ill-trained personnel, to strengthen the front at Echternach. Down south at Army Group G, Hausser watched Seventh Army's strength shifting to its right wing, away from the interarmy-group boundary, and worried that it increased the risk to his own right wing.

By 9 February, Beyer had nothing in front of XII Corps but a thin security line. The 5th Infantry Division did not detect how weak he was and showed no hurry about bursting out of its bridgehead. Fortunately for Beyer, Patton allowed VIII and XII Corps to pause from 14 to 17 February to move supplies and men up the catastrophically bad roads.

The brittle front gave way on the seventeenth when XII Corps struck again, and over several days, Beyer lost his hold over the entire area west of the Prüm. Hitler rejected Brandenberger's pleas to abandon the West Wall fortifications and form a shortened line along the Prüm. Brandenberger, therefore, improvised and quietly stripped the fortifications of all but reconnaissance troops to give himself the manpower to plug critical holes. The situation was so dire that Brandenberger performed his last act of mobile defense and, on the eighteenth, shifted the 2nd Panzer Division from Prüm to Beyer's zone, where it was able to stop the just-committed 4th Armored Division from achieving a full break-through. The shift, however, allowed VIII Corps to roll up the fortifications still held by LIII Corps, which withdrew with little but its artillery.[19]

Model relieved Brandenberger of command on 20 February 1945. "[M]y onception of the hopeless situation no longer concurred with the concep-tions and purposes of the high command of the Wehrmacht," Brandenberger commented later.[20]

Felber stepped up to take command of Seventh Army, and *General der Infanterie* Ralph *Graf* von Oriola took his place at XIII Corps. Oriola, born in Herischdorf on 9 August 1895, was the son of a junior army officer and a

Gymnasium graduate who had entered the imperial army as an enlisted man in March 1914. He was made a *leutnant* in the artillery in October, wounded in 1915, and rose to *Oberleutnant* by the war's end. Oriola remained in the artillery between the wars, married Elisabeth Trampe (product of a noble family), and had one son. He was an *Oberstleutnant* with the 18th Artillery Regiment when Hitler invaded Poland. He did not take his first infantry command until February 1943, when he was put in charge of the 72nd Infantry Division; only three months later, he took command of the 299th Infantry Division. His ratings as a division commander were excellent: an optimist, energetic, a very good tactician, beloved by his men, a good man in a crisis, hard on himself. And the key qualification: he was a convinced National Socialist.[21]

Felber's new assignment did not begin auspiciously. Only a day after Felber took charge, *jabos* bombed the army headquarters, killed most of his operations staff, and wounded Gersdorff. Things would only get worse. Felber observed that his divisions were so reduced in strength that his staff was writing the number of reported riflemen on the situation maps rather than using the flag symbols prescribed by military regulations. He also confirmed that his army had no reserve. Nothing. Supplies were inadequate, and fuel was scarce. The news about families on the home front was bleak.

Felber, the good National Socialist, chose to believe that morale nevertheless was good and that, "despite all existing serious difficulties, the situation of the army was not hopeless." (He must have known that was not true; the Third Army prisoner take in the last five days of February was 13,000, and many prisoners, including officers and noncommissioned officers in quantities never seen before, said they had just given up.) Unaware that Patton was now allowed to conduct only an "aggressive defense," Felber again wondered at Third Army's seemingly cautious advance.

Felber may have been an optimistic National Socialist, but he was also a realist about the demands of combat operations. Model, who was present at the headquarters when Felber arrived, rejected any withdrawal from the West Wall bunkers. Felber, therefore, instructed that only two or three men be left in each bunker, and the remainder be pulled back to form several new combat battalions. To that, Model assented by his silence. Felber believed that word never reached OKW, but OKW was well aware that many of the lost bunkers were barely manned.[22]

The Germans, at this point, totally misread Patton's intentions for the first time. Despite the presence of the 4th and 6th Armored Divisions in the area, OKW was under the misimpression that nothing big was in the works because it could identify no additional divisions arriving there.

By 22 February, Beyer had pulled most of his right wing back across the river under pressure from the 6th Armored Division and was deeply concerned about the setbacks suffered by Rothkirch's LIII Corps on his right. Rothkirch's leftmost division had also retreated behind the Prüm. The line offered protection in the form of some field fortifications, but they had never been completed. And the weakened divisions lacked the manpower to defend them all, anyway, a fact that became clear when the 4th Armored Division tore through the Prüm position on the twenty-fifth and advanced toward Bitburg, annihilating one of the 2nd Panzer Division's rifle battalions along the way.

Bitburg fell on 27 February, and Felber had to order the center of his line to retreat across the Kyll River. Hitler, however, forbade the withdrawal of his wings. Like the defenses along the Prüm, those of this naturally strong position were far from complete. Felber, sensing that the crisis point had shifted, ordered the staffs of XIII and LIII Corps to swap zones of responsibility, which put Oriola in charge of the most threatened center. Felber viewed Oriola, who was nearly fresh from the zone of the interior, as much more energetic than the worn-out Rothkirch.

By 3 March, the 212th Volksgrenadier Division had been pushed back southeastward almost to Trier. There were excellent West Wall fortifications to be had northwest of Trier, but the division lacked the manpower to fill them. Moreover, the Moselle Gate was already ajar: U.S. XX Corps two days earlier had captured Trier from the southwest, putting Felber's left wing in great peril.[23]

Third Army's Right Hook

This threat existed because *General der Infanterie* Walther Hahm's LXXXII Corps, the rightmost in First Army, had lost control over the Saar-Moselle triangle in a fight that was symptomatic of a slowly developing German implosion. At the beginning of February, Hahm still held the Orscholz Switch fortifications with the 416th Infantry Division, reduced by attrition to between 30 and 40 percent of its authorized strength, but reinforced by the depleted 256th Volksgrenadier Division. The latter division had come from the Vosges and was at roughly two-thirds authorized strength. With its arrival beginning 8 February, the 11th Panzer Division, which had both held part of the line and acted as the mobile reserve in the triangle, departed for Army Group B. This proved to be a fatal turn of events.

Patton had expected Sixth Army Group to take over operations in the triangle. When he found out on 2 February that this would not be the case, he was most bitter. But he later viewed it as a great fortune and used the triangle as the launching point for the capture of Trier and the invasion of the Palatinate. Patton initially approved an attack by the 94th Infantry Division on the Orscholz Switch only to battle test the outfit.

On 18 February, after two days of quiet, shelling of the western end of the fortification line gave Hahm full warning that an attack by the 94th Infantry Division was coming, but there was little he could do about it. Early the next morning, fire expanded across the line and then shifted into the German rear for a while "in order to render it difficult to bring forward any reserves (of which we had none)," recalled Hahm's Ia, *Oberst* Ingelheim. By the evening, Hahm realized he could not hold the Orscholz Switch and would have to retire behind the Saar. He was ordered to stand fast, however.

Walker, commanding XX Corps, called Patton on the nineteenth and said he thought he could take the triangle if Patton could get him an armored division. Patton wangled use of the 10th Armored Division "only for this operation."

The 10th Armored Division penetrated the fortifications on the twentieth and threatened the entire east end of the front from the rear, so Hahm ordered the troops there across the Saar. The only grace was that bad weather kept the *jabos* out of the sky. It was the last chance to get to safety in the West Wall troops that would be in good enough shape to fight.

Nevertheless, again the order came: hold! The weather cleared, the Americans attacked along the entire front, and in the course of 21 February captured Saarburg. The corps's remnants crossed the Saar that night, closely pursued by the Americans the next morning, while *jabos* and artillery, directed by spotter planes, tormented the remaining German troops. It could have been worse: the 10th Armored Division had misplaced its bridging unit and required hours to bring it up. Patton himself conceded this time that he had missed an opportunity for a rapid exploitation to Trier. By evening, the Americans had driven the *Volksturm* from the West Wall in three places, and the corps barely held a coherent line.

First Army as of late February was in bad shape, and thanks to Ultra, Patton knew it. Only two of its fifteen divisions were capable of offensive operations. Recent fighting had reduced manpower by 73 percent in the 256th Division and 81 percent in the 416th Division. The 17th SS Panzergrenadier Division's two tanks were the only ones in the entire army, but there were also 128 German and 76 Czech (almost certainly Hetzer) assault guns available, as well as 146 75mm antitank guns and 83 Jagdtiger tank killers.[24]

On 1 March, *General der Infanterie* Hermann Foertsch, commanding First Army, reported to Hausser that if Seventh Army continued to fall back and he were forced to stay put in the West Wall, he would be unable to free sufficient reserves to fight a battle on his right flank. Either he had to receive additional forces or he had to shorten his line to free some resources, specifically by abandoning the fortifications west of Saarbrücken and territory in the Pfalz Forest.

Foertsch was not a man inclined to exaggeration or panic. Born on 4 April 1895 in Drahnow, Foertsch had joined the imperial army in March 1913 as an officer cadet and been promoted August 1914 to *leutnant* just in time to go to war with the 175th Infantry Regiment. He had remained with the army between the wars, married, and had three children. He had served in the regiments and risen gradually to the rank of *Oberstleutnant*. Foertsch had held chief-of-staff jobs at the corps, army, and army-group levels for most of the war and received his first combat command only in June 1944, when he led the 21st Infantry Division on the eastern front for only three months. He had commanded X Corps in November and December and won praise for his leadership in three fierce defensive battles. Foertsch was typical of late-war Patton opponents, having little experience at his level of command and a rise to head an army doubtless having a good bit to do with the fact that he had been judged a good Nazi. His superiors considered him brave and extremely calm.

Hausser endorsed Foertsch's view and passed it up to Rundstedt. Hausser added that he required two or three mobile divisions in order to successfully wage a mobile defense west of the Rhine.

Rundstedt's Ia, Siegfried Westphal, called Army Group G and reported that Rundstedt would not pass Foertsch's analysis to OKW because Hitler had already made clear that the Saarland was to be held. Hitler would not accept "backwards." Rundstedt would, however, try to find Hausser two mobile divisions, though he should not get his hopes up because there were no reserves left in the west.

Then, said Hausser, you had better think hard about how you are going to fight west of the Rhine. He knew that experience since North Africa had shown that fortifications, like those held by First Army, were good only if they were manned with combat-effective troops backed by mobile reserves.[25]

The arrival from the Vosges front of the 2nd Mountain Division, a poorly trained outfit organized out of supply and other noncombat units, and the 6th SS Mountain Division did little but act as a speed bump. Urged on by Patton, the 10th Armored Division pushed into Trier on 1 March.

Beyer's LXXX Corps was responsible for the defense of Trier itself. Beyer's total strength in the strategic city amounted to one police and one *Volksturm* militia battalion, supported by a few guns. Beyer instructed this tiny force to defend the downtown zone and approaches to the Moselle bridges. Orders to destroy the bridges were carried out in all but one case for unknown reasons. (The reason was that an American lieutenant colonel had raced across the bridge under fire and cut the demolition wires.) That single error delivered into American hands the Kaiser Bridge.[26]

Patton's pincers soon met. The Moselle Gate stood wide open.

THE END OF THE WESTERN "FRONT"

Army Group G on 3 March took responsibility for Seventh Army in order to place the battle on both sides of the Moselle River under a single command. Army Group B's front was splintering north of Seventh Army's zone, and it could no longer direct or supply Seventh Army effectively. It was impossible to shift forces from one sector of the front to another because the pressure was heavy everywhere; the possibilities for improvisation were exhausted. OKW estimated that the Allies had committed all of their operational reserves except for three airborne divisions. Rundstedt relieved Hausser of operational responsibility for Nineteenth Army, which defended the east bank of the Rhine from its boundary with First Army to the Swiss border, to concentrate on the battle west of the Rhine. Hausser thus controlled roughly 40 percent of the fighting strength of the German army in the West.

Hausser visited Seventh Army headquarters, where Felber told him that with the exceptions of the 212th and recently arrived 246th Volksgrenadier Divisions, his nine divisions were "fought out" and were at one-third strength or less. The freed-up 2nd Panzer Division finally provided Hausser with one mobile formation, but it had only about thirty panzers and suffered from fuel shortages.[27] Hausser's Ia, *Oberst* Horst Wilutzky, recalled, "When Army Group G assumed control of Seventh Army, it was evident that the army no longer possessed any power of resistance worth mentioning and that it would be thrown back across the Moselle soon."[28]

Indeed, Felber and Gersdorff knew they could hold the Kyll line precisely as long as the American armored divisions waited to attack it. Once that happened, breakthroughs were inevitable. There were not enough troops to seal the breaches, and the troops that were left no longer saw the point in risking their lives trying. Felber told Hausser that the best he could do was wage a fighting withdrawal to the Rhine and Moselle, making certain that no large formations were cut off and destroyed. Although Felber's plan violated OKW's orders for unyielding resistance, Hausser saw there was no alternative and approved. Anticipating the possibility that he could not hold even the Moselle line, that night he quietly ordered the preparation of an alternative headquarters site east of the Rhine.[29]

COLLAPSE OF THE SAAR-PALATINATE

The American First and Ninth Armies had already reached the Rhine, as required by Eisenhower, when Patton was unleashed to wage an offensive offense. On 4 March, Patton finally threw his armored divisions right at the Germans. VIII Corps's 11th Armored Division attacked into considerable resistance.

XII Corps's 5th Infantry Division established a bridgehead across the Kyll for use by the 4th Armored Division. XX Corps's 10th Armored Division crossed the Kyll farther south and drove eastward north of the Moselle. While some German formations, such as the 5th Airborne Division, resisted with determination, Third Army recorded taking an "extraordinary number" of prisoners in the week up to the attack—a sure sign of impending collapse. The 4th Armored Division joined the party the next day and rolled more than ten miles.[30]

Felber had moved the 2nd Panzer Division opposite the 4th Armored in the XIII Corps zone near Bitburg, but the tanks lacked the fuel to maneuver. While the gunners were able to destroy a number of tanks, they could not stop the American surge.[31] In just two days, the 4th Armored Division punched thirty-five miles into Seventh Army's rear in what Bradley called "the boldest and most insolent armored blitz of the Western war."[32]

Felber observed regarding Patton:

> This extremely daring breakthrough showed that the enemy was now willing to take greater chances than up to the present. Probably he had realized the weakness and diminishing combat power of the opposing German defensive forces. The successful advance of the 4th Armored Division, which was using the same methods of combat that were first employed by the German panzer units in the campaign in the east in 1941, was initiated [by the 10th and 11th Armored Divisions]. . . . The German leadership had encountered a particularly determined and daring opponent in the person of the commander of Third U.S. Army, General Patton.[33]

The 4th Armored Division, on 6 March, plowed into the southern flank of LIII Corps, which already had lost control over the battlefield where the 11th Armored Division was carving its front into isolated pockets of resistance. Rothkirch had a company of heavy Jagdtiger tank destroyers available, but there was not enough fuel to move the panzers to the crisis point. The Americans captured Rothkirch as he was trying to organize a counterattack. Rothkirch actually met Patton face-to-face because the American wanted to ask him why the Germans kept fighting a hopeless war. Orders, replied Rothkirch. Some elements of the corps either escaped across the Moselle or north to Fifteenth Army, to which the corps was subordinated on 7 March, but most of the corps was annihilated. *Generalleutnant* Walter Botsch briefly "commanded" the shattered corps after Rothkirch and thereby earned a footnote as an enemy of Patton.[34]

The 4th Armored Division reached the Rhine near Koblenz on 7 March. First Army's 9th Armored Division took some of the shine off Third Army's achievement by capturing the Ludendorff Bridge across the Rhine at Remagen. This provoked Hitler to again sack Rundstedt as *OB West*, and he summoned *Generalfeldmarschall* Albert Kesselring from Italy to take the job. In the grim and depressing führer headquarters, Hitler on 9 March told Kesselring that he needed a younger man familiar with fighting the Western powers to restore confidence to the troops. He was most concerned about the eastern front, in part because he thought the Western Allies had suffered tremendous losses themselves. Once the situation in the east stabilized, assured Hitler, he would send more resources to the west. The situation at Remagen was to be his main concern. Otherwise, Kesselring's mission was to hang on.

When Kesselring arrived at his headquarters on 10 March to be briefed by Westphal, well known to him as his former chief of staff in Italy, he learned that the situation was far direr than had been portrayed at OKW. He faced eighty-five full-strength Allied divisions with but fifty-five of his own, each, on average, with less than half its authorized manpower. He had, perhaps, one combatant for every ten meters of front. This was not enough to create a defense in depth or to occupy the many West Wall fortifications still in German hands. The Americans were across the Rhine with an estimated force of one armored division and two infantry divisions, and he lacked the wherewithal to match even this relatively small force. The enemy had overwhelming air and materiel superiority. Kesselring decided that he would have to be an active *OB West* rather than continue Rundstedt's distant style of leadership; signs of instability were visible everywhere along the front, and he would have to be in constant contact with his forward subordinates.[35]

Kesselring's intelligence staff gave him its appreciation of the situation covering the length of the western front. Turning to 12th Army Group, the staff judged that U.S. First Army would rush resources to the Remagen bridgehead and try to break the German front. An immediate attack on the Ruhr basin appeared to be out of the question: "The U.S. Third Army will not rest on its laurels; its commander, General Patton, will see to that." It was unclear whether Patton would immediately cross the Rhine or turn south against Seventh Army below the Moselle. The latter course seemed more likely because, in light of Remagen, a second crossing would be superfluous.[36]

The answer to that question had not been clear to Patton, either, until 8 March. Eisenhower had ordered that Third Army conduct only diversionary attacks across the Moselle to help U.S. Seventh Army's attack on the southern face of the Saar-Palatinate triangle. Bradley, however, proposed that Patton be permitted to push down the Rhine, and Ike approved. Arrangements for new boundaries and coordination were worked out with Seventh Army and 6th Army Group, but

Patton already had bigger plans and orally instructed his corps commanders to establish bridgeheads across the Rhine in the vicinity of Oppenheim, Mainz, and Worms, all of which were located in Seventh Army's zone.[37]

About the time of Kesselring's briefing, Patton, judging the situation north of the Moselle nearly cleared up, was already planning to attack southeastward across the river. XX Corps was to strike from the Trier-Saarbourg area toward Kaiserslautern, while XII Corps was to drive down the Rhine toward Bingen and Bad Kreuznach and cut off the German retreat across the river. VIII Corps was to mop up north of the Moselle.[38]

On 12 March, a captured *Oberstleutnant* offered a statement during inter-rogation that Col. Robert Allen, in his memoirs about his time on Patton's staff at Third Army, inaccurately portrayed as a captured OKH analysis of Allied generals.[39] The officer declared that:

> The greatest threat . . . was the whereabouts of the feared U.S. Third Army. General Patton is always the main topic of military discussion. Where is he? Where will he attack? Where . . . ? How? With what? Those are the questions which raced through the head of every German general since the famous German counteroffensive of last December. The location of U.S. First and Ninth Armies was well known, but no one was sure where the U.S. Third Army was. . . .
>
> General Patton is the most feared general on all fronts. . . . The tactics of General Patton are daring and unpredictable. . . . He is the most modern general and the best commander of armored and infantry troops combined.[40]

This was a load of tripe, if a great contribution to the Patton legend. As we have seen, the German generals invariably knew where Third Army was and had a fairly good guess as to what Patton was about to do, where, and with what. That was true this time, too.

Third Army put Patton's latest plan in motion on 14 March.

Escape from a Mortal Wound

Hausser at Army Group G knew full well that a massive attack on the Saar-Palatinate (*Saarpfalz*) was coming. He expected a two-pronged attack, the first across the Moselle by Third Army, and the second northward out of Alsace by Seventh Army. He had not received the two or three mobile divisions that he knew he needed to mount a defense. Because of its winding course, the natural strength of the Moselle River line became a weakness because Seventh Army lacked the troops to defend its length and the mobile reserves to crush any bridgehead. All that could be done was to withdraw the fragments of the 2nd Panzer Division and meld them into a small *Kampfgruppe*; the promised "refreshing" never took place because there was no replacement equipment available.

Hausser expected, therefore, that he could only wage a fighting withdrawal to the Rhine, and in anticipation of that necessity, he requested authority over the Rhine defenses. Felber had obtained permission to withdraw Seventh Army south of the Moselle River, which, except for a few large loops of the river where the line cut across part of the north bank, constituted the German front as of 13 March.

Kesselring, having already toured the more critical parts of the front to the north, arrived at Hausser's headquarters on the 13th. Gersdorff briefed him on the state of Seventh Army. *General der Infanterie* Hoehne's LXXXIX Corps staff, which Hausser had inserted on the right wing of Seventh Army on 8 March to replace LIII Corps, controlled two or three scratch battalions in Koblenz; the 159th Infantry Division, a good but green outfit at 80 percent strength; and the 276th Volksgrenadier Division, which consisted of the staff and two scratch battalions, an SS artillery battalion, and a pioneer battalion from the 159th Infantry Division. Oriola's XIII Corps, in the center, had the 2nd Panzer Division, with few panzers and perhaps 30 percent combat value; the 9th Volksgrenadier Division, merely a regiment-sized *Kampfgruppe*; and the 246th Volksgrenadier Division, at 40 percent strength. Beyer's LXXX Corps, on the left, controlled the 352nd Volksgrenadier Division, now a regiment-sized *Kampfgruppe*; the 212th Volksgrenadier Division, virtually destroyed and now a regiment-sized *Kampfgruppe* only by virtue of having absorbed the remnants of the 560th Volksgrenadier Division; and a regiment-sized *Kampfgruppe* of the 79th Volksgrenadier Division. Seventh Army had lost its logistical reserves north of the Moselle, including its last ammunition dumps. Because of fuel shortages, it had had to abandon most of its assault guns and many artillery pieces.

Third Army at this time estimated Felber's total strength opposite XII Corps at a mere 8,500 men and twenty tanks and assault guns. It judged the force opposite XX Corps, which included the rightmost corps of First Army, as slightly weaker in manpower and the same in terms of armor.

Felber told Kesselring and Hausser that he expected Third Army to attack almost immediately on a broad front. The heretofore optimistic National Socialist later admitted to feeling the situation was hopeless. He proposed withdrawing behind the Rhine, and Kesselring flatly refused.[41]

Kesselring agreed with Hausser that Army Group G faced a probable double-envelopment. Kesselring nevertheless concluded that, because of favorable terrain, it would be possible to hold the Saar-Palatinate and its vital war industries, but only if mobile reserves were brought up. The situation at Remagen was drawing every spare resource, however, including the 11th Panzer Division, and help of that kind for Hausser looked improbable. Hausser hoped for some guidance as to what Kesselring wanted him to do in the worst case when the two spoke privately, but Kesselring offered nothing. The field marshal did set about moving some infantry formations to Seventh Army from First and Nineteenth Armies, unaware that none would arrive in time.

Kesselring mulled Hausser's idea of a fighting withdrawal—and all the other difficult decisions he faced on the western front—overnight. He concluded that First and Seventh Armies were not sufficiently mobile to conduct such an operation and would simply be smashed against the Rhine. He judged that the Saar-Palatinate was of no decisive military importance, but he could at least delay Third Army's crossing of the Rhine and exhaust its troops. Moreover, the political leadership still viewed the war industries in the Saar and along the Rhine as critically important. His answer to Hausser was a 14 March cable that read, "Hold!"[42]

Hausser says he quietly discussed with his army commanders what they should do when they had to retreat, no matter what Kesselring said. He does not say what he told them.[43]

XII Corps flattened Hoehne's shaky corps on 14 March, when the 5th and 90th Infantry and 4th Armored Divisions plunged through it toward Bingen. The inexperienced 159th Infantry Division caved under the shock. Most of LXXXIX Corps reeled back and, on orders from Felber, retreated across the Rhine. Kesselring excoriated Hausser and Felber for inflexible leadership, but it is difficult to see what they could have done with no reserves. Kesselring made up his mind to sack them both. By the next day, the path southward was open to the Americans, and XIII and LXXX Corps faced imminent encirclement.[44]

"In the open country," recalled Gersdorff, "there was nothing left but to let the armored columns roll and try to cut their lines of communication behind them." XII Corps severed Seventh Army's only supply line to Bad Kreuznach on 15 March, and the following day, the army staff escaped capture only because *jabos* gave warning of an approaching 4th Armored Division column. With Hausser's agreement, Felber ordered XIII and LXXX Corps to retreat across the Nahe River toward the Rhine; he passed his orders by phone through American lines just before the connections were cut and he lost all contact with his corps commanders. The loss of communications resulted in total confusion, as various headquarters tried to issue orders to the troops along the east bank of the Rhine.[45]

Remarkably, most of the men in the two threatened corps were able to escape through a gap northwest of Bad Kreuznach. They nevertheless had to abandon nearly all of their heavy weapons and vehicles, and morale was ebbing quickly. Hoehne, however, had done a masterful job moving his corps across the Rhine and had rescued nearly all of his heavy equipment.[46]

The situation was more critical than Kesselring could even have imagined two short days before. With Seventh Army caving in, the field marshal finally convinced Hitler, on the fifteenth to permit First Army to withdraw its right wing from the West Wall, but the decision came too late.[47]

Hahm's LXXXII Corps imploded that day under pressure from U.S. XX Corps, which imperiled LXXX Corps from the south, as well. The Americans overran the 2nd Mountain Division's line and got into its artillery positions, wiping out the heavy-artillery battalion. Two task forces led by tanks swung northward and plowed into the flank of the 256th Volksgrenadier Division. Obstfelder sent forward an infantry battalion by truck to counterattack, but it was powerless against the American armor. Contact was lost with a regiment of the 6th SS Mountain Division, which had been left behind when the division moved to the Trier area earlier in the month and had been functioning as First Army's reserve, though the SS men managed to fight their way free. Only the 416th Infantry Division held on, because it had deployed its artillery forward in an antitank role, but it, too, lost several villages.

"The entire front of the corps was pierced at numerous points by the enemy on 15 March," recalled LXXXII Corps Ia *Oberst* Ingelheim. "The Americans could now whenever they desired thrust in the general direction of Kaiserslautern, Saarbrücken, thereby setting about rolling up the West Wall."

But then Ingelheim added an observation that was an echo of so many earlier critical German assessments of Patton as an enemy in exploiting holes in the defensive line, rather than open-field running: "Most surprisingly, the enemy allowed the night of 15 March to pass without following up his successes, so that the troops of the corps had the opportunity of retiring to a new line of defense."[48]

Gersdorff, from his vantage point at Seventh Army, strongly concurred:

If at that moment XII U.S. Corps, disregarding its eastern flank—where the German XII Corps [actually a military district command that at some point in March was relabeled XII Corps, the designation that will be used here] could only fight a defensive battle—had broken through with concentrated forces along the Rhine to the south, the whole First Army and those parts of Seventh Army which were operating west of the

Rhine would have been annihilated to the last man. XII U.S. Corps, which, fanlike, was feeling its way forward from the area of [Bad] Kreuznach to the east, south, and southeast, made it possible for the weak German forces to tie the bulk of the U.S. forces down and manage to disengage sector after sector of First Army.[49]

Hausser, too, wondered why Third Army did not push down the Rhine plain and cut off his entire army group. "The enemy did not appear to have recognized this possibility! The defensive measures against that were mere improvisations," he said.[50]

Kesselring similarly observed, without mentioning Patton by name:

The enemy tank attacks were bold and, against the right wing of Seventh Army, even foolhardy. Conspicuous was the swift succession of single operations—a sign that the step-by-step methods noticeable in Italy had been abandoned—the dexterous leadership and reckless employment of tanks. . . . I was, however, surprised that having once broken through, they did not, with the support of their fighters, exploit their momentary opportunity to cut off Army Group G from the Rhine bridges and so take the first step to its annihilation. That the army group got back across the Rhine, if sadly battered, in considerable strength and was able to build up a new defense line behind the river was due to this mistake.[51]

Patton himself appeared to sense he had missed an opportunity and conceded in his memoirs, "[Third] Army did not do very well. . . ."[52] Visiting XX Corps with Ike on 16 March, Patton recorded that they found the generals "not pushing hard enough in our opinion." Eisenhower, nevertheless, over dinner, observed that Patton was not only a good general, but also a lucky one, and that Napoleon had preferred luck to greatness.[53]

While Hahm was able to patch together a security line on First Army's right wing, he lacked the wherewithal—men and ammunition—to actually defend territory. LXXXII Corps fell back in a series of delaying actions that could end only in escape or destruction.[54]

Kesselring, on 16 March, traveled to Army Group G's headquarters and told Hausser he was still required to hold the Saarland and the West Wall there, but he was not to allow formations to be cut off and destroyed. Hausser already, on his own authority, had set in motion preparations to pull back First Army's LXXXV Corps to maintain its link to LXXXII Corps, and he chose to interpret the order as permitting such a maneuver. Hausser was behaving much as he had when he evacuated Kharkov under similar instructions and thereby saved his corps to fight again. Kesselring instructed that Seventh Army, which had established poor radio communications with its LXXX and XIII Corps, was to protect First Army's right flank between Bingen and Kaiserslautern. Kesselring in his memoirs acknowledged that at this point, all issues were of local defense and there was no longer a strategic framework for German actions. This was all the more true because twice that day, Felber and Gersdorff barely evaded capture by 4th Armored Division spearheads and were in control of nothing.

Hausser exploded during a conversation with the staff at *OB West* that Kesselring overheard: "What this army group needs is help in deeds and not words, and an assignment that it's possible to accomplish!"[55]

Seventh Army, as of 18 March, could not hold a line, but only a string of strong points, in Gersdorff's view. The army's two corps had fragments of only three divisions, two of them (the 198th and 47th Volksgrenadier) just supplied by First Army. Gersdorff judged that only the fact that Eddy's XII Corps advanced "by the book," seeing to its flanks, saved Army Group G from destruction that day. Felber observed, "[T]he hesitant attitude of the enemy proved very advantageous. The continuation of the armored thrust to the Rhine, immediately after the penetration in the direction of the Nahe, would no doubt have prevented the withdrawal of Seventh and First Armies behind the Rhine." The OKW *Kriegstagebuch* recorded, "The situation on the right wing of Army Group G did not worsen further. The enemy crossed the Nahe with only weak forces."

A daring armored thrust would have ended it all, but Patton did not grasp the chance. Indeed, the 4th Armored Division had stopped to "regroup," and the 11th Armored Division, which had just entered the battle zone, had not advanced south of the Moselle as planned. Eddy told his staff that Patton was putting heat on him to get moving, but XII Corps would not really start rolling again until the nineteenth.

Fragments of Seventh Army retreated into bridgeheads at cities such as Mainz, Worms, and Ludwigshafen, where bridges offered haven east of the Rhine. One by one, the bridges were blown up, though some troops continued to escape by boat. The ruins of XIII Corps were completely across the river by the nineteenth. Other fragments pulled back along the west bank into the rapidly shrinking Army Group G bridgehead centered at Mainz.[56]

*

First Army also began to disintegrate as a unified command on 18 March. *Oberst* Horst Wilutzky, Hausser's Ia, believed that First Army as late as that day was capable of withdrawing to the Rhine and retreating across the river with battle-ready formations. Still falling back under steady American pressure, however, Hahm's LXXXII Corps lost contact with Seventh Army's LXXX Corps to its right and LXXXV Corps to its left.[57] Units were being cut off everywhere. "The eighteenth was a black day," recalled Hausser. "The next ones resembled it."[58]

American planes bombed Hausser's headquarters on the eighteenth, killed five officers and one enlisted man, and wrecked the radio center. With that, Hausser's ability to control the battle with any precision ended.[59]

Hausser ordered Kniess and his LXXXV Corps to retreat out of the West Wall step by step. For three days, beginning the twentieth, Kniess battled overwhelming American forces, namely XX Corps, descending on him from the northwest on the line Homburg-Kaiserslautern. He now controlled the 719th, 347th, and 19th Volksgrenadier Divisions. Losses were heavy, but his fairly strong divisions put up more of a fight than most along the collapsing front; the 719th Division claimed the destruction of nineteen American tanks in a single day. The operation was possible only because U.S. Seventh Army's pressure against First Army from the south was weak, and there was no danger from that quarter.

Kniess retreated southeastwards. On the twenty-third, he turned his divisions over to Simon's XIII SS Corps, and his staff left for service in Seventh Army.[60]

The View of Patton

As we have seen, the German view of Patton's generalship in the closing phase of the campaign was that, despite his demonstrated skill using armor in the advance, he missed the chance to make the Saar-Palatinate to Army Group G what the Ruhr Pocket would prove to be to Army Group B: its final resting place. Instead, it became a second Falaise Pocket, hideously destructive to the German army in the West, but permitting enough army-group, army, corps, and division staffs and elements to escape to organize a semblance of resistance east of the Rhine. Ironically, Patton's G-2, Oscar Koch, had raised the precedent of the Falaise Pocket as he assessed the impact of the 4th Armored Division's advance on 15 March, without, presumably, anticipating a pocket closing just in the nick of too late.[61] Nevertheless, as we shall now see, the destruction was so vast that the resistance could hardly slow the American advance east of the Rhine, much less stop it. One wonders, however, how many of the roughly 11,000 killed, wounded, and missing suffered by Third Army east of the Rhine would have been spared had Patton closed the trap more quickly.

PATTON CROSSES THE RHINE

The collapse in Saar-Palatinate was nearly complete on 21 March. The 90th Infantry Division reached Mainz and launched an attack on the city. The 4th Armored Division was in Worms. Hausser belatedly received authority over the east bank of the Rhine. He found that there were no resources available to defend the river other than a few ill-equipped infantry battalions and the *Volksturm* militia.[62] Hausser, on his own and against instructions from OKW, ordered Seventh Army to retreat across the Rhine to organize defenses there. Beyer's LXXX Corps was subordinated to Foertsch, and First Army, with Hoehne's LXXXIX Corps, already east of the Rhine, was placed under Army Group B in anticipation that it would become engaged against the Remagen bulge. That left Felber with the newly constituted XII Corps and XIII Corps. The former had no divisions, and the latter only one coherent formation—the 559th Volksgrenadier Division—and the "ruins and remnants" of the 9th, 159th, and 352nd Volksgrenadier Divisions and rear elements of the 2nd Panzer Division.

Army Group G's headquarters pulled back across the Rhine on 23 March, and responsibility for command of the fragments west of the river shifted to First Army for several hours.[63] First Army's staff crossed the river that night.[64]

Patton beat them to the east bank of the Rhine. The 5th Infantry Division slipped across at Oppenheim the night of 22 March and suffered only twenty-eight casualties. Patton already was planning more crossings.[65] Thanks to radio intercepts, Hausser knew the crossing was coming, but there were no resources to send to the area.[66] Seventh Army assessed that the rag-tag units available could not defend the east bank of the river, and that Third Army would cross in force south of the Main and drive through Darmstadt toward Würzburg in order to split northern from southern Germany. Felber did not learn of the crossing at Oppenheim until it had already been under way for some time.[67] Kesselring recorded that he was "dumbfounded."[68]

By this time, observed Wilutzky, the army-group headquarters had lost all authority to make autonomous decisions and was nothing but a message center for OKW, a situation that would continue through the end of the war.[69] Yet even as OKW sought to exercise increasing control over the tactical conduct of the battle—the heretofore-successful philosophy of *Auftragstaktik* was dying away, observed Felber—OKW's actual ability to do so was declining. "In general," recalled Gersdorff, "one cannot speak of operational command after the conquest of the West Wall. The technical command system continued to function, but in light of the complete hopelessness and the obvious collapse of the divisions, operational command in the sense of the former war leadership was no longer possible."[70] Army Groups B and G as of 22 March could not even communicate with one another.[71] OKW considered LXXXII, XIII SS, and LXXXV Corps to be "overrun."[72] The idea of a coherent western front, commanded and coordinated from a collective brain at OKW, was dead.

Third Army's G-2 on 23 March declared Army Group G "destroyed," which was but a slight exaggeration. Koch accurately predicted that the Germans would be able to gather nothing but makeshift elements to oppose Third Army's thrust across the Rhine. Total German reserves in the interior amounted to only nine divisions.[73]

AUTONOMIC RESPONSES

Like the autonomic nervous system in the human body, which controls functions such as breathing at a level below consciousness, the Wehrmacht fought on.

Seventh Army had less than forty-eight hours to begin organizing the fragments of divisions on the east bank (elucidated earlier) before Patton pushed across the Rhine. Seventh Army had lost most of its communications equipment and had great difficulty getting its orders to anyone. The last German battle-ready divisions had been destroyed west of the Rhine. Kesselring made Army Group G's job even harder by ordering that the 17th SS Panzergrenadier Division, the only semimobile formation available, be pulled back for rebuilding before being committed to battle. Patton's G-2 shop estimated that as of 17 March, total German tank strength on the western front amounted to the equivalent of a single full-strength panzer division. Wilutzky recalled, "We had come to the end of our strength."[74]

The Rhine, of course, represented a major water obstacle to an American advance, but it was all but indefensible without mobile reserves, which no longer existed. In the zone controlled by Hoehne's LXXXIX Corps, beginning 18 March, *Oberst* Werner Wagner, 276th Volksgrenadier Division, recalled that when his unit pulled back across the Rhine on 16 March after the collapse of LIII Corps, the men found the defensive works totally inadequate. Two more weeks of work would have been required to make them battle ready. Similarly, in the stretch under German XII Corps, where Third Army would conduct its first crossing, nothing but strongpoints had been completed and manned on the east bank.[75]

Moreover, because of the overhang of the east bank, it was nearly impossible to site weapons for direct fire on the eastern shore except in full view of the enemy. Some heavy weapons, therefore, were fully exposed. Knobelsdorff, confronted with a similar problem along the Moselle, had placed his troops out of sight beyond the crest and relied on mobile forces to seal any breaches.[76] This maneuver was far beyond Felber's capabilities.

This illustrative example of the problems posed by a theoretical defense of the Rhine, however, mattered little because no defense was going to be possible. Kesselring lamented, "As Remagen had been the grave of Army Group B, it seemed that the bridgehead at Oppenheim would be that of Army Group G. Here, too, the bulge which soon widened into a gap consumed all the forces that could be moved from other parts of the front and all replacements available in the rear."

By 24 March, Patton had the 5th Infantry and most of the 90th Infantry and 4th Armored Divisions across the Rhine at Oppenheim. OKW mistakenly thought he had added the 6th Armored Division rather than the 90th Infantry and recorded of this imagined concentration of tanks that "the tactics of General Patton were to be seen," one of only four times that OKW individually recognized Patton. The good general walked across a bridge installed by the engineers and stopped to relieve himself into the water. He had already set the 76th Infantry Division in motion to cross at St. Goar, near the site of the legendary Lorelei, the next day.

Felber planned to counterattack at Oppenheim, according to standard German practice. XII Corps was given the staff of the 159th Infantry Division and all the reserves that could be brought to bear—three corps infantry battalions, a reserve officer-candidate regiment from Frankfurt, five or six panzers and assault guns, and some artillery and flak. Kesselring, Hausser, and Felber all arrived at the operational command post to witness the event, a monumental testament to the depths to which the German army in the west had sunk. Not surprisingly, the attack was a dismal failure.

Hausser and Model urged that Kesselring withdraw the entire western front from the Rhine, but Kesselring believed that retreat would degenerate into a rout. Every day gained at the Rhine was a chance to scrape together stragglers and resources.[77]

Seventh Army's "line" caved in on the twenty-fifth, and the Americans took off toward Darmstadt. A captain-cadet regiment that took up residence in the woods south of Frankfurt was annihilated. XII Corps set about constructing a notional line along the Main River and preparing Frankfurt for defense.[78]

It was all action for action's sake. The stunned survivors were going through the motions like automatons. The visceral organs were working away without any guidance from the brain.

Some of Patton's former enemies appeared on the battlefield. Hausser gave Seventh Army the staff of Kniess's LXXXV Corps from First Army to take over from XII Corps. Kniess and his staff barely made it through the Darmstadt area on their way north before the 4th Armored Division punched through and

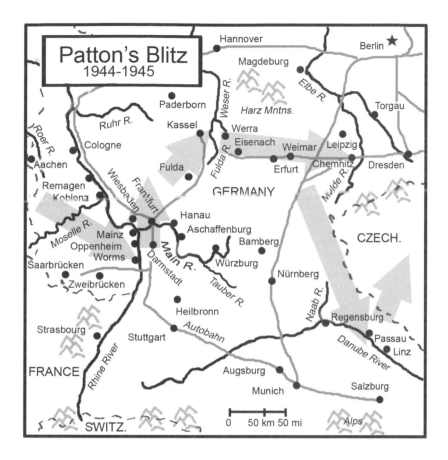

Patton's Blitz
1944-1945

severed all routes. Some corps troops following the staff had to make a lengthy detour to reach Kniess. Kesselring ordered the 11th Panzer Division, most of which had just been moved north for an aborted attempt to stop the envelopment of the Ruhr, back south to the Main to join Kniess. The division's elements still at Remagen were deeply engaged, however, and all elements were short of fuel and harassed by *jabos*. Moving troops kept bumping into American tank spearheads. Only *Generalmajor* Wietersheim and a weak reconnaissance force arrived with speed.[79]

A vast hole had emerged in Seventh Army's front. Wietersheim learned from Seventh Army that the situation south of the Main was unclear and "the only sure thing was that the Americans were advancing everywhere." Gersdorff noted that had Third Army turned southeastward, it could have rolled up all of Army Group G from the rear. Fortunately for the Germans, that was 6th Army Group's turf, and Patton was focused on wheeling north across the Main. Felber set to work on another nearly fictional blocking line from Hanau to Aschaffenburg, both important crossings on the Main River.[80]

According to Kesselring, at this stage he did not expect Third Army to turn north and cross the Main because of the amount of bridging equipment that would be required. He also was uncertain whether Third and First Armies would operate in tandem, or whether Patton would attack into southern Germany beside U.S. Seventh Army. *Oberst* Wilutzky recalled that Army Group G did expect the Americans to cross the Main and advance to the northeast, but his account is confused because he believed that it had been U.S. Seventh Army that crossed at Oppenheim and advanced on Darmstadt. Kesselring was surprised by the speed with which the Main front collapsed, which is to say that he was one more German commander surprised by the speed of Patton's attack.

Kesselring finally sacked Felber on 26 March. Felber that day was present in Frankfurt and witnessed GIs from the 6th Armored Division crossing the one bridge that had not been destroyed; soon fighting raged throughout the city center. *General der Infanterie* Hans von Obstfelder, whom Kesselring considered an energetic commander and who had briefly fought Patton in Lorraine, left his command of Nineteenth Army and took charge of Seventh Army at 1500 hours. Felber had paid the price for permitting Patton to cross the Rhine at Oppenheim. Obstfelder had the difficult task of stopping Patton's drive into central Germany. The difficulty was highlighted on the twenty-seventh, when the column conducting Patton's infamous raid on Hammelburg to rescue his son-in-law passed within a few thousand meters of Seventh Army's headquarters.

The OKW *Kriegstagebuch* reveals that, by this time, the high command's knowledge of the battle was often a day or two behind actual events. Seventh Army was in little better shape and on the twenty-seventh lost contact with Kniess's LXXXV Corps, which was now responsible for the Frankfurt sector and threatened with encirclement by U.S. XII Corps and U.S. First Army's right wing approaching from the north. Kniess controlled nothing but weak security forces and the reconnaissance battalion of the 11th Panzer Division. Kesselring that day sacked Kniess after the 4th Armored Division captured Hanau, in part because Kniess did not ensure the destruction of the bridge there across the Main.

On the twenty-eighth, the 4th Armored Division linked up with First Army north of the Main and trapped all German forces west to Wiesbaden. The OKW *Kriegstagebuch* noted that Patton had turned northward rather than continue to the east—the fourth and last time he is mentioned in the high command's account of the war. For the next week, Obstfelder had no communications with LXXXV Corps. The corps staff would eventually reemerge from the encirclement on foot and be sent to the rear under a new commander, *General der Panzertruppe* Smilo *Freiherr* von Lüttwitz. Wietersheim had been cut off from the main body of his division, which was just arriving in an assembly area, and made his way at great risk across the 4th Armored Division's line of communication to rejoin his panzers.

Hahm's LXXXII Corps (36th, 256th, and 416th Volksgrenadier Divisions) arrived by 28 March to take charge of Seventh Army's left wing. With LXXXV Corps cut off, XII Corps (11th Panzer and 159th Infantry Divisions), under *General der Artillerie* Herbert Osterkamp, was again given charge of the right wing. Born in Hamm am Sieg on 7 May 1894, Osterkamp entered the imperial army in March 1912 as an officer candidate. He rose to command an infantry company during the Great War, but shifted to the artillery when he remained with the Reichswehr between the wars. Osterkamp was serving on the armaments staff when the war in Poland broke out and remained in various staff jobs until taking command of XII Corps.81 Despite his lack of combat experience since 1918, Kesselring considered Osterkamp's command to be exemplary, judged him to have a perceptive view of the military situation, and praised him as a general willing to take independent action within the guidelines of Kesselring's overall intentions.[82]

Kesselring observed, "The fanning out of the enemy forces from the bridgeheads at Oppenheim and at Mannheim from the south towards the east and then northeast violated the principle of the concentration of effort, and its success was striking proof of the ebbing combat value of the German troops."[83] Kesselring characterized Patton's thrust across the lower Main as "partly favored by luck" and "a daring advance against vastly inferior forces" that created the "basis for far-reaching, decisive operations."[84] Indeed, all of Third Army's corps reported incidents of bitter resistance only in large towns and cities, and not all of them. Third Army's decisive operation would be to turn east and drive to Fulda.[85]

A training unit, the *Türingen* Panzer Brigade, arrived in the XII Corps area in late March. The brigade consisted of a battalion each of tanks and assault guns, a panzergrenadier regiment, and a pioneer battalion, but it lacked any supply system. The brigade was merged with the rear elements of the 2nd Panzer Division and assumed the division's name. The division joined the 11th Panzer Division, and together they prepared to make one final effort to wage a mobile defense against Third Army's XII Corps on Seventh Army's wide-open right flank.[86] When the 4th Armored Division pushed northeastward on the twenty-ninth, however, the 11th Panzer Division lacked the fuel to attack its flank, a situation the German XII Corps's chief of staff attributed to the enemy's "soldier's luck."[87]

On 30 March, Bradley ordered Patton to turn his axis northeastward and advance to the Wesser River, with further movement to the Elbe to follow.[88] This route, luckily enough, would take Third Army right up the seam between Army Groups B and G.[89] The 4th Armored Division led the charge, and Obstfelder again tried to use his armor to stop it. The 11th Panzer Division had moved to Fulda and the 2nd Panzer Division was just to its south. American control of the air and fuel shortages again frustrated all attempts to use the panzers in maneuver. The Americans overran another fresh panzer battalion just as it was detraining in Bad Hersfeld north of Fulda.[90] As of 31 March, the entire force of panzers and assault guns in Third Army's sector was estimated at only fifty-five vehicles, all opposite XX Corps in the Fulda area.[91]

At the end of the month, Seventh Army was operating in a vacuum, as Army Group G had lost any ability to direct its actions and stopped trying, leaving Obstfelder to use his own initiative.[92]

The brand-new Eleventh Army and its commander, *General der Infanterie* Otto-Maximilian Hitzfeld, subordinated to Army Group B, earned their own footnotes on the list of Patton's enemies when some of its elements fought XX Corps's 80th Infantry Division at Kassel from 3 to 4 April. The "army" had been created out of the staff of XI Corps and was to control LXVII, LXVI, and IX Corps. Kesselring personally oriented Hitzfeld, heretofore commanding LXVII Corps, on his orders to both break into the Ruhr Pocket to link up with Model and the remnants of Army Group B and use some elements to stop the American advance across the Fulda River.

In terms of numbers, Eleventh Army looked like one of the strongest armies in Germany. LXVI Corps, on its right wing, consisted largely of an SS brigade that possessed up to 4,000 men and thirty panzers, plus the 508th Heavy Tank Battalion with between twenty and thirty Royal Tigers. LXVII Corps, on the left, had the remnants of six infantry and volksgrenadier divisions, plus men from the panzer noncommissioned officers school in Eisenach and twenty panzers pulled from the Henschel works. These tanks had given the 80th Division some trouble as it approached Kassel. However, Eleventh Army had almost no reconnaissance capability, artillery, supply structure, or fuel. It had no contact with Seventh Army to its south and little idea what was going on to either flank.

Hitzfeld pondered his resources and immediately sent a radio message to Kesselring's headquarters requesting the attack order be rescinded. He knew he could not stop the Americans—who he apparently did not even know were from Third Army—in their advance across the Fulda and, in fact, probably could not even delay them. His old corps had already given up bridgeheads across the

Fulda south of Kassel on 3 April. U.S. First and Ninth Armies that same day were smashing LXVI Corps.

The 80th Division on 4 April entered Kassel. The last radio message from the commander of the city's defenses said, "Surrounded with the remnants of the garrison in the Truselturm [city center]. No ammunition, no water." The commander surrendered with 400 men.

Kesselring appeared again and told Hitzfeld the attack toward the Ruhr was off. Instead, he was to attack the Third Army's flank at Eisenach. LXVII Corps, by the evening of 6 April, had assembled some thirty tanks and assault guns and two battalions of infantry at Mülhausen to attack as ordered. The strike group moved out on the seventh, only to be shredded by the *jabos*. Third Army credited LXVII Corps with conducting a well-coordinated operation, but had no idea which German unit was involved. The survivors retreated, and thus ended Eleventh Army's real fight with Patton. Under the command of *General der Artillerie* Walther Lucht from 7 to 20 April, it continued to be a notional presence because its zone was extended to include Erfurt and Weimar, both of which Third Army easily captured, the latter without a fight.[93]

Kesselring's memoirs indicate that during April he was much more concerned with the self-effacing U.S. Seventh Army's drive through Würzburg to Nürnberg than he was with Third Army's operations. Army Group G had a new commander, *General der Panzertruppe* Karl Friedrich Wilhelm Schultz, who took command on 5 April. Schultz had been commanding general of the Seventeenth Army in Silesia when he had been summoned to Hitler's headquarters. Hitler assured him that the problems in the west were due to Allied air superiority and that he would soon have enough jets to retake control of the air. Schultz's main task in his new assignment would be to attack northward toward Würzburg to seal the American breakthrough there. Schultz, of course, immediately discovered that this goal was a fantasy. The divisions on Hitler's situation map existed, but they had the strength of battalions. At the time he took command, he still nominally controlled Seventh Army fighting Patton and thus formally joined the ranks of Patton's enemies, but in truth, he exercised no influence over the battlefield.[94]

One reason Kesselring focused on Seventh Army was that on 4 April, Patton received orders to nearly stop until First and Ninth Armies, to his left, both then involved in reducing the Ruhr Pocket, could catch up. He was given new interarmy boundaries that forced him to redraw his intercorps boundaries. Patton lamented that he was forced into "for the first time in the history of the Third Army, the act of regrouping." (He evidently had forgotten his regrouping in late November in Lorraine.) While regrouping and on a leash, his divisions advanced only a few miles a day. Nevertheless, during this period, a quarter-master unit scooped up LXXXII Corps's commanding general Hahm, who had given up the fight and sat down, waiting to be captured. Bradley loosened the leash on 12 April. By the fourteenth, XII and XX Corps surged to a hard stop line on the Mulde River, and VIII Corps caught up the following day.[95]

Hitler, five days earlier, had split *OB West* into commanders-in-chief Northwest and West in light of the total destruction of Army Group B in the Ruhr Pocket. Kesselring remained in command of operations in the south and moved his headquarters to Bavaria.[96]

The German army was engaged in nothing more than a semiorganized retreat, marked by occasional delaying battles and fights for cities where flak guns provided a base of fire. It is merely a matter of record on the list of Patton's enemies that as of 11 April, according to Gersdorff, Obstfelder's Seventh Army—now subordinated directly to Kesselring rather than Army Group G—consisted of XC Corps, commanded by *General der Flieger* Erich Petersen, on its left, control-ling three ad hoc division fragments; LXXXV Corps, commanded by *General der Panzertruppe* Smilo *Freiherr* von Lüttwitz, in the center, with Wietersheim's 11th Panzer Division and several *Kampfgruppen*; and Osterkamp's XII Corps, on the right, with the 2nd Panzer Division and several division fragments. Obstfelder's right flank was hanging in air. (Wilutzky's account states that XC Corps was still part of First Army and dates Kesselring's taking direct control over Seventh Army to "around" 25 April.)

Radio intercepts had revealed the boundary between the 12th and 6th Army groups, and Obstfelder expected Third Army and the rest of Bradley's army group to continue advancing to the northeast while 6th Army Group hooked southward. Anticipating a Third Army advance through Leipzig, Obstfelder tried to strengthen his right wing, but he lacked ammunition and reserves.[97]

Patton's enemies no longer had a frame of reference in which to judge his performance. Generally, they lacked anything but a general picture of what was occurring on the battlefield. The pace and direction of Patton's advance was limited only by higher American authorities. There was no question of Patton seizing opportunities, or failing to do so. Opportunities lay at Patton's feet, on any path he chose to travel.

Let us take the case of one German commander during the first half of April. *General der Panzertruppe* Smilo *Freiherr* von Lüttwitz represented a return of a seasoned panzer general opposite Patton. Born 23 December 1895 in Strafsburg, Lüttwitz entered the imperial army in June 1914 as an officer candidate. After fighting with the 4th Panzer Division in Operation Barbarossa, Lüttwitz had overseen the conversion of the 23rd Infantry Division into a panzer division and then, a newly minted *Generalmajor*, been given command of the 20th Panzer Division in December 1942. He had also earned the Knight's Cross.

Lüttwitz had gained considerable experience against the Western Allies in Italy while commanding the 26th Panzer Division, and then in July 1944, he returned to the east to take command of the XLVI Panzer Corps and fought in north Ukraine and Poland. Promoted to *General der Panzertruppe*, Lüttwitz, from September through early January 1945, commanded Ninth Army until he was sacked for disobedience, a charge he faced down before a court martial. In the course of his rise, he had been judged highly intelligent, earnest, a courageous leader at the front, a fine tactician, an excellent trainer, and clear in his judgments.[98]

Lüttwitz, on 29 March, had gotten orders from Obstfelder to activate the remnants of LXXXV Corps headquarters and assume control of the Werra sector on 1 April. Lüttwitz found he had at his disposal Wietersheim's redoubtable 11th Panzer Division, still at 50 percent strength, including twenty to twenty-five Panthers and Mark IVs, and with good communications. He also had a *Kampfgruppe* from the armored-troops school with five panzers and fragments of three infantry divisions. A panzergrenadier regiment of the 11th Panzer Division supported by twelve panzers formed his only reserve.

The corps was to hold U.S. XII Corps before Eisenach and block entry into the Thuringian Forest, and as best as Lüttwitz could understand the situation, the 4th Armored and 90th Infantry Divisions would arrive in his zone in the near future. Lüttwitz planned to wage a flexible defense. He kept the 11th Panzer Division southeast of Eisenach, ready to reinforce an imperiled part of his line or to counterattack any breakthrough.

The instincts were still there, but the means were not. Lüttwitz described the last serious effort by any German commander to fight Patton:

> The north wing appeared to be particularly endangered because there was the boundary of the army group and a loose communication with the units to the north of Kreuzburg existed only temporarily. Because of inadequate radio equipment available, signal communications to [Seventh] Army as well as to subordinate and neighboring units had to be established by using the postal telephone wire net, which was mostly overburdened and therefore frequently failed to transmit.
>
> At the Werra sector, only light field positions had been built during the short lapse of time, and only small defense sectors in depth along the

main roads. But artillery and antitank defense for an efficient defense were entirely lacking. . . .

By using heavy screening smoke, the American forces crossed the Werra at Kreuzburg and south of it early in the morning of 4 April. From the bridgehead newly formed by infantry, the spearhead of the American 4th Armored Division thrust past the north of Eisenach to the east. . . . In the afternoon of the 4th, the American 90th Infantry Division attacked on a wide front against the sector south of Eisenach. . . . During these engagements, the corps (exclusive of the 11th Panzer Division) lost about 60 percent of its fighting strength. [Lüttwitz had been forced to commit the 11th Panzer Division on his right flank, and so it was not available to counterattack as he had planned. By 9 April, all formations subordinate to the corps had been annihilated except for Wietersheim's division.][99]

Responding in part to the "extremely stubborn" resistance at Eisenach, the Third Army G-2, Koch, observed, "Apparently as long as the German High Command is able to conjure up personnel that will submit to commitment it is the purpose of the High Command to wage war. . . . The bulk of the enemy's armies have been shattered and his industrial power to continue large-scale warfare has been either destroyed or captured. But his will to fight and fanatical ingenuity to inflict losses on us are unshaken. The enemy is comparable to a mad beast at bay—wounded to the death but still deadly dangerous." On 11 April, Koch judged that some 16,000 men and perhaps ninety tanks and assault guns opposed the quarter million men of Third Army.[100]

Bradley on 16 April ordered Patton to turn Third Army, which had reached the outskirts of Chemnitz, southward west of the Czechoslovakian border, with XX Corps north of the Danube and XII Corps south of it. U.S. Seventh Army also was to turn due south, while First and Ninth Armies, which were just mopping up the Ruhr Pocket, went over to a defensive posture, despite there being nothing left against which to defend.[101] Leaving VIII Corps with First Amy and picking up III Corps, Third Army set off for Bavaria on 22 April to prevent the creation of a rumored National Redoubt in the Alps, where the Nazis allegedly planned to stage a last-ditch resistance. They did not so plan, though there were impractical schemes to defend the Alps militarily. The Soviets, by this time, were fighting from building to building through Berlin.[102]

The eastern and western fronts by April were extremely close. Up until 20 April, Kesselring's mission had been to protect the rear of the eastern armies in their final battles against the Soviets. From then on, his mission was to fight to allow the eastern armies to withdraw into the British and American zones.[103]

Obstfelder's Seventh Army found itself entangled with elements of Army Group Center, fighting Soviet cavalry pushing up the Elbe River while still facing U.S. First Army to its west.[104]

The change in direction took Third Army into Army Group G's rear, but the territory really fell under no effective command. No defensive forces were available in northeastern Bavaria. A provisional XIII Corps (commanded by *General der Infanterie* Karl Weisenberger), created from a military district staff, tried to build a security line along the Naab River, but was swept backward by the 11th Armored and 26th Infantry Divisions. The main effect, according to Kesselring, was to imperil the rears of Army Groups Southeast and South on the eastern front.[105] On 24–25 April, Third Army, which had fourteen divisions advancing, plus numerous corps troops, suffered but a hundred battle casualties.[106]

Lüttwitz and his LXXXV Corps staff were transferred to the Passau area on 26 April, where they were to take charge of the 11th Panzer Division—then moving to the same area—to block Third Army's advance on Linz, Austria. It was another mission impossible. The 11th Panzer Division could hardly move for lack of fuel, and Lüttwitz was taken prisoner on 5 May.[107] Patton and the 90th Infantry Division, meanwhile, permitted Wietersheim and his 11th Panzer Division to surrender to the Americans on 4 May, although they were located in the Soviet zone. The Americans had always found the 11th Panzer Division to be an honorable enemy.[108]

As of 6 May, Third Army estimated that 144,300 Germans had fought Patton and his legions since the army became active on 1 August 1944 and had paid the ultimate price of their lives. Another 385,700 were assessed to have been wounded, and 805,321 taken prisoner.[109]

Strengthened by V Corps, Third Army finished the war by turning northeastward and crossing the Czechoslovakian frontier. Simultaneous attacks on 7 and 8 May by Third Army and the Soviets forced Obstfelder to surrender Seventh Army. *General der Panzertruppe* Hermann Balck appeared on the eighth and surrendered the remnants of his Sixth Army from the eastern front—some 200,000 men, including the 1st and 3rd Panzer Divisions and 5th SS Division *Wiking*—to the 80th Infantry Division. Koch's final periodic report ended, "Enemy Capabilities. None."

"The eighth of May," Patton observed of VE Day, "marked exactly two and one-half years since we had landed in Africa."[110] Of that time, Patton had spent about seventeen months in noncombat duties. Patton's many enemies since that first shootout in San Miguelito had actually fought him for just over a year of combat time.

------------*------------

FOURTEEN

A Footnote to the Panegyric

Most of my predecessors in this place have commended him who made this speech part of the law, telling us that it is well that it should be delivered at the burial of those who fall in battle. For myself, I should have thought that the worth which had displayed itself in deeds would be sufficiently rewarded by honors also shown by deeds; such as you now see in this funeral prepared at the people's cost. And I could have wished that the reputations of many brave men were not to be imperiled in the mouth of a single individual, to stand or fall according as he spoke well or ill. . . . Thus choosing to die resisting, rather than to live submitting, they fled only from dishonor, but met danger face to face, and after one brief moment, while at the summit of their fortune, escaped, not from their fear, but from their glory.

SO SPOKE PERICLES at the funeral for Athens' fallen warriors after the first year of the Peloponnesian War.

Like the soldiers of ancient Athens, Patton has received his laudatory orations, which also have told of the ancestry and great deeds of the dead. His acts, declared Martin Blumenson, entitled him to membership in "the pantheon of military heroes."[1] Carlo D'Este places Patton in "the pantheon of authentic American heroes."[2] Patton's failings, such as whatever caused the slapping incidents in Sicily, have only made him a flawed hero. His death so soon after the war lent him the air of an Achilles, a tragic hero destined to flame brilliantly in his time, but doomed to an early grave. Patton believed that he had been born a warrior in many ages, and it's not hard to imagine that this is the fate he would have wished.

Patton's most astute American supporter, the genius who put together the American military leadership team, marked the point at which Patton established himself as a great general as his deft blow against the Bulge. General George Marshall wrote to President Harry Truman shortly after Patton's death:

> Since his action in the Meuse-Argonne battle of 1918, I had recognized him as a determined and utterly fearless battle leader. This is one of the [reasons] I selected him to lead our troops in the landing at Casablanca in November 1942. In the fighting in Africa and in Sicily he was conspicuous for the driving energy and the tactical skill with which he led his troops The breakthrough of the Third Army in Normandy and its dramatic liberation of central France was indicative of Patton, the man who led it. But it was his counterattack towards Bastogne and the tremendous thrusts to the Rhine at Koblenz and south into the center and rear of the German armies in the Saar Basin, followed by the sudden crossing of the Rhine that established General Patton as one of the greatest military leaders in our history.[3]

The collective panegyric retrofitted Patton's great moment onto the career that preceded it. Its verse swooned that even the enemy found Patton to be a great commander.

German views of Patton as collected in the immediate aftermath of the war indicated some commanders had, indeed, come to consider Patton a respected opponent, largely because of his speed of action, which had surprised German commanders since Tunisia. As we have seen, however, his opponents found him hesitant at key points in the campaigns in Tunisia, Sicily, Lorraine, and the Saar-Palatinate. Moreover, in their minds, he appeared to play second fiddle to Montgomery, as he had throughout the war, because they admired the Briton's well-organized, if deliberate, approach to victory.

"Montgomery and Patton were the two best that I met," mused Rundstedt in a prisoner-of-war compound immediately after the war. "Field Marshall Montgomery was very systematic," he added.

So it went with Blumentritt. Patton, he offered, was speedy in the advance. Montgomery, though, "was the one general who never suffered a reverse. He moved like this—," and the general stamped deliberately forward.[4] Guderian said of Patton, "He was very quick. The essential thing in panzer command is speed."[5]

Rommel, writing while convalescing from his wounds in Normandy, drafted a manuscript in which he pondered Montgomery as a commander at some length and mentioned Patton only once, which is sensible considering whom he had fought. The Desert Fox implicitly drew a key distinction from a German perspective between Montgomery and Patton: the former was a strategist and multidimensional commander, and the latter a tactician. "Montgomery was undoubtedly more a strategist than a tactician. Command of a mobile force in combat was not his strong point. . . . In the field of higher strategic planning he must be credited with outstanding achievements. . . . [Even in North Africa] the American generals showed themselves to be very advanced in the tactical handling of their forces, although we had to wait until the Patton Army in France to see the most astonishing achievements in mobile warfare."[6] The last clause is often quoted out of context to suggest a particular admiration on Rommel's part for George Patton as an individual as opposed to being the best example of a pool of tactically skilled American commanders.

There was good reason for this view. Monty, after being wounded in 1914 while leading a rifle company, had risen to serve as the operations officer of a corps and chief of staff in an infantry division and, therefore, had developed a more strategic perspective than Patton. His experiences with mass British casualties also gave him his predisposition to look for cautious, systematic, casualty-reducing ways of fighting.[7] Patton had seen little of the Great War bloodbath and had risen from regimental to corps command with no combat experience in between that would have developed his strategic-thinking abilities.

German generals thought of Patton in the narrow context of great armored commanders. Blumentritt observed, "We regarded General Patton extremely highly as the most aggressive *Panzer-General* of the Allies, a man of incredible initiative and lightning-like action. He resembled our own *Panzer-General* Guderian. His operations impressed us enormously, probably because he came closest to our own concept of the classical military commander. He even improved on Napoleon's basic tenet—*activitée, vitesse—vitesse*."[8] *Generaloberst* Alfred Jodl likewise opined, "He was the American Guderian. He was very bold and preferred large movements. He took big risks and won big successes."[9]

Guderian himself mentioned Patton only once in his memoirs, in a factual reference to "Patton's tanks."[10] He told his captors in 1945, "I hear much about General Patton, and he conducted a good campaign. From the standpoint of a tank specialist, I must congratulate him for his victory since he acted as I should have done had I been in his place."[11]

Kesselring picked out Eisenhower and Patton for special praise among American generals. "Patton had developed tank warfare into an art and understood how to handle tanks brilliantly in the field. I feel compelled, therefore, to compare him with *Generalfeldmarschall* Rommel, who likewise had mastered the art of tank warfare. Both of them had a kind of second sight in regard to this type of warfare."[12]

Oberst Hans von Luck likewise considered Patton "probably the most flexible of the Allied tank commanders." Manteuffel, according to Luck, was *almost* willing to call Patton the American Rommel.[13] Brandenberger, as we have seen, praised Patton's execution of armored warfare according to German principles during the Battle of France. Felber similarly compared Patton's actions in March 1945 to German armored advances in the east in 1941.

The Germans, however, do not appear to have viewed Patton as the multi-faceted strategist that they saw not only in Montgomery. Panzer general Fritz Bayerlein told interrogators, "In the beginning [of the campaign in France], I thought Patton was the best because of his quick and fearless exploitation of opportunities and his breakthroughs with armored forces. From our reports, we later learned to respect Bradley even more as a cool, clear, and determined commander with more directional genius. Hodges also was considered good."[14]

This specific frame of reference, the *Panzer-General*, is probably the main reason that the Germans were less impressed by Patton as an overall commander than some American historians would like to believe. Patton was the *only* American *Panzer-General* above the division level, whereas among his German contemporaries, Patton would have had a crowd of company; the number of outstanding American armored men at the division level could be counted on one hand. In contrast, 266 German officers, 241 of them from the army, commanded panzer, light, or motorized divisions; panzer corps; and panzer armies. This represented roughly 10 percent of the army's flag-rank officers. Fifty-five of these officers remained with the panzer troops for the duration of the war, most rising to the rank of *General der Panzertruppe*.[15] To these ranks must be added the *Waffen* SS and Luftwaffe panzer generals. Among this group, Patton probably would have been merely above average.

Germany's panzer generals had a high bar for judging outstanding success. Patton's biographers have argued that he had a keen strategic mind (here, though, Blumenson demurs), but such a mind was hardly uncommon among his enemies. Regarding the Germans' stunning successes in the summer of 1943 that netted 240,000 prisoners trapped in a *Kessel* at Rostov—more men than would have been taken had Patton been allowed to close the pocket at Falaise–Mellenthin described the daring decisions made by *Generalfeldmarschalle* Maximilian *Freiherr* von Weichs and Wilhelm List and commented, "[T]he conduct of armored warfare in vast spaces also requires generals with a mastery of strategy. We possessed generals of this type. . . ."[16]

Patton's drive to the Moselle with a long, open flank was his most daring operation of the war, but such a drive was old hat to the Germans. Panzer Group Kleist and Guderian's panzer corps had done the same during their drive along the Somme to the sea in France in May 1940—without the benefit of Ultra intercepts offering secure knowledge that there was no danger.[17] Sir Basil H. Liddell Hart observed, "It is clear that Guderian and his tankmen pulled the German Army along after them, and thereby produced the most sweeping victory in modern history."[18] Jodl commented that Patton's breakout at Avranches "reminded me of Rommel's lightning capture of Cherbourg in 1940."[19]

Patton claimed that, "as of 14 August [1944], the Third Army had advanced farther and faster than any army in history."[20] XV Corps in two weeks had rolled some 140 miles in its loop from Avranches around and behind Army Group B, while the 6th Armored Division had covered roughly the same distance in the opposite direction to Brest. Generously, since armies rarely get to advance in opposite directions at the same time, Third Army had covered some 300 miles. By the time Patton's gas tanks ran dry in Verdun at the end of August, his spearheads had moved some 350 miles eastward.

By comparison, Army Group North's 4th Panzer Group, commanded by *General der Panzertruppe* George-Hans Reinhardt, over the first three weeks of Germany's invasion of the Soviet Union covered more than 500 miles toward Leningrad without the benefit, for the most part, of passable roads inside Russia. In the first four days alone, *General der Infanterie* Erich von Manstein's LVI Corps (Motorized) covered 200 miles.[21] During the first six weeks of the eastern campaign, Otto von Knobelsdorff's 19th Panzer Division covered 800 miles of ground, which Knobelsdorff boasted was "unique in Prussian-German military history."[22] The Soviet resistance encountered during this period was commensurate with the German resistance faced by Third Army.

The German panzer generals had masterfully executed difficult retreats under heavy enemy pressure—tests that, like Helmuth von Moltke, Patton never faced. Each of Patton's opposing commanders in northwestern Europe had time and again fought nail-biting battles without the huge materiel superiority they all knew Patton enjoyed.

Patton may have been a master of improvisation, particularly as compared with Montgomery's set-piece approach to battle, but German panzer generals had been improvising for years. *Generaloberst* Erhard Raus, who had participated in the invasion of the Soviet Union as an *Oberst* commanding the 6th Motorized Brigade of the 6th Panzer Division and spent the war on the eastern front, recalled, "Any observer who looks at the Russian campaign in retrospect will come to the conclusion that the multitude of tactical and logistical improvisations that had to be employed to compensate for [a] lack of planning far exceeded what Field Marshal Helmuth von Moltke once designated as a 'system of expedients' in a tactical sense. In reality, our troops found themselves forced to introduce their first improvisations as soon as they crossed the Russian border."[23]

The former eastern-front generals Patton faced in France and Germany had a broad base of comparison for Patton in the form of their Soviet enemies. They had seen their Soviet counterparts become peer competitors in mobile warfare and had developed real respect for the strategic excellence of figures such as Marshall Georgi Zhukov. Mellenthin's praise for the skill of the Soviet counterblow that stopped Fourth Panzer Army's drive to relieve Stalingrad, for example, reflects an admiration exceeding anything he had to say about Patton: "The characteristic features of this dramatic battle were mobility, quick reaction, and utter perseverance on both sides. Tanks were the main weapon used, and both sides realized the main task of the armor was to destroy the opposing tanks. The Russians . . . exploited every success immediately and without hesitation. Some of the attacks were made by Russian tanks moving in at top speed. . . . [T]he tactical conduct of the battle by the Russians was on a high level."[24]

So what are we to make of the expressions of growing admiration for Patton in the decades following the war? Balck, who had stood before his situation maps during the campaign along the German border, expressing thanks for Patton's mistakes, said years later, "Patton was the outstanding tactical genius of World War II. I still consider it a privilege and unforgettable experience to have had the honor of opposing him."[25]

Likewise, Westphal, who said nothing of the sort in his immediate post-war memoirs, wrote to Patton biographer Ladislas Farago, "As far as General Patton was concerned, I was of the opinion even then that he was by far the outstanding commander in the [enemy] camp. Above all else, Patton was remarkable for his determined and bold actions. This was quite in contrast to Field Marshal Montgomery, who was known to me from North Africa. Montgomery was always extremely cautious, unwilling to take any risks."[26]

One possibility is that, looking back on events with more distance and perspective, veteran German commanders thought more of Patton with the passage of time.

But there may have been other influences, as well. By 1955, of course, the Federal Republic of Germany had become an ally of the United States against the "red menace" and a member of the North Atlantic Treaty Organization (NATO). Wartime passions had faded, and perhaps a sense of good sportsmanship had emerged on both sides regarding the achievements of opposite numbers during the conflict. Westphal, in 1957, had applied for a position in the *Bundeswehr* (German defense force) and was approved by the personnel-screening board, though ultimately passed over by the Defense Ministry.[27] Balck and Mellenthin became military consultants for NATO. Smilo von Lüttwitz became a *Generalleutnant* in the *Bundeswehr*.

Whatever Patton's enemies thought of him and his battles, in the end, he and the other Allied chieftains won, and their enemies lost. Field commanders were only one factor in determining the outcome, but they were an important one. As the French and British demonstrated in May 1940, superior means will not necessarily ensure the decision if the leadership is flawed. Patton deserves his legend, but posterity deserves history and not myth.

The Germans did not track Patton's movements as the key to Allied intentions. Hitler does not appear to have thought often of Patton, if at all. The Germans considered Patton a hesitant commanding general in the scrum of position warfare. They never raised his name in the context of worthy strategists. But they respected him in their own demanding terms as a great panzer officer. It is enough.

Table of Equivalent Ranks

U.S. Army	German Army and Air Force	German Waffen-SS
None	Reichsmarschall	None
General of the Army	Generalfeldmarschall	Reichsführer-SS
General	Generaloberst	Oberstgruppenführer
Lieutenant General	General der	Obergruppenführer
	Infanterie	
	Artillerie	
	Gebirgstruppen	
	Kavallerie	
	Nachrichtentruppen	
	Panzertruppen	
	Pioniere	
	Luftwaffe	
	Flieger	
	Fallschirmtruppen	
	Flakartillerie	
	Luftnachrichtentruppen	
Major General	Generalleutnant	Gruppenführer
Brigadier General	Generalmajor	Brigadeführer
None	None	Oberführer
Colonel	Oberst	Standartenführer
Lieutenant Colonel	Oberstleutnant	Obersturmbannführer

U.S. Army	German Army and Air Force	German Waffen-SS
Major	Major	Sturmbannführer
Captain	Hauptmann	Hauptsturmführer
Captain (Cavalry)	Rittmeister	None
First Lieutenant	Oberleutnant	Obersturmführer
Second Lieutenant	Leutnant	Untersturmführer

Source: Hugh M. Cole, *United States Army in World War II, The European Theater of Operations, The Lorraine Campaign*, Washington, DC: Historical Division, Department of the Army, 1950.

Notes

Preface

1. Ladislas Farago, *Patton: Ordeal and Triumph* (New York: Ivan Obolensky, 1963), 79. (Hereafter Farago.)

2. *Generalfeldmarschall* Albert Kesselring, "History of the 'Commander in Chief West' Part III (10 March 1945 up to the time of the surrender)," MS # T-123, July 1948, National Archives and Records Administration (NARA), 1–2. (Hereafter Kesselring, "Commander in Chief West.")

Chapter 1: From Kid to Killer

1. Martin Blumenson, *The Patton Papers: 1885–1940* (Boston: Houghton Mifflin Company, 1972), 4. (Hereafter Blumenson, *Patton Papers: 1885.*)

2. Oscar Koch with Robert G. Hays, *G-2: Intelligence for Patton* (Atglen, PA: Schiffer Military History, 1999), 155. (Hereafter Koch.)

3. *Generaloberst* Alfred Jodl, "U.S. Operations; German Defense; Ruhr; Last Days," ETHINT-52, 2 August 1945, NARA, 4. (Hereafter Jodl, "U.S. Operations.")

4. David M. Keithly and Stephen P. Ferris, "*Auftragstaktik*, or Directive Control, in Joint and Combined Operations," *Parameters*, Autumn 1999, 118–133.

5. Steve E. Dietrich, "The Professional Reading of General George S. Patton, Jr.," *Journal of Military History* 53, no. 4, Society for Military History Full Text Collection, EBSCOhost, accessed May 2010, 410. (Hereafter Dietrich.)

6. George S. Patton Jr., *War As I Knew It* (New York: Bantam Books, 1980), 141. (Hereafter Patton.)

7. Robert S. Allen, *Patton's Third Army: Lucky Forward* (New York: Manor Books, 1965), 26–27. (Hereafter Allen.)

8. Blumenson, *Patton Papers: 1885*, 3–7.

9. Ibid., 8.

10. Omar N. Bradley, *A Soldier's Story* (New York: The Modern Library, 1999), 52. (Hereafter Bradley.)

11. Martin Blumenson, *Patton: The Man Behind the Legend, 1815–1945* (New York:

William Morrow and Company, 1985), 9. (Hereafter Blumenson, *Patton*.)

12. Patton, xvi.

13. Carlo D'Este, *Patton: A Genius for War* (New York: HarperPerennial, 1995), 811. (Hereafter D'Este, *Patton: A Genius for War*.)

14. Blumenson, *Patton*, 11.

15. The Patton Society website, www.pattonhq.com, as of December 2009. Blumenson: *Patton*, 9, 34ff. D'Este, *Patton: A Genius for War*, 17ff.

16. "Los Dorados de Villa," Presidencia Municipal Ascencion website, http://www.ascencion.gob.mx/Contenido/plantilla5.asp?cve_canal=5117&Portal=ascension, as of August 2007.

17. Eileen Welsome, *The General and the Jaguar: Pershing's Hunt for Pancho Villa, A True Story of Revolution and Revenge* (New York: Little, Brown and Company, 2006), 110ff., 261. (Hereafter Welsome.)

18. Ibid., 188ff.

19. Ibid., 261.

20. Blumenson, *Patton Papers: 1885*, 329ff. Elser, Frank, "Cardenas's Family Saw Him Die at Bay," *The New York Times*, 23 May 1816, 5.

Chapter 2: All Violent on the Western Front

1. Francis A. March and Richard J. Beamish, *History of the World War* (Philadelphia: The United Publishers of the United States and Canada, 1919), 464–465. *Final Report of Gen. John J. Pershing* (Washington, DC: Government Printing Office, 1919), 5–6. (Hereafter Pershing.) Blumenson, *Patton*, 100–103.

2. Dale E. Wilson, *Treat 'Em Rough! The Birth of American Armor, 1917–20* (Novato, CA: Presidio Press, 1990), x. (Hereafter Wilson.)

3. "Operations of Tank Corps A.E.F. at St. Mihiel, in the Meuse-Argonne Operation, and with the British E.F.," General Headquarters, American Expeditionary Force, 27 December 1918, files of the General Headquarters Commander-in-Chief, RG 120/290/79/23/6, box 42, folder 388.

4. Ibid.

5. Wilson, 10.

6. "Report on the Development of the Tank Corps," undated memorandum in the files of the General Headquarters Commander-in-Chief, RG 120/290/79/23/6, box 42, folder 387. "Organization and Training, Permanent Tank Corps," memorandum from the chief of the Tank Corps to the assistant chief of staff, G-5, American Expeditionary Force, 2 December 1918, files of the General Headquarters Commander-in-Chief, RG 120/290/79/23/6, box 42, folder 388. Wilson, 13.

7. "Operations of Tank Corps A.E.F. at St. Mihiel, in the Meuse-Argonne Operation, and with the British E.F.," General Headquarters, American Expeditionary Force, 27 December 1918, files of the General Headquarters Commander-in-Chief, RG 120/290/79/23/6, box 42, folder 388.

8. Wilson, 14.

9. "Operations of Tank Corps A.E.F. at St. Mihiel, in the Meuse-Argonne Operation, and with the British E.F.," General Headquarters, American Expeditionary Force,

27 December 1918, files of the General Headquarters Commander-in-Chief, RG 120/290/79/23/6, box 42, folder 388.

10. "Report on the Development of the Tank Corps," undated memorandum in the files of the General Headquarters Commander-in-Chief, RG 120/290/79/23/6, box 42, folder 387. "Organization and Training, Permanent Tank Corps," memorandum from the chief of the Tank Corps to the assistant chief of staff, G-5, American Expeditionary Force, 2 December 1918, files of the General Headquarters Commander-in-Chief, RG 120/290/79/23/6, box 42, folder 388. Wilson, 16–20, 35.

11. "Organization and Training, Permanent Tank Corps," memorandum from the chief of the Tank Corps to the assistant chief of staff, G-5, American Expeditionary Force, 2 December 1918, files of the General Headquarters Commander-in-Chief, RG 120/290/79/23/6, box 42, folder 388. "Operations of Tank Corps A.E.F. at St. Mihiel in the Meuse-Argonne Operation, and with the British E.F.," General Headquarters, American Expeditionary Force, 27 December 1918, files of the General Headquarters Commander-in-Chief, RG 120/290/79/23/6, box 42, folder 388.

12. Pershing, 38–43.

13. *St-Mihiel: The United States Army in the World War, 1917–1919* (Washington, DC: Historical Division, Department of the Army, 1948), 12, 15, 29. (This compilation of transcribed original documents is hereafter *St-Mihiel*.)

14. "Operations of the 304th Tank Brigade, September 12th to 15th, 1918, St. Mihiel Salient," Headquarters 304th (1st) Brigade, 12 November 1918, files of the General Headquarters Commander-in-Chief, RG 120/290/79/23/6, box 42, folder 393. "Operations of Tank Corps A.E.F. at St. Mihiel, in the Meuse-Argonne Operation, and with the British E.F.," General Headquarters, American Expeditionary Force, 27 December 1918, files of the General Headquarters Commander-in-Chief, RG 120/290/79/23/6, box 42, folder 388. General order 13, General Headquarters, Tank Corps, 20 August 1918.

15. "Operations of Tank Corps A.E.F. at St. Mihiel, in the Meuse-Argonne Operation, and with the British E.F.," General Headquarters, American Expeditionary Force, 27 December 1918, files of the General Headquarters Commander-in-Chief, RG 120/290/79/23/6, box 42, folder 388.

16. "Operations of the 304th Tank Brigade, September 12th to 15th, 1918, St. Mihiel Salient," Headquarters 304th (1st) Brigade, 12 November 1918, files of the General Headquarters Commander-in-Chief, RG 120/290/79/23/6, box 42, folder 393. "Operations of Tank Corps A.E.F. at St. Mihiel, in the Meuse-Argonne Operation, and with the British E.F.," General Headquarters, American Expeditionary Force, 27 December 1918, files of the General Headquarters Commander-in-Chief, RG 120/290/79/23/6, box 42, folder 388. Blumenson, *Patton Papers: 1885*, 590.

17. "Operations of the 304th Tank Brigade, September 12th to 15th, 1918, St. Mihiel Salient," Headquarters 304th (1st) Brigade, 12 November 1918, files of the General Headquarters Commander-in-Chief, RG 120/290/79/23/6, box 42, folder 393. "Operations of Tank Corps A.E.F. at St. Mihiel, in the Meuse-Argonne Operation, and with the British E.F.," General Headquarters, American Expeditionary Force, 27 December 1918, files of the General Headquarters Commander-in-Chief, RG 120/290/79/23/6, box 42, folder 388.

18. "Special instructions for the 326 Bn. And 327 Bn.," 8 September 1918, George S. Patton papers, box 8, Library of Congress.

19. Nigel Thomas, *The German Army in World War I (3): 1917–1918* (Botley, UK: Osprey Publishing, 2004), 5.

20. Charles T. Senay, "Unlimited objective attack in the reduction of the St. Mihiel Salient, 12 Sept., 1918," study, Command and General Staff College, 1931, Combined Arms Research Library, http://cgsc.leavenworth.army.mil/carl/contentdm/home.htm, as of July 2008.

21. *Bulletin for Field Officers*, Number 6, 8 November 1918.

22. 10th Infantry Division war diary.

23. "Generalmajor Freiherr von Diepenbroick-Grüter," Axis History Forum, http://forum. axishistory.com/viewtopic.php?f=72&t=142699, as of August 2008. James Allen Knechtmann, "German Unit Locator Matrix—1914," The General Staff Library website, http://www.generalstafflibrary.com/germanarmyaugust1914/unitlocatormatrix1914. html, as of August 2008.

24. "Histories of Two Hundred and Fifty-one Divisions of the German Army Which Participated in the War (1914–1918)," Intelligence Section, General Staff, American Expeditionary Forces, 1919, 180–183. (Hereafter "Two Hundred and Fifty-one Divisions.")

25. "Max von Gallwitz on the Battle of St. Mihiel, 12 September 1918," First World War. com, primary documents, http://www.firstworldwar.com/index.htm, as of July 2008. (Hereafter von Gallwitz.)

26. *Bulletin for Field Officers*, Number 6, 8 November 1918. Lt. Gen, Van Alfred Muther, "Organization, Armament, Ammunition And Ammunition Expenditure Of The German Field Artillery During The World War," *The Field Artillery Journal*, May–June, 1935, 197–211, http://sill-www.army.mil/famag/1935/MAY_JUN_1935/MAY_ JUN_1935_PAGES_197_211.pdf, as of July 2008.

27. Ibid.

28. 10th Infantry Division war-diary annexes.

29. 10th Infantry Division war diary. Army Group Gallwitz war diary.

30. 10th Infantry Division war-diary annexes.

31. Ibid.

32. Ibid. "Extracts from the war day book, Artillery Commander 10, from 1.7.18–14.9.18," records of the 10th Infantry Division.

33. 10th Infantry Division war-diary annexes.

34. "Operations of the 304th Tank Brigade, September 12th to 15th, 1918, St. Mihiel Salient," Headquarters 304th (1st) Brigade, 12 November 1918, files of the General Headquarters Commander-in-Chief, RG 120/290/79/23/6, box 42, folder 393. Blumenson, *Patton Papers: 1885*, 584.

35. 10th Infantry Division war diary and annexes, including the AAR (after-action report) of the 2nd Battalion, 6th Grenadier Regiment. Blumenson, *Patton Papers: 1885*, 596.

36. 10th Infantry Division war-diary annexes, AAR of the 3rd Battalion, 47th Infantry Regiment.

37. Blumenson, *Patton Papers: 1885*, 584.

38. 10th Infantry Division war-diary annexes.

39. Blumenson, *Patton Papers: 1885*, 584.

40. 10th Infantry Division war-diary annexes, AAR of the 2nd Battalion, 6th Grenadier Regiment.

41. Blumenson, *Patton Papers: 1885*, 585–586.

42. "Operations of the 304th Tank Brigade, September 12th to 15th, 1918, St. Mihiel Salient," Headquarters 304th (1st) Brigade, 12 November 1918, files of the General Headquarters Commander-in-Chief, RG 120/290/79/23/6, box 42, folder 393. Blumenson, *Patton Papers: 1885*, 586–588. Patton's tactical reports and diary entry for 12 September 1918, George S. Patton papers, box 8, Library of Congress. 10th Infantry Division war-diary annexes, including AARs of the 20th Infantry Brigade and 2nd Battalion, 47th Infantry Regiment.

43. 10th Infantry Division war-diary annexes, AAR of the 2nd Battalion, 398th Infantry Regiment.

44. "Operations of the 304th Tank Brigade, September 12th to 15th, 1918, St. Mihiel Salient," Headquarters 304th (1st) Brigade, 12 November 1918, files of the General Headquarters Commander-in-Chief, RG 120/290/79/23/6, box 42, folder 393. Society of the First Division, *History of the First Division During the Worlds War: 1917–1919* (Philadelphia: John C. Winston Company, 1922), 156. (Hereafter Society of the First Division.)
10th Infantry Division war diary annexes.

45. 10th Infantry Division war diary annexes, AAR of the 2nd Battalion, 398th Infantry Regiment.

46. "Operations of the 304th Tank Brigade, September 12th to 15th, 1918, St. Mihiel Salient," Headquarters 304th (1st) Brigade, 12 November 1918, files of the General Headquarters Commander-in-Chief, RG 120/290/79/23/6, box 42, folder 393. Society of the First Division, 156. 10th Infantry Division war-diary annexes, including the AAR of the
3rd Battalion, 398th Infantry Regiment. Blumenson, *Patton Papers: 1885*, 585. Wilson, 6.

47. Blumenson, *Patton Papers: 1885*, 590.

48. 10th Infantry Division war-diary annexes.

49. "Operations of the 304th Tank Brigade, September 12th to 15th, 1918, St. Mihiel Salient," Headquarters 304th (1st) Brigade, 12 November 1918, files of the General Headquarters Commander-in-Chief, RG 120/290/79/23/6, box 42, folder 393.

50. Pershing, 38–43.

51. Commendation, files of the General Headquarters Commander-in-Chief, RG 120/290/79/23/6, box 42, folder 398.

52. Ibid.

53. "Crown Prince Wilhelm on the Battle of St Mihiel, 12 September 1918," First World War.com, primary documents, http://www.firstworldwar.com/index.htm, as of July 2008.

54. "Operations of the 304th Tank Brigade, September 12th to 15th, 1918, St. Mihiel Salient," Headquarters 304th (1st) Brigade, 12 November 1918, files of the General Headquarters Commander-in-Chief, RG 120/290/79/23/6, box 42, folder 393.

55. "Operations of the 304th Brigade, Tank Corps, from September 26th to October 15th, 1918," Headquarters 304th (1st) Brigade, 18 November 1918, files of the General Headquarters Commander-in-Chief, RG 120/290/79/23/6, box 42, folder 395. Capt. W. L. Clemenson, "A critical analysis of the operations of the I Corps in the first phase of the Meuse-Argonne Offensive," study, Command and General Staff College, 1935, Combined Arms Research Library, http://cgsc.leavenworth.army.mil/carl/contentdm/home.htm, as of July 2008. (Hereafter Clemenson.) *St-Mihiel*, 79.

56. Thomas Fleming, "Meuse-Argonne Offensive of World War I," HistoryNet.com, www.historynet.com/meuse-argonne-offensive-of-world-war-i.htm, as of July 2008. (Hereafter Fleming.)

57. Clemenson.

58. Third Army war diary and annexes.

59. "Prince Eitel Friedrich von Preussen—PlM Recipient?" Axis History Forum, http://forum.axishistory.com/viewtopic.php?t=71280, as of July 2008. "Prince Eitel Friedrich von Preussen," The Prussian Machine, http://home.Comcast.net/~jcviser/index.htm/aka/eitel.htm, as of July 2008. 1914–18.Info, http://www.1914-18.info/, as of July 2008.

60. "Two Hundred and Fifty-one Divisions," 19–21.

61. 1st Guards Division and 1st Guards Brigade war diaries.

62. Third Army war diary and annexes. 1st Guards Infantry Brigade war diary. I Corps reports, field intelligence reports received by 1st American Army during Argonne-Meuse Offensive, September 26 to November 11, 1918. Volume 1, September 26 to October 18. Clair Kenamore, *From Vauquois Hill to Exermont: A History of the Thirty-Fifth Division of the United States Army* (St. Louis, MO: Guard Publishing, 1919), 85, 89–91. (Hereafter Kenamore.) "Berlin am 4. August," Berlin von A bis Z, www.luise-berlin.de/Kalender/Tag/Aug04.htm, as of August 2008.

63. Wilson, 133.

64. "Operations of Tank Corps A.E.F. at St. Mihiel, in the Meuse-Argonne Operation, and with the British E.F.," General Headquarters, American Expeditionary Force, 27 December 1918, files of the General Headquarters Commander-in-Chief, RG 120/290/79/23/6,
box 42, folder 388.

65. Clemenson.

66. 1st Guards Infantry Brigade war diary. Kenamore, 98–121.

67. Blumenson, *Patton Papers: 1885*, 610–617. 1st Guards Infantry Brigade war diary. Kenamore, 119.

68. "Operations of Tank Corps A.E.F. at St. Mihiel, in the Meuse-Argonne Operation, and with the British E.F.," General Headquarters, American Expeditionary Force, 27 December 1918, files of the General Headquarters Commander-in-Chief, RG 120/290/79/23/6, box 42, folder 388.

69. Ibid. Wilson, 131–132.

70. I Corps reports, field intelligence reports received by 1st American Army during Argonne-Meuse Offensive, September 26 to November 11, 1918. Volume 1, September 26 to October 18. Third Army war diary and annexes. Fleming. Wilson, 139–140.

71. "Operations of Tank Corps A.E.F. at St. Mihiel, in the Meuse-Argonne Operation, and with the British E.F.," General Headquarters, American Expeditionary Force, 27 December 1918, files of the General Headquarters Commander-in-Chief, RG 120/290/79/23/6, box 42, folder 388.

72. I Corps reports, field intelligence reports received by 1st American Army during Argonnc-Meuse Offensive, September 26 to November 11, 1918. Volume 1, September 26 to October 18. Third Army war diary and annexes. Fleming.

73. Third Army war diary.

74. 1st Guards Division war diary and annexes.

75. Wilson, 141.

76. General Order 17, GHQ Tank Corps, 11 October 1918.

77. "Organization and Training, Permanent Tank Corps," memorandum from the chief of the Tank Corps to the assistant chief of staff, G-5, American Expeditionary Force, 2 December 1918, files of the General Headquarters Commander-in-Chief, RG 120/290/79/23/6, box 42, folder 388.

78. Jean Petit, "Mémoirs de Guerre 14–18," Passé Présent Futur de Stéphane website, http://passé-présent-futur-de-stéphane.com/mmoiresdejeanpet14-18/index.html, as of March 2009.

79. Dizionario Biografico Degli Italiani, LXI (Rome: Instituto Della Enciclopedia Italiana Fondata da Giovanni Treccani, 2003), 617ff. (Hereafter Dizionario Biografico Degli Italiani, LXI.) "Henri Kervarec on the Battle of the Piave River, 15–22 June 1910," FirstWorldWar.com, primary documents, www.firstworldwar.com/source/piave_kervarec.htm, as of August 2009. "G. M. Trevelyan on the Eleventh Battle of the Isonzo, 1917," FirstWorldWar.com, primary documents, www.firstworldwar.com/source/isonzo_trevelyan.htm, as of August 2009.

80. "Personalakten für Freiherr von Broich, Fritz," German Army officers 201 files, 1900–1945, supplementary file #3, A3356, box 986, NARA. "Generalleutnant Friedrich (Fritz) Freiheer von Broich," Island Farm Prisoner of War Camp: 198/Special Camp XI, Bridgend, South Wales, www.islandfarm.fsnet.co.uk, as of February 2009. Alfred Satter, Die Deutsche Kavallerie in Ersten Weltkrieg (Norderstedt, Germany: Books on Demand GmbH: 2004), 35, 111, 122–123. Friedrich von Bernhardi, Deutschlands Heldenkampf, 1914–1918 (Munich: J. F. Lehmanns Verlag, 1922), 48–49, 62, 95. (Hereafter Bernhardi.) 1914–18.Info, www.1914-18.info, as of July 2008.

81. Hasso von Manteuffel and Franz Kurowski, Panzerkampf im Zweiten Weltkrieg: Lebenserinnerungen (Schnellbach, Germany: Verlag Siegfried Bublies, 2005), 7ff. (Hereafter Manteuffel memoirs.) "Two Hundred and Fifty-one Divisions," 127ff. "Von Manteuffel, Hasso-Eccard," Lexikon der Wehrmacht, www.lexikon-der-wehrmacht.de/Personenregister/M/ManteuffelHv.htm, as of May 2009. Axis Biographical Research, www.geocities.com/%7Eorion47/, as of May 2009. Cornelli Barnett, Hitler's Generals (New York: Grove Press, 1989), 423. (Hereafter Barnett.)

82. "Two Hundred and Fifty-one Divisions," 73, 538. "Von der Chevallerie, Kurt Wilhelm Gustav Erdmann," Lexikon der Wehrmacht, www.lexikon-der-wehrmacht.de/Personenregister/C/ChevallerieKv.htm, as of May 2009. 1914–18.Info, www.1914-18.info/, as of May 2009. Bernhardi, 118–121. "General der Infanterie Kurt von der Chevallerie," Axis Biographical Research, www.geocities.com/%7Eorion47, as of March 2009. Robert M. Citino, The German Way of War (Lawrence: University Press of Kansas, 2005), 230–231. (Hereafter Citino.)

83. "Akten über von Knobelsdorff, Otto Heinrich Ernst," German Army officers 201 files, 1900–1945, A3356, box 419, NARA. "Two Hundred and Fifty-one Divisions," 37ff. "Knobelsdorff, Otto von," Lexikon der Wehrmacht, http://www.lexikon-der-wehrmacht.de/Personenregister/K/KnobelsdorffOv.htm, as of May 2009. 1914-18.Info, http://www.1914-18.info/, as of May 2009. Axis Biographical Research, http://www.geocities.com/%7Eorion47/, as of May 2009. Bernhardi, 117ff. "5. Thüringisches Infanterie-Regiment Nr. 94 (Grossherzog von Sachsen)," Verein Historische Uniformen des Deutschen Kaiserreiches 1871-1918, http://historische-uniformen.de/Truppen/IR94/IR94.HTM, as of May 2009. "French in Charge Capture Hill 304 on Verdun Font," The New York Times, 25 August 1917, 1.

84. "*Personalakten für v. Obstfelder, Hans*," German Army officers 201 files, 1900–1945, A3356, box 612, NARA.

85. Lexikon der Wehrmacht, www.lexikon-der-wehrmacht.de. "*Leib-Kürassier-Regiment 'Grosser Kurfürst' (Schlesisches) Nr. 1*," German Wikipedia, http://de.wikipedia.org, as of June 2009. "*2. Grossherzoglich Hessisches Leib-Dragoner-Regiment Nr. 24*," German Wikipedia, http://de.wikipedia.org/wiki/Leib-Dragoner-Regiment_ (2._Großher-zoglich_Hessisches)_Nr._24, as of December 2009. *Generalfeldmarschall* Gerd von Rundstedt, "Campaign in the West (1940)," MS # C-053, not dated, NARA. (Hereafter Rundstedt.)

Chapter 3: Between the Wars

1. George F. Hofmann, *Through Mobility We Conquer: The Mechanization of the U.S. Cavalry* (Lexington: University Press of Kentucky, 2006), 101–102. (Hereafter Hofmann.)

2. "The Tactical Development Section," War Department memorandum, 18 February 1928, records of the Chief of Cavalry.

3. "Progress Reports on Development Work," War Department memorandum A.G. 400.114, 23 April 1928, records of the Chief of Cavalry. Matthew Darlington Morton, "Men on 'Iron Ponies:' The Death and Rebirth of the Modern U.S. Cavalry," doctoral dissertation, Florida State University, 2004, 32–33. (Hereafter Morton.)

4. Morton, 48–50. Brig. Gen. Adna Chaffee, "Mechanized Cavalry: Lecture Delivered at the Army War College, Washington, DC, September 29, 1939." (Hereafter Chaffee.)

5. George S. Patton Jr. and C. C. Benson, "Mechanization and Cavalry," *The Cavalry Journal*, April 1930, 239.

6. Chaffee. Morton, 50–58. Hofmann, 157ff.

7. "Notes Regarding Cavalry," memorandum from Maj. Gen. Guy Henry to the chief of staff, 23 March 1931, records of the Chief of Cavalry.

8. "Progress Report on Equipment Development," memorandum from the Office of the Chief of Cavalry to the War Department executive officer, 20 February 1932, records of the Chief of Cavalry.

9. "Army Bill Goes to Hoover," *The New York Times*, 14 July 1932, 2:3. Hofmann, 140.

10. Capt. F. T. Bonsteel, "The Employment of a Mechanized Cavalry Brigade," The Cavalry Journal, September-October 1933, 24.

11. "Motorisierung und Mechanisierung im amerikanischem Heer," German military attaché in Washington, DC, 31 May 1934, T-77, roll 904, frame 5658626, NARA.

12. Siegfried Westphal, *The German Army in the West* (London: Cassell and Company, 1951), 27–28, 33–34. (Hereafter Westphal.) Citino, 238–239.

13. Heinz Guderian, *Panzer Leader* (New York: Ballantine Books, 1972), 10–12. (Hereafter Guderian.) Citino, 240ff.

14. Westphal, 20, 35, 37–38.

15. Guderian, 25.

16. Westphal, 36.

17. "Personalakten für Freiherr von Broich, Fritz," German army officers 201 files, 1900–1945, supplementary file #3, A3356, box 986, NARA. "Generalleutnant Friedrich (Fritz) Freiheer von Broich," Island Farm Prisoner of War Camp: 198/Special Camp XI,

Bridgend, South Wales, http://www.islandfarm.fsnet.co.uk/, as of February 2009.

18. "Von der Chevallerie, Kurt Wilhelm Gustav Erdmann," Lexikon der Wehrmacht, http://www.lexikon-der-wehrmacht.de/Personenregister/C/ChevallerieKv.htm, as of May 2009. "General der Infanterie Kurt von der Chevallerie," Axis Biographical Research, http://www.geocities.com/%7Eorion47/, as of March 2009.

19. "Knobelsdorff, Otto von," Lexikon der Wehrmacht, http://www.lexikon-der-wehrmacht.de/Personenregister/K/KnobelsdorffOv.htm, as of May 2009. Axis Biographical Research, http://www.geocities.com/%7Eorion47/, as of May 2009.

20. "Personalakten für v. Obstfelder, Hans," German army officers 201 files, 1900–1945, A3356, box 612, NARA.

21. "Felber, Hans-Gustav," Lexikon der Wehrmacht, http://www.lexikon-der-wehrmacht.de/Personenregister/F/FelberHansGustav.htm, as of December 2009.

22. Hermann Priess, SS personnel files, RG 242, A3343 Series SSO, 393A, frame 1023ff., NARA. Gordon Williamson and Ramiro Bujeiro, *Knight's Cross Oak-Leaves Recipients 1941–45* (Botley, UK: Osprey Publishing, 2005), 30–31. "Priess, Hermann," Lexikon der Wehrmacht, http://www.lexikon-der-wehrmacht.de/Personenregister/P/PriessH.htm, as of June 2009.

23. Max Simon, SS personnel files, RG 242, A3343 Series SSO, 138B, frame 1054ff., NARA. "Simon, Max," Lexikon der Wehrmacht, http://www.lexikon-der-wehrmacht.de/Personenregister/S/SimonM.htm, as of June 2009. "SS-Gruppenführer und General-leutnant der Waffen SS Max Simon," Island Farm Prisoner of War Camp: 198/Special Camp XI, Bridgend, South Wales, http://www.islandfarm.fsnet.co.uk/, as of June 2009. Sydnor, 38. Introduction to *General der Waffen SS* Max Simon, "XIII SS Inf Corps in the Lorraine Campaign," ETHINT-33, 17 August 1945, NARA. (Hereafter Simon, "XIII SS Corps.")

24. Paul Hausser, SS personnel files, RG 242, A3343 Series SSO, 071A, frame 880ff., NARA. Guderian, 375. *Generalleutnant* Fritz Bayerlein, "An Interview with Genlt Fritz Bayerlein: Pz Lehr Div (Jan-28 July 44)," ETHINT-66, 7–9 August 1945, NARA, 40. (Hereafter Bayerlein interview.)

25. "Translation of Taped Conversation with General Hermann Balck, 12 January 1979, and Brief Biographical Sketch," Battelle Columbus Laboratories Tactical Technology Center, 1–2. (Hereafter "Conversation with General Hermann Balck, 12 January 1979.") *General der Panzertruppe a.D.* Hermann Balck, *Ordnung im Chaos: Erinnerungen 1893–1948* (Osnabrück: Biblio Verlag, 1981), 6–9. (Hereafter Balck.) Axis Biographical Research, http://www.geocities.com/%7Eorion47/, as of May 2009.

26. Manteuffel memoirs, 21ff. Barnett, 423–425. "Von Manteuffel, Hasso-Eccard," Lexikon der Wehrmacht, http://www.lexikon-der-wehrmacht.de/Personenregister/M/ManteuffelHv.htm, as of May 2009. Axis Biographical Research, http://www.geocities.com/%7Eorion47/, as of May 2009.

27. "Lüttwitz, Smilo Freiherr von," Lexikon der Wehrmacht, http://www.lexikon-der-wehrmacht.de/Personenregister/L/LuttwitzSFv.htm, as of December 2009.

28. "Wietersheim, Wend von," Lexikon der Wehrmacht, http://www.lexikon-der-wehrmacht.de/Personenregister/W/WietersheimWv.htm, as of December 2009.

29. "Armored Cars for Cavalry Units," *The Cavalry Journal*, January 1923, 92.

30. Guderian, 72–73.

31. *Dizionario Biografico Degli Italiani*, LXI, 618ff.

32. Farago, 119–122.

33. Martin Blumenson, *The Patton Papers: 1940–1945* (Boston: Houghton Mifflin Company, 1974), 8. (Hereafter Blumenson, *Patton Papers: 1940.*)

34. Farago, 128–129.

35. "The Historical Combat Effectiveness of Lighter-Weight Armored Forces: Final Report," the Dupuy Institute, 6 August 2001, http://www.dupuyinstitute.org/pdf/mwa-2lightarmor.pdf, as of May 2007. Untitled memorandum on infantry tank strength from Lt. Col. William Crittenberger to the Chief of Cavalry, 16 June 1939, records of the Chief of Cavalry.

Chapter 4: The Enemy Goes to War

1. "Die 1. Kavallerie-Division im Westen: 10.5.40–29.6.40," records of the 1st Cavalry Division, T-315, roll 74, frame 379, NARA.

2. Lexikon der Wehrmacht, http://www.lexikon-der-wehrmacht.de. B. H. Liddell Hart, *History of the Second World War* (New York: G. P. Putnam's Sons, 1970), 26ff. (Hereafter Liddell Hart, *Second World War.*) Erich von Manstein, *Lost Victories* (Minneapolis: Zenith Press, 2004), 38. (Hereafter Manstein.)

3. "Personalakten für v. Obstfelder, Hans," German Army officers 201 files, 1900–1945, A3356, box 612, NARA.

4. Sydnor, 41. "Simon, Max," Lexikon der Wehrmacht, http://www.lexikon-der-wehrmacht.de/Personenregister/S/SimonM.htm, as of June 2009.

5. Hermann Priess, SS personnel files, RG 242, A3343 Series SSO, 393A, frame 1023ff., NARA. Gordon Williamson and Ramiro Bujeiro, *Knight's Cross Oak-Leaves Recipients 1941–45* (Botley, UK: Osprey Publishing, 2005), 30–31. John Keegan, *Waffen SS: The Asphalt Soldiers* (New York: Ballantine Books, 1970), 51–53. (Hereafter Keegan.) Charles W. Sydnor Jr., *Soldiers of Destruction: The SS Death's Head Division, 1933–1945* (Princeton, NJ: Princeton University Press, 1977), 42–54. (Herafter Syndor.) "Priess, Hermann," Lexikon der Wehrmacht, http://www.lexikon-der-wehrmacht.de/Personenregister/P/PriessH.htm, as of June 2009.

6. Chaffee.

7. Morton, 167, 178.

8. Robert Stewart Cameron, "Americanizing the Tank: U.S. Army Administration and Mechanized Development Within the Army, 1917–1943," doctoral dissertation, Temple University, August 1944, 492–493. (Hereafter Cameron.) Donald E. Houston, *Hell on Wheels, The 2d Armored Division* (Novato, CA: Presidio Press, 1977), 33–34. (Hereafter Houston.)

9. B. H. Liddell Hart, *The German Generals Talk* (New York: Quill, 1979), 108ff. (Hereafter Liddell Hart, *The German Generals Talk.*)

10. Manstein, 100ff.

11. Rundstedt, 2.

12. "Die 1. Kavallerie-Division im Westen: 10.5.40-29.6.40," records of the 1st Cavalry Division, T-315, roll 74, frame 379ff., NARA.

13. Manstein, 101, 109, 122–123.

14. Peter D. Cornwell, *The Battle of France Then and Now: Six Nations Locked in Aerial Combat September 1939 to June 1940* (Hobbs Cross, Old Harlow, Essex: Battle of Britain International, 2007), 270–71.

15. "Translation of Taped Conversation with General Hermann Balck, 13 April 1979," 2–14. (Hereafter "Conversation with General Hermann Balck, 13 April 1979.") "Conversation with General Hermann Balck, 12 January 1979," 2–3. Balck, 399ff. Guderian, 80, 85, 90, 95–108. F. W. von Mellenthin, *Panzer Battles* (New York: Ballantine Books, 1971), , 17–20. 204ff. (Hereafter Mellenthin.) Liddell Hart, *Second World War*, 71.

16. Comments by Heinz Guderian, contained in Paul Hausser, SS personnel files, RG 242, A3343 Series SSO, 071A, frame 1963ff., NARA.

17. Keegan, 62–64. Sydnor, 80ff.

18. 83rd Infantry Division, Kriegstagebuch Nr. 1, 22 Dec 1939–21 Jul 1940, T315, roll 1126, frame 000001ff., NARA. 83rd Infantry Division, Anlagenheft 1 zum Kriegstagebuch Nr. 1, 17 Nov 1939–30 Apr 1940, T315, roll 1126, frame 000050ff. NARA

19. 19th Infantry Division, Ia, Kriegstagebuch Nr. 3, 9.5.1940–8.6.1940, T315, roll 720, frame 000165ff., NARA. Otto von Knobelsdorff, *Geschichte der niedersächsischen 19. Panzer-Division: 1939–1945* (Bad Nauheim, Germany: Podzun-Verlag, 1958), 56ff. (Hereafter Knobelsdorff, *19. Panzer-Division*.) Major L. F. Ellis, *The War in France and Flanders 1939–1940* (London: Her Majesty's Stationery Office, 1953), 67. Hugh Sebag-Montefiore, *Dunkirk: Fight to the Last Man* (Cambridge, MA: Harvard University Press, 2006), 581n.

20. Knobelsdorff, *19. Panzer-Division*, 67.

21. "Akten über von Knobelsdorff, Otto Heinrich Ernst," German Army officers 201 files, 1900–1945, A3356, box 419, NARA.

22. 28th Infantry Division, Anlagen B, Ia, zum K. T. B. Nr. 1, 4.10.39–23.4.40, T315, roll 832, frame 000002ff., NARA.

23. "Personalakten für v. Obstfelder, Hans," German Army officers 201 files, 1900–1945, A3356, box 612, NARA.

24. XXIX Corps, Kriegstagebuch 1, 1.6.40–24.6.40, T314, roll 807, frame 000003ff., NARA.

25. Farago, 139.

26. David Kahn, *Hitler's Spies: German Military Intelligence in World War II* (New York: Da Capo Press, 2000), 391–392.

27. "Antitank Doctrine and Development," memorandum AG 320.2 (7-3-40) M-C, Brig. Gen. Leslic McNair to the Commandant, Command, and General Staff School, 3 July 1940.

28. Christopher R. Gabel, *The U.S. Army GHQ Maneuvers of 1941* (Washington, DC: Center of Military History, United States Army, 1991), 48ff. (Hereafter Gabel.) Blumenson, *Patton Papers: 1940*, 35.

29. Gabel, 54, 64–67. Allen, 15.

30. Gabel, 67–90.

31. Ibid., 96–111.

32. "Memorandum for General Marshall: High commanders," from Lt. Gen. Leslie McNair, 7 October 1941.

33. Gabel, 133–150.

34. Ibid., 155–156.

35. Helmut Greiner, "Operation 'Barbarossa,'" MS # C-065i, not dated, NARA, 1–6. (Hereafter Greiner, "Operation 'Barbarossa.'")

36. *Generalmajor* Burkhart Müller-Hillebrand, "Der Zusammenhang Zwischen dem deutschen Balkanfeldzug und der Invasion in Russland," MS # C-101, November 1951, NARA, 4, 12ff. (Hereafter Müller-Hillebrand.)

37. David M. Glantz, and Jonathan M. House, *When Titans Clashed: How the Red Army Stopped Hitler* (Lawrence: University of Kansas Press, 1995), 31. (Hereafter Glantz and House, *When Titans Clashed.*) Bevin Alexander, "Barbarossa," MilitaryHistoryOnline. com, http://www.militaryhistoryonline.com/wwii/articles/barbarossa.aspx, 4 February 2006, as of July 2009. Greiner, "Operation 'Barbarossa,'" 9. Guderian, 125. Müller-Hillebrand, 12.

38. "World War II Statistics," World War II website, http://www.world-war-2.info/, as of July 2009.

39. Guderian, 120–121.

40. XXIX Corps, Kriegstagebuch 1 (Ost), 15.5.1941–19.9.1941, T314, roll 810, frame 000129ff., NARA.

41. 99th Leichte Infanterie Division, Ia, Tätigkeitsbericht, 10.12.40–25.5.41, T315, roll 1212, frame 000002ff., NARA.

42. 99th Leichte Infanterie Division, Ia, Kriegstagebuch, 25.5–25.10.41, T315, roll 1212, frame 000172ff., NARA.

43. "Generalleutnant Friedrich (Fritz) Freiheer von Broich," Island Farm Prisoner of War Camp: 198/Special Camp XI, Bridgend, South Wales, http://www.islandfarm.fsnet. co.uk/, as of February 2009.

44. "Kriegstagebuch der 1. K. D., 25.5–7.11.41,", T-315, roll 74, frame 3678ff., NARA. Guderian, 123. "Lüttwitz, Smilo Freiherr von," Lexikon der Wehrmacht, http://www. lexikon-der-wehrmacht.de/Personenregister/L/LuttwitzSFv.htm, as of December 2009.

45. 19th Panzer Division, Ia, Kriegstagebuch Nr. 1, 1.11.1940–31.5.1941, T315, roll 722, frame 000002ff., NARA.

46. "Akten über von Knobelsdorff, Otto Heinrich Ernst," German Army officers 201 files, 1900–1945, A3356, box 419, NARA.

47. Knobelsdorff, *19. Panzer-Division*, 78–80.

48. Ibid., 84–89.

49. Ibid., 121–132.

50. Manteuffel memoirs, 50ff., 64–68. On Hitler's strategy, see Guderian, 158–162, 171ff. "Model, Walter Otto Moritz," Lexikon der Wehrmacht, http://www.lexikon-der-wehrmacht.de/Personenregister/M/ModelW.htm, as of August 2009. "Personalakten für Eberbach, Heinrich," German Army officers 201 files, 1900–1945, A3356, box 146, NARA.

51. AAR, 2nd SS Division, 22 June–28 July 1941, and comments by Heinz Guderian, contained in Paul Hausser, SS personnel files, RG 242, A3343 Series SSO, 071A, frame 880ff., NARA.

52. AAR, 2nd SS Division, 22 October 1941, contained in Paul Hausser, SS personnel files, RG 242, A3343 Series SSO, 071A, frame 1951ff., NARA.

53. Paul Hausser, SS personnel files, RG 242, A3343 Series SSO, 071A, frame 1896, NARA.

54. "SS-Obergruppenführer Paul Hausser," article contained in Paul Hausser, SS personnel files, RG 242, A3343 Series SSO, 071A, frame 1992ff., NARA. Gordon Williamson, *The SS: Hitler's Instrument of Terror* (St. Paul, MN: Zenith Press, 2004), 71–72. Deutsche Wochenschau, "Panzerschlacht von Borodino," http://www.youtube.com/watch?v=6wYZqRyXovk, as of August 2009.

55. Manstein, 178.

56. "Personalakten für Brandenberger, Erich," German Army officers 201 files, 1900–1945, A3356, box 70, NARA.

57. Manstein, 179ff.

58. Max Simon, SS personnel files, RG 242, A3343 Series SSO, 138B, frame 1054ff., NARA. Sydnor, 153ff. Manstein, 186–188, 199ff.

59. "Von Kluge, Günther," Lexikon der Wehrmacht, http://www.lexikon-der-wehrmacht. de/Personenregister/K/KlugeGv.htm, as of January 2009. David Irving, *Hitler's War* (New York: Avon Books, 1990), 447–448, 558–559, 580. (Hereafter Irving.)

60. Manstein, 276, 446.

61. Knobelsdorff, *19. Panzer-Division*, 136–138. "Akten über von Knobelsdorff, Otto Heinrich Ernst," German Army officers 201 files, 1900–1945, A3356, box 419, NARA.

62. Max Simon, SS personnel files, RG 242, A3343 Series SSO, 138B, frame 1054ff., NARA. Sydnor, 153ff.

63. Hermann Priess, SS personnel files, RG 242, A3343 Series SSO, 393A, frame 1023ff., NARA.

64. Sydnor, 235–254. Max Simon, SS personnel files, RG 242, A3343 Series SSO, 138B, frame 1054ff., NARA.

65. "Anlagen zum Kriegstagebuch, 25.4.42–22.6.42," 24th Panzer Division records, T-315, roll 804, frame 2, NARA.

66. "Anlagen zum Kriegstagebuch, 25.4.42–22.6.42," 24th Panzer Division records, T-315, roll 804, frame 100ff., NARA. XLVIII Panzer Corps, Kriegstagebuch, 28.6.42–31.7.42, T314, roll 1153, frame 000385ff., NARA. Mellenthin, 186–190.

67. "Personalakten für Hörnlein, Walter," German Army officers 201 files, 1900–1945, A3356, box 344, NARA. Grossdeutschland Infantry Division Kriegstagebuch, 1.4.1942–16.8.1942, T315, roll 2282, frames 000013, 000038, NARA. Horst Scheibert and Bruce Culver, ed., *Panzer Grenadier Division Grossdeutschland* (Carrollton, TX: Squadron/Signal Publications, 1987), 7, 41. (Hereafter Scheibert, *Panzer Grenadier Division*.)

68. Grossdeutschland Infantry Division Kriegstagebuch, 1.4.1942–16.8.1942, T315, roll 2282, frame 000024ff., NARA.

69. "Personalakten für Hörnlein, Walter," German Army officers 201 files, 1900–1945, A3356, box 344, NARA. Grossdeutschland, http://www.grossdeutschland.net/, as of July 2009.

70. Grossdeutschland Infantry Division Kriegstagebuch, 1.4.1942–16.8.1942, T315, roll 2282, frame 000057ff., NARA.

71. "Anlagen zum Kriegstagebuch, 5.8.42–24.10.42," 24th Panzer Division Ia records, T-315, roll 804, frame 237ff., NARA.

72. "Personalakten für Freiherr von Broich, Fritz," German Army officers 201 files, 1900–1945, supplementary file #3, A3356, box 986, NARA.

73. Andrew Roberts, "The Genocide Generals: Secret Recordings Explode the Myth They

Knew Nothing about the Holocaust," *Mail* online, 21 July 2007, http://www.dailymail. co.uk/femail/article-469883/The-Genocide-Generals-secret-recordings-explode-myth-knew-Holocaust.html, as of March 2009. (Hereafter Roberts.)

74. Percy E. Schramm, *Kriegstagebuch des Oberkommando der Wehrmacht (Wehrmachtführungsstab), 1. Januar 1942–31. Dezember 1942, Zweiter Halbband, Band 4* (Germany: Bechtermünz, 2005), 1015ff.

75. Erhard Raus, "Defensive Tactics in Breakthroughs (East)," MS # T-10, not dated, NARA, 4. (Hereafter Raus, "Defensive Tactics.")

76. Lexikon der Wehrmacht, http://www.lexikon-der-wehrmacht.de, as of March 2009.

77. William A. Webb, "Battle of Velikiye Luki: Surrounded in the Snow," HistoryNet.com, http://www.historynet.com/battle-of-velikiye-luki-surrounded-in-the-snow.htm, as of March 2009. (Hereafter Webb.) Note: Webb confuses Kurt von der Chevallerie with Hellmut von der Chevallerie, who at this time commanded the 13th Panzer Division.

78. "Anlagen zum Kriegstagebuch 4," LIX Corps, T314, roll 1506, frame 000723. Glantz and House, *When Titans Clashed*, 136–138.

79. "Anlagen zum Kriegstagebuch 4," LIX Corps, T314, roll 1506, frame 000737.

80. Webb. "Anlagen zum Kriegstagebuch 4," LIX Corps, T314, roll 1506, frame 000750ff. Percy E. Schramm, *Kriegstagebuch des Oberkommando der Wehrmacht (Wehrmachtführungsstab), 1. Januar 1942–31. Dezember 1942, Zweiter Halbband, Band 2* (Germany: Bechtermünz, 2005), 1022ff. Helmut Heiber, and David M. Glantz, eds., *Hitler and His Generals: Military Conferences 1942–1945* (New York: Enigma Books, 2004), 41–43. (Hereafter Heiber and Glantz.) "Operations of Encircled Forces: German Experiences in Russia," Department of the Army, Washington, DC, 1952, http://www.history.army. mil/BOOKS/WWII/20234/20234.html, as of March 2010.

81. Grossdeutschland Infantry Division Kriegstagebuch 18.8.42–31.3.43, T315, roll 2283, frame 000002ff., NARA.

82. Scheibert, *Panzer Grenadier Division*, 76.

83. David M. Glantz, "Counterpoint to Stalingrad, Operation Mars (November–December 1942): Marshal Zhukov's Greatest Defeat," United States Army Foreign Military Studies Office, uploaded June 1997, http://mr-home.staff.shef.ac.uk/rzhev/rzhev3.html, as of July 2009. XLI Panzer Corps, Kriegstagebuch, 13.11.42–31.12.42, T314, roll 985, frame 000471ff., NARA. Grossdeutschland Infantry Division Kriegstagebuch 18.8.42–31.3.43, T315, roll 2283, frame 000162ff., NARA. XXXIX Panzer Corps, Kriegstagebuch Band 19 der Ia, 25.11.42–27.11.42, T314, roll 933, frame 000001ff., NARA. Situation maps, Ninth Army. Manteuffel memoirs, 82.

84. 11th Panzer Division, Kriegstagebuch Nr. 4, Führungsabteilung (Ia), 21.4.42–27.6.42, T315, roll 590, frame 000352ff., NARA. 11th Panzer Division, Kriegstagebuch Nr. 5, Führungsabteilung (Ia), 28.6.42–31.10.42, T315, roll 591, frame 000246ff,. NARA.

85. Mellenthin, 204ff. XLVIII Panzer Corps, Kriegstagebuch, December 1942, T314, roll 1160, frame 000484ff., NARA. 11th Panzer Division, Kriegstagebuch Nr. 6, Führungsabteilung (Ia), 1.11.1942–31.12.1942, T315, roll 594, frame 000502ff, NARA. Gen. William DePuy, "Generals Balck and von Mellenthin on Tactics: Implications for NATO Military Doctrine," BDM Corporation, December 1980, reproduced and edited by Reiner K. Huber (Universität der Bundeswehr München, December 2004), 42–43. (Hereafter "Generals Balck and von Mellenthin on Tactics.") "Knobelsdorff, Otto von," Lexikon der Wehrmacht, http://www.lexikon-der-wehrmacht.de/Personenregister/K/ KnobelsdorffOv.htm, as of May 2009. Heiber Glantz, , 26.

86. Manstein, 363ff., 408ff. Raus, "Defensive Tactics," 5.

87. Manstein, 420. James Sydney Lucas, *Hitler's Enforcers: Leaders of the German War Machine, 1933-1945* (Leicester, UK: Brockhampton Press, 2000), 90-92. (Hereafter Lucas.) Fourth Panzer Army, Anlagen 1 zum K.T.B. C 1 Operationen I, T313, roll 365, frame 8650861.

88. Manstein, 424ff. Raus, "Defensive Tactics," 5-6. Fourth Panzer Army, Anlagen 1 zum K.T.B. C 1 Operationen I, T313, roll 365, frames 8650900ff, 8650922ff.

Chapter 5: French North Africa: *La Guerre des Trois Jours*

1. George F. Howe, *Northwest Africa: Seizing the Initiative in the West: United States Army in World War II, The Mediterranean Theater of Operations* (Washington, DC: Office of the Chief of Military History, Department of the Army, 1957), 15ff. (Hereafter Howe.)

2. Dwight D. Eisenhower, *Crusade in Europe* (Garden City, NY: Doubleday and Company, Inc., 1948), 78-80. (Hereafter Eisenhower.) Harry C. Butcher, *My Three Years with Eisenhower* (New York: Simon and Schuster, 1946), 68-84. (Hereafter Butcher.)

3. Howe, 39. Butcher, 47, 63, 87, 93.

4. Farago, 190-191.

5. Howe, 39-40.

6. Hall, 30.

7. Jensen, 19. "The 756th Tank Battalion" website, photographs, http://www.756tank.com/, as of October 2007. Col. Harry Roper, "Report on Observations Made as Observer with Task Force Brushwood (3rd Division Landing at Fédala and Subsequent Attack on Casablanca, French Morocco)," undated. Included in "Report of Observers: Mediterranean Theater of Operations," Volume 1, 22 December 1942–23 March 1943. (Hereafter Roper.)

8. Howe, 40-41.

9. Ibid., 41.

10. Ibid., 42.

11. "US Army Military History Research Collection, Senior Officers Debriefing Program: Conversation Between General Theodore J. Conway and Col. Robert F. Ensslin," U.S. Army Heritage Collection OnLine, http://www.ahco.army.mil/site/index.jsp, as of August 2007. (Hereafter Conway.)

12. *Generalmajor,* Christian Eckhard, "Study of the Situation in the High Command of the Wehrmacht Shortly Before, During and After the Allied Landing in North Africa, 1942," MS # D-066, Historical Division, Headquarters United States Army, Europe, 1947, NARA. (Hereafter Eckhard, "Study of the Situation.") *General der Artillerie* Walter Warlimont, "Stellungsnahme zu Berichten Deutscher Offiziere: Zu den Berichten Ueber die Anglo-Amerikanische Landung in Franzoesisch-Nord Afrika im November 1942," MS # C-090, Historical Division, Headquarters United States Army, Europe, 13 February 1951, NARA, 5-8. (Hereafter Warlimont, "Franzoesisch-Nord Afrika.") Helmut Greiner, "Notes on the Situation Reports and Discussions at Hitler's Head-quarters from 12 August 1942 to 17 March 1943," MS # C-065a, Historical Division, Headquarters United States Army, Europe, not dated, NARA, 85. (Hereafter Greiner, "Discussions at Hitler's Headquarters.") *Generalfeldmarschall* Albert Kesselring, "The War in the Mediterranean, Part II: The Fighting in Tunisia and Tripolitania," MS # T-3 P1, not dated, NARA, 1. (Hereafter Kesselring, "War in the Mediterranean.") Albert

Kesselring, *The Memoirs of Field-Marshal Kesselring* (St. Paul, MN: MBI Publishing, 2007), 132. (Hereafter Kesselring memoirs.)

13. Christine Levisse-Touze, *L'Afrique du Nord Dans la Guerre 1939–1945* (Paris: Albin Michel, 1998), 37–38. (Hereafter Levisse-Touze.)

14. Levisse-Touze, 16ff.

15. Ibid., 21–39. Russell Brooks (U.S. Consul General Rabat, retired), "Casablanca—The French Side of the Fence," *United States Naval Institute Proceedings*, September 1951, 912. (Hereafter Brooks.) Annex number 5 to the final report of Western Task Force on Operation Torch, 7–11 November 1942.

16. Levisse-Touze, 63ff. Brooks, 912, footnote 1.

17. Levisse-Touze, 92ff.

18. Ibid., 177ff.

19. E. N. Harmon, with Milton MacKaye and William Ross MacKaye, *Combat Commander, Autobiography of a Soldier* (Englewood Cliffs, NJ: Prentice-Hall, 1970), 71. (Hereafter Harmon.)

20. Farago, 31, 198–199, 211.

21. D'Este, *Patton: A Genius for War*, 436.

22. Levisse-Touze, 197ff.

23. Annex number 5 to the final report of Western Task Force on Operation Torch, 7–11 November 1942.

24. Ibid.

25. Brooks, 111. Steen Ammentorp, "The Generals of WWII," http://www.generals.dk/, as of August 2008.

26. Journal, High Command of Moroccan Troops, annex number 5 to the final report of Western Task Force on Operation Torch, 7–11 November 1942. (Hereafter Journal, High Command of Moroccan Troops.) Brooks, 112. Howe, 93.

27. Howe, 92. Journal, High Command of Moroccan Troops.

28. Annex number 5 to the final report of Western Task Force on Operation Torch, 7–11 November 1942. Brooks, 912. Butcher, 116.

29. Howe, 30, 45.

30. Brig. Gen. Arthur R. Wilson, "Report of Operations in North Africa," part of the final report of Western Task Force.

31. Martin Blumenson, *Patton Papers: 1940*, 97, 103.

32. Patton, 5.

33. Brooks, 913. Eckhard, "Study of the Situation." Warlimont, "Franzoesisch-Nord Afrika," 11.

34. Brooks, 915, 924.

35. General Charles Noguès' report to his staff on the events following 8 November 1942, annex number 5 to the final report of Western Task Force on Operation Torch, 7–11 November 1942. (Hereafter Noguès' report.) Brooks, 913–916. Levisse-Touze, 247.

36. AAR, Sub–Task Force Brushwood, 3rd Infantry Division.

37. Brig. Gen. Arthur R. Wilson, "Report of Operations in North Africa," part of the final report of Western Task Force.

38. Levisse-Touze, 247.

39. Journal, High Command of Moroccan Troops.

40. Ibid. "Operations for November 8 and 9. 1942," Commander Deuve, Commander of the Garrison at Safi, to the Commanding General of the Marrakech Division, 14 November 1942. Howe, 100.

41. Harmon, 79.

42. Ibid., 81.

43. Ibid., 85. Howe, 97ff.

44. "Operations for November 8 and 9. 1942," Commander Deuve, Commander of the Garrison at Safi, to the Commanding General of the Marrakech Division, 14 November 1942. Howe, 104.

45. Journal, High Command of Moroccan Troops.

46. Brooks, 912.

47. Howe, 133–134. Brooks, 916–920.

48. Patton, 6.

49. AAR, Sub–Task Force Brushwood, 3rd Infantry Division.

50. Brig. Gen. Arthur R. Wilson, "Report of Operations in North Africa," part of the final report of Western Task Force. AAR, Sub–Task Force Brushwood, 3rd Infantry Division.

51. Ibid.

52. "Activities of G-2 Personnel and Establishment of Headquarters ashore, Fédala, November 8–11, 1942," annex number 5 to the final report of Western Task Force on Operation Torch, 7–11 November 1942.

53. AAR, Sub–Task Force Brushwood, 3rd Infantry Division.

54. Brig. Gen. Arthur R. Wilson, "Report of Operations in North Africa," part of the final report of Western Task Force. AAR, Sub–Task Force Brushwood, 3rd Infantry Division.

55. Howe, 36–38.

56. Patton, 5.

57. Ibid., 7.

58. Blumenson, *Patton Papers: 1940*, 106.

59. Lucian K. Truscott, *Command Missions* (New York: E. P. Dutton and Company, 1954), 93–95. (Hereafter Truscott.)

60. Journal, High Command of Moroccan Troops. Colonel Jean Petit, account of events at Port Lyautey, November 1943, Passé Présent Futur de Stéphane website, http://passé-présent-futur-de-stéphane.com/marocnov1942/index.html, as of August 2008. (Hereafter Petit.)

61. Petit. Douglas Johnson, "Obituary: Col Jean Petit," *The Independent*, 29 December 1997, http://findarticles.com/p/articles/mi_qn4158/is_19971229/ai_n14139340, as of August 2008.

62. History, 60th Infantry Regiment, 9th Infantry Division.

63. Ibid. Petit.

64. Petit. History, 60th Infantry Regiment, 9th Infantry Division. Brig. Gen. Arthur R. Wilson, "Report of Operations in North Africa," part of the final report of Western Task Force.

65. History, 60th Infantry Regiment, 9th Infantry Division. Petit.

66. History, 60th Infantry Regiment, 9th Infantry Division.

67. Journal, High Command of Moroccan Troops.

68. Butcher, 176.

69. Truscott, 98–108. History, 60th Infantry Regiment, 9th Infantry Division.

70. Journal, High Command of Moroccan Troops.

71. Greiner, "Discussions at Hitler's Headquarters," 111.

72. Walter Warlimont, *Inside Hitler's Headquarters, 1939–45* (Novato, CA: Presidio: 1964), 270–271. (Hereafter Warlimont, *Inside Hitler's Headquarters.*)

73. Raus, "Defensive Tactics," 4–5

74. "Activities of G-2 Personnel and Establishment of Headquarters ashore, Fédala November 8–11, 1942," annex number 5 to the final report of Western Task Force on Operation Torch, 7–11 November 1942. Brig. Gen. Arthur R. Wilson, "Report of Operations in North Africa," part of the final report of Western Task Force. Conway. Blumenson, *Patton Papers: 1940,* 106.

75. Noguès' report.

76. Greiner, "Discussions at Hitler's Headquarters," 112.

77. Petit.

78. Ibid. History, 60th Infantry Regiment, 9th Infantry Division.

79. Petit. Truscott, 115. History, 60th Infantry Regiment, 9th Infantry Division. Col. James Taylor, "Narrative of Observer's Tour with W.T.F., French Morocco," not dated. Chester Hall, *History of the 70th Tank Battalion: June 5, 1940 . . . May 22, 1946* (Louisville, KY: Southern Press, 1950?), 25–26. Howe, 161–162.

80. Journal, High Command of Moroccan Troops.

81. History, 60th Infantry Regiment, 9th Infantry Division. Petit.

82. Blumenson, *Patton Papers: 1940,* 108.

83. Brig. Gen. Arthur R. Wilson, "Report of Operations in North Africa," part of the final report of Western Task Force. Howe, map, "Landings at Fédala." AAR, Sub–Task Force Brushwood, 3rd Infantry Division. Journal, High Command of Moroccan Troops.

84. Journal, High Command of Moroccan Troops.

85. Ibid. Brig. Gen. Arthur R. Wilson, "Report of Operations in North Africa," part of the final report of Western Task Force.

86. History, 60th Infantry Regiment, 9th Infantry Division. Truscott, 118. Petit.

87. Ibid.

88. Brig. Gen. Arthur R. Wilson, "Report of Operations in North Africa," part of the final report of Western Task Force.

89. History, 60th Infantry Regiment, 9th Infantry Division.

90. Ibid. Journal, High Command of Moroccan Troops. Petit.

91. Journal, High Command of Moroccan Troops.

92. Brig. Gen. Arthur R. Wilson, "Report of Operations in North Africa," part of the final report of Western Task Force. AAR, Sub–Task Force Brushwood, 3rd Infantry Division.

93. Howe, 143. Brooks, 921.

94. AAR, Sub–Task Force Brushwood, 3rd Infantry Division.

95. Brig. Gen. Arthur R. Wilson, "Report of Operations in North Africa," part of the final report of Western Task Force. AAR, Sub–Task Force Brushwood, 3rd Infantry Division.

96. Ibid. Journal, High Command of Moroccan Troops.

97. Blumenson, *Patton Papers: 1940*, 109.

98. Ibid.

99. Noguès' report.

100. Journal, High Command of Moroccan Troops.

101. History, 60th Infantry Regiment, 9th Infantry Division. Journal, High Command of Moroccan Troops. Petit.

102. Brig. Gen. Arthur R. Wilson, "Report of Operations in North Africa," part of the final report of Western Task Force.

103. "Activities of G-2 Personnel and Establishment of Headquarters ashore, Fédala November 8–11, 1942," annex number 5 to the final report of Western Task Force on Operation Torch, 7–11 November 1942.

104. Greiner, "Discussions at Hitler's Headquarters," 113–116. *Oberst* Rudolf Lang, "Battles of Kampfgruppe Lang in Tunisia (10. Pz. Div.) December 1942 to 15 April 1943, Part I," MS # D-173, not dated, NARA. (Hereafter Lang, Part I.)

105. Noguès' report.

106. Blumenson, *Patton Papers: 1940*, 110.

107. Letter from Patton to Noguès on the terms of their agreement, 15 November 1942, George S. Patton papers, box 32, Library of Congress.

108. Brooks, 923.

109. Blumenson, *Patton*, 179.

110. D'Este, *Patton: A Genius for War*, 436.

111. Farago, 198.

Chapter 6: Tunisia: Patton Tangles With Hitler's Legions

1. "Narrative of Observer's Tour with W.T.F., French Morocco," not dated. Included in "Report of Observers: Mediterranean Theater of Operations," Volume 1, 22 December 1942–23 March 1943.

2. Ernest Harmon, letter to "Dave," 27 December 1942, records of the Armored Board, Army Ground Forces, classified correspondence, RG 337, NARA.

3. *Generalmajor* Christian Eckhard, "Consideration at Supreme Headquarters Concerning the Overall Conduct of the War in North Africa After the Allied Landing in North Africa in November 1942," MS # D-145, Historical Division, Headquarters United States Army, Europe, 18 June 1947, NARA.

4. Greiner, "Discussions at Hitler's Headquarters," 118–124.

5. "Eisenhower Report on 'Torch,'" scanned copy from the Command and General Staff College Combined Arms Research Library's digital library, http://cgsc.leavenworth. army.mil/carl/contentdm/home.htm, as of August 2007. (Hereafter "Eisenhower Report on 'Torch.'") Liddell Hart, *Second World War*, 329, 335. Greiner, "Discussions at Hitler's Headquarters," 124.

6. Albert Schick, *Die Zehnte P.D.: Die Geschichte der 10. Panzer-Division 1939–1943* (Cologne, Germany: Traditionsgemeinschaft der Ehemaligen 10. Panzer-Division, 1993), 599. (Hereafter Schick.)

7. *Generaloberst* Jürgen von Arnim, "Errinerungen an Tunesien," MS # C-098, Historical Division, Headquarters United States Army, Europe, not dated, NARA, 14–22. (Hereafter Arnim.)

8. Arnim, 24. Barnett, 427. Division von Broich, Ia, Kriegstagebuch 1, 11.11.1942–31.12.1942, T315, roll 2276, frame 000002ff., NARA. Heiber and Glantz, 64. Manteuffel memoirs, 83.

9. *Tunisia* (CMH Pub 72-12) (Washington, DC: Center of Military History, not dated), 17.

10. Percy E. Schramm, *Kriegstagebuch des Oberkommando der Wehrmacht (Wehrmachtführungsstab), 1. Januar 1943–31. Dezember 1943, Erster Halbband, Band 3* (Germany: Bechtermünz, 2005), 142. (Hereafter Schramm, *Kriegstagebuch der OKW, Erster Halbband, Band 3.*)

11. *Oberst* Ulrich Buerker, "Commitment of the 10. Panzer Division in Tunisia," MS # D-174, Historical Division, Headquarters United States Army, Europe, 20 June 1947, NARA. Schick, , 513.

12. Arnim, 61–67. Kesselring, "War in the Mediterranean," 39. Schramm, *Kriegstagebuch der OKW, Erster Halbband, Band 3*, 159.

13. Manteuffel memoirs, 85.

14. Schramm, *Kriegstagebuch der OKW, Erster Halbband, Band 3*, 187–189.

15. Arnim, 72–73.

16. *General der Panzertruppe* Gustav von Vaerst, "Operations of the 5th Panzer Army in Tunisia," MS # D-001, Historical Division, Headquarters United States Army, Europe, May 1947, NARA. (Hereafter Vaerst.) Feldgrau.com, "501. Schwere Panzer Abteilung," http://www.feldgrau.com/spa501.html as of February 2009. "Vaerst, Gustav," Lexikon der Wehrmacht, http://www.lexikon-der-wehrmacht.de/Personenregister/V/VaerstGv.htm, as of August 2009.

17. Farago, 241.

18. Ibid., 241–244. Blumenson, *Patton Papers: 1940*, 180, 186.

19. Vaerst.

20. *Generalleutnant* Alfred Gause, "Military Operations Against American Troops in Africa," MS # D-145, Historical Division, Headquarters United States Army, Europe, 1946, NARA. (Hereafter Gause.)

21. Schramm, *Kriegstagebuch der OKW, Erster Halbband, Band 3*, 201, 205.

22. 18 Army Group to 2 Corps, 1/154 and 1/155, 15 March 1943, G-2 journal, II Corps.

23. Schramm, *Kriegstagebuch der OKW, Erster Halbband, Band 3*, 159.

24. Westphal, 101.

25. Stato Maggiore, *Regio Esercito, Note sulle Operazioni in Africa dall' agosto 1942 al gennaio 1943*, T821, roll 23, frame 964ff., NARA.

26. Mike Bennighof, "Centauro at Gazala," Avalanche Press, http://www.avalanchepress.com/Centauro.php, as of November 2008.

27. Freedom Fairfield to 18th Army Group and 2 Corps, 1/161, 16 March 1943, G-2 journal, II Corps.

28. II Corps G-2 summary number 5, 17 March 1943. II Corps G-2 summary number 6, 2 April 1943.

29. Gause.

30. Blumenson, *Patton Papers: 1940*, 188.

31. Ibid., 193.

32. Col. Gibb to Col. Hewitt, 0810 17 March 1943, G-2 journal, II Corps. Freedom Fairfield to 18th Army Group and 2 Corps, 1/161, 16 March 1943, G-2 journal, II Corps. Phone message from 1st Tank Destroyer Group, 1930 17 March 1943, G-2 journal, II Corps. Phone message from Gen. Gaffet, 1240 17 March 1943, G-2 journal, II Corps. Arnim, 85.

33. G-3 Operations Report, 1st Infantry Division.

34. 1st Infantry Division to II Corps, 1144 17 March 1943, G-2 journal, II Corps Commanding General II Corps to 18th Army Group, 1007 17 March 1943, G-2 journal, II Corps. Phone message from 1st Tank Destroyer Group, 1930 17 March 1943, G-2 journal, II Corps. 18 Army Group to Two Corps, 1/162, 17 March 1943, G-2 journal, II Corps. CG II Corps to all corps divisions, 1147 18 March 1943, G-2 journal, II Corps.

35. G-3 Operations Report, 1st Infantry Division.

36. Vaerst.

37. CG II Corps to 9th and 34th Infantry Divisions, 0905 18 March, G-2 journal, II Corps. G-2 Freedom 7478, 18 March 1943, G-2 journal, II Corps. G-2 journal, II Corps. Various intelligence reports on Italian formations, G-2 journal, II Corps.

38. Farago, 249–250.

39. 18 Army Group to 2 Corps, 1/177, 19 March 1943, G-2 journal, II Corps.

40. Arnim, 79–84. Liddell Hart, *Second World War*, 416.

41. G-3 journal, 1st Armored Division.

42. Ibid.

43. Blumenson, *Patton Papers: 1940*, 196.

44. G-3 journal, 1st Armored Division.

45. Schramm, *Kriegstagebuch der OKW, Erster Halbband, Band 3*, 235.

46. G-3 journal, 1st Armored Division.

47. Blumenson, *Patton Papers: 1940*, 196.

48. G-3 journal, 1st Armored Division.

49. Schramm, *Kriegstagebuch der OKW, Erster Halbband, Band 3*, 238.

50. *Oberst* Rudolf Lang, "Report of the Fighting of Kampfgruppe Lang (10. Pz. Div.) in Tunisia from December 1942 to 15 April 1943," MS # D-166, 6 June 1947, NARA. (Hereafter Lang.) Anlagen [zum Kriegstagebuch], Panzer-Armee Oberkommando 5, "Taktische Kräftegliederung," 4 March 1943. Francois de Lannoy and Josef Charita, *Panzertruppen* (Baveux, France: Editions Heimdal, 2001), 67. (Hereafter De Lannoy and Charita.) *Oberstleutnant* Hans Roschmann, "Mountain Warfare: A Brief Treatise Based on Operations of 1st Mountain Division in Caucasus, August–September 1942," MS # P-148, not dated, NARA, 18.

51. Howe, 338–344.

52. Vaerst.

53. Lang.

54. Lang. Schick, 608.

55. Vaerst.

56. Lang. Schick, 609.

57. G-3 journal, 1st Armored Division.

58. Lang.

59. Vaerst.

60. Lang. Schick, 610.

61. Blumenson, *Patton Papers: 1940*, 197–198.

62. G-3 journal, 1st Armored Division.

63. G-2 II Corps situation summary, 26 March 1943, G-2 journal, II Corps.

64. G-3 journal, 1st Armored Division.

65. Arnim, 86. Kesselring, "War in the Mediterranean," 44. Schick, 610–611.

66. Lang. Telephone message 18 Army Group to 2 Corps, 25 March 1943, G-2 journal, II Corps.

67. Arnim, 89.

68. Lang.

69. Ibid.

70. "Personalakten für Freiherr von Broich, Fritz," German Army officers 201 files, 1900–1945, supplementary file #3, A3356, box 986, NARA.

71. Peter Hoffmann, *Stauffenberg: A Family History, 1905–1944* (Montreal: McGill-Queen's University Press: 2003), 163. (Hereafter Hoffmann.) "10. Panzer-Div.–Abt Ia–Anlagen z. K.T.B. Nr. 6, 29.10.1942–19.4.1943."

72. Hoffmann, 165, 171.

73. Louis P. Lochner, ed. and trans., *The Goebbels Diary: 1942–1943* (New York: Doubleday & Company, 1948), 244–245, 291.

74. "10. Panzer-Div.–Abt Ia–Anlagen z. K.T.B. Nr. 6, 29.10.1942–19.4.1943."

75. G-3 journal, II Corps.

76. G-3 Operations Report, 1st Infantry Division.

77. "10. Panzer-Division Abt. Ic Tätigkeitsbericht 22.3–24.4.1943." "Anlagenbandgeh. Kommandosache zum Kriegstagebuch Nr. 6." AO #2, 22 March 1943, G-2 journal, II Corps. Hoffman, 175.

78. G-3 Operations Report, 1st Infantry Division.

79. Two messages, CG II Corps to divisions, not time-stamped, 22 March 1943, G-2 journal, II Corps.

80. CG II Corps to divisions, 0410, 23 March 1943, G-2 journal, II Corps.

81. Arnim, 85.

82. Arnim, 85. Various reports, 23 March 1943, G-2 journal, II Corps. G-3 journal, II Corps. G-3 Operations Report, 1st Infantry Division. Schick, 510–513.

83. AO #4, 23 March 1943, G-2 journal, II Corps.

84. G-3 journal, II Corps.

85. Ibid.

86. G-3 Operations Report, 1st Infantry Division. Lt. Col. Herschel D. Baker, "El Guettar," *TD Combat in Tunisia* (Tank Destroyer School, 1944), 17ff. Howe, 560–562. Presidential unit citation, 601st Tank Destroyer Battalion. Telephone interview with Bill Harper, 601st Tank Destroyer Battalion, April 2002. Operations report and medal citations, 899th Tank Destroyer Battalion. Rick Atkinson, *An Army at Dawn, The War in North Africa, 1942–1943* (New York: Henry Holt and Company, 2002), 439–441. (Hereafter Atkinson, *An Army at Dawn.*)

87. Operations report and medal citations, 899th Tank Destroyer Battalion.

88. G-3 Operations Report, 1st Infantry Division.

89. G-3 journal, II Corps.

90. Farago, 251.

91. ULTRA Messages VM 7591, dated 20 1959Z March 1943, and VM 7448, dated 24 0830 March 1943. HW 1/520 and HW 1/1515, The National Archives, Kew, London, cited in Robert Baumer and Mark Reardon, *American Iliad: The 18th Infantry Regiment in World War II* (Bedford, PA: Aberjona Press, 2004), 101.

92. G-3 Operations Report, 1st Infantry Division.

93. CG II Corps to divisions, 24 March 1943, G-2 journal, II Corps.

94. 18 Army Group to Two Corps, 1/197, 24 March 1943, G-2 journal, II Corps. G-3 journal, 1st Armored Division.

95. Schramm, *Kriegstagebuch der OKW, Erster Halbband, Band 3,* 239.

96. "10. Panzer-Division Abt. Ic Tätigkeitsbericht 22.3–24.4.1943." "Anlagenbandgeh. Kommandosache zum Kriegstagebuch Nr. 6." Schick, 604.

97. Hoffmann, 164.

98. Blumenson, *Patton Papers: 1940,* 202.

99. Liddell Hart, *Second World War,* 419.

100. Schramm, *Kriegstagebuch der OKW, Erster Halbband, Band 3,* 246, 248.

101. Farago, 252. Blumenson, *Patton Papers: 1940,* 200–202.

102. Allied Forces Headquarters G-2 Axis order of battle, 28 March 1943.

103. Fernspruch *Herresgruppe Afrika,* to Rommel, 29 March 1943, T-313, roll 476, frame 8774756, NARA.

104. Schick, 610. Schramm, *Kriegstagebuch der OKW, Erster Halbband, Band 3,* 249.

105. Schick, 606. Schramm, *Kriegstagebuch der OKW, Erster Halbband, Band 3,* 251–255. Ia Kriegstagebuch 1 Jan–31 Mar 1943, 21st Panzer Division, T315, roll 769, frame 192ff., NARA.

106. Freedom to 2 Corps, 9166, 26 March 1943, G-2 journal, II Corps.

107. Blumenson, *Patton Papers: 1940,* 204, 206.

108. Schramm, *Kriegstagebuch der OKW, Erster Halbband, Band 3,* 264ff.

109. Vaerst.

110. Howe, 574–575.

111. Schramm, *Kriegstagebuch der OKW, Erster Halbband, Band 3,* 284.

112. Hoffmann, 176–180. Howe, 574. Schick, 613–617. Heeresgruppe C, Ic, "H. Gr. 'C,' Pz Armee Afrika, Meldungen, Feb–May 1943," T311, roll 10, frame 7010689, NARA.

113. "10. Panzer-Division Abt. Ic Tätigkeitsbericht 22.3–24.4.1943." "Anlagenbandgeh. Kommandosache zum Kriegstagebuch Nr. 6."

114. "Personalakten für Freiherr von Broich, Fritz," German Army officers 201 files, 1900–1945, supplementary file #3, A3356, box 986, NARA.

115. De Lannoy and Charita, 67.

116. Unit history, 899th Tank Destroyer Battalion.

117. Blumenson, *Patton Papers: 1940*, 213.

118. Heeresgruppe C, Ic, "H. Gr. 'C,' Pz Armee Afrika, Meldungen, Feb–May 1943," T311, roll 10, frame 7010683, NARA.

119. Blumenson, *Patton Papers: 1940*, 215.

120. Thomas E. Griess, ed., *The West Point Military History Series, The Second World War, Europe and the Mediterranean* (Wayne, NJ: Avery Publishing Group, 1984) , 177.

121. Warlimont, *Inside Hitler's Headquarters*, 313.

122. "Überblick USA Nr. 3," 18 May 1943, Generalstab des Heeres, Abteilung Fremde Heere West, folder containing data on U.S. Army training, tactics, and equipment, T-78, roll 442, frame 6416398ff., NARA.

123. Percy E. Schramm, *Kriegstagebuch des Oberkommando der Wehrmacht (Wehrmachtführungsstab), 1. Januar 1943–31. Dezember 1943, Zweiter Halbband, Band 3* (Germany: Bechtermünz, 2005), 1442. (Hereafter Schramm, *Kriegstagebuch der OKW, Zweiter Halbband, Band 3*.)

124. "Das Wehrpotential und die Wehrmächte Grossbritanniens und der USA," Generalstab des Heeres, Abteilung Fremde Heere West, folder containing data on U.S. Army training, tactics, and equipment, T-78, roll 442, frame 6415820ff., NARA.

125. "Bewertung der britischen Führung und Truppe nach den Kampferfahrungen in Nordafrika," Generalstab des Heeres, Abteilung Fremde Heere West, folder containing data on U.S. Army training, tactics, and equipment, T-78, roll 442, frame 6415992ff., NARA. Kesselring memoirs, 140.

Chapter 7: Intermezzo: The Brotherhood of Kursk

1. Raus, "Defensive Tactics," 6ff. Mellenthin, 252–253. Lucas, 97ff. Sydnor, 278–280. Fourth Panzer Army, Anlagen 1 zum K.T.B. C 1 Operationen I, T313, roll 365, frame 8651086ff. David M. Glantz and Jonathan M. House, *The Battle of Kursk* (Lawrence: University of Kansas Press, 1999), 13. (Hereafter Glantz and House, *The Battle of Kursk*.)

2. B. H. Liddell Hart, foreword to Manstein, 15.

3. Guderian, 234. *General der Infanterie* Theodor Busse, "Operation Citadel Overview," a.k.a., "The Zitadelle Offensive, 1943," MS # T-26, 1947, NARA, retranslated and reproduced in Steven H. Newton, *Kursk: The German View* (New York: Da Capo Press, Kindle edition, 2002), location 169ff. (Hereafter Busse/Newton.) *General der Infanterie* Friedrich Fangohr, "Fourth Panzer Army," contribution to "The Zitadelle Offensive, 1943," MS # T-26, 1947, NARA, retranslated and reproduced in Steven H. Newton, *Kursk: The German View* (New York: Da Capo Press, Kindle edition, 2002), location 1049ff. (Hereafter Fangohr/Newton.) XLVIII Panzer Corps, Kriegstagebuch, July 1943, T314, roll 1170, frame 000543ff., NARA. Fourth Panzer Army, Kriegstagebuch 4, 35.3.43–31.7943, T313 roll 365, frame 8650549ff., NARA. Glantz and House, *The Battle of Kursk*, 23.

4. Busse/Newton, location 310ff. Fangohr/Newton, location 991ff. Steven H. Newton, *Kursk: The German View* (New York: Da Capo Press, Kindle edition, 2002), location 4799ff. (Hereafter Newton.) For German tank strength, see Fourth Panzer Army, Kriegstagebuch 4, 35.3.43–31.7943, T313 roll 365, frame 8650526ff., NARA.

5. George M. Nipe Jr, "Battle of Kursk: Germany's Lost Victory in World War II," HistoryNet.com, http://www.historynet.com/battle-of-kursk-germanys-lost-victory-in-world-war-ii.htm, as of July 2009. (Hereafter Nipe.)

6. Heiber and Glantz, 39. Glantz and House, *The Battle of Kursk*, 65.

7. Alan Wilson, "Kursk—July, 1943," http://www.vy75.dial.pipex.com/, as of July 2009.

8. Busse/Newton, location 322ff. Fangohr/Newton, location 1106ff. Sydnor, 284. "Abschrift," Paul Hausser, SS personnel files, RG 242, A3343 Series SSO, 071A, frame 1993ff., NARA. Die Deutsche Wochenschau (OKW), "1943-Kursk," http://www.youtube.com/watch?v=_t26XddPwMg, as of August 2009.

9. Busse/Newton, location 327ff., 340ff. Fangohr/Newton, location 1018ff. Nipe. Newton, location 4859ff. Sydnor, 286ff. Manstein, 448–449. XLVIII Panzer Corps, Kriegstagebuch, July 1943, T314, roll 1170, frame 000543ff., NARA. Fourth Panzer Army, Kriegstagebuch 4, 35.3.43–31.7943, T313 roll 365, frame 8650581ff., NARA. "Abschrift," Paul Hausser, SS personnel files, RG 242, A3343 Series SSO, 071A, frame 993ff., NARA. Hoth's report on Hausser's actions, contained in Paul Hausser, SS personnel files, RG 242, A3343 Series SSO, 071A, frame 1941ff., NARA. Glantz and House, *The Battle of Kursk*, 181–196.

10. Alan Wilson, "Kursk—July, 1943," http://www.vy75.dial.pipex.com/, as of July 2009.

11. Busse/Newton, location 400ff.

12. "Personalakten für Hörnlein, Walter," German Army officers 201 files, 1900--1945, A3356, box 344, NARA.

13. Lexikon der Wehrmacht, http://www.lexikon-der-wehrmacht.de, as of March 2009.

14. "Kriegstagebuch 7," LIX Corps, T314, roll 1519, frame 000190. Liddell Hart, *Second World War*, 495. Schramm, *Kriegstagebuch der OKW, Zweiter Halbband, Band 3*, 1290. Erhard Raus, *Panzer Operations: The Eastern Front Memoir of General Raus, 1941–1945* (Cambridge, MA: De Capo Press, 2003), 256–258. (Hereafter Raus.) Mellenthin, 304–310. Manteuffel memoirs, 107ff. Manstein, 488–489. Glantz and House, *When Titans Clashed*, 173ff.

Chapter 8: Sicily: Empty Glory

1. Warlimont, *Inside Hitler's Headquarters*, 319–320.

2. Ibid., 326.

3. Westphal, 138–139.

4. Warlimont, *Inside Hitler's Headquarters*, 332–333.

5. *Generalfeldmarschall* Albert Kesselring, "The Battle of Sicily: Concluding Comments by the Former Commander in Chief South Field Marshal Kesselring," MS # T-2 K-1, not dated, NARA, 5. (Hereafter Kesselring, "The Battle of Sicily.")

6. Commando Supremo, *Segnalzioni su Possibilita' Azioni Nemiche*, 15 Jan–19 Aug 1943, T821, roll 21, frame 899ff., NARA. Commando Supremo, *Occupazione della Sicilia*, 23 June 1943, T821, roll 348, frame 53ff., NARA.

7. Schramm, *Kriegstagebuch der OKW, Zweiter Halbband, Band 3*, 752.

8. Heeresgruppe C, Ic, summarized intelligence reports, May–Sept. 1943," T311, roll 10, frame 7010877ff., NARA.

9. Commando Supremo, *Occupazione della Sicilia*, 23 June 1943, T821, roll 348, frame 62, NARA.

10. Kesselring, "The Battle of Sicily," 11.

11. *Dizionario Biografico Degli Italiani*, LXI, 619. Kesselring, "The Battle of Sicily," 6, 16–17.

12. *General der Panzertruppe* Walter Fries, "The Battle of Sicily," MS # T-2, 11 December 1947, NARA, 7–8. (Hereafter Fries.)

13. Commando Supremo, *Ufficio Operazioni Eseruito, R. Ecercito—Quadro di Battaglia*, 1 Jan–1 July 1943, T821, roll 2, frame 657ff., NARA. Commando Supremo, *Ufficio Operazioni Stato Efficienza Divisioni*, Jan–Sept 1943, T821, roll 2, frame 834ff., NARA.

14. Ibid. Lord Carver, *The Imperial War Museum Book of the War in Italy 1943–1945* (London: Pan Books, 2002), 4–10. (Hereafter Carver.) *Sicily* (CMH Pub 72-16) (Washington, DC: Center of Military History, 1999), 6–9. (Hereafter *Sicily*.) Kesselring, "The Battle of Sicily, 13." Fries, 10. *General der Panzertruppe* Frido von Senger und Etterlin, "War Diary of the Italian Campaign (1943–45): Liaison Activities with Italian Sixth Army," MS # C-095, not dated, NARA, 14. (Hereafter Senger und Etterlin.)

15. Kesselring, "The Battle of Sicily," 9.

16. Ibid.

17. *Oberstleutnant* Eberhard Rodt, "Studie Über den Feldzug in Sizilien bei der 15. Pz. Gren. Div. Mai-August 1943," MS # C-077, not dated, NARA, 4–10. (Hereafter Rodt.) Fries, 8.

18. *Oberst i. G.* Hellmut Bergengruen, Ia of the Hermann Göring Panzer Division, "Kampf der Pz. Div. 'Hermann Goering' auf Sizilien vom 10–14.7.1943," MS # C-087a, 31 December 1950, NARA. (Hereafter Bergengruen.) *General der Fallschirmtruppen* Paul Conrath, "Stellungsnahme des seinerzeitegen Kommandeurs der Pz. Div. H. G. Generalmajor Conrath zu den Berichten ueber den Kampf der Division," MS # C-087c, 26 January 1951, NARA, 1, 9. (Hereafter Conrath.) Kesselring, "The Battle of Sicily," 9.

19. Schramm, *Kriegstagebuch der OKW, Erster Halbband, Band 3*, 716, 725.

20. Kesselring, "The Battle of Sicily," 10–11.

21. Commando Supremo, *Occupazione della Sicilia*, 23 June 1943, T821, roll 348, frame 56, NARA.

22. Fries, 9.

23. Conrath, 4. Albert Kesselring, *The Memoirs of Field-Marshal Kesselring* (St. Paul, MN: MBI Publishing, 2007), 161. (Hereafter Kesselring memoirs.)

24. Senger und Etterlin, 9.

25. Carver, 4–10. *Sicily*, 6–9.

26. Heeresgruppe C, Ic, summarized intelligence reports, May–Sept. 1943," T311, roll 10, frame 7010935, NARA.

27. Schramm, *Kriegstagebuch der OKW, Zweiter Halbband, Band 3*, 763–764.

28. Commando Supremo, *Operazioni in Sicilia del 9 al 19 Luglio* [1943], T821, roll 21, frame 5, NARA.

29. Rick Atkinson, *The Day of Battle* (New York: Henry Holt and Company, 2007), 60. (Hereafter Atkinson, *The Day of Battle*.)

30. Fries, 19–20. Commando Supremo, *Operazioni in Sicilia del 9 al 19 Luglio* [1943], T821, roll 21, frame 7, NARA.

31. Atkinson, *The Day of Battle*, 83. Howard McGaw Smyth, assisted by Martin Blumenson, *Sicily and the Surrender of Italy: United States Army in World War II, The European Theater of Operations* (Washington, DC: Office of the Chief of Military History, Department of the Army, 1993), 149–153. (Hereafter Smyth.)

32. *Sicily*, 10–11. Smyth, 149–154.

33. Journal, 45th Infantry Division. Journal, II Corps.

34. Maj. Ellsworth Cundiff, "The Operations of the 3d Battalion, 179th Infantry (45th Infantry Division) 13–14 July 1943 South of Grammicele, Sicily (Personal Experience of a Regimental S-2)," submitted for the Advanced Infantry Officers Course, 1947–1948, the Infantry School, Fort Benning Georgia (Hereafter Cundiff.) Smyth, 154–155.

35. Schramm, *Kriegstagebuch der OKW, Zweiter Halbband, Band 3*, 771.

36. Commando Supremo, *Operazioni in Sicilia del 9 al 19 Luglio* [1943], T821, roll 21, frame 8, NARA. Kesselring, "The Battle of Sicily, 23." Conrath, 8–9.

37. Smyth, 163ff.

38. Atkinson, *The Day of Battle*, 102–103.

39. Commando Supremo, *Operazioni in Sicilia del 9 al 19 Luglio* [1943], T821, roll 21, frame 8, NARA.

40. Senger und Etterlin, 28.

41. Rodt, 12–15.

42. Schramm, *Kriegstagebuch der OKW, Zweiter Halbband, Band 3*, 771.

43. Senger und Etterlin, 34ff.

44. *Generalmajor* Max Ulich, "Specialized Defensive Tactics (Sicily) (Jul–Aug 43)," MS # D-004, 26 March 1947, NARA, 2, 8–9. (Hereafter Ulich.)

45. Commando Supremo, *Operazioni in Sicilia del 9 al 19 Luglio* [1943], T821, roll 21, frame 10, NARA.

46. Heeresgruppe C, Ic, summarized intelligence reports, May–Sept. 1943," T311, roll 10, frame 7010960, NARA.

47. *Generalmajor* Hellmuth Reinhardt and *Oberst i. G.* Hellmut Bergengruen, "Division "Hermann Goering" Questionnaire (11–12 Jul. 1943)," MS # C-087d, 14 August 1951, NARA.

48. Commando Supremo, *Operazioni in Sicilia del 9 al 19 Luglio* [1943], T821, roll 21, frame 11–12, NARA.

49. Schramm, *Kriegstagebuch der OKW, Zweiter Halbband, Band 3*, 773.

50. Ulich, 3.

51. Commando Supremo, *Operazioni in Sicilia del 9 al 19 Luglio* [1943], T821, roll 21, frame 14–15, NARA. Schramm, *Kriegstagebuch der OKW, Zweiter Halbband, Band 3*, 776.

52. Senger und Etterlin, 41.

53. Westphal, 142. Senger und Etterlin, 39.

54. "Beurteilungen: Oberst Hube, Hans-Valentin," German Army officers 201 files, 1900–1945, A3356, box 346, NARA.

55. Conrath, 7.

56. Schramm, *Kriegstagebuch der OKW, Zweiter Halbband, Band 3*, 776–778. Rodt, 16ff. Fries, 22.

57. Senger und Etterlin, 43.

58. Schramm, *Kriegstagebuch der OKW, Zweiter Halbband, Band 3*, 788.

59. Senger und Etterlin, 45.

60. Fries, 23.

61. Senger und Etterlin, 46.

62. Warlimont, *Inside Hitler's Headquarters*, 337–338.

63. Commando Supremo, *Operazioni in Sicilia del 9 al 19 Luglio* [1943], T821, roll 21, frame 21–22, NARA. Schramm, *Kriegstagebuch der OKW, Zweiter Halbband, Band 3*, 795. Fries, 24. Thomas L. Jentz, ed., *Panzertruppen 2* (Arglen, PA: Schiffer Military History, 1996), 103.

64. Commando Supremo, *Operazioni in Sicilia del 9 al 19 Luglio* [1943], T821, roll 21, frame 23–24, NARA.

65. *Sicily*, 15, 17.

66. Heeresgruppe C, Ic, summarized intelligence reports, May–Sept. 1943," T311, roll 10, frame 7010972, NARA.

67. Commando Supremo, *Operazioni in Sicilia del 9 al 19 Luglio* [1943], situation maps, T821, roll 21, frame 94–96, NARA. Schramm, *Kriegstagebuch der OKW, Zweiter Halbband, Band 3*, 802–804. Senger und Etterlin, 54–55.

68. Commando Supremo, *Operazioni in Sicilia del 9 al 19 Luglio* [1943], T821, roll 21, frame 23–24, NARA.

69. Warlimont, *Inside Hitler's Headquarters*, 340.

70. Koch, 56–57.

71. Terry Brighton, *Masters of Battle: Monty, Patton and Rommel at War* (London: Penguin Books, 2008), 210. Fries, 24ff.

72. *Sicily*, 17–21.

73. Michael Reynolds, *Monty and Patton: Two Paths to Victory* (Chalford Stroud, Gloucestershire, U.K.: Spellmount Limited, 2007), 166. (Hereafter Reynolds.)

74. Commando Supremo, *Operazioni in Sicilia del 20 al 31 Luglio* [1943], T821, roll 21, frames 134, 162, 165, 168, 176, NARA.

75. Smyth, 308–309.

76. Schramm, *Kriegstagebuch der OKW, Zweiter Halbband, Band 3*, 825.

77. Commando Supremo, *Operazioni in Sicilia del 20 al 31 Luglio* [1943], T821, roll 21, frames 134, 162, 165, 168, 176, NARA.

78. Ibid.

79. Rodt, 18ff.

80. Warlimont, *Inside Hitler's Headquarters*, 342–353, 372. Schramm, *Kriegstagebuch der OKW, Zweiter Halbband, Band 3*, 839.

81. Warlimont, *Inside Hitler's Headquarters*, 359.

82. Commando Supremo, *Operazioni in Sicilia del 20 al 31 Luglio* [1943], T821, roll 21, frames 134, 162, 165, 168, 176, NARA.

83. Schramm, *Kriegstagebuch der OKW, Zweiter Halbband, Band 3*, 855.

84. Ibid., 863.

85. *Sicily*, 21.

86. Ulich, 7.

87. Schramm, *Kriegstagebuch der OKW, Zweiter Halbband, Band 3*, 868.

88. Smyth, 352.

89. Rodt, 21. Smyth, 313–315.

90. Senger und Etterlin, 56.

91. Commando Supremo, *Operazioni in Sicilia del 1 al 17 Agosto* [1943], T821, roll 21, frame 223, NARA.

92. *Sicily*, 21. Atkinson, The Day of Battle, 154.

93. Rodt, 20ff.

94. Schramm, *Kriegstagebuch der OKW, Zweiter Halbband, Band 3*, 878.

95. Rodt, 21ff. Atkinson, *The Day of Battle*, 155ff.

96. Commando Supremo, *Operazioni in Sicilia del 1 al 17 Agosto* [1943], T821, roll 21, frame 228, NARA.

97. Ibid., frame 229.

98. Rodt, 22–23.

99. Schramm, *Kriegstagebuch der OKW, Zweiter Halbband, Band 3*, 911, 915.

100. Smyth, 350ff. Heeresgruppe C, Ic, summarized intelligence reports, May–Sept. 1943," T311, roll 10, frame 7011003, NARA.

101. Schramm, *Kriegstagebuch der OKW, Zweiter Halbband, Band 3*, 919. *Sicily*, 23–24.

102. Commando Supremo, *Operazioni in Sicilia del 1 al 17 Agosto* [1943], T821, roll 21, frame 233, NARA. Schramm, *Kriegstagebuch der OKW, Zweiter Halbband, Band 3*, 924.

103. Commando Supremo, *Operazioni in Sicilia del 1 al 17 Agosto* [1943], T821, roll 21, frame 234, NARA.

104. Smyth, 388ff.

105. Commando Supremo, *Operazioni in Sicilia del 1 al 17 Agosto* [1943], T821, roll 21, frame 236, NARA. Smyth, 404–405.

106. Schramm, *Kriegstagebuch der OKW, Zweiter Halbband, Band 3*, 937ff. Commando Supremo, *Operazioni in Sicilia del 1 al 17 Agosto* [1943], T821, roll 21, frame 238, NARA.

107. Commando Supremo, *Operazioni in Sicilia del 1 al 17 Agosto* [1943], T821, roll 21, frame 239, NARA. Rodt, 26.

108. Warlimont, *Inside Hitler's Headquarters*, 379.

109. Commando Supremo, *Operazioni in Sicilia del 1 al 17 Agosto* [1943], T821, roll 21, frame 240–241, NARA. Schramm, *Kriegstagebuch der OKW, Zweiter Halbband, Band 3*, 963–964.

110. Ulich, 10.

111. "Das Wehrpotential und die Wehrmächte Grossbritanniens und der USA," Generalstab des Heeres, Abteilung Fremde Heere West, folder containing data on U.S. Army training, tactics, and equipment, T-78, roll 442, frame 6415820ff., NARA.

112. Rodt, 30.

Chapter 9: Bait and Wait

1. Gordon A. Harrison, *Cross-Channel Attack: United States Army in World War II, The European Theater of Operations* (Washington, DC: Center of Military History, 1993), 158. (Hereafter Harrison.)

2. Farago, 373–374.

3. Ibid., 362–362. Blumenson, *Patton*, 218.

4. Radio No. 536 Washington, DC, 21 October 1943, records of the War Department General and Special Staffs (RG 165), records of the Operations Division (OPD), Top Secret Message File CM-OUT-9038, NARA.

5. Larry I. Bland and Sharon Ritenour Stevens, eds., *The Papers of George Catlett Marshall* (Lexington, VA: The George C. Marshall Foundation, 1981), electronic version based on *The Papers of George Catlett Marshall*, vol. 4, "Aggressive and Determined Leadership," June 1, 1943–December 31, 1944 (Baltimore and London: The Johns Hopkins University Press, 1996), 163–164. (Hereafter *The Papers of George Catlett Marshall.*)

6. Holt, 596.

7. Radio No. WAR-29722, Washington, DC, 29 April 1944, records of the War Department General and Special Staffs (RG 165), records of the Operations Division (OPD), Executive File 1, Item 28c, NARA.

8. *The Papers of George Catlett Marshall*, 210–211.

9. George C. Marshall Papers, Pentagon Office Collection, Selected Materials, George C. Marshall Research Library, Lexington, Virginia.

10. Blumenson, *Patton*, 217.

11. OKW Kriegesschauplätze im Rahmen der Gesamt-Kriegsführung, January–March 1944, T-77, roll 1430, frame 728ff.

12. Thaddeus Holt, *The Deceivers* (New York: Scribner, 2004), 480–493. (Hereafter Holt.) OKW Kriegesschauplätze im Rahmen der Gesamt-Kriegsführung, T-77, roll 1430, frame 728ff. Percy Schramm, "OKW War Diary (1 Apr–18 Dec 44)," MS # B-034, 1947, NARA, 3. (Hereafter Schramm, "OKW War Diary [1 Apr–18 Dec 44].)

13. Holt, 531–548.

14. Ralph Bennett, *Ultra in the West: The Normandy Campaign 1944–45* (New York: Charles Scribner's Sons, 1980), 6, 43. (Hereafter Bennett.) Holt, 504.

15. "Überblick USA Nr. 19," 16 January 1944, Generalstab des Heeres, Abteilung Fremde Heere West, folder containing data on U.S. Army training, tactics, and equipment, T-78, roll 442, frame 6416306ff., NARA.

16. Farago, 407. Percy E. Schramm, *Kriegstagebuch des Oberkommando der Wehrmacht (Wehrmachtführungsstab), 1. Januar 1944–22 Mai 1945, Erster Halbband, Band 4* (Germany: Bechtermünz, 2005), 250. (Hereafter Schramm, *Kriegstagebuch der OKW, Erster Halbband, Band 4.*)

17. Blumenson, *Patton Papers: 1940*, 409. Holt, 541. Farago, 400, 408.

18. "Invasionsgenerale: Werdegang-Urteil," Luftkriegsakademie, 7 February 2944, Bundesarchiv, RL 2 IV/116.

19. "GB-USA Fliegertruppe," March 1944, Luftwaffenführungsstab Ic, T321, roll 98, frame 000226, NARA. Jodl, "U.S. Operations," 5.

20. Bennett, 43.

21. "Überblick USA Nr. 24," 1 April 1944, Generalstab des Heeres, Abteilung Fremde Heere West, folder containing data on U.S. Army training, tactics, and equipment, T-78, roll 442, frame 6416275ff., NARA.

22. Holt, 562.

23. Reynolds, 200.

24. "Lagebericht West Nr. 1348," 5 August 1944, Oberkommando des Heeres, Heeresnach-trichtenwesen, T-78, roll 453, frame 6429448ff., NARA. Holt, 565.

25. Schramm, *Kriegstagebuch der OKW, Erster Halbband, Band 4*, 302–303. Liddell Hart, *The German Generals Talk*, 237. Warlimont, *Inside Hitler's Headquarters*, 409.

26. Bennett, 51.

27. Liddell Hart, *The German Generals Talk*, 242.

28. Schramm, "OKW War Diary (1 Apr–18 Dec 44)," MS # B-034, 1947, NARA, 8–9.

29. Ibid., 2–3.

30. "Das USA-Heer," Generalstab des Heeres, Abteilung Fremde Heere West, folder containing data on U.S. Army training, tactics, and equipment, T-78, roll 442, frame 6416100, NARA.

31. Harrison, 162.

32. Allen, 15–23, 30, 56. Blumenson, *Patton*, 220.

33. Allen, 58.

34. Blumenson, *Patton Papers: 1940*, 547.

35. Farago, 397–406.

36. Koch, 68–69.

37. Allen, 61–62.

38. Koch, 73.

39. Allen, 63.

40. Farago, 427–432.

Chapter 10: Normandy: Patton Returns to War

1. Samuel W. Mitcham, *Retreat to the Reich: The German Defeat in France, 1944* (Westport, CT: Prager, Kindle edition, 2000), locations 153–157. (Hereafter Mitcham.)

2. *Normandy* (CMH Pub 72-18) (Washington, DC: U.S. Army Center of Military History, not dated), 16–17. (Hereafter *Normandy*.)

3. Ibid., 32–34.

4. Liddell Hart, *The German Generals Talk*, 244.

5. Ibid., 244–245. Schramm, *Kriegstagebuch der OKW, Erster Halbband, Band 4*, 316–317.

6. Schramm, *Kriegstagebuch der OKW, Erster Halbband, Band 4*, 324.

7. Warlimont, *Inside Hitler's Headquarters*, 297–299.

8. Schramm, *Kriegstagebuch der OKW, Erster Halbband, Band 4*, 323–324.

9. Warlimont, *Inside Hitler's Headquarters*, 297–299.

10. Kuntzen, 11. Liddell Hart, *The German Generals Talk*, 244–248. Mitcham, locations 330–333, 367–371, 392–396.

11. Anlagen zum Kriegstagebuch, Oberkommando Heeresgruppe B, Ic, 1 July–31 December 1944, T311, roll 1, frame 7000851, NARA.

12. *General der Panzertruppe* Heinrich Eberbach, "Panzergruppe Eberbach bei Alencon und beim Durchbruch aus dem Kessel von Falaise," MS # A-922, 7 February 1946, NARA, 1. (Hereafter Eberbach, "Panzergruppe Eberbach.")

13. Allen, 64.

14. Holt, 588–589.

15. Anlagen zum Kriegstagebuch, Oberkommando Heeresgruppe B, Ic, 1 July–31 December 1944, T311, roll 1, frame 7000892ff., NARA.

16. Heeresgruppe B, Ia, Lagebeurteilungen, Wochenmeldungen, T311, roll 3, frame 7002241ff., NARA.

17. Ibid., frame 7002195.

18. *Generalmajor* Kurt von Mühlen, "The Rhineland Campaign, 15 Sept 44–21 Sept 44," MS # A-972, April 1946, NARA, 1–2. (Hereafter Mühlen.)

19. Seventh Army, tactical reports, 6 June–31 July 1944, T312, roll 1568, frame 001063, NARA.

20. Schramm, "OKW War Diary (1 Apr–18 Dec 44)," MS # B-034, 1947, NARA, 55.

21. Ibid., 56–57.

22. Guderian, 267ff.

23. Anlagen zum Kriegstagebuch, Oberkommando Heeresgruppe B, Versorgungs Führung, 1 July–31 July 1944, T311, roll 1, frame 7000828, NARA.

24. Guderian, 265.

25. Anlagen zum Kriegstagebuch, Oberkommando Heeresgruppe B, Ic, 1 July–31 December 1944, T311, roll 1, frame 7000925, NARA.

26. Guderian, 272.

27. Heeresgruppe B, Ia, Lagebeurteilungen, Wochenmeldungen, T311, roll 3, frame 7002243ff., NARA.

28. Ibid., 272.

29. "Anlage zu Lagebericht West Nr. 1333 von 21.7.44," 21 September 1944, Oberkommando des Heeres, Heeresnachrichtenwesen, T-78, roll 453, frame 6429505ff., NARA.

30. Bennett, 104. Schramm, "OKW War Diary (1 Apr–18 Dec 44)," MS # B-034, 1947, NARA, 56–57.

31. Warlimont, *Inside Hitler's Headquarters*, 443.

32. 17th SS Panzergrenadier Division, Divisionsgefechtsstand, Feindlage, 22 July 1944, Anlagen zum Kriegstagebuch, Oberkommando Heeresgruppe B, Ic, 1 July–31 December 1944, T311, roll 1, frame 7000978, NARA. *Generalleutnant* Paul Mahlmann, "353 Inf Div (24 Jul-14 Sep 44)," MS # A-984, not dated, NARA, 1. Paul Hausser, SS personnel files, RG 242, A3343 Series SSO, 071A, frame 1096, NARA.

33. *Oberst i. G.* Anton Staubwasser, "The Tactical Situation of Enemy as Seen by High Command of Army Group B During the Normandy Battle: 6 Jun to 24 Jul 44," MS # B-782, 16 December 1947, NARA.

34. Heeresgruppe B, Ia, Lagebeurteilungen, Wochenmeldungen, T311, roll 3, frame 7002203, NARA. Schramm, *Kriegstagebuch der OKW, Erster Halbband, Band 4*, 326–327.

35. Bernard Law Montgomery, *The Memoirs of Field Marshall the Viscount Montgomery of Alamein, L.G.* (New York: The World Publishing Company, 1958), 200, 227–228.

36. *Northern France*, CMH Pub 72-30 (Washington, DC: U.S. Army Center of Military History, not dated), 7. (Hereafter *Northern France*.) Report of operations, First Army. AAR, VIII Corps.

37. Schramm, "OKW War Diary (1 Apr–18 Dec 44)," MS # B-034, 1947, NARA, 56.

38. Anlagen zum Kriegstagebuch, Oberkommando Heeresgruppe B, Versorgungs Führung, 1 July–31 July 1944, T311, roll 1, frame 7000805ff., NARA.

39. *General der Infanterie* Dietrich Choltitz, "Operations, beginning 16 June 1944, conducted in Normandy by the LXXXIV Armeekorps," MS # B-418, March 1947, NARA, 18ff. (Hereafter Choltitz.)

40. Ibid., 12–13.

41. Martin Blumenson, *Breakout and Pursuit: United States Army In World War II, The European Theater Of Operations* (Washington, DC: Center of Military History, 1993), 240. (Hereafter Blumenson, *Breakout and Pursuit*.)

42. Seventh Army, Zusammenstellung der Telefongespräche über Lageorientierung und Entschlüssen, 16 July–16 August 1944, T312, roll 1568, frame 000910ff., NARA.

43. *Northern France*. Report of operations, First Army.

44. *Generalleutnant* Fritz Bayerlein, "Panzer Lehr Division: 24 to 25 July 44," MS # A-902, 12 July 1949, NARA.

45. Seventh Army, tactical reports, 6 June–31 July 1944, T312, roll 1568, frame 001068, NARA.

46. Heeresgruppe B, Ia, Tagesmeldungen, T311, roll 3, frame 7002618ff., NARA.

47. LXXXIV corps order, 26 July 1944, reproduced in M. Wind and H. Günther, *Kriegstagebuch, 30. Oktober 1943 bis 6. Mai 1945, 17. SS-Panzer-Grenadier-Division "Götz von Berlichingen"* (Munich: Schild Verlag, 1993), not paginated. (Hereafter *Kriegstagebuch* 17th SS Panzergrenadier Division.)

48. Schramm, *Kriegstagebuch der OKW, Erster Halbband, Band 4*, 327.

49. *Northern France*, 89.

50. Blumenson, *Breakout and Pursuit*, 253–254.

51. Ibid., 255.

52. Heeresgruppe B, Ia, Tagesmeldungen, T311, roll 3, frame 7002625ff., NARA.

53. Schramm, "OKW War Diary (1 Apr–18 Dec 44)," MS # B-034, 1947, NARA, 58. *General der Panzertruppe* Heinrich Eberbach, "Report on the Fighting of Panzergruppe West (5th Pz Army) From July 3–9 August 1944," MS # B-840, 1 June 1948, NARA, 37. (Hereafter Eberbach, "Report on the Fighting of Panzergruppe West.")

54. *Generalmajor* Rudolf-Christoph Freiherr von Gersdorff, "The Battle in Northern France, Chapter 5, Defensive Fighting of the 5 Panzer Army from 25 July to 25 August 44," MS # B-726, Historical Division, Headquarters United States Army, Europe, not dated, NARA, 6. (Hereafter Gersdorff, "Defensive Fighting of the 5 Panzer Army.")

55. *Generalleutnant* Otto Elfeldt, "LXXXIV Inf Corps 28 Jul–20 Aug 44." MS # A-968, 19 August 1950, NARA, 2. (Hereafter Elfeldt.)

56. "Anlage zu Lagebericht West Nr. 1343 von 31.7.44," 31 July 1944, Oberkommando des Heeres, Heeresnachtrichtenwesen, T-78, roll 453, frame 6429470ff., NARA. "Anlage

zu Lagebericht West Nr. 1339 von 27.7.44," 27 July 1944, Oberkommando des Heeres, Heeresnachtrichtenwesen, T-78, roll 453, frame 6429485ff., NARA.

57. Heeresgruppe B, Ia, Tagesmeldungen, T311, roll 3, frame 7002631ff., NARA.

58. Schramm, "OKW War Diary (1 Apr–18 Dec 44)," MS # B-034, 1947, NARA, 58.

59. Elfeldt, 3.

60. Anlagen zum Kriegstagebuch, Oberkommando Heeresgruppe B, Versorgungs Führung, 1 July–31 July 1944, T311, roll 1, frame 7000823ff., NARA.

61. Blumenson, *Breakout and Pursuit*, 309–310.

62. Ibid., 310–317.

63. Elfeldt, 4–5.

64. *Major* Percy Schramm, "Avranches and Falaise Special Questions," MS # B-719, 1953, NARA. (Hereafter Schramm, "Avranches and Falaise Special Questions.") *Generaloberst (Waffen SS)* Paul Hausser, "Seventh Army 29 June to 20 August 1944," MS # A-907, 30 May 1950, NARA, 7.

65. Schramm, *Kriegstagebuch der OKW, Erster Halbband, Band 4*, 27.

66. Heeresgruppe B, Ia, Tagesmeldungen, T311, roll 3, frame 7002637ff., NARA.

67. Schramm, "OKW War Diary (1 Apr–18 Dec 44)," MS # B-034, 1947, NARA, 59.

68. Heeresgruppe B, Ia, Tagesmeldungen, T311, roll 3, frame 7002644ff., NARA.

69. Blumenson, *Breakout and Pursuit*, 262–263.

70. Schramm, "Avranches and Falaise Special Questions." Schramm, *Kriegstagebuch der OKW, Erster Halbband, Band 4*, 330–331. *Generalmajor* Rudolf-Christoph Freiherr von Gersdorff, "Normandy, Cobra, and Mortain," MS # A-894, October 1945, NARA, 1. (Hereafter Gersdorff, "Normandy, Cobra, and Mortain.") "Rudolf Christoph Freiherr von Gersdorff," Lexikon der Wehrmacht, http://www.lexikon-der-wehrmacht.de/Personenregister/G/GersdorffRv.htm, as of October 2009.

71. Heeresgruppe B, Ia, Tagesmeldungen, T311, roll 3, frame 7002644ff., NARA. Gersdorff, "Normandy, Cobra, and Mortain," 2–5.

72. Schramm, "OKW War Diary (1 Apr–18 Dec 44)," MS # B-034, 1947, NARA, 60. Heeresgruppe B, Ia, Tagesmeldungen, T311, roll 3, frame 7002650ff., NARA.

73. *Generalmajor* Eugen Koenig, "91st Airborne Division Operations in Normandy (10 July–August 1944)," MS # B-010, 17 June 1946, NARA, 8ff. Choltitz, 20.

74. Heeresgruppe B, Ia, Lagebeurteilungen, Wochenmeldungen, T311, roll 3, frame 7002213ff., NARA.

75. Heeresgruppe B, Ia, Tagesmeldungen, T311, roll 3, frame 7002657ff., NARA.

76. Seventh Army, Zusammenstellung der Telefongespräche über Lageorientierung und Entschlüssen, 16 July–16 August 1944, T312, roll 1568, frame 000629ff., NARA.

77. Schramm, "OKW War Diary (1 Apr–18 Dec 44)," MS # B-034, 1947, NARA, 60.

78. Heeresgruppe B, Ia, Tagesmeldungen, T311, roll 3, frame 7002657ff., NARA.

79. Bennett, 105.

80. Eberbach, "Report on the Fighting of Panzergruppe West," 39–40.

81. *The Papers of George Catlett Marshall*, 535–536.

82. Holt, 586–587.

83. Heiber and Glantz, 444–449.

84. Ibid., 445.

85. Tagebuch, *Generaloberst* Jodl, 13 April 1944, T-77, roll 1430, frame 893ff. Schramm, "OKW War Diary (1 Apr–18 Dec 44)," 6–7. Schramm, *Kriegstagebuch der OKW, Erster Halbband, Band 4,* 209–210.

86. Heiber and Glantz, 445–460.

87. Tagebuch, *Generaloberst* Jodl, 31 July 1944, T-77, roll 1430, frame 893ff.

88. Schramm, "OKW War Diary (1 Apr–18 Dec 44)," MS # B-034, 1947, NARA, 60.

89. Paul Carell, *Invasion: They're Coming!* (New York: Bantam Books, 1962), 270. (Hereafter Carell.)

90. Carell, 270–271. Seventh Army, Zusammenstellung der Telefongespräche über Lageorientierung und Entschlüssen, 16 July–16 August 1944, T312, roll 1568, frame 000629, NARA. Choltitz, 19.

91. Carell, 271.

92. Seventh Army, Zusammenstellung der Telefongespräche über Lageorientierung und Entschlüssen, 16 July–16 August 1944, T312, roll 1568, frame 000631ff., NARA.

93. AAR, Third Army.

94. Report of operations, First Army.

95. Chester Wilmot, *The Struggle for Europe* (Ware, England: Wordsworth Editions Limited, 1997), 394–395, 400. (Hereafter Wilmot.)

96. Gersdorff, "Defensive Fighting of the 5 Panzer Army," 9–10.

97. Heeresgruppe B, Ia, Tagesmeldungen, T311, roll 3, frame 7002664ff., NARA.

98. AAR, Third Army.

99. Allen, 67–68.

100. AAR, Third Army.

101. *General der Artillerie* Wilhelm Farmbacher, "LXXXIV Corps (12–24 Jun 1944) and XXV Corps (May 1942–10 May 1945)," MS # B-731, 26 May 1946, NARA, 9, 19ff. (Hereafter Farmbacher.)

102. AAR, Third Army.

103. Griess, 334. Blumenson, *Breakout and Pursuit,* 348–349.

104. Warlimont, *Inside Hitler's Headquarters,* 407.

105. Seventh Army, Zusammenstellung der Telefongespräche über Lageorientierung und Entschlüssen, 16 July–16 August 1944, T312, roll 1568, frame 000635ff., NARA.

106. AAR, Third Army.

107. Farmbacher, 21.

108. Carell, 288–289.

109. AAR, Third Army. Farmbacher, 52.

110. Heeresgruppe B, Ia, Tagesmeldungen, T311, roll 3, frame 7002704ff., NARA.

111. Schramm, "OKW War Diary (1 Apr–18 Dec 44)," MS # B-034, 1947, NARA, 80. Heeresgruppe B, Ia, Führerbefehle, T311, roll 3, frame 7002311, NARA.

112. Heeresgruppe B, Ia, Tagesmeldungen, T311, roll 3, frame 7002713ff., NARA. AAR, Third Army.

113. Blumenson, *Patton Papers: 1940*, 506–507.

114. "86th Chemical Mortar Battalion History: The Story of Company 'B' from The Battle History," from http://home.cinci.rr.com/chemvets/companyb.html, as of November 2008.

115. Heeresgruppe B, Ia, Tagesmeldungen, T311, roll 3, frame 7002723ff., NARA. AAR, Third Army.

116. Carell, 289.

117. AAR, Third Army. Farmbacher, 53. "Notes on Surrender of St. Malo," C.S.D.I.C. (UK) interrogation report S.I.R. 827, and "Last orders received and published by the defender of St. Malo, S.I.R. 857, RG 165, box 661, NARA.

118. Farmbacher, 55.

119. Heeresgruppe B, Ia, Tagesmeldungen, T311, roll 3, frame 7002733ff., NARA. Farmbacher, 78ff.

120. Farmbacher, 83ff.

121. Ibid., 65, 72.

122. Ibid., 54ff. *Oberst i. G.* Rudolf Kogard, "The Battles in France in 1944: Events in western Brittany, especially in the district of the Brest fortress," MS # B-427, 12 March 1947, NARA, 29–30, 33. (Hereafter Kogard.) Erwin Rommel and B. H. Liddell Hart, ed., The Rommel Papers (New York: Da Capo Press, 1982), 343. (Hereafter Rommel.)

123. Blumenson, *Patton Papers: 1940*, 532.

124. Feindlagen West, files of Fremde Heere West, T78, roll 540, frames 001055ff., NARA.

125. Farmbacher, 64.

126. Schramm, *Kriegstagebuch der OKW, Erster Halbband, Band 4*, 335.

127. *Generaloberst* Alfred Jodl, "An Interview with Genobst Alfred Jodl: Ardennes Offensive," ETHINT-51, 31 July 1945, NARA, 9. (Hereafter Jodl, "Ardennes Offensive.")

128. Schramm, "OKW War Diary (1 Apr–18 Dec 44)," MS # B-034, 1947, NARA, 60, 63.

129. Schramm, *Kriegstagebuch der OKW, Erster Halbband, Band 4*, 336.

130. "Generals Balck and von Mellenthin on Tactics," 51.

131. Irving, 673.

132. Jodl, "U.S. Operations," 5.

133. Carell, 274. Victor Brooks, *The Normandy Campaign: From D-Day to the Liberation of Paris* (New York: Da Capo Press, 2002), 240. D'Este, 815.

134. Schramm, "OKW War Diary (1 Apr–18 Dec 44)," MS # B-034, 1947, NARA, 78.

135. Blumenson, *Breakout and Pursuit*, 321. AAR, Third Army.

136. Hans von Luck, *Panzer Commander* (New York: Dell Publishing, 1989), 203. (Hereafter Luck.)

137. Wilmot, 400.

138. Heeresgruppe B, Ia, Lagebeurteilungen, Wochenmeldungen, T311, roll 3, frame 7002246, NARA.

139. *General der Panzertruppe* Adolf Friedrich Kuntzen, "Commitment of LXXXI Inf Corps During Period 2 Aug to 4 Sep 1944," MS # B-807, 3 April 1948, NARA, 1–2. (Hereafter Kuntzen.)

140. Schramm, *Kriegstagebuch der OKW, Erster Halbband, Band 4*, 356–357. Eberbach, "Report on the Fighting of Panzergruppe West," 42.

141. Gersdorff, "Normandy, Cobra, and Mortain," 12. *Generalmajor* Rudolf-Christoph Freiherr von Gersdorff, "Comments on Seventh Army War Diary," MS # A-918, December 1945, NARA, 3. (Hereafter Gersdorff, "Comments on Seventh Army War Diary.")

142. Schramm, "OKW War Diary (1 Apr–18 Dec 44)," MS # B-034, 1947, NARA, 77. Bennett, 111. AAR, Third Army.

143. G-3 operations diary, Third Army. AAR, Third Army. AAR, XV Corps.

144. *Oberst* Erich Helmdach, "Measures Taken by the German Seventh Army in the Rear Area After the Breakthrough at Avranches," MS # B-822, 25 March 1948, NARA. (Hereafter Helmdach.) Kuntzen, 2–3. Seventh Army, Zusammenstellung der Telefongespräche über Lageorientierung und Entschlüssen, 16 July–16 August 1944, T312, roll 1568, frame 000636, NARA. Seventh Army, Ia, Berichte und Befehle, Westen, 31 July–21 August 1944, T312, roll 1569, frame 000364f., NARA.

145. Seventh Army, Ia, Berichte und Befehle, Westen, 31 July–21 August 1944, T312, roll 1569, frame 000379ff., NARA.

146. G-3 operations diary, Third Army. AAR, XV Corps. Eberbach, "Report on the Fighting of Panzergruppe West," 43.

147. "Lagebericht West Nr. 1348," 5 August 1944, Oberkommando des Heeres, Heeresnachtrichtenwesen, T-78, roll 453, frame 6429448ff., NARA.

148. Anlagen zum Kriegstagebuch, Oberkommando Heeresgruppe B, Ic, 1 July– 31 December 1944, T311, roll 1, frame 7000978, NARA.

149. Heeresgruppe B, Ia, Tagesmeldungen, T311, roll 3, frame 7002699ff., NARA.

150. Schramm, "OKW War Diary (1 Apr–18 Dec 44)," MS # B-034, 1947, NARA, 78. Kuntzen, 2.

151. Seventh Army, Ia, Berichte und Befehle, Westen, 31 July–21 August 1944, roll 1569, frame 000395, NARA.

152. Seventh Army, Zusammenstellung der Telefongespräche über Lageorientierung und Entschlüssen, 16 July–16 August 1944, T312, roll 1568, frame 000638ff., NARA.

153. "Anlage zu Lagebericht West Nr. 1349 von 6.8.44," 6 August 1944, Oberkommando des Heeres, Heeresnachtrichtenwesen, T-78, roll 453, frame 6429446ff., NARA.

154. Seventh Army, Zusammenstellung der Telefongespräche über Lageorientierung und Entschlüssen, 16 July–16 August 1944, T312, roll 1568, frame 000647, NARA. AAR, 17th SS Panzerjäger Abteilung, 10 August 1944, reproduced in *Kriegstagebuch* 17th SS Panzergrenadier Division, not paginated.

155. Bennett, 114–115.

156. Schramm, *Kriegstagebuch der OKW, Erster Halbband, Band 4,* 338.

157. Heeresgruppe B, Ia, Tagesmeldungen, T311, roll 3, frame 7002704ff., NARA. Kuntzen, 6.

158. Seventh Army, Zusammenstellung der Telefongespräche über Lageorientierung und Entschlüssen, 16 July–16 August 1944, T312, roll 1568, frame 000640ff., NARA.

159. Schramm, *Kriegstagebuch der OKW, Erster Halbband, Band 4,* 339.

160. Seventh Army, Zusammenstellung der Telefongespräche über Lageorientierung und Entschlüssen, 16 July–16 August 1944, T312, roll 1568, frame 000644, NARA.

161. Bennett, 113.

162. Schramm, *Kriegstagebuch der OKW, Erster Halbband, Band 4,* 339.

163. Heeresgruppe B, Ia, Tagesmeldungen, T311, roll 3, frame 7002713ff., NARA.

164. Seventh Army, Zusammenstellung der Telefongespräche über Lageorientierung und Entschlüssen, 16 July–16 August 1944, T312, roll 1568, frame 000646ff., NARA.

165. AAR, Third Army.

166. Ibid.

167. Seventh Army, Zusammenstellung der Telefongespräche über Lageorientierung und Entschlüssen, 16 July–16 August 1944, T312, roll 1568, frame 000649, NARA. Gersdorff, "Comments on Seventh Army War Diary," 6.

168. Heeresgruppe B, Ia, Tagesmeldungen, T311, roll 3, frame 7002713ff., NARA. Bennett, 116. AAR, Third Army.

169. Schramm, "OKW War Diary (1 Apr–18 Dec 44)," MS # B-034, 1947, NARA, 82.

170. Schramm, *Kriegstagebuch der OKW, Erster Halbband, Band 4*, 340.

171. Gersdorff, "Defensive Fighting of the 5 Panzer Army," 16.

172. Schramm, "OKW War Diary (1 Apr–18 Dec 44)," MS # B-034, 1947, NARA, 79.

173. Eberbach, "Report on the Fighting of Panzergruppe West," 44.

174. Schramm, *Kriegstagebuch der OKW, Erster Halbband, Band 4*, 340.

175. "Personalakten für Eberbach, Heinrich," German Army officers 201 files, 1900–1945, A3356, box 146, NARA. Eberbach, "Report on the Fighting of Panzergruppe West," 2.

176. *Oberst i. G.* Albert Emmerich, "The Battles of the 1. Army in France from 11 Aug to 15 Sep 1944," MS # B-728, 22 September 1946, NARA, 2. (Hereafter Emmerich, "The Battles of the 1. Army in France.")

177. Seventh Army, Zusammenstellung der Telefongespräche über Lageorientierung und Entschlüssen, 16 July–16 August 1944, T312, roll 1568, frame 000651, NARA.

178. Seventh Army, Ia, Berichte und Befehle, Westen, 31 July–21 August 1944, T312, roll 1569, frame 000443, NARA.

179. Bennett, 118–119.

180. Seventh Army, Zusammenstellung der Telefongespräche über Lageorientierung und Entschlüssen, 16 July–16 August 1944, T312, roll 1568, frame 000655ff., NARA.

181. *Generalmajor* Rudolf-Christoph Freiherr von Gersdorff, "An Interview with Genmaj Rudolf Frhr von Gersdorff," ETHINT-59, 16 May 1946, NARA, 1. (Hereafter Gersdorff interview.)

182. Schramm, "OKW War Diary (1 Apr–18 Dec 44)," MS # B-034, 1947, NARA, 84. Heeresgruppe B, Ia, Lagebeurteilungen, Wochenmeldungen, T311, roll 3, frame 7002248ff., NARA. Seventh Army, Zusammenstellung der Telefongespräche über Lageorientierung und Entschlüssen, 16 July–16 August 1944, T312, roll 1568, frame 000658, NARA.

183. Heeresgruppe B, Ia, Tagesmeldungen, T311, roll 3, frame 7002750ff., NARA. Seventh Army, Ia, Berichte und Befehle, Westen, 31 July–21 August 1944, T312, roll 1569, frame 000457ff., NARA. Eberbach, "Panzergruppe Eberbach," 19. AAR, Third Army.

184. Heeresgruppe B, Ia, Lagebeurteilungen, Wochenmeldungen, T311, roll 3, frame 7002222 and 7002262, NARA. Heeresgruppe B, Ia, Führerbefehle, T311, roll 3, frame 7002315ff., NARA. Eberbach, "Panzergruppe Eberbach," 13.

185. Heeresgruppe B, Ia, Lagebeurteilungen, Wochenmeldungen, T311, roll 3, frame 7002260, NARA. Heinz Günther Guderian, *From Normandy to the Ruhr, With the 116th Panzer Division in World War II* (Bedford, PA: The Aberjona Press, 2001), 76–80.

186. Heeresgruppe B, Ia, Tagesmeldungen, T311, roll 3, frame 7002755ff., NARA.

187. Seventh Army, Ia, Berichte und Befehle, Westen, 31 July–21 August 1944, T312, roll 1569, frame 000483, NARA. Eberbach, "Panzergruppe Eberbach," 20.

188. Heeresgruppe B, Ia, Lagebeurteilungen, Wochenmeldungen, T311, roll 3, frame 7002261, NARA. Heeresgruppe B, Ia, Führerbefehle, T311, roll 3, frame 7002317, NARA.

189. Heeresgruppe B, Ia, Lagebeurteilungen, Wochenmeldungen, T311, roll 3, frame 7002224 and 7002260, NARA.

190. Heeresgruppe B, Ia, Tagesmeldungen, T311, roll 3, frame 7002759ff., NARA. Schramm, *Kriegstagebuch der OKW, Erster Halbband, Band 4*, 343.

191. AAR, Third Army.

192. Farago, 543–544. Blumenson, *Patton Papers: 1940*, 507–508.

193. Farago, 539. Blumenson, *Patton Papers: 1940*, 507–508. "Patton Reported in Brittany Battle," Pittsburgh *Post-Gazette*, 11 August 1944, 2.

194. Heeresgruppe B, Ia, Tagesmeldungen, T311, roll 3, frame 7002762ff., NARA. Gersdorff, "Defensive Fighting of the 5 Panzer Army," 23.

195. Schramm, *Kriegstagebuch der OKW, Erster Halbband, Band 4*, 344–345.

196. Heeresgruppe B, Ia, Tagesmeldungen, T311, roll 3, frame 7002768ff., NARA.

197. Schramm, *Kriegstagebuch der OKW, Erster Halbband, Band 4*, 344.

198. AAR, Third Army. Heeresgruppe B, Ia, Tagesmeldungen, T311, roll 3, frame 7002768ff., NARA.

199. Schramm, *Kriegstagebuch der OKW, Erster Halbband, Band 4*, 345. Kuntzen, 11.

200. Emmerich, "The Battles of the 1. Army in France," 2–4. *Major* Kurt Hold, "Organization and Composition of the First Army During the Period of 11 Aug 44 until 14 Feb 45 (Part I: 11 Aug–15 Sep 44)." MS # B-732, 10 November 1947, NARA, 3. (Hereafter Hold, Part I.) Schramm, *Kriegstagebuch der OKW, Erster Halbband, Band 4*, 346.

201. "Historical Study: Operations of Encircled Forces—German Experiences in Russia," Washington, DC: Department of the Army, 1952, online edition of Pamphlet 20-234, http://www.history.army.mil/books/wwii/20234/20234.html, as of April 2009.

202. Manstein, 536–545.

203. Lexikon der Wehrmacht, http://www.lexikon-der-wehrmacht.de, as of March 2009. Axis Biographical Research, http://www.geocities.com/%7Eorion47/, as of March 2009.

204. Mellenthin, 291.

205. AAR, 87th Cavalry Reconnaissance Squadron. AAR, Combat Command B, 7th Armored Division. Emmerich, "The Battles of the 1. Army in France," 5.

206. Emmerich, "The Battles of the 1. Army in France," 5. Hold, Part I, 21. Schramm, *Kriegstagebuch der OKW, Erster Halbband, Band 4*, 346–347, 357. Paul Hausser, SS personnel files, RG 242, A3343 Series SSO, 071A, frame 880ff., NARA. Gersdorff interview, 6.

207. Emmerich, "The Battles of the 1. Army in France," 7.

208. Schramm, *Kriegstagebuch der OKW, Erster Halbband, Band 4*, 358–359.

209. Heeresgruppe B, Ia, Führerbefehle, T311, roll 3, frame 7002321ff., NARA. *Generaloberst* Alfred Jodl, "Die Operationen nach dem Durchbruch von Avranches," MS # A-927, 23 July 1945, NARA, 1. (Hereafter Jodl, "Die Operationen nach dem Durchbruch von Avranches.")

210. Heeresgruppe B, Ia, Lagebeurteilungen, Wochenmeldungen, T311, roll 3, frame 7002226, NARA. Carell, 308–309.

211. Luck, 207.

212. "Directive (Confirmation of Verbal Orders Issued 14 August 1944," 15 August 1944, document reproduced in AAR, Third Army.

213. Luck, 207. Gersdorff, "Defensive Fighting of the 5 Panzer Army," 33–34.

214. Heeresgruppe B, Ia, Führerbefehle, T311, roll 3, frame 7002327ff., NARA.

215. Emmerich, "The Battles of the 1. Army in France," 8. *Kriegstagebuch* 17th SS Panzergrenadier Division, not paginated.

216. Schramm, *Kriegstagebuch der OKW, Erster Halbband, Band 4*, 360. AAR, 51st SS Brigade, reproduced in *Kriegstagebuch* 17th SS Panzergrenadier Division, not paginated.

217. Emmerich, "The Battles of the 1. Army in France," 9. AAR, Third Army.

218. Ibid., 9–10.

219. Patton, 113.

220. Anlagen zum Kriegstagebuch, Oberkommando Heeresgruppe B, Ic, 1 July– 31 December 1944, T311, roll 1, frame 7000992ff., NARA.

221. Heeresgruppe B, Ia, Lagebeurteilungen, Wochenmeldungen, T311, roll 3, frame 7002265, NARA. Schramm, *Kriegstagebuch der OKW, Erster Halbband, Band 4*, 361.

222. *General der Artillerie* Walter Warlimont, "From Invasion to the Siegfried Line," ETHINT-1, July 1949, NARA.

223. Emmerich, "The Battles of the 1. Army in France," 5–6. AAR, Third Army.

224. Emmerich, "The Battles of the 1. Army in France," 11, 25.

225. Ibid., 12.

226. Hugh M. Cole, *The Lorraine Campaign: United States Army in World War II, The European Theater of Operations* (Washington, DC: Historical Division, Department of the Army, 1950), 16. (Hereafter Cole, *The Lorraine Campaign*.)

227. AAR, Third Army. Emmerich, "The Battles of the 1. Army in France," 12.

228. Emmerich, "The Battles of the 1. Army in France," 10–11.

229. Cole, *The Lorraine Campaign*, 22.

230. Heeresgruppe B, Ia, Führerbefehle, T311, roll 3, frame 7002335, NARA.

231. Bennett, 137–139.

232. Allen, 104–105.

233. Emmerich, "The Battles of the 1. Army in France," 12–13.

234. Heeresgruppe B, Ia, Lagebeurteilungen, Wochenmeldungen, T311, roll 3, frame 7002268, NARA.

235. Jodl, "U.S. Operations," 4.

236. Heeresgruppe B, Ia, Führerbefehle, T311, roll 3, frame 7002336ff., NARA.

237. Jodl, "Ardennes Offensive," 24.

238. Cole, *The Lorraine Campaign*, 216. Rickard, 94. Farago, 640–641. Koch, 79. Don M. Fox, *Patton's Vanguard: The United States Army Fourth Armored Division* (Jefferson, NC: McFarland & Company, Kindle edition, 2003), locations 1698–1704, 2042–2049. (Hereafter Fox.) *Generalmajor* Friedrich von Mellenthin, "Comments on Patton and the U.S. Third Army (September 1944)," ETHINT-65, 16 May 1946, NARA, 1.

239. Emmerich, "The Battles of the 1. Army in France," 13.

240. Ibid., 14–15. *Oberst* Willy Mantey, "First Army (Sep–Dec 1944)." MS # B-214, not dated, NARA, 6. (Hereafter Mantey.) AAR, Combat Command A, 7th Armored Division. Schramm, *Kriegstagebuch der OKW, Erster Halbband, Band 4*, 363.

241. Emmerich, "The Battles of the 1. Army in France," 19.

242. Schramm, *Kriegstagebuch der OKW, Erster Halbband, Band 4*, 366.

243. John Nelson Rickard, *Patton at Bay: The Lorraine Campaign, 1944* (Washington, DC: Brassey's, 2004), 52–54. (Hereafter Rickard.)

244. First United States Army, Report of Operations, 1 August 1944–22 February 1945, p. 45–46, 62–63. Rickard, 54. Christopher Gabel, *The Lorraine Campaign: An Overview, September–December 1944* (Fort Leavenworth, KS: Combat Studies Institute, 1985), 5. (Hereafter Gabel.)

245. Hold, Part I, 21.

246. Cole, *The Lorraine Campaign*, 47. *Kriegstagebuch* 17th SS Panzergrenadier Division, not paginated.

247. Blumenson, *Patton Papers: 1940*, 539.

248. Schramm, *Kriegstagebuch der OKW, Erster Halbband, Band 4*, 365.

249. "Feindlage Westen," 3 September 1944, Oberkommando des Heeres, Heeresnachtrichtenwesen, T-78, roll 453, frame 6429321ff., NARA. "Hörnlein, Walter," Lexikon der Wehrmacht, http://www.lexikon-der-wehrmacht.de/Personenregister/H/HoernleinW.htm, as of June 2009. Mantey, 4. Mühlen, 2–3. *Generalmajor* Karl Britzelmayr. "Einsatz der 19. V.G.D., 15.9.44–17.4.45.," MS # B-527, 3 April 1951, NARA, 3–4. (Hereafter Britzelmayr.)

250. "Lüttwitz, Heinrich Freiherr von," Lexikon der Wehrmacht, http://www.lexikon-der-wehrmacht.de/Personenregister/L/LuttwitzHFv.htm, as of June 2009.

251. *Oberst* Kurt von Einem, "Report of the engagements of XIII SS Corps in Lorraine During the Period from 1st September to 15th November 1944," MS # B-412, 29 October 1946, NARA, 1. (Hereafter Einem, "Engagements of XIII SS Corps.")

252. Emmerich, "The Battles of the 1. Army in France," 19–20. *Oberst* Kurt von Einem, "Bericht Über die Kämpfe des XIII. SS-A. K. in Lothringen in der Zeit vom 8. Nov. 44 bis 12. Jan. 45," MS # B-780, 30 August 1951, NARA, 2. (Hereafter Einem, "XIII. SS-A. K. in Lothringen.")

253. Allen, 108.

254. Holt, 629.

255. Heeresgruppe B, Ia, Führerbefehle, T311, roll 3, frame 7002339ff., NARA.

256. "Feindlage Westen," 4 September 1944, Oberkommando des Heeres, Heeresnachtrichtenwesen, T-78, roll 453, frame 6429316ff., NARA.

257. Heeresgruppe B, Ia, Lagebeurteilungen, Wochenmeldungen, T311, roll 3, frame 7002270, NARA.

Chapter 11: Lorraine: Patton Faces Germany's Best

1. Rickard, 55. AAR, Third Army.

2. Gabel, 7.

3. First United States Army, Report of Operations, 1 August 1944–22 February 1945, 51.

4. Manstein, 23.

5. Jodl, "Ardennes Offensive," 12–13.

6. Kesselring, "Commander in Chief West," 150, 208.

7. Rundstedt.

8. Rickard, 59. AAR, Third Army.

9. AAR, Third Army.

10. "Feindlage Westen," 6 September 1944, Oberkommando des Heeres, Heeresnachtrichtenwesen, T-78, roll 453, frame 6429292ff., NARA.

11. Rickard, 78, 89. 80th Infantry Division, Combat Interviews, NARA.

12. Blumenson, *Patton Papers: 1940*, 538.

13. Rickard, 83.

14. First Army, Order No. 11, 5 September 1944, reproduced in *Kriegstagebuch* 17th SS Panzergrenadier Division, not paginated.

15. Emmerich, "The Battles of the 1. Army in France," 20.

16. Axis Biographical Research, http://www.geocities.com/%7Eorion47/, as of March 2009.

17. Heeresgruppe B, Ia, Lagebeurteilungen, Wochenmeldungen, T311, roll 3, frame 7002272, NARA.

18. Jodl, "Die Operationen nach dem Durchbruch von Avranches," 5.

19. Farago, 579.

20. Liddell Hart, *The German Generals Talk*, ix.

21. Peter Lieb, *Konventioneller Krieg oder NS-Weltanschauungskrieg?* (Munich: Oldenbourg Wissenschaftsverlag, 2007), 82–96.

22. Manstein, 511.

23. Rickard, 80–81, 89. Einem, "Engagements of XIII SS Corps," 4–5.

24. Hermann Priess, SS personnel files, RG 242, A3343 Series SSO, 393A, frame 1023ff., NARA. Gordon Williamson and Ramiro Bujeiro, *Knight's Cross Oak-Leaves Recipients 1941–45* (Botley, UK: Osprey Publishing, 2005), 30–31. "Priess, Hermann," Lexikon der Wehrmacht, http://www.lexikon-der-wehrmacht.de/Personenregister/P/PriessH.htm, as of June 2009. "SS-Gruppenführer und Generalleutnant der Waffen SS Max Simon," Island Farm Prisoner of War Camp: 198/Special Camp XI, Bridgend, South Wales, http://www.islandfarm.fsnet.co.uk/, as of June 2009.

25. Rickard, 80–81. 5th Infantry Division, Combat Interviews, NARA. AAR, 17th Panzergrenadier Division, reproduced in *Kriegstagebuch* 17th SS Panzergrenadier Division, not paginated. Clayton Donnell, *The German Fortress of Metz 1870–1944* (New York: Osprey Publishing, 2008), , 47. (Hereafter Donnell.)

26. Koch, 82.

27. *Kriegstagebuch* 17th SS Panzergrenadier Division, not paginated.

28. Aaron C. Elson, *Tanks for the Memories: An Oral History of the 712th Tank Battalion from World War II* (Hackensack, N.J.: Chi Chi Press, 1994), 74–81; AAR, September

1944, 712th Tank Battalion. "The Battle of the CPs," Combat Interviews, 90th Infantry Division, NARA. "Interview of the Assembled Members of the 712th Tank Battalion (1st Platoon Co C) at the Battalion CP (U619802) Concerning the Enemy Attack on the 90th Infantry Division CP the Morning of 8 September," Combat Interviews, 90th Infantry Division, NARA.

29. Schramm, *Kriegstagebuch der OKW, Erster Halbband, Band 4*, 367.

30. First Army, Order No. 14, 10 September 1944, reproduced in *Kriegstagebuch* 17th SS Panzergrenadier Division, not paginated.

31. XL Panzer Corps, Anlagen zum Kriegstagebuch Nr. 7 der Führungs-abt. Ia, T314, roll 974, frame 000002ff., NARA. XL Panzer Corps, Kriegstagebuch Nr. 8 der Führungs-abt. Ia, 23.7–27.11.1944, T314, roll 974, frame 000672ff., NARA. Manteuffel memoirs, 112ff.

32. XL Panzer Corps, Kriegstagebuch Nr. 7 der Führungs-abt. Ia, 21.7–22.7.1944, T314, roll 973, frame 000521ff., NARA.

33. "Akten über von Knobelsdorff, Otto Heinrich Ernst," German Army officers 201 files, 1900–1945, A3356, box 419, NARA.

34. *General der Panzertruppe* Otto von Knobelsdorff, "Estimate of Situation When I Took Over the Armee on the 10-9-44," MS # B-222, not dated, NARA, 1–3. (Hereafter Knobelsdorff, "Estimate of Situation.") *Generalmajor* Friedrich von Mellenthin and others, "Army Group G in the period of September to the beginning of December 1944," MS # A-999, 11 July 1950, NARA, 2. (Hereafter Mellenthin and others.)

35. Einem, "Engagements of XIII SS Corps," 6.

36. *Oberst i. G.* Albert Emmerich, "The Fighting of the 1. Army in Lorraine and Northern Alsace, Part I," MS # B-363, 13 January 1947, NARA, 1. (Hereafter Emmerich, "The Fighting of the 1. Army.") Mellenthin and others, 5.

37. Mantey, 1–3, 8, 22–23. Mellenthin and others, 5. Einem, "Engagements of XIII SS Corps, 1." Donnell, 6, 45.

38. Knobelsdorff, "Estimate of Situation," 12–15. Cole, *The Lorraine Campaign*, 45.

39. Feindlagen West, files of Fremde Heere West, T78, roll 540, frames 001055ff., NARA. Obkdo. Arneegruppe G, Kriegstagebuch Nr. 2 (Führungsabteilung), 1.7–30.9.1944, T311, roll 140, frame 7185294ff., NARA.

40. Mellenthin, 382.

41. *Generaloberst* Johannes Blaskowitz, "An Interview with *Genobst* Johannes Blaskowitz: The Defense of Mctz," ETHINT-32, 20 July 1945, NARA, 1. (Hereafter Blaskowitz.)

42. Mellenthin, 382.

43. Oberkommando der Heeresgruppe G: Anlagen zum Kriegstagebuch Nr. 2 (Führungsabteilung) 1.9–30.9.1944.

44. Jeffrey J. Clarke and Robert Ross Smith. *Riviera to the Rhine: United States Army in World War II, The European Theater of Operations* (Washington, DC: Office of the Chief of Military History, Department of the Army, 1993), 183–184. (Hereafter Clarke and Smith.) Obkdo. Arneegruppe G, Kriegstagebuch Nr. 2 (Führungsabteilung), 1.7–30.9.1944, T311, roll 140, frame 7185271ff., NARA.

45. Blaskowitz, "Fighting By Armeegruppe 'G' in Southern France until the middle of September 1944," 23ff.

46. Obkdo. Arneegruppe G, Kriegstagebuch Nr. 2 (Führungsabteilung), 1.7–30.9.1944, T311, roll 140, frame 7185271ff., NARA.

47. Ibid., frame 7185288ff.

48. Ibid., frame 7185297ff. Knobelsdorff, "Estimate of Situation," 10. Mühlen, 4. Emmerich, "The Battles of the 1. Army in France," 24. Mantey, 5, 12.

49. Tagebuch, *Generaloberst* Jodl, "9. Abends," T-77, roll 1430, frame 893ff.

50. Obkdo. Arneegruppe G, Kriegstagebuch Nr. 2 (Führungsabteilung), 1.7–30.9.1944, T311, roll 140, frame 7185294ff., NARA.

51. *Major* Kurt Hold, "Organization and Composition of the First Army During the Period of 11 Aug 44 until 14 Feb 45 (Part II: from 15 Sep 44 until 14 Feb 45," MS # B-821, not dated, NARA, 8–9. (Hereafter Hold, Part II.) Einem, "Engagements of XIII SS Corps," 6–7.

52. Knobelsdorff, "Estimate of Situation," 14–15.

53. Mantey, 2.

54. Rickard, 86–89.

55. *General der Panzertruppe* Hasso-Eccard von Manteuffel, "The Commitment of the Fifth Panzer Army West of the Vosges within the Framework of Army Group 'G,' from About 15 September to 15 October 1944," MS # B-757, 15 November 1947, NARA, 1. (Hereafter Manteuffel.)

56. Luck, 211–212. Manteuffel, 1–6. Manteuffel memoirs, 126–135. XL Panzer Corps, Anlagen zum Kriegstagebuch Nr. 7 der Führungs-abt. Ia, T314, roll 974, frame 000002ff., NARA. XL Panzer Corps, Kriegstagebuch Nr. 8 der Führungs-abt. Ia, 23.7–27.11.1944, T314, roll 974, frame 000672ff., NARA.

57. "Personalakten für Krüger, Walter," German Army officers 201 files, 1900–1945, A3356, box 455, NARA.

58. Cole, *The Lorraine Campaign*, 142ff. 5th Infantry Division, Combat Interviews, NARA.

59. Emmerich, "The Battles of the 1. Army in France," 24. Rickard, 90.

60. Cole, *The Lorraine Campaign*, 74.

61. *Oberst* Wolf von Kahlden, "Einsatz des Panzer-A.O.K. 5 Westlich der Vogesen in der Zeit von 15.9. bis 15.10.44." MS # B-472, 20 March 1947. NARA, 17–18. (Hereafter Kahlden.) Manteuffel, 11. Einem, "Engagements of XIII SS Corps," 7–8. Cole, *The Lorraine Campaign*, 77–81, 86–87. 80th Infantry Division, Combat Interviews, NARA.

62. Kahlden, 17–18. Manteuffel, 11. Einem, "Engagements of XIII SS Corps," 7–8. Cole, *The Lorraine Campaign*, 86–87.

63. Gyldenfeldt, 9. Emmerich, "The Fighting of the 1. Army," 1–2, 24. Mantey, 13. Manteuffel, 11ff. Manteuffel memoirs, 130–140. *Generalleutnant* Edgar Feuchtinger, "21st Panzer Division in Combat Against American Troops in France and Germany," MS # A-871, 17 December 1949, NARA, 11. (Hereafter Feuchtinger.) *Generalleutnant* Ernst Häckel, "Der Feldzug im Rheinland 15.9.-Anf. Dez. 44," MS # B-452, not dated, NARA, 3.

64. Gyldenfeldt, 3–4.

65. Rickard, 104–107.

66. Obkdo. Arneegruppe G, Kriegstagebuch Nr. 2 (Führungsabteilung), 1.7–30.9.1944, T311, roll 140, frame 7185314ff., NARA. Schramm, *Kriegstagebuch der OKW, Erster Halbband, Band 4*, 372.

67. Obkdo. Arneegruppe G, Kriegstagebuch Nr. 2 (Führungsabteilung), 1.7–30.9.1944, T311, roll 140, frame 7185324ff., NARA.

68. Ibid., frames 7185315ff., 7185335. Knobelsdorff, "Estimate of Situation," 14. Emmerich, "The Fighting of the 1. Army," 2–3. Britzelmayr, 5. Jodl, "U.S. Operations," 3.

69. "Amendment No. 2 to Operational Directive, 5 September 1944," reproduced in AAR, Third Army.

70. Mellenthin, 375.

71. Patton, 127.

72. Heeresgruppe B, Ia, Führerbefehle, T311, roll 3, frame 7002349, NARA.

73. Schramm, *Kriegstagebuch der OKW, Erster Halbband, Band 4*, 393–394.

74. Obkdo. Arneegruppe G, Kriegstagebuch Nr. 2 (Führungsabteilung), 1.7–30.9.1944, T311, roll 140, frame 7185328ff., NARA.

75. Ibid., frame 7185333ff.

76. Manteuffel, 16.

77. Emmerich, "The Fighting of the 1. Army," 4. Mantey, 4, 13ff.

78. Cole, *The Lorraine Campaign*, 221.

79. History, 603rd Tank Destroyer Battalion.

80. Feuchtinger, 14.

81. Obkdo. Arneegruppe G, Kriegstagebuch Nr. 2 (Führungsabteilung), 1.7–30.9.1944, T311, roll 140, frame 7185329, NARA.

82. Richard R. Buchanan, Richard D. Wissolik, David Wilmes, Gary E. J. Smith, et al, eds., *Men of the 704th: A Pictorial and Spoken History of the 704th Tank Destroyer Battalion in World War II* (Latrobe, PA: Saint Vincent College Center for Northern Appalachian Studies, 1998), 46. Richard D. Wissolik and Gary E. J. Smith, eds., *Reluctant Valor, The Oral History of Captain Thomas J. Evans* (Latrobe, PA: Saint Vincent College Center for Northern Appalachian Studies, 1995), 83. AAR, CCA, 4th Armored Division. 4th Armored Division, "The Tank Battle 19–22 September as related by Lt. Col. Hal Pattison," Combat Interviews, NARA.

83. Patton, 129.

84. Obkdo. Arneegruppe G, Kriegstagebuch Nr. 2 (Führungsabteilung), 1.7–30.9.1944, T311, roll 140, frame 7185340ff., NARA. Feuchtinger, 15.

85. AAR, CCA, 4th Armored Division.

86. Obkdo. Arneegruppe G, Kriegstagebuch Nr. 2 (Führungsabteilung), 1.7–30.9.1944, T311, roll 140, frame 7185340ff., NARA.

87. Mellenthin and others, 12.

88. Obkdo. Arneegruppe G, Kriegstagebuch Nr. 2 (Führungsabteilung), 1.7–30.9.1944, T311, roll 140, frame 7185343, NARA. Raus, 262–268.

89. Patton, 130.

90. Mellenthin, 373.

91. "Conversation with General Hermann Balck, 13 April 1979," 2–14. "Conversation with General Hermann Balck, 12 January 1979," 2–3. Balck, 399ff.

92. Guderian, 296, 301.

93. "Generals Balck and von Mellenthin on Tactics," 9.

94. Mellenthin, 304, 373.

95. "Conversation with General Hermann Balck, 13 April 1979," 30–31, 41–42.

96. Ibid., 42.

97. Ibid., 42. Mellenthin, 26–27.

98. Balck, 560.

99. "Conversation with General Hermann Balck, 13 April 1979," 34.

100. Obkdo. Arneegruppe G, Kriegstagebuch Nr. 2 (Führungsabteilung), 1.7–30.9.1944, T311, roll 140, frame 7185348ff., NARA.

101. Balck, 572.

102. Obkdo. Arneegruppe G, Kriegstagebuch Nr. 2 (Führungsabteilung), 1.7–30.9.1944, T311, roll 140, frame 7185348ff., NARA. XL Panzer Corps, Anlagen zum Kriegstagebuch Nr. 7 der Führungs-abt. Ia, T314, roll 974, frame 000002ff., NARA. Einem, "Engagements of XIII SS Corps," 9. Mühlen, 5. Britzelmayr, 7.

103. Blumenson, *Patton Papers: 1940*, 552.

104. Schramm, *Kriegstagebuch der OKW, Erster Halbband, Band 4*, 394–395.

105. Ibid., 431.

106. Obkdo. Arneegruppe G, Kriegstagebuch Nr. 2 (Führungsabteilung), 1.7–30.9.1944, T311, roll 140, frame 7185352ff., NARA.

107. AAR, CCA, 4th Armored Division.

108. Mellenthin, 379–380.

109. Patton, 130.

110. Schramm, *Kriegstagebuch der OKW, Erster Halbband, Band 4*, 396.

111. Mellenthin and others, 13. Obkdo. Arneegruppe G, Kriegstagebuch Nr. 2 (Führungsabteilung), 1.7–30.9.1944, T311, roll 140, frame 7185357ff., NARA.

112. Obkdo. Arneegruppe G, Kriegstagebuch Nr. 2 (Führungsabteilung), 1.7–30.9.1944, T311, roll 140, frame 7185359ff., NARA.

113. Kahlden, 28–29. *Generalleutnant* Wend von Wietersheim, "Rhineland, Part I: The Employment of the 11th Panzer Division in Lorraine," MS # C-090, 13 February 1951, NARA, 2. (Hereafter Wietersheim, Part I.) A. Harding Ganz, "The 11th Panzers in the Defense, 1944," *Armor*, March–April 1994, 31. (Hereafter Ganz.)

114. Mellenthin and others, 13–14. Mellenthin, 380–381. Kahlden, 32. Wietersheim, Part I, 16. Ganz, 33. Einem, "Engagements of XIII SS Corps," 9. Schramm, *Kriegstagebuch der OKW, Erster Halbband, Band 4*, 397.

115. Emmerich, "The Fighting of the 1. Army," 5–7. Mellenthin and others, 13. Einem, "Engagements of XIII SS Corps," 10.

116. Mantey, 14.

117. Manteuffel, 33.

118. Guderian, 299.

119. Obkdo. Arneegruppe G, Kriegstagebuch Nr. 2 (Führungsabteilung), 1.7–30.9.1944, T311, roll 140, frame 7185369ff., NARA.

120. Emmerich, "The Fighting of the 1. Army," 5.

121. Ibid., 5–6.

122. Mellenthin, 382.

123. "Letter of Instructions No. 4," 25 September 1944, reproduced in AAR, Third Army.

124. Schramm, *Kriegstagebuch der OKW, Erster Halbband, Band 4*, 396–397.

125. Sixth Army Group history.

126. Rickard, 54–55.

127. "Defense of the West Wall," interview with *Major* Herbert Büchs, aide to *Generaloberst* Alfred Jodl, ETHINT-37, 28 September 1945, NARA. *Major* Percy Ernst Schramm, "OKW War Diary (1 Apr–18 Dec 1944)," MS # B-034, not dated, NARA, 189. (Hereafter Shramm, "OKW War Diary [1 Apr–18 Dec 1944].")

128. First United States Army, Report of Operations, 1 August 1944–22 February 1945, 57.

129. Schramm, "OKW War Diary (1 Apr–18 Dec 1944)," 192–193.

130. Charles B. MacDonald, *The Battle of the Bulge* (London: Guild Publishing, 1984), 62. (Hereafter MacDonald, *The Battle of the Bulge*.)

131. First United States Army, Report of Operations, 1 August 1944–22 February 1945, 55.

132. Schramm, *Kriegstagebuch der OKW, Erster Halbband, Band 4*, 434.

133. Mellenthin, 14, and others. Obkdo. Heeresgruppe G, Anlagen (Chefsachen) zum Kriegstagebuch Nr. 3 der Führungsabteilung, 1.10–31.12.1944, T311, roll 142, frame 7187976, NARA.

134. Rickard, 136.

135. Knobelsdorff, "Estimate of Situation," 7.

136. Obkdo. Arneegruppe G, Kriegstagebuch Nr. 2 (Führungsabteilung), 1.7–30.9.1944, T311, roll 140, frame 7185327, NARA.

137. Donnell, 48.

138. Emmerich, "The Battles of the 1. Army in France," 19. Einem, "Engagements of XIII SS Corps," 11.

139. Emmerich, "The Battles of the 1. Army in France," 23. Mantey, 4–5. Knobelsdorff, "Estimate of Situation," 9. *Generalleutnant* Heinrich Kittel, "An Interview with Genlt Heinrich Kittel: Defense of Metz," ETHINT-77, 10 January 1946, NARA, 1.

140. Rickard, 136.

141. Cole, *The Lorraine Campaign*, 264–265.

142. Ibid., 266.

143. *Armored Special Equipment*, the General Board, United States Forces, European Theater, 14 May 1945, 10.

144. Cole, *The Lorraine Campaign*, 275. Patton, 141. Emmerich, "The Fighting of the 1. Army," 17.

145. Charles B. MacDonald, *The Battle of the Bulge* (London: Guild Publishing, 1984), 21ff.

146. Balck, 557–560. Mellenthin, 372, 406.

147. Mellenthin and others, 16–17. Hold, Part II, 5. Knobelsdorff, "Estimate of Situation," 12.

148. "Conversation with General Hermann Balck, 13 April 1979," 28. Mellenthin and others, 30.

149. Heeresgruppe B, Ia, Führerbefehle, T311, roll 3, frame 7002351ff., NARA.

150. Emmerich, "The Fighting of the 1. Army," 9, 12.

151. Hold, Part II, 9.

152. Mellenthin and others, i.

153. Obkdo. Arneegruppe G, Kriegstagebuch Nr. 2 (Führungsabteilung), 1.7–30.9.1944, T311, roll 140, frame 7185375, NARA.

154. Balck, 560–565. Mellenthin, 21, 221–222.

155. Obkdo. Heeresgruppe G, Kriegstagebuch der Führungsabteilung Nr. 3a, 1.10–30.11.1944, T311, roll 142, frame 7188093ff., NARA. Obkdo. Heeresgruppe G, Anlagen (Chefsachen) zum Kriegstagebuch Nr. 3 der Führungsabteilung, 1.10–31.12.1944, T311, roll 142, frame 7187977, NARA.

156. Balck, 560. Obkdo. Heeresgruppe G, Kriegstagebuch der Führungsabteilung Nr. 3a, 1.10–30.11.1944, T311, roll 142, frame 7188114ff., NARA.

157. Obkdo. Heeresgruppe G, Kriegstagebuch der Führungsabteilung Nr. 3a, 1.10–30.11.1944, T311, roll 142, frame 7188114ff., NARA.

158. Mantey, 16.

159. Mellenthin, 384.

160. Mellenthin and others, 17–22. Obkdo. Heeresgruppe G, Kriegstagebuch der Führungsabteilung Nr. 3a, 1.10–30.11.1944, T311, roll 142, frame 7188086ff., NARA.

161. "Conversation with General Hermann Balck, 12 January 1979," 16–17.

162. Balck, 567.

163. Mellenthin and others, 15.

164. Emmerich, "The Fighting of the 1. Army," 8.

165. Obkdo. Heeresgruppe G, Kriegstagebuch der Führungsabteilung Nr. 3a, 1.10–30.11.1944, T311, roll 142, frame 7188076ff., NARA.

166. Obkdo. Heeresgruppe G, Anlagen (Chefsachen) zum Kriegstagebuch Nr. 3 der Führungsabteilung, 1.10–31.12.1944, T311, roll 142, frame 7187979, NARA.

167. "Conversation with General Hermann Balck, 13 April 1979," 24.

168. Balck, 567–568.

169. Obkdo. Heeresgruppe G, Anlagen (Chefsachen) zum Kriegstagebuch Nr. 3 der Führungsabteilung, 1.10–31.12.1944, T311, roll 142, frame 71888157ff., NARA. Mellenthin, 386–387. *Oberstleutnant i. G.* Karl Redmer, "Kaempfe der 416. I. D. Zwischen Mosel und Saar vom 5.10.44–17.2.45," MS # B-573, 31 May 1947, NARA, 4–5. (Hereafter Redmer.) "Pflieger, Kurt," Lexikon der Wehrmacht, http://www.lexikon-der-wehrmacht.de/Personenregister/P/PfliegerKurt.htm, as of November 2009.

170. Raus, 275–277.

171. Mellenthin, 386–387. Einem, "Engagements of XIII SS Corps," 11–12. Obkdo. Heeresgruppe G, Anlagen (Chefsachen) zum Kriegstagebuch Nr. 3 der Führungsabteilung, 1.10–31.12.1944, T311, roll 142, frame 71888160ff., NARA.

172. Obkdo. Heeresgruppe G, Anlagen (Chefsachen) zum Kriegstagebuch Nr. 3 der Führungsabteilung, 1.10–31.12.1944, situation map for 5 November 1944, T311, roll 142, frame 71888196, NARA.

173. "Personalakten für Hörnlein, Walter," German Army officers 201 files, 1900–1945, A3356, box 344, NARA.

174. Emmerich, "The Fighting of the 1. Army," 13–16. Mantey, 17ff. Mellenthin and others, 17. Obkdo. Heeresgruppe G, Kriegstagebuch der Führungsabteilung Nr. 3a, 1.10–30.11.1944, T311, roll 142, frame 7188087ff., NARA.

175. Mellenthin and others, 19–20, 27–28. Obkdo. Heeresgruppe G, Kriegstagebuch der Führungsabteilung Nr. 3a, 1.10–30.11.1944, T311, roll 142, frame 7188150, 7188201ff., NARA. "Freiherr von und zu Gilsa, Werner-Albrecht," Lexikon der Wehrmacht, http://www.lexikon-der-wehrmacht.de/Personenregister/G/GilsaWAFv.htm, as of July 1943.

176. Mellenthin and others, 28, 37. Obkdo. Heeresgruppe G, Kriegstagebuch der Führungsabteilung Nr. 3a, 1.10–30.11.1944, T311, roll 142, frame 71888171, NARA.

177. Balck, 571–575. Obkdo. Heeresgruppe G, Kriegstagebuch der Führungsabteilung Nr. 3a, 1.10–30.11.1944, T311, roll 142, frame 71888157ff., NARA.

178. Obkdo. Heeresgruppe G, Kriegstagebuch der Führungsabteilung Nr. 3a, 1.10–30.11.1944, T311, roll 142, frame frame 71888183ff., NARA.

179. "Outline Plan for the Resumption of the Offensive," 18 October 1944, reproduced in AAR, Third Army.

180. "Operational Directive," 3 November 1944, reproduced in AAR, Third Army.

181. Obkdo. Heeresgruppe G, Anlagen (Chefsachen) zum Kriegstagebuch Nr. 3 der Führungsabteilung, 1.10–31.12.1944, T311, roll 142, frame 7187982ff., NARA. Schramm, Kriegstagebuch der OKW, Erster Halbband, Band 4, 389, 403. General der Infanterie Kurt von Tippelskirch, "Die Kaempfe der 1. Armee in Lothringen vom 1. bis 12.11.1944," MS # B-491-492, 1 March 1947, NARA, vol. 1, 2. (Hereafter Tippelskirch.) Generalleutnant Wend von Wietersheim, "Rhineland, Part II," MS # B-416, 1 October 1946, NARA, 1. (Hereafter Wietersheim, "Rhineland, Part II.") Ganz, 34. "General der Infanterie Kurt Oskar Heinrich Ludwig Wilhelm von Tippelskirch," Axis Biographical Research, http://www.geocities.com/%7Eorion47/, as of June 2009.

182. Obkdo. Heeresgruppe G, Kriegstagebuch der Führungsabteilung Nr. 3a, 1.10–30.11.1944, T311, roll 142, frame 7188151, NARA.

183. Mellenthin and others, 33–36. "Generals Balck and von Mellenthin on Tactics," 45–46. Einem, "XIII. SS-A. K. in Lothringen," 5. Obkdo. Heeresgruppe G, Anlagen (Chefsachen) zum Kriegstagebuch Nr. 3 der Führungsabteilung, 1.10–31.12.1944, T311, roll 142, frame 7187984ff., NARA.

184. Cole, The Lorraine Campaign, 306, citing OKH numbers.

185. AAR, Third Army.

186. Tippelskirch, vol. 1, 3–4. Mellenthin, 387. Rickard, 171.

187. Mellenthin and others, 40–41. Patton, 158.

188. "Personalakten für v. Tippelskirch, Kurt," German Army officers 201 files, 1900–1945, A3356, box 852, NARA. "Von Tippelskirch, Kurt Oskar Heinrich Ludwig Wilhelm," Lexikon der Wehrmacht, http://www.lexikon-der-wehrmacht.de/Personenregister/T/TippelskirchKv.htm, as of December 2009.

189. Schramm, Kriegstagebuch der OKW, Erster Halbband, Band 4, 425. Emmerich, "The Battle of the 1. Army in Lothringen and Northern Elsass, from 15 Sep. 1944 to 15 Feb. 1945, Part II," 7. Wietersheim, "Rhineland, Part II," 5ff. Tippelskirch, vol. 2, 2ff. Einem, "Engagements of XIII SS Corps," 12–14. Mühlen, 7. Feuchtinger, 28. Obkdo. Heeresgruppe G, Kriegstagebuch der Führungsabteilung Nr. 3a, 1.10–30.11.1944, T311, roll 142, frame 71888201ff., NARA. Obkdo. Heeresgruppe G, Anlagen (Chefsachen) zum Kriegstagebuch Nr. 3 der Führungsabteilung, 1.10–31.12.1944, T311, roll 142, frame 7187989, NARA. Mellenthin, 390. Ganz, 34. Kriegstagebuch 17th SS Panzergrenadier Division, not paginated. AAR, 4th Armored Division, Combat Command B. Rickard, 177ff. Blumenson, Patton Papers: 1940, 571ff. Patton, 159.

190. Tippelskirch, vol. 1, 6–7.

191. Mellenthin and others, 44. Donnell, 53.

192. Tippelskirch, vol. 2, 6. Redmer, 19.

193. Obkdo. Heeresgruppe G, Kriegstagebuch der Führungsabteilung Nr. 3a, 1.10–30.11.1944, T311, roll 142, frame 7188215ff., NARA.

194. Obkdo. Heeresgruppe G, Anlagen (Chefsachen) zum Kriegstagebuch Nr. 3 der Führungsabteilung, 1.10–31.12.1944, T311, roll 142, frame 7187992ff., NARA. Obkdo. Heeresgruppe G, Kriegstagebuch der Führungsabteilung Nr. 3a, 1.10–30.11.1944, T311, roll 142, frame 7188216, NARA. Rickard, 179–180.

195. Redmer, 19–20.

196. Schramm, *Kriegstagebuch der OKW, Erster Halbband, Band 4*, 439.

197. Obkdo. Heeresgruppe G, Anlagen (Chefsachen) zum Kriegstagebuch Nr. 3 der Führungsabteilung, 1.10–31.12.1944, T311, roll 142, frame 7187992ff., NARA. Obkdo. Heeresgruppe G, Kriegstagebuch der Führungsabteilung Nr. 3a, 1.10–30.11.1944, T311, roll 142, frame 7188216, NARA. Mellenthin, 390. Wietersheim, "Rhineland, Part II," 6ff. Ganz, 35. 6th Armored Division, Combat Interviews, NARA. AAR, 4th Armored Division, Combat Command A. AAR, 4th Armored Division, Combat Command B. AAR, 6th Armored Division. Albin F. Iryzk, *He Rode Up Front for Patton* (Raleigh, NC: Pentland Press, 1996), 174. (Hereafter Iryzk.) Fox, location 2885–2976.

198. Balck, 575.

199. Emmerich, "The Battle of the 1. Army in Lothringen and Northern Elsass, from 15 Sep. 1944 to 15 Feb. 1945, Part II," 4.

200. Obkdo. Heeresgruppe G, Anlagen (Chefsachen) zum Kriegstagebuch Nr. 3 der Führungsabteilung, 1.10–31.12.1944, T311, roll 142, frame 7187995, NARA.

201. AAR, 4th Armored Division, Combat Command A. AAR, 4th Armored Division, Combat Command B.

202. Iryzk, 176.

203. AAR, 6th Armored Division.

204. Feuchtinger, 30.

205. "Personalakten für Feuchtinger, Edgar," German Army officers 201 files, 1900–1945, A3356, box 434, NARA. "Feuchtinger, Edgar," Lexikon der Wehrmacht, http://www.lexikon-der-wehrmacht.de/Personenregister/F/FeuchtingerEdgar.htm, as of December 2009. Luck, 167.

206. Emmerich, "The Battle of the 1. Army in Lothringen and Northern Elsass, from 15 Sep. 1944 to 15 Feb. 1945, Part II," 8.

207. Sixth Army Group history. Clarke and Smith, 368ff. Mellenthin and others, 60–61.

208. Mellenthin and others, 63, 72–73. Obkdo. Heeresgruppe G: "Anlagen (Chefsachen) zum Kriegstagebuch Nr. 3 der Führungsabteilung v. 1.10–31.12.44, T311, roll 142, frame 7187995, NARA. Patton, 155.

209. Einem, "Engagements of XIII SS Corps," 14–15.

210. Fox, locations 3106–3181.

211. Obkdo. Heeresgruppe G, Kriegstagebuch der Führungsabteilung Nr. 3a, 1.10–30.11.1944, T311, roll 142, frame 7188237ff., NARA. Schramm, *Kriegstagebuch der OKW, Erster Halbband, Band 4*, 443. Wietersheim, "Rhineland, Part II,"

7. Feuchtinger, 131. Einem, "Engagements of XIII SS Corps," 15–16. Einem, "XIII. SS-A. K. in Lothringen," 11. *Generalmajor* August Wellm, "Bericht über das Einsatz der 36. Volks-Grenadier-Division in Lothringen vom 12.XI.1944–27.XII.1944," MS # B-223, 15 November 1946, NARA, 8ff. (Hereafter Wellm.) 6th Armored Division, Combat Interviews, NARA. AAR, 6th Armored Division.

212. Emmerich, "The Battle of the 1. Army in Lothringen and Northern Elsass, from 15 Sep. 1944 to 15 Feb. 1945, Part II," 5.

213. Schramm, *Kriegstagebuch der OKW, Erster Halbband, Band 4*, 415.

214. Emmerich, "The Battle of the 1. Army in Lothringen and Northern Elsass, from 15 Sep. 1944 to 15 Feb. 1945, Part II," 8–9. Obkdo. Heeresgruppe G, Kriegstagebuch der Führungsabteilung Nr. 3a, 1.10–30.11.1944, T311, roll 142, frame 7188242ff., NARA. Schramm, *Kriegstagebuch der OKW, Erster Halbband, Band 4*, 416. AAR, 4th Armored Division, Combat Command B.

215. Mellenthin and others, 53–54. Obkdo. Heeresgruppe G, Kriegstagebuch der Führungsabteilung Nr. 3a, 1.10–30.11.1944, T311, roll 142, frame 7188259ff., NARA.

216. Obkdo. Heeresgruppe G, Kriegstagebuch der Führungsabteilung Nr. 3a, 1.10–30.11.1944, T311, roll 142, frame 7188250ff., NARA.

217. *General der Waffen SS* Hermann Priess, "The Commitment of I SS Panzer Corps during the Ardennes Offensive: December–January, 1944–1945," MS # A-877, March 1946, NARA, 6, 16. (Hereafter Priess.) *General der Waffen SS* Max Simon, "Report on the Rhineland and South Germany Campaigns," MS # C-023, March 1947, NARA, 4. (Hereafter Simon, "South Germany Campaigns.") Einem, "XIII. SS-A. K. in Lothringen," 11. Max Simon, SS personnel files, RG 242, A3343 Series SSO, 138B, frame 1054ff., NARA.

218. Simon, "XIII SS Corps," 1.

219. "SS-Gruppenführer und Generalleutnant der Waffen SS Max Simon," Island Farm Prisoner of War Camp: 198/Special Camp XI, Bridgend, South Wales, http://www.islandfarm.fsnet.co.uk/, as of June 2009.

220. Simon, "South Germany Campaigns," 8.

221. Simon, "XIII SS Corps," 2.

222. Simon, "South Germany Campaigns," 5–7.

223. Obkdo. Heeresgruppe G, Kriegstagebuch der Führungsabteilung Nr. 3a, 1.10–30.11.1944, T311, roll 142, frame 7188254ff., 7188263ff., NARA. Feuchtinger, 32.

224. Simon, "XIII SS Corps," 3–4.

225. Ibid., 4ff. Emmerich, "The Battle of the 1. Army in Lothringen and Northern Elsass, from 15 Sep. 1944 to 15 Feb. 1945, Part II," 5–6, 9. Mellenthin and others, ii, 71–72. Einem, "XIII. SS-A. K. in Lothringen," 2. Obkdo. Heeresgruppe G, Kriegstagebuch der Führungsabteilung Nr. 3a, 1.10–30.11.1944, T311, roll 142, frame 7188273ff., NARA. Obkdo. Arneegruppe G, Anlagen zum Kriegstagebuch Nr. 3a der Führungsabteilung, 16.11–30.11.1944, T311, roll 143, frame 7189319, NARA.

226. Patton, 166.

227. Emmerich, "The Battle of the 1. Army in Lothringen and Northern Elsass, from 15 Sep. 1944 to 15 Feb. 1945, Part II," 6.

228. Patton, 167–168.

229. Einem, "XIII. SS-A. K. in Lothringen," 13–14. Simon, "XIII SS Corps," 5. Simon, "South Germany Campaigns," 14. Feuchtinger, 32–33.

230. Mühlen, 8.

231. Army Group G situation maps.

232. *Generalmajor* Friedrich von Mellenthin, "Kaempfe in Lothringen und in den Vogesen im Herbst 44 Teil IV," MS # B-078, not dated, NARA, 13–14, 17. Emmerich, "The Battle of the 1. Army in Lothringen and Northern Elsass, from 15 Sep. 1944 to 15 Feb. 1945, Part II," 14–15. Feuchtinger, 33–35. Redmer, 21ff. Obkdo. Heeresgruppe G, Anlagen (Chefsachen) zum Kriegstagebuch Nr. 3 der Führungsabteilung, 1.10–31.12.1944, T311, roll 142, frame 7187999ff., NARA. Obkdo. Heeresgruppe G, Kriegstagebuch der Führungsabteilung Nr. 3a, 1.10–30.11.1944, T311, roll 142, frame 7188299ff., NARA. Cole, *The Lorraine Campaign*, 409.

233. Feuchtinger, 35. "Personalakten für Hörnlein, Walter," German Army officers 201 files, 1900–1945, A3356, box 344, NARA.

234. Emmerich, "The Battle of the 1. Army in Lothringen and Northern Elsass, from 15 Sep. 1944 to 15 Feb. 1945, Part II," 14–15. *General der Infanterie* Gustav Hoehne, "LXXXIX Corps (22 Nov 1944–13 Jan 1945)," MS # B-075-077, 9 May 1946, NARA, 2ff. Obkdo. Heeresgruppe G, Anlagen (Chefsachen) zum Kriegstagebuch Nr. 3 der Führungsabteilung, 1.10–31.12.1944, T311, roll 142, frame 7187999ff., NARA. Obkdo. Heeresgruppe G, Kriegstagebuch der Führungsabteilung Nr. 3a, 1.10–30.11.1944, T311, roll 142, frame 7188301ff., NARA. AAR, 6th Armored Division.

235. Helmut Ritgen, *West-Front 1944* (Stuttgart: Motorbuch Verlag, 2001), 194ff. J. Dugdale, *Panzer Divisions, Panzer Grenadier Divisions, Panzer Brigades of the Army and the Waffen SS in the West; Autumn 1944–February 1945, Ardennes and Northwind, Volume 1 [Part 4A]*, (Milton Keynes, England: The Military Press, 2002), 7. (Hereafter Dugdale.)

236. Army Group G situation maps.

237. Einem, "XIII. SS-A. K. in Lothringen," 15. Obkdo. Heeresgruppe G, Kriegstagebuch der Führungsabteilung Nr. 3a, 1.10–30.11.1944, T311, roll 142, frame 7188314ff., NARA.

238. Bennett, 174.

239. Obkdo. Heeresgruppe G, Anlagenmappe, Karten, zum Kriegstagebuch Nr. 3 der Führungsabteilung, 1.10–31.12.1944, T311, roll 142, frame 7187910, NARA.

240. Simon, "South Germany Campaigns," 16. Obkdo. Heeresgruppe G, Kriegstagebuch der Führungsabteilung Nr. 3a, 1.10–30.11.1944, T311, roll 142, frame 7188334ff., NARA.

241. Obkdo. Heeresgruppe G, Kriegstagebuch der Führungsabteilung Nr. 3a, 1.10–30.11.1944, T311, roll 142, frame 7188339ff., NARA. Feuchtinger, 36.

242. Emmerich, "The Battle of the 1. Army in Lothringen and Northern Elsass, from 15 Sep. 1944 to 15 Feb. 1945, Part II," 15. Feuchtinger, 36. Obkdo. Heeresgruppe G, Kriegstagebuch der Führungsabteilung Nr. 3a, 1.10–30.11.1944, T311, roll 142, frame 7188347ff., NARA.

243. Einem, "XIII. SS-A. K. in Lothringen," 16. Obkdo. Heeresgruppe G, Kriegstagebuch der Führungsabteilung Nr. 3a, 1.10–30.11.1944, T311, roll 142, frame 7188339ff., NARA.

244. Simon, "South Germany Campaigns," 18.

245. "Akten über von Knobelsdorff, Otto Heinrich Ernst," German Army officers 201 files, 1900–1945, A3356, box 419, NARA.

246. Emmerich, "The Battle of the 1. Army in Lothringen and Northern Elsass, from 15 Sep. 1944 to 15 Feb. 1945, Part II," 15. Einem, "XIII. SS-A. K. in Lothringen," 17ff. Feuchtinger, 39. Obkdo. Heeresgruppe G, Kriegstagebuch der Führungsabteilung Nr. 3b, 1.12–31.12.1944, T311, roll 143, frame 719655ff., NARA.

247. *Oberst i. G.* Ludwig *Graf* von Ingelheim, "Engagements Fought by LXXXII A.K. During the Period 2 Dec 1944 to 27 Mar 1945," MS # B-066, 30 May 1946, NARA, ii. (Hereafter Ingelheim.)

248. "Personalakten für Hahm, Walter," German Army officers 201 files, 1900-1945, A3356, box 263, NARA.

249. Obkdo. Heeresgruppe G, Kriegstagebuch der Führungsabteilung Nr. 3b, 1.12–31.12.1944, T311, roll 143, frame 719665ff., NARA.

250. Ibid., frame 719671ff. Ingelheim, 4–6.

251. Obkdo. Heeresgruppe G, Kriegstagebuch der Führungsabteilung Nr. 3b, 1.12–31.12.1944, T311, roll 143, frame 719678ff., NARA. Feuchtinger, 41–43. Ingelheim, 5.

252. Obkdo. Heeresgruppe G, Kriegstagebuch der Führungsabteilung Nr. 3b, 1.12–31.12.1944, T311, roll 143, frame 719681ff., NARA. OKH/GenStdH/Org.Abt. Nr. I/20981/44 g.Kdos v. 1.12.1944, Tagesstärken der Divisionen auf OKW-Kriegsschauplätzen Ende November 1944 cited in Hermann Jung, *Die Ardennen-Offensive 1944/45 – Ein Beispiel für die Kriegführung Hitlers* (Frankfurt: Musterschmidt Gottingen, 1971), 295–296. (Hereafter Jung.) Dugdale, 8.

253. "Operational Directive," 4 December 1944, reproduced in AAR, Third Army.

254. Blumenson, *Patton Papers: 1940,* 587.

255. Emmerich, "The Fighting of the 1. Army," 1. Obkdo. Heeresgruppe G, Kriegstagebuch der Führungsabteilung Nr. 3b, 1.12–31.12.1944, T311, roll 143, frame 719686ff., NARA. Simon, "South Germany Campaigns," 20.

256. *General der Infanterie* Günther Blumentritt, "Engagements of the LXXXVI A K on and west of the Lower Maas between the 3 and 20 Oct 44," MS # B-634, August 1947, NARA, 7.

257. "Personalakten für v. Obstfelder, Hans," German Army officers 201 files, 1900-1945, A3356, box 612, NARA.

258. Emmerich, "The Battle of the 1. Army in Lothringen and Northern Elsass, from 15 Sep. 1944 to 15 Feb. 1945, Part II," 23. Britzelmayr, 19–20.

259. Einem, "XIII. SS-A. K. in Lothringen," 18. Obkdo. Heeresgruppe G, Kriegstagebuch der Führungsabteilung Nr. 3b, 1.12–31.12.1944, T311, roll 143, frame 719708ff., NARA. Britzelmayr, 19–20.

260. 4th Armored Division, Combat Interviews, NARA. 6th Armored Division, Combat Interviews, NARA.

261. Ingelheim, 6–7.

262. Obkdo. Heeresgruppe G, Kriegstagebuch der Führungsabteilung Nr. 3b, 1.12–31.12.1944, T311, roll 143, frame 719730, NARA.

263. Ibid., frame 719728ff.

264. Ibid., frame 719743ff.

265. Manteuffel memoirs, 158.

266. Jodl, "Ardennes Offensive," 25.

267. Balck, 586–587.

268. Emmerich, "The Battle of the 1. Army in Lothringen and Northern Elsass, from 15 Sep. 1944 to 15 Feb. 1945, Part II," 24. Einem, "XIII. SS-A. K. in Lothringen,"19. Obkdo. Heeresgruppe G, Kriegstagebuch der Führungsabteilung Nr. 3b, 1.12–31.12.1944, T311, roll 143, frame 719749ff., NARA.

269. Obkdo. Heeresgruppe G, Kriegstagebuch der Führungsabteilung Nr. 3b, 1.12–31.12.1944, T311, roll 143, frame 719758ff., NARA. Simon, "South Germany Campaigns," 24. Ingelheim, 6–9.

270. Obkdo. Heeresgruppe G, Anlagen (Chefsachen) zum Kriegstagebuch Nr. 3 der Führungsabteilung, 1.10–31.12.1944, T311, roll 142, frame 7188004, NARA. Obkdo. Heeresgruppe G, Kriegstagebuch der Führungsabteilung Nr. 3b, 1.12–31.12.1944, T311, roll 143, frame 719653ff., NARA.

271. Allen, 148–153. Patton, 179.

272. Balck, 576.

273. Emmerich, "The Battle of the 1. Army in Lothringen and Northern Elsass, from 15 Sep. 1944 to 15 Feb. 1945, Part II," 25–26.

274. Simon, "South Germany Campaigns," 25.

275. Patton, 178–179.

276. Balck, 595.

277. Balck, 595–596. Mellenthin, 404.

Chapter 12: Battle of the Bulge: Patton's Greatest Moment

1. Farago, 699–700. Schramm, *Kriegstagebuch der OKW, Erster Halbband, Band 4*, 440.

2. "Personalakten für Brandenberger, Erich," German Army officers 201 files, 1900–1945, A3356, box 70, NARA. "Brandenberger, Erich," Lexikon der Wehrmacht, http://www.lexikon-der-wehrmacht.de/Personenregister/B/BrandenbergerE.htm, as of August 2009.

3. *General der Panzertruppe* Erich Brandenberger, "Ardennes Offensive of Seventh Army (16 Dec 1944–25 Jan 1945)," MS # A-876, not dated, NARA, enclosure 4. (Hereafter Brandenberger, "Ardennes Offensive of Seventh Army.")

4. *General der Panzertruppe* Erich Brandenberger, "Seventh Army from 16 December 944 to 16 January 1945; Nineteenth Army from 28 March to 5 May 1945," MS # A-934, May 1950, NARA, 1, 16. Hereafter Brandenberger, Seventh and Nineteenth Armies.) Brandenberger, "Ardennes Offensive of Seventh Army," vol. 1, 22.

5. *General der Infanterie* Baptist Kniess, "An Interview with Gen Inf Baptist Kniess: LXXXV Inf Corps (Nov–26 Dec 44)," ETHINT-40, 11 August 1945, NARA, i. (Hereafter Kniess interview.) "Kniess, Baptist, Gen. d. Inf.," German Army officers 201 files, 1900–1945, A3356, box 419, NARA.

6. Kniess interview, 1ff.

7. "Heilmann, Ludwig," Lexikon der Wehrmacht, http://www.lexikon-der-wehrmacht.de/Personenregister/H/HeilmannL.htm, as of September 2009. Samuel W. Mitcham and Friedrich von Stauffenberg, *The Battle of Sicily: How the Allies Lost Their Chance for Total Victory* (Mechanicsburg, PA: Stackpole Books, 2007), 159. (Hereafter Mitcham and Stauffenberg.) Jung, 349.

8. Brandenberger, Seventh and Nineteenth Armies, 1–3, 13. Brandenberger, "Ardennes Offensive of Seventh Army," vol. 1, 33, 48. *Generalmajor* Ludwig Heilmann, "Fifth Parachute Division (1 Dec 44–12 Jan 45)," MS # B-023, not dated, NARA. (Hereafter

Heilmann.) *Generalmajor* Erich Schmidt, "Ardennen (16.12.44–25.1.45)," MS # B-067, June 1946, NARA, 2ff. (Hereafter Schmidt.)

9. Brandenberger, Seventh and Nineteenth Armies, 1. Brandenberger, "Ardennes Offensive of Seventh Army," vol. 1, 49. *General der Infanterie* Franz Beyer, "The Last Battle of LXXX Corps: From the Marne to the Danube, part 2," MS # B-081, not dated, NARA, 28ff. (Hereafter Beyer, "The Last Battle of LXXX Corps.")

10. "Personalakten für Beyer, Franz," German Army officers 201 files, 1900–1945, A3356, box 434, NARA. "Beyer, Dr. jur. Franz," Lexikon der Wehrmacht, http://www.lexikon-der-wehrmacht.de/Personenregister/B/BeyerF.htm, as of September 2009.

11. Brandenberger, Seventh and Nineteenth Armies, 1. Oberst i. G. Werner Bodenstein, "Report of my activities during the Americans' campaign on the west front: Ardennes (16 Dec 44–25 Jan 45)," MS # B-032, 17 April 1946, NARA, 1ff. (Hereafter Bodenstein.)

12. Brandenberger, "Ardennes Offensive of Seventh Army," vol. 1, 17.

13. Brandenberger, Seventh and Nineteenth Armies, 13.

14. Guderian, 308.

15. Brandenberger, Seventh and Nineteenth Armies, 12. Brandenberger, "Ardennes Offensive of Seventh Army," vol. 1, 25–27.

16. Koch, 88–97.

17. *Ardennes-Alsace*, CMH Pub72-26 (Washington, DC: U.S. Army Center of Military History, not dated), 16ff. (Hereafter *Ardennes-Alsace.*)

18. Priess, 10–11.

19. Jodl, "Ardennes Offensive," 17.

20. Patton, 180.

21. Bennett, 211.

22. Patton, 181–182.

23. Ibid., 185–188.

24. Jodl, "Ardennes Offensive," 18.

25. Brandenberger, "Ardennes Offensive of Seventh Army," vol. 2, 20–22, 42–43.

26. Beyer, "The Last Battle of LXXX Corps," 37.

27. Brandenberger, Seventh and Nineteenth Armies, 16.

28. Brandenberger, "Ardennes Offensive of Seventh Army," vol. 2, 24–26, 44–45. Kniess interview, 3ff. Beyer, "The Last Battle of LXXX Corps," 38. "Kniess, Baptist, Gen. d. Inf.," German Army officers 201 files, 1900–1945, A3356, box 419, NARA.

29. "Sixth Pz Army in the Ardennes Offensive," ETHINT-16. Historical Division, Headquarters United States Army, Europe, 1945. This is an interview with *Generaloberst* (*Waffen SS*) Josef "Sepp" Dietrich, 8–9 August 1945. NARA.

30. Jodl, "Ardennes Offensive," 2–3.

31. Brandenberger, "Ardennes Offensive of Seventh Army," vol. 2, 26–27, 45. Beyer, "The Last Battle of LXXX Corps," 38ff.

32. Brandenberger, "Ardennes Offensive of Seventh Army," vol. 2, 29.

33. "Personalakten für Graf von Rothkirch und Trach, Edwin," German Army officers 201 files, 1900–1945, A3356, box 434, NARA.

34. Roberts.

35. Brandenberger, "Ardennes Offensive of Seventh Army," vol. 2, 30.

36. Kokott, 112.

37. Brandenberger, "Ardennes Offensive of Seventh Army," vol. 2, 30–32. Heilmann, 37–38. Bodenstein, 4ff. Schmidt, 6. *General der Panzertruppe* Heinrich Freiherr von Lüttwitz, "Einsatz des XXXXVII. Panzer-Korps in den Ardennen 1944/1945," MS # A-939, not dated, NARA, 10–13. (Hereafter Lüttwitz, "Einsatz des XXXXVII. Panzer-Korps in den Ardennen 1944/1945.") *Generalmajor* Heinz Kokott, "Ardennes Offensive: Battle of Bastogne, part 1," MS # B-040, not dated, NARA, 1ff. (Hereafter Kokott.)

38. Brandenberger, Seventh and Nineteenth Armies, 14. Brandenberger, "Ardennes Offensive of Seventh Army," vol. 2, 51ff.

39. Patton, 188–189.

40. Brandenberger, "Ardennes Offensive of Seventh Army," vol. 2, 65ff. Guderian, 309. Heilmann, 39ff. Kokott, 116ff., 130ff. *Generalmajor* Heinz Kokott, "An Interview with Genmaj Heinz Kokott," ETHINT-44, 29 November 1945, NARA, passim. Lüttwitz, "Einsatz des XXXXVII. Panzer-Korps in den Ardennen 1944/1945," 15–18. AAR, 4th Armored Division, Combat Command A. AAR, 4th Armored Division, Combat Command B. Mitcham and Stauffenberg, 159. Patton, 191.

41. Blumenson, *Patton Papers: 1940*, 607.

42. Brandenberger, Seventh and Nineteenth Armies, 1, 14. Brandenberger, "Ardennes Offensive of Seventh Army," vol. 2, 49.

43. Lüttwitz, "Einsatz des XXXXVII. Panzer-Korps in den Ardennen 1944/1945," 21–22. *General der Panzertruppe* Heinrich Freiherr von Lüttwitz, "XXXXVII. Panzer-Korps in den Ardennen-Schlacht," MS # A-940, 27 February 1946, NARA, 10–11. (Hereafter Lüttwitz, "XXXXVII. Panzer-Korps in den Ardennen-Schlacht.")

44. Priess, 46–48.

45. *General der Panzertruppe* Hasso-Eccard von Manteuffel, "An Interview with Gen Pz Hasso von Manteuffel," ETHINT-46, 29 and 31 October 1945, NARA, 3. (Hereafter Manteuffel interview.)

46. Priess, 21.

47. Lüttwitz, "Einsatz des XXXXVII. Panzer-Korps in den Ardennen 1944/1945," 23.

48. Patton, 197.

49. AAR, 4th Armored Division, Combat Command A. Third Army G-2 periodic report, 30 December 1944. Heilmann, 44.

50. Lüttwitz, "Einsatz des XXXXVII. Panzer-Korps in den Ardennen 1944/1945," 24. Patton, 197, 202. AAR, 11th Armored Division.

51. Bodenstein, 6ff.

52. Priess, 48ff. Lüttwitz, "Einsatz des XXXXVII. Panzer-Korps in den Ardennen 1944/1945," 25. Lüttwitz, "XXXXVII. Panzer-Korps in den Ardennen-Schlacht," 12. Patton, 202.

53. Priess, 53ff.

54. Third Army G-2 periodic report, 4 January 1945.

55. Patton, 203. Blumenson, *Patton Papers: 1940*, 615.

56. Priess, 55ff.

57. Ibid., 56.

58. Blumenson, Patton Papers: 1940, 616.

59. Priess, 56–57. Third Army G-2 periodic report, 8–9 January 1945.

60. Lüttwitz, "Einsatz des XXXXVII. Panzer-Korps in den Ardennen 1944/1945," 26.

61. Patton, 206–207.

62. Schramm, *Kriegstagebuch der OKW, 1. Januar 1944–22 Mai 1945, Zweiter Halbband, Band 4*, 1002, 1009.

63. AAR, 4th Armored Division, Combat Command A. AAR, 4th Armored Division, Combat Command B. Patton, 207.

64. Bodenstein, 8ff. Heilmann, 49ff. Brandenberger, Seventh and Nineteenth Armies, 13–15.

65. Priess, 57–58. Manteuffel memoirs, 182.

66. Lüttwitz, "Einsatz des XXXXVII. Panzer-Korps in den Ardennen 1944/1945," 26.

67. Brandenberger, "Ardennes Offensive of Seventh Army," vol. 2, 87ff. Bodenstein, 9ff. Manteuffel memoirs, 178. Schramm, *Kriegstagebuch der OKW, 1. Januar 1944–22 Mai 1945, Zweiter Halbband, Band 4*, 1032. Blumenson, *Patton Papers: 1940*, 625ff.

68. Lüttwitz, "Einsatz des XXXXVII. Panzer-Korps in den Ardennen 1944/1945," 27.

69. Blumenson, *Patton Papers: 1940*, 630.

70. Manteuffel memoirs, 176, 179–180.

71. Generalstab des Heeres, Abteilung Fremde Heere West, folder containing data on U.S. Army training, tactics, and equipment, T-78, roll 442, frame 6415526ff., NARA.

Chapter 13: Patton Flattens Germany's Remnants

1. Manteuffel memoirs, 181–184.

2. Schramm, *Kriegstagebuch der OKW, 1. Januar 1944–22 Mai 1945, Zweiter Halbband, Band 4*, 1042-1043. *Generalmajor* Carl Wagener, "Die Folgen der Ardennen-Offensive," MS # A-964, 4 February 1946, NARA, 5. (Hereafter Wagener.) Guderian, 335, 245–246.

3. Wilmot, 663–664.

4. Wagener, 9–10. Third Army G-2 periodic report, 4 February 1945.

5. Patton, 216, 219.

6. Bradley, 499–501.

7. Patton, 225. Blumenson, Patton Papers: 1940, 635–636.

8. *Generaloberst* (*Waffen SS*) Paul Hausser, "Rheinland: Heeres-Gruppe 'G,'" MS # B-600, June 1947. NARA, 2. (Hereafter Hausser, "Rheinland: Heeres-Gruppe 'G.'")

9. *Oberst i. G.* Horst Wilutzky, "Der Kampf der Heeresgruppe G im Westen. Der Zusammenbruch der Westfront (20.2–22.3.45)," MS # B-450, not dated, NARA, 4. (Hereafter Wilutzky, "Der Zusammenbruch der Westfront.")

10. *Generalmajor* Rudolf-Christoph Freiherr von Gersdorff, "Zwischen Westwall und Rhein: Die Kaempfe der 7. Armee vom 1. Febr.-21. Maerz 45," MS # B-123, February 1946, NARA, 1ff. (Hereafter Gersdorff, "Zwischen Westwall und Rhein.") Felber, "XIII A. K.: Bericht ueber den Ardennenfeldzug—III. Teil, Zeit von 25.1. bis 20.2.45," 14.

11. Wilutzky, "Der Zusammenbruch der Westfront," 4. *General der Infanterie* Baptist Kniess, "Saar-Rhein-Pfalz: 21.1.45–23.3.1945," MS # B-121, 3 May 1946, NARA, 1–2. (Hereafter Kniess, "Saar-Rhein-Pfalz: 21.1.45–23.3.1945.")

12. Wilutzky, "Der Zusammenbruch der Westfront," 3–5.

13. Gersdorff, "Zwischen Westwall und Rhein," 7. Hausser, "Rheinland: Heeres-Gruppe 'G,'" 8.

14. *General der Infanterie* Hans Felber, "XIII A. K.: Bericht ueber den Ardennenfeldzug— III. Teil, Zeit von 25.1. bis 20.2.45," MS # B-494, 25 April 1947, NARA, 14–15. (Hereafter Felber, "XIII A. K.: Bericht ueber den Ardennenfeldzug—III. Teil, Zeit von 25.1. bis 20.2.45.")

15. "Personalakten für Felber, Hans-Gustav," German Army officers 201 files, 1900–1945, A3356, box 1177, NARA. "Felber, Hans-Gustav," Lexikon der Wehrmacht, http:// www.lexikon-der-wehrmacht.de/Personenregister/F/FelberHansGustav.htm, as of November 2009.

16. Felber, "XIII A. K.: Bericht ueber den Ardennenfeldzug—III. Teil, Zeit von 25.1. bis 20.2.45," 16, 32.

17. Gersdorff, "Zwischen Westwall und Rhein," 9–12. Felber, "XIII A. K.: Bericht ueber den Ardennenfeldzug—III. Teil, Zeit von 25.1. bis 20.2.45," 16–20.

18. *General der Infanterie* Franz Beyer, "The Final Fighting of LXXX Corps: From the Marne to the Danube, part 3," MS # B-082, not dated, NARA, 3–4. (Hereafter Beyer, "The Final Fighting of LXXX Corps.")

19. Ibid., 5. Gersdorff, "Zwischen Westwall und Rhein," 7, 13, 15–17. Hausser, "Rheinland: Heeres-Gruppe 'G,'" 20. Blumenson, *Patton Papers: 1940*, 638–639. Third Army G-2 periodic report, 10–12 February 1945.

20. *General der Panzertruppe* Erich Brandenberger, "Questions for the 7. Army," MS # B-447, May 1946, NARA, 46.

21. "Personalakten für Graf von Oriola, Ralph," German Army officers 201 files, 1900– 1945, A3356, box 620, NARA.

22. Schramm, *Kriegstagebuch der OKW, 1. Januar 1944–22 Mai 1945, Zweiter Halbband, Band 4*, 1115. *General der Infanterie* Hans Felber, "Seventh German Army: Fighting Between the West Wall and the Main (from 20 Feb to 26 Mar 1945)," MS # B-831, not dated, NARA, 11–15. (Hereafter Felber, "Seventh German Army.") Third Army G-2 periodic report, 28 February 1945.

23. Schramm, *Kriegstagebuch der OKW, 1. Januar 1944–22 Mai 1945, Zweiter Halbband, Band 4*, 1118. Beyer, "The Final Fighting of LXXX Corps," 5–9. Felber, "Seventh German Army," 14, 18ff. Gersdorff, "Zwischen Westwall und Rhein," 7, 13, 17–18. Kesselring, "Commander in Chief West," 150, 213–214.

24. Ingelheim, 24ff. Redmer, 48ff. Patton, 223, 231, 234. Blumenson, *Patton Papers: 1940*, 645. Bennett, 238.

25. Wilutzky, "Stellungsnahme zu der Bearbeitung des ehemaligen Generalfeldmarschalls Kesselring 'Geschichte des Oberbefehlhaber West, III Teil,'" MS # C-036, November 1948, NARA, 4–8, 12, 17–18. (Hereafter Wilutzky, "Stellungsnahme zu der Bearbeitung") "Personalakten für Foertsch, Hermann," German Army officers 201 files, 1900–1945, A3356, box 146, NARA.

26. Beyer, "The Final Fighting of LXXX Corps," 13. Patton, 236.

27. Schramm, *Kriegstagebuch der OKW, 1. Januar 1944–22 Mai 1945, Zweiter Halbband, Band 4*, 1138. *Oberst i. G.* Horst Wilutzky, "Stellungsnahme zu der Bearbeitung" 17. Wilutzky, "Der Zusammenbruch der Westfront," 17–20. Beyer, "The Final Fighting of LXXX Corps," 16. Third Army G-2 periodic report, 15 March 1945.

28. *Oberst i. G.* Horst Wilutzky, "The Fighting of Heeresgruppe 'G' in the West: The Final Battle in the Central and Southern Germany Until the Surrender (22 Mar 45–6 May 45)," MS # B-703, not dated, NARA, 3. (Hereafter Wilutzky, "The Fighting of Heeresgruppe 'G.' ")

29. Gersdorff, "Zwischen Westwall und Rhein," 25. Wilutzky, "Der Zusammenbruch der Westfront," 19–20, 23.

30. Patton, 238–239. Third Army G-2 periodic report, 4 March 1945.

31. Gersdorff, "Zwischen Westwall und Rhein," 26. Wilutzky, "Der Zusammenbruch der Westfront" 25

32. Bradley, 509.

33. Felber, "Seventh German Army," 24–25.

34. Patton, 239. Blumenson, *Patton Papers: 1940*, 652. Gersdorff, "Zwischen Westwall und Rhein," 26–28. Felber, "Seventh German Army," 26.

35. Kesselring memoirs, 237–240. Kesselring, "Commander in Chief West," 25, 208.

36. Kesselring, "Commander in Chief West," 82.

37. Charles B. MacDonald, *The Last Offensive: United States Army in World War II, The European Theater of Operations* (Washington, DC: Office of the Chief of Military History, Department of the Army), 1993, 239–241. (Hereafter MacDonald, *The Last Offensive.*)

38. Patton, 239–240.

39. Allen, 31.

40. Blumenson, *Patton Papers: 1940*, 654.

41. Wilutzky, "Stellungsnahme zu der Bearbeitung" 4–8, 12, 17–18. Felber, "Seventh German Army," 31–32. Schramm, *Kriegstagebuch der OKW, 1. Januar 1944–22 Mai 1945, Zweiter Halbband, Band 4*, 1166. Third Army G-2 periodic report, 14 March 1945.

42. Hausser, "Rheinland: Heeres-Gruppe 'G,' " 28. Wilutzky, "Stellungsnahme zu der Bearbeitung" 11. Wilutzky, "Der Zusammenbruch der Westfront," 25, 28. Felber, "Seventh German Army," 26. Kesselring memoirs, 241–244. Kesselring, "Commander in Chief West," 94ff.

43. Hausser, "Rheinland: Heeres-Gruppe 'G,' " 28.

44. Beyer, "The Final Fighting of LXXX Corps," 20ff. Gersdorff, "Zwischen Westwall und Rhein," 29. Felber, "Seventh German Army," 33. Kesselring, "Commander in Chief West," 117ff.

45. Gersdorff, "Zwischen Westwall und Rhein," 39ff.

46. *Generalmajor* Rudolf-Christoph Freiherr von Gersdorff, "The Final Phase of the War," MS # A-893, 20 March 1946, NARA, 2. (Hereafter Gersdorff, "The Final Phase of the War.")

47. Kesselring memoirs, 244–245. Kesselring, "Commander in Chief West," 116ff.

48. Ingelheim, 35ff.

49. Gersdorff, "The Final Phase of the War," 5.

50. Hausser, "Rheinland: Heeres-Gruppe 'G,'" 32.

51. Kesselring memoirs, 247. Kesselring, "Commander in Chief West," 140.

52. Patton, 247.

53. Blumenson, *Patton Papers: 1940*, 656–657.

54. Ingelheim, 35ff.

55. Wilutzky, "Stellungnahme zu der Bearbeitung des ehemaligen Generalfeldmarschalls Kesselring 'Geschichte des Oberbefehlhaber West, III Teil,'" 25–26. Gersdorff, "Zwischen Westwall und Rhein," 42. Felber, "Seventh German Army," 34. Kesselring memoirs, 245.

56. Gersdorff, "Zwischen Westwall und Rhein," 44–48. Gersdorff, "The Final Phase of the War," 6. Felber, "Seventh German Army," 38. Schramm, *Kriegstagebuch der OKW, 1. Januar 1944–22 Mai 1945, Zweiter Halbband, Band 4*, 1181. MacDonald, *The Last Offensive*, 256–258.

57. Wilutzky, "Stellungnahme zu der Bearbeitung" 22. Ingelheim, 40.

58. Hausser, "Rheinland: Heeres-Gruppe 'G,'" 33.

59. Wilutzky, "Der Zusammenbruch der Westfront," 33–34.

60. Kniess, "Saar-Rhein-Pfalz: 21.1.45–23.3.1945," 4. Kesselring, "Commander in Chief West," 128.

61. Third Army G-2 periodic report, 15 March 1945.

62. Wilutzky, "Stellungnahme zu der Bearbeitung" 29. Patton, 251.

63. Wilutzky, "Stellungnahme zu der Bearbeitung" 27. Wilutzky, "The Fighting of Heeresgruppe 'G,' " 5. Beyer, "The Final Fighting of LXXX Corps," 26. Gersdorff, "The Final Phase of the War," 7–8.

64. Beyer, "The Final Fighting of LXXX Corps," 28.

65. Patton, 258–259.

66. Wilutzky, "The Fighting of Heeresgruppe 'G,' " 12–13.

67. Felber, "Seventh German Army," 45–47.

68. Kesselring memoirs, 248.

69. Wilutzky, "The Fighting of Heeresgruppe 'G,' " 5.

70. Gersdorff, "Zwischen Westwall und Rhein," 24. Felber, "Seventh German Army," 59.

71. Wilutzky, "The Fighting of Heeresgruppe 'G,'" 5.

72. Schramm, *Kriegstagebuch der OKW, 1. Januar 1944–22 Mai 1945, Zweiter Halbband, Band 4*, 1192.

73. Third Army G-2 periodic report, 23 March 1945.

74. Wilutzky, "Stellungnahme zu der Bearbeitung" 31–33. Gersdorff, "Zwischen Westwall und Rhein," 23–24. Third Army G-2 periodic report, 17 March 1945.

75. *Generalleutnant* Ernst Fäckenstedt, "Der Feldzug in Mitteldeutschland vom 22.3–11.5.45 aus dem Abschnitt Koblenz-Speyer bis in die Erzgebirgs-Stellung," MS # B-404, 1947, NARA, 3. (Hereafter Fäckenstedt.)

76. *Oberst* Werner Wagner, "Einsatz der 276. Volksgrenadier-Division: 17–27 Mar 1945," MS # B-124, not dated, NARA, 1–5.

77. Kesselring memoirs, 249. Patton, 259. Gersdorff, "The Final Phase of the War," 10–11. Fäckenstedt, 9–10. Felber, "Seventh German Army," 47ff. Schramm, *Kriegstagebuch der OKW, 1. Januar 1944–22 Mai 1945, Zweiter Halbband, Band 4*, 1196.

78. Gersdorff, "The Final Phase of the War," 12.

79. Ibid., 13–14. *Generalleutnant* Wend von Wietersheim, "Die Kämpfe der 11. Panzer-Division Zwischen Rhein und tschechischer Grenze (21.3–15.4.45; Teil I)," MS # B-755, 16 December 1947, NARA, 2-4. (Hereafter Wietersheim, "Die Kämpfe der 11. Panzer-Division.")

80. Gersdorff, "The Final Phase of the War," 15–17. Wietersheim, "Die Kämpfe der 11. Panzer-Division," 3. Patton, 260ff.

81. "Personalakten für Osterkamp, Herbert," German Army officers 201 files, 1900–1945, A3356, box 622, NARA.

82. Schramm, *Kriegstagebuch der OKW, 1. Januar 1944–22 Mai 1945, Zweiter Halbband, Band 4*, 1200, 1209. Gersdorff, "The Final Phase of the War," 18–21. Felber, "Seventh German Army," 51–54. Kesselring, "Commander in Chief West," 150, 157. Wilutzky, "The Fighting of Heeresgruppe 'G,'" 13–18. Kesselring, "Commander in Chief West," 159, 185. Wietersheim, "Die Kämpfe der 11. Panzer-Division," 5–6. AAR, Third Army.

83. Kesselring memoirs, 250.

84. Kesselring, "Commander in Chief West," 189.

85. AAR, Third Army. Third Army G-2 periodic reports, March 1945.

86. Gersdorff, "The Final Phase of the War," 21–22.

87. Fäckenstedt, 20.

88. Patton, 264.

89. Schramm, *Kriegstagebuch der OKW, 1. Januar 1944–22 Mai 1945, Zweiter Halbband, Band 4*, passim.

90. Gersdorff, "The Final Phase of the War," 22–26. Fäckenstedt, 20–21.

91. Third Army G-2 periodic report, 31 March 1945. Army Ground Forces Report No. 808, "Tank Destroyer Information Letter No 8," 4 April 1945.

92. Wilutzky, "The Fighting of Heeresgruppe 'G,'" 23–24.

93. Schramm, *Kriegstagebuch der OKW, 1. Januar 1944–22 Mai 1945, Zweiter Halbband, Band 4*, 1225ff. *Oberst* Fritz Estor, "Kaempfe der 11. Armee April 1945 in Mitteldeutschland," MS # B-581, 3 January 1947, NARA, passim. Third Army G-2 periodic report, 1–12 April 1945.

94. Kesselring memoirs, 271ff. *General der Infanterie* Friedrich Schultz, "Bericht ueber Lage, Auftrag und Massnahmen (im Grossen) der Heeresgruppe 'G' im April 1945," MS # B-583, May 1946, NARA, 1ff.

95. Patton, 269–271, 279–281. Gersdorff, "The Final Phase of the War," 37.

96. Kesselring, "Commander in Chief West," 290.

97. Gersdorff, "The Final Phase of the War," 34ff. Wilutzky, "The Fighting of Heeresgruppe 'G,'" passim.

98. "Personalakten für Frhr. v. Lüttwitz, Smilo," German Army officers 201 files, 1900–1945, A3356, box 515, NARA. "Lüttwitz, Smilo Freiherr von," Lexikon der Wehrmacht, http://www.lexikon-der-wehrmacht.de/Personenregister/L/LuttwitzSFv.htm, as of December 2009.

99. *General der Panzertruppe* Smilo Freiherr von Lüttwitz, "Combat Report of the LXXXV. 'Armeekorps,'" MS # B-617, June 1947, NARA, 1ff. (Hereafter Lüttwitz, "Combat Report of the LXXXV. 'Armeekorps.'")

100. Third Army G-2 periodic reports, 5 and 11 April 1945.

101. Patton, 286–287. Third Army G-2 periodic report, 17 April 1945.

102. AAR, Third Army. Kesselring, "Commander in Chief West," 340–341.

103. Kesselring, "Commander in Chief West," 349.

104. Gersdorff, "The Final Phase of the War," 43ff.

105. Kesselring, "Commander in Chief West," 352–357.

106. Patton, 295.

107. Lüttwitz, "Combat Report of the LXXXV. 'Armeekorps,'" 25ff. Wilutzky, "The Fighting of Heeresgruppe 'G,'" 46.

108. Third Army G-2 periodic report, 5 May 1945. Brig. Gen. (ret.) Raymond E. Bell Jr., "Giving Up the Ghost," *World War II History* magazine online, http://www.wwiihistorymagazine.com/2005/sep/fea-ghost.html, as of November 2009.

109. Third Army G-2 periodic report, 6 May 1945.

110. Patton, 312. Kesselring, "Commander in Chief West," 405. Third Army G-2 periodic report, 8 May 1945.

Chapter 14: A Footnote to the Panegyric

1. Blumenson, *Patton*, 11.

2. D'Este, *Patton: A Genius for War*, 2.

3. George C. Marshall Papers, China Mission, General, George C. Marshall Research Library, Lexington, Virginia.

4. Liddell Hart, *The German Generals Talk*, 257–258.

5. *Generaloberst* Heinz Guderian, "Panzer Employment, Western Front." ETHINT-39, 16 August 1945, NARA, 10. (Hereafter Guderian, "Panzer Employment, Western Front.")

6. Rommel, 521–523.

7. Reynolds, 42–45.

8. Farago, 505.

9. Jodl, "U.S. Operations," 4.

10. Guderian 355.

11. Guderian, "Panzer Employment, Western Front," 13.

12. *Generalfeldmarschall* Albert Kesselring, "An Interview with Genfldm Albert Kesselring: General Questions," ETHINT-72, 6 May 1946, NARA, 6.

13. Luck, 203, 212.

14. Bayerlein interview, 19.

15. De Lannoy and Charita, 7ff.

16. Mellenthin, 190–192. Farago, 401–406, 559ff. Blumenson, *Patton*, 17.

17. Mellenthin, 21.

18. Liddell Hart, *Second World War*, 73.

19. Jodl, "U.S. Operations," 2.

20. Patton, 104.

21. Raus, 84.

22. Knobelsdorff, *19. Panzer-Division*, 96–97.

23. Raus, 2.

24. Manstein, 438–439. Mellenthin, 233–237.

25. Farago, 505.

26. Ibid., 505.

27. Alaric Searle, *Wehrmacht Generals, West German Society, and the Debate on Rearmament, 1949–1959* (New York: Praeger Publishers, 2003), 207–208.

Glossary

Ia	Operations officer (German)
Ic	Intelligence officer (German)
Brig. Gen.	Brigadier General
Capt.	Captain
Col.	Colonel
Cpl.	Corporal
ETO	European Theater of Operations
Führerbefehl	Personal order from Hitler
G-2	Intelligence officer/staff
G-3	Operations officer/staff
Gen.	General
GPF	Grande Puissance Filloux, 155mm rifles
Goumiers	French Arab colonial troops
HE	High-explosive
Jeep	1/4-ton truck
Kampfgruppe	Task-organized battle group
Kriegstagebuch	War diary; American equivalent: G3 journal
Los Dorados	"The Golden Ones," Pancho Villa's bodyguard
Lt.	Lieutenant
Lt. Col.	Lieutenant Colonel
Lt. Gen.	Lieutenant General
Maj.	Major

Maj. Gen.	Major General
Panzer	Tank
Panzergrenadier	Armored infantry
Pfc.	Private First Class
Pvt.	Private
RACM	Regiment d'Artillerie Coloniale du Maroc, Moroccan Colonial Artillery
RCT	Regimental Combat Team, an infantry regiment with attachments
REC	Regiment Etranger de Cavalerie, Foreign Legion Cavalry
REI	Regiment Etranger d'Infanterie, Foreign Legion
RICM	Regiment d'Infanterie Coloniale du Maroc, Moroccan Colonial Infantry
RSM	1st Regiment de Spahis Marocains, Moroccan Spahis (cavalry)
RTA	Regiment Tirailleurs Algeriens, Algerian Rifle Regiment
RTM	Regiment of Tirailleur Marocains, Moroccan Rifle Regiment
Schwerpunkt	Main point of effort
Sgt.	Sergeant
S/Sgt.	Staff Sergeant
SHAEF	Supreme Headquarters Allied Expeditionary Force
Volksartillerie	People's Artillery

Bibliography

Books and Booklets

Allen, Robert S. *Patton's Third Army: Lucky Forward*. New York: Manor Books, 1965.

Ardennes-Alsace. CMH Pub72-26. Washington, DC: U.S. Army Center of Military History, not dated.

Atkinson, Rick. *An Army at Dawn: The War in North Africa, 1942–1943*. New York: Henry Holt and Company, 2002.

———. *The Day of Battle: The War in Sicily and Italy, 1943–1944*. New York: Henry Holt and Company, 2007.

Balck, Hermann. *Ordnung im Chaos: Errinerungen 1893–1948*. Osnabrück, Germany: Biblio Verlag, 1981.

Barnett, Cornelli. *Hitler's Generals*. New York: Grove Press, 1989.

Baumer, Robert, and Mark Reardon. *American Iliad: The 18th Infantry Regiment in World War II*. Bedford, PA: Aberjona Press, 2004.

Bennett, Ralph. *Ultra in the West: The Normandy Campaign 1944–45*. New York: Charles Scribner's Sons, 1980.

Bernhardi, Friedrich von. *Deutschlands Heldenkampf, 1914–1918*. Munich: J. F. Lehmanns Verlag, 1922.

Blumenson, Martin. *Breakout and Pursuit: United States Army in World War II, The European Theater of Operations*. Washington, DC: Center of Military History, 1993.

———. *Kasserine Pass*. New York: Jove Books, 1983.

———. *Patton: The Man Behind the Legend, 1815–1945*. New York: William Morrow and Company, 1985.

———. *The Patton Papers: 1885–1940*. Boston: Houghton Mifflin Company, 1972.

———. *The Patton Papers: 1940–1945*. Boston: Houghton Mifflin Company, 1974.

———. *Salerno to Cassino*. Washington, DC: Office of the Chief of Military History, 1969.

Bradley, Omar N. *A Soldier's Story*. New York: The Modern Library, 1999.

Bradley, Omar N., and Clay Blair. *A General's Life*. New York: Simon and Schuster, 1983.

Brighton, Terry. *Masters of Battle: Monty, Patton and Rommel at War*. London: Penguin Books, 2008.

488

Brooks, Victor. *The Normandy Campaign: From D-Day to the Liberation of Paris.* New York: Da Capo Press, 2002.

Buchanan, Richard R., Richard D. Wissolik, David Wilmes, and Gary E. J. Smith, eds. *Men of the 704th: A Pictorial and Spoken History of the 704th Tank Destroyer Battalion in World War II.* Latrobe, PA: Saint Vincent College Center for Northern Appalachian Studies, 1998.

Butcher, Harry C. *My Three Years with Eisenhower.* New York: Simon and Schuster, 1946.

Carell, Paul. *Invasion: They're Coming!* New York: Bantam Books, 1962.

Carver, Lord. *The Imperial War Museum Book of The War in Italy 1943–1945.* London: Pan Books, 2002.

Citino, Robert M. *The German Way of War.* Lawrence: University Press of Kansas, 2005.

Clarke, Jeffrey J., and Robert Ross Smith. *Riviera to the Rhine. United States Army in World War II, The European Theater of Operations.* Washington, DC: Office of the Chief of Military History, Department of the Army, 1993.

Cole, Hugh M. *Battle of the Bulge: United States Army in World War II, The European Theater of Operations.* Washington, DC: Center of Military History, 1993.

———. *The Lorraine Campaign: United States Army in World War II, The European Theater of Operations.* Washington, DC: Historical Division, Department of the Army, 1950.

Cornwell, Peter D. *The Battle of France Then and Now: Six Nations Locked in Aerial Combat September 1939 to June 1940.* Hobbs Cross, Old Harlow, Essex: Battle of Britain International, 2007.

Gabel, Christopher. *The Lorraine Campaign: An Overview, September–December 1944.* Fort Leavenworth, Kansas: Combat Studies Institute, 1985.

De Lannoy, Francois, and Josef Charita. *Panzertruppen.* Baveux, France: Editions Heimdal, 2001.

D'Este, Carlo. *Patton: A Genius for War.* New York: Harper Perennial, 1995.

Dizionario Biografico Degli Italiani. Rome: Instituto Della Enciclopedia Italiana Fondata da Giovanni Treccani, 2003.

Donnell, Clayton. *The German Fortress of Metz 1870–1944.* New York: Osprey Publishing, 2008.

Dugdale, J. *Panzer Divisions, Panzer Grenadier Divisions, Panzer Brigades of the Army and the Waffen SS in the West; Autumn 1944–February 1945, Ardennes and Northwind, Volume 1 (Part 4A).* Milton Keynes, England: The Military Press, 2002.

Eisenhower, Dwight D. *Crusade in Europe.* Garden City, NY: Doubleday and Company, 1948.

Elson, Aaron C. Tanks for the Memories: An Oral History of the 712th Tank Battalion from World War II Hackensack, N.J.: Chi Chi Press, 1994.

Farago, Ladislas. *Patton: Ordeal and Triumph.* New York: Ivan Obolensky, 1963.

Fox, Don M. *Patton's Vanguard: The United States Army Fourth Armored Division.* Jefferson, NC: McFarland & Company, Kindle edition, 2003.

Frankel, Nat, and Larry Smith. *Patton's Best: An Informal History of the 4th Armored Division.* New York: The Berkley Publishing Group, 1984.

Gabel, Christopher R. *The U.S. Army GHQ Maneuvers of 1941.* Washington, DC: Center of Military History, United States Army, 1991.

Glantz, David M. and Jonathan M. House. *The Battle of Kursk*. Lawrence: University Press of Kansas, 1999.

———. *When Titans Clashed: How the Red Army Stopped Hitler*. Lawrence: University Press of Kansas, 1995.

Griess, Thomas E., ed. *The West Point Military History Series, The Second World War, Europe and the Mediterranean*. Wayne, NJ: Avery Publishing Group, 1984.

Guderian, Heinz. *Panzer Leader*. New York: Ballantine Books, 1972.

Guderian, Heinz Günther. *From Normandy to the Ruhr, With the 116th Panzer Division in World War II*. Bedford, PA: The Aberjona Press, 2001.

Hall, Chester. *History of the 70th Tank Battalion: June 5, 1940. . . May 22, 1946*. Louisville, KY: Southern Press, 1950.

Harmon, E. N., with Milton MacKaye and William Ross MacKaye. *Combat Commander, Autobiography of a Soldier*. Englewood Cliffs, NJ: Prentice-Hall, Inc., 1970.

Harrison, Gordon A. *Cross-Channel Attack: United States Army in World War II, The European Theater of Operations*. Washington, DC: Center of Military History, 1993.

Heiber, Helmut, and David M. Glantz, eds. *Hitler and His Generals: Military Conferences 1942–1945*. New York: Enigma Books, 2004.

Hofmann, George F. *Through Mobility We Conquer: The Mechanization of the U.S. Cavalry*. Lexington: University Press of Kentucky, 2006.

Hoffmann, Peter. *Stauffenberg: A Family History, 1905–1944*. Montreal: McGill-Queen's University Press: 2003.

Holt, Thaddeus. *The Deceivers*. New York: Scribner, 2004.

Howe, George F. *Northwest Africa: Seizing the Initiative in the West: United States Army in World War II, The Mediterranean Theater of Operations*. Washington, DC: Office of the Chief of Military History, Department of the Army, 1957.

Irving, David. *Hitler's War*. New York: Avon Books, 1990.

Iryzk, Albin F. *He Rode Up Front for Patton*. Raleigh, NC: Pentland Press, 1996.

Jentz, Thomas L., ed. *Panzertruppen 2*. Arglen, PA: Schiffer Military History, 1996.

Jung, Hermann *Die Ardennen-Offensive 1944/45—Ein Beispiel für die Kriegführung Hitlers*. Frankfurt: Musterschmidt Gottingen, 1971.

Kahn, David. *Hitler's Spies: German Military Intelligence in World War II*. New York: Da Capo Press, 2000.

Keegan, John. *Waffen SS: The Asphalt Soldiers*. New York: Ballantine Books, 1970.

Kenamore, Clair. *From Vauquois Hill to Exermont: A History of the Thirty-Fifth Division of the United States Army*. St. Louis, MO: Guard Publishing, 1919.

Kesselring, Albert. *The Memoirs of Field-Marshal Kesselring*. St. Paul, MN: MBI Publishing, 2007.

Knobelsdorff, Otto von. *Geschichte der niedersächsischen 19. Panzer-Division: 1939–1945*. Bad Nauheim, Germany: Podzun-Verlag, 1958.

Koch, Oscar, with Robert G. Hays. *G-2: Intelligence for Patton*. Atglen, PA: Schiffer Military History, 1999.

Levisse-Touze, Christine. *L'Afrique du Nord Dans la Guerre 1939–1945*. Paris: Albin Michel, 1998.

Lieb, Peter. *Konventioneller Krieg oder NS-Weltanschauungskrieg?* Munich: Oldenbourg Wissenschaftsverlag, 2007.

Liddell Hart, B. H. *The German Generals Talk.* New York: Quill, 1979.

———. *History of the Second World War.* New York: G. Putnam's Sons, 1970.

Lochner, Louis P., editor and translator. *The Goebbels Diary: 1942-1943.* New York: Doubleday & Company, 1948.

Lucas, James Sydney. *Hitler's Enforcers: Leaders of the German War Machine, 1933-1945.* Leicester, UK: Brockhampton Press, 2000.

Luck, Hans von. *Panzer Commander.* New York: Dell Publishing, 1989.

MacDonald, Charles B. *The Battle of the Bulge.* London: Guild Publishing, 1984.

———. *The Last Offensive: United States Army in World War II, The European Theater of Operations.* Washington, DC: Office of the Chief of Military History, Department of the Army, 1993.

———. *The Siegfried Line Campaign: United States Army in World War II, The European Theater of Operations.* Washington, DC: Office of the Chief of Military History, Department of the Army, 1993.

Manstein, Erich von. *Lost Victories.* Minneapolis: Zenith Press, 2004.

Manteuffel, Hasso von, and Franz Kurowski. *Panzerkampf im Zweiten Weltkrieg: Lebenserinnerungen.* Schnellbach, Germany: Verlag Siegfried Bublies, 2005.

March, Francis A., and Richard J. Beamish. *History of the World War.* Philadelphia: The United Publishers of the United States and Canada, 1919.

Mellenthin, F. W. von. *Panzer Battles.* New York: Ballantine Books, 1971.

Mitcham, Samuel W. *Retreat to the Reich: The German Defeat in France, 1944.* Westport, CT: Prager, Kindle edition, 2000.

Mitcham, Samuel W., and Friedrich von Stauffenberg. *The Battle of Sicily: How the Allies Lost Their Chance for Total Victory.* Mechanicsburg, PA: Stackpole Books, 2007.

Montgomery, Bernard Law. *The Memoirs of Field Marshall the Viscount Montgomery of Alamein, L.G.* New York: The World Publishing Company, 1958.

Newton, Steven H. *Kursk: The German View.* New York: Da Capo Press, Kindle edition, 2002.

Normandy. CMH Pub72-18. Washington, DC: U.S. Army Center of Military History, not dated.

Northern France. CMH Pub72-30. Washington, DC: U.S. Army Center of Military History, not dated.

Patton, George S., Jr. *War As I Knew It.* New York: Bantam Books, 1980.

Raus, Erhard. *Panzer Operations: The Eastern Front Memoir of General Raus, 1941–1945.* Cambridge, MA: De Capo Press, 2003.

Reynolds, Michael. *Monty and Patton: Two Paths to Victory.* Chalford Stroud, Gloucestershire: Spellmount Limited, 2007.

Rhineland. CMH Pub72-25. Washington, DC: U.S. Army Center of Military History, not dated.

Rickard, John Nelson. *Patton at Bay: The Lorraine Campaign, 1944.* Washington, DC: Brassey's, 2004.

Ritgen, Helmut. *West-Front 1944*. Stuttgart: Motorbuch Verlag, 2001.

Rommel, Erwin, and B. H. Liddell Hart, ed. *The Rommel Papers*. New York: Da Capo Press, 1982.

Satter, Alfred. *Die Deutsche Kavallerie in Ersten Weltkrieg*. Norderstedt, Germany: Books on Demand GmbH: 2004.

Scheibert, Horst, and Bruce Culver, ed. *Panzer Grenadier Division Grossdeutschland*. Carrollton, TX: Squadron/Signal Publications, 1987.

Schick, Albert. *Die Zehnte P.D.: Die Geschichte der 10. Panzer-Division 1939–1943*. Cologne, Germany: Traditionsgemeinschaft der Ehemaligen 10. Panzer-Division, 1993.

Schramm, Percy E. *Kriegstagebuch des Oberkommando der Wehrmacht (Wehrmachtfüh-rungsstab), 1. Januar 1942–31. Dezember 1942, Zweiter Halbband, Band 2*. Germany: Bechtermünz, 2005.

———. *Kriegstagebuch des Oberkommando der Wehrmacht (Wehrmachtführungsstab), 1. Januar 1942–31. Dezember 1942, Zweiter Halbband, Band 4*. Germany: Bechtermünz, 2005.

———. *Kriegstagebuch des Oberkommando der Wehrmacht (Wehrmachtführungsstab), 1. Januar 1943–31. Dezember 1943, Erster Halbband, Band 3*. Germany: Bechtermünz, 2005.

———. *Kriegstagebuch des Oberkommando der Wehrmacht (Wehrmachtführungsstab), 1. Januar 1943–31. Dezember 1943, Zweiter Halbband, Band 3*. Germany: Bechtermünz, 2005.

———. *Kriegstagebuch des Oberkommando der Wehrmacht (Wehrmachtführungsstab), 1. Januar 1944–22 Mai 1945, Erster Halbband, Band 4*. Germany: Bechtermünz, 2005.

Searle, Alaric. *Wehrmacht Generals, West German Society, and the Debate on Rearmament, 1949–1959*. New York: Praeger Publishers, 2003.

Sebag-Montefiore, Hugh. *Dunkirk: Fight to the Last Man*. Cambridge, MA: Harvard University Press, 2006.

Sicily. CMH Pub 72-16. Washington, DC: Center of Military History, 1999.

Smyth, Howard McGaw, assisted by Martin Blumenson. *Sicily and the Surrender of Italy: United States Army in World War II, The European Theater of Operations*. Washington, DC: Office of the Chief of Military History, Department of the Army, 1993.

Society of the First Division. *History of the First Division During the Worlds War: 1917–1919*. Philadelphia: John C. Winston Company, 1922.

Southern France. CMH Pub72-31. Washington, DC: U.S. Army Center of Military History, not dated.

St. Lô, facsimile reprint of CMH Pub 100-13. Washington, DC: U.S. Army Center of Military History, 1983.

St-Mihiel: The United States Army in the World War, 1917–1919. Washington, DC: Historical Division, Department of the Army, 1948.

Sydnor, Charles W., Jr. *Soldiers of Destruction: The SS Death's Head Division, 1933–1945*. Princeton, NJ: Princeton University Press, 1977.

Thomas, Nigel. *The German Army in World War I (3): 1917–1918*. Botley, UK: Osprey Publishing, 2004.

Truscott, Lucian K. *Command Missions.* New York: E. P. Dutton and Company, 1954.

Tunisia. CMH Pub 72-12. Washington, DC: U.S. Army Center of Military History, not dated.

Warlimont, Walter. *Inside Hitler's Headquarters, 1939–45.* Novato, CA: Presidio Press, 1964.

Welsome, Eileen. *The General and the Jaguar: Pershing's Hunt for Pancho Villa, A True Story of Revolution and Revenge.* New York: Little, Brown and Company, 2006.

Westphal, Siegfried. *The German Army in the West.* London: Cassell and Company, 1951.

Williamson, Gordon. *The SS: Hitler's Instrument of Terror.* St. Paul, MN: Zenith Press, 2004.

Williamson, Gordon and Ramiro Bujeiro. *Knight's Cross Oak-Leaves Recipients 1941 15.* Botley, UK: Osprey Publishing 2005.

———. *Knight's Cross Oak-Leaves Recipients 1941–45: The Southern Fronts, 1941–45.* Botley, UK: Osprey Publishing, 2005.

Wilmot, Chester. *The Struggle for Europe.* Ware, England: Wordsworth Editions, 1997.

Wilson, Dale E. *Treat 'Em Rough! The Birth of American Armor, 1917–20.* Novato, CA: Presidio Press, 1990.

Wind, M., and H. Günther. *Kriegstagebuch, 30. Oktober 1943 bis 6. Mai 1945, 17. SS-Panzer-Grenadier-Division "Götz von Berlichingen."* Munich: Schild Verlag, 1993.

Wissolik, Richard D., and Gary E. J. Smith, eds. *Reluctant Valor: The Oral History of Captain Thomas J. Evans.* Latrobe, PA: Saint Vincent College Center for Northern Appalachian Studies, 1995.

Zaloga, Steven J. *George S. Patton: Leadership, Strategy, Conflict.* New York: Osprey Publishing, 2010.

Articles

"Armored Cars for Cavalry Units," *The Cavalry Journal,* January 1923, 92.

Bonsteel, Capt. F. T. "The Employment of a Mechanized Cavalry Brigade." The Cavalry Journal, September–October 1933, 19–26.

Brooks, Russell (U.S. Consul General Rabat, retired). "Casablanca—The French Side of the Fence." *United States Naval Institute Proceedings,* September 1951, 909–925.

Chaffee, Brig. Gen. Adna. "Mechanized Cavalry: Lecture Delivered at the Army War College, Washington, DC, September 29, 1939."

Dietrich, Steve E. "The Professional Reading of General George S. Patton, Jr." *Journal of Military History* 53, no. 4: 387–418. Society for Military History Full Text Collection, EBSCOhost, accessed May 2010.

Ganz, A. Harding. "The 11th Panzers in the Defense, 1944." *Armor,* March–April 1994, 26–37.

Keithly, David M., and Stephen P. Ferris. "*Auftragstaktik,* or Directive Control, in Joint and Combined Operations." *Parameters,* Autumn 1999, 118–133.

Patton, Maj. George S. Jr., and Maj. C.C. Benson. "Mechanization and Cavalry," *The Cavalry Journal,* April 1930, 234–240

Unpublished Studies

Arnim, *Generaloberst* Jürgen von. "Errinerungen an Tunesien." MS # C-098, not dated. NARA.

Bayerlein, *Generalleutnant* Fritz. "An Interview with Genlt Fritz Bayerlein: Pz Lehr Div (Jan–28 July 44)." ETHINT-66, 7–9 August 1945. NARA.

———. "Panzer Lehr Division: 24 to 25 July 44," MS # A-902, 12 July 1949, NARA.

Bergengruen, *Oberst i. G.* Hellmut, Ia of the Hermann Göring Panzer Division. "Kampf der Pz. Div. 'Hermann Goering' auf Sizilien vom 10.–14.7.1943." MS # C-087a, 31 December 1950, NARA.

Beyer, *General der Infanterie* Franz. "The Final Fighting of LXXX Corps: From the Marne to the Danube, part 3." MS # B-082, not dated, NARA.

———. "The Last Battle of LXXX Corps: From the Marne to the Danube, part 2." MS # B-081, not dated, NARA.

Blaskowitz, *Generaloberst* Johannes. "An Interview with Genobst Johannes Blaskowitz: The Defense of Metz." ETHINT-32, 20 July 1945. NARA.

Blumentritt, *General der Infanterie* Günther. "Engagements of the LXXXVI A K on and west of the Lower Maas between the 3 and 20 Oct 44." MS # B-634, August 1947, NARA.

Bodenstein, *Oberst i. G.* Werner. "Report of my activities during the Americans' campaign on the west front: Ardennes (16 Dec 44–25 Jan 45)." MS # B-032, 17 April 1946, NARA.

Brandenberger, *General der Panzertruppe* Erich. "Ardennes Offensive of Seventh Army (16 Dec 1944–25 Jan 1945)." MS # A-876, not dated, NARA.

———. "Questions for the 7. Army." MS # B-447, May 1946, NARA.

———. "Seventh Army from 16 December 1944 to 16 January 1945; Nineteenth Army from 28 March to 5 May 1945." MS # A-934, May 1950, NARA.

Britzelmayr, *Generalmajor* Karl. "Einsatz der 19. V.G.D., 15.9.44–17.4.45." MS # B-527, 3 April 1951, NARA.

Buerker, *Oberst* Ulrich. "Commitment of the 10. Panzer Division in Tunisia." MS # D-174, 20 June 1947. NARA.

Cameron, Robert Stewart. "Americanizing the Tank: U.S. Army Administration and Mechanized Development Within the Army, 1917–1943," doctoral dissertation, Temple University, August 1944.

Choltitz, *General der Infanterie* Dietrich. "Operations, beginning 16 June 1944, conducted in Normandy by the LXXXIV Armeekorps." MS # B-418, March 1947. NARA.

Conrath, *General der Fallschirmtruppen* Paul. "Stellungsnahme des seinerzeitegen Kommandeurs der Pz. Div. H. G. *Generalmajor* Conrath zu den Berichten ueber den Kampf der Division." MS # C-087c, 26 January 1951. NARA.

"Defense of the West Wall." Interview with *Major* Herbert Büchs, aide to *Generaloberst* Alfred Jodl. ETHINT-37, 28 September 1945. NARA.

DePuy, Gen. William. "Generals Balck and von Mellenthin on Tactics: Implications for NATO Military Doctrine," BDM Corporation, December 1980, reproduced and edited by Reiner K. Huber, Universität der Bundeswehr München, December 2004.

Eberbach, *General der Panzertruppe* Heinrich. "Panzergruppe Eberbach bei Alencon und beim Durchbruch aus dem Kessel von Falaise." MS # A-922, 7 February 1946. NARA.

——. "Report on the Fighting of Panzergruppe West (5th Pz Army) From July 3–9 August 1944." MS # B-840, 1 June 1948. NARA.

Eckhard, *Generalmajor* Christian. "Consideration at Supreme Headquarters Concerning the Overall Conduct of the War in North Africa After the Allied Landing in North Africa in November 1942." MS # D-385, Historical Division, Headquarters United States Army, Europe, 18 June 1947. NARA.

——. "Study of the Situation in the High Command of the Wehrmacht Shortly Before, During and After the Allied Landing in North Africa, 1942." MS # D-066, Historical Division, Headquarters United States Army, Europe, 1947. NARA.

Einem, *Oberst* Kurt von. "Bericht Über die Kämpfe des XIII. SS-A. K. in Lothringen in der Zeit vom 8. Nov. 44 bis 12. Jan. 45." MS # B-780, 30 August 1951. NARA.

——. "Report of the engagements of XIII SS Corps in Lorraine During the Period from 1st September to 15th November 1944." MS # B-412, 29 October 1946. NARA.

Elfeldt, *Generalleutnant* Otto. "LXXXIV Inf Corps 28 Jul–20 Aug 44." MS # A-968, 19 August 1950. NARA.

Emmerich, *Oberst i. G.* Albert. "The Battles of the 1. Army in France from 11 Aug to 15 Sep 1944," MS # B-728, 22 September 1946, NARA.

——. "The Fighting of the 1. Army in Lorraine and Northern Alsace, Part I," MS # B-363, 13 January 1947, NARA.

——. "The Battle of the 1. Army in Lothringen and Northern Elsass, from 15 Sep. 1944 to 15 Feb. 1945, Part II," MS # B-443, 3 July 1947, NARA.

Estor, *Oberst* Fritz. "Kaempfe der 11. Armee April 1945 in Mitteldeutschland." MS # B-581, 3 January 1947. NARA.

Fäckenstedt, *Generalleutnant* Ernst. "Der Feldzug in Mitteldeutschland vom 22.3–11.5.45 aus dem Abschnitt Koblenz-Speyer bis in die Erzgebirgs-Stellung." MS # B-404, 1947. NARA.

Farmbacher, *General der Artillerie* Wilhelm. "LXXXIV Corps (12–24 Jun 1944) and XXV Corps (May 1942–10 May 1945)." MS # B-731, 26 May 1946. NARA.

Felber, *General der Infanterie* Hans. "Seventh German Army: Fighting Between the West Wall and the Main (from 20 Feb to 26 Mar 1945)." MS # B-831, not dated. NARA.

——. "XIII A. K.: Bericht ueber den Ardennenfeldzug—III. Teil, Zeit von 25.1. bis 20.2.45." MS # B-494, 25 April 1947. NARA.

Feuchtinger, *Generalleutnant* Edgar. "21st Panzer Division in Combat Against American Troops in France and Germany." MS # A-871, 17 December 1949. NARA.

Fries, *General der Panzertruppe* Walter. "The Battle of Sicily." MS # T-2, 11 December 1947. NARA.

Gäbelein, *Major* Wolfgang. "XIII Corps (21 Mar.–2 May 1945)." MS # B-173, not dated. NARA.

Gause, *Generalleutnant* Alfred. "Military Operations Against American Troops in Africa." MS # D-145, 1946. NARA.

Gersdorff, *Generalmajor* Rudolf-Christoph Freiherr von. "An Interview with Genmaj Rudolf Frhr von Gersdorff." ETHINT-59, 16 May 1946. NARA.

——. "The Battle in Northern France, Chapter 5, Defensive Fighting of the 5 Panzer Army from 25 July to 25 August 44." MS # B-726, not dated. NARA.

———. "Comments on Seventh Army War Diary." MS # A-918, December 1945. NARA.

———. "The Final Phase of the War." MS # A-893, 20 March 1946. NARA.

———. "Normandy, Cobra, and Mortain." MS # A-894, October 1945. NARA.

———. "Zwischen Westwall und Rhein: Die Kaempfe der 7. Armee vom 1. Febr.–21. Maerz 45." MS # B-123, February 1946. NARA.

Greiner, Helmut. "Notes on the Situation Reports and Discussions at Hitler's Headquarters from 12 August 1942 to 17 March 1943." MS # C-065a, not dated. NARA.

———. "Operation 'Barbarossa.'" MS # C-065i, not dated. NARA.

Guderian, *Generaloberst* Heinz. "Panzer Employment, Western Front." ETHINT-39, 16 August 1945. NARA.

Gyldenfeldt, *Generalleutnant* Heinz von. "Die Kaempfe der Heeres-Gruppe 'G' vom 15. bis 25.9.1944." MS # B-589, June 1947. NARA.

Häckel, *Generalleutnant* Ernst. "Der Feldzug im Rheinland 15.9.-Anf. Dez. 44." MS # B-452, not dated. NARA.

Hausser, *Generaloberst* (*Waffen* SS) Paul. "Rheinland: Heeres-Gruppe 'G.'" MS # B-600, June 1947. NARA.

———. "Seventh Army 29 June to 20 August 1944." MS # A-907, 30 May 1950. NARA.

Heilmann, *Generalmajor* Ludwig. "Fifth Parachute Division (1 Dec 44–12 Jan 45)." MS # B-023, not dated. NARA.

Hoehne, *General der Infanterie* Gustav. "LXXXIX Corps (22 Nov 1944–13 Jan 1945)." MS # B-075, 9 May 1946. NARA.

Hold, *Major* Kurt. "Organization and Composition of the First Army During the Period of 11 Aug 44 until 14 Feb 45 (Part I: 11 Aug–15 Sep 44)." MS # B-732, 10 November 1947. NARA.

———. "Organization and Composition of the First Army During the Period of 11 Aug 44 until 14 Feb 45 (Part II: from 15 Sep 44 until 14 Feb 45)." MS # B-821, not dated. NARA.

Ingelheim, *Oberst* i.G. Ludwig Graf von. "Engagements Fought by LXXXII A.K. During the Period 2 Dec 1944 to 27 Mar 1945)." MS # B-066, 30 May 1946. NARA.

Jodl, *Generaloberst* Alfred. "Die Operationen nach dem Durchbruch von Avranches." MS # A-927, 23 July 1945. NARA.

———. "An Interview with Genobst Alfred Jodl: Ardennes Offensive." ETHINT-51, 31 July 1945. NARA.

———. "U.S. Operations; German Defense; Ruhr; Last Days." ETHINT-52, 2 August 1945. NARA.

Kahlden, *Oberst* Wolf von. "Einsatz des Panzer-A.O.K. 5 Westlich der Vogesen in der Zeit von 15.9. bis 15.10.44." MS # B-472, 20 March 1947. NARA.

Kesselring, *Generalfeldmarschall* Albert. "The Battle of Sicily: Concluding Comments by the Former Commander in Chief South Field Marshal Kesselring." MS # T-2 K-1, not dated. NARA.

———. "History of the 'Commander in Chief West' Part III (10 March 1945 up to the time of the surrender)." MS # T-123, July 1948. NARA.

———. "An Interview with Genfldm Albert Kesselring: General Questions." ETHINT-72, 6 May 1946. NARA.

———. "The War in the Mediterranean, Part II: The Fighting in Tunisia and Tripolitania." MS # T-3 P1, not dated. NARA.

Kittel, *Generalleutnant* Heinrich. "An Interview with Genlt Heinrich Kittel: Defense of Metz." ETHINT-77, 10 January 1946. NARA.

Kniess, *General der Infanterie* Baptist. "An Interview with Gen Inf Baptist Kniess: LXXXV Inf Corps (Nov–26 Dec 44)." ETHINT-40, 11 August 1945. NARA.

———. "Ardennen (16.12.44–12.1.45)." MS # B-030, 21 May 1946. NARA.

———. "Saar-Rhein-Pfalz: 21.1.45–23.3.1945." MS # B-121, 3 May 1946. NARA.

Knobelsdorff, *General der Panzertruppe* Otto von. "Estimate of Situation When I Took Over the Armee on the 10-9-44." MS # B-222, not dated. NARA.

Koenig, *Generalmajor* Eugen. "91st Airborne Division Operations in Normandy (10 July–August 1944)." MS # D-010, 17 June 1946. NARA.

Kogard, *Oberst i. G.* Rudolf. "The Battles in France in 1944: Events in western Brittany, especially in the district of the Brest fortress." MS # B-427, 12 March 1947. NARA.

Kokott, *Generalmajor* Heinz. "An Interview with Genmaj Heinz Kokott." ETHINT-44, 29 November 1945. NARA.

———. "Ardennes Offensive: Battle of Bastogne, part 1." MS # B-040, not dated. NARA.

Kuntzen, *General der Panzertruppe* Adolf Friedrich. "Commitment of LXXXI Inf Corps During Period 2 Aug to 4 Sep 1944." MS # B-807, 3 April 1948. NARA.

Lang, *Oberst* Rudolf. "Battles of Kampfgruppe Lang in Tunisia (10. Pz. Div.) December 1942 to 15 April 1943, Part I." MS # D-173, not dated. NARA.

———. "Report of the Fighting of Kampfgruppe Lang (10. Pz. Div.) in Tunisia from December 1942 to 15 April 1943." MS # D-166, 6 June 1947. NARA.

Lüttwitz, *General der Panzertruppe* Heinrich Freiherr von. "XXXXVII. Panzer-Korps in den Ardennen-Schlacht." MS # A-940, 27 February 1946. NARA.

———. "Einsatz des XXXXVII. Panzer-Korps in den Ardennen 1944/1945." MS # A-939, not dated. NARA.

———. "An Interview with Gen Pz Heinrich von Luettwitz: XLVII Pz Corps (16 Dec-24 Dec 44)." ETHINT-41, 29 and 13 October 1945. NARA.

Lüttwitz, *General der Panzertruppe* Smilo Freiherr von. "Combat Report of the LXXXV. 'Armeekorps.'" MS # B-617, June 1947. NARA.

Mahlmann, *Generalleutnant* Paul. "353 Inf Div (24 Jul–14 Sep 44)." MS # A-984, not dated. NARA.

Manteuffel, *General der Panzertruppe* Hasso-Eccard von. "An Interview with Gen Pz Hasso von Manteuffel." ETHINT-46, 29 and 31 October 1945. NARA.

———. "The Commitment of the Fifth Panzer Army West of the Vosges within the Framework of Army Group 'G,' from About 15 September to 15 October 1944." MS # B-757, 15 November 1947. NARA.

Mantey, *Oberst* Willy. "First Army (Sep–Dec 1944)." MS # B-214, not dated. NARA.

Mellenthin, *Generalmajor* Friedrich von. "Comments on Patton and the U.S. Third Army (September 1944)." ETHINT-65, 16 May 1946. NARA.

———. "Kaempfe in Lothringen und in den Vogesen im Herbst 44 Teil IV." MS # B-078, not dated. NARA.

Mellenthin, *Generalmajor* Friedrich von, and others. "Army Group G in the period of September to the beginning of December 1944." MS # A-999, 11 July 1950. NARA.

Morton, Matthew Darlington. "Men on 'Iron Ponies:' The Death and Rebirth of the Modern U.S. Cavalry," doctoral dissertation, Florida State University, 2004.

Mühlen, *Generalmajor* Kurt von. "The Rhineland Campaign, 15 Sept 44–21 Sept 44." MS # A-972, April 1946. NARA.

Müller-Hillebrand, *Generalmajor* Burkhart. "Der Zusammenhang Zwischen dem deutschen Balkanfeldzug und der Invasion in Russland." MS # C-101, November 1951. NARA.

Priess, *General der Waffen SS* Hermann. "The Commitment of I SS Panzer Corps during the Ardennes Offensive: December-January, 1944–1945." MS # A-877, March 1946. NARA.

Raus, *Generaloberst* Erhard. "Defensive Tactics in Breakthroughs (East)." MS # T-10, not dated. NARA.

Redmer, *Oberstleutnant i. G.* Karl. "Kaempfe der 416. I. D. Zwischen Mosel und Saar vom 5.10.44–17.2.45." MS # B-573, 31 May 1947. NARA.

Reinhardt, *Generalmajor* Hellmuth, and *Oberst i. G.* Hellmut Bergengruen. "Division 'Hermann Goering' Questionnaire (11–12 Jul. 1943)." MS # C-087d, 14 August 1951. NARA.

Rodt, *Oberstleutnant* Eberhard. "Studie Über den Feldzug in Sizilien bei der 15. Pz. Gren. Div. Mai–August 1943." MS # C-077, not dated. NARA.

Roschmann, *Oberstleutnant* Hans. "Mountain Warfare: A Brief Treatise Based on Operations of 1st Mountain Division in Caucasus, August–September 1942." MS # P-148, June 1951. NARA.

Rundstedt, *Generalfeldmarschall* Gerd von. "Campaign in the West (1940)." MS # C-053, not dated. NARA.

Schmidt, *Generalmajor* Erich. "Ardennen (16.12.44–25.1.45)." MS # B-067, June 1946. NARA.

Schramm, *Major* Percy. "Avranches and Falaise Special Questions." MS # B-719, 1953. NARA.

———. "OKW War Diary (1 Apr–18 Dec 44)." MS # B-034, 1947. NARA.

Schultz, *General der Infanterie* Friedrich. "Bericht ueber Lage, Auftrag und Massnahmen (im Grossen) der Heeresgruppe 'G' im April 1945." MS # B-583, May 1946. NARA.

Senger und Etterlin, *General der Panzertruppe* Frido von. "War Diary of the Italian Campaign (1943–45): Liaison Activities with Italian Sixth Army." MS # C-095, not dated. NARA.

Simon, *General der Waffen SS* Max. "Report on the Rhineland and South Germany Campaigns." MS # C-023, March 1947. NARA.

———. "XIII SS Inf Corps in the Lorraine Campaign." ETHINT-33, 17 August 1945. NARA.

"Sixth Pz Army in the Ardennes Offensive." ETHINT-16. Historical Division, Headquarters United States Army, Europe, 1945. This is an interview with *Generaloberst* (*Waffen SS*) Josef "Sepp" Dietrich, 8–9 August 1945. NARA.

Staubwasser, *Oberst i. G.* Anton. "The Tactical Situation of Enemy as Seen by High Command of Army Group B During the Normandy Battle (6 Jun to 24 Jul 44.)" MS # B-782, 16 December 1947. NARA.

Tippelskirch, *General der Infanterie* Kurt von. "Die Kaempfe der 1. Armee in Lothringen vom 1. bis 12.11.1944." MS # B-491-492, 1 March 1947. NARA.

"Translation of Taped Conversation with General Hermann Balck, 12 January 1979, and Brief Biographical Sketch." Battelle Columbus Laboratories Tactical Technology Center.

"Translation of Taped Conversation with General Hermann Balck, 13 April 1979." Battelle Columbus Laboratories Tactical Technology Center.

Ulich, *Generalmajor* Max. "Specialized Defensive Tactics (Sicily) (Jul–Aug 43)." MS # D-004, 26 March 1947. NARA.

Vaerst, *General der Panzertruppe* Gustav von "Operations of the 5th Panzer Army in Tunisia." MS # D-001, May 1947. NARA.

Wagener, *Generalmajor* Carl. "Die Folgen der Ardennen-Offensive." MS # A-964, 4 February 1946. NARA.

Wagner, *Oberst* Werner. "Einsatz der 276. Volksgrenadier-Division: 17–27 Mar 1945." MS # B-124, not dated. NARA.

Warlimont, *General der Artillerie* Walter. "From Invasion to the Siegfried Line." ETHINT-1, July 1949. NARA.

———. "Stellungsnahme zu Berichten Deutscher Offiziere: Zu den Berichten Ueber die Anglo-Amerikanische Landung in Franzoesisch-Nord Afrika im November 1942." MS # B-364, 10 January 1947. NARA.

Wellm, *Generalmajor* August. "Bericht über das Einsatz der 36. Volks-Grenadier-Division in Lothringen vom 12.XI.1944–27.XII.1944." MS # B-223, 15 November 1946. NARA.

Wietersheim, *Generalleutnant* Wend von. "Die Kämpfe der 11. Panzer-Division Zwischen Rhein und tschechischer Grenze (21.3–15.4.45; Teil I)." MS # B-755, 16 December 1947. NARA.

———. "Rhineland, Part I: The Employment of the 11th Panzer Division in Lorraine." MS # C-090, 13 February 1951. NARA.

———. "Rhineland, Part II." MS # B-416, 1 October 1946. NARA.

Willemer, *Oberst i. G.* Wilhelm. "Divisional Operations During the German Campaign in Russia." MS # P-143c, not dated. NARA.

Wilutzky, *Oberst i. G.* Horst. "The Fighting of Heeresgruppe 'G' in the West: The Final Battle in the Central and Southern Germany Until the Surrender (22 Mar 45–6 May 45)." MS # B-703, not dated. NARA.

———. "Der Kampf der Heeresgruppe G im Westen. Der Zusammenbruch der Westfront (20.2–22.3.45)." MS # B-450, not dated. NARA.

———. "Stellungsnahme zu der Bearbeitung des ehemaligen Generalfeldmarschalls Kesselring 'Geschichte des Oberbefehlhaber West, III Teil.'" MS # C-036, November 1948. NARA.

Online Resources

1914-18.Info, http://www.1914-18.info/, as of July 2008.

"5. Thüringisches Infanterie-Regiment Nr. 94 (Grossherzog von Sachsen)," Verein

Historische Uniformen des Deutschen Kaiserreiches 1871-1918, http://historische-uniformen.de/Truppen/IR94/IR94.HTM, as of May 2009.

"86th Chemical Mortar Battalion History: The Story of Company 'B' from The Battle History." From http://home.cinci.rr.com/chemvets/companyb.html, as of November 2008.

Alexander, Bevin. "Barbarossa." MilitaryHistoryOnline.com, http://www.militaryhistory-online.com/wwii/articles/barbarossa.aspx, 4 February 2006, as of July 2009.

Ammentorp, Steen. "The Generals of WWII," http://www.generals.dk/, as of August 2008.

Axis Biographical Research. Website at http://www.geocities.com/%7Eorion47/, as of March 2009.

Bell, Brig. Gen. (ret.) Raymond E. Jr. "Giving Up the Ghost." *World War II History* magazine online, http://www.wwiihistorymagazine.com/2005/sep/fea-ghost.html, as of November 2009.

Bennighof, Mike. "Centauro at Gazala," Avalanche Press, http://www.avalanchepress.com/Centauro.php, as of November 2008.

Clemenson, Capt. W. L. "A critical analysis of the operations of the I Corps in the first phase of the Meuse-Argonne Offensive," study, Command and General Staff College, 1935, Combined Arms Research Library, http://cgsc.leavenworth.army.mil/carl/contentdm/home.htm, as of July 2008.

Feldgrau.com. http://www.feldgrau.com/spa501.html, as of February 2009.

First World War.com, primary documents, http://www.firstworldwar.com/index.htm, as of July 2008.

Fleming, Thomas. "Meuse-Argonne Offensive of World War I." HistoryNet.com, http://www.historynet.com/meuse-argonne-offensive-of-world-war-i.htm, as of July 2008.

Glantz, David M. "Counterpoint to Stalingrad, Operation Mars (November-December 1942): Marshal Zhukov's Greatest Defeat." United States Army Foreign Military Studies Office, uploaded June 1997, http://mr-home.staff.shef.ac.uk/rzhev/rzhev3.html, as of July 2009.

Grossdeutschland, http://www.grossdeutschland.net/, as of July 2009.

"Historical Study: Operations of Encircled Forces—German Experiences in Russia." Washington, DC: Department of the Army, 1952. Online edition of Pamphlet 20-234, http://www.history.army.mil/books/wwii/20234/20234.html, as of April 2009.

Island Farm Prisoner of War Camp: 198/Special Camp XI, Bridgend, South Wales, http://www.islandfarm.fsnet.co.uk/ as of February 2009.

Johnson, Douglas. "Obituary: Col Jean Petit." *The Independent*, 29 December 1997, http://findarticles.com/p/articles/mi_qn4158/is_19971229/ai_n14139340, as of August 2008.

Lexikon der Wehrmacht. http://www.lexikon-der-wehrmacht.de, as of March 2009.

"Los Dorados de Villa." Presidencia Municipal Ascencion website, http://www.ascencion.gob.mx/Contenido/plantilla5.asp?cve_canal=5117&Portal=ascension, as of August 2007.

Muther, Lt. Gen, Van Alfred. "Organization, Armament, Ammunition and Ammunition Expenditure of the German Field Artillery During the World War." *The Field Artillery Journal*, May–June, 1935, 197–211, http://sill-www.army.mil/famag/1935/MAY_JUN_1935/MAY_JUN_1935_PAGES_197_211.pdf, as of July 2008.

Nipe, George M. Jr. "Battle of Kursk: Germany's Lost Victory in World War II." HistoryNet.com, http://www.historynet.com/battle-of-kursk-germanys-lost-victory-in-world-war-ii.htm, as of July 2009.

"Operations of Encircled Forces: German Experiences in Russia." Department of the Army, Washington, DC, 1952, http://www.history.army.mil/BOOKS/WWII/20234/20234.html, as of March 2010.

The Patton Society website. http://www.pattonhq.com/, as of December 2009.

Petit, Colonel Jean. Account of events at Port Lyautey, November 1943, Passé Présent Futur de Stéphane website, http://passé-présent-futur-de-stéphane.com/marocnov1942/index.html, as of August 2008.

———. "Mémoirs de Guerre 14-18," Passé Présent Futur de Stéphane website, http://passé-présent-futur-de-stéphane.com/mmoiresdejeanpet14-18/index.html, as of March 2009.

"Prince Eitel Friedrich von Preussen." The Prussian Machine, http://home.Comcast.net/~jcviser/index.htm/aka/eitel.htm, as of July 2008.

"Prince Eitel Friedrich von Preussen—PlM Recipient?" Axis History Forum, http://forum.axishistory.com/viewtopic.php?t=71280, as of July 2008.

Roberts, Andrew. "The Genocide Generals: Secret Recordings Explode the Myth They Knew Nothing about the Holocaust." *Mail* online, 21 July 2007, http://www.dailymail.co.uk/femail/article-469883/The-Genocide-Generals-secret-recordings-explode-myth-knew-Holocaust.html, as of March 2009.

Senay, Charles T. "Unlimited objective attack in the reduction of the St. Mihiel Salient, 12 Sept., 1918," study, Command and General Staff College, 1931, Combined Arms Research Library, http://cgsc.leavenworth.army.mil/carl/contentdm/home.htm, as of July 2008.

Webb, William A. "Battle of Velikiye Luki: Surrounded in the Snow," HistoryNet.com, http://www.historynet.com/battle-of-velikiye-luki-surrounded-in-the-snow.htm, as of March 2009.

Williams, J. J. Bethurum. "Situation, the Allied plans, and a brief outline of operations of the First American Army," study, Command and General Staff College, 1933, Combined Arms Research Library, http://cgsc.leavenworth.army.mil/carl/contentdm/home.htm, as of July 2008.

Wilson, Alan. "Kursk—July, 1943," http://www.vy75.dial.pipex.com/, as of July 2009.

"World War II Statistics." World War II website, http://www.world-war-2.info/, as of July 2009.

Index